JOHN BURNS
MARTIN QUINN
LIZ WARREN
JOÃO OLIVEIRA

MANAGEMENT ACCOUNTING

MANAGEMENT ACCOUNTING

**McGraw-Hill
Higher Education**

London   Boston   Burr Ridge,   IL Dubuque,   IA Madison,   WI New York   San Francisco
St. Louis   Bangkok   Bogotá   Caracas   Kuala Lumpur   Lisbon   Madrid   Mexico City   Milan
Montreal   New Delhi   Santiago   Seoul   Singapore   Sydney   Taipei   Toronto

Management Accounting
John Burns, Martin Quinn, Liz Warren, João Oliveira
ISBN-13 9780077121617
ISBN-10 0077121619

Published by McGraw-Hill Education
Shoppenhangers Road
Maidenhead
Berkshire
SL6 2QL
Telephone: 44 (0) 1628 502 500
Fax: 44 (0) 1628 770 224
Website: www.mcgraw-hill.co.uk

British Library Cataloguing in Publication Data
A catalogue record for this book is available from the British Library

Library of Congress Cataloguing in Publication Data
The Library of Congress data for this book has been applied for from the Library of Congress

Acquisitions Editor: Leiah Batchelor
Development Editor: Stephanie Frosch
Senior Production Editor: James Bishop
Marketing Manager: Alexis Thomas

Text Design by HL Studios
Cover design by Adam Renvoize
Printed and bound in Singapore by Markono Print Media Pte Ltd

ISBN-13 9780077121617
ISBN-10 0077121619

Dedication

To my wife Nichola and my daughters Catherine and Rachel – John Burns

To my family, Regina, Josephina and Eric – Martin Quinn

To Lee, Chloe and Jasmine for their all support. I would also like to give thanks to all my students for teaching me so much – Liz Warren

To my wife, Mónica, my children, Beatriz and Inês, and my parents – João Oliveira

Brief Table of Contents

Detailed Table of Contents

Detailed Table of Contents (continued)

Detailed Table of Contents (continued)

Detailed Table of Contents (continued)

Detailed Table of Contents (continued)

Detailed Table of Contents (continued)

Detailed Table of Contents (continued)

Detailed Table of Contents (continued)

About the Authors

John Burns is Professor of Management & Accountancy at the University of Exeter where he formerly held the position of Head of Department in the University's Accounting faculty. Prior to this he has taught at the University of Manchester and the University of Colorado, Denver (USA), and he was previously Dean of the School of Accounting and Finance at the University of Dundee. Throughout his career he has taught extensively on management accounting courses, covering all levels from introductory undergraduate level through to advanced and postgraduate. He received his PhD in management accounting from the University of Manchester in 1996.

John's research interests rest primarily in management accounting, organizational change, sustainable development, and strategic and change management. He has published extensively in these subject areas, in both academic and professional journals, such as *Organization Studies*, *Accounting, Organizations and Society*, *Management Accounting Research*, *European Accounting Research*, *Accounting, Auditing and Accountability Journal*, *Critical Perspectives on Accounting*, *Qualitative Research in Accounting and Management*, *Journal of Management Control*, and *Financial Management (CIMA)*. John has been Associate Editor for the international academic journal *Management Accounting Research* since 1999, and he is a member of the editorial board for several other leading journals such as *Accounting, Auditing and Accountability Journal*, *Accounting and Business Research*, *Journal of Management and Governance*, and *Journal of Accounting and Organizational Change*. He has been a member of the Research Board for the Chartered Institute of Management Accountants (CIMA) since 2004; and is co-founder and principal coordinator of the European Network for Research of Organizational and Accounting Change. John has held visiting positions at WHU Otto Beisheim School of Management (Germany) and Örebro University (Sweden).

Martin Quinn is a Lecturer in Accounting at Dublin City University, Ireland where he teaches at undergraduate and postgraduate level. He has also taught accounting at the university of Oviedo, Spain and to students of professional accounting bodies. He is a registered Chartered Management Accountant, and started his career as a management accountant in manufacturing firms and worked in both accounting and information systems roles in a number of local and global firms. He has worked on, for example, implementations of SAP throughout Europe.

He has a BA(Hons) in Business Studies, an MSc in Management and Applications of IT in Accounting, and he completed his PhD at the University of Dundee. His research interests include ERP systems and management accounting, management accounting in small and medium sized enterprises, processual change in management accounting, organizational routines, institutional theory, and cloud accounting.

He has written a number of basic accounting books like *Brilliant Book-keeping* and *Brilliant Accounting* and has previously contributed case material to academic textbooks such as Seal's, *Management Accounting*, also by McGraw-Hill. Martin has also published articles in *Journal Of Management Control*, *Journal of Accounting & Organizational Change* and *Accountancy Ireland*.

Martin regularly writes about accounting related issues on his blog www.martinjquinn.com.

About the Authors (continued)

Liz Warren is a Principal Lecturer in Management Accounting at the University of Greenwich where she teaches Management Accounting at both the undergraduate and postgraduate level. She has previously lectured at the University of Lincoln and has also taught in Hong Kong, Malaysia and France. Before joining academia she started her career in the automobile industry as an accountant. She holds a BA in Accounting and Finance from the University of Lincolnshire and an MRes in Finance from the University of Greenwich. She is currently waiting for the final stages of her PhD to be completed.

Her current research interests include investment decisions, the UK electricity generation industry structuration theory, sustainability and uncertainty in regulatory systems.

João Oliveira is an Assistant Professor at the School of Economics and Management, University of Porto in Portugal, where he teaches management accounting and control at undergraduate and postgraduate levels. He is a visiting professor in HEC Paris in 2013 and he has previously taught at the Porto Business School and at the University of Dundee, UK. He is a chartered accountant and he has worked in the banking and in the consumer products industries. He has an MSc in Business Administration (Specialization in Accounting) from the School of Economics and Management, University of Porto and a PhD in Accounting from the University of Dundee. He received the IBM PhD Fellowship Award and a PhD scholarship from the Calouste Gulbenkian Foundation.

His research interests include organizational change, information systems, shared services centres, institutional theories and power, and he published chapters on Research in Management Accounting and on Enterprise Resource Planning systems.

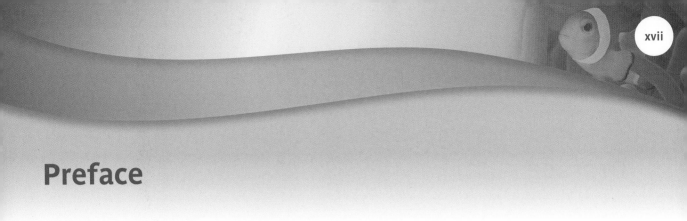

Preface

Management accounting seeks to provide information and insight to assist organizational managers in their decision-making. It comprises multiple tools and techniques which together form a fluid portfolio of organization-specific information that focuses on both the short and long-term and which, through careful planning and monitoring can help an organization pursue its goals.

The gathering and use of such information for decision-making in organizations has never been so crucial, it is the life blood of sustainable organizational practice. The recent and continuing global financial crisis has revealed many challenges, possibly the most important of all being that all organizations, no matter their size, location or sector, need an abundance of both financial expertise and broad business acumen to help guide decision makers towards achieving their long-run objectives and with this, the knowledge and competency of management accountants has become increasingly important.

This textbook is written for a new generation of management accountants who will command multi-faceted roles in tomorrow's organizations. It is contemporary in its approach but respectful of the classics and presents students with a broad coverage of both well-established and new management accounting tools and techniques and most importantly, it places such tools and techniques in the fast-changing contexts in which they operate.

There are new skills and capabilities which tomorrow's management accountants must equip themselves with if they are to continue being 'masters' of useful business information. Such new skills require both hard skills (e.g. accounting techniques, IT awareness, broad business understandings) and soft skills (e.g. communication, interpersonal, and critical thinking). It is the intention to permeate these new skills throughout the proposed textbook by taking the students beyond accounting calculations and numbers *per se*, to place accounting information and the roles of management accountants in the context of broader organizational themes and challenges. That is, whilst it remains crucial for students to emerge from their studies with a sound comprehension of all the relevant management accounting techniques, it is nowadays equally important for students to comprehend how such techniques integrate within broader and continually changing organizational and environmental settings.

Accordingly, this cutting-edge textbook provides a definitive education for tomorrow's advisory management accountants, as well as finance-literate managers. Theoretically rigorous but useful to practitioners, we believe this text is an essential companion for undergraduate management accounting students, as well as those studying at masters-level.

Key features of the textbook:

- Broad coverage of both traditional and contemporary management accounting tools and techniques.
- Emphasis throughout on the roles and skills required from tomorrow's management accountants.
- Positions the role of management accountants in tomorrow's organizational dilemmas, looking at contemporary issues such as sustainable development, ethics, hyper-competition, 'Big Data' and more.
- Exploration of the more technical aspects of management accounting in its broader organizational, institutional and social context.
- An underlying focus on the drivers and consequences of management accounting, viewed as a relatively stable yet changeable aspect of organizational life.
- Offering a wealth of real-life and research-informed examples, including well-known companies such as Apple Inc., Wikipedia, Facebook, Handelsbanken, Netflix, Tesco, Innocent, Procter & Gamble, Novo Nordisk, SAP, Coca-Cola and more.

Preface (continued)

Approach and Aims:

The book is intended to be useful to students who are new to the subject of management accounting, but there are particular features which aim to make the book a 'must have' for intermediate and advanced students as well, such as:

- Consistent and unwavering attempt to connect the technical aspects of management accounting to the 'bigger picture' in which organizations design, implement and use management accounting. Reinforced through the inclusion of many real-world illustrations such as 'Management Accounting in Practice' and using the most recent and cutting-edge research in the 'Management Accounting Insight' exhibits and end-of-chapter case studies.
- An integrated approach whereby each individual chapter or topic can be taken in its own right but where considerable attention is drawn to how different individual themes inter-connect and overlap. Management accounting is a holistic and broad-sweeping feature of organizational life, and this is reflected in how we present our textbook.
- Significant opportunities for students to test their knowledge, with worked examples and mini-case questions throughout the text. Also, at the end of each chapter, there are review questions, group discussion and activities questions, exercises and case-study-based problems (all organized by level of difficulty to help both the student and lecturer) that have a contemporary and modern feel and resonate with the skills required by tomorrow's management accountants.
- Comprehensive readings and references in each chapter, comprising the latest research and practitioner-oriented literature, for inspiration and to encourage students to broaden their knowledge and understanding.
- The text is accompanied by a high-quality resource package which comprises full online instructor and student support – including brand new Excel video walkthroughs and McGraw-Hill's fully integrated assessment package Connect™. Extending this innovative resource package further still, there is also an authors' blog at **www.burnsetal.com** which will be updated weekly by the authors, as well as a twitter account at: **https://twitter.com/Burnsetal**.

Overview of the Book

The textbook comprises six sections which together represent a comprehensive insight into management accounting – its technical attributes, changeable wider context, and the multiple roles of management accountants. The sections cover: (1) an introduction to management accounting, (2) how organizations account for their costs, (3) the importance of tools and techniques which assist organizational planning and control, (4) the various dimensions of making business decisions, (5) the complex issues surrounding measurement of organizational performance, and (6) accounting for an organization's strategic aims and future. Spread across these sections, there are twenty-two chapters, the key focus of which can be summarized as follows:

Chapter 1 – Introduction to management accounting and its changing context sets the scene for tomorrow's world of management accounting, including its definition and an understanding of the key drivers of change. We also explore the roles and skills required by tomorrow's so-called 'advisory' management accountants. Such background is important for students to be able to comprehend both traditional and new tools and techniques that comprise much of this book.

Chapter 2 – Information and management accounting highlights the importance of management accounting information in organizations, and how such information constitutes much more than 'just' the outputs of tools and techniques for presenting data to managers. We establish how powerful management accounting information can be, as well as emphasizing a need to carefully manage the information process.

Preface (continued)

Chapter 3 – The classification of cost(s) introduces key cost terms and concepts, as essential grounding for later chapters. We discuss how costs can be captured, identified and categorized in multiple ways, and how such different views can shape a variety of approaches towards decision-making.

Chapter 4 – Costing systems covers how organizations assign costs to products and services, which then form the basic cost data that managers use to plan, control and make decisions. We consider three types of costing system – job, process and contract costing.

Chapter 5 – Cost reporting explores the differences between two costing techniques (variable and absorption costing), emphasizing its application to internal performance measurement and reporting. We also briefly cover the potential of some novel management concepts when reporting internally.

Chapter 6 – Activity based costing explores a technique which offers a more sophisticated approach for allocating indirect costs (or overheads) to products, services or other 'cost objects'. We pay particular attention to the role(s) of management accountants in designing and implementing this technique, and highlight some of its common problems.

Chapter 7 – Planning and control: ideas, theories and principles considers some of the underlying reasons why and how organizations engage in planning and control, and we illustrate the usefulness of management accounting techniques in doing so.

Chapter 8 – Traditional budgeting examines budgeting techniques which are still popular in many organizations across multiple sectors. We consider the role of budgets and their different functional types, and highlight the management accountant's role in the budgeting process.

Chapter 9 – Standard costing, flexible budgets and variance analysis covers techniques which are commonly used in organizations for planning, control, decision making and product costing. Such techniques are amongst the most widely used in organizations, we also apply them to innovative real-world settings.

Chapter 10 – Beyond traditional budgeting examines alternative and more contemporary techniques such as rolling forecasts and activity-based budgeting. We consider the management philosophy known as 'beyond budgeting', and explore the role of management accountants to find a budgeting system that aligns with an organization's strategy and operating style.

Chapter 11 – Short-term decision making: cost-volume-profit analysis explores the main tools used by management accountants when making short-term decisions, assisting managers to tackle dilemmas such as how much sales volume is needed to cover their costs.

Chapter 12 – Cost behaviour and estimation shows how an understanding of cost behaviour can help estimate business costs. We explore for example how, by being able to predict how costs behave in response to changing activity levels, managers can anticipate the cost impacts of alternative strategies and decisions.

Chapter 13 – Decision making: relevant costs and revenues presents more techniques available to management accountants when providing information for decision-making across different time horizons.

Preface (continued)

In particular, it extends knowledge on how and when some costs or revenues may or may not be relevant to a particular decision-making scenario.

Chapter 14 – Pricing covers both the basic calculations for, and the wider implications of, pricing decisions for organizations. We use real-world examples to illustrate how some leading organizations utilize pricing strategies in a proactive way.

Chapter 15 – Capital investment decisions introduces some of the financial techniques available for analysing capital investments. We explain how financial numbers alone do not determine the final decision on whether an investment project goes ahead or not, and we stress the strategic nature of a management accountant's role in such activity.

Chapter 16 – Performance measurement and management: ideas, theories and principles is a general overview of how, why and when management accounting can facilitate performance measurement and management, and considers the potential contribution that management accountants have in this respect.

Chapter 17 – Accounting for strategic management explores contemporary ways in which managers have attempted to align organizational behaviour and decision-making with strategic goals. In particular, we consider and critically review the strategic-facing management accounting tool known as the 'balanced scorecard'.

Chapter 18 – Financial performance measurement and transfer pricing is a synthetic, yet rigorous analysis of the main techniques for performance measurement in divisionalised and multinational organizations. We expose the multiple challenges faced by management accountants when working in such complex settings.

Chapter 19 – Cost management, value creation and sustainable development explores managing and balancing costs and value. We present new techniques for informing decisions that ensure future costs will be supported by generated value, but also with aims for sustainable development.

Chapter 20 – Managing quality and time looks at two increasingly essential characteristics for competing in today's markets: quality and time. We provide numerous examples of how management accountants play an important role in measuring and managing quality and time, hence creating value for their organizations.

Chapter 21 – Information systems and management accounting discusses how information systems are increasingly relevant for tomorrow's management accountants. It covers key issues a management accountant needs to know about information systems and technology, and reviews some major trends and developments such as ERPs, cloud accounting and 'Big Data'.

Chapter 22 – Managing change and challenges for the future explores the complexities of management accounting change, as well as teasing out the multiple challenges faced when managing change. We look at specific areas for change in the future, and explore their ramifications for management accountants.

Acknowledgements

Authors' acknowledgements:

We would like to thank Orla Feeney, Dublin City University Business School, and Gerhard Kristandl, University of Greenwich, for their contributions to the online resources.

We would also like to thank the following people for their contributions to the text:

Annie Bladen, University of Greenwich, UK

Raul Dores, University of Minho, Portugal

Dr Barbara Flood, Dublin City University Business School, Ireland

Dr Agnieszka Herdan, University of Greenwich, UK

Bill Hugill, University of Greenwich, UK

Wendy Humphries, University of Greenwich, UK

Rui Leite, School of Economics and Management, University of Porto, Portugal

Gerhard Kristandl, University of Greenwich, UK

Graça Maciel, School of Economics and Management, University of Porto, Portugal

Dr Ruth Mattimoe, Dublin City University Business School, Ireland

José Neto, School of Economics and Management, University of Porto, Portugal

Gary Owen, University of Greenwich, UK

Samuel Pereira, School of Economics and Management, University of Porto, Portugal

João Rebello de Andrade, IBM Portugal

Jorge Sá Couto, Eurogroup Consulting, Portugal

Kevin Williams, University of Greenwich, UK

Publisher's acknowledgements:

Our thanks also go to the following reviewers for their comments at various stages in the text's development:

Dila Agrizzi, University of Southampton

Graham Ball, Nottingham Trent University

Paul Claes, Vrije Universiteit Amsterdam, Netherlands

Christopher Coles, University of Glasgow

Hilary Coyle, University of Derby

Johan de Kruijf, Universiteit Twente, Netherlands

Miles Gietzmann, City University London

Dimitrios Gounopoulos, University of Surrey - Guildford

Abeer Hassan, University of the West of Scotland

Douglas Howcroft, Nottingham University

Shahed Imam, University of Warwick

Ingrid Jeacle, University of Edinburgh

Christian Lukas, Universität Konstanz

Patricia Martyn, National University of Ireland, Galway

Messaoud Mehafdi, University of Huddersfield

Jodie Moll, University of Manchester

Kristian Møller, Aarhus Universitet, Denmark

Helen Oakes, Keele University

Jatin Pancholi, Middlesex University

Finn Porsgaard, Aarhus Universitet, Denmark

Haider Shah University of Hertfordshire

Alan Somerville, Bradford University

Teerooven Soobaroyen, Aberystwth University

Chandres Tejura, London Metropolitan University

Ian Thomson, University of Strathclyde

Androniki Triantafylli, University of Manchester

David Trodden, London Metropolitan University

Mathew Tsamenyi, University of Birmingham

Hassan Yazdifar, University of Glasgow

We are grateful to the Association of Chartered Certified Accountants (ACCA), the Chartered Institute of Management Accountants (CIMA), the Institute of Incorporated Public Accountants (IIPA), and the Institute of Certified Public Accountants in Ireland (CPA Ireland) for permission to reproduce past examination questions. The suggested ACCA solutions that are available to lecturers have been prepared by us.

Acknowledgements (continued)

This publication contains references to the products of SAP AG. SAP, R/3, SAP NetWeaver, Duet, PartnerEdge, ByDesign, SAP BusinessObjects Explorer, StreamWork, and other SAP products and services mentioned herein as well as their respective logos are trademarks or registered trademarks of SAP AG in Germany and other countries.

Business Objects and the Business Objects logo, BusinessObjects, Crystal Reports, Crystal Decisions, Web Intelligence, Xcelsius, and other Business Objects products and services mentioned herein as well as their respective logos are trademarks or registered trademarks of Business Objects Software Ltd. Business Objects is an SAP company. Sybase and Adaptive Server, iAnywhere, Sybase 365, SQL Anywhere, and other Sybase products and services mentioned herein as well as their respective logos are trademarks or registered trademarks of Sybase, Inc. Sybase is an SAP company. SAP AG is neither the author nor the publisher of this publication and is not responsible for its content. SAP Group shall not be liable for errors or omissions with respect to the materials. The only warranties for SAP Group products and services are those that are set forth in the express warranty statements accompanying such products and services, if any. Nothing herein should be construed as constituting an additional warranty.

Every effort has been made to trace and acknowledge ownership of copyright and to clear permission for material reproduced in this book. The publishers will be pleased to make suitable arrangements to clear permission with any copyright holders whom it has not been possible to contact.

Guided Tour

Chapter outline

- A closer look at management accounting
- Drivers of management accounting change
- The accounting department and accountants' roles

Learning outcomes

On completion of this chapter, students will be able to:

LO1 Define management accounting and its role in the

LO2 Explain the main objectives of management accounti

LO3 Appreciate the complex nature of global managemen

LO4 Convey knowledge of the main drivers of manageme

LO5 Distinguish management accounting from financial

Chapter Outlines and Learning Outcomes

Each chapter opens with a list of topics to be covered in the chapter along with a set of learning objectives, summarizing what you will learn from each chapter.

Key Terms

These are highlighted in bold type throughout the text, with page number references at the end of each chapter so they can be found quickly and easily. A full glossary of definitions can also be found at the end of the book.

Key terms

Data Facts and figures (p. 31)
Decentring of accounting knowledge A process whereby financial knowledge is spread through an organization, among managers and workers, who can connect a 'bottom-line effect' to localized activities (p. 37)
Forecasting Using tools and techniques to make predictions about the future, as opposed to planning which is more about what the future 'should' look like (p. 38)
Information When raw data comes to be useful and meaningful to its owner(s), and subsequently has potential to influence their decision-making (p. 31)
Information integration The bringing together of a broader business perspective, as expressed through both financial and non-financial measures (p. 36)
Information overload The potential danger of producing too much management

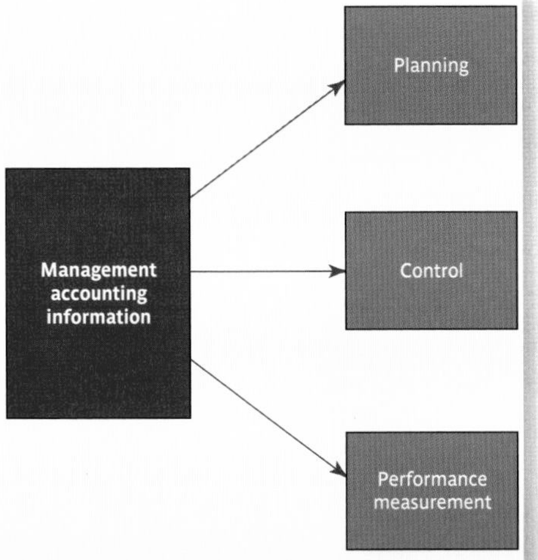

Exhibit 1.3: Objectives of management accounting

Exhibits

Each chapter presents a number of figures and tables to help you to visualize the material being covered and to illustrate and summarize important concepts.

Guided Tour (continued)

12.1: Management Accounting in Practice

Some examples of cost structures
The following examples give some indication of the varying cost st

iPhone/iPad apps
In early 2012, there were more than 300,000 apps available for the
Some are free, some require payment. In 2010, the top-grossing p
app can be downloaded for €0.79. The app is developed by a Finn
likely to have a high level of fixed costs in its cost structure. The co
as is the cost of the information technology infrastructure used to
developers. Arguably, the distribution costs on the app store are a
$99 annual fee plus 30 per cent of all revenues. The variable costs
or even close to zero.

Mars Inc.
US-based Mars Inc. is a well-known global food and confectionary
Snickers, Uncle Ben's, Wrigley and Whiskas. Foods products such a
produced in a complex manufacturing process, the costs of which
over time (that is, depreciation). Other typical fixed costs like salar
However, at the product level, variable costs occur too. Thinking a
variable costs would include ingredients and process labour costs.
structure of Mars Inc. is likely to have a relatively higher proportio
development company.

'Management Accounting in Practice' examples

This feature provides illustrations to show how management accounting affects real companies. Each illustration is accompanied by an exercise so you can analyse the content.

'Management Accounting Insight' examples

This feature provides an insight into real accounting research that is relevant to the chapter topics.

10.1: Management Accounting Insight

Is the beyond budgeting philosophy turning tradi
Although most individuals recognize the concepts of the beyond budget
Dugdale and Lyne (2010) questioned whether this philosophy has resulte
Within a field study based survey, Dugdale and Lyne (2010) examined eig
companies are provided in the table:

Business	Ownership
Aerospace	Part of aerospace multinatic
Food ingredients manufacture	Irish group listed stock exch
Construction	Part of UK construction gro
Frozen food manufacture	German private company
Food manufacture	Part of large UK food group
Plastic and glass product manufacture	Part of South African divers
Systems engineering	Private UK-based company
Wholesale, retail and leisure	Private UK-based company

Worked Example 4.2

Reallocating service centre costs
Beco Manufacturing produce heavy duty plasti
The factory floor has two large machines, an
Mitsubishi ME III Injection Molding (MIM). Ea
There are also two service departments, maintenance and q
centres.

The management accountant and other managers have
overheads for the coming year as follows

Cost centre	Total ov
AIM	1,200
MIM	1,450
Maintenance	280
Quality	160
	3,090

The supervisors in both maintenance and quality estimate t
machine as follows:

	AIM
Maintenance	20%
Quality	40%

Worked Examples

Worked examples help you learn how to apply theory in practice by explaining how to solve problems in a step-by-step format.

Guided Tour (continued)

Chapter summary

This chapter has detailed one set of techniques used by mana
managers in general, namely CVP analysis. These techniques ca
ways:

Determine the output required to break even or achieve a target prof
learned that fixed cost divided by contribution per unit gives the
fixed and variables costs, that is, break to even.

Apply CVP analysis to a multiple-product setting. In multiple produ
assumed sales mix can be utilized to effectively convert the scenar
even bundle of products can be calculated, but is should be re
change and this effects any previous calculations performed.

Prepare CVP and PV graphs. Several assumptions are made in CV
used when calculating break-even and also to graph the relat
volume and profit. The CVP graph can be used to quickly ascerta
on costs and revenues, while the PV graph relates output to pro
analysis and graphs include: (1) costs and revenues are linear;
within a relevant range of output; (3) there are no inventories; (
constant sales mix is assumed known; and, (5) all costs and price

Risk and uncertainty. Measures of risk and uncertainty, such as the
and sensitivity analysis can be used to help managers gain mor
cost, volumes and profits. By incorporating risk and uncertainty, t
variables and assumptions can be seen.

Chapter Summaries

These boxes provide an opportunity to recap and review the main topics presented in each chapter, to ensure you have acquired a solid understanding as you work through the book.

The following end-of-chapter question materials are ordered and highlighted by level of difficulty to ensure that all readers have questions appropriate to their stage of learning.

Review Questions

These questions encourage you to review the key principles and apply the knowledge you have acquired from each chapter.

Group discussion and activity que

1.10 This question will require some research. Search for,
the Chartered Institute of Management Accountant
Management Accountants (IMA). Seek out, compare
definitions of management accounting. [LO1]

1.11 Browse as many job descriptions as you can find for
Search employment agencies on the Internet, look a
accountancy bodies (for example), and list the most
which the job descriptions include. Which of these
been a requirement for many years, and which do y
[LO1, LO6, LO7]

1.12 Describe some of the likely differences between mana
in: (1) a private sector commercial business, for exam
sector organization, for example a hospital, and (3) a
UNICEF. [LO1, LO2, LO3]

1.13 What is management accounting, and critically appra
has changed in recent decades? [LO1, LO2, LO4]

1.14 Which is most important to organizations – financial
accounting? [LO5]

1.15 Having undertaken some research, for example via th
describe what you predict to be the important skills fe
management accountants? [LO1, LO2, LO3, LO4, L

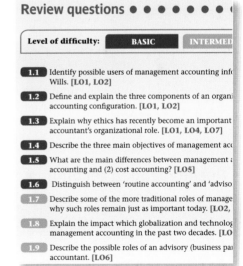

Review questions ● ● ● ● ● ● ●

| Level of difficulty: | BASIC | INTERMED |

1.1 Identify possible users of management accounting inf
Wills. [LO1, LO2]

1.2 Define and explain the three components of an organi
accounting configuration. [LO1, LO2]

1.3 Explain why ethics has recently become an important
accountant's organizational role. [LO1, LO4, LO7]

1.4 Describe the three main objectives of management acc

1.5 What are the main differences between management a
accounting and (2) cost accounting? [LO5]

1.6 Distinguish between 'routine accounting' and 'adviso

1.7 Describe some of the more traditional roles of manage
why such roles remain just as important today. [LO2,

1.8 Explain the impact which globalization and technolog
management accounting in the past two decades. [LO

1.9 Describe the possible roles of an advisory (business pa
accountant. [LO6]

Group Discussion & Activity Questions

These questions promote in-class discussion and encourage you to actively research a topic. Ideal for use in seminars.

Guided Tour (continued)

4) Variable costs in each division: no change in the average varia[...] the wholesale division. In the retail division, a variable cos[...] projected by changing the packaging used for the items sold.

5) Fixed costs are expected to change as follows in each division:

	Wholesale
Building and occupancy costs	Increase by 2%
Other administrative costs	Unchanged
Interest and financial costs	Increase by 1%

Required:

a) Using the values shown for the year end 31 March 2015, calcul[...] to sales margin for the wholesale division, the retail division a[...]

b) Prepare the budgeted sales and costs for each division and th[...] end 31 March 2016 using the same layout as shown for the year[...] account of the anticipated changes outlined above.

c) Using the figures for the company overall which you have c[...] prepare a break-even chart, clearly identifying each of the follc[...]

The revenue line

Exercises

This end-of-chapter feature is the perfect way to practise the techniques you have been taught and apply methodology.

Case Study Problem

Each chapter features one case study with its own set of questions, designed to test how well you can apply the main techniques learned.

Case study problem ● ● ● ● ● ●

C5.1 Cost reporting at Skanva Papers [LO1, LO2, LO[...]

Skanva Papers are a medium-sized Swedish pulp and paper compa[...] and packaging products from heavy cardboard to office papers. [...] Sweden, one in Örebro and one in Uppsala, both of which manu[...] years ago, a new information system was installed at these two [...] performs a number of functions as follows, some of which were [...]

Customers and products are defined in the software.

Processes customer orders.

Each product/customer order is costed in the software, usir[...]

Production is planned and monitored. Actual production [...] operator input (using a keyboard) or captured automaticall[...]

Completed inventory is recorded and tracked.

Deliveries to customers are recorded and invoices generatec[...]

Actual production data, namely material usage, labour tin[...] and all customer orders are 're-costed' based on this inform[...]

At the time of installing the information system at these two [...] centralize sales and production planning at Örebro, but botl[...] accounting function. The Örebro facility has typically being mc[...]

In the past 12 months or so, the management accountant at l[...] the profitability of the operation. He believes sales levels can be [...] understanding of the cost structure of the business. Production [...]

Recommended reading ●

- Dugdale, D., C. Jones and S. Green (2006) C[...] *Manufacturing*, London: CIMA.

This CIMA report provides some useful insights into[...] also some information in the use of throughput cost.[...]

References ● ● ● ● ● ●

Bragg, S. (2007) *Throughput Accounting – a Guide[...]*

CIMA (2009) 'Management Accounting survey –[...] Thought-leadership/Research-topics/Manageme[...] accounting-survey/ (accessed on 26 June 2012).

Cunningham, J. and O. Fiume (2003) *Real Numl[...]* Durham, NC: Managing Times Press.

Dugdale, P. C. Jones and S. Green (2006) *Cor[...] Manufacturing*, London: CIMA.

Goldratt, E.M. and J. Cox (2004) *The Goal*, 4th e[...]

Recommended Reading and References

Each chapter features a list of comprehensive readings and references, comprising the latest research and practitioner-oriented literature, to broaden your knowledge and understanding of the chapter topics.

 ## STUDENTS...

Want to get **better grades**? *(Who doesn't?)*

Prefer to do your **homework online**? *(After all, you are online anyway.)*

Need **a better way** to **study** before the big test? *(A little peace of mind is a good thing...)*

With **McGraw-Hill's** *Connect*™ *Plus Accounting*,

STUDENTS GET:

- **Easy online access** to homework, tests, and quizzes assigned by your instructor.

- **Immediate feedback** on how you're doing. (No more wishing you could call your instructor at 1 a.m.)

- **Quick access** to lectures, practice materials, eBook, and more. (All the material you need to be successful is right at your fingertips.)

- A Self-Quiz and Study tool that **assesses your knowledge** and **recommends** specific readings, supplemental study materials, and additional practice work.

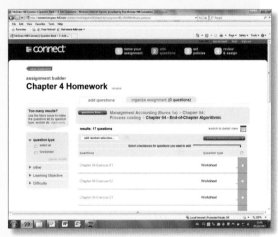

Less managing. More teaching. Greater learning.

INSTRUCTORS...

Would you like your **students** to show up for class **more prepared**?
(Let's face it, class is much more fun if everyone is engaged and prepared...)

Want an **easy way to assign** homework online and track student **progress**?
(Less time grading means more time teaching...)

Want an **instant view** of student or class performance relative to learning objectives? *(No more wondering if students understand...)*

Need to **collect data and generate reports** required for administration or accreditation? *(Say goodbye to manually tracking student learning outcomes...)*

Want to **record and post your lectures** for students to view online?

With **McGraw-Hill's *Connect™* Plus Accounting,**

INSTRUCTORS GET:

- Simple **assignment management**, allowing you to spend more time teaching.
- **Auto-graded** assignments, quizzes, and tests.
- **Detailed Visual Reporting** where student and section results can be viewed and analysed.
- Sophisticated **online testing** capability.
- A **filtering and reporting** function that allows you to easily assign and report on materials that are correlated to accreditation standards, learning outcomes, topic and difficulty
- An easy-to-use **lecture capture** tool.
- The option to **upload course documents** for student access.

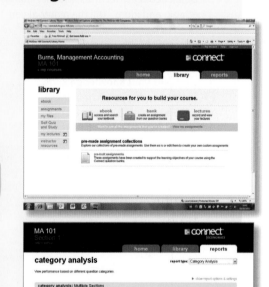

Want an online, **searchable version** of your textbook?

Wish your textbook could be **available online** while you're doing your assignments?

Connect™ Plus Accounting eBook

If you choose to use *Connect™ Plus Accounting*, you have an affordable and searchable online version of your book integrated with your other online tools.

Connect™ Plus Accounting eBook offers features like:

- Topic search
- Direct links from assignments
- Adjustable text size
- Jump to page number
- Print by section

Want to get more **value** from your textbook purchase?

Think learning accounting should be a bit more **interesting**?

Check out the STUDENT RESOURCES section under the *Connect™* Library tab.

Here you'll find a wealth of resources designed to help you achieve your goals in the course. You'll find things like **quizzes, PowerPoints, and weblinks** to help you study. Every student has different needs, so explore the STUDENT RESOURCES to find the materials best suited to you.

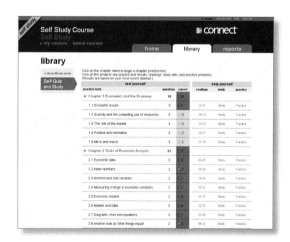

Online Learning Centre

Visit www.mcgraw-hill.co.uk/textbooks/burns today!

Student - Helping you to Connect, Learn and Succeed

We understand that studying for your module is not just about reading this textbook. It's also about researching online, revising key terms, preparing for assignments, and passing the exam. The website above provides you with a number of **FREE** resources to help you succeed on your module, including:

- Self-test MCQ's
- Excel Templates
- Excel Application Videos
- Web Links
- Links to Case Articles
- Learning Outcomes
- Glossary

Lecturer support - Helping you to help your students

The Online Learning Centre also offers lecturers adopting this book a range of resources designed to offer:

- **Faster course preparation**- time-saving support for your module
- **High-calibre content to support your students**- resources written by your academic peers, who understand your need for rigorous and reliable content
- **Flexibility**- edit, adapt or repurpose; test in EZ Test or your department's Course Management System. The choice is yours.

The materials created specifically for lecturers adopting this textbook include:

- Solutions Manual
- Instructors Manual
- PowerPoint Slides
- Testbank
- Artwork from the Book
- YouTube Video Links

To request your password to access these resources, contact your McGraw-Hill representative or visit:

www.mcgraw-hill.co.uk/textbooks/burns

Test Bank Available in McGraw-Hill EZ Test Online

A test bank of hundreds of questions is available to lecturers adopting this book for their module. For flexibility, this is available for adopters of this book to use through Connect or through the EZ Test online website. For each chapter you will find:

- A range of multiple choice, true or false, fill-in-the blank and short answer essay questions
- Questions identified by type, difficulty, and topic to help you to select questions that best suit your needs

McGraw-Hill EZ Test Online is:

- **Accessible** anywhere with an Internet connection – your unique login provides you access to all your tests and material in any location
- **Simple** to set up and easy to use
- **Flexible,** offering a choice from question banks associated with your adopted textbook or allowing you to create your own questions
- **Comprehensive,** with access to hundreds of banks and thousands of questions created for other McGraw-Hill titles
- **Compatible** with Blackboard and other course management systems
- **Time-saving**- students' tests can be immediately marked and results and feedback delivered directly to your students to help them to monitor their progress.

To register for this FREE resource, visit **www.eztestonline.com**

Make our content your solution

At McGraw-Hill Education our aim is to help lecturers to find the most suitable content for their needs delivered to their students in the most appropriate way. Our **custom publishing solutions** offer the ideal combination of content delivered in the way which best suits lecturer and students.

Our custom publishing programme offers lecturers the opportunity to select just the chapters or sections of material they wish to deliver to their students from a database called CREATE™ at

www.mcgrawhillcreate.co.uk

CREATE™ contains over two million pages of content from:
- textbooks
- professional books
- case books – Harvard Articles, Insead, Ivey, Darden, Thunderbird and BusinessWeek
- Taking Sides – debate materials

Across the following imprints:
- McGraw-Hill Education
- Open University Press
- Harvard Business Publishing
- US and European material

There is also the option to include additional material authored by lecturers in the custom product – this does not necessarily have to be in English.

We will take care of everything from start to finish in the process of developing and delivering a custom product to ensure that lecturers and students receive exactly the material needed in the most suitable way.

With a **Custom Publishing Solution**, students enjoy the best selection of material deemed to be the most suitable for learning everything they need for their courses – something of real value to support their learning. Teachers are able to use exactly the material they want, in the way they want, to support their teaching on the course.

Please contact **your local McGraw-Hill representative** with any questions or alternatively contact Warren Eels **e: warren_eels@mcgraw-hill.com.**

BACKGROUND AND CONTEXT

CHAPTER 1

INTRODUCTION TO MANAGEMENT ACCOUNTING AND ITS CHANGING CONTEXT

Chapter outline

- A closer look at management accounting
- Drivers of management accounting change
- The accounting department and accountants' roles

Learning outcomes

On completion of this chapter, students will be able to:

LO1 Define management accounting and its role in the management process

LO2 Explain the main objectives of management accounting

LO3 Appreciate the complex nature of global management accounting practice

LO4 Convey knowledge of the main drivers of management accounting change

LO5 Distinguish management accounting from financial accounting and cost accounting

LO6 Describe the main purpose of an accounting (or finance) department

LO7 Discuss the current and potential future roles and skills of management accountants

Introduction

Accounting is concerned with the provision of financial and non-financial **information** to help its users make decisions. The particular branch called **management accounting** is a professional practice that seeks to provide information to assist organizational *managers* in their decision making. Management accounting thus involves information which is internal to an organization, and allows managers to plan for both the short- and the long-term futures. It also helps to ensure that such plans are put into action, and monitored, so that an organization remains on track to achieve its goals.

Much of the management accounting practice that we see in today's organizations mirrors the practices of many decades ago. If you compared a 1970s management accounting textbook to a present-day textbook, for instance, there would be significant overlap in their content. In particular, you would soon appreciate that many of the tools and **techniques** described in today's textbooks, as well as those tools and techniques actually being used in today's organizations, remain more or less the same as they were several decades ago.

A recent survey of the main tools and techniques used by management accountants, undertaken by the Chartered Institute of Management Accountants (CIMA, 2009a – see *Management Accounting in Practice 1.1*), confirms the continued popularity of such long-established tools and techniques as budgeting, variance analysis, and payback investment appraisal methods. These long-standing tools of the trade remain central to the management accounting profession, and will be given plenty of coverage in this textbook.

However, there have been changes too, in particular with respect to the broader social and organizational context in which management accounting operates. These broader developments, and the new tools and techniques which they have stimulated, will also be given considerable coverage in this textbook. The CIMA survey mentioned in *Management Accounting in Practice 1.1*

1.1: Management Accounting in Practice

CIMA's survey on management accounting tools

In 2009, the Chartered Institute of Management Accountants (CIMA) reported a survey which explored current and intended usage of more than 100 management accounting (and closely related) tools. The survey was completed by 439 professional members, and here we summarize two of the key findings. First, the survey asked CIMA members which were the 10 most used management accounting tools/techniques, the results of which were as follows:

	% respondents
Financial year forecasting	86
Profit before tax	82
Cash forecasting	78
Variance analysis	72
Strategic planning	71
Gross margin	69
Overhead allocation	67
Rolling forecast	66
SWOT analysis	65
Net profit margin	63

Second, the respondents were also asked which management accounting tools they were most likely to adopt in the next two years, the results of which were as follows:

	No. respondents
Balanced scorecard	50
Customer profitability analysis	36
Rolling forecast	34
Activity-based management	31
Environmental management accounting	29
Product/service profitability analysis	28
Activity-based costing	25
Post-completion audits	25
Business process reengineering	24
CIMA's strategic scorecard	22

Source: CIMA (2009a).

Exercises

1) Numerous academics (and consultants) have argued, over the last two decades in particular, that long-established management accounting tools and techniques such as budgeting and 'payback' investment appraisal methods are dated and unfit for purpose in modern organizations. Yet most evidence confirms that such traditional tools remain as popular as ever. Why do you think that traditional management accounting tools and techniques remain so popular?

2) In which sector would you expect organizations to use the most management accounting tools and techniques – the manufacturing sector, the public sector or the services sector? Explain your choice.

suggests that such contemporary tools as the balanced scorecard, rolling forecasts and activity-based management will become more popular in the short term.

In summary, management accounting practice still comprises many of the traditional tools and techniques which have been used, and remained largely unchanged, for many decades. But there have also been some innovations and change in recent years, driven by the shifting context in which management accounting operates. Rapid advances in both information technology (for example, databases, the Internet, digital, wi-fi, big-data) and production technology (for example, automation, robots) have had a profound impact on the capabilities and capacity of management accounting practice – see below for more discussion of the main **drivers of management accounting** change.

Although many of the long-established management accounting tools and techniques still feature prominently in most organizations, a great deal of the traditional tools and techniques are nowadays performed 'automatically' by advanced software, as well as being used in different ways than in the past. For instance, traditional budgets remain as popular as ever in most organizations. However, nowadays, compared to say 20 years ago, far more budgeting is performed by business managers rather than by management accountants, and today's budgets tend also to form only a part of broader **planning** and **control** architecture which now usually includes greater emphases on forecasting. These latter and more subtle changes, as well as the marrying of new and more traditional management accounting practices, will be highlighted throughout this textbook.

For many management accountants, their organizational role has also changed in recent years. Evidence suggests that many of today's management accountants undertake advisory **roles** within their place of work, as **business partners** whose primary task is to solve business problems and to help instil more commercial astuteness in both day-to-day and strategic decision-making situations (CIMA, 2009b). These management accountants have moved on from so-called traditional 'scorekeeping' roles (although data capture and analysis remains as important as ever – see

Management Accounting in Practice 1.4), and have adopted broader organizational roles, which entail interaction with colleagues across an array of decision-making scenarios.

The remainder of this chapter presents additional background to the shifting context within which management accounting operates. But, first, we extend our definition of management accounting, including clarification of what it is not. Next, we explore some of the main change drivers of management accounting, which constitute factors that might influence shifts in the information requirements of organizational managers and other decision makers. We also explore the role(s) of the accounting function within organizations, as well as the likely skills required for tomorrow's management accountants.

A closer look at management accounting

Extending our definition of management accounting

We began this textbook with a broad definition of management accounting: 'a professional practice that seeks to provide information to assist organizational *managers* in their decision-making'. This definition is intentionally broad, and should not be regarded as set in stone or as being universal, not least because management accounting differs across organizations, but also because management accounting does not constitute an exact science.

An examination of different definitions of 'management accounting' over the years makes for an interesting read. Scanning through different management accounting textbooks over multiple generations would reveal some definitional changes, especially in terms of the respective primary focus. However, three aspects that consistently appear in definitions over time are that management accounting is in some way closely linked to: (1) *information provision* that (2) *assists management decision making*, and thereby (3) helps towards the *attainment of organizational goals*. Management accounting is thus an enabling feature of organizations.

Organizational goals can take many forms, depending upon the type of organization. For example, private-sector organizational goals would normally constitute seeking continuous improvement in competitiveness and long-run profitability. On the other hand, the goals for public-sector organizations, charities and other not-for-profit organizations would normally constitute the provision of services via cost-effective and sustainable means.

Most organizational decisions rely to an extent on the information that is fed into the decision-making process, including historical, analytical and predictive information. **Information** is a building block of knowledge accumulation and organizational learning. But information is also simultaneously the foundation of both stability *and* change in organizations (Burns and Scapens, 2000). Such information can be financially oriented or non-financial, and its users can be situated across multiple parts of an organization (see Exhibit 1.1). Such is its importance to the whole topic of management accounting, we explore the issue of 'information' in its own right in the next chapter.

Examples of where management accounting might feature in different parts of an organization include (but are by no means exhaustive):

- Calculating the costs of design in a jet-ski manufacturing company
- Evaluating 'on-time delivery' rates for the despatch department of an Internet retailer
- Assessing product quality for the production unit in a mobile phone producer
- Comparing a charity organization's running costs against its revenues and donations
- Assisting a marketing department to set prices for a range of new designer clothing
- A wholesale wine supplier analysing the net profitability of individual customers
- Compiling revenue forecasts for an executive board meeting in the regional council

Exhibit 1.1: Dispersion of management accounting information around an organization

Effective decisions would be those which can make positive impacts towards achieving organizational goals. The decision-making process comprises, for example, the formulation of an organization's strategic intentions, assessing the related risks, and designing the routine procedures and structures that will hopefully guide the organization in the right direction towards its strategic goals. Given their expertise and skills, management accountants normally have potential to support such decision-making processes, at various junctures. We will return to the subject of management accountants' roles and skills requirements later in this chapter.

Traditionally, management accounting would be focused to a large extent on the provision of *financially* oriented information, for instance an array of information which correlates with profits, cash-flow and financial ratios. However, increasingly *non-financial* information carries at least as much importance in management accounting practice, albeit still alongside financial information. So, for instance, management accountants are involved in the provision of information relating to customers, product quality, employee well-being, environmental issues, and much more. Further, financial and non-financial information increasingly becomes interconnected, and in recent times many organizations have tried to integrate financial and non-financial goals through such tools as a balanced scorecard (see Chapter 17).

What organizational decision makers require is accurate, relevant and timely information that can assist them to make sensible decisions and which, in turn, they hope will lead them towards attaining their goals. The precise nature of organizational information at any point in time will depend on numerous factors, including the type of organization (for example, profit-seeking commercial enterprise, public sector organization, or other not-for-profit organizations such as charities), the size and complexity of an organization (for example, a multinational corporation, a small local business, or a virtual organization), the purpose for which such information is needed (for example, planning, control, evaluation of past performance, short-term decisions or strategic decisions), the level of detail required (for example, aggregated, or drilled down to individual business processes), and more.

There is no such thing as an 'optimal package' of management accounting components, neatly fitting the requirements of all its users. Nevertheless, it is always possible to design a management accounting system which 'does enough' to provide relevant and useful information for specific local needs, aligned with careful and detailed forward planning, as well as ongoing reassessments and review. These difficulties should be regarded as part of the appeal and strength of management accounting rather than a weakness; that is, *management accounting can to an extent be just what an organization wants it to be.*

It does not necessarily follow that more information will lead to better decision making; simple and basic management accounting **systems** might, in some instances, be 'good enough' and fit for purpose. Organizational decision-making is complex, frequently ad hoc, and sometimes relies on hunch and instinct. It is more often than not encased in conditions of uncertainty and volatility which, in turn, means that taking risks is not uncommon. Thus, an important aspect of the management accountant's role is to provide information that can assist its users to cope under such conditions of uncertainty and volatility. At this point we should also recognize the importance of an organization's informal (as opposed to formal) information base, for example the routines, norms and shared experiences which transport information over time.

Three components together constitute an organization's formal management accounting configuration, and it is the combination of these different components (alongside informal channels of information and knowledge) that makes management accounting a key provider of information for organizational decisions. We define this formal configuration of components as follows:

- *Management accounting systems:* the hardware and software which facilitates the collation of data and the processing of information

- *Management accounting techniques:* an array of calculative methods that allow organizations to structure their problems and offer alternative actions

- *Management accountants' roles:* the ways in which accountants become involved in, and assist, organizational decision-making.

There are many available information systems and techniques from which management accountants can choose, and then mobilize them in such a way that the chosen configuration provides useful information for, and assists, organizational decision making. Having said this, management accounting does not represent some neutral bundle of systems and techniques that *guarantee* success or optimal decision making. Management accounting is far from being 'neutral' in an organization, and its use can frequently have significant ramifications both within and outside that stretch beyond merely the calculative or technical dimension. Management accounting, and its influence on the information used by managers in all organizations, is a mixture of both informal and formal phenomena (see Exhibit 1.2).

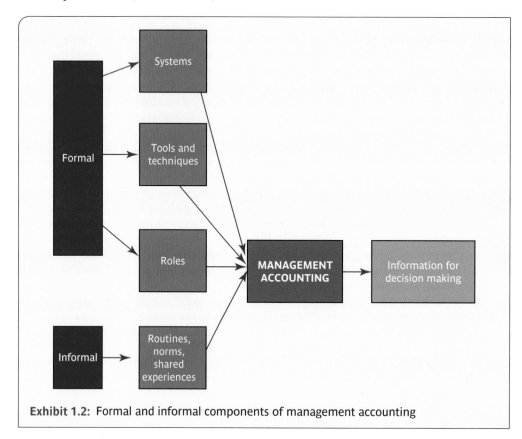

Exhibit 1.2: Formal and informal components of management accounting

For instance, management accounting information can act as an organizational language, a currency through which colleagues communicate with each other, as well as through which they assess each others' respective performance (Roberts and Scapens, 1985). It can also be a source of trust within organizations (Busco et al., 2006), a mechanism for exerting power (Collier, 2001), and much more. We will explore such non-technical (social, political, institutional) properties of management accounting information throughout the textbook – see especially the 'constitutive aspects of management accounting information' section in Chapter 2.

Objectives of management accounting

Having defined management accounting, we can now consider some examples of where organizational decisions are made and, thus, where management accounting information has a potential important role to play, as follows.

- Organizational planning is where managers select from alternative options such that their decisions (combined) will assist towards achievement of organizational goals. Management accounting information will usually form a key component of what constitutes the various options upon which such decisions are made.

- Organizational control denotes the process through which managers seek to ensure that their plans are being put into action, for example through monitoring and reporting activities. Such monitoring and reporting usually comprises information which management accountants aim to provide.

- **Performance measurement** describes where managers assess an organization's actual performance against its planned activity, as well as continually gauging the likelihood of achieving organizational goals. Traditionally management accountants have normally provided the information to facilitate such a process, and increasingly such information is both non-financial and financial in nature.

Planning, control and performance measurement (see Exhibit 1.3) will all feature in later chapters of this book, as well as tools and techniques to facilitate such aspects of organizational life.

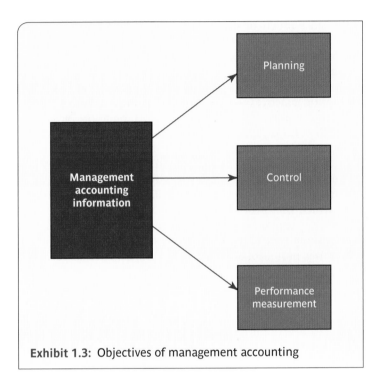

Exhibit 1.3: Objectives of management accounting

What management accounting is not?

Before leaving our definitions, we should probably also clarify what management accounting is *not*. That is, we should make a clear distinction between management accounting and two other important strands of accounting which are closely related to but distinct from management accounting, namely: (1) financial accounting and (2) cost accounting.

Financial accounting

Financial accounting describes the process of collating information for the purpose of external financial reports, the most obvious of which would be the 'glossy' annual financial statements. By contrast, management accounting is concerned with the production of information used primarily for internal reports (or simply for informal discussion) that feeds into organizational decision making.

The production of financial statements is legally binding (that is, required by company statute) for many organizations. And, the format and content of such statements is significantly guided by professional accounting standards, as well as directives such as those issued by the International Accounting Standards Board (IASB). Management accounting, on the other hand is entirely optional, although professional management accounting bodies issue guides and professional codes of conduct to their practising members.

Financial statements present an aggregated view of mostly the financial well-being of an entire organization at a particular point in time – for example, the year-end or interim financial statements. Whereas, management accounts will more frequently, sometimes ad hoc, focus on general analysis of organizational performance. That is, as well as presenting aggregated performance at defined points in time, management accounting can also drill down to specific areas of an organization at any particular point in time – for example, an analysis of customers, products, markets, machinery, divisions or outsourced operations. Monthly management accounts are still commonplace today; however, in fast-changing business environments, and with the availability of higher-capacity information systems, ad hoc analysis and real-time management reporting is on the increase.

Eventually, decisions that emerge from the management accounting process will feed through to the financial well-being, or converse, of an organization. In many organizations, management accounting is nowadays a 'performance maker' rather than merely a historical portrayal of past performance. And therefore much of today's management accounting practice exhibits 'feed-forward' characteristics, for example, forecasting, in comparison with financial accounting which is predominantly historical and 'feed-backward' in its nature.

Although financial accounting is of paramount importance to many organizations, its functioning is significantly rules and regulations led. As such, there is a sizeable degree of commonality across global financial accounting practices, something that is only likely to intensify in the future. The rules and regulations, as mentioned above, are a combination of government statute and professional standards. In contrast, although there are numerous common techniques and rules underpinning management accounting practice, technically speaking organizations have the opportunity to design their management accounting in any which way they choose.

Management accounting information is produced by employees within an organization, so its users can potentially (re)shape its content, detail and format. Users can also try to influence the validity and meaning which they will attach to such information. There is thus a considerable ability in organizations to create management accounting practices (hence, the information derived from them) in whichever way they choose. This contrasts with financial accounting information which, governed by various professional laws and principles, external users and decision makers must more or less accept as received.

Cost accounting

Cost accounting is a narrower application (a subset) of management accounting. It concentrates on an organization's acquisition or consumption of resources, normally how much it costs to make particular products and/or provide a particular service. Such information is critical in most organizations – for instance, when calculating the value of stock or work-in-progress that a business has.

While part of the remit for management accounting is to focus on an organization's costs, it tends to be carried out in a broader business and management context than is cost accounting. Also, the malleability of management accounting practice allows for potential analysis of different cost measures for different decision-making scenarios (see Chapter 3). For example, organizations might wish to explore the costs associated with particular customers, of using particular suppliers, the costs associated with outsourcing part of a commercial business, or the set-up costs of a potential new project. Then, based upon such analyses, decisions about the future can be made.

Importantly, management accounting also focuses on issues that are not directly (but often can still be *in*directly) cost related, such as quality, customer satisfaction, employee well-being, new product development and business growth (see Chapters 19 and 20). There is accounting-for-costs, which is techniques-led attention on desirable financial performance, and which is also necessary to meet the requirements for external financial statements (for example, stock valuation). But, there is also management-of-costs in its broader context (see *Management Accounting in Practice 1.2*). In this textbook we explore both old and new costing techniques, but we also highlight the uncertainty and complex issues relating to the management of costs over time.

Chapter 3 of this textbook will cover the basic definitions and more technical aspects of costs per se. Such background is essential for any management accounting student or practitioner – not least because there are so many different ways to categorize, define and interpret costs. But, that aside, we must also bear in mind that today's costs are intertwined with so much more of an

1.2: Management Accounting in Practice

Managing costs for multiple organizational (and wider) benefits

There have been some fascinating innovations in recent years that aim to improve (which usually means decrease) cost inefficiencies but which, for example, also improve an organization's performance in respect of sustainable development (see below, and in several later chapters, especially Chapters 19 and 22). Briefly, **sustainable development** is a term which describes how some organizations attempt to develop their activities in a financially rewarding way but not at the expense of costs incurred on society or the environment, thus preserving life opportunities for future generations. So, in transport activities for example, we have seen such innovations as the following:

- Some organizations (for example, L'Oréal) have acquired supplier businesses (for example, bottling suppliers). This has significantly cut the cost of freight miles but also decreased CO_2 emissions.

- Philips utilizes freight barges on canals and rivers, rather than trucks on roads, to carry its export goods to busy Dutch ports. Again, this has had a beneficial impact on travel (fuel) costs and CO_2 emissions.

- In Spain, the car manufacturer SEAT has resurrected an old train line to transport cars from its Martorell factory to the port of Barcelona.

- McDonald's (Europe) is recycling about 80 per cent of its used frying oil, and has biodiesel specialists convert this waste into engine fuel which is then used by their long-haul trucks.

- US food giant, Cargill, has helped develop more economical and more environmentally friendly ways of shipping, by designing a huge kite for the front of its cargo ships.

- Global delivery organizations such as Deutsche Post (DHL Germany) and La Poste (France) have been investing heavily in more economical and eco-friendly transport, such as all-electric and hybrid vehicles.

Source: Schiller, B. (2012).

Exercise

The above discussion highlights how some leading organizations are introducing new innovations in their transport activities in order to improve both cost efficiency *and* sustainable development. Can you think of and provide evidence for other areas of activity where organizations can innovate to simultaneously improve cost performance and sustainable development?

organization's activities. In particular, today's organizations do not just seek to measure or calculate costs, but also need to *manage* costs (see Chapter 19 for further discussion), and to do so in a way that is reinforcing of broader and long-term goals. This, in particular, is how management accounting goes further than cost accounting.

Drivers of management accounting change

As we have established, the management accounting practices in use today are largely driven by the informational demands of decision makers within organizations. It follows that changes in management accounting can be influenced by shifts in these information demands. Change is an all-pervading feature of most organizations nowadays, an expected and normal part of the day-to-day organizational fabric. And, management accounting is no exception. For instance, tomorrow's management accounting can be shaped by changes in the global economic and financial environment, new technology, new managerial styles, new organizational forms, new regulation, and more. We now explore some of these drivers of management accounting change in more detail, although each (and more!) of these change drivers will be further discussed at various junctures of the textbook. The following is merely an introduction to important themes in connection with how management accounting changes over time.

The global economic and financial environment

The globalization of products, services and capital markets is one of the main drivers of management accounting change. Far from being a new phenomenon, it is the intensity of globalization in recent decades that has had such a significant impact on management accounting.

With global distribution networks, faster and more economical transportation, and immediate access to all manner of information via the Internet and digital communication, the competition faced by most of today's organizations is international rather than merely national or local. We live in a huge global marketplace, with relatively few barriers to trade, and where much more nowadays is instantaneously known about one's competitors. Products in general do not last as long as they once did, as new innovations and 'the next best thing' abound. Also, many products now have shorter product life cycles – that is, the period of time from research and development until when after-sales support is no longer offered. Many organizations now also face shorter periods of competitive advantage over their potential rivals, and must exploit these situations quickly and with faster reaction times. Importantly, such developments as these all have important ramifications for management accounting, not least because it creates a need for faster, real-time and increasingly 'feed-forward'-type information to inform decisions (CIMA, 2008a).

Not unrelated, and still as a consequence of growing international competition, most profit-seeking organizations are highly focused on issues such as quality and customer satisfaction. Today's customers can be much more choosy and discriminating, and will take as given the variety of products on offer; they need not be loyal. As such, customer or client satisfaction, which means both keeping those customers you have but also attracting new ones, is a priority in many organizations with which management accountants become directly involved.

Today compared, say, to just 10 years ago, there is much greater complexity surrounding organizations of all kinds – for example, in relation to stakeholders and governance matters, there is also increased economic and financial uncertainty, epitomized by market volatility, economic downtimes and more significant financial 'shocks' (see *Management Accounting in Practice 1.3*). With this background, organizations explicitly recognize, and try to allow for volatility and risk as part of their ongoing management process (Wilson, 2011). Again, management accountants have a key role to play in this respect.

1.3: Management Accounting in Practice

The changing context in which management accounting operates

Recent times have asked serious questions of the nature of information being used by managers in all kinds of organizations. The global economic and financial crisis that began in 2008 has especially forced many managers to reconsider their information base, thus having major implications for management accounting. Hopwood (2009) captured the essence of how the altered economic and financial climate has considerably reshaped the context(s) in which management accounting operates. More specifically, Hopwood argued that the significant changes in context were driving organizations to:

- Continually set aside and reformulate budgets

- Question and revise expectations for revenues and costs

- Carefully manage cash flows, and also be ready to convert assets into cash

- Revise strategy in a more frequent manner, more about 'being strategic'

- Engage in more ad hoc analyses of an organization's business

- Treat management accounting as a process operating in continuous time.

There are many examples in today's world that can be used to illustrate the sorts of thing which Hopwood highlighted. One recent example would be how the already struggling holiday operator in the UK, Thomas Cook, has been forced to abandon its premium holiday packages for the 2012 Olympic Games in London. The company was granted a licence as an official provider by the Olympics Organizing Committee several years before the games would take place and, more importantly, before the global financial/economic collapse.

One particular aspect of what Thomas Cook offered was a high-priced corporate package, costing £6,500 per person. This package would include not only tickets for leading events at the games but also five-star hotel accommodation and fine dining in the UK capital city.

However, then the economic crash happened, and the demand for such expensive corporate packages did not materialize – in the suddenly changed economic conditions, the corporate market simply could not afford such luxuries. With only two months remaining before the event began, nearly a quarter of Thomas Cook's ticket allocation were unsold. Consequently the travel operator had to revisit its original plans, and began selling much cheaper packages, with no-frills deals reported to be starting at around £99 per person.

Source: based on author's own research and Hopwood, A. (2009).

Exercises

1) Explain why organizations might continually set aside and reformulate their budgets. Give more examples of, and discuss, organizations which you suspect may have (and why?) continually set aside and reformulated their plans in recent years.

2) What do you think Hopwood meant when he wrote that 'strategies are being constantly recast' and that organizations should be 'strategic rather than merely having a strategy'? Discuss the implications that such developments can have for management accounting.

Information technology

Over the past few decades, technological change has had a profound impact on management accounting. First, there has been considerable advance in production technology, including advanced manufacturing technologies (AMTs) such as computer-aided design and computer-aided manufacture (CAD/CAM), robotics (that is, automation) and flexible manufacturing systems. Also, there have been considerable advances in the way products and services are supplied and delivered to customers or clients. Such important developments in ways of working often require changes in organizational information, and will be highlighted throughout the textbook.

Information technology has also advanced significantly over recent decades. First, information preparation and dissemination is so much easier than it once was, less expensive and with incredible capacity nowadays. The extent and sheer pace of development in information technology really cannot be overstated. Personal computers, laptops, tablets and hand-held devices are liberally scattered around organizations, and computer-based technology is taken for granted.

Just a few decades ago, printing the monthly management accounting reports, comprising, say, 50 pages of mostly financial information, would normally require leaving a mainframe computer (roughly the size of a small university seminar room) to run overnight, and even longer in some cases (see Exhibit 1.4). Nowadays, given the appropriate software and adequate data source, a laptop or tablet can produce a management information pack within seconds! Then, the same networked laptop can also send this information to colleagues on the other side of the world, also within seconds. And, further still, many organizational managers nowadays can access specific real-time information systems from their desktop. To the student reader, many of whom have free access to networked Personal Computers (PCs) at their halls of residence such description of technological advance might simply be dismissed. And, yet, such descriptions should not be underestimated; they relate to a technological landscape that has undergone revolutionary change in a relatively short space of time.

The increased capacity of organizational computing has had a profound effect on the nature of work, information flows and, hence, on management accounting. And, this is set to expand further, and rapidly, in the immediate future due to such incredible innovations as 'cloud accounting' (see Chapter 21). In addition, organizations have a wealth of communication technologies at their disposal, for example, the Internet, intranets, email, mobile devices, tablets, social networking, video conferencing and e-business tools. Information today is extremely portable and can be as transparent as organizations allow.

Exhibit 1.4: A mainframe computer in the 1960s
Photo: @HultonArchive

Further advances in information technology (IT), is something that tomorrow's management accountants can take for granted, and they must keep up with new (and fast-emerging) developments – we will cover some of the latest technology throughout this textbook. But management accountants must also bear in mind what they are about where such technology is concerned. That is, although the future is bound to offer considerable new sources of data, as well as different ways to present information, it will be important to maintain that what matters is the provision of useful and relevant information to inform decision making – see Chapter 2 for elaboration of these points.

Management styles and organizational forms

Corporate trends, even fads, can have an impact on an organization's information needs and, by implication, on the demands of its management accounting practice. For instance, the type of organization, particularly its structure and normal 'ways of working' can have a significant bearing on the nature of management accounting practice within that organization. And, over time, organizational structures and ways of working can, and usually do, change.

For example, since the 1970s in particular, much of the industrialized corporate world has experienced a multitude of mergers and acquisitions, creating large global conglomerates. In recent decades, some extremely large organizations, including multinationals, have been created. This, in turn, has led to changes in the way that such organizations collate and use management information (see Chapter 18). More recently, a spate of organizational alliances, networks and outsourcing have incited new informational demands, hence new management accounting practices. Some organizations share common costs with their competitors, for instance when airline companies share airport facilities and provisions; and other organizations collaborate in their research and development activities. Some organizations link up formally with their suppliers to help ease their supplies process, while others readily share information with their customers.

Other developments in organizational forms that have an impact on informational requirements include the privatization of state-owned organizations, and the deregulation of public services. For instance, UK service organizations such as the utilities (gas, electricity and water suppliers) moved into unfamiliar territory during the 1980s and 1990s especially, where cost management and financial sustainability became more critical than ever before. At the same time, their markets were opened up, and competition rose markedly. The trend consequently has been for many of these service industries to move closer to the management accounting practices of private sector organizations.

Environmental and ethical matters

Ethics and environmental concerns have become a more significant feature of day-to-day organizational practice. Both have had an impact on the nature of information required in organizations and, thus, have had an effect on management accounting practice.

There has been increased attention to ethics particularly in the wake of various business and financial collapses and scandals, especially during the past decade. New and tighter regulations have emerged, including the Sarbanes–Oxley Act of 2002, demanding new and tighter quality standards which have to be adhered to in an organization's internal and external reporting processes.

The past decade has also witnessed an increased focus on, and a general concern for, the environment. The requirement for organizations to be managed in a sustainable way is something that has been embraced across the accounting profession, and embedding sustainable development in organizations is an area in which management accountants are becoming increasingly involved (Hopwood et al., 2010).

This concludes our summary of some of the key drivers of management accounting change over recent decades. It is the magnitude and intensity of such drivers that makes more recent times so different. That is, while things such as technological change and global competition were important in, say, the 1950s, such factors were nowhere near the scale or intensity of recent (or future!) times.

The accounting department and accountants' roles

The accounting department

Management accounting's boundaries have been extended considerably over the years, particularly so in the last two decades. Having said this, and as mentioned already, much of the so-called 'traditional' management accounting practices that first appeared nearly a century ago remain as popular as ever. Future economic, technological and organizational development more or less guarantees further changes in management accounting. And, being able to meet the ongoing challenge of both identifiable and less obvious informational and decision-making needs will be a key role for tomorrow's management accountants. In the remainder of this chapter, we consider these roles more closely, as well as the skills required by tomorrow's management accountants. But, first, we focus our attention more broadly on the accounting department.

Until quite recently, most organizations would have an accounting department (also commonly referred to as 'the finance function') that comprised all manner of accountants, including: financial accountants, management accountants, financial ledger managers, tax experts, internal auditors, and more. Such departments would comprise a mixture of professional accountants and accounting clerks. More often than not, the accounting department would also be somewhat remote in an organization, interacting only occasionally with others, for instance to discuss monthly accounting reports.

However, the past decade in particular has delivered significant change in this situation (Simons, 2007). Accounting departments nowadays can comprise different (and potentially separated) parts, namely:

- **Routine accounting** which consists of a relatively small number of specialists who oversee the more routine accounting tasks like external financial reporting, transaction processing, ledger management, simple accounting calculations such as costing or budgeting, taxation and internal audit. Such tasks nowadays are no less important; indeed some of these tasks have probably never been *so* important. However, advances in information technology mean that probably fewer individuals are now required to undertake such tasks and, in many instances, business managers themselves rather than accountants will undertake them. Some medium to large organizations will concentrate their entire routine accounting process in a common 'shared service', while other organizations have even outsourced routine accounting tasks to external partners (CIMA, 2008b).

- **Advisory accounting** which describes the increase of accountants' roles within management teams, and 'out in the field' as so-called business partners (CIMA, 2008a, 2008b). An increasing number of management accountants are using their financial astuteness and their expertise in producing and analysing information to assist all kinds of decision makers in *their* local activities. In other words, management accountants are plying their skills towards assisting multiple colleagues to understand and integrate both financial and non-financial implications of what they do in their parts of the organization.

Management accounting has become quite different, though clearly still connected, to other forms of accounting such as financial accounting. Yet, even if much of the day-to-day work of these advisory management accountants is alongside the business managers, as partners, some organizations still charge out the cost of these people (as costs of the accounting function) to the different business users. Whereas, other organizations have formally integrated their advisory management accountants within the various business units, therefore treating them as localized (business-unit) costs, and leaving a much smaller and more specialist centralized accounting department.

Accountants' roles

Management accountants perform an integrating role between day-to-day organizational activity and the pursuit of strategic goals. In so doing, this demands the provision of information to assist integration across multiple functions and departments – quite frequently spanning multiple country settings – and mobilizing both financial and non-financial aspects of organizational performance. The role of management accountants is thus crucially important for organizations who aim to make sensible decisions that will help the organization reach its strategic goals (see Chapter 17).

Management accountants are experts in the preparation, interpretation and use of organizational information. As such, they are often situated at the hub of intra- and extra-organizational flows of information. Traditionally their roles might have involved lengthy spells of score keeping; that is, routinely collating data, measuring and 'policing' colleagues against predominantly financial targets, and so on. In addition this traditional role would usually entail strict adherence to, and involvement in, a reporting cycle of routine accounting reports, budgets and more. However, as mentioned above, information technology advance has taken over a significant chunk of this kind of work; nowadays management accountants usually have the opportunity for more advisory and business-analytical roles, providing a broad range of management information in easily accessible formats. Accounting information compared, say, to the 1960s, is generally more proactive, feed-forward and strategic, and mixes both financial and non-financial outlooks to facilitate sound management decisions. In this respect there have been some important recent innovations in management accounting such as the balanced scorecard and rolling forecasts, both of which will be covered in more detail in later chapters.

However, traditional score-keeping roles have not disappeared. Other more traditional accountants' roles and traits – for example, stewardship, compliance, integrity, controllership and governance – are also no less important. Indeed, following the numerous highly publicised corporate scandals of the past decade, the sudden demise of well-known corporations, as well as the enduring global financial and economic instability, such traditional roles, especially cash-flow management, have probably never been more critical (Baldvinsdottir et al., 2009).

1.4: Management Accounting in Practice

The role of senior accountants in Tesco's

Many of today's management accountants are engaged in advisory roles which position them 'in the field', day to day, with fellow business managers and executives. However, as the following words from a senior finance executive in Tesco's, a large UK retail organization, indicate, this does not preclude the continuation of more long-standing accountants' roles such as 'keeping the score':

You have always got to do the basics. First of all, at the more junior levels in the organisation, our accountants do collate the numbers, they do keep the accounts. They do old-fashioned things like paying the bills and producing the management accounts. You have to keep the score, you have got to do the

basics in everything, and it is a big part of the job. But then, the hope is that they are part of the management team which runs the business, just another manager around the table. You are collectively responsible for the business, and I think every manager should have a view on everything else. As Finance Director, I sit around the table as an equal business person, with all the other Executives. And I have my say on things, the same as everybody else, on everything, ranging from the marketing of the business, to customers and more. But, at the same time, I am also responsible for the funding of the business. I have to go to the City, I have to talk to shareholders, and I have to do the nitty-gritty finance bits as well.

Source: based on author's own research and Baldvinsdottir, G., J. Burns, H. Norreklit and R. W. Scapens (2009).

Exercise

What do you think are some of the typical roles and activities for the Finance Executive of a mobile phone business, say for example, O2 mobile phones?

Tomorrow's advisory accountants work alongside their non-accounting colleagues, as integral members of eclectic management teams. They relate financial *and* non-financial accounting information to wider information flows within the organization, including strategic information, while also recognizing the potential limitations of management accounting, as well as exploiting and nurturing *informal* information and communication mechanisms. Supra-information systems, such as enterprise resource planning (ERP) systems (see Chapter 2), stacked up with powerful data management software such as 'business intelligence' (CIMA, 2008a), have also assisted in this process of redeveloping an accountant's role.

A typical view of today's roles for management accountants would include the following elements, few of which would have been in their job description 10 years ago:

- *Corporate strategy* – Composing, driving, overseeing and leading organizational strategy, on a global basis, rather than merely supporting the strategy process with routine/historic accounting information. Being close to the strategic heart of an organization and linking the 'strategic' (what we want to achieve) to the 'operational' (what we actually do).

- *Change management* – Driving, leading and managing organizational change, for example organizational restructuring, new systems implementation, or the acquisition of another organization. Again, management accountants will frequently do such things in a proactive rather than merely a supportive manner.

- *Customer-relationship management* – Not only working on ways to sustain the existing customer and client base, but also targeting and driving new markets and identifying new value-creating products or services. Most of all, management accountants would produce and communicate relevant information to the appropriate people, to better understand the needs of an organization's customers or clients.

- *Systems development* – Alongside information technology experts and statisticians, management accountants will design and oversee business systems development including, but not exclusively, the accounting systems. They lie at the hub of an organization's information flows and, as such, they will normally have an influence on the design, management and potential redevelopment of the information systems, with overall aim being to capture quality data that informs decision making.

- *Risk management* – Another key role for management accountants is identifying, measuring and monitoring risks, and, where possible, they will also help to avert such risks and/or minimize their damage. Organizations face multiple and often unpredictable risks – for instance, as a consequence of economic crises, wars, natural disasters, and more. And, part of a management accountant's role is to try and integrate such factors into their organization's financial and non-financial plans – if possible, before they happen.

All organizations differ, and so will the roles of management accountants. Although this list is far from exhaustive, it nevertheless gives a flavour of some of the roles which management accountants now engage in, alongside some of their more traditional roles like stewardship, control and internal audit. In practice, the future role of management accountants is likely to comprise a combination of the above as well as other, existing and emerging dimensions.

In many organizations, such roles can take place within and across the whole spectrum of organizational activities. As advisory members of the organizational team, or as 'business partners', management accountants are key players in driving new strategies and moulding value-adding activities throughout an organization, as well as instilling an ethos and 'ways of working' that are embedded in efficiency seeking and continuous improvement (see Chapter 16). Today's management accountants are experiencing and, in some cases, driving the shift from routine to more proactive accounting, and many hold central and dynamic roles within the broader management process. Many management accountants are no longer just support staff but are important generators of business value.

Having said that, and just to reiterate some of the key issues raised above, technical accounting expertise remains fundamental. Although nowadays we see greater empowerment of employees, and local business managers' ownership of accounting numbers, management accountants must still draw on their technical expertise to integrate both financial and non-financial performance measures into a coherent and comprehensive picture of overall business performance (Baldvinsdottir et al., 2010).

1.5: Management Accounting in Practice

The roles and skill-set of management accountants

One of the world's major professional bodies for management accounting is the Chartered Institute of Management Accountants (CIMA), who define the roles and skill-set of today's management accountants as follows:

Roles:

- Advise managers about the financial implications of projects.

- Explain the financial consequences of business decisions.

- Formulate business strategy.

- Monitor spending and financial control.

- Conduct internal business audits.

- Explain the impact of the competitive landscape.

Skill-set:

- Analysis – they analyse information and using it to make business decisions.

- Strategy – they formulate business strategy to create wealth and shareholder value.

- Risk – they identify and manage risk.

- Planning – they apply accounting techniques to plan and budget.

- Communication – they determine what information management needs and explain the numbers to non-financial managers.

Source: CIMA website, http://www.cimaglobal.com.

Exercise

Critically discuss the roles and skill-set as defined by CIMA (above). Do you disagree with any of these suggestions, or see problems or challenges in their application within particular organizational settings?

Skill requirements

It follows that as traditional roles remain important for management accountants, then traditional (or 'technical') accounting skills also remain important. Although these technical skills are by no means dominant nowadays, they are still assumed to be part of a management accountant's skill-set. Although powerful IT hardware and software programmes (combined) today perform much of the accounting techniques that not so long ago would normally entail significant manual calculation, it is still important to know the underlying mechanics. Just as students should learn the rudimentary principles of mathematics before falling back on the comfort of a calculator, all management accountants should understand the core principles of management accounting techniques.

Technical skills, some of which have existed for many decades and others which are more recent, borne out in the various tools and techniques that are presented in this textbook, are essential acumen for tomorrow's management accountants. But, by themselves such technical skills are insufficient for tomorrow's management accountant. The following extract highlights some of the important non-technical aspects of a management accountant's skills-set:

> *Making sensible choices about adopting (management accounting) innovations and driving those choices to the implementation stage is likely to become a key role for management accountants. It may well stretch their technical abilities and also require a grasp of the broader implementation issues involved – e.g., how they affect the way organisations behave. [...] one CFO reflected on a failed attempt to introduce a new management accounting technique to his company: 'The intellectual merit of the (accounting) technique was hard to question; it's not that it was flawed. But you have got to be able to marry two things up. One is that the technique actually leads you to the right conclusion – and it certainly did. The other is that it's something that will work within your organisation'.*
> *(Baldvinsdottir et al., 2009, p. 34)*

Accordingly, in this textbook we will cover a significant amount of the technical and calculative tools and techniques which management accountants need to master, but we will also supplement these with broader understandings, and the sorts of broader issues facing today's advisory management accountant. Today's management accountants also require both hard and soft skills, such as the following.

Hard skills

- *IT proficiency* – Ability to assist information technology experts and statisticians in the design and development of information systems, integrating the latest (and best suited) technologies. This includes, but is not exclusive to, the accounting systems; which, for an increasing number of organizations, forms part of supra-integrated information systems (see Chapter 21) such as enterprise resource planning systems, packaged with data management software and tools.

- *Broad business understandings* – As described above, management accountants oversee a great deal of the information that flows within and between different parts of an organization. They therefore need a broad organizational acumen, while not necessarily needing to master everything, so that they are then able to help their less quantitative or financially astute colleagues to assess local performance and make key local decisions.

Soft skills

- *Communication* – As management accountants will be collaborating with colleagues from all around an organization, they will also need to be able to communicate effectively. This includes an ability to relate management accounting information to the various users in an organization, and in a manner that is understood by those users.

- *Interpersonal* – Not unrelated, management accountants interact frequently with non-accountants. And, if they are expected to contribute towards the activity and decisions of management teams, they need strong interpersonal skills, as well as an ability to nurture good relationships and trust with colleagues across the organization.

- *Conviction* – The expertise of management accountants can often place them in situations where they can influence very important (for example, high-level, strategic) decisions. They must therefore show strong conviction, and be convincing, in pushing through their ideas which, in turn, requires dealing with different personalities, levels of seniority, and mindsets.

Aspiring management accountants

Over the past decade or so we have probably been witnessing the emergence of 'something different', something removed from traditional management accounting. The role of many management accountants has to an extent become removed from score keeping (though the latter has by no means disappeared) and is more about support for managerial decision making and problem solving at multiple organizational levels, as well as working in a forward-looking advisory capacity.

What should aspiring management accountants therefore be learning in their education and/ or training, especially as groundwork for a rewarding career in one of the advisory or business-partner roles? First, a solid grasp of management accounting techniques, both traditional and new, is essential; these techniques remain the foundational tools-of-the-trade. But, such technical know-how is by itself insufficient. Management accountants increasingly work in cross-functional management teams; thus, second, they require a broad knowledge of organizations and management-type issues. In other words, tomorrow's management accountants need to be able to apply their technical accounting skills and know-how to multiple (and changing) aspects of organizational life. This may therefore require the core techniques of management accounting to be used differently, or even changed, as situations or settings change.

No single textbook can cater for all such skills and knowledge. However, this textbook provides a starting point for the aspiring management accountants of today. It thus covers:

1) Both traditional and more recent management accounting techniques.

2) Non-technical aspects of accounting and, more broadly, organizational activity.

3) The interface between (1) and (2).

Chapter summary

The intention of this chapter was to set the scene for tomorrow's world of management accounting, including its definition and an understanding of the key drivers of change. We have also explored the roles and skills requirements of tomorrow's advisory management accountants. Such background is important to be able to position both the traditional and the new management accounting techniques that make up a substantial part of this textbook.

Key terms

Advisory accounting Where management accountants work as integral members of management teams, as 'business partners', using their financial astuteness and analytical skills to assist all kind of decision making (p. 15)

Business partners A recent description of some management accountants' role, one of being adviser (consulting-like) to organizational managers outside of the accounting department (p. 5)

Control The process through which managers seek to ensure that their plans are being put into action, for example through monitoring and reporting activities (p. 5)

Cost accounting A narrower application (subset) of management accounting, which concentrates on an organization's acquisition or consumption of resources (p. 10)

Drivers of management accounting change Factors which cause shifts in the information requirements of business managers, hence affecting and potentially changing management accounting (p. 5)

Financial accounting The process of collating information for the purpose of external financial reports, the most obvious of which would be the 'glossy' annual financial statements (p. 9)

Information Assists business managers in making decisions; a building block of organizational knowledge and learning, the production of which rests to a large extent with management accountants (p. 4)

Management accounting The provision of information to assist organizational decision making (p. 4)

Performance measurement Where managers assess an organization's actual performance against its planned activity, as well as continually gauging the likelihood of achieving organizational goals (p. 9)

Planning Where managers select from alternative options such that their decisions (combined) will assist towards achievement of organizational goals (p. 5)

Roles The ways in which accountants become involved in, and assist, organizational decision-making (p. 5)

Routine accounting Tasks that nowadays are largely organized automatically via advances in IT and software, for example, financial reporting, transaction processing, ledger management, taxation and internal audit (p. 15)

Sustainable development A term which describes organizations attempting to develop its activities in a financially rewarding way but not at the expense of costs incurred on society or the environment (p. 11)

Systems The hardware and software which facilitates the collation of data and the processing of information (p. 7)

Techniques An array of calculative methods that allow organizations to structure their problems and offer alternative actions (p. 4)

Review questions • • • • • • • • • • • • connect • • • •

Level of difficulty:	BASIC	INTERMEDIATE	ADVANCED

1.1 Identify possible users of management accounting information in the retail companies, for example, Jack Wills. **[LO1, LO2]**

1.2 Define and explain the three components of an organization's formal management accounting configuration. **[LO1, LO2]**

1.3 Explain why ethics has recently become an important aspect of a management accountant's organizational role. **[LO1, LO4, LO7]**

1.4 Describe the three main objectives of management accounting. **[LO2]**

1.5 What are the main differences between management accounting and (1) financial accounting and (2) cost accounting? **[LO5]**

1.6 Distinguish between 'routine accounting' and 'advisory accounting'. **[LO6, LO7]**

1.7 Describe some of the more traditional roles of management accountants, and explain why such roles remain just as important today. **[LO2, LO6, LO7]**

1.8 Explain the impact which globalization and technological advance have had on management accounting in the past two decades. **[LO3, LO4]**

1.9 Describe the possible roles of an advisory (business partner) management accountant. **[LO6]**

• • • Group discussion and activity questions • • • • • • • • •

1.10 This question will require some research. Search for/take a look at the websites for the Chartered Institute of Management Accountants (CIMA) and the Institute of Management Accountants (IMA). Seek out, compare and contrast their respective definitions of management accounting. **[LO1]**

1.11 Browse as many job descriptions as you can find for 'management accountants'. Search employment agencies on the Internet, look at the websites of professional accountancy bodies (for example), and list the most common skills and attributes which the job descriptions include. Which of these skills listed do you think have been a requirement for many years, and which do you think are quite recent? **[LO1, LO6, LO7]**

1.12 Describe some of the likely differences between management accounting undertaken in: (1) a private sector commercial business, for example Philips Electronics, (2) a public sector organization, for example a hospital, and (3) a charity organization, for example UNICEF. **[LO1, LO2, LO3]**

1.13 What is management accounting, and critically appraise to what extent, how, and why it has changed in recent decades? **[LO1, LO2, LO4]**

1.14 Which is most important to organizations – financial accounting or management accounting? **[LO5]**

1.15 Having undertaken some research, for example via the Internet and/or via articles read, describe what you predict to be the important skills for tomorrow's 'business partner' management accountants? **[LO1, LO2, LO3, LO4, LO7]**

• • • Exercises • • • • • • • • • • • • • • • connect™ • • •

E1.1 **Defining management accounting [LO1, LO2]**

Cost accounting is a broader and more complex discipline than management accounting: true or false?

E1.2 **Objectives of management accounting [LO1, LO2]**

Fill in the missing word:

Three major objectives of using management accounting information are for (1) planning, (2) performance measurement, and (3) _____.

E1.3 **Management accountants' roles [LO6, LO7]**

Which of the following would not normally be a primary role associated with management accountants?

a) The provision of information to organizational managers

b) Reporting financial performance to external stakeholders

c) Assisting managers to make business decisions

d) Partnering with senior managers to achieve strategic goals.

E1.4 **Management accountants' roles [LO1, LO2, LO6, LO7]**

Fill in the missing word:

A management accountant, when acting in the capacity as an adviser (or consultant) to managers outside of the accounting department is known as a business _____.

E1.5 **Drivers of management accounting change [LO4]**

Listed below are some causes that drove the changes in management accounting.

1) Fewer barriers to trade allowing access to more information about one's competitors.

2) Emergence of stricter and tighter regulations such as Sarbanes–Oxley Act of 2002.

3) Increased focus on quality and customer satisfaction as today's customers are choosy and discriminating.

4) Improved dissemination of financial data owing to innovations such as cloud accounting.

5) Newer informational demands due to the growth in organizational alliances, networks and outsourcing.

Required:

Identify each of them as caused by changes in:

- Global economic and financial environment
- Information technology
- Management styles and organizational forms
- Environmental and ethical concerns.

E1.6 **Drivers of management accounting change [LO4]**

Which of the following is least likely to be a key driver of change and development in management practice?

a) Environmental and ethical regulation

b) Information technology

c) International financial reporting standards

d) The economic and financial environmental.

E1.7 **Skill requirements of the management accountant [LO7]**

Listed below are some of the hard and soft skills that management accountants need to possess. Categorize each skill as either a hard or a soft skill. Furthermore, identify the category of hard or soft skill that each one falls into from the following: Broad business understanding, communication, conviction, interpersonal or IT Proficiency.

Description	Hard skill/Soft skill	Category
1) Ability to provide information in a manner which is easily understood by the users		
2) Ability to design the accounting system that is to be implemented in the organization		
3) General understanding of each process of the organization		
4) Ability to influence the decision-making process with new and better ideas		
5) Ability to nurture good relationships with colleagues across the organization		

E1.8   **Terms and definitions in management accounting [LO1,2,4,5,6]**

Match the following descriptions with the terms provided in the table below.

Description	Term
1) A subset of management accounting that concentrates on an organization's acquisition or consumption of resources	a) Balanced scorecard
2) Factors which cause shifts in the information requirements of business managers, hence affecting and potentially changing management accounting	b) Cost accounting
3) One of the contemporary tools of management accounting that helps in integrating financial and non-financial goals of an organization	c) Drivers of management accounting change
4) The management accounting objective where managers select from alternative options such that their decisions are geared towards achieving organizational goals	d) Financial accounting
5) The process of collating information for the purpose of external financial reports at a particular point in time	e) Organizational control
6) The process through which managers seek to ensure that their plans are being put into action	f) Organizational planning

E1.9   **Objectives of management accounting [LO2]**

Management accounting information plays a major role in organizational planning, organizational control and performance measurement.

Required:

Which of the following exhibits the use of management accounting information in organizational planning? (Select all that apply.)

a)   Jumbo Cola planned a production of 2.4 billion cans this year, implying a monthly production target of 0.2 billion per month. The production department manager implemented a daily production report to monitor the production level on a daily basis. This was done to ensure they hit production targets every month.

b)   Playons Ltd. is considering various regions for expanding its operations. The management accounting report shows the Philippines as the most profitable region among all the alternatives being considered, as the cost of operations will be low.

c)   The compensation structure of managers of Dice Decorators entitles them to receive 10% of profits that are above the set target as bonus. This year, profits were expected to be 10 million, but actual profits were only 7.5 million. As a result, the managers did not receive any bonus.

d)   Knight Ltd. is a producer of a variety of roller skates in Manchester, U.K. The company received a merger proposal from Hood Ltd., which produces Heelys and other complimenting sporting goods in Dublin. Knight is now considering whether to accept or reject the merger proposal.

E1.10   **The nature of management accounting information [LO1, LO2, LO3]**

Give an example of management accounting information which could possibly assist a manager to make decisions in respect to the following scenarios:

a)   The Marketing Director of a medium-sized retail company in Argentina is considering whether or not to launch a website for the purpose of starting Internet sales.

b)   Owners of a well-known (but in recent times, poorly performing) football team in the premier division of the Netherlands.

c) Executives of (high-class) car manufacturers in Italy, who are considering the outsourcing of after-sales services.

d) The Vice-Chancellor of a lead university in Belgium who is being pressured to utilize, at considerable financial and other cost, scarce 'green areas' to build necessary additional student accommodation on campus.

e) The manager of a fairly new 'sensation' boy band (already with two No. 1 hits in the UK music charts) who is considering taking this band (4 male singers, all under the age of 19) on a three-month tour of Europe, playing gigs at large arena stadiums.

f) The organizers of a large football tournament in Germany (involving global celebrities and ex/retired professional footballers), being held to raise as much cash as possible for a well-known developing-world charity.

E1.11 Outsourcing [LO2, LO3, LO6]

Outsourcing is where an organization allows an outside party to provide goods or services that used to be provided inside the organization. Take a medium-sized orange-juice manufacturer in Spain which is considering whether to outsource its canteen in a factory where 150 employees work. From a management accountant's perspective, assess the potential positives and negatives of implementing such change.

E1.12 Drivers of management accounting change [LO4]

Explain how globalization, advanced technologies, management styles, organizational forms, sustainable development and ethics can impact or change an organization's management accounting practices.

E1.13 Sustainable development and management accounting [LO1, LO2, LO4, LO6, LO7]

According to the Bruntland Report, sustainable development is about 'meeting the needs of the present without compromising the ability of future generations to meet their own needs' (World Commission on Environment and Development, 1987, p. 8). With this statement as context, critically assess how tomorrow's management accountants can contribute towards making progress in sustainable development.

E1.14 The external image of accountants [LO1, LO2, LO6, LO7]

In recent years there has been a not-insignificant amount of, and sometimes quite critical, academic and professional literature on the external/society image of management accountants and the management accounting profession in general. Basically, so the story goes, the 'dull and boring scorekeeper' of 20 years ago and more has, it is argued, been largely replaced by more proactive, dynamic and consulting-like business partners. Do some research, via the Internet and articles (for example, Baldvinsdottir et al., 2010) and critically assess whether you think there is a 'best' type of image for management accountants to portray of themselves in society.

E1.15 Management accounting and financial accounting [LO5]

Élan is a newly established, industrial design company. To fill the roles in its accounting department, the company recently hired Katie as the financial accountant and Joshua as the management accountant.

Required:

The following table lists various roles of Katie and Joshua. Identify and mark the roles of each of these employees. (Mark "X" in the applicable column; select only one)

Roles	Katie	Joshua
1) Collating information for the purpose of external reporting and to feed into organizational decision making		
2) Identifying new value-creating products or services		
3) Designing business systems and overseeing their development		
4) Ensuring that taxes are duly and correctly filed		
5) Identifying, measuring and monitoring risks		
6) Ensuring compliance with accounting rules and regulations		
7) Collecting information from financial statements and other sources to measure performance		
8) Preparing financial statements to present an aggregated view of the financial well-being of the organization at a particular point in time		

E1.16   **The rules and routine nature of management accounting [LO1, LO2, LO7]**

Read the article J. Burns and R. W. Scapens (2000) 'Conceptualizing management accounting change: an institutional framework', *Management Accounting Research*, 11(1), pp. 3–25* and answer the following questions:

a)   Define, and give examples, of how an organization's management accounting practices can be underpinned to an extent by formal rules, then over time become routine and institutionalized.

b)   What is the real significance for an organization when (at least part of) its management accounting practice becomes routine and institutionalized?

c)   How do extra-organizational factors (for example, global economic conditions, IT, regulation) impact and change management accounting rules and routines?

d)   In your view, what should management accountants be wary of, and do, in organizations where management accounting practices appear on the face of it to have become highly institutionalized?

* *A link to the article is available online at www.mcgraw-hill.co.uk/textbooks/burns.*

• • • • **Case study problem** • • • • • • • • • • • **connect**™ • • •

C1.1   **Butt PLC [LO1, LO2, LO3, LO4, LO6, LO7]**

Butt PLC is the UK manufacturing business for a multinational pharmaceuticals organization. It is an example of where there has been significant change in management accountants' roles, but where changes in management accounting techniques and systems have been minimal. In this organization, management accountants now spend a great deal of their time assisting the business managers on a daily basis, in an advisory capacity.

During much of the 1990s, Butt PLC enjoyed a near-monopoly position in its markets, due to patents on several very profitable medicines. However, such a powerful position was altered by a number of significant external factors, namely:

1)   Cessation of the patents of Butt PLC's two most profitable products

2)   Increased government restrictions on health spending in the UK

3)   Intensified global competition (including mergers among major competitors).

Butt PLC's response was a radical change programme, which included business process re-engineering, various IT projects, new product innovation, activity analysis and, importantly, process ways of working (PWW). Process ways of working involved the reorganization and realignment of individual products to individual sites, where each would also fall under the control of a unique 'process leader'. Previously, Butt PLC had been a rather functionally based organization, with various functions located at different sites across the UK. However, following the introduction of PWW, individual products were now entirely dedicated to one site, from receipt of a product's original order through to the final customer delivery. As a result, many functional departments were either radically reduced in size, or else completely disbanded, and most staff were redeployed in the process/product stream. Only three centralized departments retained their non-process-stream status: accounting, IT and quality assurance. These three departments charge the respective process streams for any specialist services provided.

Prior to the introduction of PWW, the accounting function had been quite centralized, with most of their accountants performing such duties as transaction processing, financial reporting and clerical-type financial management. Post-PWW, however, the nature of accountant's roles changed markedly. Overall the number of staff within the accounting department rapidly declined from 120 to 60 staff, a hit that was mostly taken by staff involved in transaction processing and financial reporting. The bulk of remaining accountants (post-PWW) worked within the process streams, alongside managers in such expertise areas as sales, marketing, operations and engineering. These people combined their accounting knowledge with a growing understanding of process stream business. They particularly advised process stream leaders on strategic business issues, and assisted other managers with local process-stream-oriented decisions.

Much of the data used by the accountants was managed within the process streams. A primary task for the accountants was to collate such data in a form which satisfied the managers' information needs, and in a format which could be widely understood. Particular emphasis was placed on forecasting, or 'feed-forward-oriented' information that would help managers to continually gauge where their activities were likely heading as opposed to merely confirming what they had been doing. Budgets remained as an overall management framework for the year, but forecasts received most day-to-day management attention. Moreover, as the forecasts were generated internally from within the process streams rather than imposed from outside, there was a greater feeling of ownership about this information, as well as a commitment to do better in forecast terms.

Post-PWW, one of the main challenges faced by the accounting department was how best to (re)structure itself, and particularly where the accountants working in process streams should be physically located. There was, for instance, much debate over whether these accountants should report directly to senior managers in the accounting department or to the process stream leader(s). Also, there was questioning as to whether these accountants should be charged out as an overhead by the accounting department to the process streams, or be classified as indirect costs within the process streams.

Source: Case summary adapted from Burns, J. and G. Baldvinsdottir (2005).

Required:

1) What kind of external factors had a changing influence on the role(s) of Butt PLC's management accountants, and why?

2) Should accountants working within process streams be located alongside the process stream managers, rather than being physically more remote in a centralized accounting office?

3) Describe in more detail what you think 'PWW' involved, and how you think it affected the nature of management accounting (systems, techniques and roles) in Butt PLC?

4) Following the implementation of PWW, do you think that the process stream managers (with backgrounds in engineering, operations, research, marketing, and so on) will have a different perception of the accountants who aligned themselves to the process streams?

● ● ● ● Recommended reading ● ● ● ● ● ● ● ● ● ● ● ● ● ● ● ● ● ●

- Burchell, S., C. Clubb, A. Hopwood and J. Hughes (1980) 'The roles of accounting in organizations and society', *Accounting, Organizations and Society*, 5(1), pp. 5–27.

A classic academic article which in the early 1980s went against the grain, and viewed management accounting as much more than a technique for 'optimal' business solutions, and alerted its readers to a wider perspective on the issues at stake.

- CIMA (2008a) 'Improving decision making in organisations: unlocking business intelligence', The Chartered Institute of Management Accountants, September, London: CIMA.

A paper on IT developments (in particular, 'business intelligence'), and its implication for decision making in organizations.

- CIMA (2008b) 'Improving decision making in organisations: the opportunity to transform finance', The Chartered Institute of Management Accountants, December, London: CIMA.

An overview of contemporary issues in management accounting, and specifically in relation to management accountants' roles.

- Hopwood, A. and P. Miller (1994) *Accounting as Social and Institutional Practice*, Cambridge: Cambridge University Press.

The entire collection of articles are extremely worth the read in respect of digesting accounting as more than just a technical/calculative phenomena, but at least read the 'Introduction' chapter by P. Miller, outstanding views of accounting.

- IFAC (2008) 'The crucial roles of professional accountants in business in mid-sized enterprises', an information paper published by the International Federation of Accountants, Professional Accountants in Business Committee, New York, September, downloaded from http://www.ifac.org.

This paper is a useful and interesting collection of practitioner-written commentaries on the roles of accountants. Particularly helpful in this paper, however, is the focus on medium-sized organizations whereas most other literature tends to focus on large organizations.

● ● ● References ●

Baldvinsdottir, G., J. Burns, H. Nørreklit and R. W. Scapens (2009) 'The management accountant's role', *Financial Management* (CIMA), September, pp. 33–4.

Baldvinsdottir, G., J. Burns, H. Nørreklit and R. W. Scapens (2010) 'Risk manager or risqué manager: the new platform for the management accountant', CIMA Research Executive Summary Series, 6(2).

Burchell, S., C. Clubb, A. Hopwood and J. Hughes (1980) 'The roles of accounting in organizations and society', *Accounting, Organizations and Society*, 5(1), pp. 5–27.

Burns, J. and G. Baldvinsdottir (2005) 'An institutional perspective of accountants' new roles – the interplay of contradictions and praxis', *European Accounting Review*, 14(4), pp. 725–57.

Burns, J. and R. W. Scapens (2000) 'Conceptualizing management accounting change', *Management Accounting Research*, 11(1), pp. 3–25.

Busco, C., A. Riccaboni and R. W. Scapens (2006) 'Trust for accounting and accounting for trust', *Management Accounting Research*, 17(1), pp. 11–41.

CIMA (2008a) 'Improving decision making in organisations: unlocking business intelligence', Chartered Institute of Management Accountants, September, London: CIMA.

CIMA (2008b) 'Improving decision making in organisations: the opportunity to transform finance', Chartered Institute of Management Accountants, December, London: CIMA.

CIMA (2009a) 'Management accounting tools for today and tomorrow', Chartered Institute of Management Accountants, November, London: CIMA.

CIMA (2009b) 'Improving decision-making in organisations: the opportunity to reinvent finance business partners', July, London: CIMA.

Collier, P. (2001) 'The power of accounting: a field study of local financial management in a police force', *Management Accounting Research*, 12(4), pp. 465–86.

Hopwood, A. and P. Miller (1994) *Accounting as Social and Institutional Practice*, Cambridge: Cambridge University Press.

Hopwood, A. (2009) 'The economic crisis and accounting: implications for the research community', *Accounting, Organizations and Society*, 34, pp. 797–802.

Hopwood, A., J. Unerman and J. Fries (2010) *Accounting for Sustainability*, Earthscan.

IFAC (2008) 'The crucial roles of professional accountants in business in mid-sized enterprises', an information paper published by the International Federation of Accountants, Professional Accountants in Business Committee, New York, September.

Roberts, J. and R. W. Scapens (1985) 'Accounting systems and systems of accountability – understanding accounting practices in their organisational context', *Accounting, Organizations and Society*, 10(4), pp. 43–56.

Schiller, B. (2012) 'Transport's cleaner future', *Financial Management* (CIMA magazine), February, pp. 26–30.

Simons, P. (2007) 'Transforming finance', *Financial Management* (CIMA), November, pp. 36–7.

Wilson, E. (2011) 'Managing volatility', *Financial Management* (CIMA), June, pp. 26–30.

World Commission on Environment and Development (1987) *Our Common Future*, (Brentland Report), Oxford: Oxford University Press.

When you have read this chapter

Log on to the Online Learning Centre at **www.mcgraw-hill.co.uk/textbooks/burns** to explore chapter-by-chapter test questions, links and further online study tools for Management Accounting.

CHAPTER 2

INFORMATION AND MANAGEMENT ACCOUNTING

Chapter outline

- The emergence of management accounting

- More contemporary developments

- The information process

- Constitutive aspects of management accounting information

- Information technologies

Learning outcomes

On completion of this chapter, students will be able to:

LO1 Appreciate the importance of management accounting information

LO2 Convey some knowledge of the historical development of management accounting

LO3 Know and be able to explain key aspects of the *Relevance Lost* thesis

LO4 Discuss more contemporary developments in management accounting information

LO5 Describe essential qualities and characteristics of management accounting information

LO6 Explore the more constitutive nature of management accounting information

LO7 Recite the key users, and multiple demands of management accounting information

LO8 Highlight key sources of management accounting information

LO9 Appreciate the significance of *non*-financial management accounting information

Introduction

In Chapter 1, we highlighted the importance of *information* to an organization and its external stakeholders. Moreover, we described the pivotal role played by management accountants in designing, implementing and overseeing an organization's information base. It would seem sensible at an early stage to consider more deeply this notion of information.

The term **information** describes when **data**, that is raw facts and figures, come to be useful and meaningful to its users, and subsequently has potential to influence their decision making. Typically, management accounting information is said to be especially useful for informing decisions (and, subsequently, actions) relating to organizational planning, control and measurement.

Management accounting information constitutes a key component of an organization's overall stock of information. It sits alongside other key sources of information, for instance information deriving from an operations department, the marketing unit, research and development, distribution, packaging, and more. Normally management accounting information comprises part of an integrated (or enterprise-wide) information system, stacked up with data management software such as 'business intelligence' tools (CIMA, 2008).

No more than 20 years ago, most organizations would comprise multiple localized information systems, attached to various parts of the organization. For instance there could be a production information system, a marketing system, a materials procurement system, an accounting system and a personnel system. While all of these systems were crucially important to the functional locale in which they were situated, the respective systems rarely connected or 'spoke' to one another – there was no integration of systems, and software technology was not advanced enough at that time for such things to occur.

During and before this time, accountants commanded a general perception of being 'information experts' within an organization, not least because they were the people who gathered data and produced the information which encapsulated how well or how badly an organization was performing in financial/monetary terms. To most organizations, this financially oriented perspective was ultimately what mattered the most.

Nowadays the situation is very different. Database technology, and supra-information systems offer massive information capacity in an organization, and information which is increasingly integrated, holistic, real time and accurate. Furthermore, today's information systems comprise the accounting or finance element as only a part (albeit an important part) of their whole, and more managers are conversant in such information systems, not just accountants. At the same time there is anecdotal evidence that non-accounting business managers in today's organizations know much better than their contemporaries of 20 years ago *what* information they want, and how to get it. This could be accessed via the management accountants, but is not necessarily the case as much as it was. The management accountant probably still has the mantle of a 'font of information' in many organizations, but he or she likely needs to work harder, adapt, and develop, to maintain the assumption of 'information expert' in the future.

All too frequently, in our everyday lives we take for granted the information at our disposal. Nowadays, there is a raft of ways to access information, not least via the power and capacity presented by computing, digital, wi-fi and Internet technologies. As mentioned above, traditionally management accountants have a reputation for being experts of information. That is, they are the assumed by many to be masters, gatekeepers and innovators of an organization's information base. This, in turn, can position management accountants at the front end of information technology design and implementation, although usually in collaboration with IT specialists and statisticians.

Management accountants must understand and manage intra- and extra-organizational information flows and requirements (including the interface between the two), in their broad context. We will focus on some of these broader aspects to an organization's management accounting information in this chapter. In later chapters, we will then be better equipped to position some of the tools and techniques that actually produce management accounting information within organizations.

Our coverage in this chapter is as follows. First, we begin by providing some background to how management accounting has evolved through time to a situation of being one of the main sources of information in organizations. This first part of the chapter also describes key arguments of a book entitled *Relevance Lost* (Johnson and Kaplan, 1987) which represents a milestone in the development of present-day management accounting. Next, we discuss some of the more contemporary developments for management accounting information within today's organizations. Then, we explore the information process in more detail and, finally, we cast light on some of the main sources of management accounting information in today's organizations.

The emergence of management accounting

As was explained in Chapter 1, both the reshaping *and* endurance of particular aspects of management accounting practice in recent decades have to a large extent been driven by the changing context in which such practice operates. And, all through this process, the main anchor is business managers' demands for *information*.

However, prevalent management accounting practices have probably not always reflected the current information demands of business managers (albeit maybe not knowingly). In fact, as we discuss below, there was a stage in the history of management accounting, more specifically around the mid-1980s, where influential scholars at Harvard Business School claimed that management accounting practices at that time were providing anything but useful or relevant information to business managers. In this part of the chapter, we provide a brief overview of the development of management accounting practices and especially highlight the extent to which its development has (or has not) been influenced by managers' changing information needs.

Historical development of management accounting practice

The origins of management accounting probably date back to the first quarter of the nineteenth century, with the start of the Industrial Revolution, in developed countries such as parts of Western Europe, the USA and Japan. Organizations emerged, as business trading became more complex, owners employed managers to run their businesses, managers employed staff to do the work, new scientific management techniques started to appear, and more. In a nutshell, the birth of organizations, and the whole growing complexity surrounding them, meant there was a need for more business management information that could suitably inform decision making in much more complicated scenarios. So, for the next century or so, multiple new management tools were developed that would present managers with useful and relevant information which their organizations required. This was the beginnings of management accounting as we now know it.

From the early 1800s until the 1920s most of the basic management accounting tools and techniques, which still exist to this day, had been designed and were being used by organizations at that time. For instance, businesses discovered that they had greater need to control their costs of production, to measure their efficiency (or inefficiency) in operations, to calculate returns on their investments, and more. So from the early 1800s until the early 1900s is when basic management accounting tools such as budgeting, standard costing, variance analysis and payback calculations were invented – see later chapters in the book for more details on such tools. By the 1920s, management accounting had well and truly taken shape, and its constituent parts to that point had been influenced by the changing and growing informational demands of organizational managers.

The *Relevance Lost* debate

Then there followed a period of stagnation in the development of management accounting, lasting some 60 years, as claimed by Johnson and Kaplan in their influential book ***Relevance Lost*** (Johnson and Kaplan, 1987). No new management accounting tools or techniques had emerged in the period from the mid-1920s to the mid-1980s. However, during the same 60-year period, the landscape in which organizations operated had altered substantially. For example, there had been considerable growth in international competition and trade, significant advances in technology, and much more. The information requirements of business managers by the 1980s were so different and more complex than they had been in the 1920s (even if many managers did not necessarily realize this at the time). Hence the title of Johnson and Kaplan's book – management accounting had *lost its relevance* in terms of providing useful information to inform managers' decision making.

Management accounting had failed to develop in a manner which would continue to support (changing) managers' informational demands.

There were several key reasons why this had happened, according to Johnson and Kaplan. First, it was claimed that management accounting had become subservient to financial accounting, and that a 'financial accounting mentality' had become dominant in most organizations. Financial accounting continued to be shaped (*and* constrained) by professional regulations and company statute in the twentieth century, whereas management accounting remained subject to professional guidelines but was not heavily regulated or controlled through company law.

During this time it was not feasible for an organization to have two accounting systems (that is, one for financial accounting and another for management accounting). The information technology which exists today and which allows both financial and management accounting to be carried out using the same single set of data was not yet available. And, to have two separate accounting systems would be just too expensive an option for the majority of organizations at that time. So, there was little choice but to adopt accounting systems which were geared primarily towards financial accounting, since the latter was required by law. Importantly, this meant that organizations were making business decisions based on information which, as Johnson and Kaplan stressed, was not ideal and was potentially quite damaging.

A second reason, it is claimed, for the stagnation of management accounting in the sixty years since the 1920s was a general lack of pressure to change and innovate. The period was one of incredible growth and economic success for many of the countries (and their indigenous organizations) which had been using management accounting tools and techniques. Fast-expanding markets, plus competition that was mostly localized, meant that many organizations in the USA, Japan and Western Europe were able to mass produce and undercut any potential competitors. Thus, during this time there was little incentive to change, among the organizations which might have been expected to drive innovation in management accounting tools and techniques.

In their book, Johnson and Kaplan alerted the global business world to the dangers of having no innovation in management accounting since the 1920s. The information being drawn from (financial accounting-dominated) accounting systems, they argued, was not fit for purpose in respect of informing managers' decision making: 'Today's management accounting information, driven by the procedures and cycle of the organization's financial reporting system, is too late, too aggregated, and too distorted to be relevant for managers' planning and control decisions' (Johnson and Kaplan, 1987, p. 1). They called for more innovation in management accounting. In particular they called for the development of new management accounting tools that would provide more accurate costing information (rather than basic cost information which is geared towards financial accounting), improved techniques for measuring and evaluating business performance, identifying operational efficiencies and for better control of far more complex and diversified organizations. This was essentially their call for such new management accounting techniques as activity-based costing (see Chapter 6) and the balanced scorecard (see Chapter 17), and on which Kaplan later had considerable influence in their original design.

Relevance Lost is a milestone book in the history of management accounting, a book which seemingly re-channelled the profession back towards the provision of useful and relevant information for business managers. By the late 1980s, the landscape for organizations was incomparable to what it had been in the 1920s when most 'traditional' management accounting tools and techniques had already been devised. As we covered in the previous chapter, such change drivers as globalization, competition, information technology and new organizational forms had carved out an organizational world where the information requirements of managers had become something very different. Since then, we have witnessed the design and introduction of numerous new management accounting tools and techniques, although as was explained in the previous chapter these seem to have supplemented traditional tools, plus management accounting tools are by no means nowadays the *only* source of management information.

More contemporary developments

Having described the historical development of management accounting, in this section we now explore some of the more recent developments in the nature and use of management accounting information in organizations.

The management accounts

The management accounts traditionally comprised documentation and reports which accountants presented on a regular basis to senior managers in an organization, say in time for the monthly executive meeting. They should be distinguished from the 'financial accounts' which, by comparison, are presented on an annual (or sometimes bi-annual or quarterly) basis to shareholders, investors and other interested parties.

The **management accounts** are an aggregated depiction of an organization's (monthly, year-to-date) financial and non-financial results that help managers to keep in touch with their organization's underlying short- and long-run position. Traditionally they have represented a rather historical and *feed-backward* depiction of organizational performance (see Exhibit 2.1), and comprised predominantly financially oriented data. Thus, the management accounts traditionally would have been rather limited in so far as indicating and informing whether or not an organization is developing in a sustainable (and, for commercial enterprises at least, a profit-generating) way.

An important distinction to be made is that between what we call 'feed-backward information' and 'feed-forward information'. Feed-backward information is that which is used *after the event*. This kind of information assists managers to evaluate how well or how badly their organization has performed against previously set targets. A traditional budgeting system (see Chapter 8) would be an example of a feed-backward information system, whereby managers compare actual results (for example, turnover, costs) to original targets in the budget.

Feed-backward information undoubtedly still has its purpose today, confirmed by the continual popularity of traditional budgeting systems – in particular, such information is an important part of any planning and/or control system. However, such is the capacity of information (real-time) reporting nowadays, feedback information (which waits for things to happen) is at best usually only confirming what managers already know.

Moreover, feedback information is slow and static in nature. It lacks the dynamic, future-oriented characteristics that tomorrow's management accountants need from their information. This is

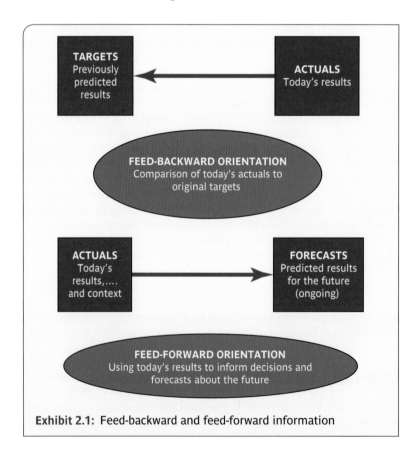

Exhibit 2.1: Feed-backward and feed-forward information

where feed-forward information comes in; feed-forward information is that which contributes to decisions about the future. A feed-forward information orientation is one that emphasizes the ongoing use of (new) information such that forward-looking plans are continually updated with the latest assumptions, data, and so on. A rolling forecast (see Chapter 10) would be an example of a tool from which management accountants try to nurture a feed-forward orientation, an organization which is *facing into* the future, rather than looking back and checking how things have gone.

Whether labelled the 'management accounts', the 'monthly business report', or other, most organizations do still produce some form of monthly internal accounting-generated report that is used for passing information upwards and/or across the organization, but also as the basis for discussions at more localized and business unit levels. Usually such monthly management reports will comprise financial statements, including cash flow, but additional detail than might be expected in, say, a set of financial accounts – for example, information on production, equipment utilization, customers and market trends, health and safety issues, staff matters and more.

Management accounts are frequently still used in high-level (for example, executive-level) meetings to 'set the scene' for the subsequent discussion – for example, as a starting point for debate and analysis of organizational performance. However, today's management accounts rarely contain information which is unfamiliar to its users. This is because information included within the management accounts will usually have been available and continually monitored, real-time, from the desktops of executives, managers and other workers.

Nowadays, the management accounts usually have more feed-forward-orientation by which, it is intended, information conveys where the organization is 'going' as opposed to where it has been. Information presented in the management accounts is also nowadays usually handled in the context of wider sets of available information. For example, today's management accounts would comprise a significant amount of detail relating to *non*-financial performance in organizations, and the user will be invited to interpret financial information in the broader context of non-financial performance measures, such as measures relating to customer satisfaction, quality of service/product, employee satisfaction and impact on the society/environment. Traditionally, the management accounts in most organizations provided only a partial (that is, financially oriented) view of performance. Today, however, they might, for example, highlight correlations between short-run profitability and potential long-term decline in customer or employee satisfaction.

Information integration

Traditional management accounting reports would likely be incomplete as far as today's organizations are concerned. However, their mostly historical and financially oriented information would still provide a useful overall summary of an organization's financial position at any point in time. Importantly, the interpretation and use of management accounts nowadays is usually carried out in the context of broader and increasingly non-financial dimensions of an organization. Thus, the financial part of an organization's management accounts can be kept relatively simple, but with broader information drawn upon to interpret the financial results in its wider business context.

One of the key roles of today's management accountants is to bring together the broader business perspective, as expressed through a manageable number of performance measures. Management accountants aim to link financial performance with the strategic consequences of activities that have been undertaken in an organization. In so doing, it is also within the remit of management accountants to reconcile the monthly management accounts to a wider set of organizational information that is available to the management team. This wider information set will comprise both financial and non-financial measures, as well as both long-term and short-term performance measures.

As mentioned previously, for this purpose a management accountant needs to develop a broad understanding of the organization and its interconnected activities and operations. This is something quite different to traditional score-keeping roles, when the general perception of a management accountant would be as a colleague who undertook independent and objective monitoring of financial performance across an organization. Management accountants are usually challenged to integrate information from different functional parts of an organization, as well as explain the interconnectivity between non-financial performance measures and the more conventional financial measures in the management accounts.

Such **information integration** is particularly important because it should enable business managers to 'see' the linkages between day-to-day localized activities, how such activities feed into the management accounts, and make the connection to broader and more strategic concerns of an organization (as reflected in the non-financial measures). There are tools and techniques which assist management accountants to engage in such integrating roles, and to nurture more organization-wide perspectives on organizational performance, such as the balanced scorecard (see Chapter 17).

Non-financial information

To some extent, the preceding discussion about integration reflects a shift in the nature of monitoring performance in organizations. Traditionally, the management accounts for most organizations would include predominantly financial and usually quantitative information – for example, profit-related indicators, percentage capital returns, fixed asset valuations and variances against budgets. However, in recent years, management accounting has increasingly involved drawing upon *non*-financial and qualitative measures, which are used alongside rather than replacing financial measures. The underlying principle here is that improvements in non-financial outputs, such as product or service quality and customer satisfaction, will eventually feed through to improvements in financial outputs.

This reorientation of the management accounts towards a more even mixture of both financial and **non-financial information** is sometimes shaped both by an organization's strategic concerns and its aim to increase the financial astuteness of business managers. This notion of financial astuteness captures the organizational requirement to continue in the future which, for commercial enterprises at least, means achieving long-run profitability as opposed to seeking short-run gains. This implies a more strategic outlook that stresses the capacity to achieve long-run organizational goals, and with a focus on the expectations of multiple stakeholders.

The shift of management accounting towards relatively more non-financial measurement does not usually imply less quantitative measurement. Indeed, it may actually bring more measurement, but across a broader range of performance-related information. In addition, organizations are likely to undertake ongoing comparisons between measures that capture actual performance, original targets and forecasts. Such analysis, moreover, need not take place over time periods that

2.1: Management Accounting in Practice

Information changes in UK universities

In Chapter 1, we discussed the various key drivers of change in management accounting practices, and concluded that future change for the context in which management accounting operates is guaranteed. Thus we can also rely upon changes in the future for the information requirements of an organization and its managers and workers, a situation that demands the attention of management accountants.

One recent example of where significant change has taken place is in the UK university sector (but, more specifically, universities in England). In 2012, most of the universities in England began for the first time charging sizeable fees to its 'home' (English) students. Until this point, home students had been largely subsidized by government funds. But this type of state funding has now been taken away, and at the same time government funding for academic research was also slashed drastically. In other words, the entire funding model for universities in England has been revolutionized into something it never was.

The consequence of these changes is that university leaders will need to manage their organizations in very different and untested ways. And, in turn, their *information* requirements will become very different.

There is now a significant chunk of funds which these universities can no longer rely upon, which once was taken for granted. So universities have needed to devise new information to manage ways to maintain existing and attract new student numbers. Very quickly, universities have become involved in *information-laden* activities that were not as prioritized (if done at all) in the recent past – for example, such activities as degree pricing, marketing for new student catchments, analysing the relative success of different degree programmes, programme mix, and much more.

At the same time, a university now must have a much improved understanding of its degree programme costs – even lower-level analyses such as the cost of running a particular module. Again this requires a much greater amount (and level of sophistication) of information than has traditionally been associated with the management of the UK university sector.

Students of universities in England are moving ever closer to becoming 'customers' in the same sense as private-sector enterprises and their customers. With that comes significant changes in the required information base of such organizations. This promises to have significant implications for management accountants in English (and possibly other UK) universities, because traditionally in such public-sector organizations management accounting has been fairly marginalized. Prior to the recent funding changes imposed by the UK government, university accountants generally were little more than score-keepers and did little in respect of strategizing, forecasting, cost management, profitability analysis and the like. There are some very serious challenges ahead.

Source: ideas taken from Clarke, P. (2012).

Exercises

1) What sort of information do you think senior managers of UK universities focused on primarily before the government-imposed changes to student fees and research funding?

2) Following the imposed changes, what sort of new information do you think the universities will be seeking?

3) Should management accountants assume that they will be looked upon in UK universities to lead the necessary 'information revolution'?

strictly adhere to traditional accounting cycles, as much management accounting nowadays can be ad hoc.

The use of broader performance measurement systems is likely to increase, the reasons for and likely nature of which we will explore throughout this textbook (see especially Chapter 16). Globalized competition in particular means that most organizations are devoting additional time and resource to strategic matters. Many organizations are also directing relatively more attention to 'outside' matters rather than a predominant focus on 'inside' matters such as traditional cost control.

However, this is not to say that cost control or other financial-oriented management is unimportant; far from it. Indeed, cost control, cash flow and other predominantly financial-oriented tools remain crucially important for any organization, and it is an area that we give coverage in several chapters of this textbook. However, as an example, increasingly nowadays organizations will endeavour to manage costs *over time*, aligned to long-run strategic goals rather than as an independent or exclusive focus on cost reduction (see Chapter 19). Importantly, this has led many organizations to identify what they believe to be their strategy-linked key performance measures.

Decentring of accounting knowledge

Another recent development for management accounting information, facilitated by advances in information technology, is a **decentring of accounting knowledge** (or financial astuteness) among non-accountants. In recent times there has been more diffusion throughout organizations of a basic understanding of the financial implications of localized decisions, as well as how management accounting information might be utilized in making such decisions.

Management accounting knowledge is being pushed outwards into the organization, at different levels and across different nodes of the organizational process. Managers and workers in all manner of organizations are becoming more financially literate, the intention being that they are able to connect a financial perspective to localized activities such as operations that are frequently measured and understood in non-financial terms. Management accounting information is nowadays more widely available, understood and used outside the accounting function, subject to appropriate security. Non-accounting managers access the management accounting systems, undertake localized analysis and use the information to inform local decisions.

There remains an important role here for management accountants, who design and oversee the management accounting information systems, and who must ensure that such information is being used correctly. Also, as mentioned above, the management accountant will likely be expected by many to have the expertise required to reconcile what the management accounting reports convey, actual organizational activities and long-run organizational goals.

Forecasting

Forecasting concerns making predictions about what the future will hold, whereas planning is more about what the future 'should' look like. Management accounting information increasingly feeds into an organization's **forecasting** process and tools (see Chapter 10). Ongoing comparison between budgeted (planning) performance measures, actual outcomes or results, and forecasts is becoming an important procedure for many organizations. There has been some criticism in recent years directed at traditional planning and control mechanisms, such as the annual budgeting tool, claiming that very quickly into the annual cycle they can become out of date, as changing external or internal circumstances affect underpinning assumptions. So, simultaneously there have been increased calls for forecasting in organizations.

Having said this, many organizations continue to adopt traditional planning tools such as budgets because, some would claim, they still provide a useful overarching framework for planning ahead at a particular point of time. Most evidence suggests that today's organizations are placing more emphasis on forecasts, but they are doing so alongside traditional budgets.

Forecasts usually require considerable data input from across an entire organization, so that the necessary detailed and local information can be produced. To this extent, managers can develop a greater feeling of ownership over such information compared to a traditional budget which would tend to be driven by, and generally perceived to be 'owned by', the accountants.

The information process

Useful information and information overload

The capacity of information technology is vast, and future advancement is guaranteed. However, this should not conceal the fact that, for organizations, it is not necessarily more information that matters but what organizations can do with the information at their disposal. Management accounting concerns the provision and use of information, but this needs to be information that its users perceive and experience to be helpful in the complex organizational world (Young, 2011). Without such boundaries, **information overload** is a very real possibility for today's organizations, and avoidance of such overload is a key remit for management accountants. In this context we should consider some of the important features of the information process.

2.1: Management Accounting Insight

Information to reduce the complexity that organizations operate within

Management accounting provides information that assists managers to steer their organizations through the complexities in which they operate. An interesting article in *Financial Management* outlines ways to ensure that information can reduce such complexity to manageable levels, as follows:

- Grasp the extent of any complexity problem, in particular the complexity of an organization's structures, systems and processes.

- Management accountants should take ownership of, and lead, the management (and reduction) of complexity.

- Undertake information audits to ensure that information is still valuable and has both short- and long-term purposes.

- Ensure that information is still (promising to) contribute towards long-run strategic success.

- Be alert to possible 'over-engineering' of information systems – sometimes simpler versions may be most appropriate.

- Work on colleagues to try to identify and eradicate costly and unnecessary complexities, and assist them to understand the benefits from such a proactive approach.

- Be prepared to 'savagely prune' complex situations which appear intuitively at least to be inefficient and costly but where it is difficult to pinpoint the complexity.

Source: adapted from Young, R. (2011).

Exercise

As a management consultant, you have been invited by the head of finance (and accounting) of a major European airline to investigate the information produced and used in their organization, more specifically their internal management information. Assuming that you accept this invitation, outline some of the initial investigations that you would undertake (for example, what would you look for, how and with whom?) before implementing any actual change.

Consistent with our earlier premise that we do not regard management accounting to be an exact or optimizing science, there is no general template for what constitutes 'right' or 'proper' management accounting information for an organization. However, certain qualities and characteristics might be generalizable to an extent (see Exhibit 2.2). Managers attempt to make 'right' decisions based on the information at their disposal. But this scenario does not guarantee the 'right' (or 'successful') outcome. On the basis of information at their disposal, managers can make what they think is the 'right' decision but which leads to below-expectation outcomes; conversely they can make seemingly 'poor' decisions which lead to better-than-expected outcomes.

What constitutes relevant and useful information is unique and specific to every organization, its stakeholders and its different actors; and these things can also change over time and in response to multiple outside factors. However, overlaps and common practice inevitably exist in some management accounting – for instance, it is not unusual to observe common management accounting practices among the different subsidiaries of a multinational organization. There is

- **Accuracy**: Information is only as good as the data used, and its interpretation
- **Timely**: Today's information can often be too late for decisions about tomorrow
- **Global**: Information that connects organizations all over the world
- **Trusted**: Without trust, information can be a source of tension, distrust, and even conflict
- **Practicality**: Useable, understood, and tailored to particular requirements
- **Holistic**: All-encompassing of organizational activities, balanced and integrated
- **Flexible**: Permitting adaptability in fast-moving organizational contexts
- **Contextual**: Aligned to the idiosyncrasies of a particular organization
- **Secure**: Not all information should be made available to everyone

Exhibit 2.2: The qualities and characteristics of useful management accounting information

also evidence of international convergence in particular aspects of global management accounting practice (Busco et al., 2007).

Every organization will still have specific information needs which, in turn, shape the idiosyncratic nature of what constitutes 'relevant' information. One approach to decipher what might constitute relevant management accounting information in a particular context might be to consider two aspects: (1) what is the purpose of such information, and (2) who are the main users of information.

Purpose of management accounting information

While not necessarily an exhaustive list, a typical portrayal of the purpose of management accounting information could be a combination of the following:

- *Score keeping*: Routine recording and calculation of organizational activity over time, now increasingly undertaken 'automatically' by computer systems.

- *External reporting*: Provision of some management accounting information for use in external reports such as the 'Annual Report'.

- *Attention directing*: Routine reporting and analysis of performance across different organizational activities, and identifying areas that might warrant some action.

- *Problem solving*: Routine and ad hoc investigation of different courses of action in an organization, judging different potential outcomes and choosing the preferred option.

Key users of management accounting information

When considering the main users of management accounting information, we might think of the following:

- *Line workers:* This concerns either routine or ad hoc use of information to assist those below management level to undertake their localized and day-to-day activities, but still aligned to broader and strategic organizational goals.

- *Operational managers:* This concerns information normally used by middle/lower management to oversee that short-term organizational activities are in line with more strategic objectives.

- *Strategic decision makers:* This concerns information for the executives and managers at the higher level of an organization, whose primary task is to establish and monitor the goals and achievements of an organization over longer periods.

We should however, at this point, remind ourselves that management accounting information comprises only a part of an organization's entire information base. Whereas 20 years ago, management accounting information tended to constitute the bulk of an organization's information set, nowadays information is dispersed throughout organizations. Notwithstanding that information provision still forms the backbone of their organizational role, management accountants are no longer sole proprietors of business information, a situation that can potentially lead to professional competition and conflict between accountants and other functional parts of an organization.

Constitutive aspects of management accounting information

Much has been written, particularly in the academic accounting literature, about the numerous constitutive aspects of management accounting information. Management accounting constitutes much more than simply a set of tools and techniques to produce information which subsequently feeds into organizational decision making. Some of these constitutive, *beyond-the-technical* aspects are covered throughout the textbook, but the following presents a brief introduction to some of them:

- The application of management accounting techniques in many organizations constitutes a largely routinized and frequently unquestioned 'way of doing things' (Burns and Scapens, 2000). As routines, expressed in management reports and other communications, management accounting can define what is, or should be, deemed 'acceptable' and 'proper' information within an organization.

- Particularly when routinized practice, management accounting has the potential to promote stability, sometimes a level of predictability in organizational activity, although routines can change (Lukka, 2007). In today's fast-paced and generally *un*predictable economic and social environment, such continuity can be a useful organizational attribute; however a degree of flexibility in management accounting practices can also be useful in particular circumstances.

- Management accounting information can provide a coherent basis upon which people in organizations make sense of, interpret and predict their actions and the action of others (Macintosh and Scapens, 1990). Thus, management accounting can constitute an important ingredient in processes of accumulating organizational knowledge and learning.

- Management accounting information can shape the meanings which people within organizations attach to different phenomena, therefore assisting them in making sense of complex situations (Tillmann and Goddard, 2008). This is not to say, however, that different people necessarily attach the same meaning to things – for example, an engineer's interpretation of 'costs' may differ from an accountant's interpretation.

- Management accounting information can underpin organizational language (Roberts and Scapens, 1985), meaning that many people within an organization, not just accountants, can converse (think, act, plan, control, evaluate) in terms of the language 'currency' which management accounting information provides.

- Management accounting information can shape, and be shaped by, an organization's identity or how an organization views itself (Abrahamsson et al., 2011), which also links closely to its external image and what an organization believes outsiders think of them.

Some commentators, particularly in 'alternative' management accounting research (Baxter and Chua, 2003), have for several decades argued strongly that management accounting, and the roles of management accountants, stretches considerably beyond tools and techniques per se. For many years, most professional-oriented and consultancy publications have 'sold' management accounting tools as unproblematic *solutions* to business problems, and most business and management courses in universities all over the world have reinforced such mainstream thinking by stressing the appeal of *optimizing* tools and techniques.

But, even an organization's *selection* of which tools and techniques to adopt goes further than being merely some technical exercise, and will demand more than technical knowledge and expertise from management accountants:

> *We believe that tomorrow's management accountants should try to understand the varied opportunities that new methods can offer. They should use their understanding to shape how such innovations are modified and applied locally [...] It may well stretch their technical abilities and also require a grasp of the broader implementation issues involved – e.g., how they affect the way organizations behave [...]. One-size-fits-all methods fail because they ignore far too much of the stuff of life, such as organisational culture, values, norms and power. We believe that a key role for management accountants is to be discriminating and circumspect when considering the many new approaches on offer. They need to be more critical and try to understand innovations in their wider contexts. Great new ideas can mean little when the situation to which they are being applied is rife with complexity. (Baldvinsdottir et al., 2009a, p. 34).*

While change may be slower to take place in academia, there appears to be some increase (though not enough) recently among the practitioner-led media in a recognition that management accounting encapsulates much more than just the technical, and that a management accountant nowadays must have a broad understanding of such 'non-technical' phenomena as culture, politics, trust, ethics and much more which lie outside of the techniques per se.

If you are particularly interested in further exploring the constitutive aspects of management accounting, as well as exploring more of the non-technical dimensions to management accounting practice, you should especially consult articles in such academic journals as *Management Accounting Research* (Elsevier), *Accounting, Auditing and Accountability Journal*, (Emerald), *Accounting, Organizations and Society* (Elsevier), *Journal of Accounting and Organizational Change* (Emerald), *Qualitative Research in Accounting and Management* (Emerald) and *Critical Perspectives on Accounting* (Elsevier).

Information technologies

There are numerous **information technologies** supporting management accounting practices, several of which we will highlight in the textbook (see especially Chapter 21). Here, as an introduction, we briefly highlight some technologies that have had a particular impact on the nature and use of management accounting information during recent decades:

- *Computers*: Most students have probably grown up with computers everywhere in their lives, and now take the power of computers for granted. However, the substantial role that computers (also laptops, tablets and hand-held devices) now play in organizations, and life in general has only been that way for the past 25 years or so.

- *Spreadsheets*: These tabulate numbers, for example accounting numbers, in an ordered and integrated way. The significant thing about spreadsheets is that they permit managers to set out their plans and forecasts, for instance cash-flow forecasts, over a particular period of time, but then they are also able to consider different scenarios and new assumptions caused by changes in external and/or internal context, and to recalculate the effect.

- *Database/data warehouses*: A database is a means for organizations to systematically record their data, store such data in convenient and useful formats, and permit easy but secure access for its user. A database management system (DBMS) is the main software required to operate a database. Frequently, though not always, an organization will centralize its databases at a single corporate location, or at some external data storage facility.

- *Enterprise resource planning systems (ERPs)*: These are built on databases that essentially include all the data used within an organization's information system. Typically, its software integrates the accounting systems with the information systems underpinning other organizational functions such as human resources, manufacturing, distribution and sales systems. Thus, with ERP systems, 'common' information is shared and flows between and across different parts of the business process. They are integrated, process-oriented and organization-wide information systems.

- *Business intelligence*: This describes the combined use of present-day data technologies such as data warehousing and data management for collecting, storing and providing access to a considerable mass of data that can then be used to inform decisions.

- *The Internet*: We are all familiar with the impact *in still relatively recent times* of the Internet. Management accounting has been no exception; for instance, many organizations now advertise and sell their products via the Internet. Numerous Internet-based organizations such as the internet retailer Amazon.com have evolved and very quickly challenged the once-dominant market leaders of the high street. *Intranets* are now also being used by many organizations – that is, a web system that allows access only to users within a particular organization and not to outsiders. Importantly, intranets facilitate the organization-wide accessibility of management accounting information, at the click of a mouse or the touch of a screen. The vast capability of new Internet-based technology, such as cloud computing and a whole lot more, will be returned to in later chapters (especially Chapter 21).

Technologies such as those listed above have fostered a revolution in management accounting. Compared to, say, 10 years ago, there has been a significant capacity increase in the technologies underpinning management accounting information, faster processing speeds, and the opening-up of wider and anytime accessibility. As mentioned above, the impact of current and future IT development on management accounting will feature in many of the remaining chapters of this textbook.

Management accountants need not necessarily be experts on information technology – IT technicians and statisticians will continue to serve this role. However, management accountants will work alongside such colleagues in driving and implementing new information systems designs (including, but not exclusively, the management accounting systems). Hence, a management accountant will need to be IT proficient to the extent that they are aware of the latest software, what this software can achieve, its compatibility with other information systems in their organization, the scale of local knowledge required, the necessity for training, and more.

Chapter summary

In this chapter, we have highlighted not only how important management accounting information is within organizations, but also how such information constitutes much more than just techniques and the 'simple' tasks of presenting data in management reports. As we have established, management accounting information is a very powerful phenomena in all organizations, and appropriate and careful management of the information process is paramount. We will continue to highlight both technical and non-technical aspects of management accounting throughout the remainder of the textbook.

Key terms

Data Facts and figures (p. 31)

Decentring of accounting knowledge A process whereby financial knowledge is spread through an organization, among managers and workers, who can connect a 'bottom-line effect' to localized activities (p. 37)

Forecasting Using tools and techniques to make predictions about the future, as opposed to planning which is more about what the future 'should' look like (p. 38)

Information When raw data comes to be useful and meaningful to its owner(s), and subsequently has potential to influence their decision-making (p. 31)

Information integration The bringing together of a broader business perspective, as expressed through both financial and non-financial measures (p. 36)

Information overload The potential danger of producing too much management accounting information to the extent that it becomes unmanageable, rather than focusing on relevant and useful information for managers' decision-making needs (p. 38)

Information technologies An array of computing and telecommunications tools which assist management accountants to collate, store, retrieve and use information in their day-to-day role (p. 42)

Management accounts An aggregated depiction of an organization's (monthly, year to date) financial and non-financial results, (p. 34)

Non-financial information Information such as quality and customer satisfaction, and the management of which is deemed by some to be a precursor to financial success (p. 36)

Relevance Lost A milestone book published in 1987, which claimed that management accounting had ceased to provide business managers with useful information (p. 32)

Review questions • • • • • • • • • • • • connect • •

| Level of difficulty: | BASIC | INTERMEDIATE | ADVANCED |

2.1 Why do you think that forecasting is becoming more popular in today's organizations? **[LO1, LO4, LO5]**

2.2 Explain what is meant by 'information overload'. **[LO1, LO4, LO5, LO7, LO8]**

2.3 Why did the development of management accounting stagnate from the 1920s to the 1980s? **[LO2, LO3]**

2.4 Describe some of the main qualities of 'good' management accounting information. **[LO5]**

2.5 Describe some of the key IT-related sources of management accounting information to date. **[LO8]**

2.6 What does it mean to say that management accountants try to *integrate* financial and non-financial information? **[LO4, LO6, LO9]**

2.7 What does 'decentring of accounting knowledge' mean, and what do you think management accountants should do to facilitate such a thing? **[LO4, LO7]**

Group discussion and activity questions • • • • • • • •

2.8 The more information that is available to an organization, the better. Discuss. **[LO1, LO5]**

2.9 Information produced in non-accounting areas of an organization (for example, production, marketing, research and development) are irrelevant to management accountants. Discuss. **[LO1, LO4, LO6, LO7, LO9]**

2.10 Critically evaluate whether or not the most important information for managers in any commercial enterprise is financial information. **[LO1, LO4, LO6, LO9]**

2.11 With illustrations and real examples, discuss how, and through which technology, organizations might best capture data for management accounting information purposes. **[LO5, LO7, LO8]**

2.12 Do some additional research into the *Relevance Lost* thesis, and discuss whether the suggested 'crisis' in management accounting has been quashed and rectified. **[LO2, LO3]**

2.13 Discuss, and illustrate with real examples, how management accounting tools and techniques might become a routine part of day-to-day organizational activity, and what effect does this have? **[LO5, LO6]**

Exercises • • • • • • • • • • • • • • • • • • connect • •

E2.1 **The management accounts [LO2]**

The 'management accounts' are presented on an annual (or sometimes bi-annual, or quarterly) basis to shareholder, investors and other interested parties: true or false?

E2.2 **The information process [LO5, LO7]**

Fill in the missing words:

We call it _____ _____ when too much management accounting information is being produced to the extent that it becomes unmanageable.

E2.3 **Characteristics of useful management accounting information [LO5]**

Listed below are the main characteristics and qualities of management accounting information.

Global	Accuracy
Holistic	Contextual
Secure	Flexible
Timely	

Required:

For the following, select the quality or characteristic of management accounting information that best suits the description.

1) Information should be aligned to the idiosyncrasies of a particular organization

2) Today's information can often be too late for decisions about tomorrow

3) Information should permit adaptability in fast-moving organizational contexts

4) Information should connect organizations all over the world

5) Information is only as good as the data used, and its interpretation

6) Not all information should be made available to everyone

7) Information should encompass all organizational activities and should be balanced and integrated.

E2.4 **Management accounting information [LO5]**

For each of the following situations, identify whether the organization is exhibiting a feed-backward orientation or a feed-forward orientation. (Select one)

Situation	Feed-Backward Orientation	Feed-Forward Orientation
Net profit of Foley PLC was £150 million this year, much better than its competitors. However, the management expected profits to be £180 million. The management now wants to investigate this variance.		
Rex Ltd. budgets to produce and sell 5,500 units next month, as it anticipates a 10% increase in market demand. It sold 5,000 units in the current month.		
Bubbles Ltd. uses a two-year rolling forecast for budgeting. By the end of April 2014, it will be working on the budget for April 2016.		
Frank PLC had set target net profits for 5 years with 15% increment each year. However, it revised its budgeted net profit for the next year, accounting for the recent economic downturn.		
Pyrex Ltd. spent €130 million to purchase 5,000,000 units of raw material. The standard price of such material was €24. The purchase manager is asked to investigate the unfavourable variance.		

E2.5 **Users of management accounting information [LO7]**

Management accounting information can be used by multiple users including line workers, operational managers and strategic decision makers. The following pieces of information can be found in various management accounting reports:

1) Market potential of a new product to decide whether to launch the product.

2) Contribution margin per unit of constraint, for the bottlenecks processes, to determine the unit level of production of a particular product.

3) Day-to-day budgeted production level, to help in producing the expected amount of production.

4) Comparison of standard price versus actual price per unit of material, to help investigate the reasons for variances.

5) Market value of the company, to evaluate acquisition proposals.

Required:

Identify the most likely user from those identified above for each piece of information.

E2.6 **The Relevance Lost debate [LO3]**

a) According to Johnson and Kaplan, which of the following are reasons for the loss of relevance of management accounting? (Select all that apply.)

  a) Management accounting had become subservient to financial accounting.

  b) Financial and management accounting used a single set of data.

  c) Management accounting was only providing non-financial information to decision makers.

  d) Strict regulations and controls were imposed on management accounting.

  e) Management accounting faced very little pressure to change and innovate techniques.

b) Which of the following are changes suggested in Johnson and Kaplan's book titled *Relevance Lost*? (Select all that apply.)

  a) Develop new management accounting tools to provide more accurate costing information.

  b) Ignore traditional management accounting tools and techniques as they have lost relevance.

  c) Identify operational efficiencies that increase utilization of existing resources.

  d) Use separate sets of data for financial and management accounting.

  e) Develop new financial accounting methods to comply with managerial accounting rules and regulations.

E2.7 **Contemporary developments in management accounting information provision [LO4]**

Which of the following words most suitably complete this sentence?

A traditional budgeting system would be an example of a feed-_____ information system, whereby managers compare actual results (for example, turnover or costs) to original targets in the budget.

a) Data

b) Backward

c) Strategic

d) Forward

E2.8 **Feed-back versus feed-forward tools and techniques [LO3, LO4, LO5]**

Explain, with illustrations, what you understand by the distinction between management accounting tools which provide a *feed-backward* perspective and those which are more *feed-forward* oriented?

E2.9 **Information for business managers in production [LO4, LO5, LO7, LO8, LO9]**

This question will require some research. What sorts of information would be needed, and how frequently, by the production manager of a factory that produces digital radios? Moreover, in what ways might a management accountant assist this production manager?

E2.10 **Non-financial information [LO4, LO5, LO7, LO9]**

Non-financial information has grown substantially in popularity in recent years, and usually a management accountant will have main responsibility for overseeing its provision. Critically appraise why the status of non-financial information has increased considerably in most organizations, relative to financial information.

E2.11 **Management accounting information [LO5]**

Match the following descriptions with the terms provided below.

Descriptions	Terms
1) A web system that allows access only to users within a particular organization and not to outsiders	a) Business intelligence
2) A feature of information system design that compares today's actuals to original targets	b) Forecasting
3) Using tools and techniques to make predictions about the future	c) Enterprise resource planning systems
4) Routine recording and calculation of organizational activity over time	d) Feed-backward
5) The combined use of present-day data technologies for collecting, storing and providing access to a considerable mass of data that can then be used to inform decisions	e) Intranet
6) Information system that uses today's results to inform decisions and forecasts about the future	f) Feed-forward
7) The systems through which 'common' information is shared between and across different parts of the business process	g) Score-keeping

E2.12 **Information for airlines [LO1, LO4, LO5, LO6, LO7, LO8, LO9]**

You have been asked by the Chief Finance Officer (CFO) of an airline in South East Asia to investigate their management accounting and their information base, then to make some suggestions for improvement. The airline is a reasonably successful company, though not a big world competitor – it predominantly charters routes within the South East Asian region. For many years the organization has been run mostly on extremely traditional management accounting practices, and the information used by managers is generally financially oriented and historical. You are invited to write a two-page brief on potential new features of a new way to approach their management accounting.

E2.13 **Information and management accountants [LO1, LO4, LO5, LO9]**

Plenty of professional *and* academic literature in recent years has elevated management accounting to an *exciting* 'business partner' role which means no longer doing as much of the traditional and less exciting tasks. However, some authors have warned against too much innovation and change in management accountants' roles, and recommended caution. Baldvinsdottir et al. (2009b) wrote:

> *Tomorrow's management accountants can still drive fast cars, sky-dive and pursue other exciting pastimes. But their fundamental business role is still to be a logical analyser of management decisions and a provider of relevant information to ensure long-term performance and proper conformance. Long live the dull, pessimistic management accountant! (p. 35).*

a)   When referring to 'fast cars, sky-diving and exciting pastimes', Baldvinsdottir et al. (2009b) were referring to recent images being used for management accountants in professional magazines such as *Financial Management* (CIMA), websites and more. How important do you think the external image of management accountants is?

b)   Explain in detail what Baldvinsdottir et al. (2009b) mean in respect of a management accountant's 'fundamental business role'.

c)   In respect of their 'fundamental role', why do you think Baldvinsdottir et al. called for longevity of the 'dull, pessimistic management account', and what would this mean in respect of the *information* which management accountants should prioritize in their organizations?

E2.14 **Purpose(s) of management accounting information [LO3, LO5, LO7]**

In the main text of this chapter, we listed the purpose of management accounting as comprising: (1) score keeping, (2) external reporting, (3) attention directing, and (4) problem solving. Describe briefly what each of these mean. Then, undertaking some background research, and with plenty of imagination, describe what you expect to become the main purpose(s) of management accounting by the year 2020, and why?

• • • • **Case study problem** • • • • • • • • • • • **connect** • • •

C2.1 **Relevant management accounting information can be *simple* [LO1, LO5, LO6, LO7]**

Becks Ltd is a small, privately owned chemicals manufacturer based in the UK. The business is managed using a simple management accounting system, which suggests that sometimes management accounting does not need to be sophisticated – sometimes, *simplicity is best*. Becks Ltd sells a range of chemical products, but the majority of their revenue comes from 'captive products', which are chemicals produced under (approximately five-year, but renewable) contracts with particular customers, and usually products that are made to the customer's specification.

Management accounting is an integral part of Becks' management process, and involves managers from all areas of the business; in fact, most of the information comprising 'the management accounts' originates from the managers rather than the accountants. Management accounting information reinforces the knowledge and understanding that Becks' workers and managers have about the various activities of the organization. It focuses multiple personnel on the underlying profitability implications of local activities, and influences decisions in all areas. There is particular emphasis on cost control in this organization, and it is simple *contributions-based* management accounting information which underpins much of the organizational knowledge.

Contribution is a traditional financial measure, specifically defined in the organization as sales less materials costs. Materials constituted around 90 per cent of total costs in Becks over the years, so the managers had become comfortable with 'more or less' managing the organization on such bases. The remainder of total cost is mostly accounted for by labour costs and utilities costs. Across different departments, and at all levels of the organizational hierarchy, staff converse in terms of 'contributions earned'; they are monitored by contributions; and plans are formulated in terms of expected contribution earnings. *Contribution per product* is a well-established source of knowledge used throughout the company; and the ongoing use of contribution routines assists many to make sense of their activities and the activities of others, and to make decisions based on such understandings.

Every week, there is a meeting to discuss the business plan and decide what is possible, production-wise, in the short term. Participants attend this meeting from the sales, production, technical, quality and engineering departments. However, the accountants do not attend these meetings but they do summarize the business activities, mostly in contribution terms, at the monthly board meeting.

Contribution routines, and the language that they underpin, enable personnel throughout Becks to control their own part of the business in the short term. For example, a key document for the Operations Department is a 12-week production plan which provides information on cost variance against standards and, importantly, expected contributions per product or per vessel. Also, short run control in Becks rests with a basic forecast model that comprises target contribution levels.

The widespread adoption of contribution routines in Becks was part of an initiative to disperse financial acumen in the organization. This initiative emerged from the lessons learned during a serious cash-flow crisis in the 1990s, and formed part of the resultant new strategic objectives to broaden Becks' product base beyond 'captive' contracts and towards more generic products that might attract multiple customers. Managers were expected to have a clear picture of the expected contribution earnings from all products, and a grasp of how the organization was progressing, or not, in respect of short-term profitability.

Contribution routines had become embedded in Becks, but there had been difficulties in reaching this stage. For example, the Sales and Marketing Director had said that 'accounting does not find you markets'. Also, the Production Director stressed that 'whereas the accountants may be pleased that we have made excellent contributions in one particular month, they might be completely unaware that, for various reasons, it has been an absolute nightmare down on the plant'.

Source: adapted from Burns, J. (2000).

Required:

1) Why can Becks Ltd rely upon a simple contributions-based management accounting system? What is the context of this organization that makes simplicity the better alternative?

2) Which of the qualities and characteristics of 'good' management accounting information, as per Exhibit 2.1, do you think Becks' contributions-based information exhibits?

3) Can you think of ways through which Becks might be able to improve their management accounting information further?

4) What do you think the management accountants' role is in Becks? How might the management accountants become more proactive?

5) What kind of information technologies do you think Becks could implement?

6) Why and how does contribution-based information underpin the organizational language through which personnel understand and organize activities?

7) As the management accountant, how would you approach the problems raised by the Sales and Marketing Director and the Production Director?

• • Recommended reading • • • • • • • • • • • • • • • • • •

- Baxter, J. and W. F. Chua (2003) 'Alternative management accounting research – whence and whither', *Accounting, Organizations and Society*, 28(2–3), pp. 97–126.

An overview of decades of non-mainstream 'alternative' academic literature studying management accounting as a practice which stretches further than being merely a portfolio of optimizing tools and techniques.

- Hall, M. (2010) 'Accounting information and managerial work', *Accounting, Organizations and Society*, 35(3), pp. 301–15.

An insightful investigation of the nature and significance of accounting information in day-to-day management.

- Loft, A. (1995) 'The history of management accounting: relevance found', in D. Ashton, T. Hopper and R. W. Scapens (eds), *Issues in Management Accounting*, 2nd edn, New York: Prentice Hall, pp. 21–44.

A useful account of the origins and development of management accounting up to the 1990s, including some focus on the Relevance Lost debate during the 1980s.

• • • References •

Abrahamsson, G., H. Englund and J. Gerdin (2011) 'Organisational identity and management accounting change', *Accounting, Auditing and Accountability Journal*, 24(3), pp. 345–76.

Baldvinsdottir, G., J. Burns, H. Nørreklit and R. W. Scapens (2009a) 'The management accountant's role', *Financial Management*, (CIMA), September, pp. 33–4.

Baldvinsdottir, G., J. Burns, H. Nørreklit and R. W. Scapens (2009b) 'The management accountant's role', *Financial Management*, (CIMA), July–August, pp. 34–5.

Baxter, J. and W. F. Chua (2003) 'Alternative management accounting research – whence and whither', *Accounting, Organizations and Society*, 28(2–3), pp. 97–126.

Burns, J. (2000) 'The dynamics of accounting change: the inter-play between new practices, routines, institutions, power and politics', *Accounting, Auditing and Accountability Journal*, 13(5), pp. 566–96.

Burns, J. and R. W. Scapens (2000) 'Conceptualising management accounting change: an institutional framework', *Management Accounting Research*, 10(1), pp. 3–25.

Busco, C., E. Giovannoni and A. Riccaboni (2007) 'Globalisation and the international convergence of management accounting', in T. Hopper, D. Northcott and R. W. Scapens (eds), *Issues in Management Accounting*, 3rd edn, pp. 65–92, Harlow: FT/Prentice Hall.

CIMA (2008) 'Improving decision making in organisations: unlocking business intelligence', a report by the Chartered Institute of Management Accountants, September.

Clarke, P. (2012) 'How an understanding of profitability and costs can help universities to face the unknown', *Financial Management* (CIMA), February, pp. 50–3.

Hall, M. (2010) 'Accounting information and managerial work', *Accounting, Organizations and Society*, 35(3), pp. 301–15.

Johnson, H. T. and R. Kaplan (1987) *Relevance Lost: The Rise and Fall of Management Accounting*, Boston MA: Harvard Business School Press.

Loft, A. (1995) 'The history of management accounting: relevance found', in D. Ashton, T. Hopper and R. W. Scapens (eds), *Issues in Management Accounting*, 2nd edn, New York: Prentice Hall, pp. 21–44.

Lukka, K. (2007) 'Management accounting change and stability: loosely coupled rules and routines in action', *Management Accounting Research*, 18(1), pp. 76–101.

Macintosh, N. and R. W. Scapens (1990) 'Structuration theory in management accounting', *Accounting, Organizations and Society*, 15(5), pp. 455–477.

Roberts, J. and R. W. Scapens (1985) 'Accounting systems and systems of accountability – understand accounting practices in their organisational context', *Accounting, Organizations and Society*, 10(4), pp. 43–56.

Tillmann, K. and A. Goddard (2008) 'Strategic management accounting and sense-making in a multinational company', *Management Accounting Research*, 19(1), pp. 80–102.

Young, R. (2011) '8 ways to reduce complexity', *Financial Management* (CIMA), July/August, pp. 36–7.

When you have read this chapter

Log on to the Online Learning Centre at **www.mcgraw-hill.co.uk/textbooks/burns** to explore chapter-by-chapter test questions, links and further online study tools for Management Accounting.

ACCOUNTING FOR COSTS

CHAPTER 3

THE CLASSIFICATION OF COST(S)

Chapter outline

- Accounting for costs – in general
- Cost objects
- Cost accumulation and cost assignment
- Cost classifications
- Technology and cost gathering

Learning outcomes

On completion of this chapter, students will be able to:

LO1 Appreciate different perspectives and classifications of cost

LO2 Define and illustrate a cost object

LO3 Explain the principles of cost accumulation, cost assignment and cost allocation

LO4 Define and distinguish between direct costs and indirect costs

LO5 Define and distinguish between fixed costs and variable costs

LO6 Have a basic knowledge of how product costs are treated in different organizational and sector types

LO7 Define and distinguish between job and process costing

LO8 Identify which costs are (not) relevant to a particular decision-making situation

LO9 Define and distinguish between absorption costing and variable costing

LO10 Recite some technological developments that have impacted cost accounting

LO11 Appreciate the importance of measuring and managing costs in an organization

Introduction

In the previous two chapters you learned how important management accounting information is to organizations, including cost information. Some would argue that managing costs is *the* most fundamental dimension to running an organization. Cost information is critical for numerous aspects of organizational activity, including planning, control and evaluation; and is also at the heart of many decisions.

In this chapter we explore the concept of **cost** – defined as the monetary value of the resources forgone or sacrificed in order to achieve a specific objective such as acquiring a good or service. We introduce key cost terms and concepts, as essential grounding for later chapters where we go into further detail on particular aspects. This groundwork is important – before we can actually calculate and measure costs, we need to learn more about what costs mean, not least because the reality is that costs can have multiple meanings, and different outlooks on cost can be used according to different scenarios. Thus, one of the main aims of this chapter is to undertake a classification of costs that can then form a foundation for later, more detailed chapters on specific aspects of accounting for costs.

Accounting for costs – in general

There are multiple purposes (and users) of an organization's cost information. Examples of how and when cost-related information might be used by organizations, although decisions will not necessarily be made on the basis of cost information alone, are:

- What price should we set for our new product?
- Who are our most profitable customers?
- Which of our services achieve greatest margins on average?
- How should we best finance our new acquisition?
- Which of our various departments are the least economical?
- What are the social and environmental costs of our products?

Cost reduction is a process of attempting to decrease the amount of financial outlay in conducting business so as to enhance the chance for increasing earned profits or surplus. It is also usually a key part of the strategic objectives of most organizations nowadays (see Chapter 19), especially when such reductions can emerge via the achievement of efficiencies within an organization's activities.

Traditionally in most organizations, accounting for costs would rest with management accountants, gathering the necessary data to generate usable cost information in what could be a painstaking and largely manual activity. Nowadays, however, most cost accounting is undertaken automatically through advanced and increasingly integrated information systems and other new technologies. Thus, design and some knowledge of the technology underlying a cost system would be as important for today's management accountants as the routine mechanics of costing techniques.

Accountants will usually be involved in such design, often in collaboration with IT specialists. But, automation of much of the cost accounting process means that a significant chunk of routine cost accounting is now performed by managers rather than by accountants, although the latter are still available to consult and advise.

Cost objects

First, we can define a **cost object**. A cost object is something for which a separate cost measurement is required. If someone wishes to know the cost of something, that 'something' is the cost object.

A cost object can be numerous things – for example, a product or service, a customer, a supplier, a project, a new product launch, an acquisition, and more, see Table 3.1 for further examples.

Table 3.1: Examples of cost objects	
Cost object	**Examples**
Product	SAAB motor car
	A new (downloadable) iPod tune
Service	Flight from Stockholm to St Petersburg
	A heart-bypass operation in hospital
Activity	Quality inspections in one of Shell's oil refineries
	Maintenance of machinery in a SMART-TV manufacturer
Project	Building construction – e.g., a large dam, or a bridge
	New stadium for a major sports event such as the Olympics
Department	Merchandising department in H&M retail stores
	Research and development (R&D) unit for Proctor and Gamble
Customer	Internet-only customers for Sony
	Long-standing customers who receive loyalty discounts at Singapore Airlines
Supplier	Outsourced catering in the canteen of a distribution depot for NIKE
	Bulk-purchasing of product components for Harley Davidson

Probably the most obvious cost objects are products and services because, depending on the type of organization, information relating to products and services can be useful for many purposes such as pricing, budgeting or more strategic decision making. Organizations measure the costs associated with a particular cost object, following which that cost object then becomes the focal point of analysis, monitoring and cost management.

3.1: Management Accounting in Practice

London Olympic Games, 2012: the new velodrome project

As part of the London Olympic Games 2012, one major project was the building of a new velodrome which would be the location for all the cycling events. The stadium, seating 6,000 spectators, cost somewhere in the region of £100 million, and was one of the first major projects to be completed in the run-up to the Olympiad event. The project would be treated as a cost object by its managers, until completion. Most of the costs incurred for a project such as this are probably agreed in advance (subject to certain clauses), so the cost object overall is relatively easy to calculate in terms of its expected monetary value. Examples of individual costs that would form part of the overall cost for the project include: architect fees, legal fees, ground preparation, raw materials, equipment hire including large cranes, skilled labour, administrative support services and much more.

Exercise

Think of the other types of cost objects listed in Table 3.1 – a product, a service, an activity, a department, a customer, a supplier. Think of a real example and list some individual costs that would likely be part of the cost calculation for each particular cost object.

Cost accumulation and cost assignment

A **cost system** is a form of accounting system which captures cost data that will then form the basis of cost information for managers' use. Chapter 4 will discuss cost systems in much greater detail, but we should consider the basics here. Typically, a cost system would comprise two key stages, as follows:

1) **Cost accumulation**, whereby cost data is organized according to a classification system that identifies a group of costs in a particular (and usually obvious) way. For example, it is common to see categories like labour costs, materials costs, packing costs, advertising costs, distribution costs and utilities costs. In this respect, there is some overlap with financial accounting, in which expenses are similarly categorized.

2) **Cost assignment**, whereby the accumulated costs (above) are attributed to specific cost objects. Assignment requires two sub-stages, namely: (i) 'tracing' accumulated costs to a cost object, and (ii) 'allocating' accumulated costs to a cost object. As will be explained below, (i) refers to accounting for direct costs, whereas (ii) refers to accounting for indirect costs.

The systems used to capture, accumulate and assign costs are fundamental to organizations, and there are multiple questions to consider. For instance, should an organization accumulate actual costs, budgeted costs, forecast costs or a mixture? Increasingly organizations have relied on database-grounded technology which allows managers to alternate between purposes from the same overall bank of cost data. Advance in information technology has fundamentally improved the capacity and speed through which costs can be accounted for and analysed, as will be discussed at the end of this chapter.

Cost classifications

As was mentioned at the outset of this chapter our purpose here is to provide an introduction to the different ways in which costs can be classified, as well as explain the kind of situations where a particular classification is most suitable. Table 3.2 lists the various classifications that we will cover.

Assigning costs to cost objects

Direct and indirect costs

In attempting to measure a cost object, an important distinction to make is that between direct and indirect costs:

- **Direct costs** can be easily associated with a particular cost object.
- **Indirect costs** evidently support more than one cost object.

Table 3.2: Cost classifications	
Cost classification	**Purpose of the cost classification**
Direct and indirect costs	Assigning costs to a cost object
Product and period costs	Preparing financial statements
Manufacturing, merchandising or service sector costing	Different costs for different sector types
Absorption and variable costing	Valuation of inventory for reporting purposes
Job costing and process costing	Costing systems for different organizational types
Variable and fixed costs	Predicting cost behaviour when output/activity levels change
Standard costs	Costs to assist planning and evaluation
Controllable and uncontrollable costs	Costs to assist planning and evaluation
Relevant costs	Costs used in different decision-making scenarios
Opportunity costs	Costs used in different decision-making scenarios

Direct costs tend not to be difficult to identify because, by definition, they are incurred as a direct consequence of the cost object's existence or occurrence. The terminology normally used is that direct costs are assigned to a particular cost object through **tracing** – that is, identified to a specific cost object with ease, without contention or doubt. An example would be the music system inside a high-performance motor car, the cost data for which can be obtained from the bill of materials issued by the supplier.

On the other hand, indirect costs (sometimes referred to as overheads) can be more problematic. Indirect costs are so called because they are costs that support more than one cost object. They are costs which cannot be identified with a single cost object. An example would be the electricity costs in a factory which produces several different styles of fashionable ladies' shoes; where the cost object is one particular style of shoe there will be a need to calculate the proportion of total electricity costs in the factory which are specifically attributable to the production of that shoe (not an easy task!).

So, in measuring the total cost of a particular cost object, we must include a proportion of indirect costs and, as far as possible, must do this in a manner that accurately reflects the cost object's actual usage of total indirect cost inputs. Thus, we need a way to reasonably and accurately assign indirect costs to different cost objects; this is done through a process of **cost allocation**. There are two main methods for allocating indirect costs, namely: (1) absorption costing (see Chapter 5); and, (2) activity-based costing (see Chapter 6).

In summary, once accumulated, all costs are then assigned to cost objects. The assignment of direct costs is done via tracing, whereas the assignment of indirect costs is via cost allocation. It is important to remind ourselves, however, that the same cost can be both a direct and an indirect cost at the same time – depending on what the cost object is. For instance, think of the salary costs of a service engineer at Rolls-Royce aero-engines, who services the manufacture of different types of engines for aircraft. If our cost object is the engineering department, the engineer's salary would be classified as a direct cost. However, if our cost object is specifically a T900 aero-engine, the engineer's salary would be classified as an indirect cost.

Ideally organizations would prefer to be able to classify as much of their costs as possible as direct costs. Because, by definition, direct costs are more accurate in terms of the actual resources used by particular cost objects, and thus rely on little or no arbitrary spreading of costs (or allocation) over different cost objects. Accounting for indirect costs has long been a challenging area for management accounting. Inappropriate techniques and ill-designed systems can produce misleading information which, in turn, has potential to drive poor decision making. Nevertheless, many contemporary organizations have witnessed sharp increases in indirect costs over recent times, so the challenge is not likely to disappear. Organizations normally have two choices, as follows:

1) To design more sophisticated accounting methods for dealing with the assignment (or allocation) of indirect costs to different cost objects (see Chapter 6), or;

2) Endeavour to 'convert' as many indirect costs as possible into direct costs. This is not always easy to achieve, and is often very costly to do so. But, for example, an organization might choose to install electricity or other utility meters with every factory machine, to capture exactly how much electricity is being used by a particular machine (see *Management Accounting in Practice 3.2*).

3.2: Management Accounting in Practice

Converting indirect costs to direct costs

Contract Chemicals is a leading independent UK-based manufacturer of fine and speciality chemicals, established in 1977. The company has grown significantly in the last decade, and produces chemicals for customers all over the world. In their line of business, the bulk of costs for producing the chemicals are direct costs, in particular raw material and labour costs. The main indirect costs are utility costs, especially water and electricity. The manufacture of individual chemicals is normally designated to particular reactor-vessels, and so it is a relatively easy task to monitor and measure the amount of direct costs being incurred per vessel (or chemical). However, it was less easy to calculate the amount of water (mostly for vessel-cooling purposes) and electricity that was being consumed by individual vessels in the manufacturing plant. In the 1990s, therefore, the company installed meters on all vessels for both water and electricity supplies, so that it became possible to accurately measure such quantities, and previously hard-to-measure indirect costs for their chemical products were now calculated accurately. These indirect costs were now more or less 'direct' in that a high level of accuracy was guaranteed with respect to measuring how much water and electricity was being consumed by each individual vessel.

Source: based on author's own research.

Exercise

Can you think of any other situations in any other type of organization where indirect costs might be 'converted' into direct costs?

Preparing financial statements

Product costs and period costs

Another important aspect of management accounting is how and when to recognize the costs of making, acquiring or providing products and services. Knowing the cost of products is critical for organizations – for example in setting product prices, in compiling the annual report, in seeking operational efficiencies, and more. And, having inaccurate information on the cost of products or service can lead to potentially damaging decisions.

An **expense** is a cost that has been incurred when an asset is used up or sold for the purpose of generating revenues. There are two different ways to treat costs in respect of their conversion to an expense, as follows.

A **product cost** is a cost that is assigned to goods either purchased or manufactured for (re)sale. They are treated as current assets when incurred, and posted to the statement of financial position as inventory until the final product is sold. This method resonates with the requirements of financial accounting to 'match' costs with associated revenues in the relevant time period. Upon sale, product costs are recognized as an expense in the income statement, as 'the costs of good sold'.

A cost that is not a product cost is called a **period cost**. Period costs are not specifically related to making or acquiring a product, or providing a service that generates revenues. They are not costs of good sold (or services provided), but relate to other organizational activities such as selling and administration. Period costs are recognized in the income statement as an expense at the time they are incurred, and are therefore not included as inventory in the statement of financial position.

Different costs for different sector types

Next, we consider three different sectors and highlight how the identification and treatment of product costs differ across each; but it should be noted that the following are rather broad descriptions. Many organizations span more than one sector – for example, many manufacturers also provide services such as after-sales and finance services. Given the relatively more complex process of inventorying costs from direct materials, to work in progress, to finished goods (see Exhibit 3.1), proportionately more attention is given here to manufacturing organizations.

Manufacturing

Manufacturing organizations purchase materials and components, and then convert them into finished products – examples include food processing companies, quad-bike producers and mobile phone organizations. In such organizations, all manufacturing costs are product costs, including direct materials, direct labour and indirect manufacturing costs (overheads). Costs are accumulated, and presented in the statement of financial position at different stages of the inventory process. Manufacturers will normally have up to three types of inventory:

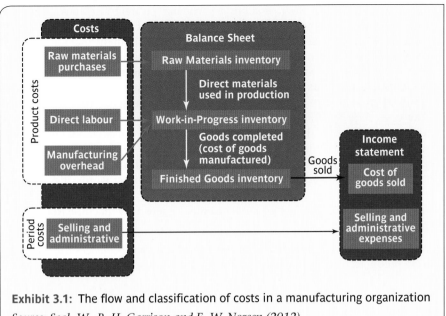

Exhibit 3.1: The flow and classification of costs in a manufacturing organization

Source: Seal, W., R. H. Garrison and E. W. Noreen (2012).

1) Direct materials inventory – direct materials in stock, awaiting use in the manufacturing process (for example, integrated circuits for the manufacturer of Amazon's Kindle)

2) Work-in-progress inventory – goods that have been partially worked on, but which are not yet complete (for example, the shells of a motor car which still have to be spray-painted, and the internal decor and electrics fitted)

3) Finished goods inventory – finished and completed goods, but not yet sold (for example, laptops, ready for sale at one of Dell's manufacturing plants).

Traditionally, manufacturing organizations will accumulate their costs (for example, direct materials, direct labour and indirect manufacturing costs), the total of which is held as an asset in the statement of financial position until the finished product is sold. Upon the sale of a product, the manufacturing costs are charged to the organization's income statement as costs of goods sold. Importantly, this means that even though direct materials and other direct inputs may be incurred in an earlier period, they are still held as an asset (rather than charged as an expense to the income statement) until the final product is sold in a subsequent period.

Manufacturing costs comprise the following:

- *Direct materials* – materials that are easily identified with a finished product. For example, this might include the aluminum used to make cookery pans, yeast used to make beer, or the plastic casing for an iPod.

- *Direct labour* – labour that can be easily identified with (traced) a finished product. For example, this might include a machinist who makes a cutting tool, the salary of a painter who hand-paints a rare set of dinner plates, or the remuneration of a carpenter who plies her trade on a building site. Particularly with increased automation in production, there have been significant drops in direct labour costs in recent times, whereas the proportion of indirect labour costs has tended to be on the increase.

The term 'easily' (used twice, above) means that such costs are physically possible and convenient to identify. Any cost that is difficult to trace to a particular cost object would normally be treated as an indirect cost (see below). This indirect category might also include proportionately insignificant direct costs, such as the glue used in making a child's wooden toy.

All the direct costs incurred when making a particular product also have a name – **prime costs**. In most cases this is the sum of all direct material and direct labour costs, but can sometimes include additional direct expenses. For example, a direct expense might include the employment of an external consultant, or hiring a specialist machine, for a specific product.

Another term which seems worthy of a mention here is **conversion cost**. Conversion costs comprise all manufacturing costs other than direct materials costs. Some organizations adopt this term to simplify their accounts. It can be a useful term in the sense that it represents all the manufacturing costs required to convert direct materials into finished goods. Such methods are most common in organizations that have relatively insignificant direct labour commitments, such as highly automated and machine-intensive organizations.

Indirect manufacturing costs (or manufacturing overhead) – all manufacturing costs other than direct materials, direct labour and any other direct expenses. In other words, it comprises:

- Indirect materials, such as the maintenance costs for a factory machine that is used to make several products

- Indirect labour, such as the wages of a factory supervisor who oversees the manufacturing of multiple products, or factory-wide health and safety officers

- Indirect manufacturing expenses, such as the rent or electricity costs incurred in a factory.

In summary, manufacturing costs are inventorized as products move from direct materials to work in progress, and then to completed goods. An important distinction is made between direct and indirect manufacturing costs; and, the manner in which such costs are captured and recorded is fundamental to any cost system. How to account for costs in manufacturing organizations will be given more coverage in Chapter 4.

Merchandising

Merchandising organizations purchase and then sell tangible products without altering their basic form. They generate profits or surplus by selling their merchandise for a price that is higher than its cost of purchase.

Examples of merchandising organizations include wholesalers and retailers (for example, sportswear stores and bookshops). In general, wholesalers purchase products from manufacturers or other wholesalers, and then sell on to the retailers. Retailers buy from wholesalers or manufacturers, and then sell these products to final consumers.

Merchandisers hold only one type of inventory, that is, they hold merchandising inventory, which constitutes the purchased products in their original form. The product costs recorded for inventory will be the actual price paid, in addition to any incoming freight costs and any insurance or handling costs that were incurred in getting the goods on site and ready for resale to customers. Following the purchase of goods, there are potentially quite negligible additional costs to be incurred in preparation for resale. Thus, in merchandising organizations product cost normally constitutes a significant proportion of total costs.

Finally, product costs in merchandising do not include costs incurred after a product is ready for resale. For instance, in a retail organization product costs would not include the wages of store sales assistants; such costs would in fact be treated as period costs.

Service sector

Service-sector organizations provide services and/or intangible products to their customers – for example, in this category we might think of professional accounting firms, lawyers, health-care organizations, airlines and Internet service providers.

Service organizations do not normally hold inventories of any tangible products that are for sale or resale. Although service organizations can still be viewed as providing products to customers – for instance, in respect of the organizations mentioned above, we can think in terms of an audit, a legal case, an operation, a flight to Australia, an anti-spam facility – these services lack any physical substance. There is no need to inventory costs in service organizations, and all such costs are charged as an expense to the current period.

Valuation of inventory for reporting purposes

Absorption costing and variable costing

Another distinction to make for costs is that between absorption costing and variable costing. Both costing methods establish a way to value inventory in the management accounts, but there are differences between them. Importantly, as these methods have different impacts on inventory valuation, they potentially have different impacts on profit or surplus calculations. This topic receives considerable coverage in Chapter 5; however we provide a brief introduction here.

- **Absorption costing** describes when all manufacturing costs are regarded as being inventoriable. That is, all manufacturing costs are absorbed into the valuation of inventory, whereas;

- **Variable costing** describes when only variable manufacturing costs are inventoried, and fixed manufacturing cost is treated as an expense at the time period in which it is incurred (that is, period costs).

Since the variable costing method means inventorying only variable manufacturing costs, income statements under this approach have a 'contributions' focus, where contribution is equal to sales less variable costs. And, in this scenario, operating profits are driven entirely by the units of sales, whereas under absorption costing, units of production are also relevant for profit calculation. Some organizations regard the latter as being an advantageous dimension to variable costing, and that variable cost information is more useful across a broader range of decision-making scenarios. On the other hand, some organizations hold a view that absorption costing is most appropriate because it does not underplay the importance of fixed costs, and because it shows consistency with financial reporting requirements.

In most countries, it is a professional requirement for organizations to use absorption costing; that is, organizations must treat fixed manufacturing costs as able to be inventoried, but any non-manufacturing costs can be treated as period costs. The absorption – variable distinction is 'however' probably more compelling in financial reporting; indeed, it is not unusual to observe organizations adopting absorption costing in the annual financial statements yet adopt variable costing for management accounting purposes.

Costing systems for different organizational types

Job costing and process costing

As you have learned already, determining product costs in manufacturing organizations is usually more complicated than organizations in other sectors, not least because of the different stages of inventory and the multiple inputs to a production process.

For manufacturing organizations, we need to briefly highlight two different methods for determining the cost of products (see Chapter 4 for more in-depth consideration), namely: (1) job costing, and (2) process costing.

Job costing accumulates the costs incurred in the production of a single unit or a single batch of units. Importantly, the unit produced for one job is dissimilar from the unit produced for another job. Thus, cost information is gathered for each individual job in production, and the cost for each unit is calculated separately. Examples where job costing would be appropriate include the production of a cruise liner, a Grand Prix motor racing car or the construction of a new hospital. Job costing would also be applicable to the services of professional accounting or legal firms, whose work entails customizing their expertise towards different customer needs.

Process costing is most appropriate when an organization's units of production are identical, or almost identical, such that each individual unit of production consumes the same amount of manufacturing input resource. In such cases, rather than calculate separate costs for each unit, an average per unit cost can be applied across the board.

The advantage of process costing, where applicable, is its accuracy and simplicity, based on an average per unit of production cost figure. Examples where process costing would be appropriate include the production of canned drinks, tinned foods and beers. It should be noted that many diversified and multi-product organizations nowadays adopt both job and process costing systems. However, the two are not interchangeable.

A key task for management accountants is the selection and design of a cost system which most appropriately serves an organization's information needs. A rule of thumb would be that where average cost per unit of product represents a reasonably accurate reflection of the cost of an individual product, then process costing is likely to be appropriate. That is, process costing tends to be appropriate for an organization whose individual products all consume roughly equal amounts of resource. As mentioned above, we will cover the job-process costing distinction in more detail in the next chapter.

Predicting cost behaviour when output/activity levels change

Variable costs and fixed costs

The distinction between variable costs and fixed costs underpins how we might view costs changing in response to changes in organizational activity. It is thus a very important distinction for organizational decision making and will be given plenty of coverage in Chapters 11 and 12, but first we provide a summary of the core issues here.

Organizational activity can be measured in various ways – for instance, units of production, sales, labour hours, members' subscriptions and a whole lot more. The types of decisions which might require information on how costs can change in response to shifts in activity levels include:

- How much output do we plan to produce next year?

- What price should we charge next year for product X?

- How will profitability change if we offer customers a 10 per cent discount next month?

- Is it more effective to pay our sales staff by fixed salaries, or by commission?

A **variable cost** changes (in total) in proportion to the level of activity. An example of a variable cost would be the cost of windscreens for an Audi A4 motor car (see *Worked Example 3.1*). We can portray a variable cost as shown in Exhibit 3.2.

> **Worked Example 3.1**
>
> ## Variable costs – windscreens for a car manufacturer
>
> Assume that Audi A4 windscreens cost €400 each and, if next month Audi sell 100 A4 cars, the total cost of windscreens would be €40,000. If Audi sell 200 cars, total windscreen cost would be €80,000; if they sell 250 cars, total cost would be €100,000, and so on. In other words, as activity (that is, the number of cars sold) changes, there is a proportionate change in the *total cost* of windscreens; for every new car sold, the total cost of windscreens will increase by €400.

A **fixed cost** does not change (in total) as activity levels fluctuate. An example of a fixed cost is the factory rent for a motor car manufacturing plant. If we assume there is an agreed annual fee for rent (say €300k), then future changes in the number of cars produced will have no impact on the total cost of rent, it will remain at €300k. We can portray a fixed cost as shown in Exhibit 3.3.

Relevant range

There is a particular period over which the definition of variable and fixed costs holds, called the **relevant range**. This relevant range is specific to a particular organization, and can also change over time for the same organization. Beyond any relevant range period, the basic principles of variable and fixed costs do not necessarily hold and thus cannot be relied upon in decision making.

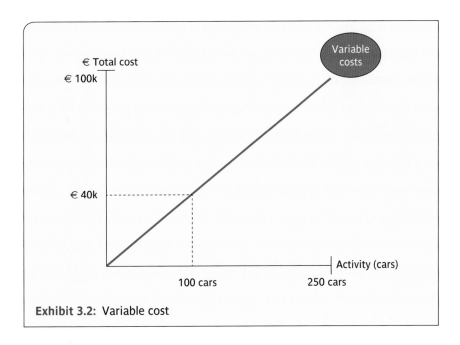

Exhibit 3.2: Variable cost

Costs to assist planning and evaluation

Standard costs

On the basis of careful analysis and estimation, **standard costing** establishes an array of acceptable costs that an organization expects to incur, and monitors actual costs against these standards. Traditionally standard costing systems would assist planning, would help to establish performance targets, and would be used routinely to evaluate actual performance against these targets.

The process of standards setting is complex and varied (see Chapter 9 for more discussion). Suffice to say at this stage, that standard costing gathers as much information as possible about what appears to be an appropriate cost (that is, *standard*) for a particular aspect of organizational activity. So, for example, manufacturing organizations would establish a standard cost for materials that would be used to produce one unit of output, and another standard for the labour hours expected to produce one unit of output. This process would normally be continual and iterative, such that organizations would make comparisons between standard and actual cost figures, undertake evaluations, premise future decisions on these evaluations, and so on.

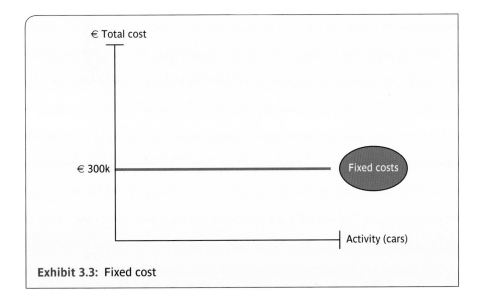

Exhibit 3.3: Fixed cost

Controllable costs and uncontrollable costs

Another important distinction to make when looking at costs, particularly when making business plans and evaluating subsequent performance against those plans, is that between controllable and **uncontrollable costs**.

Controllable costs are those costs which can be influenced by the actions of a particular person (or group) in relation to a particular undertaking. Many organizations establish responsibility centres, including a **cost centre**, which are held responsible for the costs incurred within the centres's area of activity and over which it has influence. Most variable costs are controllable costs – for instance a cost centre in a typical manufacturing organization might be made responsible for direct materials, direct labour, direct expenses and some indirect costs if there is felt to be sufficient influence held over such indirect costs. Another example might be the costs of stationery; if an organization believes that the prices being charged by a stationery supplier are too high then, subject to contract terms, it will be able to pressure the supplier into offering a better (lower cost) deal or else it can seek a new supplier.

Uncontrollable costs are those costs which cannot be influenced by the actions of an individual (or group) for a particular undertaking. Many fixed costs are deemed as uncontrollable, at least in the short term, for example factory rent or council charges. Uncontrollable costs tend to be externally oriented; that is, they are imposed on an organization. There will be more discussion of the controllable–uncontrollable distinction in Chapter 17.

Costs used in different decision-making scenarios

Relevant costs

In making decisions, organizations have a wealth of cost-related information that is potentially available to them, particularly with advanced information technologies at their disposal. However, it is important to keep abreast of that which constitutes relevant information. Relevant information will vary across organizations, decision-making scenarios and time periods. The subject of relevant costs is an important one for management accountants and there will be more detailed discussion in Chapter 13; however, here we briefly present some of the key aspects.

Relevant information is that which is pertinent to a particular decision in so far as it will influence which decision alternative is chosen. Extrapolating from this, a **relevant cost** is a cost (or cash outflow) that would influence the choice among decision alternatives. Relevant costs exhibit two main properties:

1) It is a cost which will be incurred in the future, and;

2) There must be cost differentials between decision alternatives.

Sunk costs

In relation to (1), an organization's current decisions have no bearing on prior expenditure, and expenditures associated with the past (called **sunk costs**) cannot be altered through current or future decisions. Therefore, because sunk costs are unaltered by current and future decisions, they are irrelevant to current and/or future decisions.

Although sunk costs are irrelevant to current decision making, they should always be considered independently from irrelevant costs, because not all irrelevant costs are sunk costs. For instance, consider a bistro café that is deciding which of two coffee-making machines it should purchase, but where both machines actually cost the same to purchase. In such a case, the (purchase) cost is irrelevant because there is no differentiation; but the cost is not a sunk cost but rather a cost to incur in the future.

Cost differentials

In relation to property (2) above, future costs must differ between decision alternatives if they are to be treated as relevant to a particular decision scenario. Where future costs are the same regardless of alternative choices made, they are deemed irrelevant (as in the example of coffee makers, above).

> **Worked Example 3.2**
>
> ## Sunk costs – irrelevance for decisions about the future
>
> One year ago, an Italian ice cream manufacturer had spent €150,000 on constructing a car park at the rear of its manufacturing plant. One year on, the same organization is considering whether to extend its plant over about half of the car park space, for an estimated total cost of €360,000. On the face of it, last year's expenditure on a car park would seem to be important when considering whether or not to erect the proposed plant-extension; surely if the ice cream manufacturer chose to proceed with the plant extension, last year's expenditure of €150k would represent a waste of resource and should be included in some way in the cost of proposed extension?
>
> However, if we approach this situation in relevant-cost terms, last year's car park costs are irrelevant for the purpose of deciding whether or not to erect an extension to the plant. Why? Because the car park has already been paid for, or at least the payment is committed to and is unavoidable, and the proposed extension to the plant would have no impact on that car park cost. Put another way, whether or not the ice cream manufacturer decides to proceed with the plant extension, the cost of the car park is sunk and nothing can be done to change that.

And, referring also to the ice cream manufacturer example (*Worked Example 3.2*), if the total heating costs of the plant with-extension were the same as heating costs without-extension, heating costs would then be irrelevant to the decision over building an extension. Sometimes, relevant costs are referred to as *avoidable costs* and irrelevant costs referred to as *unavoidable costs*. The overlap is intuitive; that is, avoidable costs can be saved if a particular decision alternative is not adopted, whereas unavoidable costs, by definition, cannot be saved.

Opportunity costs

Another important definition to make is opportunity cost. **Opportunity cost** is the value of something that a decision maker gives up as one decision option is selected over another. It is equal to the benefits forgone by electing one decision alternative over another, and can be a cost that implies no cash outlay.

The concept of opportunity cost is premised in resource scarcity. That is, given an organization's portfolio of resource (for example, its workforce, materials, capital, finance), there is a limit to how much it can actually achieve with such resources. So, for instance, if an organization is working to full capacity, in other words it is utilizing its resources to the maximum, a significant change in work patterns will mean lost opportunities elsewhere. As an example, when an organization which is running at full capacity chooses to launch a new product, they run the risk of losing income that is earned on existing products.

If a particular resource has no use, there is zero opportunity cost. However, where a resource has an alternative use, and especially when such resource is scarce, we can say that an opportunity cost exists. Moreover, this opportunity cost should be taken into consideration for any decision about whether or not to engage in an alternative use of the resource.

The opportunity cost perspective is an attempt to integrate 'the bigger picture' into organizational decision-making scenarios, rather than basing judgement entirely on financial or cash implications. While its philosophy might not always be appropriate for organizational decision scenarios, some managers in some circumstances do still take opportunity costs into account.

Technology and cost gathering

Having covered different classifications of cost, most of which will be expanded upon in later chapters, we now finish this chapter with a short discussion of the technology via which cost data is captured. Developments in information technology, particularly over the past two decades, have fundamentally extended the capacity and speed at which organizations can process cost information (and more significant technology is on its way!). We give a brief insight into some of these developments now.

Bar-coding

Bar-coding is a means of gathering cost information at source, and works on the same (code and scanning) principles used in supermarkets. Among other things, bar-coding allows an organization to immediately recognize and account for the cost of goods (or services) acquired as they are bought. Consider a construction organization which makes new homes, and which purchases bricks in bulk from a brick manufacturer. A common bar-coding system can be established so that, upon delivery to the building site or warehouse, bricks will be immediately registered into the respective information systems via bar-code identification. And, as far as the construction organization is concerned, the cost of bricks will be immediately accumulated in the accounting system and assigned to different cost objects (for example, bricklayer staff, an individual building site, or a particular house design).

Such real-time data capture, and simultaneous accumulation and assignments of costs, significantly increase the pace at which transactions can be accounted for; hence, such technology considerably augments the timeliness of information for decision making. Bar-coding has made a significant contribution to current business activity; however, this kind of 'recognition' technology is advancing fast, such as radio frequency identification (see *Management Accounting in Practice 3.3*), and it is likely that bar-coding will soon become technology of the past.

3.3: Management Accounting in Practice

Radio frequency identification

Radio frequency identification (RDIF) is the next generation on from bar codes. It promises to have a fundamental impact on the way that information (including cost information) is gathered, collated and presented. With RDIF, bar codes are replaced by 'smart labels' which connect wirelessly to a networked system that instantly records usage or purchase of any items that you consume or purchase. One example where this technology will likely be used soon is in supermarkets. So, with RDIF technology, the labels (or 'tags') will communicate with an electronic reader that will instantly detect every item in your shopping cart. The electronic reader will be connected to a network that sends your purchase information to the retailer and product manufacturers. Your bank will also be notified how much your total shopping bill amounts to, and this total will be deducted from your account. In other words, you will have been into a large supermarket, taken all the goods that you wanted, then left the store without queuing, waiting or even 'physically' paying!

Source: 'How stuff works, a Discovery company', http://electronics.howstuffworks.com/gadgets/high-tech-gadgets/rfid.htm (accessed on 15 November 2012).

Exercise

How else might RDIF technology be used in the future by organizations?

Database technology

Database technology is information technology that supports storage of vast amounts of data, including cost and cost-related data, being stored in a coherent way via the codification and classification of different cost items. From this core set of data, managers can extract the specific cost information they require, at a particular time. For example, a database system could accommodate two separate reports from the same core data based on the two different perspectives of absorption and variable costing, as described above. There are many and varied possibilities with a good database system.

Powerful database software from the likes of Oracle, Microsoft and IBM can pull out relevant (cost and other) data, in various formats and according to the various users' specific requirements. In other words, it is possible for cost data to be 'cut and slice' in multiple ways from the same core database, to suit different decision-making needs. As well as acquiring the software, its design is also important and is likely to be something that tomorrow's management accountants will engage in.

Enterprise resource planning systems

Enterprise resource planning systems (ERPs) comprises multiple, integrated software applications, called 'modules'. These modules service different organizational areas, including aspects of accounting such as inventory, cash flow and procurement.

At the heart of ERP systems is a common database, and authorized people are able to access a raft of information, real time, covering multiple dimensions of the organization. Being a common database for an integrated system, data needs only be entered once. So, although the quantity of labour hours worked on a particular product during a week is likely to be relevant data for several ERP system modules, like stock valuation, operations and personnel, the data need only be entered on one occasion. Once entered, this data is then automatically and immediately posted to other integrated modules.

Enterprise resource planning systems have had a significant impact on management accountants' roles. Owing to their integrating and real-time nature, much of the collation and processing of routine organizational information is now done automatically, thus freeing up time for more advisory roles.

Chapter summary

Knowledge of costs is critical for any organization, especially in today's highly competitive, volatile and fast-moving economic and social setting. Cost information has many purposes – setting product prices, inventory valuation, seeking to improve process efficiency, preparing bids for an acquisition, to name a few.

In this chapter, we have explored multiple meanings of, and different ways to categorize and accumulate, costs. In today's organization, multiple costs are incurred and there are multiple perspectives from which they can be viewed. Costs can be captured, identified and categorized in many ways. And, these alternative views will shape different perspectives in respect of managers' decision making.

As with all management accounting, accounting for costs is not an exact science; there is not necessarily any 'best' way to configure an organization's cost systems. Every organization has its own specific cost information needs, which evolve and can change over time. Identifying appropriate means to capture, collate and use cost information is a key task for management accountants, one that is likely to intensify in the future, and one that requires broad understanding beyond simply cost techniques per se.

Key terms

Absorption costing A method when all manufacturing costs are regarded as being inventoriable (p. 61)

Bar-coding A bar-code is an optional display of data, the contents of which can be read by scanning devices. Their most commonly known application is in the automation of processing food and other products through supermarket checkouts (p. 66)

Controllable costs Costs which can be influenced by the actions of a particular person (or group) in relation to a particular undertaking (p. 64)

Conversion costs All manufacturing costs other than direct materials costs (p. 60)

Cost Typically, this is some monetary measure of the resources sacrificed or forgone in order to achieve a specific objective, such as acquiring a good or service. But, it is usually more complex than this – there are different costs for different purposes (p. 54)

Cost accumulation Where cost data is organized according to a classification system that identifies a group of costs in a particular (and usually obvious) way (p. 56)

Cost allocation A method to reasonably and accurately assign indirect costs to different cost objects (p. 57)

Cost assignment Where accumulated costs are attributed to specific cost objects, via 'tracing' and allocating accumulated costs to a cost object (p. 56)

Cost centre A group which has responsibility for the costs incurred in a particular activity, normally headed up by a main responsibility manager (p. 64)

Cost objects Something for which a separate cost measurement is required (p. 54)

Cost reduction A process undertaken by an organization to decrease costs. This can involve a variety of strategies and target different measures of 'cost' (p. 54)

Cost system A form of accounting system which captures cost data that will then form the basis of cost information for managers' use (p. 55)

Database technology Information technology that supports the storage of vast amounts of data (p. 66)

Direct costs Costs which can be easily associated with a particular cost object, (p. 56)

Expense A cost that has been incurred when an asset is used up or sold for the purpose of generating revenues (p. 58)

Fixed costs Do not change (in total) as activity levels fluctuate (p. 62)

Indirect costs Costs which evidently support more than one cost object (p. 56)

Job costing A method which accumulates the costs incurred in the production of a single unit or a single batch of units, (p. 61)

Opportunity cost The value of something that a decision maker gives up as one decision option is selected over another (p. 65)

Period costs Costs that are not related to making or acquiring a product, or providing a service that generates revenues (p. 58)

Prime costs All the direct costs incurred when making a particular product (p. 60)

Process costing A method used when an organization's units of production are identical, or almost identical, in which case average per unit costs can be applied to product costing (p. 61)

Product cost A cost that is assigned to goods either purchased or manufactured for (re)sale (p. 58)

Relevant costs Those costs which are pertinent to a particular decision in so far as they will influence which decision alternative is chosen (p. 64)

Relevant range The period over which the definition of variable and fixed costs is assumed to hold and can be relied upon (p. 62)

Standard costing The process of establishing cost standards that an organization expects to incur, then to monitor actual costs against such standards (p. 63)

Sunk costs are associated with the past, and are unaltered by current and future decisions, so they are irrelevant to current and/or future decisions (p. 64)

Tracing The process of assigning direct costs to a particular cost object (p. 57)

Uncontrollable costs Costs which cannot be influenced by the actions of an individual (or group) for a particular undertaking (p. 64)

Variable cost A change (in total) in proportion to the level of activity (p. 62)

Variable costing When only variable manufacturing costs are inventorized, and fixed manufacturing cost is treated as an expense at the time period in which it is incurred (p. 61)

Review questions ● ● ● ● ● ● ● ● ● ● ● ● connect ● ● ● ●

Level of difficulty:	BASIC	INTERMEDIATE	ADVANCED

3.1 **Accounting for costs [LO1, LO2]**

Fill in the missing words:

Something for which a separate cost measurement is required is known as a

_____ _____ .

3.2 Define what is meant by 'cost'. **[LO1, LO2]**

3.3 Identify two real-life examples for each of the following different types of cost objects: (i) product, (ii) service, (iii) activity, (iv) project, (v) department, (vi) customer, (vii) supplier. **[LO2]**

3.4 What is meant by tracing a cost to a cost object? **[LO2, LO4]**

3.5 Define and relate between cost accumulation and cost assignment. **[LO3]**

3.6 Would the salary of a night-time security guard in a factory be classified as a direct or indirect cost? **[LO4]**

3.7 What is the relevant range for an organization? **[LO5]**

3.8 Describe the main difference between job and process costing. **[LO7]**

3.9 Describe some of the main advances in information technology over the past two decades that have fundamentally extended the capacity and speed at which organizations can process cost information. **[LO10]**

3.10 Describe how manufacturing organizations inventory their costs. **[LO6]**

3.11 Why is the salary of a machinist in a textiles business classified as an inventory cost, yet the salary of a shop assistant regarded as a period cost? **[LO6]**

Group discussion and activity questions ● ● ● ● ● ● ● ● ● ●

3.12 The distinction between direct and indirect costs is very important. For the following cost objects, identify three direct costs and three indirect costs: **[LO1, LO2, LO3]**

- The canteen for a primary school in Frankfurt, Germany.
- A boxing event, with four fights, held in a large complex in Las Vegas.
- A charity cycle ride from Paris to Amsterdam.

3.13 All costs attached to an organization are primarily the management accountants' responsibility. Discuss. **[LO11]**

Exercises ● ● ● ● ● ● ● ● ● ● ● ● ● ● ● ● connect ● ● ●

E3.1 **Cost classification [LO1]**

Discuss the main purposes of collecting and classifying cost information in a business organization.

E3.2   **Cost classification [LO1, LO6, LO8]**

Your friend is considering setting up her own manufacturing business, and has commenced a business management course, which involves a short module on management accounting. As outlined below, she is confused by some of the issues presented in her course. She is seeking you to clarify things for her and has asked you to email her some responses to the following questions:

1) How can the same cost be classified in different ways? Surely each cost can simply be described as one thing!

2) Please explain the following cost terms for me: period cost, product cost, sunk cost.

E3.3   **Indirect costs [LO4]**

Which one of the following should be classified as indirect labour:

a) Assembly workers on a car production line?

b) Bricklayers in a construction company?

c) Machinists in a factory producing clothes?

d) Forklift truck drivers in the stores of an engineering company?

E3.4   **Cost behaviour when activity levels change [LO5]**

Performance Cars Ltd spends £1000 per audio system on its 2013 sports model. If the company sells 30 cars in its first quarter of the current year, what is the total cost of audio system?

a) £1,000

b) £30,000

c) £3,000

d) £300,000

E3.5   **Product and period costs [LO6]**

Classify each of the following costs as either a product cost or period cost by inserting a tick in the correct column.

	Product cost	Period cost
Wood used to make a chair		
The touchscreen of a smart phone		
Quality control inspectors salary		
Business insurance		
Sales Managers expenses		
Rent of office space		
Labour costs of process workers in a pharmaceutical company		
Repairs to sales representative's car		
Power costs in a factory		
Cost of installing seats in an aircraft by aircraft manufacturer		

E3.6 **Relevant costs and decision-making [LO8]**

There are two parts to this question:

1) Explain the following terms:

a) Opportunity costs

b) Sunk costs.

2) Management accounting aims to assist managers in their decision-making process. Explain briefly why conventional financial accounting could mislead managers.

E3.7 **Cost classification and relevant costs [LO1, LO4, LO6, LO8]**

Henderson Ltd produces and sells bikes. They have been approached by an overseas customer to supply them with a one off order of 10,000 bikes that are custom-made to their own specific requirements. The customer is willing to pay €100 per bike. As the management accountant you have gathered the cost information for producing the 10,000 bikes:

	€
Metal	200,000
Rubber	100,000
Other variable costs	100,000
Production team wages	50,000
Supervision salaries	30,000
Managers' salaries	30,000
General manufacturing overheads	500,000
Administration expenses	20,000
	1,030,000

Further information:

For a one-off contract the already existing supervisors could cover supervisory roles for this contract. However, as a gesture of goodwill a one-off bonus payment would be made of €2,000.

Required:

1) From the cost information provided, identify the direct and indirect costs.

2) From the cost information provided, identify the prime costs, product cost and period costs.

• • Case study problem • • • • • • • • • • • • connect • • •

C3.1 **Low-cost airlines [LO11]**

Low-cost (or 'low frills') airlines began to appear in the 1970s, and many still exist today, including Ryanair, easyJet and flybe. Their business model is essentially to eradicate some of the costs associated with flying with mainstream airlines, but to do this they offer a service which is far more basic. These airlines can advertise extremely low air fares; in fact it is not uncommon to see fares advertised for nil price. However, when passengers go further in their booking they must pay for extras such as baggage allowance, airport landing fees, flight taxes, seating choice, and more. So, eventually, the ticket prices can eventually become not so low. Ryanair has even recently considered charging passengers to use the toilets when in flight, or at least replacing some of the toilets on their planes with more passenger seats. Overall, low-cost airlines do still tend to undercut their more-frills competitors, but the experience on low-cost flights is frequently a cause for dissatisfaction among those who use them. And, in recent years there have been a number of low-cost airlines who have ceased to do business.

Required:

Do some research into low-cost airlines.

a)   How risky is the low-cost airline business model?

b)   Should low-cost airlines be able to advertise their prices without prior inclusion of ancillary charges such as airport taxes, baggage fee and food/beverages?

c)   Think of any industry. What might your business plan include if you decided to establish a company in this industry as a low-cost competitor to established (mainstream) companies?

● ● ●   Recommended reading   ● ● ● ● ● ● ● ● ● ● ● ● ● ● ● ●

- CIMA (2005) *Management Accounting Official Terminology*, Oxford: Elsevier/CIMA.

A useful collection of terminology in management accounting – including cost terminology and classifications.

● ● ●   References   ●

CIMA (2005) *Management Accounting Official Terminology*, Oxford: Elsevier/CIMA.

Seal, W., R. H. Garrison and E. W. Noreen (2012) *Management Accounting*, 4th edn., Maidenhead: McGraw-Hill.

When you have read this chapter

Log on to the Online Learning Centre at **www.mcgraw-hill.co.uk/textbooks/burns** to explore chapter-by-chapter test questions, links and further online study tools for Management Accounting.

CHAPTER 4

COSTING SYSTEMS

Chapter outline

- Cost systems

- Overview of a job costing system

- Manufacturing overhead allocation – traditional approach

- Non-manufacturing overhead

- Overview of contracting and process costing systems

- Job costing in the service sector

Learning outcomes

On completion of this chapter, students will be able to:

LO1 Understand and explain different approaches to product and service costing

LO2 Understand how labour and material costs can be traced to jobs

LO3 Calculate a manufacturing overhead rate to assign jobs

LO4 Calculate a job cost and understand its use in decision making

LO5 Deal with under or over allocated manufacturing overhead

LO6 Understand how non-manufacturing overheads are treated

LO7 Understand how job costing can be used in contracting and service businesses

LO8 Record job costs and how these relate to the accounting system

Introduction

All business owners and managers need to know the underlying cost of the products or services they offer. If information on cost is not readily available, making even the most basic business decisions becomes very difficult and a business manager would have no idea of the profitability of a product or service.

In Chapter 3, you learned various ways costs can be classified. With this knowledge, in this chapter you will learn how to assigns costs to products and services, which in turn, provides the basic cost data used by managers to plan, control and make day-to-day decisions. How costs are assigned to products depends on the type of business. This chapter focuses mainly on job costing, but also mentions cost assignment in process and contract-type businesses. Job costing implies a unique product, service, order or job is identified as the cost object. In practice, this means a job could be a customer order, a single product, a batch of products or the provision of a service. For now, let's assume job costing means assigning costs to a product/order in a manufacturing setting. Cost assignment for the service sector will be mentioned later in the chapter.

In this chapter, an **absorption costing** approach is used to calculate costs for jobs. Using this traditional approach, all costs of manufacture are assigned to a product, that is, materials, labour and a portion of manufacturing overhead. As absorption costing includes all manufacturing costs, it is also called the full cost approach. As this chapter progresses, you will learn how costs are assigned to products using this approach. Chapter 5 will discuss alternatives to absorption costing.

Before getting into the detail of costing jobs using absorption costing, a brief outline of differing cost accumulation systems is given, namely job, contract and process costing systems. Some more detail on the latter two is given towards the end of the chapter.

Cost systems

Costs are assigned to products or services using some recognized method which reflects the interrelationship with the cost object and how a business or organization runs. The term **cost system** has already been defined in Chapter 3. There are three cost system types typically associated with manufacturing companies and in some service-sector organizations: job costing, process costing and contract costing.

As you have learned in Chapter 3, a **job costing** system (sometimes called a job-order costing system) is one where many uniquely identifiable products/services are the norm. A job may consist of a single unique product or a group of identical products referred to as a batch. In practice, this means that some unique product identifier, code or order number is used as the basis for tracking and assigning costs. For example, if an individual orders one laptop from Dell, this order (job) has a unique order number. Similarly, if a business were to order a batch of 50 laptops, a unique order number would also be assigned. In both cases, a 'job' exists to which costs can be assigned. You will see later how all direct costs are typically assigned to a job, with some indirect costs also assigned.

A **contract costing** system is similar to job costing in that a unique job can be identified. In this case, the job is typically longer term in nature and unique in that it is for a contracted product of service. Engineering or construction-type companies typically use a contract costing system whereby costs are assigned to each construction contract. More direct costs are normal in contracting-type businesses. For example, construction projects may have specific plant and equipment used on one contract–depreciation on this can be treated as a direct cost. Likewise, the salary of a construction site supervisor is often directly assigned to a single project. As contracting-type businesses may have contracts spanning many years, it is important to track costs accurately to determine their long-term profitability. In financial accounting, International Accounting Standard (IAS) 11 deals specifically with construction contracts and specifies how and when costs, revenues and profits/losses are to be recognized in financial statements. Although this is not required in management accounting, the internal costs assigned to contracts are based on the requirements of IAS11. A brief example of contract costing is given later in this chapter.

A **process costing** system was also briefly outlined in Chapter 3. A process costing system is used when a manufacturing process exists in which a unique product or unit cannot be identified. The easiest way to think of a 'process' in manufacturing terms is to think of it as a formula or recipe where the output cannot be broken down into its original components. For example, baking a cake involves mixing flour, eggs, milk and other ingredients which results in the final cake(s). Once mixed and baked, the cake cannot be broken down to the original ingredients. In other words, the output or 'unit' from a process does not materialize until the end of the process. Thus, it is not possible to calculate costs for a unit so the process itself is costed. A cost of a unit of output is derived by dividing the process cost by the expected output from the process. Again, a brief example of how costs are assigned in a process costing system is given later in this chapter.

Management Accounting in Practice 4.1 gives some examples of companies that are likely to use each type of costing system mentioned. The exhibit also shows that a mixture of cost systems can be used by certain types of business.

4.1: Management Accounting in Practice

Job costing

John Dennis Coachbuilders, based in Guildford, UK, designs and builds fire engines and related components. The company uses truck and coach bodies from Volvo, MAN, Scania and Mercedes. It supplies local and city authorities throughout the UK. When such an authority places an order for, say, 15 new engines, this would be considered a job. The cab and chassis are purchased from one of the auto manufacturers mentioned above, and this is a primary material cost. Other materials include the necessary equipment needed on a fire engine, the majority of which is likely to be purchased. Labour costs are likely to be recorded by job, and overheads such as supervisors' salaries and insurance are also likely to be allocated to jobs in some way.

Contract costing

According to their website, Laing O'Rourke is the UK's largest privately owned construction solutions provider with a turnover of £5 billion in 2009. Construction projects due for completion between 2010 and 2015 include: the Olympic and Paralympic Park, London, UK and Mass Transit Railway Maintenance, Hong Kong. Projects like these are effectively long-term 'jobs'. Costs associated with each contract will be carefully recorded and monitored. Costs will include all materials, labour and other direct costs (like project managers' salaries). A portion of Laing O'Rourke's head office and management costs might be assigned to each contract.

Process costing

Bertolli is a well-known brand of Italian olive oil. The brand is owned by global food company Unilever, but is still produced under careful supervision in Italy. Producing olive oil like Bertolli involves an extraction process to remove the oil present in olives. The process uses an industrial scale decanter, into which crushed olives and water are placed. The decanter is rotated at speed and centrifugal force separates the paste into oil, water and solids. The oil can then be drained off and bottled. No job is identified in this example until the end of the process; rather the extraction process is the cost object. The cost of olives, process labour and overhead costs of the process can be assigned to each process run.

Job and process costing

Some industries feature elements of both job and process costing systems. Global packaging industry firms like Smurfit Stone (USA) and SCA (Europe) typically face what they refer to as a V-type production flow. This means that part of the production process uses undifferentiated raw materials, such as cardboard. This element of the production process is typically costed as a process. Then, as the cardboard is cut to size from large sheets to make boxes, a customer job can be identified which is costed as a job. Other industries with similar part-process, part-job structures include dairy processing and metal fabrication.

Exercise

Can you think of other organizations or industries that may use each type of costing system?

Sources: Company websites: johndennisfire.co.uk, laingorourke.com, bertolli.com, smurfit.com and sca.com.

Overview of a job costing system

Job costing systems are typically associated with manufacturing business, although it is also used in the service sector. For the purposes of explanation, a manufacturing operation is assumed to help you understand job costing. The service sector is examined later in the chapter. Manufacturing costs are generally classified as materials, labour and manufacturing overhead (see Chapter 3). Before looking at how each of these three cost classifications are measured and assigned to products, it is first useful to visualize how costs are accumulated as products 'flow' through a typical production process. Exhibit 4.1 depicts such a process, using the example of assembling a notebook computer.

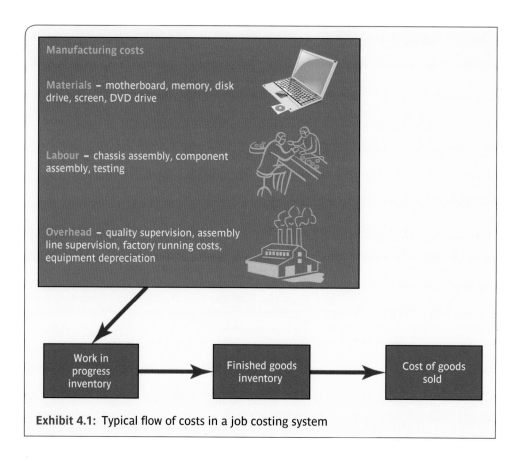

Exhibit 4.1: Typical flow of costs in a job costing system

Looking at Exhibit 4.1, you can see how the cost of a product is accumulated as the manufacturing process occurs. Skilled assembly operators put the necessary materials together in sequence. The assembly operators' labour cost is also included, plus a proportion of overhead. At any point in time, it should be possible to put a reasonably accurate value on any notebook computers which are partially assembled, that is, obtain a valuation of work in progress. Capturing and allocating these costs is not without issue, so below you will learn how costs can be traced to a job. You could also think of each cost and stage in Exhibit 4.1 as a ledger account – a materials cost account, a labour cost account and an overhead cost account. In turn, as materials, labour and overhead are 'used', the costs are recorded in a work-in-progress account. Once products are fully produced, the cost is credited in the work-in-progress account and debited to a finished goods account. Finally, when sold the goods would be debited to a cost of goods sold account from the finished goods account. You do not normally see these accounts in practice, but they are still there in the background of the information systems used to capture and accumulate costs.

Two key questions in a manufacturing environment are (1) when to produce? and, (2) what to produce? Both questions may be answered by customer and/or market requirements, but if enough materials and labour are not readily available, any manufacturer will face problems satisfying customers' orders. Thus, ensuring ample production capacity is a key task for a manufacturing operation. This planning is usually achieved through production planning software, which will typically include detailed data on materials and labour. Management accountants often use this data to help them establish a job or product cost. While ensuring ample production capacity is not normally the responsibility of a management accountant, by interacting with production systems management accountants may be able to assist production managers through the provision of accurate costs. These costs help production managers appreciate, for example, the cost of holding excessive materials in stock, or having employees idle. Thus, a good two-way data flow between management accountants and production management may ensure good costing information and efficient operations. An output of production planning is a **production schedule** which is the plan for what is to be manufactured, when it needs to be done and how it is to be done. The schedule is collated from customer orders, which originate from a sales ordering system.

A key goal of any production manager is to produce efficiently, so jobs may be combined as a job lot, which means multiple products are referred to as a single job lot. For example, if a large business ordered 500 notebook computers from Dell, this order would be in their production schedule using a single reference number or code. Such a job lot is also typically costed as such, rather than as single jobs. Finally, costs for a job or lot are accumulated in some form of cost record. Traditionally, a paper **job card** is attached to each order as it passes through a manufacturing facility. The job card can be used to record costs of materials, labour hours worked on a job, and so on. This data is more likely to be collected electronically nowadays; more detail is provided below.

Next let's see the issues faced by management accountants specifically in a typical manufacturing-based job costing system.

Material cost

The materials necessary to make any products are usually purchased by a centralized purchasing or materials management function. The quantity to be purchased is determined by a number of factors, as follows:

- The quantity of materials in stock, taking into account any policy on minimum inventory levels and delivery lead time from suppliers.

- The price and/or availability of price discounts.

- The quantity needed to produce customer orders.

You might be thinking, how is the quantity of materials needed for customer orders calculated? The production schedule is usually used as a base point, and this, combined with a **bill of materials** for each product helps determine what materials are needed and in what quantities. A bill of materials is a simple list of the materials needed for any product and it is typically a component of production planning software used by a company. The quantity of materials needed per product is multiplied by the quantity of products to be produced to work out the material requirements for production.

Once material requirements for production have been determined, existing stock is checked and, if necessary, material can be ordered from suppliers using a **purchase order**, which shows the quantity to be supplied, an agreed price and a delivery date. Once goods have been received from a supplier, they are checked upon receipt against the purchase order and discrepancies noted. The quantity received is recorded to inventory, and in turn can be issued to production. There are many linked processes in obtaining materials for production, so Exhibit 4.2 provides a useful summary, which should help you understand the issues arising for management accountants.

The processes shown in Exhibit 4.2 are usually replicated in the information systems of an organization. This may be an enterprise resource planning system, which is a large-scale integrated system which aims to streamline as many business processes as possible. You can also see that the

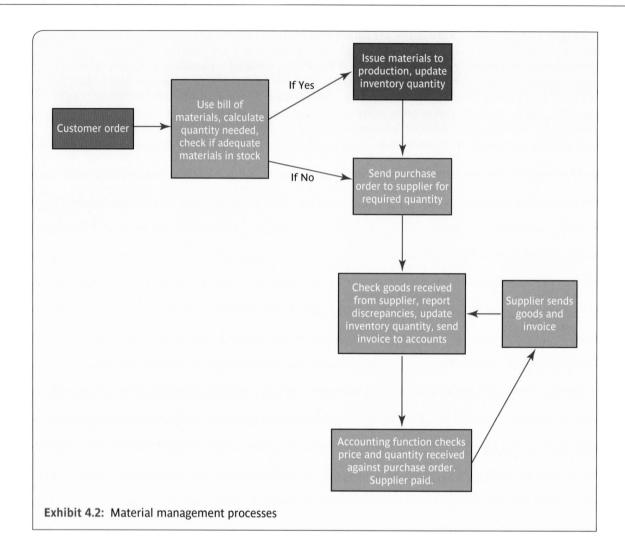

Exhibit 4.2: Material management processes

accounts function is near the end of the process, where the supplier's invoice is paid once goods have been received and the price charged by the supplier is correct.

The price of materials is actually a key issue to be addressed in tracing material costs to products. Let's assume a customer places an order for a notebook computer. The necessary materials are determined from the bill of materials, so to trace the material cost we need only attach a price for each material used. Correct? Yes, but what price? It is possible that materials have been bought from different suppliers and/or at different prices. In other words, it may not always be possible to determine the actual cost of all materials used in any product as it is not possible to physically trace materials to individual products. When this happens, assumptions can be made on the movement of materials, which in turn assists the tracing of material costs to a product. The three alternative assumptions used are termed (1) **first in, first out (FIFO)**, (2) **last in, first out (LIFO)** and (3) **average cost (AVCO)**. Each is briefly explained in *Worked Example 4.1*. Remember however, these are assumptions for accounting purposes and are not related to how materials physically move or flow in reality.

You can see from *Worked Example 4.1* how each assumed method gives a slightly different valuation of the materials issued for use in production and to closing inventory. International accounting standards do not permit the use of the LIFO method, as it has the effect of reducing profits (through lower stock valuations). Remember, these are only assumptions for accounting purposes. The physical movement of goods might follow a FIFO or LIFO system, depending on the business. Of course, if a business has information systems and processes capable of capturing each unique material movement, then actual cost can be used instead of the above assumptions.

Worked Example 4.1

Assumptions for tracing material costs to product

Assume a computer manufacturer buys disk drives from a supplier in the Far East. Here are some recent purchases and the associated purchase price:

Date	No. of drives bought	Price £ each	Total cost
02/09/2013	1,000	5.00	£5,000
12/09/2013	1,300	5.10	£6,630
25/09/2013	2,200	5.20	£11,440

Disk drives were issued from the stores to the production line as follows for two large customer orders:

Date	No. of drives issued
14/09/2013	1,500
28/09/2013	1,000

Now let's see how each of the three methods affects the material costs:

1) FIFO

Using FIFO, the oldest disk drives are assumed to be used first. The cost of the drives assuming FIFO is shown below:

Date	No. of drives issued	Cost £
14/09/2013	1,500	$(1,000 \times £5.00) + (500 \times £5.10) = £7,550$
28/09/2013	1,000	$(800 \times £5.10) + (200 \times £5.20) = £5,120$

There would be 2,000 drives left in stock, valued at £5.20 each as they all come from the stock bought on 25th September. Thus, the value of materials in stock at the end of September is £10,400.

2) LIFO

Using LIFO, the newest drives are assumed to be used first. The costs would now be as follows:

Date	No. of drives issued	Cost £
14/09/2013	1,500	$(1,300 \times £5.10) + (200 \times £5.00) = £7,630$
28/09/2013	1,000	$(1,000 \times £5.20) = £5,200$

Again there would be 2,000 drives in stock but this time 1,200 from the delivery of 25th September and 800 from the delivery of 2 September. Thus, the value of materials in stock is £10,240 at the end of the month.

3) AVCO

The AVCO method differs slightly in that an average unit cost is calculated for units in stock. Here is what would happen:

Date	No. drives bought/used	No. drives in stock	Total cost of purchase/usage	Value of stock	Unit cost £
02/09/2013	1,000	1,000	£5,000	£5,000	5.00
12/09/2013	1,300	2,300	£6,630	£11,630	5.06
14/09/2013	(1,500)	800	£7,590	£4,040	5.06
25/09/2013	2,200	3,000	£11,440	£15,480	5.16
28/09/2013	(1,000)	2,000	£5,160	£10,320	5.16

The average unit cost is calculated by dividing the total value of the materials stock by the number of units held. As you can see, the value of materials in stock is now £10,240.

Labour cost

Labour costs in a job-costing system typically refer to the costs of employees directly working on the manufacture of a product. Labour costs are comprised of the gross (before tax) pay, plus any additional benefits paid to employees, such as pension costs, social clubs, club membership or life assurance. These costs are collated by employee in payroll software, which in turn is typically linked automatically to time and attendance software, that is, software and/or a time clock which records the time an employee enters and leaves a facility. For job-costing purposes however, the time worked on each job/order needs to be captured. Traditionally, the time worked was captured on a job card, along with materials as mentioned. Today, more technologically sophisticated methods are more likely to be used in larger manufacturing operations, as portrayed in the *Management Accounting in Practice 4.2*. These methods usually involve either the employee recording time worked on a job, or automatic capture of the time spent on a job. For example, jobs on a factory floor may be labelled with a bar code or use a radio frequency tag. Sensors on machines can use the label/tag to identify the time a job started and the completion time. The time captured may also be linked to an employees' record in a payroll system and matched to the relevant rate of pay, thus easily calculating the labour cost for a job.

4.2: Management Accounting in Practice

Capturing job times in a manufacturing setting

The manufacture of cardboard boxes (or corrugated containers) by firms like Smurfit-Kappa, Mondi and Saica entails costing each customer job. As orders are manufactured, the time spent on each order can be captured automatically at the process machinery. Industry specific software like Kiwiplan can capture 'start and finish times, thus eliminating the need for manually recording them. It also records set-up time, quantity produced and downtime information for each job run' (www.kiwiplan.com). This means that the time each job takes on a machine is accurately captured, and this is turn is used to establish the labour time, for example 30 minutes on a machine with a two-person crew = 1 labour hour. The labour time can then be costed to the job accordingly. Such systems are not perfect in that machine operators may be paid differing rates of pay, or they may work on several machines. However, the information captured is deemed accurate enough for decision-making purposes.

Exercise

Do you think it is possible to capture totally accurate labour costs per job/product in a typical manufacturing type firm?

When tracing labour costs, a problem faced by all manufacturing operations has been hinted at in the above example. The problem is what to do with labour hours that are not or cannot be traced to a particular job. For example, downtime on a machine, idle time or time spent on normal work breaks cannot be traced to a particular job, but must be paid for. To ensure the labour cost of items such as these are included in a job/product cost, they are usually treated as part of manufacturing overhead (see next section). Other labour costs, such as supervisor or maintenance crew wages are usually treated as indirect labour costs and are also included in manufacturing overhead. The next section explains how manufacturing overhead is traced to products.

Manufacturing overhead allocation – traditional approach

Any manufacturing operation will have costs other than material and labour which cannot be traced directly to products. These indirect costs are typically referred to as manufacturing overhead. Costs like depreciation of manufacturing equipment, utilities (power, oil, gas and water), rent, factory insurance, equipment maintenance and salaries of factory supervisors are all likely to be classed as manufacturing overhead. It is not possible to trace such costs directly to a product in the same way as materials and labour. On the other hand, if manufacturing overheads are not traced to products in some way, then it is not possible to determine the product cost. Also, international accounting standards require a proportion of manufacturing overhead be included in the valuation of inventory. The question is how to trace or allocate a portion of overhead to a product. The accounting standards do not provide a solution and how management accountants in practice allocate manufacturing overhead can vary considerably. Broadly speaking, however, there are two general approaches used which are (1) the traditional approach and (2) an activity-based approach. The latter will be dealt with in Chapter 6. The remainder of this section explains the traditional approach.

Manufacturing overhead allocation

When management accountants refer to 'allocating overhead' or 'absorbing overhead', they are referring to some method used to divide manufacturing overheads costs to each product produced. Two principal questions need to be answered before this can be done. First, the costs to be classified as manufacturing overhead must be agreed. Typically all indirect manufacturing costs are easily identified, but some subjectivity is always possible. For example, is the cost of a quality manager's salary a manufacturing cost or a selling cost? Quality issues are often related to after-sales service. Working together with production managers and staff can help a management accountant identify and correctly attribute costs to a manufacturing process. The second question is how to divide up the costs to products? In an ideal world, all products would use exactly the same quantity of materials, use the same labour and be identical in every way. Thus, it would be possible to give an equal portion of overhead to each product. Although some manufacturing operations may just make a single product, it is highly unlikely each customer order would be for the exact same quantity. Therefore, management accountants must find some way to allocate overheads to products in a manner which reflects the 'amount' of overhead a product 'absorbs' as it passes through the manufacturing process. You will see below how this problem has been traditionally solved. Building a job or product cost using this traditional method of 'absorbing' overhead and adding this to direct material and direct labour costs is termed absorption costing or **normal costing**.

Steps in manufacturing overhead allocation

The allocation of manufacturing overhead follows the steps outlined below. Before allocation occurs however, a choice must be made on whether to use a plant-wide rate or a cost-centre rate. A **plant-wide rate** means that the same overhead rate is used for all products manufactured in a particular facility. While this is a simpler method, it does not reflect how, for example, some products might use more or less manufacturing machines or process steps compared with others. It also assumes overheads are evenly incurred throughout a facility – this may not be the case as, for example, some manufacturing equipment might use a lot more energy than others, meaning energy costs would be higher in that particular part of the manufacturing process. A **cost-centre rate** means that overhead costs are first attributed to cost centres and then an overhead rate is calculated for each cost centre. Let's see first how an overhead rate is calculated and allocated to products.

Step 1 – Estimate total manufacturing overhead

Chapter 8 'Traditional budgeting' will give you more details on budgets, but for now let's define a budget as a plan for the coming year (or month/quarter). Let's assume the budget for manufacturing overhead is prepared for the coming year. Therefore, a management accountant has an estimate of what the manufacturing overhead to be allocated to products is. If a plant-wide overhead rate is being used, there is no need to have any more detail than a total figure. However, if a cost-centre rate is to be used, a more detailed budget for each cost centre is needed (additional comment is given below). Let's assume a company uses a plant-wide rate and the total budgeted manufacturing overhead is £10 million.

Step 2 – Select an allocation base

In step 1 it has been assumed that £10 million of overhead needs to be carved up some way to products. A *basis* for allocating the cost needs to be selected. Traditionally, labour hours or machine hours are used as the basis – a machine hour represents one hour of running time on a machine, which may be more than one labour hour as for example a machine with a crew of five incurs five labour hours for each machine hour. Ideally, the base for allocation should be what 'drives' the costs (see Chapter 6, 'Activity-based costing'). Traditionally, the more labour worked and the more time machinery operated, the higher the costs. Thus, labour hours and machine hours were normally used as an allocation base. It is also relatively easy to record labour hours worked for a particular job/product and/or time spent on machines. As in step 1, an estimate of the allocation base for the coming years needs to be made. Let's assume labour hours are selected as the basis for allocation, and 40,000 labour hours are budgeted.

Step 3 – Calculate the manufacturing overhead rate

The overhead rate can now be calculated as follows:

$$\text{Overhead rate} = \frac{\textbf{Planned manufacturing overhead cost}}{\textbf{Planned quantity of allocation base}}$$

Using the figures assumed in steps 1 and 2, the overhead rate would be:

$$\text{Overhead rate} = \frac{£10,000,000}{40,000 \textbf{ labour hours}} = £250 \textbf{ per labour hour}$$

Step 4 – Allocate overhead to jobs/products

The final step uses the overhead rate calculated in step 3 to a job/product. For example, if a customer order actually took 10 labour hours to manufacture, the overhead for this order would be:

$$10 \textbf{ hours} \times £250 = £2,500$$

Labour hours are recorded as mentioned previously on either a job card or in an information system. These hours are then used to calculate the manufacturing overhead for each job.

If a cost-centre overhead rate is used, then steps 1 and 2 need to be repeated for each cost centre, that is, the overhead attributable to each cost centre needs to be estimated and a suitable cost base for each cost centre selected. Estimating the manufacturing overhead cost for each cost centre may be a simple or more difficult task, depending on how the organization structures itself for cost collection and cost control. Remember a cost centre is one type of responsibility centre (see Chapter 8, 'Traditional budgeting', for more detail), where a manager is responsible for costs which can be readily traced to the cost centre. In a manufacturing facility, each machine, for example, might be considered a cost centre – a machine foreman might be responsible for all material, labour and all other costs traceable to the machine. If a company has a detailed cost-centre structure, then it is likely it has devised methods to trace as many costs as possible directly to cost centres – information systems like enterprise resource planning systems (ERP) usually require companies to set up a reasonably detailed cost centre structure, so any such company using ERP could readily trace and plan costs by cost centre which would be very useful in determining an overhead rate. If complex systems are not available, some costs like energy, light or rent for example, may be allocated to cost centres by management accountants on the basis of floor area or some other method.

There may also be cost centres such as maintenance or materials handling, both of which are manufacturing overheads. These types of cost centres are often called service centres in that they provide a 'service' to other cost centres. Of course, this creates a problem for the traditional approach to allocating overhead as described above if direct labour hours or machine hours are used as a base. The problem is how to incorporate the service centre costs into other cost centres. If the service centre costs are ignored, then a sizeable portion of manufacturing overhead will not get allocated to products. Consider the example in *Worked Example 4.2*.

<table>
<tr><td>**Worked Example 4.2**</td><td colspan="2">### Reallocating service centre costs</td></tr>
</table>

Beco Manufacturing produce heavy duty plastic products used in industrial products. The factory floor has two large machines, an Arburg Injection Molder (AIM) and a Mitsubishi ME III Injection Molding (MIM). Each machine is treated as a cost centre. There are also two service departments, maintenance and quality inspection, which are also cost centres.

The management accountant and other managers have prepared a plan for manufacturing overheads for the coming year as follows

Cost centre	Total overhead £
AIM	1,200,000
MIM	1,450,000
Maintenance	280,000
Quality	160,000
	3,090,000

The supervisors in both maintenance and quality estimate the portion of time they spend on each machine as follows:

	AIM	MIM
Maintenance	20%	80%
Quality	40%	60%

Using these percentages to allocate the service department costs yields the following:

	AIM	MIM
Given costs	1,200,000	1,450,000
Maintenance	56,000	224,000
Quality	64,000	96,000
Total overhead costs	1,320,000	1,770,000

As you can see in *Worked Example 4.2*, the costs of each service department have been apportioned to each machine cost centre. An overhead for each of AIM and MIM cost centres can now be calculated using a suitable basis. By apportioning the service centre costs in this way (based on the supervisor's estimates in *Worked Example 4.2*) or some other manner, the resulting allocation of manufacturing overhead to products is improved. The method used in *Worked Example 4.2* is known as the direct allocation method, in that the overheads of the service departments are simply directed allocated to production departments There are several more complex methods of apportioning service department costs such as the repeated distribution method and the simultaneous equation method. These methods recognize that service departments may actually do some work for other service departments and thus perform several iterations of the type of allocation shown in *Worked Example 4.2* until eventually all overheard gets allocated to production departments. However, the key issue is to ensure as much overhead as possible is eventually allocated to products.

Thus far, you have learned that manufacturing overhead allocation involves a lot of estimation on the part of management accountants and managers. First, why not use actual overhead costs you might ask? The answer is that it is not possible to know actual manufacturing overhead cost until after the end of an accounting period – which might be the end of the accounting year. A business cannot wait this long to cost and/or price its products, so by using a budgeted overhead rate as a 'best guess' a reasonably accurate product cost is determined. Second, the allocation of overhead as described above is also an estimation of how products might 'incur' overhead costs.

Given the estimating that occurs, you might be thinking how are actual manufacturing overhead costs reflected in the accounting systems of a business? The next section details what happens when actual manufacturing overheads differ from the planned figure, as is normally the case.

Under/over-allocation of manufacturing overhead

You now know that the allocation of manufacturing overhead to jobs is an estimation exercise and does not reflect actual overhead costs. Yet, actual costs will be accumulated in the accounts of any business, so let's now see how the difference between actual costs and the predetermined overhead which is allocated to jobs is accounted for in *Worked Example 4.3*.

Worked Example 4.3

Under/over-allocated manufacturing overhead

Let's assume a company has manufacturing overheads of £500,000 and uses direct labour hours as a basis to allocate overhead. For the next financial year, it is planned to work 125,000 labour hours.

Therefore the predetermined overhead rate is:

$$\text{Manufacturing overhead rate} = \frac{£500,000}{125,000 \text{ hours}} = £4 \text{ per labour hour}$$

At the end of the year actual overhead costs were recorded as £527,300 and 131,000 labour hours were worked. We can now see if enough or too much overhead has been allocated to products.

Overhead allocated = 131,000 hours × £4 per hour = £524,000
Actual overhead cost = £527,300
Difference = £3,300

As the overhead allocated to products is less than the actual cost, this means overhead has been under-allocated.

Looking at Worked Example 4.3, let's assume that actual labour hours worked were 134,000, which means the allocated overhead would have been £536,000 (134,000 × £4). In this case, an over-allocation of overhead occurred in the amount of £8,700. The over- or under-allocation of overhead is not traced to products in any way. It is instead treated as a period cost (that is, shown in the income statement as an expense) rather than included in cost of goods sold.

Looking back to Exhibit 4.1 (p. 72), you have seen how job costs (materials, labour and overhead) are accumulated in a work-in-progress account. For manufacturing overhead it is the allocated overhead that is recorded in this account. The actual overhead is recorded in a separate overhead cost account, with the allocated overhead cost credited to the work-in-progress account. Exhibit 4.3 uses the data from *Worked Example 4.3* to prepare a cost account for manufacturing overhead.

Overhead cost account			
Bank (actual costs)	527,300	Work in progress	524,000
		Under-allocated	3,300
	527,300		527,300

Exhibit 4.3: An overhead cost account

As you can see in Exhibit 4.3, the actual overhead costs are debited to the account in the same way as any other expense account. As jobs occur, a portion of the overhead is credited out of the account and debited to the work-in-progress account. This achieves the objective of including a portion of overhead cost in the value of work in progress and, in turn, finished goods, which is particularly useful for financial accounting purposes. You are unlikely to see any manual ledger accounts in a modern business, but what is portrayed in Exhibit 4.3 occurs in the background of any information system which tracks product costs and is linked to financial accounting reports like the income statement or statement of financial position. The term **integrated ledger** is often used to describe the type of information system which links costs gathered for internal use, with the underlying ledger accounts used for financial accounting. ERP systems and other large-scale information systems typically adopt an integrated ledger as standard.

Non-manufacturing overhead

The focus of the chapter so far has been on manufacturing overhead. Traditionally, manufacturing businesses using a job costing system tend to assign only manufacturing costs to products /jobs. There are two main reasons why this is so. First, accounting standards only require an element of manufacturing overhead, and no other overhead, to be included in the cost of inventory. Other overhead costs are viewed as period costs and thus treated as an operating expense rather than a component of cost of sales. A second reason is that, traditionally, manufacturing overhead costs probably were the most significant overhead costs, with selling and administration overhead significantly less proportionately. This has changed in more recent times, as factors such as increased manufacturing automation, automated process control and growing numbers of customer support staff have increased the proportion of non-manufacturing overhead.

Regardless of the requirements of accounting standards, business managers still need to know the full cost of a job to guide business decisions. For example, it would be difficult to determine the profitability of a product, or set a sales price, without some knowledge of the total cost of manufacture. How are non-manufacturing overheads traced or allocated to jobs? It is possible to use the same steps identified earlier for manufacturing overhead, where costs are traced to cost centres and then an overhead rate is calculated. It is also possible that some other costs, such as delivery costs, can be traced directly to a product. If non-manufacturing overhead costs are allocated to cost centres, the obvious question is, on what basis? Labour hours, machine hours or units output are typically not related to non-manufacturing costs, but are sometimes utilized. The best base to use would be one which best relates the non-manufacturing cost to the job. This is not simple, and often results in a somewhat arbitrary allocation of costs. For example, selling overhead might be allocated to products based on a percentage of total sales value in a business, as shown in *Worked Example 4.4*.

Worked Example 4.4

Example of allocation of non-manufacturing overhead

Meridian Manufacturing has three products. Planned sales and production figures for 2014 are shown below:

Product	Sales £	Production/sales units
AD45	5,000,000	100,000
HY789	30,000,000	200,000
JKR4	15,000,000	180,000

A total sales overhead cost of £200,000 is planned. This figure could be allocated to each unit using percentage of total sales value as shown:

Product	% Total sales	Allocated sales overhead (£)	Sales overhead per unit (£)
AD45	10	20,000	0.20
HY789	60	120,000	0.60
JKR4	30	60,000	0.33

While the example shown in *Worked Example 4.4* seems a plausible method, the allocation of the sales overhead cost has no cause-and-effect relationship with the units produced and sold. For example, product HY789 sells more than the other two products but may in fact involve little selling effort on the part of the sales staff at Meridian Manufacturing. If this were so, then it is likely that too much sales overhead has been allocated to the product HY789.

Overview of contract and process costing systems

You now know how jobs are costed, including the difficult task of allocating overhead to a product or job. As outlined at the beginning of the chapter, some companies may accumulate costs in a slightly different way as their methods of operation vary from a typical job-costing scenario. *Management Accounting in Practice 4.1* gave examples of the type of companies that might have a contract-based costing system or a process-based one. The differences of each compared to a job costing system are outlined below.

Contract costing

A contract-costing system is similar to a job-costing system in that a uniquely identifiable cost object is present, that is, a contract. Typically, a contract refers to something like a construction or engineering project which is to be completed according to an agreed specification or plan; for example, a contract from a local council to build a bridge or a motorway. It might also be a contract for services spanning multiple years; for example, Mears Group (http://www.mearsgroup.co.uk/) provides housing maintenance services to UK local authorities under long-term contracts.

There are two main differentiating factors in a contract costing system: (1) the longer time frame causes issues for reporting revenues and costs, and (2) there are more direct costs. The first point is more related to financial accounting. In fact as mentioned previously, an international accounting standard (IAS11) is solely dedicated to the issues around long-term contracts. The standard is not discussed in detail here, but the basic accounting concepts of accruals and prudence are applied by the standard. This means that it is permissible to report a portion of revenues in financial statements as a contract proceeds, together with associated costs. This in effect means a portion of contract profit is recognized. IAS11 also requires any contract losses to be recognized immediately and requires certainty of a contract outcome before any profits can be recognized. The portion of any revenues or profits to be recognized is usually determined using some method which approximates the degree of completion of a contract. A typical example is to use the valuation of work done provided by an architect or engineer and express this as a portion of the agreed contract price. *Worked Example 4.5* gives a short example.

Worked Example 4.5

Apportioning contract costs and revenues

The following data relates to a motorway construction contract that Road Contractors plc are undertaking for a local authority. All data is at 31 December 2014, the financial year end.

Agreed contract price	£50 million
Progress invoices to date	£30 million
Costs incurred to date	£20 million

The company apportions profit on the basis of progress work invoiced as a percentage of total contract price.

First, the contract so far has made a notional profit of £10 million (£30 million – £20 million). Then, based on the information given, the portion of this profit to be recognized in the financial statements is as follows:

$$£10 \text{ million} \times \frac{£30 \text{ million}}{£50 \text{ million}} = £6 \text{ million}$$

The financial statements would thus include:

	£ million
Revenue	26 (balancing figure)
Costs	20
Profit	6

There are methods other than that shown in *Worked Example 4.5* to attribute costs and revenues to several accounting periods, and the accounting standards do not define a particular method. The key point is to recognize a loss straight away and some fair portion of profit. A calculation similar to that shown in *Worked Example 4.5* should be performed each accounting period to ascertain a profit or loss. Normally, cumulative profits are easiest calculated, so any previously recognized profits would be deducted to work out current year figures.

The other distinctive feature of a contract-costing system is the prevalence of direct costs. A contract is like a job in that it is a unique cost object, but it is much easier to trace costs directly to a contract. Costs like supervisors' wages, depreciation of equipment and insurance are much more likely to be direct costs of a particular contract. For example, all larger construction sites would normally have a site foreman, site safety office and site engineers dedicated purely to the particular contract site. Also, equipment may even be specifically purchased or designed for a contract, for example tunnel-boring machines. Thus, accountants and managers do not have to spend as much time allocating indirect costs to contracts. In many large construction companies for example, the only indirect cost may be the cost of running a head-office building. This might include centralized services like payroll, accounting and legal staff. This cost might be allocated to each contract on the basis of contract value or number of employees on site. Finally, as contracts may span several years, stock of materials may exist at the end of an accounting year. The value of any stock is treated in the same way as any other inventory, that is, the accruals concept is applied and the value is matched against the following years' cost.

Process costing

As mentioned at the beginning of this chapter, a process environment means that the output of the manufacturing process does not become a 'physical' product until the end of the process. Instead, the process itself has costs which can be identified, that is, the process is the cost object. However, it is highly unlikely that the output of a process is sold in one large lot; it is normally split up into identifiable products. Thus the problem for management accountants is to find some form of 'unit' as a cost object to help identify costs and profits. *Worked Example 4.6* gives a simple example to help you understand the problem and a simple solution.

> **Worked Example 4.6**
>
> ## Process costing – simple example
>
> Sunblest Ingredients is a large-scale food ingredient manufacturer based in the UK. One of their process lines makes powered egg protein, which is used in the food and restaurant sector. The process entails separating the egg white from eggs and adding several ingredients. The resulting product is a white powder. A typical process run follows a standard recipe as below:
>
> | | |
> |---|---|
> | Eggs | 3,000 kg |
> | Water | 900 litres |
> | Emulsifier | 100 kg |
>
> The cost of these ingredients is £1,250. Labour costs of £150 are incurred each time this recipe is baked and the management accountant has allocated £100 of overhead. Following this recipe yields 4,000 kg of powered egg white.
>
> The costs of the process are £1,500, but a cost per kilogram would be very useful for decision-making purposes. This could be calculated as follows:
>
> $$\frac{\text{Process costs}}{\text{Expected output}}$$
>
> In this example, the cost per kg would be:
>
> $$\frac{£1,500}{4,000 \text{ kg}} = 37.5 \text{ p/kg}$$

As you can see in *Worked Example 4.6*, a simple cost per unit can be calculated from the total process costs and the expected output of a process. The process cost will include direct costs like material and labour, but again some method to allocate indirect costs (that is, manufacturing overhead) is required. It could be on the basis of process hours, the area of factory space used by a process or some other method. In practice, there are more complications to processes than the example in *Worked Example 4.6* shows. There is usually an input loss due to waste in a process, as the output of a given process 'recipe' cannot be guaranteed each time. Processes can have a normal loss and an abnormal loss. For example, the recipe in *Worked Example 4.6* might say a normal loss of 5 per cent is expected, meaning that the output would be 3,800 kg (4,000 kg × 95 per cent). As a normal loss is expected, the cost of this is reflected in the normal good output. Thus, the cost per kg of powdered egg white in *Worked Example 4.6* would now be 39.5p (£1,500/3,800 kg). An abnormal loss occurs when the loss is greater than expected. Such a loss is treated as a period cost. It is also possible that the process loss is less than expected, and this is referred to as an abnormal gain.

A further complication arises if, at the end of an accounting period, a process is incomplete. The problem is how to value the 'units' within the partially completed process. Take a look at *Worked Example 4.7*.

> **Worked Example 4.7**
>
> ## Process costs with closing inventory
>
> Suppose Sunblest Ingredients runs the process as described in Worked Example 4.6 100 times per annum. However, at year end the final process run is not fully complete and the following data is available:
>
> All ingredients are added at the start of the process.
>
> The factory supervisor estimates the process to be 60 per cent complete.

Remember we are trying to calculate a cost per kg. To calculate the cost, we need to include the costs of the completed goods and the partially completed final process. The table below shows how this is done, by working out equivalent fully completed units for work in progress.

Cost element	Total cost £	Completed kg[1]	WIP kg	Total kg	Cost per kg £
Ingredients	125,000	396,000	4,000	400,000	0.3125
Labour	15,000	396,000	2,400	398,400	0.0375
Overhead	10,000	396,000	2,400	398,400	0.0250
					0.3750

Note: 1. The process is run 100 times per annum. Thus $100 \times 4,000$ kg $= 400,000$ kg should be complete. The final run is not complete as stated, so $400,000 - 4,000 = 396,000$ kg are deemed complete.

Note how the cost per kg equals the cost as calculated in *Worked Example 4.6*. As per the advice of the factory supervisor, 60 per cent of the final process output is being deemed as complete, hence this is equivalent to 2,400 kg completed (4,000 kg × 60 per cent). As all ingredients are added at the start of the process, then all units are considered as complete for this cost element. Now that we have costs for each element of the process, we can split costs between completed units and closing work in progress as follows:

	£
Completed (396,000 kg × 37.5p)	148,500
Value of closing WIP:	
Ingredients (4,000 kg × 31.25p)	1,250
Labour (2,400 kg × 3.75p)	90
Overhead (2,400 kg × 2.5p)	60
	1,500

The calculation of units costs is further complicated when opening work in progress is present. The problem then is that an assumption must be made on how the partially completed units are pushed through the process. A First-in, First Out approach can be used where the costs of completing opening work in progress units are calculated first. A weighted average approach is also possible, where opening work in progress is grouped together with all other units to calculate a unit cost. *Worked Example 4.8* depicts both approaches to dealing with opening inventory in a process.

Worked Example 4.8

Process costs with opening inventory

The following data relates to process A for a month

Opening inventory	2,000 units 50 per cent complete
Units started in month	7,000 units
Closing inventory	1,000 units, 20 per cent complete

Prior month costs attached to opening inventory were £500, all conversion cost

Costs for the month were: materials £12,000, conversion costs £9,000.

Materials are added at the end of the process and conversion costs are incurred uniform throughout the process.

It is useful to first ascertain how many units were completed in the month, as follows:

Opening inventory units	2,000
Units started	7,000
Closing inventory units	(1,000)
Completed units	8,000

We can now prepare an equivalent units table.

	Units	Equivalent units	
		Material costs	**Conversion costs**
Completed (8,000)			
–from opening inventory	2,000	2,000	1,000
–started and complete	6,000	6,000	6,000
Closing inventory	1,000	0	200
Units		8,000	7,200
Current period cost		£12,000	£9,000
Cost per equivalent unit		£1.50	£1.25

The opening inventory has not yet had materials added–materials are added at the end of the process, hence 2,000 equivalent units under the material cost column. Similarly, opening inventory has had 50 per cent of the conversion done in the previous month, so 1,000 equivalent units (2,000 × 50 per cent). Now, we can cost the completed units for the process using the FIFO method:

Cost of completed units	**£**
2,000 units from opening inventory	
Prior month cost	500
Materials (2,000 × 1.50)	3,000
Conversion (1,000 × 1.25)	1,250
6,000 units started and complete	
(6,000 × 2.75)	16,500
Total cost	21,250

Cost of closing inventory	**£**
Materials	0
Conversion (200 × 1.25)	250
Total	250

You can see how the opening inventory is assumed to be completed first and included separately in the cost calculations.

Using the weighted average method, the opening inventory units are not identified separately. The cost calculations are a little different as follows:

	Units	Equivalent Units	
		Material costs	Conversion costs
Completed	8,000	8,000	8,000
Closing inventory	1,000	0	200
Equivalent units		8,000	8,200
Cost prior period		0	£500
Cost current period		£12,000	£9,000
		£12,000	£9,500
Cost per equivalent unit		£1.50	£1.16

As you can see, the weighted average method makes no attempt to separate the opening inventory units. Instead they are incorporated within the completed units. The value of the completed units and closing inventory is as shown below:

Cost of completed units	£
8,000 × £2.66	21,280

Cost of closing inventory	£
Materials	0
Conversion costs 200 × £1.16	£232
	£232

Job costing in the service sector

This chapter so far has concentrated on job costing in a typical manufacturing company. Some service-type companies too can adopt job-costing techniques. Professional firms like firms of accountants, legal firms, consultants and architects have readily identifiable jobs in the form of work done for clients. Costs in such firms will consist typically of labour and overhead. Capturing the labour cost of a client job can be achieved using a time-recording system. For example, in a consulting firm each labour hour worked by a consultant is recorded to a client. A pay rate will be available as shown in *Worked Example 4.9*.

Labour cost in a consulting firm

FGT Associates are a business consulting firm. They are currently working on a project for ABC plc, which involves one senior consultant and one junior consultant. Their salaries are £100,000 and £40,000 per annum respectively.

Ignoring social insurance and other employment costs, a cost per hour for each consultant as follows:

	Senior consultant	Junior consultant
Annual salary	£100,000	£40,000
Working days per annum	250	250
Rate per day	£400	£160
Rate per hour (8 hr day)	£50	£20

The rates per hour above could then be charged to clients based on hours worked to determine a cost for each client job.

As with the previous manufacturing examples, in a service-sector firm an overhead rate also needs to be calculated. Keeping with the consulting firm example, overhead costs might include expenses such as office running costs (phone, light, heat), support staff salaries, rent and advertising. As with the previous manufacturing examples, budgeted overhead figures are used and allocated using a suitable base. The total labour hours planned for all consultants in a firm could be used, and an overhead rate per labour hour calculated. This, in turn, could be used to allocate overhead costs to clients. Thus, job costing in a service sector firm may be quite similar to that in a manufacturing firm.

However, many services firms have relatively low labour costs and high overheads, which means that using labour hours as a basis to allocate overhead is questionable. Take a bank for example: while customer service staff and bank managers do deal with customers and banks do have lots of employees, labour cost is a relatively small portion of total costs. The larger component of cost in a bank consists of the costs of running the many supporting systems and process which keep the bank running, for example Internet banking, ATMs and payment-processing systems. Thus, using labour hours as a basis to allocate the overhead costs in a bank might result in costs which are unreflective of the service provided. For example, a consultation with a bank manager on a loan application does involve some labour hours, but paying a bill through online banking does not. The latter however, uses costly information systems resources. If labour hours were used as a basis to allocate overhead, the consultation will be charged some overhead, whereas the online bill payment will not although it 'consumes' some overhead cost.

Additionally, the existence of a 'product' or 'service' may even be questionable in some service companies, which in turn raises questions on the usage of techniques mentioned in this chapter. Bhimani and Bromwich (2010, pp. 83–84) point out that companies like Facebook or Google do not have a product or service in the traditional sense as consumers of the services of such companies typically pay nothing. In companies like these, the focus is more on raising enough revenue to cover a largely fixed cost base. In other words, the product consumed – a Google search or a Facebook post – is disassociated with any price and underlying costs of providing the service. Instead, the longer-term viability of companies like Facebook and Google is more dependent on building a very large user base which may in turn be used to market services which are revenue generating. Of course, these companies do generate revenue from advertising and add-on services, but the price charged is not reflective of the cost of maintaining the large supporting information technology infrastructure.

In summary, job costing as shown in this chapter may not be a suitable solution for service-sector companies, particularly in relation to overhead allocation. However, you will learn about activity-based costing in Chapter 6. This technique offers a potentially improved way to allocate overheads and removes the traditional focus away from labour or machine hours as an allocation base. As you will see, using activity-based costing allows management accountants to continue to use job-costing concepts in service-sector companies.

Chapter summary

This chapter introduced three types of costing system–job, process and contract. The mechanics of costing a job in a manufacturing firm were detailed. Material, labour and manufacturing overhead costs were identified as three major cost classifications in a typical job. Issues with costing materials and manufacturing overhead were addressed. In particular, how overheads costs are traditionally allocated to products using budget data was detailed. Differences between contract costing and process costing systems were highlighted and a brief overview of the calculation of costs in both systems was given. Finally, how job-costing might be used in service-sector companies was outlined, together with some potential shortcomings.

Key terms

Absorption costing A cost system which allocates all costs to products/services (p. 74)

Average cost The cumulative average cost of inventory (p. 78)

Bill of materials A list of all material components of a product (p. 77)

Contract costing A cost accumulation system used in contracting-type business (p. 74)

Cost system An accounting system to capture information on costs (p. 74)

Cost-centre rate An overhead absorption rate for a cost centre (p. 81)

First in, first out A term used in inventory management, whereby the oldest inventories are assumed as sold first (p. 78)

Integrated ledger A single ledger which is used for internal and external reporting purposes (p. 85)

Job card A card or report which details the cost of a job/order (p. 77)

Job costing A cost accumulation system used in a business where individual jobs/orders are identifiable (p. 74)

Last in, first out A term used in inventory management, whereby the newest inventories are assumed sold first (p. 78)

Normal costing See absorption costing (p. 81)

Plant-wide rate A single overhead absorption rate for a production plant/facility (p. 81)

Process costing A cost accumulation system used in a process-type business, that is, where units are not identifiable until the end of the process (p. 74)

Production schedule A plan for production (p. 77)

Purchase order A document raised to a supplier/vendor to confirm the purchase of goods or services (p. 77)

Review questions ● ● ● ● ● ● ● ● ● ● ● connect ● ● ● ● ●

Level of difficulty:	BASIC	INTERMEDIATE	ADVANCED

4.1 What sort of costing system would an advertising agency use – job or process? [LO1]

4.2 How is the costing system of a contracting-type business similar to a job costing business? [LO1]

4.3 Which of the following businesses would be more likely to use a job costing system rather than a process costing system: [LO1]

   a) Steel manufacturing?

   b) Firm of architects?

   c) Beer company?

   d) Oil refining?

4.4 What is the difference between the FIFO and LIFO methods used in calculating material costs of a job? [LO2]

4.5 What is the formula used to calculate a predetermined manufacturing overhead rate? [LO3]

4.6 Why is budgeted manufacturing overhead, rather than actual overhead, used when calculating and overhead rate for manufacturing overhead? [LO3]

4.7 Can the techniques normally used to allocate manufacturing overhead be used for other overheads? [LO3]

4.8 What happens when manufacturing overhead absorbed by products is more or less than budgeted overhead? [LO5]

4.9 Job costing is normally associated with manufacturing firms. Can it be used in the service sector? [LO7]

4.10 In a service sector firm, can direct labour hours be used as a base to allocate overhead? Are there any problems using labour hours as a base? [LO7]

Group discussion and activity topics

4.11 Discuss the type of costing systems which might be used by some businesses you know. Discuss the nature of the business and why you think a particular costing system would be most suited. **[LO1]**

4.12 Discuss why it would not be advisable for a custom motorcycle shop like Orange County Choppers (http://www.orangecountychoppers.com/) to use process costing. **[LO1]**

4.13 Discuss why managers need to know the full cost of an order/job. **[LO4]**

4.14 Go to www.youtube.com and search for clips on how a product is made. Food products are usually a good example. Watch the video clip and then discuss the materials used in the product (direct and indirect), the direct and indirect labour costs and the likely elements of manufacturing overhead. **[LO2]**

Exercises   connect

E4.1   **Under/over-absorption of overhead [LO1, LO5]**

The following information is available for two production cost centres in a factory owned by Makers Ltd for the month of July:

	Cost centre X	Cost centre Y
Budgeted costs	£28,556	£54,264
Budgeted hours	1,210 machine hours	6,460 labour hours
Predetermined absorption rate	£23.60 per machine hour	£8.40 per labour hour
Actual costs	£29,609	£52,567
Actual hours	1,235 machine hours	6,395 labour hours

Required:

a)   Calculate the over- or under-absorption of overhead for the period in each cost centre.

b)   Explain two advantages of using predetermined, as opposed to actual, overhead absorption rates.

Source: adapted from Association of Chartered Certified Accountants, Certified Accounting Technician, Paper T4.

E4.2   **Material cost and job costs [LO1, LO3, LO4]**

BRC Ltd, manufactures power generation units for wind turbines. The company was founded five years ago by Brian Williams, an engineer. In the past 18 months, production of the units has increased dramatically due to a large increase in demand from other EU countries. The increased demand has resulted in the hiring of additional staff, both production and administrative. Brian recently approached the company bankers to seek additional finance for further expansion. The bankers are willing to grant the required finance, provided BRC Ltd engage a full-time management accountant to implement good accounting controls – an area which has been lacking due to Brian's engineering focus.

You have been hired by BRC Ltd as a management accountant. It quickly emerges that the companies highest cost component is materials and no inventory control system exists to value inventory or identify the quantities in stock. Brian commented to you: 'We only ever do a stock count once a year when the auditor arrives. Otherwise, I have no idea what's in stock or what it's worth.' You immediately set to work implementing an inventory system.

You make contact the person who has responsibility for ordering new items and issuing stock to production. You find that one item, a 10kw motor, has a very high value relative to others, so you decide to implement controls on this item first. The following inventory movements relate to the 10kw motors for the month of April:

Goods inwards		
Date	*Qty*	*Price £*
2 April	60	200
9 April	80	240
16 April	75	275
21 April	40	290

Goods issued to production	
Date	*Qty*
11 April	110
18 April	90
23 April	50

You have also ascertained that each complete power generation unit has a labour cost of £85 per unit and an overhead allocation of £35 per unit. The selling price of each unit is £500.

Required:

a) Write a brief memo to Brian Williams outlining the three major product cost components and why it is necessary to calculate product cost.

b) Identify and briefly explain three possible methods which could be used for pricing and valuing inventory at BRC Ltd. (No calculations are required for this section.)

c) Calculate the cost of each inventory issue of 10kw motors for April and the value of closing stock at the end of April using the FIFO and AVCO methods.

d) Using the average unit cost of a 10kw motor as at the end of April and other information given, calculate the product cost and profit for each complete power generation unit using each of the two methods of valuing inventory you used in part (c).

E4.3 **Job cost in manufacturing company [LO3, LO4]**

Oracle Consulting Ltd has three production departments, X, Y and Z. It currently uses a single overhead absorption rate expressed as a percentage of direct wages cost. The management accountant at the company has suggested that a departmental overhead absorption rate would give more accurate job costs. The data in the tables gives budget information for 2014 and actual data for order 285.

Budget data	Direct labour £	Labour hours	Machine hours	Manufacturing overheads £
Dept X	400,000	32,000	72,000	300,000
Dept Y	300,000	54,000	57,000	500,000
Dept Z	500,000	30,000	65,000	30,000
Total	1,200,000	116,000	194,000	830,000

Order 285 cost data

	Material £	Wages £	Labour hours	Machine hours
Dept X	98.00	225.00	18	17
Dept Y	110.00	105.56	19	19
Dept Z	75.00	216.67	13	1
Total cost £	283.00	547.22		

A profit margin of 11 per cent is added to full cost to obtain a selling price.

Required:

a) Calculate the current overhead absorption rate.

b) Using the current overhead rate calculate the full cost, expected profit and selling price for order 285.

c) Calculate department absorption rates using the dominant activity in each department.

d) Using the departmental overhead rates calculate the full cost, expected profit and selling price for order 285.

E4.4 **Job cost in service company [LO4, LO6, LO7]**

PMG are a medium-sized accounting, auditing and consulting firm. They employ 130 staff across four departments: Audit, Tax, Management Information Systems consulting (MIS) and Compliance. Staff at the firm complete timesheets for each job, but the firm does not allocate all costs to its jobs in a detailed manner.

The following summary of costs has been complied by one of the firm's managing partners for the month of June:

	Total	Audit	Tax	MIS	Compliance	Unallocated
	£000's*	£000's	£000's	£000's	£000's	£000's
Costs						
Staff salaries	6,000	2,020	1,040	520	540	1,880
Indirect staff costs						
Office managers	250					250
HR staff	200					200
Library and research	160					160
Professional development	1,200	500	200			500
Other costs						
Supplies and stationery	36	5	5	16		10
Travel	500	130	50	160		160
Office running costs	140					140
Information systems cost	1,615	50	20	10	35	1,500
Total costs	10,101	2,705	1,315	706	575	4,800
No. of jobs		95	1,800	45	140	

* 000's is to show that the numbers in the table are in thousands.

The partner then allocates the costs depicted above as unallocated to the four departments as a proportion of the staff salary cost. The resulting costs are then divided by the number of jobs undertaken for clients by each department to determine a cost per job. A cost report is circulated each month to senior partners in the firm

Required:

Calculate a cost per job for each department using the partners original method of allocating costs (that is, as a proportion of staff cost)

E4.5 **Journal entries for job costs [LO8]**

Camprint are a campus-based publishing company. Most of their work is for the university's various faculties, but it does publish and sell some books to the general public. All work for the faculties is charged at full cost plus an agreed profit margin. It uses a job-costing system and has two direct costs (materials and labour) and one indirect costs (manufacturing overhead, allocated as 150 per cent of direct manufacturing labour costs). The company keeps a stock of printing and binding materials and also has a stock of books for resale on hand.

Required:

a)   Draw an overview diagram of the cost system at Camprint.

     The following data relates to 2015 for Camprint:

	£000's
Paper and binding materials bought on credit	400
Paper and binding materials used	350
Paper (bought as material) used by administrative departments	10
Direct manufacturing labour, all paid in cash	625
Depreciation of equipment	100
Indirect labour, all paid in cash	250
Other manufacturing overhead, all on credit	620
Manufacturing overhead (150 per cent as detailed above)	?
Paper and binding materials returned to suppliers	5

b) Prepare journal entries to summarize the above transactions in the Camprint job-costing system (narratives are not required).

c) Prepare a journal entry to dispose of the under/over allocated manufacturing overhead as a cost of sale.

E4.6 Service department overheads and job cost [LO1, LO3, LO4]

AM Appliances Ltd manufactures and distributes a wide range of household appliances. The company is organized into various cost centres and management calculate product costs based on the number of cost centres that a typical product passes through during its production cycle. The company produces one basic dishwasher using five different cost centres for accounting purposes. There are three production departments (Machining, Assembling and Finishing) and two service departments (Materials Handling and Production Control). Costs of these five cost centres for last year, when 2,000 machines were produced, were as follows:

Materials	£
Machining	240,000
Assembly	160,000
Finishing	40,000
Materials handling	4,000

Wages	£
Machining	10,000 hours at £3.72 each
Assembly	5,000 hours at £2.88 each
Finishing	3,000 hours at £3.60 each
Materials handling	£8,000
Production control	£11,200

Other costs	£
Machine shop	41,920
Assembly	12,960
Finishing	7,920
Materials handling	8,000
Production control	2,400

It is estimated that the benefit derived from the service departments are as follows:

	Materials handling	Production control
Machine shop	60%	40%
Assembly	30%	30%
Finishing	10%	20%
Materials handling	n/a	10%

Required:

a) Prepare a schedule showing the overhead only which should be incurred by each of the five departments.

b) Prepare a schedule showing the overhead re-apportioned from the service departments to the production departments.

c) Calculate an overhead absorption rate for each of the three production departments using a rate per unit basis (to two decimal places).

d) Prepare a schedule showing the components of total production cost for one dishwasher.

e) Assuming that AM Appliances Ltd use 'production cost plus' as a pricing mechanism, estimate the selling price (to the nearest £) using both a margin of 20 per cent and a mark-up of 25 per cent.

Source: adapted from The Institute of Certified Public Accountants in Ireland, Formation 2, Management Accounting.

● ● ● ● ● **Case study problem** ● ● ● ● ● ● ● ● ● ● **connect** ● ● ●

C4.1 **Flight costs and prices at low-cost carriers [LO1, LO3, LO4, LO6, LO7]**

You work as an accountant for a diverse investment and capital company and have been reading the following excerpt from a local newspaper:

> Low-cost airlines like Ryanair and easyJet are taking on Europe's traditional airlines and seem to be making good profits even in leaner economic times. Traditional (sometimes flag) carriers have been reporting major losses in recent times. For example, in their three most financial years to 2010, EasyJet and Ryanair reported profits of about £240 million and £800 million respectively, with profits made each year. In the same period British Airways made profits of £123 million, but with losses of approx £750 million in 2009 and 2010.

Just yesterday, your boss mentioned the idea of buying some passenger aircraft and setting up an airline as he believes he has seen an opening in the market for a low-cost but 'with frills' airlines, that is a cheap fare, but offering the services of more traditional airlines. You show him the article above. This encourages him, as he sees a major gap as more passengers are getting 'tired' of the low-cost model. You have been asked to do an initial analysis on the costs of flights to a number of key routes to assess whether of not they would be profitable and how profits would be affected by the number of passengers per flight, that is the load factor. The routes under considering are:

Route	Distance
London–Vienna	1,250 km
London–Paris	340 km
London–Rome	1,450 km

Two aircraft are under consideration for the new airline (1) a Boeing 737-900ER which costs $90 million (assume a GBP:USD rate of $1.50) and (2) an Airbus A321 costing $105 million. The Boeing 737 can carry 163 passengers while the Airbus A320 carries 195 passengers.

Both aircraft will be expected to fly on average 5,000 km per day on an average of 320 days per year for the next 15 years. Current jet fuel prices are approximately 40 pence per litre and both aircraft consume on average 15 litres per kilometre flown.

Currently, the following prices are charged on the above mentioned routes:

Route	Low cost carrier price (one-way)	Traditional carrier price (one-way)
Vienna	£90	£95–340
Paris	£85	£100–280
Rome	£110	£130–450

(The highest price for traditional carriers is the business class fare.)

The aircraft will have a complement of six cabin crew with an annual total salary cost of £30,000 each. The captain's salary cost will be £100,000 and the co-pilot's £70,000. The on-board service offerings (food, drinks, and so on) will cost £5 per passenger.

Required:

Compile a report for your boss which addresses the following:

a) Based on the above data, calculate an approximate total cost of each flight for each aircraft type assuming a 100 per cent load factor.

b) Calculate the revenue generated for each flight assuming a 100 per cent load factor and a one-way fare price of the average of the traditional carriers.

c) Calculate the profit for each flight and aircraft type.

d) Calculate the minimum load factor for each aircraft type to generate a profit on each flight based on the average fare of the traditional carriers.

e) Assuming a 75 per cent load factor, calculate the minimum average fare required to generate a profit on each flight for each aircraft type.

f) Assuming you present your analysis of costs and revenues (in (a) to (e) above) to your boss, what limitations of your analysis would you highlight?

g) Assuming your cost analysis depicts a profit on routes, and taking into account your all your calculations, recommend an aircraft type. Indicate what further information about the aircraft would be needed to make a final decision.

● ● Recommended reading ● ● ● ● ● ● ● ● ● ● ● ● ● ● ● ● ● ●

- Bhimani, A. and M. Bromwich (2010) *Management Accounting: Retrospect and Prospect*, London: CIMA.

This book gives some food for thought on more modern business models, where products or services may be more difficult to construe.

- Dugdale, D., T. Colwyn-Jones and S. Green (2006) *Contemporary Management Accounting Practices in UK Manufacturing*, London: CIMA.

This is a good and comprehensive survey report of actual UK management accounting practices.

Reference

Bhimani, A. and M. Bromwich (2010) *Management Accounting: Retrospect and Prospect*, London: CIMA.

International Accounting Standard 11, Construction Contracts, available at www.ifrs.org.

When you have read this chapter

Log on to the Online Learning Centre at **www.mcgraw-hill.co.uk/textbooks/burns** to explore chapter-by-chapter test questions, links and further online study tools for Management Accounting.

CHAPTER 5

COST REPORTING

Chapter outline

- Absorption versus variable costing

- Profit reporting

- Impact on managers

Learning outcomes

On completion of this chapter, students will be able to:

LO1 Illustrate differences between absorption costing and variable costing

LO2 Calculate and compare profits based on absorption and variable costing principles

LO3 Explain the use of absorption costing in financial accounting

LO4 Discuss the advantages and disadvantages of absorption and variable costing

LO5 Interpret the impact of a JIT philosophy on absorption and variable costing methods

LO6 Discuss the impact of absorption and variable costing on the role managers and accountants

Introduction

In Chapter 3, you were introduced to typical cost classifications, which included variable and fixed costs. Chapter 4 detailed how a typical job costing scenario includes costs of making a product or delivering a service, including a portion of overhead. While this seems quite logical, it could be said that any fixed costs are in fact not relevant to short-term decisions and thus can be excluded from product/service costs for internal reporting purposes (Chapter 13 will provide greater detail on relevant costs and revenues for decision-making purposes). While financial accounting requires a portion of overhead to be included in the valuation of inventory (per IAS2), remember that management accounting does not necessarily have to follow any particular rules.

This chapter describes how internal reports can be prepared using only variable costs as an alternative to using full (absorption) cost. As you will learn, using variable product costs is arguably more relevant to internal decision making and performance reporting, as fixed costs are incurred regardless of output volume. You will learn how management accountants could use either absorption or variable costing to prepare internal profit reports and you will also learn to explain differences in the profits reported under both approaches. Before reading this chapter, you may find it useful to reread Chapter 3 to ensure you understand the nature of variable and fixed costs.

Absorption costing versus variable costing

In Chapter 4, you learned the basic techniques of absorption costing as applicable to individual products or services. Of course, any business using absorption costing methods will need to accumulate product costs into meaningful profit reports which show the costs for a period of time. As you know from Chapters 3 and 4, absorption costing means all production costs are absorbed into products. This means that the cost of production, or the cost of sales in financial accounting terms, will be measured according to absorption costing techniques and include a portion of fixed manufacturing overhead cost. In variable costing only variable manufacturing costs are included in product costs and fixed costs are treated as a period cost. The choice of method – absorption or variable costing – for reporting purposes will depend on the use of the information by managers, but you may have guessed that profit figures will vary depending on the method adopted. The rest of this chapter explains how and why the differences occur and the reasons for choosing one method over the other, with the remainder of this section showing you how both methods work by means of an illustrative example.

Some management accountants and management accounting textbooks use the term **marginal costing** in place of variable costing. The term marginal costing is more often used by economists, where marginal cost means the cost of one additional unit of output. Economists argue that fixed costs would increase as new productive equipment or resources may be required to increase output, that is, fixed costs are stepped. While this may be true, management accounting typically views costs as fixed within a relevant range of output, thus the marginal cost of one extra unit of output does not include any fixed costs. The term variable costing is used in this chapter, but it can be taken as interchangeable in practice with the term marginal costing.

Absorption costing

You already know the techniques of absorption costing from Chapter 4. In Exhibit 5.1 you will see how these techniques are used to prepare a profit report, which includes all costs of production and values inventory at full cost. Remember that absorption costing defines full cost as all variable manufacturing costs plus a portion of fixed manufacturing overhead. In other words, fixed manufacturing overhead is treated as a product cost. Let us see how the technique is used to report on costs and profits using the sample data presented in Exhibit 5.1. The budget and actual data in Exhibit 5.1 relates to PoshNosh Ltd, who prepare luxury ready meals for major retailers. You can assume that all fixed overhead costs relate to meal preparation and exclude selling and administration overhead and that actual overheads incurred are the same as budget.

Budget data	£				
Sales price per meal	5.50				
Ingredients	1.25				
Labour	0.70				
Fixed costs per month £25,000	(based on 10,000 meals per month)				
Actual data					
	January	February	March	April	May
Meals prepared	11,000	12,000	12,000	11,000	11,000
Meals sold	10,500	12,200	12,000	11,200	11,100
Meals in stock at month end	500	300	300	100	0

Exhibit 5.1: PoshNosh Ltd

First, from Exhibit 5.1, we need to calculate the budgeted fixed cost per meal that is, the absorption rate.

$$\frac{\text{Fixed Costs}}{\text{Budgeted output}} = \frac{£25,000}{10,000} = £2.50 \text{ per meal}$$

Using the variable costs given above, we now know the full cost of each meal is £4.45 (£1.25 + £0.70 + £2.50). We also have the selling price of each meal and the units prepared and sold. Based on this information, we can prepare profit statements for the months of January to May, as shown in Exhibit 5.2.

Profit using absorption costing	January	February	March	April	May
Meals sold	10,500	12,200	12,000	11,200	11,100
	£	£	£	£	£
Sales	57,750	67,100	66,000	61,600	61,050
Cost of meals prepared					
Meals prepared	11,000	12,000	12,000	11,000	11,000
	£	£	£	£	£
Opening inventory @ £4.45	0	2,225	1,335	1,335	445
Preparation cost @ £4.45	48,950	53,400	53,400	48,950	49,395
Under/(over)-absorbed overhead	(2,500)	(5,000)	(5,000)	(2,500)	(2,500)
Closing inventory @ £4.45	(2,225)	(1,335)	(1,335)	(445)	0
	44,225	49,290	48,400	47,340	47,340
Profit	13,525	17,810	17,600	14,260	13,710

Exhibit 5.2: Profit statement of PoshNosh Ltd using absorption costing

Looking at Exhibit 5.2, you can see how the full unit cost of £4.45 is used to both calculate the costs of preparing meals and valuing inventory. Note also how overhead is over-absorbed in all months as we are told that actual overhead costs were as planned. Remember from Chapter 4 that under- and over-absorbed over head occurs when actual output varies from planned output. Now let's see how a profit statement would look using variable costing.

Variable costing

Based on the data in Exhibit 5.1, we can work out the variable costs per meal at £1.95 (£1.20 + £0.70). Exhibit 5.3 shows a profit statement for PoshNosh Ltd adopting variable costing techniques. You will notice how fixed costs are treated as a period cost in the profit statement.

Profit using variable costing	January	February	March	April	May
Meals sold	10,500	12,200	12,000	11,200	11,100
	£	£	£	£	£
Sales	57,750	67,100	66,000	61,600	61,050
Cost of meals prepared					
Meals prepared	11,000	12,000	12,000	11,000	11,000
Opening inventory @ £1.95		975	585	585	195
Preparation cost @ £1.95	21,450	23,400	23,400	21,450	21,450
Closing inventory @ £1.95	(975)	(585)	(585)	(195)	0
Variable cost of meals sold	20,475	23,790	23,400	21,840	21,645
Contribution	37,275	43,310	42,600	39,760	39,405
Fixed costs	(25,000)	(25,000)	(25,000)	(25,000)	(25,000)
Profit	12,275	18,310	17,600	14,760	14,405

Exhibit 5.3: Profit statement of PoshNosh Ltd using variable costing

The layout of this profit statement is slightly different from the one using absorption costing in Exhibit 5.2. It shows the **contribution**, which is calculated as sales less variables cost (see Chapter 11 for more detail). Fixed costs are then deducted from contribution to derive a profit figure. You can also see that the meal preparation costs are calculated using variable cost per unit and inventory is valued similarly using variable unit cost.

5.1: Management Accounting in Practice

Fixed costs in road haulage

In the road haulage industry, fuel costs represent a major variable cost. In recent years, increasing oil prices and emissions legislation have seen fuel costs increase dramatically for the UK haulage business. The result is increasingly tight profit margins. To add to their woes, European haulage firms, who have lower fixed costs and possibly lower fuel costs, are competing with UK firms. Accordingly, haulage firms are being selective in the jobs they take on, trying to accept only work which provides a suitable margin above variable costs. The following quote by a haulage company owner from an article in the *Birmingham Post* newspaper (1 November 2010) summarizes the difficulties:

The rates are just too thin and the rise in diesel is a big consideration. I was doing the sums each week and it became clear I could make more money driving for an agency. Every day I had off I was canvassing all the industrial estates across the West Midlands area but everyone is battening down – there is no investing.

The quote above suggests this haulage company owner was comparing variable costs (mainly fuel) with the prices available for haulage work. The resulting margin appears to have been insufficient to cover fixed costs and generate an adequate profit. As fuel prices are likely to continue on an upward trend – due to fuel tax increases – this haulier closed the business.

Sources: http://www.expressandstar.com/news/2010/10/28/midlands-hauliers-in-fuel-prices-warning/ and http://www.birminghampost.net/birmingham-business/birmingham-business-news/other-uk-business/2010/11/01/west-midlands-transport-bosses-feeling-the-squeeze-as-fuel-prices-keep-rising-65233-27579677/ (all accessed on 15 November 2012).

Exercise

Can you think of other industries or sectors that may incur similarly high variable costs over which they have little or no control?

In Chapters 8 and 16 you will learn about planning and how managers are held to account for their performance compared to the plan/budget. The term **responsibility centre** is used to describe any organizational unit (for example a department, function, branch) for which a manager can be held accountable. While, you will learn more about responsibility centres later, for this chapter you need to consider the effect responsibility centres can have on profit statements.

Consider the example in Exhibit 5.4, which shows a variation on a typical variable costing profit statement.

	Product A	Product B	Total
	£000	£000	£000
Sales	32,500	85,000	117,500
Production cost of sales	10,000	36,000	46,000
Gross profit	22,500	49,000	71,500
Variable administration costs	2,300	22,600	18,900
Contribution	20,200	26,400	46,600
Specific fixed costs			
Marketing costs	4,000	6,000	10,000
Contribution towards general fixed costs	16,200	32,400	36,600
General fixed costs			
Administration costs			10,000
Production overhead			15,000
Profit			11,600

Exhibit 5.4: Product specific fixed costs

Each product has specific marketing campaigns, which cost £4,000,000 and £6,000,000 for products A and B respectively. A product manager is accountable for the profitability of each of the two products.

Looking at the data presented in Exhibit 5.4, you will notice that the product specific fixed cost are shown separately. Although these costs are fixed, the fact that a product manager is responsible for each product line would suggest they are accountable for all costs (fixed or variable) associated with the products. On the other hand, the product managers could not be held accountable for general administration or other overheads over which they have no control. Thus, Exhibit 5.4 shows a figure called 'contribution toward general fixed costs'. This contribution is the controllable contribution for each product manager, and is thus useful to report on. The example profit statement shown in Exhibit 5.4 may vary according to the context of a particular organization. However, where it is possible to identify some specific fixed costs to products, processes or organizational units, this is commonly reflected in the internal profit statement to assist with management performance and control reviews.

5.2: Management Accounting in Practice

Fixed costs in pharmaceuticals

The pharmaceutical sector incurs high research and development cost bringing new drugs to market – as high as $1.3billion in 2009, according to a 2011 article in *BioSocieties*. The vast majority of this cost would have been incurred on developing a new chemical which would form the backbone of new drug. These costs although most likely easily identifiable to an individual drug, are according to the article's authors, difficult to estimate. For example, the period for the drug to be 'discovered' could range from three months to 30 years. There are also the costs of trialling the new drug to be considered, as well as profits forgone on other potential products. As noted in the article, it is quite difficult to get accurate costs of drug development as pharmaceutical firms do not necessarily disclose detailed information. However, it is highly probable that internally, pharmaceutical firms may have product specific type fixed costs as costs for developing and trialling new drugs are likely to be readily attributable as specific. For example, the Swine Flu outbreak of 2009 saw pharmaceutical firms rapidly develop specific vaccines, even developing new production methods.

Sources: Light, D.W. and R. Warburton (2011), pp. 34 – 50; 'How big pharma profits from Swine Flu', http://www.spiegel.de/international/business/0,1518,663357,00.html (accessed on 15 November 2012).

Exercise

Can you think of any other product specific fixed costs which may be incurred in other sectors?

Profit reporting

Looking back to Exhibits 5.2 and 5.3 you may have noticed a difference in the profit figures calculated under absorption and variable costing methods. For internal reporting purposes management accountants can choose either absorption or variable costing to prepare profit statements or other cost reports. However, we need to explore a number of aspects of the costing method used. To do this, we will use the data from PoshNosh Ltd to (1) explain the differing profit figures, (2) understand the impact the costing method has on managers and decision making, and (3) help choose the appropriate method for decision making purposes.

Explaining the difference

Exhibit 5.5 shows the difference in the profits of PoshNosh Ltd calculated under absorption and variable costing.

As you can see in Exhibit 5.5, the difference in profits can be explained with reference to the movements in inventory levels. Take a look at what has occurred in January. The opening inventory was nil, but this increased to 200 meals at the end of the month. Under absorption costing, this increase in inventory is valued at the full cost of £4.45, which includes £2.50 fixed overhead. Two hundred meals in inventory at month end, with an additional £2.50 cost per unit, will defer this amount to the following month. This explains why the profit in January is £500 higher (£2.50 per meal fixed cost × 200 meals) under absorption costing. Similarly, the profit in February is higher under absorption costing for the same reason. In March, the profits are the same under both methods. In this case, the opening inventory was 300 meals, and the closing inventory was also 300 meals, thus there are no extra inventory costs between the two methods. In April and May, inventory levels have decreased in both months. The effect of decreasing inventory is the opposite of increasing inventory levels. Taking April as an example, you can see in Exhibit 5.5 that the profit using absorption costing is £500 less than under variable costing. This is due to cost of

	January £	February £	March £	April £	May £
Profit under absorption costing	12,775	17,390	17,600	14,260	14,155
Profit under variable costing	12,275	16,890	17,600	14,760	14,405
Difference	500	500	0	(500)	(250)
Inventory increase	200	200	0	(200)	(100)
Fixed overhead per meal	2.50	2.50	2.50	2.50	2.50
Profit difference	500	500	0	(500)	(250)

Exhibit 5.5: Differences in calculated profits of PoshNosh Ltd

sales being increased by the amount of fixed overhead included in the decreased inventory levels that is, 200 meals at £2.50. In effect, the fixed overhead included in inventory has been 'released' to cost of sales. Similarly, the profit in May is less using absorption costing as inventory levels have decreased in the month. Table 5.1 summarizes how we can explain differences in profits resulting from the costing methods chosen.

Table 5.1: Effects of costing methods on profits	
Inventory movement in reporting period	*Relationship between profit using absorption costing versus variable costing*
Sales = production, no movement	Absorption costing profit = variable costing profit
Sales > production, inventory decreases	Variable costing profit > absorption costing profit
Production > sales, inventory increases	Absorption costing profit > variable costing profit

Also, looking at Exhibit 5.1, you can see that the inventory levels have increased over the five month from nil to 100 meals. The total profit for the five months using absorption costing is £76,180; using variable costing the total profit is £75,930. The difference between the two profits is £250, which is a result of the fixed costs incorporated in the increased inventory, that is, 100 meals × £2.50 = £250.

As summarized in Table 5.1, when sales and production levels are the same, profit will be the same under absorption and variable costing. This is because the cost of sales to the income statement does not vary, as the fixed manufacturing overhead expensed is the same using either method. When sales exceeds production, then more fixed manufacturing overhead is expensed under absorption costing, so the profit will be lower than variable costing. When the reverse occurs, production exceeds sales, more fixed manufacturing overhead is deferred to later periods, so the expensed overhead is less using absorption costing, thus yielding a higher profit than variable costing.

Over time however, the profit figures under absorption costing and variable costing will tend to be the same. This is because over time sales and production levels will tend to be the same. Thus, any differences in profits reported internally under either method will be short term.

Impact on managers

Chapter 7 will introduce you to some behavioural issues encountered in management accounting, particularly in the area of planning and control. Looking at Exhibits 5.2 and 5.3, if you were a manager you might be inclined to choose the reporting method most favourable to the context. If the objective of a division or business unit is to maximize profit, then it is easy to see how a manager could use absorption costing and choose to increase production to maximize profit in the current period. Of course, any increased profit under absorption costing is a temporary difference and will wash out over the longer term. Thus, any efforts to 'manipulate' profits by using absorption costing would be quite fruitless.

In Chapter 1, management accounting was set out with a primary objective of assisting organizational decision-making. The profit statements seen in the earlier exhibits are part of the decision-making tools used on a regular basis by managers. In order to make sound business decisions, managers need to have information presently to them in a clear, understandable format suitable to the decision purpose. As we have seen, in terms of profit statements, this may mean preparing separate profit statements for internal use. As these internal profit statements are not subject to any external regulation like income statements prepared for publication, their usefulness to managers is determined by the impact on decision making. Thus the choice of absorption or variable costing for internal profit reporting is an important one, which we will now explore.

Choosing a costing method

Absorption costing has a major advantage in that it meets the requirements of International Financial Reporting Standards. IAS 2 (Inventories), paragraph 12 states: 'the cost of conversion of inventories include costs directly related to the units of production, such as direct labour. They also include a systematic allocation of fixed and variable production overheads that are incurred in converting materials into finished goods'. The requirements of IAS 2 implies that all external reporting must calculate production and inventory costs using absorption costing techniques. Thus all companies will use absorption costing at least once per year when preparing annual financial statements. However, as noted earlier absorption costing could lead to undesirable inventory building, particularly if managers are incentivized on the basis of profits.

It can be argued that absorption costing gives managers an incorrect view of product costs for day-to-day decision making, such as product pricing for example. Absorption costing attributes an even amount of fixed manufacturing overhead to each similar product. Thus, for example, if the absorption base is machine hours, two products using six machine hours each would incur the same overhead (see more on this in Chapter 6, 'Activity-based costing'). However, as production output increases, the unit fixed cost actually declines as the fixed cost is spread over more units. If managers cannot quickly assess the effects of increases or decreases in production output on costs, then incorrect pricing decisions could be made, for example a product is priced too high, or a profitable product is dropped (see Chapter 11, 'Cost-volume-profit analysis' for more detail). A further issue with absorption costing is the base used to allocate overheads. From Chapter 4, you know that the denominator in the formula for calculating an overhead absorption rate is based on a budgeted figure. While using a budget figure is necessary, the question of which denominator to use can arise. For example, a manufacturing plant could base the denominator used for the overhead absorption rate based on budgeted plant capacity or the utilization of that capacity. Take a look at *Worked Example 5.1*, which describes a scenario of a bottling plant.

Worked Example 5.1	**Bottling plant capacity and utilization**

BM Bottling own a highly automated bottling plant and offer services to distillers, breweries and wine-makers. Their plant can bottle a maximum of 1,500,750 ml bottles per hour. The plant runs two 8-hour shifts and works 20 days each month. Fixed manufacturing overhead is £70,000 per month.

Taking the above capacity, the maximum output level would be:

$$1,500 \text{ bottles} \times 8 \text{ hours} \times 20 \text{ days} = 240,000 \text{ bottles.}$$

This capacity level is referred to as the **theoretical capacity**. Assuming theoretical capacity, the overhead rate per 750 ml bottle would be £0.292 (£70,000/240,000). In practice, the theoretical capacity level is not achieved due to reductions in output caused by equipment maintenance, downtime, and so on. The **practical capacity** of a plant takes such issues into account. Assuming 1.5 days per month is lost at the BM Bottling plant, then its practical capacity is now:

$$1,500 \text{ bottles} \times 8 \text{ hours} \times 18.5 \text{ days} = 222,000 \text{ bottles.}$$

▶

Thus, at the practical capacity level, the overhead rate per bottle would be £0.315 (£70,000/222,000).

Now let's assume the production manager at BM Bottling gives us some more information on how the capacity of the bottling plant is used i.e. customer demand. According to the production manager, the current year budget has predicted customer demand at 180,000 bottles per month. This level is below **normal utilization** due to a generally poor economic outlook for the current year. Normally, demand is 210,000 bottles on a monthly basis and this demand level is expected to return in the next 12 months.

The additional information given by the production manager provides two further possible denominators which may be used to calculate an overhead rate. Using the budgeted demand (or **budgeted utilization**) of 180,000 bottles per month, the overhead rate can be calculated as £0.389 per bottle (£70,000/180,000). If the normal utilization is used as a denominator, the overhead rate can be calculated as £0.333 (£70,000/210,000).

As shown by *Worked Example 5.1*, the denominator used affects the overhead absorption rate, and in turn the profit calculated using absorption costing. And, we know from earlier in this chapter that a higher unit product cost will increase inventory value and profits if absorption costing is used internally. Usually, the budget utilization is used in the calculation, as you have seen in Chapter 4. In the data shown above in *Worked Example 5.1*, this happens to be the highest absorption rate, which will imply the highest profit if inventory is allowed to build up. However, using an overhead rate which is calculated on theoretical or practical capacity is unlikely to reflect reality. It can be argued that normal utilization might be a useful denominator for overhead rate calculation in businesses which are subject to longer-run demand cycles. However, it may also be overly optimistic and thus budget utilization is the normal denominator used.

Variable costing offers a number of advantages for internal reporting purposes over absorption costing, as follows:

- Variable costing techniques are more useful in reporting profitability of products, customers and business segments. This is due to the somewhat arbitrary nature of allocation fixed costs using absorption costing techniques (see Chapters 4 and 6).

- The fixed costs are easily identifiable on variable costing profit statements whereas absorption costing includes fixed costs in unit cost. Fixed costs are not relevant to many managerial decisions (see Chapter 13).

- Using variable costing, managers see the actual unit costs which are controllable in the short term. Using absorption costing, a manager cannot easily separate the costs into fixed and variable components.

- As shown in earlier examples, variable costing does not affect profitability to the same extent as absorption costing when inventory levels are increased. Assuming sales price and variable costs remain constant, profit will increase or decrease in tandem with sales levels when variable costing is used. With absorption costing, for example, sale levels may remain static, but increasing production (and thus inventory) levels will increase profits without any corresponding increase in sales.

- Arguably, the profit reported under variable costing is closer to the actual cash flows generated by business operations. This information may be particularly important if a business is experiencing tight cash flows.

- Variable costing profit statements may be more easily understood by junior managers and other employees. This may be particularly important in organizations where larger information systems distribute cost information to a broad audience.

Looking at the above advantages, you might think why would a company use absorption costing at all? Traditionally, as absorption-costing is required for external reporting purposes, accounting information systems were designed according to absorption-costing techniques. A view held in the past may have been that the extra expense of running additional systems or software to extract variable costing profit statements was not worthwhile. Another view on maintaining a single accounting system is to use variable costing and when required for external reporting, adjust costs and profits to an absorption-costing basis. Nowadays, accounting and business information systems offer quite powerful information processing and analysis capabilities, particularly at the higher end of the market, and can provide cost information in multiple formats. For example, the Product Cost Controlling Information System (or CO-PC-IS) module of SAP (an enterprise resource planning system) can display product costs as fixed, variable or full.[1] Thus, with systems like SAP, a business can produce profit statements using either variable or absorption costing in a few mouse clicks, so no addition effort is required once product costs are input to the system. However, in smaller organizations absorption cost may be more prevalent. Dugdale et al. (2006) reported that 68 per cent of companies they surveyed used variable costing profit statements. More recently, CIMA's Annual Management Accounting survey (CIMA, 2009) reported that approximately 45 per cent of 439 respondent organizations used absorption costing as the main operational costing tool, with approximately 35 per cent using variable costing. The choice of method is thus mixed according to this research. Ultimately, the costing method used will depend on organizational context and the nature of decision making within the organization – for example, more frequent short-term decisions may imply more use of variable costing.

JIT environment

You have learned how inventory levels affect profits throughout this chapter, particularly when absorption-costing techniques are adopted. If an organization uses **just-in-time** (JIT) techniques the choice of costing method is less relevant. Chapter 20 will give you more detail on the nature of JIT, but for now we can summarize JIT as a philosophy whereby customer orders are made on request. In a JIT environment, a customer order is a trigger for production to start, which in turn triggers orders to suppliers for materials, and so on. One of the main goals of a JIT environment is to dramatically reduce, or even eliminate, materials inventory and work in progress. In such an environment with little or no inventory, the profits reported under variable and absorption costing will be very similar. This does not mean that product costs are the same, as absorption costing includes fixed manufacturing costs, but any difference in reported profits are likely to disappear as no inventory is allowed to build up.

Lean organizations and throughput accounting

Many manufacturing operations, as well as adopting JIT principles, may adopt a **lean manufacturing** approach. A 'lean' approach can be applied in manufacturing or service organizations. Essentially, a lean approach eliminates all forms of waste in an organization and focuses on delivery the product or service as quickly and efficiently as possible. In lean manufacturing, there are three key underlying tenets (Cunningham and Fiume, 2003):

- A pull-demand approach – producing the product as customers require rather than to inventory.

- Flow production – production should flow as individual products/order rather than in batches. Product movements should be minimized and any wait times eliminated.

- Takt (or cycle) time – the manufacturing process should be altered to match the cycle time required to meet customer demand. This typically means reducing the time.

In a similar way to JIT, a lean approach is likely to reduce inventory and would imply little difference in reported profits regardless of the costing method used. Lean principles can be applied to other management accounting tasks like budgeting and performance measurement. According to Cunningham and Fiume (2003), this not only changes the focus of these tasks more towards measuring value than cost or revenue, but also offers an alternative presentation of internal profit statements which provides more meaningful information. One alternative method to present profit statements is to use **throughput accounting**. This chapter introduces the basic concepts

5.3: Management Accounting in Practice

Lean accounting in practice

Lean accounting is typically deployed as part of lean manufacturing initiatives. For example, Watlow Electric Manufacturing Co (based in St. Louis, Missouri, USA) adopted lean accounting approaches in 2009 following changes to a lean manufacturing plant. A business unit controller at the firm notes how the simpler approach of lean accounting has not only provide more relevant and useful cost reports to managers, but also provided a clearer understanding of real costs. And, as the accounting has been simplified, weekly financial data is available. The lean accounting/manufacturing approach has actually allowed the company to grow, despite an economic slowdown – the business unit control puts this down to understanding costs better.

Source: http://www.industryweek.com/articles/watlow_electric_finds_value_in_lean_accounting_19837.aspx (accessed on 15 November 2012).

Exercise

Do you think lean accounting could be used in a service sector organization?

of throughput accounting and highlights some differences compared to traditional methods of product costing and cost/profit reporting. Chapter 20 will provide more detail.

Throughput accounting is based on the ideas of Goldratt (see Goldratt and Cox, 2004) which were first revealed in his book *The Goal* in 1984. Goldratt presented his theory of constraints, which is based on the concept that for an organization to achieve its overriding goal, it must define the primary constraint which allows it to achieve or maximize that goal. For example, in a manufacturing process involving several machines, the maximum output of a factory may be constrained by the slowest machine. By increasing the throughput of this machine, overall output and profit may be increased. This example conveys one of the key objectives of the theory of constraints, which is to manage bottlenecks and improve the efficiency of the systems as a *whole*. Although initially a concept to improve the operation and processes of organizations, the theory of constraints also has some financial aspects which are briefly outlined below:

1) Totally variable costs – this means a cost which is incurred only when a product is produced. In practice, this often means only material costs. Labour costs are not totally variable, as employees are typically paid even when production is halted. Some transportation, subcontracting or commissions may be totally variable. All overhead costs are not totally variable.

2) Throughput – this refers to revenue less totally variable costs. Thus, a contribution using throughput accounting is likely to be higher than in a traditional sense.

3) Operating expenses – this refers to all costs other than totally variable costs. Operating expenses are not distinguished into categories such as fixed or variable, or allocated to products in any way. In a way, operating expenses are similar to period costs, as they are costs which are more associated with the passage of time than with products.

4) Net profit – in throughput accounting, the net profit is simply throughput minus operating expenses.

Arguably, a key advantage of throughput accounting is that is overcomes the problem of overhead cost allocation associated with both traditional absorption costing and activity-based costing (see Chapter 6). As only totally variable costs are including in a calculation of contribution/product margin, then any product which has revenue greater than the totally variable cost adds to the overall profitability of the organization. This is because all other operating expenses are incurred regardless of whether a product is produced or not. Under traditional costing methods, many of the expenses classified as operating expenses in throughput accounting are allocated to products, resulting in a higher product cost. In turn this higher product cost, may be used a basis to reject products which have a 'negative' contribution in the traditional sense. However, such products may actually contribute to overall profitability as many of the operating expenses will be incurred anyway. Thus, as Bragg puts it, in throughput accounting the focus is taken away from 'product costing' and put to 'system profitability' (2007, p. 41). Despite its apparent simplicity, according to CIMA's 2009 survey of management accounting practices, only 5 per cent of respondent firms use throughout accounting techniques, compared to approx 35 per cent who use variable costing. This may be due to its incompatibility with **Generally Accepted Accounting Principles (GAAP)**, which is typically integrated into accounting information systems. As mentioned in Chapter 4, under GAAP inventory must be valued at a cost which includes a proportioning of production overhead incurred.

As you can see from Table 5.2, the resulting net profit is the same under GAAP and throughput methods. However, the contribution using throughout methods is considerably higher than the gross profit under GAAP principles – regardless of whether activity-based costing or a traditional absorption method is used. And, the contribution would be higher than a profit statement prepared using variable costing as direct labour and other variable costs are excluded from totally variable costs. Although not shown in Table 5.2, it should be noted that any closing inventory of finished goods in throughput accounting is valued at totally variable cost i.e. material cost typically.

Table 5 2: Profit Statement		
	GAAP **£000**	**Throughput accounting** **£000**
Revenue	8,250	8,250
Cost of goods sold		
Materials	1,650	1,650
Direct labour	825	
Overhead	2,050	
	4,525	1,650
Gross margin	3,725	
Contribution		6,600
Operating expenses		
Advertising	75	
Commissions	50	
Depreciation	80	
Contracted services	20	
Salaries	3,005	
Supplies	60	
Utilities	35	
Total operating expenses	3,325	6,200
Net profit	400	400

Note: the figure for operating expenses in throughput accounting is £3,325,000 plus direct labour and overhead

Source: adapted from Bragg (2007).

Chapter summary

This chapter has introduced you to two costing methods used to report on profits internally, namely, variable and absorption costing. Variable costing assumes only variable costs are included in unit costs and treats fixed costs as period costs. Absorption costing includes fixed manufacturing overhead in unit costs, which is a requirement of accounting regulations, and thus more suited to external reporting. You have learned how to prepare profit statements using both methods and how to explain differences in reported profits between the two methods, that is, fixed manufacturing costs absorbed in inventory. You also learned how the choice of denominator in the calculation of an overhead absorption rate effects the profit calculation when absorption costing is used. However, over the longer term, both variable and absorption costing methods will produce similar profit figures. Variable costing offers several advantages over absorption costing, but research indicates the latter is still commonly used. This may be due to traditional or the possibility that present-day information systems can produce profit statements using either method. Finally, the effects of some more novel management concepts like JIT and throughput accounting on cost and profit reporting were outlined briefly.

Key terms

Budgeted utilization The planned usage of the capacity of a production facility (p. 109)
Contribution Sales revenue less variable costs (p. 104)
Generally Accepted Accounting Principles (GAAP) A combination of accounting standards and accepted conventions which define how accounting information is recorded and reported (p. 112)
Just-in-time A Japanese management philosophy which aims to produce/deliver products when required, and thereby reduce inventories (p. 110)
Lean manufacturing An approach to manufacturing which aims to eliminate unnecessary process and production waste (p. 110)

Marginal costing A costing technique in which only variable costs are attributed to products/services (p. 102)
Normal utilization The capacity of a production plant that is typically utilized under normal business/economic conditions (p. 109)
Practical capacity The likely maximum possible output of a production facility, taking into account expected normal delays like down time (p. 108)
Responsibility centre An organizational unit for which a manager can be held accountable/responsible (p. 105)
Theoretical capacity The maximum possible output of a production facility (p. 108)
Throughput accounting An alternative to traditional cost accounting which takes into account operational constraints which limit the capacity, and hence profitability, of an organization (p. 110)

Review questions • • • • • • • • • • connect • • • •

Level of difficulty: BASIC   INTERMEDIATE   ADVANCED

5.1 What is the main difference between variable and absorption costing? [LO1]

5.2 What are the limits of variable costing? [LO1]

5.3 Which costing method is likely to be found in the published accounts of a company? [LO1, LO2]

5.4 What arguments can be made for treating fixed manufacturing overheads as a period cost? **[LO1, LO3]**

5.5 How are selling and administration overheads treated when variable costing is used to prepare profit statements? **[LO2]**

5.6 Explain why absorption and variable costing can result in different profit figures. **[LO2]**

5.7 Will the profit under absorption costing be higher or lower when inventories increase? **[LO2]**

5.8 Which costing method might encourage managers to increase inventory levels? Why? **[LO4, LO6]**

5.9 Over the longer term, which costing method will give the greater profit? **[LO4]**

5.10 How relevant is the choice of costing method in a JIT environment? **[LO5]**

• • • Group discussion and activity topics • • • • • • • • • • •

5.11 Read this article* from *The Economist*, which describes issues of increasing energy costs for business: http://www.economist.com/node/17314626. Think about how energy costs would be reflected in internal profit statements. Do you think absorption costing or variable costing would be most suited? (Hint: try to think about how energy costs could be attributed to products.) **[LO1]**

5.12 Read this article* from the *Guardian* newspaper: http://www.guardian.co.uk/uk/2010/jul/19/olympic-delivery-authority-savings-economic-report. In the article it states 'The Olympic Delivery Authority today announced they had successfully absorbed a £27m reduction in their budget'. What does this mean? Discuss what kind of internal profit statement the Authority might prepare. (Hint: assume the Authority has income from the sale of broadcasting rights.) **[LO1, LO2]**

   If, after the London 2012 games, some of the facilities (for example, a swimming pool) are run on a commercial basis by sub-letting to commercial organizations, what kind of internal profit statement would you think the commercial organizations might use?

The links to these articles are available online at www.mcgraw.hill.co.uk/textbooks/burns

• • • Exercises • • • • • • • • • • • • • • • • • • connect • •

E5.1 Basic profit statements [LO2]

Envirocare Ltd manufacture plastic composting bins. The company prepares profit statements every six months and the following data relates to the two six-month periods in the year ending 31 December:

	Six months ending	
	30 June	**31 December**
	Units	**Units**
Opening stock	10,000	14,000
Units produced	50,000	56,000
Units sold	46,000	60,000

The selling price achieved in both periods was £70 per bin. As in the prior year, variable manufacturing costs amounted to £22 per unit in both periods, whereas variable non-manufacturing costs were £14. Fixed manufacturing overhead costs of £400,000 per six-month period were incurred, which was exactly as budgeted and as was incurred in the prior period. Fixed selling and administration overhead costs were £300,000 in each period. For absorption costing purposes, a predetermined rate to absorb fixed manufacturing overhead to units of product is calculated, based on a production activity of 50,000 units per six-month period.

Required:

a) Prepare an operating profit statement for both six-month periods using absorption costing and variable costing.

b) Reconcile any difference in the profits for the six months ended 31 December.

E5.2 Budget profit statements [LO1, LO2]

Jones Ltd makes and sells a single product. The budgeted costs and selling price per unit are as follows:

	£
Selling price	140
Materials	50
Labour	40
Variable manufacturing overhead	10
Fixed manufacturing overhead	8
Selling variable overhead	4
Selling fixed overhead	8
Fixed administration overhead	6

Activity levels (in units) are estimated as follows for the next three months:

	Sales (units)	Production (units)
September	9,500	10,000
October	11,000	12,000
November	13,000	14,000

All fixed overhead costs are budgeted on the basis of projected annual output levels of 150,000 units and all costs are incurred evenly over the year. There is no inventory on hand on 1 September.

Required:

a) Prepare a budgeted profit statement for each of the three months using absorption and variable costing.

b) Explain the difference in total profits over the three-month period.

E5.3 Absorption costing [LO1, LO2]

A manufacturing company uses a standard costing system. Extracts from the budget for April are as follows:

Sales	1,400 units
Production	2,000 units
Direct costs	£15 per unit
Variable overhead	£4 per unit

The budgeted fixed production overhead costs for April were £12,800. The budgeted profit using variable costing for April was £5,700.

Required:

a)   Calculate the budgeted profit for April using absorption costing.

b)   Briefly explain two situations where marginal costing is more useful to management than absorption costing.

Source: adapted from Chartered Institute of Management Accountants, P1 Management Accounting, Performance Evaluation.

E5.4   Cost methods [LO1, LO4]

An enterprise can choose to use either variable costing or absorption costing for internal reporting purposes. These are significantly different systems and in certain circumstances may lead to differences in reported profits.

Required:

a)   Clearly explain the different treatment of costs used by each costing method.

b)   Outline the arguments in favour of using each costing method.

c)   Explain the effect on short-term results where sales and production are not equal.

Source: adapted from The Institute of Certified Public Accountants in Ireland, Formation 2, Management Accounting.

E5.5   Profit statements [LO2]

MK produces and sells two high performance motor cars; Car X and Car Y. The company operates a standard absorption costing system. The company's budgeted operating statement for the year ending 30 June and supporting information is given below:

	Car X £000's	Car Y £000's	Total £000's
Sales	52,500	105,000	157,500
Production cost of sales	40,000	82,250	122,250
Gross profit	12,500	22,750	35,250
Administration costs			
Variable	6,300	12,600	18,900
Fixed	7,000	9,000	16,000
Profit/(loss)	(800)	1,150	350

The production cost of sales for each car was calculated using the following values:

	Car X		Car Y	
	Units	£000's	Units	£000's
Opening inventory	200	8,000	250	11,750
Production	1,100	44,000	1,600	75,200
Closing inventory	(300)	(12,000)	(100)	(4,700)
Cost of sales	1,000	40,000	1,750	82,250

Production costs

The production costs are made up of direct materials, direct labour, and fixed production overhead. The fixed production overhead is general production overhead (it is not product specific). The total budgeted fixed production overhead is £35,000,000 and is absorbed using a machine hour rate. It takes 200 machine hours to produce one Car X and 300 machine hours to produce one Car Y.

Administration costs

The fixed administration costs include the costs of specific marketing campaigns: £2,000,000 for Car X and £4,000,000 for Car Y.

Required:

a) Produce the budgeted operating statement in a variable costing format.

b) Reconcile the total budgeted absorption costing profit with the total budgeted variable costing profit as shown in the statement you produced in part (a).

Source: adapted from Chartered Institute of Management Accountants, P1 Management Accounting, Performance Evaluation.

E5.6 **Marginal and absorption costing [LO2]**

MZ produces and sells two types of motorcycle: X and Y. The company operates an absorption costing system. The management accountant has prepared a budgeted profit statement for the year ended 31 December 201X. This and other relevant information is given below:

Profit statement for the year ended 31 December 201X			
	X	Y	Total
	€000's	€000's	€000's
Sales	105,000	210,000	315,000
Production costs	80,000	164,500	244,500
Gross profit	25,000	45,500	70,500
Admin costs – variable	12,600	25,200	37,800
Admin costs – fixed	14,000	18,000	32,000
Profit/(loss)	(1,600)	2,300	700

The production costs were calculated using the following data:

	X		Y	
	Units	€000's	Units	€000's
Opening inventory	400	16,000	500	23,500
Produced	2,200	88,000	3,200	150,400
Closing inventory	600	24,000	200	9,400
Cost of production	2,000	80,000	3,500	164,500

Production costs consist of direct materials, direct labour and fixed overhead. Fixed overhead is budgeted at €70,000,000 and is absorbed using a machine hour rate. Motorcycle X takes 200 machine hours to produce, with Y needing 300 machine hours.

Required:

a)   Redraft the budgeted profit statement using a marginal (variable) costing format.

b)   Reconcile the budgeted profit per the absorption costing profit statement and the marginal costing profit computed in part (a).

• • • Case study problem • • • • • • • • connect • • •

C5.1   **Cost reporting at Skanva Papers [LO1, LO2, LO4, LO6]**

Skanva Papers are a medium-sized Swedish pulp and paper company. They manufacture several paper and packaging products from heavy cardboard to office papers. The have two facilities in southern Sweden, one in Örebro and one in Uppsala, both of which manufacture cardboard packaging. Three years ago, a new information system was installed at these two facilities. The information system performs a number of functions as follows, some of which were previously done manually:

– Customers and products are defined in the software.

– Processes customer orders.

– Each product/customer order is costed in the software, using standard costs.

– Production is planned and monitored. Actual production data is recorded by either factory
– operator input (using a keyboard) or captured automatically using bar-code technology.

– Completed inventory is recorded and tracked.

– Deliveries to customers are recorded and invoices generated.

– Actual production data, namely material usage, labour time and machine time are captured and all customer orders are 're-costed' based on this information.[2]

At the time of installing the information system at these two facilities, a decision was made to centralize sales and production planning at Örebro, but both retained a separate finance and accounting function. The Örebro facility has typically being more profitable than Uppsala.

In the past 12 months or so, the management accountant at Uppsala has been trying to improve the profitability of the operation. He believes sales levels can be increased if sales staff have a better understanding of the cost structure of the business. Production at Uppsala is not at full capacity, so output can be increased. To this end, he is trying to educate sales staff on variable costing. He also wants to introduce the use of profit statements based on variable costs, which he will obtain from the information system. To be as accurate as possible, he wants to use the costs post-production (that is, order costs re-costed to reflect actual usages and times as described above). Before designing the new profit statements he has meeting with the production manager at Uppsala to help classify costs as either fixed or variable. To gather his thoughts, he is using a sample customer order produced in that past week, which is shown below:

Order no. K134567, date due 31 January, selling price SEK5,000 per 1,000.	
Post-production costs per 1,000 boxes	
	SEK
Material costs	1,370
Labour cost	1,200
Manufacturing overhead	1,330
Selling and administration overhead	500
Total production costs	4,400

The information shown above is available to sales staff for any new (unproduced) or old (produced) customer orders, the difference with the latter being they reflect actual costs and usages. The management accountant has jotted down some notes on the above cost report, where he mentions material and labour costs as variable and all other costs as fixed. He will use this classification to prepare monthly profit statements and to educate sales staff of how to use variable cost information. He presents the above to the production manager at their meeting. The production manager immediately disagrees. He says: 'The only variable cost we have is material. The machine operators get paid whether they are busy or idle, so this has to be a fixed cost. It costs SEK 4,000 a week to employ them regardless of our output. The only way to avoid this cost is close the factory.' The management accountant is surprised by this, but can see the production manager's point. Later the production manager says: 'Look I am not a sales person, so you need to chat to them about the price, but as far as I am concerned, we can increase output to full capacity with no fixed cost increases. So, if we can get a price that is higher than our material costs and customers will buy at this price, then are we not adding to the contribution?'

Again, the management accountant can see the production manager's argument, so he decides to reflect for a short while before training sales staff and introducing profit statements based on variable costs.

Required:

1) Do you agree with the production managers' assessment of the variable costs of production at the Uppsala facility? Briefly explain your reasoning.

2) If you were the management accountant, briefly explain if you would convey the production managers' approach to variable costs to sales staff?

3) Why do you think it is important to agree costs at the Uppsala facility as either fixed or variable for the purposes of profit reporting using variable costing techniques?

4) Explain if you think the management accountant should consult with sales staff before finalizing his decision or not.

Recommended reading

- Dugdale, D., C. Jones and S. Green (2006) *Contemporary Management Accounting Practices in UK Manufacturing*, London: CIMA.

This CIMA report provides some useful insights into the prevalence of absorption and variable costing, but also some information in the use of throughput costing in practice.

References

Bragg, S. (2007) *Throughput Accounting – a Guide to Constraint Management*, Hoboken, NJ: Wiley.

CIMA (2009) 'Management Accounting survey – 2009 results', http://www.cimaglobal.com/Thought-leadership/Research-topics/Management-accounting-in-different-sectors/Management-accounting-survey/(accessed on 26 June 2012).

Cunningham, J. and O. Fiume (2003) *Real Numbers - Management Accounting in Lean Organisations*, Durham, NC: Managing Times Press.

Dugdale, P. C. Jones and S. Green (2006) *Contemporary Management Accounting Practices in UK Manufacturing*, London: CIMA.

Goldratt, E. M. and J. Cox (2004) *The Goal*, 4th edn, Great Barrington, MA: North River Press.

Light, D. W and R. Warbuston (2011) 'Demythologizing the high costs of pharmaceutical research', *Biosocieties*, 6.

● ● ● ● **Notes** ●

1 Product Cost Controlling Information System (CO-PC-IS) manual, SAP AG (2005).
2 Before production starts, all customer orders are costed based on standard costs and usages, both of which are regularly updated. Once an order is produced, it is costed again, based on actual labour times, actual machine time and actual material usage. In each case, the actual usages and standard prices are used.

When you have read this chapter

Log on to the Online Learning Centre at **www.mcgraw-hill.co.uk/textbooks/burns** to explore chapter-by-chapter test questions, links and further online study tools for Management Accounting.

CHAPTER 6

ACTIVITY-BASED COSTING

Chapter outline

- Philosophy of ABC

- Relevance of ABC

- Designing the ABC system

- ABC versus other costing systems

- Activities and cost drivers

- Calculating the ABC numbers

- ABC in practice

- Shared services and internal markets outsourcing of overheads

- Problems with ABC

- Time-driven ABC

- Customer profitability analysis

- What can you do with customer profitability?

Learning outcomes

On completion of this chapter, students will be able to:

LO1 Understand the difference between a traditional costing system and ABC

LO2 Understand the process of developing an ABC system

LO3 Critically analyse the design stage of an ABC systems

LO4 Calculate the cost of a cost object using the ABC method

LO5 To be able to discuss the implications ABC has for companies using the ABC system

LO6 Critically discuss the limitations of ABC

LO7 Illustrate the difference between ABC and TD-ABC

LO8 Calculate CPA and analyse the numeric outcomes

Introduction

In Chapter 3 we discussed the concept of costs, you were introduced to the idea that costs can be categorized into direct and indirect costs. Direct costs are those which can be easily associated with a particular cost object and indirect costs are those which support more than one cost object. As part of the discussion of indirect costs you learned that the process of allocating indirect costs to specific cost objects can be a very difficult process. In Chapter 4 you learned that all business owners and managers need to know the underlying cost of the products or services they offer. This chapter will focus on one of the techniques available that allow you to calculate those costs, **activity-based costing (ABC)**.

The chapter will examine the technical process of ABC and in addition will examine the role of the management accountant in this process by examining the design and implementation process. As stated in Chapter 3, the process of calculating cost objects is now typically incorporated into an information system, and in many cases analysed by general managers. Therefore, it is important to understand the role in which the management accountant has within the ABC process.

With the main focus of the chapter relating to the technical process of allocating indirect costs to cost objects, we will focus on organizations with existing products or services. Later, in Chapter 19, you will learn about alternative techniques for examining costs of new products or services such as target costing. When discussing ABC most literature will refer to the **traditional costing method** (TCM); this technique has already been examined in Chapter 4. If you need to refresh your memory it would be useful to refer back to that chapter at this point. Chapter 4 provides a contextual background for this chapter.

Philosophy of ABC

Traditional costing became central within a discussion on the relevance of management accounting in the 1980s. Johnson and Kaplan (1987) examined the existing costing systems, in the 1980s,[1] against the then current needs of organizations. The conclusion of their analysis, and the debates which followed, highlighted that the TCM was designed in a business era when overheads were much more concentrated and the main activities within an organization were either related to labour or the use of machinery. On the whole, costing systems were designed for manufacturing businesses, which dominated in terms of employment when the costing systems were designed. Therefore, simplified costing systems which focused on products consuming resources were based upon allocation systems of labour and machine hours.

However, the transition of the business environment, with industry moving from being dominated by local manufacturing companies to large international organizations resulted in the TCM becoming obsolete. The business environment had not only changed, in terms of location and size, but service-centred organizations became a more significant part of the employment pool. The TCM was identified as providing inaccurate costing information because the systems were based on inappropriate assumptions.

The content and complexity of overheads for a typical organization had changed since the introduction of the TCM. In addition, the percentage of indirect costs as opposed to direct costs had changed. Indirect costs associated with individual products and services had increased. The complexity of organizations and the portfolio of products they produce had also expanded. Therefore, tracing overhead costs to individual products had become much more difficult. All of these changes resulted in the cost of a product and service using the TCM, being inaccurate. It was very difficult for organizations to analyse which products or services were profitable and which were not. We started this chapter by referring back to the introduction in Chapter 3 where we stated that 'all business owners and managers need to know the underlying cost of the products or services they offer' – using TCM most organizations did not know this basic information.

One of the most fundamental roles of a management accountant is to ensure that the information and cost systems used within their own organization are fit for purpose. Meaning that management accountants must ensure the systems used recognize the complexity of the organization and are designed appropriately to produce relevant data and effective information. The aim is to design a system that can be used to generate information that will improve strategic decisions. If an organization does not reflect the assumptions of the TCM, it is the management accountants' role to find a system that does.

Following the debate on relevant systems, ABC was exposed to the majority of the business world in two articles by Cooper and Kaplan (1988a, 1988b), although the ideas initially emerged in the 1970s. The two professors argued that the TCM, which relied on labour, machine hours and material costs to allocate the overheads, did not reflect the true nature of the overheads they were allocating. Cooper and Kaplan (1988a, 1988b) noted that the use of labour and machine hours were in fact distorting costs. Products and services that were produced in low volumes were not allocated enough indirect costs, whereas those produced in high-volume were being over-charged. The result being, that high-volume products and services were subsidizing the low-volume products.

Relevance of ABC

A variety of organizations have implemented ABC and this chapter will provide some examples. ABC is used in public and private sectors, emerging and developed countries (although it is documented that it is used more in developed countries), different types of industries and different-sized industries.

Although ABC is used within a variety of industries and geographic locations, the tool is incredibly resource intensive. It is resource intensive because it takes a significant amount of time to design, implement and maintain; the costs associated with this tend to be very high. The costs and complexity explain why larger organizations use ABC more than smaller ones. CIMA (2009) supports these findings and reported that only 22 per cent of their respondents from smaller organizations used ABC, whereas 46 per cent of the larger organizations used this tool. However, CIMA (2009) also suggested that the complexity of the larger organization could also be a contributing factor for larger organizations using this tool, rather than smaller organizations. Although the CIMA survey was international, 61 per cent of the main respondents were from the UK.

Examining a separate geographical area from the CIMA report (2009), Stratton et al. (2009) provided a survey analysis on the relevance of ABC which was also internationally based but with the dominant sample of respondents from North America. They also found that fewer than 50 per cent of respondents used ABC as a form of allocating indirect overhead costs.

The Stratton et al. (2009) survey also examined how ABC is used along the value chain. This survey provided data which showed that ABC was more commonly used in shared service centres and customer service centres. ABC was least used in areas such as research and design and product and process design departments. The survey demonstrates that although ABC is used in many types of organizations, the system can be useful in individual business units and centres within the organizations.

Designing the ABC system

The cost object is the start of the ABC process. The cost object can be a product, service, end consumer or region. Remember that ABC is and has been used in many different industries and sectors; therefore, the cost object will fit the needs of the information required by the individual organization. As discussed in Chapter 3 a cost object is something for which a separate cost measurement is required.

Table 6.1 summarizes the design process for an ABC system. On paper, the exercise seems very straightforward but remember that the larger the organization, the more complex each stage becomes. Identifying the cost object is the easiest stage. Once the cost object is identified the organization needs to create a work flow for the cost object. The work flow will identify all the processes and support activities that are used to produce the cost objects. In other words, the entire value chain needs to be analysed. This is where the complex nature of the design stage begins. Some organizations will use their management accounting team, others will hire in consultants to work alongside either their management team or accounting team to establish the cause and effects of activities and drivers. Understanding the cause and effect of work flows requires intense knowledge of the business practice, otherwise the wrong drivers can be identified.

In the process of identifying activities, work flow maps are very useful, as they prevent activities being missed. Work-flow maps are diagrams which represent the processes involved within an organization. Cross-matching the work-flow map with the payroll of the organization often helps to identify all support activities. In large international organizations there can be thousands of

Table 6.1: Stages in the design process of an ABC system		
Cost object	Identify your cost object, e.g. product, service, consumer, region	This will be determined by the type of industry you are in
Activities	From the cost objects a work flow must be identified to trace all activities, including support activities	Work-flow mapping and payroll can help in this stage to ensure all activities and employees are included.
Resources	Activities must be examined in terms of how they consume resources, establishing the resource drivers	Work surveys are usually used to determine how the resources are consumed by the activities. Detailed surveys and interviews with key members of staff can help to determine how much resource each activity uses
Allocating resources to activities	The resources are allocated to the activities	The resource drivers are used as a means of allocating the resources to the activities. When the activities have resources attached to them they are known as activity pools
Cost drivers	The activities must be examined in terms of what drives the costs within the activity pools	Cost drivers are the driving force which connect the activities to the cost objects. Clear and easy to measures cost drivers must be allocated to each activity

activities within a work-flow map; however, by analysing the work flow, prominent activities will emerge and these will become the focus of the **activity pools** within the ABC system.

Once the activities are established the organization will then engage in a process which identifies how activities consume resources. This can be a complicated process which includes lengthy surveys or interview processes. Identifying how the resources are consumed by the activities is known as identifying the resource drivers. Once the resources are traced to the activities then the resources can be allocated to the activity pools, identified in the previous stage, through the use of the resource drivers. In many cases, time is used to allocate the costs based upon the surveys used.

The final stage is to collect data which relates to the cost drivers. The cost drivers connect the activity pools and the cost objects. The cost drivers represent how the cost objects consume resources from within the activity pools. There is a causal relationship between activity pools and cost objects, and this relationship is represented through the cost driver. There are no perfect cost drivers; using the business experience of the team involved they must approximate the nearest measurement that fits the relationship.

Problems within the design stage

Many of the criticisms of ABC rest within the design stage. As you have learned, ABC uses surveys and interviews to collect information relating to work flows. It is possible for individuals within the organization to distort the collection process by manipulating the information they provide. Rowe et al. (2012) argue that systems such as ABC are based upon subjective information provided by employees, who sometimes have it in the own best interests to distort information to hide inefficiencies and prevent excessive change. Unless the collection of data is sufficiently audited, this can lead to biased and unreliable information being generated from systems such as ABC.

ABC versus other costing systems

ABC is a refined methodology based upon the basic calculations of TCM. The TCM assumes that resources are allocated to cost objects. In contrast, ABC, presumes that the cost objects use activities during the process of being produced and the activities use the resources of the organization. Based on this methodology, the indirect costs, that is, the overheads, are allocated into activity pools rather than cost centres. When comparing the TCM and ABC, typically you will see many more activity pools within an ABC than you will cost centres within the TCM. The activity pools are created based upon a set of tasks that are connected within an organization.

Once the activity pools are established, an analysis will take place to consider the drivers of the resources within the activity pools. The cost driver is something which can measure the cost object's use of the activity; in other words, it is what drives the consumption of the costs associated with the activity. There are many types of cost drivers but the main consideration when designing a system is that they must be easy to measure and be identifiable with the type of activity pool they are associated with. Activity pools and cost drivers will be discussed in more detail later in this chapter.

The main philosophy behind ABC is that different cost objects consume varying amounts of resources because each has different demands. Rather than costs being analysed in broad functions such as cost of sales and selling expenses as listed on the income statement, ABC analyses the consumption of resources through activities to identify patterns at the operational level.

Is ABC used in all industries?

Although ABC was designed to fit the current business needs of organizations this does not mean it is a perfect fit for all industries/sectors. For example, Lin (2012) found that in the international air industry, ABC provides a very useful way of controlling and reducing costs. The use of ABC in the air industry has provided a way for large carriers to analyse the way they operate and they have created new business models following the data provided from the ABC system. ABC allows individual air carriers to identify inefficiencies and then remove or reduce them, which has improved profitability and, in the low-cost airlines, allowed them to maintain low pricing.

In contrast to the airline industry, within the financial services industry (UK), the use of ABC is now limited (Soin and Scheytt, 2009). Soin and Scheytt (2009) explain that although the banking industry in the first wave of regulation used ABC intensively to seek ways of reducing costs, this was subsequently replaced by risk management systems due to the new regulation approach based on risk measures. ABC was not found to be an effective way of managing the industry and the regulation focused on risk-based measures rather than on cost-based measures. This demonstrates that the use of management accounting can be influenced by the internal needs of an organization and external pressures such as regulation.

Activities and cost drivers

Activities come in many forms and they can be presented as a hierarchy. Exhibit 6.1 highlights the fact that every organization will have different types of activities. Analysing the activities into units, batches, products and facility levels is not just a paper exercise. By identifying activities in different categories, it provides managers with an understanding that these activity costs can only be reduced by focusing on the type of activity it is categorized under. For example, if batch-level activities were identified as consuming the most resources, managers may be required to make this activity more efficient and thus reduce costs. The manager, in this case, would need to analyse the work flow of the batch production not the unit production. Individual units, in this case, do not increase the costs allocated to batch activities; it is the number of batches which increase the costs at batch activity. **Pareto analysis** provides us with the 80/20 rule suggesting that 80 per cent of the overheads of an organization are generally caused by 20 per cent of the activities. Therefore by identifying and controlling the 20 per cent of key activities the organization should theoretically be able to control 80 per cent of the overheads.

In the previous section we explained that activities are related to cost objects through **cost drivers**. All organizations will need to design their own system of activities and cost drivers to reflect the nature of their own organization; however, there are some standard activities and cost drivers which most organizations will use. *Management Accounting in Practice 6.1*, provides an example of a telecommunication company's dictionary of activities and cost drivers.

The methodology behind the ABC costing system using activities and cost drivers, can certainly represent a more accurate portrayal of how a cost object accumulates costs. However, it would be misleading to say that ABC produces more accurate costing of a cost object – its accuracy will depend on the design of the system. Examining *Management Accounting in Practice 6.1*, if Marconi designed or implemented the ABC system incorrectly then the system would provide inaccurate cost information. It is the role of the management accountant to ensure the design accurately reflects the business model of the individual organization.

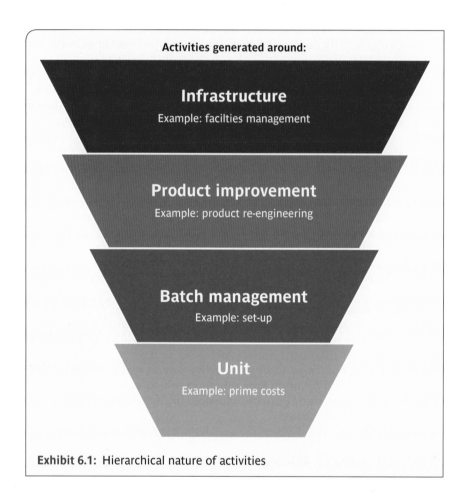

Exhibit 6.1: Hierarchical nature of activities

6.1: Management Accounting in Practice

Identifying activity pools and activity drivers

Major and Hopper (2005) examined a Portuguese telecommunications company, Marconi, that implemented ABC. Marconi created a dictionary of activities and cost drivers. The activities were categorized into three broad groups; activities oriented to customers, activities oriented to the network and supporting activities. Being a service industry they had adjusted the hierarchy as presented in Exhibit 6.1 to represent their own organizational business model. Below is a summary extract of some of the key activities identified, relating to customers:

Activities orientated to customers

- Defining strategies in telecommunications business

- Researching and analysing new business opportunities

- – Elaborating and controlling marketing plan

- – Researching markets and customers

- – Developing products and services

- – Commercializing products and services

- – Billing

- – Management of customers' debts

- – Maintenance of customers' services

- – Assuring the quality of services. (Major and Hopper, 2005, p. 215)

In total, the company identified 71 key activities. The cost drivers that were seen to be the key drivers of many of the activities identified included labour hours, equipment capacity and traffic volumes. Additional cost drivers were identified when these were not appropriate:

Drivers of activities:

Driver 1	Number of invoices valued by effort
Driver 2	Number of document (incoming traffic) × 80% = number of open positions > 6 months × 20%
Driver 3	Number of invoices per product/service
Driver 4	Number of invoices × 70% = number of open positions > 6 months × 30%
Driver 5	Setups (broadcasting – accidental services)
Driver 6	Number of processes valued by duration
Driver 7	Number of alterations in network valued by the type of service
Driver 8	Routes valued by number of circuits
Driver 9	Similar allocation for the respective pseudo-department
Driver 10	Reallocation of computing applications/machines DDS. (Major and Hopper, 2005, p. 217)

Driver 1 named 'number of invoices valued by effort' related to the billing invoice received by the customer and this was valued in terms of how many rows of information were printed on the invoice.

Exercise

Consider a business who manufactures smart phones; identify three possible activity pools and three possible cost drivers which would connect the smart phone (the cost object) to the activity pool.

Calculating the ABC numbers

So far we have discussed the design of, and the issues around, ABC. What we now need to do is have a look at the technical aspects of ABC. The basic concepts of overhead allocation which are behind ABC have already been addressed in Chapter 5. However, *Worked Example 6.1* shows how the approach to ABC calculations differs from what you have learned so far.

<table>
<tr><td rowspan="2">

Worked Example 6.1
</td><td>

Computation of ABC

Elviso Ltd manufactures parts for medical equipment. The details of the two parts and relevant information are given below for one period:
</td></tr>
</table>

Product parts	Alpha	Beta
Output in units	12,000	14,000
Costs/cost drivers		
Direct material	£240,000	£350,000
Direct labour	£168,000	£147,000
Total machine hours	2,100	2,400
Orders executed	150	110
Number of production runs	90	40
Number of shipments	50	15
Number of product returns	90	40

The production overhead is currently absorbed by using units, and the total of the production overhead for the period has been analysed as follows:

Activity pools	Annual costs £	Cost driver	
Production	180,000	Machine hours	4,500
Material handling	78,000	Orders executed	260
Quality enhancing and inspection	130,000	Number of production runs	130
Delivery	26,000	Number of shipments	65
Production returns management	52,000	Number of production returns	130
	466,000		

It is possible with this example to compare the cost for both Alpha and Beta using the traditional costing method and ABC.

We begin with the traditional costing method below:

	Alpha £	Beta £
Direct material	240,000	350,000
Direct labour	168,000	147,000
Overhead	215,040*	250,880*
Total cost	623,040	747,880
Total cost per unit	**51.92**	**53.42**

Note: *There are rounding errors; therefore if you add these together they do not equal the original £466,000.

You can see that the start of the process is to include the prime costs: direct material and direct labour. These have been provided in the example so you are not calculating anything at this point. You then add the overhead. In this example, we assume the overheads are currently absorbed on a 'per unit' basis. To calculate the overhand absorption rate you simple divide the total number of units of both Alpha and Beta added together into the total overheads:

$$£466,000/(12,000 \text{ units} + 14,000 \text{ units}) = £17.92$$

(This is where the rounding error is created, presenting the answer to two decimal places.)

At this point, to calculate the total overhead for all the units produced for Alpha you multiply the absorption rate of £17.92 by the number of units produced, which in this case is 12,000 units: £17.92 × 12,000 = £215,040.

▶

The ABC approach is more involved because instead of having one absorption rate, this time you will calculate a cost driver rate for each of the activities. In this example it means you will need to calculate the five cost-driver rates because we have five activities: production, material handling, quality enhancing and inspection, delivery and product return management.

The process of calculating each cost driver rate is simply:

Costs of the activity/cost driver

In this example the five cost driver rates would be as follows:

Activity	Annual cost £	Cost driver	£	Cost-driver rate
Production	180,000	Machine hours	4,500	40 per hour
Material handling	78,000	Orders executed	260	300 per order
Quality enhancing and inspection	130,000	Number of production runs	130	1,000 per run
Delivery	26,000	Number of shipments	65	400 per shipment
Product returns management	52,000	Number of production returns	130	400 per return
	466,000			

For production costs we divide the £180,000 by the 4,500 machine hours, £180,000/4,500 = £40 per hour.

Once you have the cost driver rates you then need to apply them to the individual products, in this case Alpha and Beta.

	Alpha	Beta	Total
	£	£	£
Production costs			
Alpha: £40 × 2,100 machine hours	84,000	96,000	180,000
Beta: £40 × 2,400 machine hours			
Material handling			
Alpha: £300 × 150 orders	45,000	33,000	78,000
Beta: £300 × 110 orders			
Quality improvement and product inspection			
Alpha: £1,000 × 90 production runs	90,000	40,000	130,000
Beta: £1,000 × 40 production runs			
Delivery			
Alpha: £400 × 50 shipments	20,000	6000	26,000
Beta: £400 × 15 shipments			
Production returns management			
Alpha: £400 × 90 production runs	36,000	16,000	52,000
Beta: £400 × 40 production runs			
Total overhead	**275,000**	**191,000**	**466,000**
Number of units	**12,000**	**14,000**	
Overhead per unit (rounded to two decimal places)	**22.92**	**13.64**	

To calculate these values, you simply take the cost driver rate you have calculated previously, and multiply it by the use of that driver for each product. For example Alpha uses 2,100 machine hours for all 12,000 products produced, so you multiply the 2,100 hours by the costs driver rate of £40 per machine hour which we calculated earlier, 2,100 × £40 = £84,000.

You are now ready to produce a cost budget for the two products. The prime costs remain the same but this time the overheads change to represent the use of the activities.

	Alpha £	Beta £
Direct material	240,000	350,000
Direct labour	168,000	147,000
Overhead	275,000	191,000
Total cost	**683,000**	**688,000**
Total cost per unit (rounded to two decimal places)	56.92	49.14

ABC in practice

Cooper and Kaplan (1991) argued that one of the main features of ABC is to provide an organization with a clearer picture of how their cost objects produce profits. Analysing cost objects by both the revenue they generate and the resources they consume provides an opportunity to improve efficiency and profitability. An overwhelming amount of research agrees that ABC is at its best when implemented to work alongside business processes of a strategic nature. Rather than using ABC to simply produce the costing structure of the cost objects, the system should be used to identify areas of performance improvement.

6.2: Management Accounting in Practice

JEA using ABC

JEA are a large American municipal utility company. Waldrup et al. (2009) analysed the ABC system within this company and found that ABC, which was once used only to provide basic cost structure had changed. JEA moved the focus of ABC, to examine activities in hierarchies. The hierarchies related to levels of management. By analysing the activities into hierarchies of this nature, the managers who could influence the costs at that level were identified. Thus, connecting the ABC data to the managers' performance improved the performance of the company.

Source: Waldrup et al. (2009).

Exercise

Read the Waldrup et al. (2009) article and discuss how the use of ABC helped to improve the performance of the company. A link to the article is available online at www.mcgraw-hill.co.uk/textbooks/burns.

By focusing on activities it is possible for organizations to identify the activities which have the biggest impact on the end profit and by doing so can work on improving the efficiencies within these activities. However, moving the data produced into a strategic tool moves ABC to activity-based costing management (ACBM) which will be discussed more in detail in Chapter 19.

There is a large body of research examining ABC, including those who have found organizations who have implemented ABC with success and are continuing to use this system. Debate continues on what variables create a successful ABC system (see Pike et al. (2011) for an overview of the debates in this research area).

Research provides us with numerous examples of companies trying to implement ABC, those that have completed the implementation of ABC, and examples where they have tried using the technique but it has not been successful. Table 6.2 provides a few of the studies analysing ABC in different geographical locations:

Table 6.2: ABC studies around the world		
Country	Author and year	Content of study
China	Lui and Pan (2011)	This study examines the introduction of ABC within a large Chinese manufacturing company. Examining the implementation of ABC within a culture where standardization is not common practice and where advance IT systems within manufacturing companies is lower than in the western culture. Within an autocratic style management system this study provides an opportunity to consider how ABC can influence additional IT developments and how the autocratic style management successfully encouraged corporate-wide learning in terms of using ABC.
Tunisia	Salem-Mhamdia and Ghadhab (2011)	This paper is set within the service sector in Tunisia, restaurants. Within this setting the paper explores how value management and ABC were used to improve the estimation of profit margins of the food offered in these restaurants. The research was extended to see how these tools can be used to explore customer satisfaction. Out of 11 restaurants examined, it was found that both techniques helped the owners of six restaurants to improve decision making through improved analysis of profitability and customer satisfaction.
Jordan	Nassar et al. (2011)	Set within a Jordanian industrial sector, this paper explores the diffusion process of ABC. This case study investigates the motivations of implementing ABC and the reasons for not implementing the technique. In this geographical area it was found that the implementation process was based on the classic S-shape and that consultants played a significant role in the adoption process.
France	La Villarmois and Levant (2011)	An example of ABC in France, this paper compared the usefulness of *unité de valeur ajoutée* (UVA – added value unit) implemented within small companies compared to the use of ABC. This paper found that although the resource implications of implementing UVA were much less than ABC, the technique was limited in comparison to ABC as a management tool. The authors believed this could be due to the size of the organizations using the UVA method.
Australia	Ratnatunga and Waldmann (2010)	Examining the transparent costing (TC) framework of Australian Competitive Grant research projects, the process of identifying indirect costs and full costs (FC) was analysed. Set in the Australian Higher Education sector, it was found that TD-ABC was preferable to ABC when analysing FC in research-only departments. However, within teaching and learning departments FCs were understood better through analysing the workload models and interviewing the people involved within the department.
Malaysia	Majid and Sulaiman (2008)	Although ABC is not widely used within companies in Malaysia, this paper examines the problems and advantages of implementing ABC in two companies, one a multinational based Malaysian company and one a multinational Malaysian company. The research focuses on the managerial aspects of implementation, rather than the technical issues. From the analysis of these two companies they found that for successful implementation several factors needed to be present: management support, a simplified implementation process, finding software that was suitable and a solid training process for all those involved in the process and use of ABC.

Shared services and internal markets

We have discussed some of the ways ABC can add value to organizations throughout this chapter. You have learned that ABC can identify activities which need to be streamlined; **shared service centres** can be one way of achieving this. Shared service centres are now common across different industries, bringing together administration processes across large organizations into one centre. These centres include activities such as IT, HRM and accounting. The primary aim is to create efficiencies in administrative processes by bringing together the expertise spread across organizations. Creating pockets of expertise can drive down costs, which will improve profits. By establishing shared services the organization creates what is known as an **internal market** because each centre will provide services for the other centres within the same company. Internal markets create the need to transfer the costs of the shared service centres to the cost objects; here is the link to ABC. The organization has to trace these overheads from the shared service centres and this can be achieved through ABC.

You have already learnt that ABC is a system which can help organizations to trace the use of overheads. Tracing overheads is achieved by identifying activities, and then through the use of cost drivers absorbing these overhead costs to the business units (the cost objects in this case). The use of ABC in business models, which use shared service centres, prevent some business units cross-subsidizing the activities of other business units. One key area which the management accountant needs to address, where relevant, relates to maximizing shared service centre capacity. As with any other overhead which is not fully utilized, the system must be designed to ensure idle time is still accounted for.

Although the concept of shared services will be discussed in more detail in Chapter 18 it is important to link business models with systems. It is vital to gain a deeper understanding of how the overall role of a management accountant involves much more than the numbers. The management accountant must understand both the internal business model and, as you will learn next, the business environment within which they work.

Outsourcing of overheads

In the previous section we discussed the business model of using internal markets through the use of shared service centres, this can also be considered to be a form of internal outsourcing. By implementing ABC and identifying activities which are not efficient in terms of resource consumption an organization may choose to restructure their organization to use new business models such as shared service centres or they may choose to outsource to external companies. By outsourcing the activity, the costs can theoretically be reduced. However the design of the ABC will still include these activities. The cost of outsourcing still needs to be traced to the cost objects.

6.3: Management Accounting in Practice

Chrysler and ABC

Chrysler, is an American car manufacturer that uses ABC. They reported that they discovered some of the manufacturing processes had been underestimated for years. Some were calculated to be 30 times more expensive than they had originally thought. By using ABC they identified the activities that had been underestimated in terms of cost, and the activities which could not be improved internally. The activities which could not be improved internally were then outsourced to external specialists.

Chrysler is not the only car manufacturer to respond to new data in this way; others such as Toyota have followed similar business models. Although it should be recognized that the outsourcing encountered in the car manufacturing industry has developed into strategic partnerships rather than a simple contact between two organizations.

Source: Anon (2008, 2009).

Exercise

Strategic partnerships within the car industry can reduce costs; however, they can create problems for the branding of the company. Using examples, discuss.

Problems with ABC

Throughout this chapter you have learned about some of the potential problems of using ABC; we will now consider these issues in more detail. Originally ABC was designed for organizations which were located in one location only, or designed to be used in one department. As the idea of ABC was accepted more within industry, larger international organizations began to take on the concept. The larger organizations tried to implement this system within much more complex organizational settings. These companies had more processes, which translated into more activities. This, of course, resulted in very complicated systems in terms of time required to collect the data and resources used.

One of the key issues identified by Kaplan and Anderson (2004) with the traditional ABC system relates to how quickly the design system of the activities and cost drivers become out of date. Businesses change, and so do the environments within which they operate. Changes to business processes and environments equate to changes in the activities and cost drivers identified in the original design stage. Either organizations fail to update their systems or they try to maintain updates, but the process of doing so becomes both time-consuming and very expensive. Waldrup et al. (2009) agree with Kaplan and Anderson (2004) and argue that many of the problems with ABC are due to the fact that they become outdated very quickly. In *Management Accounting in Practice 6.1*, Marconi's system was designed so that most customers would receive their billing invoices through the post. Therefore, drivers such as driver 1 named 'number of invoices valued by effort' would be a driver that reflects the ability to increase the cost of the billing activity. However, in today's business environment where sustainability is a central business strategic objective, paperless billing is now encouraged. Thus, the content of an invoice may not be the key trigger of increasing the cost of the billing activity; the customers' choice to use paperless billing or traditional billing may be more appropriate.

The accuracy of the system is dependent on many variables such as system design and updates of the system. There have been many examples of companies where ABC has been heavily critiqued. The critiques include examples of scenarios where ABC has failed after years of use, and companies have stopped using ABC. For a good overview of the literature which includes some of the problems within the implementation process and use of ABC see Pike et al. (2011), Stratton et al. (2009) and, for a very detailed examination of a problematic implementation process, Major and Hopper (2005).

Management Accounting in Practice 6.4 represents an organization that tried and failed to maintain system updates.

6.4: Management Accounting in Practice

ABC and the Metropolitan Police Authority, UK

The Metropolitan Police Authority (MPA), United Kingdom, was required by the Home Office (HO) to provide information relating to key expenditure using ABC from 2003/4. Data from 43 forces across the UK was collected using a costing methodology set by the HO. The data was collected by each force by using a two-week activity survey; the individual boroughs were only surveyed on average every three years. The model was able to rank and identify the proportion of resources spent on different activities. While the police could see the benefits of using the information as a management tool, the result within the police was not successful. The cost of implementing and maintaining the system was expensive and time-consuming – having to complete the two-week surveys. Therefore, following a review of the costing system the HO ceased asking for the information from 2008/9. The individual forces were then asked to consider using alternative methods.

Source: www.policeauthority.org/metropolitan/.

Exercise

Find other examples of companies who have started to use ABC but then stopped; discuss the reason for ABC being abandoned.

The use of surveys to identify resources is a problem we considered earlier in this chapter. We learned that most survey respondents do not document any idle time. Not reporting accurate timing, results in the resource use being inaccurately represented. Therefore, the role of the management accountant would be to devise a system whereby this information can be collected without it impeding the day-to-day activities of an organization. The management accountant also needs to ensure that the system is streamlined so that the maintenance is manageable.

The manageability of a system is fundamental in management accounting. Some organizations which are still using the ABC systems, find that the level of detail needed to facilitate such a system is now becoming an issue; storage space on the software programmes is becoming a problem. Companies have reported that monthly documents are taking up to three days to generate, due to the sophistication within the design of the system (Kaplan and Anderson, 2004).

The sophistication of the system can be a result of the complexity of the organization or the IT systems used. Pike et al. (2011) examined how the performance of an ABC system within organizations can be influenced by type of system used. The organization used in the Pike et al. (2011) research was a large provider of information and communications products in South East Asia. Although the findings of this study were contradictory to some previous studies, they found that this company preferred a stand-alone system which was not integrated with the other business systems, thus reducing complexity. This demonstrates that a management accountant needs to consider the type of system they use within their own organization.

Although there are many identified problems with the initial ABC concept, as stated earlier in this chapter, many organizations across the world are still using the system. Many have found it helpful, especially, when used within a strategic concept to improve profitability.

Time-driven ABC

Following the many criticisms of traditional ABC, including cost, design problems and maintenance issues as discussed earlier, Kaplan and Anderson (2004) provided an analysis of how ABC could be used in practice to overcome some of these issues. They introduced time-driven activity-based costing (**TD-ABC**). TD-ABC simplifies the ABC process, resulting in the process becoming more suitable for complex organizations. As you read in *Management Accounting in Practice 6.4*, the UK MPA found one of the biggest inconveniences of ABC was having to complete the employee surveys. Surveys are both costly and time-consuming and this interfered with the MPA's daily activities. Kaplan and Anderson (2004) found that many other companies were experiencing similar issues. TD-ABC does not require individual employees to carry out detailed and complicated surveys to track the use of resources. Instead, TD-ABC relies more on managerial estimates; it bypasses the stage of allocating resources to activities.

Managerial estimates can be used to identify two key components of this systems:

1) The cost time unit of supplying each resource

2) The unit time of consumption of each resource by cost object.

Managers estimate how much time each resources has in theory and then estimates how much time is actually available in practice. Unlike the survey method in the original ABC where idle time is rarely documented, this method accepts that resources are not used to their full capacity. Although time is used in many cases, hence the name TD-ABC, other units of analysis can also be used, such as space. Once the cost time unit of each resource is calculated, the manager then needs to estimate how much time (or other method of measurement) it takes to complete each activity. At this stage the cost time unit of resources is multiplied by the time taken to complete one activity to calculate the cost driver. For a technical guide of how to apply TD-ABC, refer to Kaplan and Anderson (2004).

6.5: Management Accounting in Practice

TD – ABC and DHL

One of biggest claims made for TD-ABC is that it enables managers to identify inefficiencies in processes. Holton (2007) followed DHL, an international delivery company which is a division of the Deutsche Post, Germany. DHL uses TD-ABC to reduce the cost for its customers. DHL focused on investigating why it was taking varying amounts of time to deal with individual customers. By analysing the time, rather than the weight of the packages, DHL was able to design a more realistic costing system.

Source: Holton (2007).

Exercise
Research other companies who are using TD-ABC. Did they use ABC prior to this system and why did they change?

Analysing individual customers can be a very important source of data for companies. The methodology of ABC has been transported into a technique called customer profitability analysis, which we will consider next.

Customer profitability analysis

Customer profitability analysis (CPA) draws upon the ABC principles discussed earlier in this chapter. Rather than a product or service being the object of tracking the consumption of costs through activities they use, in this case the customers themselves become the object of the cost consumption. By analysing the resources and activities which individual customers use it is possible to trace the profitability of each customer by offsetting their costs with the revenues they bring to the company. This analysis can be used for individual customers or customer segments.

The focus behind CPA is to increase the profitability of each customer or to remove them from the customer base if they cannot be improved, unless there is a strategic reason for allowing them to be part of the business process. The aim is to increase profit by reducing the cost structure of each customer rather than increasing the price. The need to analyse customer profitability relates to the notion that customers have an uneven distribution of profit due to the different way each customer proceeds with business. Some will be more time/resource-consuming than others due to their own business models. *Worked Example 6.2* helps to explain this.

 Mossmart Ltd

Mossmart Ltd sells specialist electrical components to four customers. At the present time, Mossmart Ltd is reviewing its customer base by reviewing the profits it earns from each of its customers. It uses customer profitability analysis and customer profitability review to determine whether to continue with the current mix of sales to its existing customers: A, B, C and D.

Demand for activities by the customers for the period, using relevant cost drivers are given below:

Cost driver/Customer	A	B	C	D
Number of sales orders	200	100	50	30
Number of service calls	20	10	5	5
Number of normal deliveries	180	50	50	30
Number of special deliveries	20	50	0	0
Number of after sales support requests	20	10	5	3

The customer overhead costs for the period total £211,100 and have been analysed as follows:

Customer activity costs	Annual budgeted costs £	Cost driver
Sales order processing	100,700	Number of sales orders
Customer database maintenance	10,000	Number of service calls
Normal delivery	69,750	Number of normal deliveries
Special delivery	19,250	Number of special deliveries
After-sales support	11,400	Number of after sales support requests

Required:

a)   Compare the total costs attributable to each customer.

Assume that the operating profit contributed by the customers are £90,000, £130,000, £70,000 and £180,000 for A, B, C and D respectively:

b)   Determine the level of profitability for each customer.

Solutions

a)   The first part of this process is based on the same principles you go through with ABC (see earlier in this chapter) in that you need to calculate the cost driver rates for the individual activities.

Customer overhead costs	Annual budgeted costs £	Cost driver	Total	Per unit of cost driver £
Sales order processing	100,700	No. of sales orders	380	265
Customer database maintenance	10,000	No. of service calls	40	250
Normal delivery	69,750	No. of normal deliveries	310	225
Special delivery	19,250	No. of special deliveries	70	275
After sales support	11,400	No. of after sales support requests	38	300

Therefore as you can see above for each of the activities you would identify the total cost driver which is related to the activity and divide the total cost driver into the total activity. So for example if we take 'Sales order processing' as an example, you are told in the question that the cost driver for this activity is the number of sales orders. In the question you are provided with a data table for each customer, A, B, C and D:

Cost driver/Customer	A	B	C	D
Number of sales orders	200	100	50	30

You need to add all the sales orders from all of the customers so you have the total number of sales orders (we are assuming there are only four customers). In this case the total number of sales orders is 200 + 100 + 50 + 30 = 380 sales orders.

In the question you are told the 'sales order processing activity has £100,700 of overheads allocated to it so you need to take this value and divide by the total number of sales orders we have just calculated:

£100,700/380 orders = £265 per sales order

You should perform this calculation for each activity.

The second stage is to analyse how much of the activities the individual customers are using so we will take the cost-driver rates and multiply them by the related driver use of each customer.

Customer attributable costs	A £	B £	C £	D £	Total £
Sales order processing	53,000	26,500	13,250	7,950	100,700
Customer database maintenance	5,000	2,500	1,250	1,250	10,000
Normal deliveries	40,500	11,250	11,250	6,750	69,750
Special deliveries	5,500	13,750	0	0	19,250
After sales support	6,000	3,000	1,500	900	11,400
Totals	**110,000**	**57,000**	**27,250**	**16,850**	**211,100**

In the table above the process is very logical. If we take Sales Order processing for customer A, you can see the table above shows that customer A uses £53,000 of this resource. This was calculated by taking the cost driver rate which we have previously calculated, £265 per order and multiplying it by the number of sales orders which customer A places in this period which in this case is 200 orders, £265 × 200 orders = £53,000. By following through these calculations you reach a point where you know how much of each activity each customer is using.

It is then possible to work out the total overhead use of each customer by simply adding each activity use together so for customer A this would be £53,000 + £5,000 + £40,500 + £5,500 + £6,000 = £110,000.

b) Part B of the question asks you to determine the level of profitability for each customer which means you need to take the operating profit for each customer, as given in the question, and subtract the total activity overhead use that you have just calculated.

	A	B	C	D
Operating profit	90,000	130,000	70,000	180,000
Customer attributable costs	110,000	57,000	27,250	16,850
Profit	**(20,000)**	**73,000**	**42,750**	**163,150**

It is possible to observe, through this one period of analysis, that customer A is not profitable; however, do note that we have only analysed one period in this example. In reality a management accountant would be expected to identify trends in profitability by analysing other periods as well because the period analysed here may not reflect a typical period. Customer D is a very profitable company so it would be advisable to consider how to strengthen this relationship; you would ask yourself if a customer loyalty programme would help to lock this customer into your business.

What can you do with customer profitability?

Worked Example 6.2 highlighted that not all customers are profitable and some are more profitable than others. With customer profitability you can rank in order and using Pareto analysis, it is often found that around 20 per cent of the customers account for the most value brought into the organization. The role of the management accountant is not only to perform a CPA; the data then needs to be addressed, and there are then several ways in which the company would go forward. The accountant must analyse the cost structure of each customer and determine if it is possible to reduce the costs of those customers that are currently unprofitable or those which provide very little profit margin. If the analysis highlights some significantly valuable customers then the company may want to direct more of the resources to those customers to ensure they retain customers.

Roslender and Hart (2010) argue that CPA is one of the techniques available that provides a business the opportunity to bring customers into account, bringing them into the heart of the business rather than seeing them as an end product. However, more often than not it is simply used as a numeric exercise rather than a strategic tool. Using management accounting techniques such as CPA successfully requires a good relationship between the management accountant and the marketing manager (Roslender and Hart, 2010), which is difficult to achieve. CPA can be extended to analyse customers as assets by using models to discount future value the customers may bring under different scenarios, using discounted value-based models, discounting (will be discussed in Chapter 15). In addition to analysing customers and identifying required returns for customers, the information from CPA can also be considered within the balanced scorecard, which will be considered in Chapter 17.

Chapter summary

In this chapter we have focused on the technique of ABC, its design and implementation. It is important to understand that ABC is a technique which provides costing data. However, the basic ABC methodology can be used to add value to organizations in many ways; budgeting (to be discussed in Chapter 8), to analyse customers (discussed in this chapter) and as part of the management system which is something known as activity-based management ABM, to be examined in Chapter 19).

Throughout this chapter we have considered the advantages of using ABC and we have critically evaluated ABC by highlighting some of the problems associated with this technique. Considering some of the problems, you then learned that using TD-ABC can avoid some of these problems. However, this is not the end of our discussion on TD-ABC; in Chapter 19 we will also consider the management aspects of using TD-ABC.

Key terms

ABC A costing techniques that uses activity pools to store overheads, these are then traced to cost objects through the use of cost drivers (p. 122)

Activities The name of a collection of tasks or processes which are linked in terms of overheads (p. 125)

Activity pools The collection point for overheads related to specific activities (p. 124)

Cost drivers Drivers that connect the activity pools and the cost objects. The cost drivers represent how the cost objects consume resources from within the activity pools (p. 125)

Internal markets A market which exists within an organization (p. 131) **Pareto**

analysis 80/20 rule that enables you to see what 20 per cent of cases are causing 80 per cent of the problems within a scenario, or how 20 per cent of cases are creating 80 per cent of the profits (p. 125)

Shared service centre A centre that is responsible for specific tasks, providing expertise in one area to the remaining part of the organization (p. 131)

TD-ABC A version of ABC which works on estimating time rather than identifying cost drivers through lengthy surveys or interviews (p. 134)

Traditional costing method Based on an old business model where the consumption of overheads was typically absorbed on the basis of labour hours, machine hours or units (p. 122)

• • • • ● Review questions • • ● ● ● ● ● ● ● ● ● ● connect ● •

Level of difficulty:	BASIC	INTERMEDIATE	ADVANCED

6.1 What is an activity pool? **[LO2]**

6.2 Explain the main difference between traditional costing systems and ABC. **[LO1]**

6.3 Traditional costing had the tendency to over-charge low volume products, true or false? **[LO1]**

6.4 Provide an example of an activity and a potential cost driver that may be associated with that activity. **[LO2]**

6.5 ABC allocates overheads directly to the cost objects, true or false? **[LO1]**

6.6 In a manufacturing environment list the hierarchy of activities. **[LO3]**

6.7 Provide three problems encountered by organizations when using ABC. **[LO3]**

6.8 Explain the difference between ABC and TD-ABC. **[LO7]**

6.9 Define a cost driver. **[LO2]**

Group discussion and activity questions ● ● ● ● ● ● ● ● ● ● ●

6.10 Activity-based costing (ABC) provides more accurate costing data for an organization – critically discuss. **[LO3]**

6.11 ABC costing is not suitable for a small organization – critically discuss. **[LO5]**

6.12 Time-driven activity-based costing (TD-ABC) resolves most of the problems associated with the original ABC – critically discuss. **[LO7]**

6.13 In the design stage of ABC what should the management accountant consider? **[LO3]**

Exercises ● ● ● ● ● ● ● ● ● ● ● ● ● ● ● ●connect ● ● ●

E6.1 ABC and Pareto analysis [LO4]

W is a manufacturing company that produces three products: X, Y and Z. Each uses the same resources but in different quantities as shown in the table of budgeted data for 201X below:

Product	X	Y	Z
Budgeted production	1,500	2,500	4,000
Direct labour hours per unit	2	4	3
Machine hours per unit	3	2	3
Batch size	50	100	500
Machines set-up per batch	2	3	1
Purchase orders per batch	4	4	6
Material movements per batch	10	5	4

W's budgeted production overhead costs for 201X are €400,000 and current practice is to absorb these costs into product costs using an absorption rate based on direct labour hours. As a result the production overhead cost attributed to each product unit is:

Product X €32   Product Y €64   Product Z €48

The management of W are considering changing to an activity-based method of attributing overhead costs to products and as a result have identified the following cost drivers and related cost pools:

Cost Pool	€	Cost driver
Machine maintenance	100,000	Machine hours
Machine set-ups	70,000	Machines set-ups
Purchasing	90,000	Purchase orders
Material handling	60,000	Material movements

The remaining €80,000 of overhead costs are caused by a number of different factors and activities that are mainly labour related and are to be attributed to products on the basis of labour hours.

Required:

a)   Calculate the production overhead cost attributed to each product unit using an activity-based approach.

b)   Explain how W has applied Pareto analysis when determining its cost drivers and how it may continue to use Pareto analysis to control its production costs.

Source: adapted from Chartered Institute of Management Accountants, Specimen paper P2.

E6.2   **ABC analysis [LO4]**

Sweden PLC makes and sells products: A, B and C. Estimated details for the next year are as follows:

	Product A	Product B	Product C
Production/sales (units)	10,000	20,000	80,000
Total direct material costs	160,000	600,000	4,040,000
Total direct labour costs	80,000	200,000	1,320,000

Variable overhead cost is £1,500,000; 40 per cent is material related and the remainder is labour related.

The following absorption bases are currently used to absorb variable overheads into product units:

1)   Material related variable overhead as a percentage of total direct material costs (for all products), applied to direct material cost

2)   Labour related variable overhead as a percentage of total direct labour costs (for all products), applied to direct labour cost.

Required:

a)   Prepare estimated unit product costs for products A, B and C, where variable overhead is charged to product units, using the absorption basis outlined above.

b)   Prepare estimated unit product costs for products A, B and C, using ABC, with regard to the following cost drivers:

	Product A	Product B	Product C
No. of material bulk purchases per unit	4	1	1.5
No. of labour operations per unit	6	1	2

c)   Comment on your findings in (a) and (b) above.

E6.3   **ABC principles [LO4]**

MZ is considering changing to an activity-based costing system. The management accountant has analysed the fixed production overhead as follows:

	€
Machining costs	14,000
Set-up costs	24,000
Quality,inspections	14,040
Stores,receiving	6,960
Stores,issuing	11,000
Total	70,000

The analysis also revealed the following:

	X	Y
Budgeted production (motorcycles)	2,200	3,200
Motorcycles per production run	10	40
Inspections per production run	40	160
Component deliveries during the year	984	1,800
Issues from stores during the year	8,000	14,000

Motorcycle X uses 200 machine hours per bike and Y 300 machine hours.

Required:

a) Calculate the budgeted fixed production cost of motorcycle X using activity-based costing techniques.

Source: Association of Chartered Certified Accountants F5.

E6.4 **Traditional costing and ABC [LO4, LO5]**

Alfresco Limited manufactures picnic tables for the Irish market. Since its inception, it has allocated overhead costs based on labour hours. The Managing Director is happy with this approach as he can understand the calculations and it is relatively quick to calculate the overhead rate per labour hour. Despite this, the accountant is eager to adopt an activity-based costing approach to overhead allocation. The accountant has already studied the 'cost drivers' of Alfresco Limited and identified the following:

Activity	Cost driver	Cost pool
Assembly costs	Number of labour hours	€56,000
Purchasing department	Number of purchase orders	€44,000
Delivery costs	Number of deliveries	€42,000
Machine maintenance	Machine hours	€45,000

Alfresco Limited manufactures three different styles of picnic tables: 'Round', 'Square' and 'Octagon'. Information relating to the manufacturing process is as follows:

	Round	Square	Octagon
Direct material cost	€157,500	€157,500	€210,000
No. of machine hours required	1,200	400	1,400
No. of labour hours	3,000	4,000	3,000
No. of purchase orders	3	2	6
No. of deliveries required	10	30	20
Production (units)	1,500	1,500	2,000
Selling price (mark-up on cost)	30%	30%	40%

Required:

a) Calculate the selling price for each of the three products, using the traditional approach to costing.

b) Calculate the selling price for each of the three products, using activity-based costing.

c) Describe the circumstances where traditional costing systems are likely to report distorted costs. You should include appropriate reference to your calculations performed in parts (a) and (b) when describing such circumstances.

Note: Figures should be rounded to two decimal places.

Source: Institute of Certified Public Accountants in Ireland, Formation 2, MA.

E6.5   **Revised costing using ABC [LO4, LO5]**

You have been hired by Maxitron Limited, a company which manufactures a range of sophisticated products, the biggest seller of which is the 'Obashton' (annual sales of this item amount to 8,000 units per annum).

A long-standing customer has offered to purchase a large volume of 'Obashton'. However, the customer is seeking a 30% discount off the normal selling price. The cost card (direct costs only) for the product is as follows:

	Notes	€
Material	0.5 kilos	45
Labour	1 labour hour	15
Finishing costs	1 machine hour	8
Direct costs		68

Note: The current basis of charging fixed overheads to units of production is explained later in the question. To compute a product's selling price, the company adds fixed overheads to direct costs to compute manufacturing cost and then adds a mark-up of 30% to the manufacturing cost.

- The Chief Financial Officer (CFO) is opposed to accepting the deal under the proposed terms. He notes that since the selling price of this product is calculated using a mark-up of 30% of cost, the company cannot agree to the pricing terms requested by the customer. He has publically dismissed the deal to be "a non-runner".

- The Chief Manufacturing Officer (CMO) however, disagrees with the Chief Financial Officer and feels there may be scope for accepting the deal. He feels that since the customer has been (and continues to be) a "key-account" customer for many years, that extra effort ought to be made to meet the demand. He fears a refusal might be seriously detrimental to the ongoing relationship between the customer and Maxitron Limited.

Your task is to resolve the disagreement between the CFO and the CMO and report your proposed resolution to each of these officers.

In your efforts to resolve the dispute, you have collected the following information:

1. The company currently uses an absorption costing system to charge overheads to products. These overheads total €700,000 per year. The current basis of charging fixed overheads to units of production is summarized in the following table:

	Overheads charged using labour hours €	Overheads charged using machine hours €
Total annual overhead	400,000	300,000
Total annual hours	20,000	25,000

2. A study by external consultants identified the following drivers of the annual fixed overheads incurred by the company:

	Total number of cost driver events per annum	Total amount of overhead cost €
Purchasing/goods inward costs	1,200	30,000
Machine set-up/retooling	6	90,000
Quality control inspections	8,000	500,000
Despatch/goods outward costs	5,000	80,000
Total annual overhead cost		700,000

You have analysed the activities referable to the 'Obashton' product for the past year and have determined the following information:

Cost driver	Number of cost-driver events per annum
Purchasing/goods inward costs	120
Machine set-up/retooling	2
Quality control	2,000
Despatch/goods outward costs	500

Required:

a) Calculate the current fixed overhead absorption rates used by the company.

b) Calculate the current selling price of the 'Obashton' product.

c) Calculate the total overheads which would be charged to the annual production of 'Obashton' using activity-based costing principles and the amount per unit.

d) Calculate the revised manufacturing cost of an 'Obashton' using activity-based costing principles.

e) Prepare a brief memorandum (not to exceed approximately 1 page) to the CFO and CMO setting out your findings. Your memorandum should include reference to possible factors which they may wish to consider when deciding whether the terms should be accepted.

Source: adapted from Certified Public Accountants, Formation 2, MA.

E6.6 **Improving the profitability of products using ABC [LO4, LO5]**

The Gadget Co produces three products, A, B and C, all made from the same material. Until now, it has used traditional absorption costing to allocate overheads to its products. The company is now considering an activity-based costing system in the hope that it will improve profitability. Information for the three products for the last year is as follows:

	A	B	C
Production and sales volume (units)	15,000	12,000	18,000
Selling price per unit	€7.50	€12	€13
Raw material usage (kg) per unit	2	3	4
Direct labour hours per unit	0.1	0.15	0.2
Machine hours per unit	0.5	0.7	0.9
Number of production runs per annum	16	12	8
Number of purchase orders per annum	24	28	42
Number of deliveries to retailers per annum	48	30	62

The price for raw materials remained constant throughout the year at €1.20 per kg. Similarly, the direct labour cost for the whole workforce was €14.80 per hour. The annual overhead costs were as follows:

	€
Machine set up costs	26,550
Machine running costs	66,400
Procurement costs	48,000
Delivery costs	54,320

Required:

a) Calculate the full cost per unit for products A,B, and C under traditional absorption costing, using direct labour hours as the basis for appointment.

b) Calculate the full cost per unit of each product using activity-based costing.

c) Using your calculations from (a) and (b) above, explain how activity-based costing may help the Gadget Co improve the profitability of each product.

Source: adapted from Association of Chartered Certified Accountants, Paper F5.

E6.7 Pricing strategies and ABC [LO4, LO5]

Brick by Brick (BBB) is a building business that provides a range of building services to the public. Recently they have been asked to quote for garage conversions (GC) and extensions to properties (EX) and have found that they are winning fewer GC contracts than expected.

BBB has a policy to price all jobs at budgeted total cost plus 50 per cent. Overheads are currently absorbed on a labour hour basis. BBB thinks that a switch to activity-based costing (ABC) to absorb overheads would reduce the cost associated to GC and hence make them more competitive.

You are provided with the following data:

Overhead category	Annual overheads €	Activity driver	Total number of activities per year
Supervisors	90,000	Site visits	500
Planners	70,000	Planning documents	250
Property related	240,000	Labour hours	400,000
Total	400,000		

A typical GC costs €3,500 in materials and takes 300 labour hours to complete. A GC requires only one site visit by a supervisor and needs only one planning document to be raised. The typical EX costs €8,000 in materials and takes 500 hours to complete. An EX requires six site visits and five planning documents. In all cases labour is paid €15 per hour.

Required:

a) Calculate the cost and quoted price of a GC and of an EX using labour hours to absorb the overheads.

b) Calculate the cost and the quoted price of a GC and of an EX using ABC to absorb the overheads.

c) Assuming that the cost of a GC falls by nearly 7 per cent and the price of an EX rises by about 2 per cent as a result of the change to ABC, suggest possible pricing strategies for the two products that BBB sells and suggest two reasons other than high prices for the current poor sales of the GC.

d) One BBB manager has suggested that only marginal cost should be included in budget cost calculations as this would avoid the need for arbitrary overhead allocations to products. Briefly discuss this point of view and comment on the implication for the amount of mark-up that would be applied to budget costs when producing quotes for jobs.

Source: adapted from Association of Chartered Certified Accountants, Paper F5.

E6.8 Customer profitability analysis [LO8]

a) Below you will find an extract from a non-financial company's customer profitability analysis covering a 12-month period. From this data you are requested to:

i) Rank the customers in their order of profitability once customer attributed costs are applied. (The customer with the highest profitability being number 1.) Clearly showing your calculations in arriving at their ranking.

ii) Explain your findings and provide details on how customer profitability can be increased. Does the Pareto view apply in this instance?

Activity	Cost driver rate £	
Sales order processing	200	per sales order
Sales visits	400	per sales visit
Normal delivery costs	1.50	per delivery miles travelled
Special orders	600	per delivery
Credit collection costs	12%	per annum on average payment time

Customer	A	B	Y	Z
No. of sales orders	300	150	60	20
No. of sales visits	30	12	6	8
Miles per delivery	280	170	125	40
Number of deliveries	130	100	45	20
Special orders	50	10	1	0
Average collection period (days)	105	90	0	5
Annual sales	£2,100,000	£2,000,000	£780,000	£1,750,000
Annual operating profit contribution	£180,000	£150,000	£50,000	£125,000

● ● Case study problem ● ● ● ● ● ● ● ● ● ● ● connect ● ● ●

C6.1 National Health Service, UK and ABC [LO5, LO6]

The National Health Service (NHS) system, in the UK, has a costing system called the patient-level information and costing system (PLICS). This costing system is based upon ABC principles. Prior to the implementation of this system they had a traditional system based upon allocation costs using averages and apportionments. They moved away from this system because they wanted a costing system that reflected reality, based on the patients. Therefore, the cost object in this case would be considered as 'the patient'.

The system

The costing system is designed around the patient (cost object) and the resources are allocated to activities that the patients use. These activities are centred on events or services that the patients use. The system is designed so that 'in-patient' costs are calculated from the time of admission through to the time of discharge, while 'out-patients' are charged on the basis of the service they require.

The principles of ABC are used to calculate the costs of patients on a basis which is clinically meaningful and results in resources being traced to clinical activities. The design of the system ensures that there are a minimum number of activities which include: wards, pathology, imaging, pharmacy services and drugs, prostheses, therapies, critical care, operating theatres, special procedure suites, other diagnostics, emergency department and outpatients.

They claim the benefits of this system are as follows:

1) An ability for an organization to truly understand their economic and financial drivers. PLICS can provide transparency to an organization of their income and costs at a service and sub service level on a monthly basis. It provides the capability to benchmark, analyse, investigate and evaluate the make-up of the organizations service costs. There is a further ability to benchmark individual cost elements (e.g. nursing costs, drugs, theatre cost) and patient cost profiles against other providers.

2)   Dramatically improved clinical ownership of operating information. Dialogue can be had about resources consumed by individual patients with similar diagnoses and comparisons can be made against peer groups, teams, individuals as well as care pathways.

3)   Provides crucial information to inform any future change in the grouping and classification of patients. A detailed knowledge of the cost distribution of individual patients rather than the average cost is a necessary precondition for best in class classification.

4)   Provides necessary and crucial information to inform funding policy for payment of high and low outliers for each HRG. Distribution of patient cost is again a prerequisite to ensure the calculation and payment of a long-term sustainable price to an efficient provider – a critical goal of Payment by Results (PbR).

5)   Provides valuable data in discussions with commissioners.

Source: www.nhs.uk

Required:

The PLICS system has been designed to provide accurate information for patients using the services of the NHS.

a)   Discuss some of the main problems which may be encountered by the NHS when using such as system.

b)   Although the patient is the 'cost object' in this case, consider what other cost objects could be used within the NHS.

c)   Discuss the problems of using costing systems, originally designed for the private sector, in public-sector organizations.

● ● ● ● **Recommended reading** ● ● ● ● ● ● ● ● ● ● ● ● ● ● ● ● ●

- Hoozée, S. and W. Bruggeman (2010) 'Identifying operational improvements during the design process of a time-driven ABC system: the role of collective worker participation and leadership style', *Management Accounting Research*, 21, pp. 185–198.

This article examines a Belgium-based, warehousing company, who implemented TD-ABC. This paper follows the implementation process from two distinct perspectives: a participative design process and a non-participative design process. The paper concludes that worker participation with appropriate leadership style is indispensable to the successful implementation of TD-ABC.

- Kaplan, R. and S. Anderson (2004) 'Time-driven activity-based costing', *Harvard Business Review*, November pp. 131–138.

A very practical explanation of TD-ABC, Kaplan and Anderson, provide an example of how TD-ABC can overcome some of the problems highlighted in critiques of traditional ABC. Throughout their discussion they provide examples of companies where they have made the change from ABC to TD-ABC.

- Major, M. and T. Hopper (2005) 'Managers divided: implementing ABC in a Portuguese telecommunication company', *Management Accounting Research*, 16, pp. 205–229.

This is a detailed case study which follows the implementation process of ABC within a Portuguese telecommunications company. Examining the process from a manager's perspective – production managers, production personal and commercial managers – this case study investigates how the ABC systems was perceived from different sets of employees within this one organization. The findings show that there were varying levels of acceptance of the new ABC systems between operating and corporate levels, with resistance from the operations side creating major problems.

- Pike, R., M. Tayles and N. Mansor (2011) 'Activity-based costing user satisfaction and type of system: a research note', *The British Accounting Review*, 43(1), pp. 65–72.

Based in South East Asia this paper examines how user perceptions and system types impact on the ABC performance. This research surveys 54 developers and 181 users spanning 16 different types of ABC systems. The systems type is analysed as three types – embedded, stand-alone and ad hoc – with the findings demonstrating that the perceptions of the users were driven by the type of systems used; therefore system type is a valid contributor to ABC performance.

- Stratton, W., D. Desroches, R. Lawson, and T. Hatch (2009) 'Activity-based costing: is it still relevant?', *Management Accounting Quarterly*, Spring, pp. 31–40.

This paper explores whether ABC is still relevant in the current economic climate and needs of organizations. Surveying 348 manufacturing and service sector companies, they find that ABC still has value to offer companies from both strategic and operational aspects of companies.

References

Anon. (2008) 'Outsourcing', *The Economist*, 29 September, www.economist.com (accessed on 8 March 2011).

Anon. (2009) 'Activity-based costing', *The Economist*, 29 June, www.economist.com (accessed on 8 March 2011).

CIMA (2009) 'Management accounting tools for today and tomorrow', www.cimaglobal.com/resources (accessed on 15 May 2012).

Cooper, R. and R. Kaplan (1988a) 'How cost accounting distorts product costs', *Management Accounting*, April, pp. 20–27.

Cooper, R. and R. Kaplan (1988b) 'Measure costs right: make decisions right', *Harvard Business Review*, September–October, pp. 96–103.

Cooper, R. and R. Kaplan (1991) 'Profit priorities from activity-based costing', *Harvard Business Review*, May–June, pp. 130–5.

Holton, M. (2007) 'Implementing ABC in a service-driven business – DHL worldwide express', in J. A. Smith (ed.) *Handbook of Management Accounting*, 4th edn, London: CIMA and Elsevier, pp. 543–54.

Johnson, H. and R. Kaplan (1987) *Relevance Lost: The Rise and Fall of Management Accounting*, Cambridge, MA, Harvard Business School Press.

Kaplan, R. and S. Anderson (2004) 'Time-driven activity-based costing', *Harvard Business Review*, November, pp. 131–8.

La Villarmois, O. and Y. Levant (2011) 'From adoptions to use of a management control tool, case study evidence of a costing tool', *Journal of Applied Accounting*, 12(3), pp. 234–59.

Lin, Wen-Cheng (2012) 'Financial performance and customer service: an examination using activity-based costing of 38 international airlines', *Journal of Air Transport Management*, 19, pp. 13–15.

Lui, L. and F. Pan (2011) 'Activity based costing in China: a case study of Xu Ji Electric Co Ltd', *CIMA Research Executive summary series*, 7(13), www.cimaglobal.com/resources (accessed on 15 May 2012).

Majid, J. and M. Suliman (2008) 'Implementation of activity based costing in Malaysia. A case study of two companies', *Asian Review of Accounting*, 16(1), pp. 39–55.

Major, M. and T. Hopper (2005) 'Managers divided: implementing ABC in a Portuguese telecommunication company', *Management Accounting Research*, 16, pp. 205–29.

Nassar, M., H. Al-Khadash and A. Sangster (2011) 'The diffusion of activity-based costing in Jordanian industrial companies', *Qualitative Research in Accounting and Management*, 8(2), pp. 180–200.

Pike, R., M. Tayles and N. Mansor (2011) 'Activity-based costing user satisfaction and type of system: a research note', *The British Accounting Review*, 43(1), pp. 65–72.

Ratnatunga, J. and E. Waldmann (2010) 'Transparent costing: has the emperor got clothes?', *Accounting Forum*, 34(3–4), pp. 196–210.

Rowe, C., M. Shields and J. Birnberg (2012) 'Hardening soft accounting information: games for planning organizational change', *Accounting, Organizations and Society*, 37(4), pp. 260–79.

Salam-Mhamdia, A. and B. Ghadhab (2011) 'Value management and activity based costing model in the Tunisian restaurant', *International Journal of Contemporary Hospitality Management*, 24(2), pp. 1–17.

Soin, K. and T. Scheytt (2009) 'Management accounting in financial services', *Handbook of Management Accounting Research*, vol. (3), Oxford: Elsevier, pp. 1385–92.

Stratton, W., D. Desroches, R. Lawson and T. Hatch (2009) 'Activity-based costing: is it still relevant?', *Management Accounting Quarterly*, Spring, pp. 31–40.

Waldrup, B., J. MacArthur and J. Michelman (2009) 'Does your costing system need a tune up?', *Strategic Finance,* June, pp. 47–61.

● ● ● Note ●

1 This is when it became internationally recognized as a problem. Discussions had taken place as early as the 1970s.

When you have read this chapter

Log on to the Online Learning Centre at **www.mcgraw-hill.co.uk/textbooks/burns** to explore chapter-by-chapter test questions, links and further online study tools for Management Accounting.

PART 3

PLANNING AND CONTROL

CHAPTER 7

PLANNING AND CONTROL: IDEAS, THEORIES AND PRINCIPLES

Chapter outline

- Organizational planning
- Organizational control
- Management control systems
- Complexity in organizations
- Ways to conceptualize control
- Important features of planning and control mechanisms
- The roles of management accountants in planning and control

Learning outcomes

On completion of this chapter, students will be able to:

LO1 Conceptualize how planning and control mechanisms might assist organizations in their decision making over time

LO2 Convey the important role(s) of management accountants for (re)designing holistic and integrated planning and control systems

LO3 Have a feel for the complexity of organizational life, and discuss how planning and control can help to manage such complexity

LO4 Explain the basics of three main (behavioural, cultural and output) perspectives on control

LO5 Recite some of the key features of any planning and/or control mechanism

LO6 Explain how planning and control mechanisms are intended to express and achieve an organization's objectives

Introduction

In previous chapters, you have learned the importance of management accounting *information* in today's organizations. More specifically, we highlighted how important management accounting information is for facilitating (1) planning, (2) control, and (3) performance measurement.

Chapter 2, in particular, explored how significant management accounting is for contributing towards an organization's overall information base. Information is a vernacular that binds together potentially chaotic organizations; it provides a corporate language; informs managers' interpretations and understandings; and, most of all, it facilitates a degree of coherence into managerial decision making. Decision making takes place throughout organizations, not just among the most senior managers. Many organizations empower their employees to make local decisions, within a broader strategic framework, because employees have comparative advantage over others on understanding the traits and routines of their locality within an organizational setting. In situations of **employee empowerment**, employees are usually also designated **responsibility** for their local decisions and actions.

Management accounting information serves both as an integrative mechanism used to co-ordinate diverse business activities, and as a measure of overall performance and viability; it therefore has central place in the control of organizational activity. In this chapter we explore the concepts of planning and control in a broad sense, and also what such concepts mean from a management accounting perspective. In Chapters 8 to 10 we will look more closely at specific tools and techniques generally used by management accountants to facilitate planning and control. Following that, we will explore the concepts, tools and techniques underlying performance measurement.

Although the respective themes of planning, control and performance measurement appear in two different sections within this textbook, it is important to stress that all three dimensions are closely connected. Planning, control and performance measurement can all be investigated as stand-alone themes, but we should not lose sight of how all three are integral and interconnected aspects of an organization's decision-making process. Furthermore it is also very important that we remind ourselves of the key roles for management accounting, and management accountants, in mobilizing and often leading such activities that feed management decision making.

By way of context, this chapter discusses both established and more recent ideas, theories and principles underpinning the planning and control processes within organizations. First, however, we should revisit and define what we actually mean by 'planning' and 'control'.

Organizational planning

Planning describes how an organization selects from alternative options, such that all decisions combined will assist in the achievement of its goals. The goals (or objectives) of an organization can take many different forms and rarely do they remain static over time (see *Management Accounting in Practice 7.1*). For instance, the goals of a private-sector chemicals research company would likely be different in multiple ways (yet probably overlapping in other ways) to a government-owned chemicals research laboratory. For instance, the former will be more likely than the latter to gear its planning process towards maximization of economic profits. In broad terms, most organizations will have both short-run (operational) and long-run (strategic) goals, and management accounting plays a key role in defining and making visible such goals. Commercial businesses will normally target the maximization of economic profits (although other goals such as social and environmental impact, long-run financial security, capital investment, customer satisfaction and many more objectives can also take priority, at different times). Organizational goals are of course varied and changeable, and each organization's context should be taken into consideration at a particular point in time.

Few could deny that planning is almost always a useful tactic. We all engage in planning at some stage in our lives, some more than others. On occasions this might be financial planning (for example, putting monies aside each month for next year's holiday, or to purchase the latest tablet from Apple), or more general planning (for example, mapping out your intended career progression over the next 10 years). Well-informed planning can help organizations steer through the often unpredictable and changeable business environment to which they are exposed. It is frequently management accounting information that underpins this process, and providing useful data to inform sound planning decisions is a key role for all management accountants.

Management accounting information will establish the alternative options available for decision makers, providing its users with more knowledge about the planning problems and issues. We assume that greater knowledge about the potential impact of decisions for an organization will enable managers to make more informed decisions, though not necessarily the 'best' decision. Options in today's organizations tend to be complex and changeable, thus in recent times we have begun to see more sophistication in the management accounting techniques and tools that are adopted for these purposes. For instance, many organizations have introduced more dynamic and flexible features into their planning and control processes, for example rolling forecasts (see Chapter 10), and the management accounting which feeds the planning and control processes in many organizations will nowadays comprise as much *non*-financial information as it will financial information (see Chapter 17). Indeed, a feature of useful management accounting would be the integration of both non-financial and financial data/information to provide a comprehensive view of the organization.

7.1: Management Accounting in Practice

Planning new flights

Airlines need to undertake significant investigation when considering the adoption of new travel routes. The decision as to which new travel routes to adopt (if any) during a particular year will take into account a number of factors, many of which will be informed by management accounting information. For instance, the choice between alternative new flights to be adopted will be informed (non-exclusively) by such things as:

- Predicted size, and potential growth, of the new customer base

- Competitor airlines who already operate similar flights

- Projected costs of both launching and operating the potential new flights

- Knock-on effects for other flights operated by the airline.

Management accountants will build a plan for each alternative new flight and/or for a combination of different new flights, and will attempt to quantify not only expected revenues and costs for each new potential option, but will also incorporate non-financial costs and benefits, opportunity costs, and more. In the end, decision makers within an airline will opt for a particular course of action based on an informed and balanced assessment of both tangible and intangible (estimated) costs and revenues, plus usually a slice of 'gut, sense and general know-how'. Once the decisions are made, however, these plans will become more formalized into the day-to-day organizational machinery (for example, via budgets and forecasts).

Exercise

You are an executive decision-maker in the following situations. Describe the kind of information that you would ask your management accountants to collate in helping you to investigate whether or not you would support a particular proposal:

a) You are Finance Director for a local government in the Netherlands; a well-known accountancy firm has offered, at a considerable cost, to undertake all of your routine accounting tasks such as payroll, general ledger, taxation and annual reporting.

b) You are the owner of a small cakes manufacturer in the South of England. Marks and Spencer (M&S), a large retailer, has approached you to see if your company will supply them with cakes; if you agree, M&S's requirements will more or less take up the whole of your production capacity.

c) You are Vice-Chancellor (V-C) of a major University in Australia. The V-C of a less well-known university in the same city has approached you to gauge your interest in a merger between both universities.

Sometimes it can prove quite difficult to produce the necessary data to inform sound planning decisions. For example, successful planning in some organizations might rely upon data that is difficult to source, for instance if it is data relating to your competitors' affairs. Or, data can simply be hard to quantify, for instance when trying to predict the market share for a new product launch in unfamiliar territory. However, recent developments in data storage and retrieval, and predictive analysis, promise to offer organizations *considerably* more capacity to plan and make future-oriented decisions (see Chapter 22 for more detail).

In extreme and highly unusual cases, some organizations are faced with situations that are nigh impossible to predict or plan for. For example, only a handful of commentators predicted the global financial crisis that began with the USA's sub-prime mortgage crisis in 2007 and has since had adverse ramifications on a massive scale. Few organizations predicted or planned for the emergent global financial crisis and economic downturn. Consequently, for most organizations at this time, financial and other business plans were 'shot' and immediately became meaningless, and reformulation and repositioning became a general necessity.

There will always be shocks and major unpredictable occurrences that impact organizations, and a key role for management accountants is to react to such things in a way that reorients their organization towards a revised strategy that is bedded in the new and emerging environmental context. Better, but harder, still is to 'see' shocks before they actually happen, and therefore have alternative or contingency plans in place before the event.

Notwithstanding the fragile nature of business plans, as described above, the general consensus would be that it is still better to have plans than to not have plans. The contemporary approach in many lead organizations is to engage in more holistic, forward-looking and flexible planning tools. Contingencies or buffers built into business plans 'for a rainy day' would also seem to be a routine aspect of many organizations' strategy nowadays.

Organizational control

Control describes how managers seek to ensure that their plans are being followed in practice. We should make a distinction between control and controls, as follows:

- **Control** – the process of ensuring that what is actually done in an organization correlates with its objectives

- **Controls** – the package of tools, techniques, artefacts which produce and comprise the information necessary to assist the control process.

Once organizations have made their decisions, and plans are in place, there needs to be both encouragement and monitoring to ensure that the plans are acted upon. This process, including the provision of alerts where there is any divergence from original plans, sparking rectification where necessary, is engaged via an organization's **management control system**.

Management control systems

A management control system (MCS) is a system which gathers and uses information to plan, control and monitor the decisions and subsequent actions of an organization.

Exhibit 7.1 portrays a management control system in fairly simple terms, although the fundamental thing to bear in mind is that this caption is meant to be interpreted in a *cumulative* sense – that is, the process shown is ongoing and continual. An organization makes plans, which will incite particular decisions and appropriate actions, to reach its strategic goals. These strategic goals are changeable over time, mostly as they will be (re)shaped by broader economic, social and political factors which impinge on an organization's situation at any point in time. The frequency and magnitude of such broader change is not really generalisable and is certainly not uniform across organizations and through time; many such changes can come in the shape of unpredictable 'shocks'.

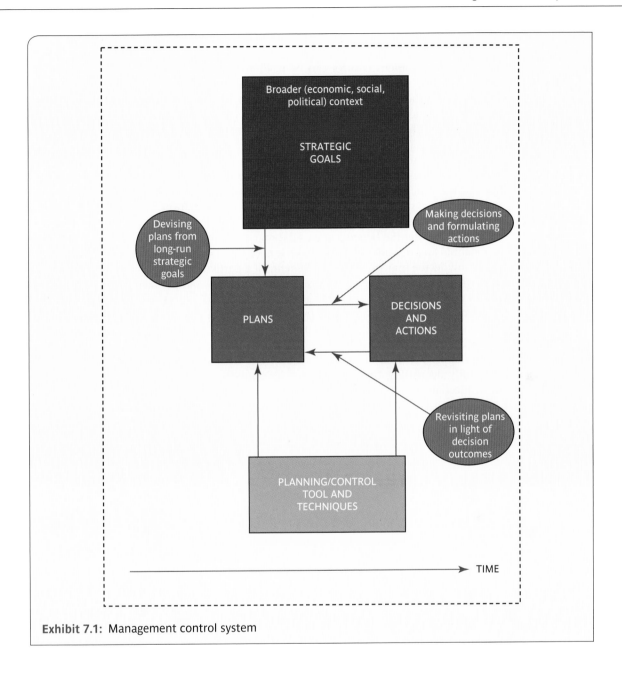

Exhibit 7.1: Management control system

An organization's plans, decisions and actions need to be monitored at particular points in time, and there are numerous planning and control tools and techniques which can assist in this, covered in more detail in Chapters 8 to 10. At particular intervals, the frequency of which is not uniform but is entirely organization-specific, questions need to be asked, such as are the actions achieving what was planned and, in turn, do such plans still appear to adhere to the strategic goals?

Some of the planning and control tools and techniques used by management accountants compare actual results to plans after the event (that is, a *feed-backward* orientation), while others plan continuously with today and tomorrow's information for future scenarios (*feed-forward* orientation). Once again, we stress the *ongoing* nature of the management control system presented in Exhibit 7.1, depicted by the time line included at the bottom of the diagram. Also, there are double arrows between plans and decisions/actions, signifying that although plans will shape decisions and actions, the nature and outcome of any actions at any particular point in time can (re) shape future plans. And, as mentioned above, we also stress that an organization's strategic goals will be continuously open to influence and change from broader developments in, for example, the economic, social and political spheres, and this can also have ramifications for an organization's plans.

At a basic level, management control can be facilitated via performance reports whereby, at particular points in time senior managers review actual performance against original plans. However, management control systems are becoming increasingly holistic in nature. That is, control systems today generally seek to manage (monitor, etc.) an organization through ongoing analysis of both financially oriented *and* non-financial information. It is no surprise therefore that 'balanced scorecards' (see Chapter 17) have in many organizations become an integral and important part of the control systems, but also that they are frequently interconnected to planning tools such as budgets and forecasts. The design of an organization, its governance and the matrix of responsibilities is also something that inextricably gets woven into the control process. The design of management control systems, sourcing of data, analysing information, and more, constitutes a key role for today's management accountants.

However, for all the potential benefits of a well-designed management control system, there are usually both potential and real adverse effects which need to be set against the benefits. Sometimes an organization will decide that the potential benefits of a particular type of control system would likely be outweighed by various expected negative impacts. For example, when one organization (parent) acquires another (subsidiary) the former might choose to impose its management control systems on the latter, bringing consistency in group reporting. The advantages of this consistency in group practices, however, need to be stacked up against potential adverse impact, such as resistance in the subsidiary against top-down-imposition and a perceived loss of local control.

An alternative approach would be for the acquiring company to engage in a more light-touch approach, hopefully decreasing the potential for resistance and conflict. Having said this, such slighter-control mechanisms could be risky if there were underlying problems in the subsidiary, because it may be too late before the new parent company becomes aware of such problems. Decisions over the nature of control and planning systems are usually complex, and require a balanced view of the particular organizational situation.

Complexity in organizations

Most organizations are complex, in respect of their structure, stakeholders, business processes, and much more. There are a multitude of people within an organization, populating different functional areas, different levels on the corporate hierarchical ladder, different backgrounds, and more. Take a look at the organizational chart in Exhibit 7.2, for example. This is the organizational chart for Coca-Cola Hellenic, one of the world's largest bottling companies for Coca-Cola products, based in Athens (Greece). The chart shows positions of responsibility at the higher levels of the organization but it is quite clear just how complex the web of cross-functional interests is.

At the top of the hierarchical ladder is the board of directors, which is monitored by various stakeholder-led committees such as the audit committee and the social responsibility committee. The board appoints an overall main business manager, the chief executive officer (CEO). The latter in turn oversees a selection of regional and group-based divisions or directorships, each of which will have direct reporting lines into the CEO. Such complexity, which is considerable in many organizations makes the achievement of management control, ensuring that organizational behaviour aligns to top-level goals and objectives, an incredibly difficult task.

In effect we can think of the array of control mechanisms in an organization as constituting a web of interconnected gateways and check-points for different individuals and/or groups within, or connected to an organization, to monitor the behaviour of others in the context of the overall goals. For instance, control-oriented tools and techniques can be used as a means to monitor all of the following (and more):

- The owners and other stakeholders monitoring the behaviour of managers in whom they entrust to maximize benefits (for example, profits) to the former.

- Heads of business units and departments monitoring the behaviour of other, less senior, colleagues.

- Managers monitoring the behaviour of connected but outside parties, such as suppliers, or outside parties 'brought-in', such as outsourced services.

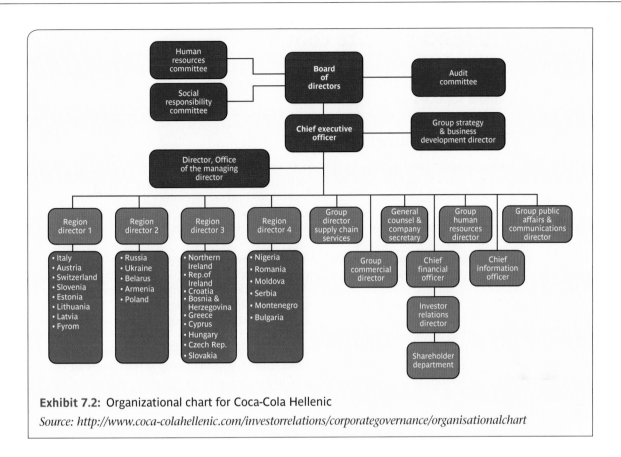

Exhibit 7.2: Organizational chart for Coca-Cola Hellenic

Source: http://www.coca-colahellenic.com/investorrelations/corporategovernance/organisationalchart

Some commentators have highlighted that where there is more trust within an organization, there is likely to be less need for strict and formalized control systems (Johansson and Baldvinsdottir, 2003) Others have highlighted the importance of informal (as opposed to formalized) controls for binding together an organization and its multiple stakeholders (Lukka, 2007).

Extending the concept and nature of organizational control even further, many organizations will nowadays adopt tools and techniques which are able to facilitate and support both operational and strategic goals. Indeed, it is through planning and control techniques and tools, in particular, that organizations are able to devise, implement and monitor the journey from operational matters to strategic goals. Planning and control mechanisms have the capacity to link an organization's strategic objectives to things that are actually done on a day-to-day basis.

Management accounting tools and techniques which assist an organization's planning and control are integral features of the broader management process. However, it should be acknowledged that they constitute only part, albeit an important part, of this process. If we take a generic definition of control as constituting 'the monitoring of actual behavior against objectives', it is easy to understand why there would need to be control in many other areas of an organization – for example, production controls (product quality, health and safety regulations), research and development controls (trials time-utilization, materials requisition), stock controls (records of delivery, in and out of stock control), and more. One of the fundamental advancements of recent times is that high-capacity information technology now permits a powerful cocktail of holistic and integrated controls, thereby offering sophisticated and detailed recording and analysis.

Notwithstanding that management accounting constitutes only part of an organization's overall configuration of controls, the control-facing management accounting tools and techniques adopted by an organization will be important, especially those controls which are output or performance related. Management accounting tools for control, for instance budgets or forecasts, have an immediate appeal in the sense that they are able to convey aspects of organizational performance against the corporate plans in both monetary and quantitative terms. Undoubtedly, in the long run, and especially where profit-seeking organizations are concerned, the establishment of monetary targets and monitoring their (non-)achievement is fundamental to helping to assure long-run sustainability of all types of organization.

Ways to conceptualize control

Conceptually there are different ways that we can portray and think about types of control within an organization. We now briefly consider three particular ways to conceptualize control, highlighting the negative and positive aspects of each.

1. Action/behavioural control

Action/behavioural controls are usually established when desirable (or undesirable) actions are known, but they can also be observed or monitored in practice. The control mechanism can take various forms, including: (1) behavioural constraints and preventive measures such as laws, rules and/or passwords, (2) pre-action reviews, scrutiny and approval processes, such as authorization, directives and formal agendas, and (3) action-accountability and codes of conduct, such as upper limits to spending and post-event reviews.

An obvious advantage of action-oriented controls is that because actions are usually observable, it should be no problem to measure the effect. However, in order to have any impact through such control mechanisms, there needs to be direct link between them and the action per se; in other words, the control mechanism should prevent and/or encourage action(s). Moreover, the cause-and-effect relationship between control and action needs to be easily understood by all those parties implicated in its workings.

The (potential) disadvantage of an action-oriented control mechanism is twofold: (1) that such controls are probably best suited to stable situations, and (2) if such control mechanisms are overly-rigid and inflexible, they might discourage creativity and innovation.

2. Personnel/cultural control

Personnel/cultural controls are grounded in an underlying belief that organizations can mobilize and nurture solidarity and commitment towards organizational goals. Employees can, it is assumed, be socialized into particular ways of working, an organizational culture, and norm behaviours. In practice, organizations might try to embed a culture via its corporate values which it tries to instill organization-wide through such means as training, development and targeted recruitment of employees.

An obvious advantage of culture-geared controls in an organization is that in comparison with other types of control mechanisms they tend to be relatively inexpensive to design and operate; there are probably also relatively less potential harmful side effects. However, on the negative side, culture controls will normally be more difficult to achieve as the complexity of an organization increases, and especially in situations where there is incongruence between local (for example, a subsidiary) and broader (for example, parent company) organizational goals.

7.2: Management Accounting in Practice

Corporate values and culture

Novo Nordisk is a Danish pharmaceuticals company, has been in existence for nearly a century, and specializes mostly in diabetes care. It employs approximately 33,000 people across 75 countries, and sells its products in nearly 200 countries. All staff and other stakeholders are fully aware of, and trained in, 'the Novo Nordisk Way', which encapsulates the corporate culture and Novo Nordisk's way of doing business. All business activities must be aligned to this Novo way. The Novo Nordisk way is summarized, by means of its 'essentials', as:

- Create value from a patient-centred business approach.
- Set ambitious goals and strive for excellence.
- Be accountable for financial, environmental and social performance.

● Provide innovation to the benefit of our stakeholders.

● Build and maintain good stakeholder relations.

● Treat everyone with respect.

● Focus on personal performance and development.

● Maintain a healthy and engaging working environment.

● Optimize the way we work and strive for simplicity.

● Never compromise on quality and business ethics.

Source: based on author's own research and Novo Nordisk's web pages, see http://www.novonordisk.com/default.asp.

Exercise

You are chief executive for a well-known (global) car manufacturer with headquarters in Germany, and make cars to serve both 'everyday, family' and 'high-class' automobile markets. It has been suggested by some senior colleagues that your company lacks identity, so you have agreed to review and work on enhancing the corporate values and culture. Describe some of the things that you will do.

3. Results/output control

Results/output control is undertaken through measuring outcomes. This could take various specific forms, including: (1) measures that minimize undesirable behaviour, (2) measuring performance against financial and non-financial targets, and (3) establishing a system of rewards for successful outcomes, and/or disincentives against poor outcomes.

Such an outputs-oriented approach can be particularly worthwhile when the knowledge of (un)desirable action is thin. Also, since the focus of this approach is on outcomes there is potentially small restriction on individual autonomy. On the negative side, however, output controls might, if not carefully designed and monitored, encourage too much focus on quantitative measures, as well as nurturing a short-term perspective that might serve the interest of individuals or groups involved but not the organization as a whole. Moreover, while there is no doubting the *potential* usefulness of an outputs-geared control system, probably the most significant danger for such systems, especially where they become interconnected to incentive systems, is that they become open to data manipulation or can cause dissatisfaction among staff.

Important features of planning and control mechanisms

While there is no universal 'best' way to design or implement planning and control mechanisms for an organization, there are particular features that would seem important in most cases, for example:

● *Clear objectives and targets* – without such clarity there would be uncertainty and tension as to who does what, when, and so on.

● *Strategic relevance* – all organizational activities should ultimately be aligned with its strategic intent.

● *Accuracy and measurability* – inaccurate data makes for unhelpful information which, if used, might make for risky decision making.

● *Timeliness* – the pace of organizational life is now ultra-fast and unrelenting; today's information is frequently too late for decisions about tomorrow.

- *Flexibility* – external factors in particular can change rapidly and unexpectedly; planning and control systems need to absorb and quickly move on from such occurrences.

- *Understandability* – planning and control systems are used widely across an organization; its outputs must be broadly comprehensible to be of real use.

- *Open for corrective action* – as with flexibility, tomorrow's planning and control mechanisms should not be overly rigid or static

- *Appropriate incentives* – planning systems aim to identify where an organization wants to be, while control systems help to check that a organization gets there. For this journey to happen, there usually needs to be appropriate incentives to the employees implicated in making this happen

The roles of management accountants in planning and control

In Chapter 1 you learned how management accounting practice was increasingly being pushed 'out into the field' such that business managers were themselves engaged in planning and control tools and techniques such as budgets and forecasts. That said, in most organizations the management accountants will likely remain as guardian and overseer of planning and control systems, in particular the financial systems.

Management accountants will normally lead the (re)design of planning and control systems which could, for example, result from the acquisition of another organization, a merger, joint venture or alliance, outsourcing, or a corporate restructuring. An important aim of such (re)design in organizations is to engage the financial planning and control systems with other *non*-financial systems, as well as engage the accountants with the other parts of the organizational process. In other words, holistic and integrated systems design is an objective for many of today's organizations. In addition, many organizations will likely nowadays intend to implement planning and control systems which have some feed-forward orientation (for example, forecasts) as well as appropriate incentives for those implicated in the new systems.

There always will be a limit to just how much any tools and techniques, no matter how sophisticated, can achieve in terms of planning and controlling for the future. The opening chapter of this book highlighted just how changeable the organizational environment can be, with multiple drivers fuelling an inherent uncertainty and unpredictability in both short- and long-run activities and, hence, the broader contexts to such activities. As we mentioned at the start of this chapter, taken to its extreme there will always be occurrences that cannot be planned for, and/or which are incredibly difficult to build in controls for. Again, how many airlines had planned for the 9/11 'twin towers' disaster in 2001, how many banks had foreseen the global financial crash in 2007/08, how many insurers were prepared for the Japanese tsunami of 2011, or the earthquake in Christchurch, New Zealand, in February 2011?

Of course the answer to all these extreme occurrences is probably 'nil'; but such extreme events *will* always happen. Organizations will not be able to plan for or control such things. Nevertheless, it is usually better to try to plan and control than to not do so. And, the more responsive and flexible that planning and control tools can be in the face of extreme and shock occurrences, normally the better in terms of usefulness for management decision making.

Chapter summary

This chapter has discussed underlying theories, ideas and principles which influence how and why organizations engage in planning and control, to a large extent via their management accounting techniques and systems. As highlighted, the implementation and use of planning and control systems is an ongoing, challenging and important task for most organizations. In practice, as with much of the context in which management accounting operates, an understanding of management accounting needs a broader lens than merely a techniques-oriented focus. A need for such broader lens and more holistic understandings will be borne out in the following chapters when we investigate the traditional budgeting process (Chapter 8), flexible budgeting and variance analysis (Chapter 9) and the 'beyond budgeting' debate (Chapter 10).

Key terms

Action/behavioural controls Are normally established when desirable (or undesirable) actions are known, and can also be observed in practice (p. 158)

Control The process of ensuring that what is actually done in an organization correlates with its objectives (p. 154)

Controls Are the package of tools, techniques and artefacts which produce and comprise the information necessary to assist the control process (p. 154)

Employee empowerment Where organizations give managers and workers the right to independently make local decisions (p. 152)

Management control system Systems which gather and use information to plan, control and monitor the actions of organizations (p. 154)

Personnel/cultural controls Are grounded in an underlying belief that organizations can mobilize and nurture solidarity and commitment towards organizational goals (p. 158)

Planning When organizations select from alternative options, such that all decisions combined will assist in the achievement of its goals (p. 152)

Responsibility The notion that when employees are empowered, they also become accountable for (and will have monitored) their actions and decisions (p. 152)

Results/output controls Are undertaken through measuring outcomes, and can be particularly worthwhile when the knowledge of (un)desirable action is sparse (p. 159)

Review questions ● ● ● ● ● ● ● ● ● ● ● ● connect ● ● ●

Level of difficulty: | BASIC | INTERMEDIATE | ADVANCED |

7.1 Define both organizational *planning* and organizational *control*. **[LO1, LO3]**

7.2 Explain why today's organizations place more emphasis on non-financial measures in their plans and controls. **[LO1, LO3, LO5]**

7.3 Why do you think that trust and informal controls might lessen the imperative for formal planning and control systems? **[LO1, LO3, LO5]**

7.4 What are some of the key features for today's planning and control systems? **[LO1, LO5]**

7.5 What are some of the key roles for management accountants in facilitating an organization's planning and control processes? **[LO2]**

7.6 Critically appraise the relative advantages and disadvantages of: (1) behavioural controls, (2) cultural controls and (3) output controls. **[LO5]**

● ● ● ● Group discussion and activity questions ● ● ● ● ● ● ● ● ● ●

7.7 In this chapter you have seen that for some organizations it is impossible to plan for every eventuality. Sometimes things happen, both inside and external to an organization, which are simply unpredictable yet incredibly significant. Discuss, as management accountants, how you might approach the following corporate dilemmas. (*Hint: Would you look to revise your business plans, and what controls might you put in place? How would you implement such changes? What new forms of data/information would you seek? What broader investigations and/or changes might you consider initiating?*) **[LO1, LO2, LO3, LO4, LO5]**

a) You are a management accountant for the council/municipality in Madrid, Spain. Faced with a need to cut the national debt, and in a time of global austerity, the Spanish government passes a law that, in 8 months' time it will drastically reduce funding to all city councils, by at least 40 per cent.

b) You are a management accountant for a professional football team in the North West of England. Unfortunately your team has just been relegated from the Premiership, and now faces the prospect of significantly less revenues than you have become used to in recent times. There is a 'buffer fund' available for relegated teams, but this only lasts for one season and at £20 million it constitutes only about a quarter of the revenues you had been receiving from Sky television rights for playing in the Premiership. Up to this point you have not been particularly successful in terms of global brand and marketing, and you expect your paying fans base to almost halve next season (this season's average home game attendance was 22,000 supporters). Even more worryingly, an independent consultant, appointed by you, recently recommended that your ground, with a full capacity of 30,000 supporters, is in a serious state of disrepair and is actually very close to contravening the world football authority's health and safety regulations.

7.8 You are management accountant for a small manufacturing company in Belgium, a producer of speciality beer. Your company has recently acquired a competitor speciality beer producer, for what you believe to be a fair purchase price. It is your task to review the planning and control tools and techniques in the acquired company, and thereafter to design and lead a change programme that will bring the newly acquired organization's planning and control mechanisms in line with those of your (parent) company. **[LO1, LO2, LO3, LO4, LO5]**

The parent company (for whom you have worked 10 years) has highly formalized planning and control mechanisms in place, which have successfully assisted the management process over the years. There is a detailed but unsophisticated budget tool, updated every 12 months, an overarching annual budget cycle and a basic forecast tool. These planning and control systems are well regarded by the executives of your company, and they are expected to retain their usefulness in future years – even if some might think them traditional and simplistic. Some other local organizations (non-competitors) with which you have good corporate relations have emulated your planning and control systems as an example of best practice.

To your surprise, as you start to investigate the planning and control systems of the acquired company, it quickly becomes clear that their systems are radically different; in fact their planning and control systems do not really exist at all! Very little is formally structured – for instance, written down in manuals – about the subsidiary's planning or control process. The CEO of the acquired business said, while you chatted over a coffee break: 'We have never had a need for formal planning and control systems, ever since we set the organization up two years ago. We *know* our business, we *just know it*. So we just get on with things, we all just do what we need to do in our different parts of the organization. And *it works*! Our turnover has gone from near €500k in our first year of business to just over €750k this year. Net profit each year has been in the region of €100k. Now, I'm not an accountant – and we don't have an accountant in the organization, we are too small – but I would say that for a new company with just four staff, these are good numbers.'

Required:

You are concerned, and also alarmed at the CEO's comments. Your task is to arrange a meeting with the CFO of the parent company, articulating your concerns and making a case for the changes that you are suggesting in terms of new planning and control practices in the subsidiary company.

• • • Exercises • • • • • • • • • • • • • • • connect • • • •

E7.1   Control versus controls [LO1, LO2]

Controls are the collection of tools and techniques which produce and comprise the information necessary to assist the control process: true or false?

E7.2   Adverse effects of a well-designed management control system [LO2]

Lemonade PLC is a manufacturer of concentrated lime juice in Glasgow. Lemonade has a well-designed management control system that involves tools and techniques to provide an analysis of both financial and non-financial information.

    In the coming year, the company plans to acquire Berries PLC, a manufacturer of concentrated berry juices. Berries' control system is considerably basic and only reviews actual performance against original plans. William, the chief operating officer of Lemonade, has suggested implementing the advanced management control system of Lemonade in Berries too.

Required:

What adverse effects should the management keep in mind before implementing the advanced management control system in Berries? (Select all that apply.)

a)   It may lead to inconsistencies in group reporting.

b)   Berries' employees might resist the top-down imposition.

c)   It might de-motivate the employees of Lemonade PLC.

d)   Berries' existing employees might perceive a loss of local control in the company.

e)   The market value of Lemonade's stock may fall.

E7.3   Different perspectives on control [LO4]

Fill in the missing words:

Management controls that are grounded in an underlying belief that organizations can mobilize and nurture solidarity and commitment towards organizational goals are normally referred to as _____ or _____ controls.

E7.4   Important features of planning and control mechanisms [LO5]

Which of the following do you think would be important to consider when designing or implementing planning and control mechanisms?

A)   Strategic relevance

B)   Flexibility

C)   Timeliness

D)   All of the above.

E7.5 **Management planning and control system [LO1, LO2, LO4]**

Fill in the blanks with the appropriate terms given below:

Balanced scorecard	Cultural controls
Behavioural controls	Feed-forward orientation
Management control systems	Output controls

1) Management accounting techniques that change the plans continuously with new information are said to have a _____.

2) _____ are established or written based on desirable and undesirable actions, and can be observed in practice.

3) _____ is a management accounting tool that uses both financial and non-financial information in an integrated way to assist managers in decision-making.

4) _____ gathers and uses information to plan, control and monitor the decisions and subsequent actions of an organization.

5) _____ are grounded in an underlying belief that organizations can nurture commitment towards organizational goals.

6) _____ are particularly worthwhile when the knowledge of an action is thin.

E7.6 **Planning for proposed business expansion [LO1, LO2, LO5]**

You are chief management accountant for a well-known chain of gymnasia/health spas in major Austrian cities. Company executives are considering expansion into the German market, with a suggestion of opening five new gyms in major German cities over the next two years. You have been asked to put together a feasibility study. What information, discussion, and areas for further detailed investigation do you think should be included in this study, and how will you obtain such information?

E7.7 **Multinational organizations and control mechanisms [LO2, LO3, LO4]**

Describe some of the advantages and disadvantages for a multinational organization at having strict and formalized financial controls over its subsidiaries which are located across multiple continents.

E7.8 **Informal controls [LO3, LO4, LO5]**

What do you think is meant by 'informal controls' (as opposed to 'formal controls'), and are they a better type of management control?

E7.9 **Incentives and rewards [LO4, LO5, LO6]**

In the main text of this chapter we considered how important it is to establish appropriate rewards and incentives to encourage employees to undertake activities in the manner that will assist an organization to achieve its objectives. If you were the Chairman of a major rugby union team in New Zealand, what different kinds of incentives (for example, bonuses) would you offer to the squad players in addition to their flat salary?

E7.10 **Ways to conceptualize control [LO4]**

Conceptually, there are three different types of control within an organization – behavioural controls, cultural controls and output controls.

Required:

Identify the type of control mechanism that each of the following situations exhibits.

1) The production manager of Phoenix Ltd. received 40% of his annual salary as bonus for achievement of his yearly target.

2) The success of Tangent's training programme depends largely on how the trainees observe and adapt their mentor's behaviour to carry out tasks assigned. This is because very few rules exist to guide and restrict their actions.

3) Employees of A to Z Marketing are required to seek approval from the HR department if they start work after 9:30 A.M.

4) With the level of sophistication in training technologies these days, employees at Titus Ltd. are able to manufacture high-quality products with a low degree of supervision.

5) Lifestyle PLC prepares a productivity chart of each employee on a monthly basis. Employees with lower than average productivity are sent a show-cause notice by their respective managers.

6) Due to increased instances of theft in the recent past, Trump Card Ltd. has decided to provide individual lockers to their employees to keep their valuables.

E7.11 **Important features of planning and control mechanisms [LO5]**

Identify the feature of planning and control mechanisms that each of the following situations exhibit:

Flexibility	Strategic relevance
Appropriate incentives	Understandability
Timeliness	Accuracy and measurability

1) All departments of Ozone Ltd. aim to provide the best quality products to customers at affordable prices. Ozone's corporate goal is to increase customer loyalty by improving customer satisfaction.

2) Tulip's yearly sales and marketing targets are adjusted for changes in economy every quarter.

3) The output of Georgia PLC's planning system is broadly comprehensible by employees at all levels.

4) The planning and control system of Best Frappé PLC is designed to provide a cash bonus to any employee who achieves more than 110% of his target.

5) Rosemary Ltd. has set a review process to ensure that the data used for planning and decision-making is error free.

6) Wester Ltd. sets yearly productions targets. The planning system of the company is designed to provide a daily production update to the department managers. This helps them resolve any shortcomings in meeting the yearly target.

E7.12 **Organizational culture [LO6]**

You will need to do some research – via the Internet and/or via articles and papers. Investigate the *objectives* for up to five organizations, covering at least one private-sector organization, one in the public sector and one not-for-profit organization. Compare and contrast the detail in their objectives, and compare also to the objectives of Novo Nordisk (see *Management Accounting in Practice 7.2*)

E7.13 **Action/behavioural controls [LO1, LO3, LO4]**

The potential disadvantage of action-oriented controls are two fold: (1) that such controls are best suited to stable conditions, and (2) that if such controls are overly rigid and inflexible they might hinder innovation and change. Give real-world examples/illustrations for each potential situation, and for each of your examples suggest possible alternative controls

Case study problem ● ● ● ● ● ● ● ● ● ● ● connect ● ● ●

C7.1 Implementing 'simple' control mechanisms with significantly adverse behavioural consequences [LO1, LO2, LO4, LO5]

Fashion Plc is a well-known high-street clothing retailer in Australia. Its performance has been declining over recent years, along with its share price. Things have also not been helped in the past few years by several high-profile incidents of bad national press which have considerably tarnished the corporate image. There is a sense of realization and acceptance at executive level that the company is facing a serious crisis, and that there needs to be some fundamental changes.

One area of the business that has become very costly is holding stocks of saleable products in the high-street stores. Storage and handling of stocks can be an expensive operation in any organization, and thus the accountants want this aspect of the business to be better controlled than it has been to date. At the same time the organization intends to implement new divisional depots which can hold stocks for multiple stores located in their divisional area and supply-on-demand via an integrated ordering system. However it is expected to be at least a year before such a divisional-based storage and deliveries system might be fully operational.

As a new and more immediate mechanism for control within the business, the accountants decide to introduce a charge into the profit statements of individual stores. Every store has its own profit statement which broadly speaking records revenues and costs attributable to that store. These are internal management reports, compiled by the management accountants, and constituting an important part of how executive and divisional managers assess store performance over time. Importantly, the senior managers in each store, including the store manager, have a not insignificant proportion of their salary and annual bonus based on a percentage of their store's net profit figure. The new charge is to be based on the amount of stocks being held on average, over a year, by a particular store. The higher the average stocks held, the higher the charge in a store's profit statement and, consequently, the lower the net profit. All other employees of a store (retail assistants, administrators and storeroom staff) also receive an annual 'Christmas bonus' that is calculated in relation to their store's net profitability.

The accountants will implement the changes to stores reporting within two months, in time for the start of the new financial year. The changes, approved recently by majority vote at executive level, will be 'sold' to employees mostly via memos and email on the basis that the organization is facing a serious crisis, costs *must* be cut drastically, and that the introduction of a charge for holding stocks in stores was a sensible way to improve control over this particular element of business costs.

No further consultation was planned, and the accountants intended to run brief training courses for their store managers, at which the technicalities of calculating the new charges for stock-holding (but not much else) would be explained.

Source: based on author's own research, company anonymized and disguised.

Required:

You are a senior management accountant in Fashion Plc, although you are not actually leading this particular change programme. You have serious reservations about what is being proposed. Write a memo to the CFO of Fashion Plc explaining the reasons why you have serious reservations about the proposed changes, and describe alternative options (not just accounting related) that might be considered during this extremely testing time for the organization.

● ● ● ● Recommended reading ● ● ● ● ● ● ● ● ● ● ● ● ● ●

● Berry, A. J., A. F. Coad, E. P. Harris, D. T. Otley and C. Stringer (2009) 'Emerging themes in management control: a review of recent literature', *British Accounting Review*, 41, pp. 2–20.

A captivating and recent review of some of the more contemporary and emerging themes in the realm of management control.

● Malmi, T. and D. A. Brown (2008) 'Management control systems as a package – opportunities, challenges and research directions', *Management Accounting Research*, 19(4), pp. 287–300.

An interesting taxonomy of the management control (academic) literature, focusing particularly on planning, cybernetic, reward and compensation, administrative and cultural controls.

- Nixon, W. A. J. and J. Burns (2005) 'Management control in the 21st century', *Management Accounting Research*, 16(3), pp. 260–8.

This paper is another fairly comprehensive review of the academic literature on management control.

References

Berry, A. J., A. F. Coad, E. P. Harris, D. T. Otley and C. Stringer (2009) 'Emerging themes in management control: a review of recent literature', *British Accounting Review*, 41, pp. 2–20.

Johansson, I.-L. and G. Baldvinsdottir (2003) 'Accounting for trust: some empirical evidence', *Management Accounting Research*, 14(3), pp. 210–34.

Lukka, K. (2007) 'Management accounting change and stability: loosely coupled rules and routines in action', *Management Accounting Research*, 18(1), pp. 76–101.

Malmi, T. and D. A. Brown (2008) 'Management control systems as a package – opportunities, challenges and research directions', *Management Accounting Research*, 19(4), pp. 287–300.

Nixon, W. A. J. and J. Burns (2005) 'Management control in the 21st century', *Management Accounting Research*, 16(3), pp. 260–8.

When you have read this chapter

Log on to the Online Learning Centre at **www.mcgraw-hill.co.uk/textbooks/burns** to explore chapter-by-chapter test questions, links and further online study tools for Management Accounting.

CHAPTER 8

TRADITIONAL BUDGETING

Chapter outline

- What is budgeting?

- The budgeting process

- Functional budgets

- Different roles of budgeting

- Focus of budgets

- Budget (system) automation and devolved budgeting responsibilities

- Appendix 8A – worked example, cash budget

Learning outcomes

On completion of this chapter, students will be able to:

LO1 To explain the nature of a budget

LO2 To be able to discuss the process of budgeting

LO3 To analyse the functions of budgets within various contexts

LO4 To prepare functional budgets

LO5 To appreciate the devolved nature of budgeting systems

LO6 To critically analyse the human behaviour aspects of budgeting

LO7 To explain the various roles of the budget

Introduction

Chapter 7 introduced planning and control systems, of which budgeting is a key component. This chapter will introduce some basic budgeting techniques. Chapters 9 and 10 will examine further issues relating to budgeting. In this chapter we will consider some of the **functional budgets** that are used within organizations, such as the sales **budget** and the material budget. In addition to examining a typical budgeting process for a manufacturing company, we will also consider how budgets are used within government planning processes, thus demonstrating that budgets are not just about profit generation. Through analysing budgets we will discuss the different types of budgets, different uses of budgets and also different styles of budgeting.

Following the discussion of the basic process of budgeting, this chapter will then proceed to examine how the management accountants' role has evolved within the budgeting process. This will be analysed by examining the devolved nature of the budgeting process.

There is a current debate about whether budgeting is a useful tool within organizations or is more of a hindrance (see Chapter 10). This chapter will focus on the process and technical aspects of budgeting. Although some problems will be highlighted as we go through the points of budgeting, a full critique will be postponed until Chapter 10. Therefore, the focus of this chapter will be on traditional budgeting. The issues of beyond budgeting, rolling budgets and other approaches will be addressed later in Chapter 10.

What is budgeting?

A budget is a financial plan which considers income and expenditure. At its basic level, budgeting is something which we all do. We may not formulate complex budgets on a spreadsheet, but we all plan how we can save up for something or how we can afford to cover our expenses in the following month. Budgeting can be formal, where you can see the numbers in black and white and informal where individuals create a mental calculation.

The budgeting process is simply translating a situation or plan into numbers. We examine the impact of an event or a process in the future. It is important to remember that budgets are estimates; they are targets that we would like to achieve. Just because an organization or individual creates a target, it does not mean they will actually achieve it. Budgeting has become such an everyday part of our lives that even most smartphones offer applications which help you budget your own finances. Following the financial crisis, budgeting has became the focus of a lot of attention, for individuals, businesses and public-sector organizations.

Although *Management Accounting in Practice 8.1* considers individuals using budgets, within businesses and public organizations they tend to be far more complex. Budgeting is a long-established

8.1: Management Accounting in Practice

Financial crisis and personal budgeting

Following the financial crisis in 2008, individual households within the UK had to budget their personal finances with much more care (personal budgets, typically, include both income and expenses). In 2011, only one in four workers received pay rises, and one in 20 actually suffered pay cuts – this was a significant reduction in planned income for these individuals. At the same time as these individuals were dealing with the consequences of having less income, their expenses also increased. For example, food prices increased by 5.2 per cent in 2011. Budgeting can help anyone or any business plan adjust their spending habits to counteract reductions in real cash.

Source: Hawkes (2011).

Exercise

Consider your own budget for this year. What income and expenses do you have? How do you estimate your future expenses? What plans do you have in place in case your predications are not correct?

8.2: Management Accounting in Practice

Government budgets

In 2011, many individual countries were experiencing deficits in their budgets. A deficit occurs when expenses are higher than the income being generated. Within government budgets the majority of the income is gained through taxes. However, with the financial downturn, many countries such as the USA, Ireland, Portugal, Spain, Italy and the UK, found that their budgets came under intense scrutiny.

Deficits in one country can create significant problems for other countries. If one country cannot repay its debt, this can affect all other countries that share the same currency or have investments within that country. For example, in 2011, the US government had to find £1.5 trillion of cuts within their government budget. With budgets showing they were unable to pay off current debts, the USA had to find additional borrowing. Although they secured additional borrowing eventually, this resulted in a reduction of their credit rating. The market had little faith in their ability to respond at an appropriate speed.

Source: Przybyla and Rubin (2011).

Exercise

Research other countries hit by the financial crisis, what budget measures did they put in place?

tool. In an international survey covering all sectors (CIMA, 2009), it was reported that financial forecasting was the most commonly used tool provided by management accounting. This was the finding for companies of all sizes and all sectors.

In 2011, there were many examples where the budgets of countries were under intense speculation. A government budget is different from most other budgets because it is a legal document.

The budgeting process

So far you have learned about budgets in general; however, it is important to understand that in business, when using budgets there is often a formal process to create them. The steps taken to form budgets will depend on the size of the organization; the process discussed in Exhibit 8.1 often relates to medium and large-sized organizations. In such organizations there are more resources and multiple levels of management involved. The process of creating and using budgets should directly relate to the needs of an organization. What is relevant for one organization may not be relevant for another. For example, some organizations will have a **budget manual** that would include the processes and requirements, but others will not.

The budgeting process typically consists of six steps that are summarized in Exhibit 8.1.

1) **Setting objectives** – every organization has a strategy and from this they will set objectives which will help achieve them. It is important for each organization to have clear objectives before they begin the budgeting process, providing an opportunity for resources to be placed in areas where they will achieve the desired goals. It is key to remember, at this point, that the objectives of the company must consider any external factors that relate to their strategies and the budgets required.

2) **Analysing resources** – The resources of an organization are analysed so that a **master budget** can be created. The company will use past master budgets and variance reports to formulate the predicted cash budget, income statement and statement of financial position, which are created through the use of functional budgets.

The master budget is simply the total budget, the sum of all the individual budgets used in individual departments or processes – known as functional budgets. Functional budgets will be examined later in this chapter.

3) **Negotiating operational requirements** – stage 1 of the budgeting process refers to the strategic objectives of the organization, in stage 3, the process includes the operational needs of the various departments, processes or units. The negotiation process will be dependent on the type of organization you work within. In some organizations no negotiation is required because the top-level managers will determine the allocation of resources. The budgets will simply bypass this stage, with operational managers not engaging in any form of discussion regarding their own budgets. This is referred to as the **top-down budget**.

   Other organizations will include negotiation and allow operational managers to participate in meetings and put forward budget proposals for the forthcoming year. This participation is based on their knowledge of what is required within their own budget or function. This is known as the **bottom-up budget**.

4) **Co-ordinating resources** – with the resources analysed, the available money for the forthcoming year predicted and the strategic and operational objectives understood, the process of co-ordination can now begin. The **budget committee**, (if the organization is large enough to have one) or a manager/ management accountant (if not), will co-ordinate the resources and needs of the organization. They will ensure that the resources are allocated, theoretically, in the most effective manner. At this stage they will consider individual budgets for departments, processes or units, and match the resources available.

5) **Obtaining approval** – the approval stage will be dependant once again on the size and nature of the organization. In some smaller organization this will be a process for the accountant or the owner agreeing the budgets. In larger organizations, where a budget committee exists, it will be their role to approve the annual budget. Although the budget committee has this responsibility, in most large international organizations, this is overseen by the finance committee (who report directly to the board of directors).

6) **Distributing budgets** – the final stage communicates the approved budgets to the relevant managers.

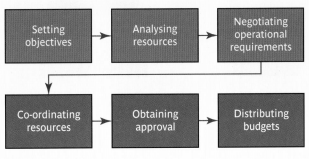

Exhibit 8.1: Summary of the budgeting process

Although Exhibit 8.1 shows the process as linear, in reality this is not always the case. Some of these processes will take place at the same time, following negotiation. It is sometimes necessary to return to one of these stages. Reviewing stages can occur because new information is established. It is also important to understand that the detail of these processes, as described in Exhibit 8.1, may not be the same in all organizations.

8.1: Management Accounting Insight

The Turkish Hospitality Industry

Research on the Turkish hospitality industry conducted by Uyar and Bilgin (2011), found that most hotels in their study, incorporated the use of both budget manuals and committees as part of the budgetary process. However, an alternative study by Jones (2008) found that, in UK hotels, the use of a budget manual was rare. This shows that each industry and country will have their own style when it comes to the budgeting process.

Functional budgets

Just as the process of the budgeting system will be shaped by the individual company, the structure of the budgeting system will also be determined by the business model used within that organization. These individual budgets which refer to a department, process or unit are known as functional budgets.

Within manufacturing, the functional budgets are often based around processes and operations such as research and development, sales, materials and marketing (see Exhibit 8.2). However, in the public sector, they would create budgets based upon specific policies and programmes. Government bodies such as the Department of Energy and Climate Change (DECC), in the UK, create budgets based upon targets they need to achieve, driven by government policies and programmes.

Within manufacturing, the types of functional budgets you will often be exposed to are:

- Sales
- Purchases
- Production
- Direct materials
- Direct labour
- Production overheads
- Administration expenses
- Marketing expenses
- Research and development
- Inventory
- Accounts payable
- Accounts receivable
- Working capital
- Cash
- Capital projects

Exhibit 8.2: Typical functional budgets (within a manufacturing setting)

As stated previously, the functional budgets form the master budget. Exhibit 8.3, diagrammatically represents the relationship of the predicted financial statements and functional budgets.

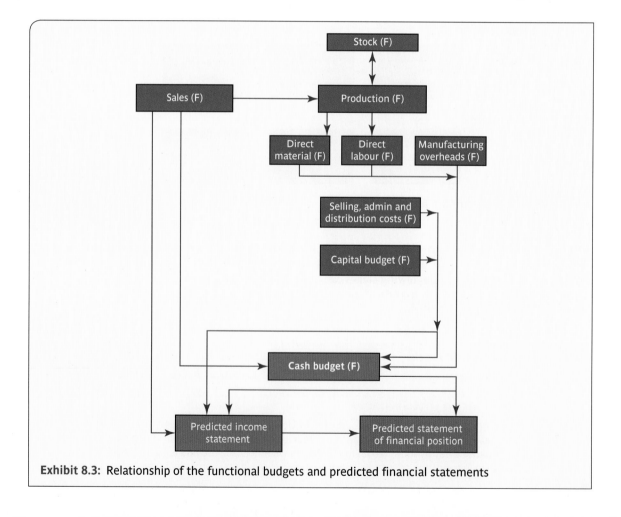

Exhibit 8.3: Relationship of the functional budgets and predicted financial statements

Exhibit 8.3 depicts the relationship of the functional budgets with the cash budget being central to this process. *Worked Example, 8.1*, will take you through a numeric example which demonstrates this relationship.

Worked Example 8.1

Detailed functional budgeting exercise culminating in the formulation of a master budget

The number of individual functional budgets, including those relating to sales, production, materials, labour and overheads, are combined into the master budget. The central budget here will be the cash budget, which will show the cumulative impact of the functional budgets upon the pattern of cash receipts and expenditure.

This simplified example illustrates the main procedures involved. In practice a typical budgetary process is likely to be more detailed.

Alehouse Rock Limited manufactures metal vats, of a single capacity, for the distilling industry. The company's one model is named the 'Deepdraft'. The following information relates to the preparation of the budget for the year to 31 July 201X.

1) Sales budget details for the 'Deepdraft'.

   Expected selling price per vat: £200
   Expected sales: 10,000 vats
   All sales are proposed to be on credit terms.

2) Each 'Deepdraft' produced requires 5 kgs of copper and 10 kgs of aluminium.

3) The purchasing director has forecast that copper is expected to cost £6.00 per kg and aluminium £8.00 per kg. The company's purchasing director also intends to purchase all metals on credit terms.

4) Two departments are involved in the manufacture of the 'Deepdraft', 'Pressing' and 'Machining and Finishing'.

5) The production director has provided the following relevant information:

	Direct labour hours per 'Deepdraft'	Direct labour rate per hour
Pressing	1.00	£12.00
Machining and finishing	0.50	£16.00

6) The finishing production overhead costs are expected to amount to £200,000.

7) At 1 August 201X, 800 completed vats of 'Deepdraft' are expected to be in inventory at a value of £104,000.

8) 4,500 kgs of copper at a value of £27,000, and 12,000 kgs of aluminium at a value of £96,000 are also expected to be held in inventory.

9) The production director has requested that the inventory of both finished goods and raw materials, throughout the budget period, should be planned to be 10 per cent above the expected opening inventory levels as at 1 August 201X.

10) Administration, selling and distribution overhead is expected to amount to £300,000 for the budget period.

11) Other relevant information provided to the company's budget committee is as follows:

   a) Opening accounts receivable are expected to be £160,000. Closing accounts receivable are expected to amount to a sum equivalent to 15 per cent of the budgeted total sales for the year.

   b) Opening accounts payable are expected to be £56,000. Closing accounts payable are expected to amount to a sum equivalent to 10 per cent of the purchases for the year.

   c) All other expenses will be paid in cash during the year.

   d) Other balances from the previous statement of financial position are as follows:

	£	£
Share capital: ordinary shares		450,000
Retained profits		35,000
Proposed dividend		150,000
Non-current assets at cost		500,000
Less accumulated depreciation	(200,000)	300,000
Cash at bank and in hand		4,000

12) Capital expenditure for the year is expected to amount to £100,000 payable in cash on 1 August 201X.

13) Non-current assets are depreciated on a straight line basis at a rate of 20 per cent per annum on cost.

Even with this simplified budgeting exercise, there is clearly a great deal of work involved in preparing budgets. To enable you to understand the process more easily, the procedure will be outlined step-by-step.

Step 1: Prepare the Sales Budget

Sales Budget for period beginning 1 August 201X

Units of 'Deepdraft'	Selling price per unit	Total sales value
	£	£
10,000	200	2,000,000

This data has been extracted from point (1) of the worked example scenario.

Step 2: Prepare the Production Quantity Budget

You can complete the production quantity budget by relating to the Sales Budget, the expected period opening stock of finished units of output, and the desired closing stock level.

Production Quantity Budget for period beginning 1 August 201X

	Units
Budgeted Sales of 'Deepdraft'	10,000
Less: Opening inventory	800
	9,200
Add: desired closing inventory	
[opening inventory + 10%] [800 × 1.1]	880
Production required (units)	10,080

This data has been extracted from the sales budget and points (7) and (9) of the worked example scenario.

Step 3: Prepare the Direct Materials Usage Budget

Once you have the budgeted production quantity you can now work out the amount of each type of raw material that will be required to achieve that production target.

Direct Materials Usage Budget

Direct materials:		
Copper	5 kg × 10,080	50,400 kg
Aluminium	10 kg × 10,080	100,800 kg

This data has been extracted from point (2) of the worked example scenario and production units from the Production Quantity Budget.

Step 4: Prepare the Direct Materials Purchase Budget

Now that you have the quantity of raw materials to be used in production, by adjusting for the budgeted opening and closing inventory of raw materials you can formulate the Direct Materials Purchases Budget. You will obtaine the following calculations:

Direct Materials Purchases Budget

	Copper	Aluminium
	kg	kg
Usage [as per Direct Material usage budget]	50,400	100,800
Less: opening inventory	4,500	12,000
	45,900	88,800

Add: desired closing inventory		
[opening inventory + 10%]	4,950	13,200
	50,850	102,000
× unit cost	× £6	× £8
Total value of purchase of materials	£305,100	£816,000

This data has been extracted from the Direct Material Usage Budget and points (3), (8) and (9) of the worked example scenario.

Step 5: Prepare Direct Labour Hours Usage Budget

Using the production quantity budget as your base, you can now work the Direct Labour Budget for the two processes of 'Pressing' and 'Machining and finishing' by using the information on labour hours required for each unit of finished output in each process. Your calculation will be as follows:

Direct Labour Hours Usage Budget

	'Pressing'	'Machining and finishing'
Production units of 'Deepdraft'		
[as per Production Quantity Budget]	10,080	10,080
× direct labour hours required	× 1 DLH	× 0.5 DLH
	10,080 DLH	5,040 DLH

This data has been extracted from the Production Quantity Budget and point (5) of the worked example scenario.

Step 6: Direct Labour Cost Budget

You can now work the total budgeted direct labour costs based upon the budgeted Direct Labour Hours requirement. Your budget will be:

Direct Labour Cost Budget

	'Pressing'	'Machining and finishing'
Total direct labour hours required	10,080 DLH	5,040 DLH
× direct labour wage rate per hour	× £12	× £16
Total budgeted direct labour cost	£120,960	£80,640

This data has been extracted from the Direct Labour Hours Budget and point (5) of the worked example scenario.

Step 7: Prepared Fixed Production Overhead Budget

Given as £200,000, point (6) of the worked example scenario.

Step 8: Calculate the value of the Budgeted Closing Raw Material Inventory

You can work the budgeted closing raw materials inventory value based upon budgeted closing inventory quantity.

Budgeted closing inventory of raw materials

Raw material	Closing inventory kg	Cost per kg	Total value
	£	£	29,700
Copper	4,950	6	105,600
Aluminium	13,200	8	135,300

This data has been extracted from the Direct Material Purchase Budget and point (3) of the worked example scenario.

Step 9: Calculate the value of Closing Inventory of finished units of 'Deepdraft'

You will have determined the following valuation to the budgeted level of Closing Inventory:

Closing Inventory of finished units budget

		£	£
Unit cost :			
Direct materials : Copper 5 kg × £6 per kg		30	
Aluminium 10 kg × £8 per kg		80	110
Direct labour : Pressing 1 hour × £12 per hour		12	
Machining and finishing 0.5 hr × £16 per hr		8	20
Total direct cost			130
× Units of 'Deepdraft' in inventory			× 880
			£114,400

This data has been extracted from the Production Quantity Budget and points (2), (3) and (5) of the worked example scenario.

You will note that this is a 'marginal cost' valuation including only prime costs of direct materials and labour, but no proportion of production overheads absorbed into the valuation. The 'absorption cost' valuation would include:

$$\frac{£200,000}{10,080} \times 880 = £17,460$$

with a total closing inventory valuation of £131,860.

Step 10: Prepare the Administration, Selling and Distribution Budgets

Given as combined figure of £300,000, point (10) of the worked example scenario.

Step 11: Prepare the Capital Expenditure Budget

Given as £100,000, point (12) of the worked example scenario.

Step 12: Calculate the cost of 'Deepdrafts' sold

Cost of Goods Sold Valuation

	£
Opening inventory	104,000
Manufacturing cost:	
Production units	
= 10,080 × £130	1,310,400
	1,414,400
Less: Closing inventory	
[from 8 : 880 units × £130]	114,400
Cost of units of 'Deepdraft' sold [10,000 units]	1,300,000

This data has been extracted from the Production Quantity Budget, closing inventory of finished units budget and point (7) of the worked example scenario.

You are now ready to begin the assembly of the Master Budget comprising:

- A Cash Budget
- A Forecast Income Statement
- A Forecast Statement of Financial Position.

Step 13: Prepare the Cash Budget

You will have prepared the following Cash Budget for the period:

	£
Receipts:	
Opening accounts receivables	160,000
Sales [£2,000,000 × 85%]	1,700,000
	1,860,000
Payments:	
Opening accounts payable	56,000
Purchases [from 4 : (£305,100 + 816,000) × 90%]	1,008,990
Wages [from 6 : £120,960 + 80,640]	201,600
Fixed Production Overhead	200,000
Administration, selling and distribution overhead	300,000
Capital expenditure	100,000
Proposed Dividend	150,000
	2,016,590
Net receipts:	[156,590]
Add: Opening cash	4,000
Budgeted closing cash balance	[152,590]

Step 14: Prepare the Budgeted Income Statement

Your completed Income Statement will have the following outcome:

	£	£
Sales [from 1]		2,000,000
Less: Variable cost of sales [from 12]		1,300,000
Gross profit		700,000
Less: Fixed Production Overhead [from 7]	200,000	
Depreciation [£500,000 + 100,000 × 20%]	120,000	320,000
		380,000
Less: Administration, selling and distribution expenses		300,000
Budgeted net profit		80,000

Step 15: Prepare the Budgeted Statement of Financial Position

	£	£
Non-current Assets	280,000	
Accounts receivable [£2,000,000 × 15%]	300,000	
Inventory:		
Raw Materials [from 8]	135,300	
Finished inventory [from 9]	114,400	
		829,700
Accounts payable		
[from 4 : 10% × (£305,100 + 816,000)]	112,110	
Bank Overdraft [from 13]	152,590	
		264,700
Net Assets		565,000
Financed by:		
Share Capital Ordinary shares	450,000	
Retained Profit [£35,000 + £80,000]	115,000	
		565,000

Summary of the important aspects arising from this worked example:

1) You have worked a simplified budgeting process to produce agreed budget statements.

2) You can see how functional budgets, such as the Direct Materials Cost Budget and the Direct Labour Cost Budget, have been based upon, for example, the assumptions of a standard amount of direct material content per unit, a standard price per unit for direct materials, a standard number of hours of direct labour time within each activity within the production process, and a standard wage rate per hour for similar units of direct labour. You will discuss this concept of 'standards' in Chapter 9.

3) It is clear that on the basis of the budgets prepared, the projected profit and cash position at the end of the budget period are not the same. There is a substantial budgeted cash deficit (overdrawn) position at the period end. Does this need some corrective action now? Should the budgets be agreed or should the assumption upon which the budgets are based be reviewed?

Source: with thanks to Mr Bill Hugill, University of Greenwich.

Why are functional budgets important?

Functional budgets provide an opportunity for companies to scrutinize individual aspects of the organization. *Worked Example 8.1*, demonstrated the relationship between the various functional budgets and the master budget. Although the worked example only considered one time period, these functional budgets will normally analyse monthly data and year-end data to identify any variance from the predicted budgets. Below we will examine three key functional budgets; sales, production and cash budgets to consider how they can improve planning and control within a business.

Sales budgets

The sales budget is very important because it can help you plan your production patterns and is often linked to key targets within an organization; in the previous worked example the sales budget was the first functional budget we produced. The sales budget will look different in every organization due to the range of products being sold, size of the company and the company's organizational structure. If you are examining an international organization, sometimes sales are reported in terms of geographical area.

The way sales are reported will be determined by the purpose of the budget. If the budget is related to sales targets, then the sales are normally recorded as they are invoiced because the budget can be analysed against these targets. If the sales budget is used to feed directly into the cash budget, the sales may be recorded when the sales transactions convert into cash received.

Production budget

The production budget, or operating budget as it will be known in a service-sector organization, considers the 'units' of production rather than the cost. Therefore, the budget value is normally units not currency. In step 2 of the worked example we produced a production budget and to begin this budget we started with the data from the sales budget.

This budget is linked to your inventory accounts and your sales account. It will also include any normal loss that is anticipated during the production and include contingency policies. This budget is useful in two ways: to manage the production rate and to help maintain the company policy on stock levels. If a company uses philosophies such as just in time (JIT) then they will want to maintain very low stock levels, and this will mean their control on the production budget will be essential, ensuring correct items are purchased at precisely the right time.

Cash budgets

Cash is the heart of every organization. Regardless of the millions of pounds presented on the Income Statement and the Statement of Financial Position, if they cannot pay their debts they will go bankrupt. Student often get the profit and the cash position confused. One example to demonstrate the difference is to consider sales value, on the Income Statement. The sales value on the Income Statement represents the recorded number of sales in an accounting year. However, the value shown does not represent the cash received for these sales. The sales will include the accounts receivable, that is, those who have received the goods or services but have not yet settled their invoices. This is exactly why the cash budget is essential within any business. Keeping a close eye on the cash flow can save a business.

The management of cash is fundamental in any business or public organization; it is in terms of spending too much money and not spending enough. Management accounting uses cash budgets as a technique to manage this process. In the previous worked example the cash budget collated all the information relating to cash transactions from the other functional budgets. For a more detailed example of a cash budget you should refer to the appendix at the end of this chapter.

Functional budgets within the public sector

As mentioned earlier, not all functional budgets are based on the production processes because not all organizations produce products. The service sector and in the public sector will have functional budgets that fit with the needs of their organizations.

As the *Management Accounting in Practice 8.3* shows, budgets can be *incredibly* useful in providing detail which can be used for planning purposes. Whether it is a sales budgets or a carbon budget, it provides the users with a target.

8.3: Management Accounting in Practice

The Department of Energy and Climate Change, UK, and budgets

The Department of Energy and Climate Change (DECC), within the UK, use budgets to achieve targets based on protecting the environment under the Climate Change Act 2008. An example of this is the carbon budget. Under the Climate Change Act 2008 the government is legally bound to achieve a reduction in greenhouse gas emissions. The Act itself states that on an annual basis the emissions within the UK must be reported.

Therefore, the department responsible for these targets have created long-term budgets based upon individual budgets, set at different stages. The targets are to be achieved by 2050. In June 2011 four budgets had been created, covering 2008–12, 2013–17, 2018–22 and 2023–27. For each budget a total emission limit has been created, imitating a master budget. Each budget is divided into industries which contribute to the emissions. It is the DECC's responsibility to balance the emissions from each industry. If emission limits increase in one industry they need to find reductions in another. Resulting in emission limits in these budgets, replacing the units or money in other functional budgets.

The predicted budgets are published by DECC, however, it is the information provided by the various industries which form the data in the actual budget. The data is subject to accounting regulation, Carbon Accounting (amendment) regulations 2009 (SI 2009/3146).

Source: www.decc.gov.uk – extract (accessed on 12 May 2012).

Exercise

Find other examples of either service-sector or public-sector organizations that use functional budgets. What names do they give them? What information is important to them?

Different roles for budgeting

Although we have already mentioned planning and control in terms of budgeting, they can play many roles within an organization; they can be used for planning, communicating, control, motivation and co-ordination. You need to understand all the roles that budgets can play within an organization to understand the problems that can arise when they are not used effectively.

Planning

Organizations that have money to invest in new projects may use budgets to model the financial outcome or effectiveness when choosing a particular option. Also budgets are used to plan ahead and analyse the financial position of a company in one, two and sometimes 15 years ahead. By planning ahead it is possible to predict labour as well as material requirements. Planning also includes predicting future problems.

When preparing budgets you must have contingency plans for the unexpected. Take the riots in the UK in August 2011. The local councils and businesses would not have expected this to happen, however, both were left with the cost of recovering. These riots occurred at the same time as the second dip of the recession so it is unlikely that they had prepared a contingency fund to cover this kind of cost. Instead, it is highly likely that funds were transferred from other less immediate concerns. This of course is a smaller problem compared with the US sub-prime mortgage crisis in 2007, as discussed in Chapter 7.

Communication

Budgets enable organizations to work towards common financial goals. As all departmental (functional) budgets will together form the master budget, it is possible to ensure cost control at an organization level. Communication within large organizations can often be neglected. A budget can provide a means of fostering communication across the organization, by ensuring employees and managers both understand the goals of the organization. This only works if the members of the organization know how budgets work. Communicating budgets across the organization allows all managers to understand what and why resources are being used in different areas of the business.

Co-ordination

Using a master budget provides a structured framework for the financial needs of the whole organization. If a master budget was not used you could end up with different departments working towards their own goals, rather than the targets of the company. Co-ordinating through the use of budgets can result in resources being used effectively in the right areas.

Motivation

Using budgets to aid motivation is a topic which has long been discussed by academics. It has been recognized that if budgets are used appropriately they can be motivational. In general it is agreed that managers who are educated and are involved in the budget-setting process will work harder towards achieving the goals of the organization. Motivational benefits depend on whether the budgets are viewed as a threat or as a challenge.

Control

Organizations that use budgets to monitor performance are using the budget as a control device. They set targets at the beginning of the year and assess how the individual managers have performed that year by using variance analysis; this will be discussed in detail in Chapter 9. Of course, if used incorrectly, this technique can in fact demotivate employees and managers.

There are many roles of budgeting, it should be noted that not all budgets are expected to deliver all of these roles. In fact many organizations will have different budgets for different purposes. *Management Accounting in Practice 8.4* focuses on the National Health Service and demonstrates that every organization will choose what role the budget will play.

8.4: Management Accounting in Practice

Budgets in the NHS, UK

A report from the public sector in the UK, analysing the use of budgets in the National Health Service (NHS), reported that budgets should serve a multi-purpose role. The report indicated that, in addition to financial control, the budget in this sector was expected to deliver strategy implementation, control, empowerment and performance improvement.

The report argued that budgets should form part of the longer-term strategic direction of the NHS, with doctors playing key roles in managing this success. The use of budgets to facilitate empowerment should be established by budgets allowing NHS staff to take decisions at the point of action. In other words the budget should be flexible enough for the patients' needs to be addressed and decisions to be taken at that stage. The final factor of budgeting within this report revolved around performance improvement and it was suggested that the budgeting system should be a key driver of continuous improvement.

Source: Harradine et al. (2011).

Exercise

Read this report to analyse whether the budgeting system did in fact deliver what was expected. A link to the report is available online at www.mcgraw-hill.co.uk/textbooks/burns.

Focus of budgets

The role of budgeting can vary in organizations and its purpose can also different. Budgets can be short term or long term. Many organizations use monthly or quarterly budgets to focus on short-term goals and ensure the operational side of their business is successful. As we have seen with the cash budget, keeping a close eye on the cash flow of a business or organization allows the managers to use feed-forward control and prevent a cash-flow crisis. Another example would be the short-term sales forecast budgets. With software like Excel it is possible for organizations to link in all the individual live sales reports from individual sales managers to keep a real-time view of current sales. A reduction in the anticipated sales can result in urgent conference calls being held to strategize how, in the short term, they can rectify the problem.

Companies also use long-term budgets, which usually link to strategic plans. When an organization decides on new strategic direction the budget, in turn, will change the resource allocation to meet these new demands.

8.5: Management Accounting in Practice

Examples of short-term and long-term budgets

Within the electricity generation industry, for assets such as the combined cycle gas turbines (CCGT) power stations, there are many levels of budgets. Typical budgets are as follows:

- A 35-year budget which covers the life of the plant up to decommissioning, this covers the capital budgeting
- A 10-year budget which covers both capital and revenue
- A two-year budget which covers operational issues
- A one-year budget which is the focus of reporting, covering operational issues
- A quarterly budget which is forecast towards the one-year budget, operational.
- A one-month budget which is the reported targets, operational.

Source: based on author's own research.

Exercise

Consider your own future. Can you list different budgets you would need for different purposes? Are they short-term budgets or long-term budgets?

Management Accounting in Practice 8.5 shows that the budgeting process is a mixture of short-term and long-term goals. Of course, these budgets are also subdivided into their functions. If a specific function is identified as a key component in achieving long-term goals the role of the budget committee will be to ensure that sufficient resources are allocated to the relevant function.

Budget (systems) automation and devolved budgeting responsibilities

Control through budgeting, as we have just seen, can be through short-term and long-term budgets. Although budgets are still central to the control aspect of most organizations the role of the management accountant in the process of budgeting has changed over the years. Baldvinsdottir et al. (2010) reported that although control is still fundamental, recently the role of the management accountant has become more strategically focused. This leaves the question of who is actually involved in the creating and facilitating of the budget itself?

In Chapter 1 we revealed how many of the traditional management accounting responsibilities have been devolved into other job roles and the management accounting role has become more strategically focused. Budgeting is one of the areas which is often seen as an automated system. With accounting information systems (AIS) now providing pre-populated and formatted templates, accountants spend very little time on this process. Individual managers of the functions are often part of the process of either negotiating budgets or preparing them. However, following the recent financial crisis in 2008, and the failure of many international and smaller organizations, questions are now been raised as to whether the role of the management accountant should go back to basics. Should the management accountant go back to being the bean counter, the one who oversees the management control systems, such as the budgeting system (Baldvinsdottir et al. 2010)?

Chapter summary

This chapter has examined what are known as traditional budgets, which are still being used in many organizations. We have analysed the role of budgets and the different types of functional budgets that can be found within organizations. We have placed a big emphasis on the relationship of the functional budgets and the master budget.

In the Chapter 9 you will learn about flexible budgets and standard costing – where budgets are used as both a control feature and a motivational tool. In Chapter 10, we will then turn our attention to some current debates on budgeting, considering whether traditional budgeting is still relevant.

Key terms

Bottom-up budgets Budgets which are created through a process of negotiation with the operational managers (p. 171)

Budget A financial plan which considers the income and expenditures (p. 169)

Budget committee A formal committee within an organization who oversee the budgeting process and approval of the final budgets (p. 171)

Budget manual A document explaining how all the budgets relate. Containing information on coding items within the budgets (p. 170)

Functional budgets Day-to-day operational budgets which focus on specific functions or aspects of the process or service (p. 169)

Master budget A collection of all the data from all the individual functional budgets, typically in the form of the cash budget, predicted Incomes Statement and Statement of Financial Position (p. 170)

Top-down budgets Budgets which are formulated by top managers and imposed on the operational managers (p. 171)

Review questions • • • • • • • • • • • • connect • • •

• • •

Level of difficulty:	BASIC	INTERMEDIATE	ADVANCED

8.1 Explain what a budget is. **[LO1]**

8.2 Describe how the budget is developed within an organization. **[LO2]**

8.3 How can budgets be used to motivate employees? **[LO5]**

8.4 Name five functional budgets in a manufacturing setting. **[LO4]**

8.5 List three roles of budgeting within an organization. **[LO7]**

Group discussion and activity questions • • • • • • • • •

8.6 In groups, critically analyse the use of top-down budgeting within organizations. **[LO2]**

8.7 Discuss the advantages and disadvantages of using traditional budgeting within an organization. **[LO6]**

8.8 Providing examples, explain how the feed-forward control systems can be more effective than simply relying on feedback control. **[LO3]**

8.9 Debate the most important role of the budgeting system within an organization. **[LO7]**

8.10 Management accountants are no longer required in the budgetary systems – discuss. **[LO5]**

Exercises • • • • • • • • • • • • • • • • • connect • • • •

E8.1 **Cash budgeting [LO4]**

Speed Limited is considering investing in new equipment and the management needs to estimate how much cash will be available to the company at the end of the year.

From the administration department you have received the following information:

1) Cash available at the end of June was £2,000.

2) Sales were £10,000 in May and were £15,000 in June.

3) Selling price will remain constant and all stock will be sold at the end of each month.

4) Monthly purchases are 60 per cent of the previous month's sales.

5) 30 per cent of sales are collected cash, the remaining 70 per cent is collected with two months credit.

6) 50 per cent of purchases are paid in cash, the remaining 50 per cent are paid after one month.

7) Wages consists of £3,000 paid each month.

8) The sales representatives are paid a 4 per cent commission on each month sales. The commission is paid one month in arrears.

9) The company has set up a standing order to pay the rent. The payments will start in September and the amount is £1,500 every two months.

10) Telephone, heating and electricity bills to pay are estimated to be £100 every month.

11) The company has scheduled a 1p per share dividend payment to shareholders in December 2007. Company equity consists of 10,000 £1 ordinary shares.

12) The depreciation charge for the companies fixed assets is £400 a month.

13) A loan has been taken in January this year. The total repayable amount for this loan (including interest) is £600 a year. The loan is paid in equal monthly instalments over 12 months.

14) The tax bill is £200 and it has to be paid in November.

15) Sales forecast is reported in this table:

	Jul	Aug	Sep	Oct	Nov	Dec
Sales (unit)	100	140	150	140	100	120
Unit price	100	100	100	100	100	100

Required:

a) Produce a cash budget from July to December.

b) Discuss how the company can improve its cash flow.

c) Explain why cash and profit are different concepts and then explain how to treat depreciation expenses in cash budgeting.

E8.2 **Budget preparation and behavioural issues [LO1, LO6]**

You have been appointed group finance director of a medium-sized company, effective May 201X. You have examined the budget prepared by your predecessor and the budget preparation process. Following your examination, you would like to propose a new budget preparation process. Previously, budgets for the calendar year were prepared after the current year's September actual results became available. You believe this time frame is too short to prepare a reliable budget before the start of the next year. You therefore propose to start budget preparation after the current year's June results are available, leaving more time for all managers involved to participate.

In the current year, there are some problems in the company:

● Division X has no managing director. He resigned after poor trading results for the first quarter of the year. The finance director at the division is assuming the duties of managing director until a replacement is found.

● Division Y has launched a new product range aimed at completely new markets. The marketing effort began in the first quarter.

● Division Z are constructing a new plant, which they initially predicted would be operational in the third quarter. Numerous delays during the construction process means the plant may not be fully operational until next year.

Required:

As group finance director, prepare a report for presentation to the board of directors which:

a) Explains why your proposed changes to the extend the budget preparation are beneficial.

b) Discusses the three problems mentioned, and any other anticipated difficulties in formulating your budget, and advise how they may be resolved.

E8.3 **Responsibility centres [LO1, LO7]**

a) A responsibility centre can be defined as a business unit of a firm where an individual manager is held responsible for that unit's performance.

Identify and briefly describe the types of responsibility centre. Give a practical example of each centre type.

b)   Can a responsibility centre manager be held totally responsible for all revenue and costs? Explain why or why not.

c)   Controls may be defined as feed-back or feed-forward. Explain each type, citing one example of each.

E8.4   **Direct labour budgets [LO4]**

You are currently helping the head of an arts department with a college in the UK. Your main responsibilities are to ensure that core units within your department have teaching coverage. You are provided with a budget of £151,000 at the beginning of the year. This budget must cover the teaching costs of all core units and any additional courses that the department chooses to provide for the local community.

You are provided with the predictions for this coming year in relation to the teaching responsibilities:

Course	A-level	GNVQ	Adult education
No. of students	110	70	40

You have two art rooms that can hold a maximum of 20 students each. The college policy is to have one teacher per 10 pupils; however, the second teacher in a classroom can be a teaching technician or a part-time member of staff. The college waives this policy for adult education classes where one teacher per class is acceptable.

The average cost of the teachers used is as follows:

Job title	Number available	£
Head of department	1	40,000
Full-time teaching staff	2	28,000
Teaching technician	1	8,000
Part-time staff (per group)	As many as needed	1,500

The head of department can only cover one group throughout the year due to administration responsibilities. Full-time teaching staff are able to cover four groups each, while the teaching technician is able to cover six groups as he or she has no administration responsibilities.

The head of the department has been asked to provide a foundation degree in collaboration with a local university but this would result in having to recruit a new full-time member of staff who could specialize in this.

Required:

a)   Prepare a report for the head of department answering if the department can afford to take on one new full time member of staff. The report should include the budget for teaching costs using the most efficient use of available staff. Your budget must include one head of department, and two full time teaching members.

b)   Within a large organization explain the process of creating functional budgets.

c)   'When creating a labour budget it is always essential that you prepare your needs based on the most cost effective use of available of staff'. Discuss.

E8.5   **Material budget [LO4]**

You are the purchase manager for a national garden supplier. You are currently producing a material budget for the stone section of the business. You are provided with the following information.

Last year's information:

Material	Cost per tonne	Amount purchased
Plum slate	£100	20,000 tonne
Green slate	£80	15,000 tonne
White stone	£90	16,000 tonne
Mixed pebbles	£110	18,000 tonne

Stock levels at present:

Material	Tonnes
Plum slate	600
Green slate	5,000
White stone	900
Mixed pebbles	300

All costs from your supplier have increased by 3 per cent since last year. At the beginning of the year it is normal for you to predict a purchase that will ensure stock levels of 21,000 tonnes at the beginning of the year for every kind of material.

However, based on last year's sales you have noticed that green slate is not as popular as it had been in previous years, so you have decided to cut the normal beginning of the year stock levels by 50 per cent.

At the Chelsea Flower Show this year, many gardens used mixed pebbles and you have therefore predicted an increase in demand for this particular product. You have decided to increase beginning of the year stock levels by 25 per cent.

This year you have been offered a one-off contract with a local garden supplier to purchase 5,000 tonnes of white stone at a cost of only £50 per tonne because they are shutting down their business. You have decided to accept this contract but the rest of the material will come from your normal supplier.

Required:

Create a material budget for this year.

E8.6 **Budget-setting process [LO6]**

A firm of solicitors is preparing its budgets for 201X. The structure of the firm is that it has a managing partner who is responsible for client and staff management, the firm's accounts and compliance matters and three other partners who each take responsibility for case matters depending on the branch of law that is involved in each case.

For a number of years the managing partner has prepared the budgets for the firm. These include budgets for fee income and costs analysed by each partner, and a cash budget for the firm as a whole. The firm has overdraft facilities which are renewable in June each year and sets cash balance targets for each month that reflect the seasonality of some of its work. At the end of each month there is a partners' meeting at which the managing partner presents a statement that compares the actual results of the month and the year to date with the corresponding budget. At this meeting all partners are asked to explain the reasons for the variances that have arisen.

The managing partner recently attended a course on 'Budget Planning and Cost Control' at which the presenter argued that each of the partners in the firm should be involved in the budget-setting process. However, the managing partner is not convinced by this argument as she believes that this could lead to budget manipulation.

Required:

a) Explain feed-back and feed-forward control systems, and give an example of each in the context of the firm of solicitors.

b) Discuss ONE potential beneficial consequence and ONE potential adverse consequence of involving the firm's other partners in the budget setting process of the firm.

Source: Chartered Institute of Management Accountants, P2 specimen paper.

E8.7 Cash budget [LO4]

Manna Limited has been in business for 12 years. It has traded successfully since its inception. The company manufactures two products, namely, 'Basic' and 'Opulent'. Most of the company's success has been due to the sale of 'Opulent' which targeted high-income earners who were not price sensitive. In recent months, Manna Limited has seen a change in sales demand, with the 'Basic' product now becoming the most popular product for the company.

The following table summarizes cost and selling price information:

	Note	Basic €	Opulent €
Selling price		50	75
Raw materials:			
Basic 3kg @ €4		12	
Opulent 3kg @ €5			15
Labour 2 hrs @ €10		20	20
Variable Overhead 2 hrs @ €3	1	6	6
Fixed overhead (per unit)	2	10	10

Note 1: Variable overheads are absorbed on a labour hour basis.

Note 2: Fixed overhead per unit cost has been calculated using a budgeted production of 240,000 units and includes total fixed costs of €2,400,000.

The Management Accountant has alerted the Managing Director to the change in sales mix and its effect on the cash flows of the business. They have reviewed the management accounts for the eight-month period ending 31 August 201X and discussed methods of cost reduction for the remaining four months of their accounting year.

Cost reduction strategies include:

1) Following a review of recent market research, Manna Limited forecasts the following sales mix and demand levels for September 201X to December 201X:

'Basic'	80 per cent
'Opulent'	20 per cent

	September 201X	October 201X	November 201X	December 201X
Total sales units	20,000	18,000	18,000	14,000

2) In order to ensure the increased sales of 'Basic', Manna Limited has offered a 'price discount' coupon with the national Sunday newspapers. The coupon offers 10 per cent off the recommended retail price. This price promotion will run for the two months of September and October 201X. It is estimated that 20 per cent of 'Basic' customers will take up the discount offer.

Long-standing customers of 'Opulent' are offered credit terms of one month. seventy per cent of 'Opulent' customers will qualify and use these credit terms. Total sales of 'Opulent' for the month of August 201X amounted to €285,715.

3) Manna Limited's purchasing manager has renegotiated prices with their materials suppliers and agreed a discount of 10 per cent on all material prices. However, in order to secure this discount, Manna Limited will have to pay for materials in the month of purchase. There were no opening trade creditors in September 201X.

4) The company has reviewed all fixed overheads and has decided to change the accounting policy for depreciation. This has resulted in an annual reduction of fixed overheads of €20,000. (Depreciation has not been included in the fixed overheads outlined in table above.)

5) Labour and variable overhead costs are both paid in the month incurred.

6) Manna Limited has ordered new machinery costing €100,000. The machine will be delivered in October 201X and will have to be paid for immediately. Machinery is depreciated on a straight-line basis, at a rate of 10 per cent per annum. The company has applied for a capital grant to assist with the funding of the machine. The grant, totalling €30,000, will be transferred directly in the company's bank account on the 1st December 201X.

7) There is €15,000 in the company's bank account as at 1 September 201X.

Required:

a) Prepare a cash budget for Manna Limited for the four month period of September to December 201X.

b) Manna Limited's management accountant is eager to increase the involvement of departmental managers in the budgeting process. He would like to issue a 'checklist' to the sales and purchasing managers which would give an overview of the stages in the budgeting process. Prepare this checklist for the departmental managers, briefly outlining the stages of the budgeting process.

Source: adapted from Institute of Certified Public Accountants in Ireland, Formation 2, Management Accounting.

• • • Case study problem • • • • • • • • • • • • connect • • •

C8.1   Rapid technologies and forecasting growth [LO3, LO7]

Rapid Technologies is one of the UK's fastest-growing IT and communications companies. The company has recorded strong growth in their market, which is encouraging, but has created a number of problems, both financially and strategically. With strong growth there is always the potential for overtrading.

The strong growth was a result of the company diversifying into new areas such as Internet services and education. While diversifying they were very aware that there was potential for growing too quickly, where the working capital could not keep up with the growth. With knowledge of this they made sure they had good purchasing and general financial controls in place, so they could keep a close eye on sales, cash, assets, liabilities, accounts payable and accounts receivable.

> 'Reviewing the figures, we realised that while sales calls were flooding in, we were in danger of not having the people or financial resources to fulfil orders or provide ongoing services. Profit margins were also being squeezed as we cut prices to compete with new competitors.' (Managing Director, Mark Stevens)

At the same time as profit margins being squeezed they realized that inventory was becoming an increasing problem; they imported most of their inventory. To keep up with the increase in sales demand they need to buy more. Most of their inventory was purchased using letters of credit. Mark Stevens explained:

'Letters of credit (LCs) offer assurance to the exporter that their invoices will be paid when certain documents, such as signed delivery notes, are submitted to them. However banks treat LCs as a commitment to pay and deduct the outstanding amount from the importer's bank facilities. We could see that our letters of credit would soon eat up our entire overdraft facility, further reducing our working capital.'

To avoid overtrading and using up their bank overdraft facility they examined ways in which they could overcome this problem. They started offering discounts to their own customers and negotiating new credit terms with their own suppliers. At the same time they spent more resources on their own payment recovery system. While analysing their own budgets and managing their cash-flow system as best they could, with currency resources, they realized they needed additional help.

'We needed to inject some capital too, but like most owner-operators we didn't have a lot of cash sitting in the bank and we didn't generate enough cash flow to finance growth from monthly profits. We didn't want to introduce new equity partners, as this would reduce control. In agreement with the bank, we borrowed money from our self-managed pension fund with a detailed plan for repayment, which we have subsequently achieved.' (Managing Director, Mark Stevens)

With the cash flow under control they then turned their attention to the strategic direction of the company, to try and avoid this problem in the future. They recognized that current trading was not under control and this had to be managed in line with their cash-flow facilities. After analysing all functions within their organization they decided to reorganize. They eventually closed their retail area and focused on telesales which targeted niche markets that they considered strategically important. By doing this they could choose the type of customers with when they entered into business agreements. They chose to enter emerging technologies which were more profitable and reduced their involvement in hardware and software, focusing on sales to customers who requested large orders only. Large orders in this area were more cost-effective, in terms of after-sale care, than small orders.

The cash-flow analysis and restructuring worked, with growth averaging 25 per cent every year. Mark Stevens stated: 'Given our time again, we would put better forecasting processes in place to match cash requirements to sales forecasts at a much earlier stage.'

Source: adapted from www.businesslink.gov.uk (accessed on 12 May 2012).

Required:

a) Discuss how cash-flow budgeting helped this company to meet their growth strategy.

b) Critically analyse why the previous business model was restricting the performance of this company.

c) Discuss the concept of overtrading and the implications of companies doing this.

Appendix 8A

Worked Example 8A.1 ## Cash budget

Elton plc is considering investing in new equipment and the management needs to estimate how much cash will be available to the company at the end of the accounting year. From the administration department you have received the following information:

1) Cash available at the end of the previous year was £8,000.

2) Sales in the previous year were £17,000 in October, £15,000 in November and £23,000 in December.

3) Selling price will remain constant and all inventory will be sold at the end of each month.

4) Monthly purchases are 70 per cent of the previous month's sales.

5) Forty per cent of sales are collected in cash, and the remaining 60 per cent is collected with two months credit.

6) Forty per cent of purchases are paid cash, and the remaining 60 per cent is paid after two months.

7) Wages consists of £3,000 paid each month.

8) The company pays sales representative a five per cent commission on each month's sales. The commission is paid one month in arrears.

9) The company has set up a standing order to pay the rent. The payments will start in February and the amount is £3,000 every two months.

10) Heating and electricity bills are estimated to be £300 every month, payable quarterly, with the first amount to be payable in March this year.

11) The company as scheduled a 5p per share dividend payment to shareholders in the forthcoming June. Company equity consists of 20,000 £1 ordinary shares.

12) The depreciation charge for the companies fixed assets is £400 a month.

13) The next tax bill is £1,500 and it has to be paid in May.

14) Sales forecast for the next six months, January to June is reported in Table 8.A1.

Table 8A.1

	Jan	Feb	Mar	Apr	May	Jun
Sales (unit)	160	250	260	220	210	240
Unit price	100	100	100	100	100	100

Required:

Produce a cash budget for the next six months, January to June. All relevant workings must be shown.

Solution

We will now work together through this problem so you can appreciate the step-by-step process of constructing such a budget. The completed budget is shown in Table 8.A2, and the workings are explained below.

Table 8A.2

Elton plc		Jan £	Feb £	Mar £	Apr £	May £	Jun £
Opening bank balance		8,000	5,670	11,890	10,080	12,580	14,320
Sales cash	40%	6,400	10,000	10,400	8,800	8,400	9,600
Sales credit	60%	9,000	13,800	9,600	15,000	15,600	13,200
		23,400	29,470	31,890	33,880	36,580	37,120
Purchases cash	40%	6,440	4,480	7,000	7,280	6,160	5,880
Purchases credit	60%	7,140	6,300	9,660	6,720	10,500	10,920
Wages		3,000	3,000	3,000	3,000	3,000	3,000
Sales commission	5%	1,150	800	1,250	1,300	1,100	1,050

Rent		3,000		3,000		3,000
Heating and lighting			900			900
Dividends 5p per share						1,000
Tax bill					1,500	
Total cash payments	17,730	17,580	21,810	21,300	22,260	25,750
Closing bank balance	5,670	11,890	10,080	12,580	14,320	11,370

Explanation of workings

Opening balance

In January the opening balance is presented as £8,000. This information is found in point 1 of the question. The remaining opening balances are determined by the previous month's closing balance. So if you look at the closing balance of January you will see it is £5,670 and the opening balance of February is exactly the same, £5,670. What cash you finish with at the end of one month must be the same as you begin with in the next.

Sales cash 40% and Sales credit 60%

This takes a little more explanation but once you have analysed it this is very logical. The question provides sales data in point 2 of the question and also in Table 8.A1. Therefore the first thing to prepare is the actual sales values from October of the previous year through to June of forthcoming year:

Sales	Oct	Nov	Dec	Jan	Feb	Mar	Apr	May	June
£	17,000	15,000	23,000	16,000	25,000	26,000	22,000	21,000	24,000

The sales for October to December are provided in full in point 2 of the question but for the remaining months you need to calculate these from the data provided in Table 8.A1 of the question. So for example:

January: The sales (units) are recorded as 160 and the unit price is recorded as £100.

Therefore the total sales for January are 160 units × £100 = £16,000.

Once you have the sales you now need to determine how much each month will be paid in cash. The solution splits the sales into two categories because you have two types of customers: those who pay cash at the point of sale and those who at the point of sale sign up for credit which means they take your goods or receive your service but do not pay you until later, in this case two months. Point 6 of the questions provides this information and also tells you that you have 40 per cent cash buyers and 60 per cent credit buyers (these become your accounts receivable in the Statement of Financial Position). Therefore, the 60 per cent credit buyers will not give you cash for two months.

You have been asked to prepare a budget from January to June which means we will need the sales information from November because credit buyers who purchased in November will not pay cash until January. Below are the workings for the sales collection for the six months.

Sales	Jan £	Feb £	Mar £	Apr £	May £	Jun £
Cash buyers	6,400	10,000	10,400	8,800	8,400	9,600
Credit buyers	9,000	13,800	9,600	15,000	15,600	13,200

So if we examine the values for January we can see through sales cash collection we have collected £6,400 from the cash buyers who bought items in January and £9,000 from the credit buyers who bought goods in November. These are calculated as follows:

£6,400: The sales in January were £16,000. Of these £16,000 40 per cent represent buyers who paid cash which means £16,000 × (40/100) = £6,400.

£9,000: The sales in November were £15,000 of this 60 per cent of these sales represented credit buyers which means £15,000 × (60/100) = £9,000. As these credit buyers get two months credit they will pay the £9,000 two months later, that is in January.

Purchase cash and purchase credit

In point 4 of the question it states that purchases are directly related to sales, in that for the next six months you will purchase 70 per cent of the previous month's sales. In point 6 of the question it explains that of these purchases you will pay for 40 per cent of them in cash on the day of purchase and the remaining 60 per cent you will take two months to pay. This means the 60 per cent of purchases will show up on your Statement of Financial Position as Accounts Payable because you will receive the good or service on the day of sale but you will not pay for them for two months.

The first stage is to calculate the purchases:

Purchases	Nov	Dec	Jan	Feb	Mar	April	May	June
£	11,900	10,500	16,100	11,200	17,500	18,200	15,400	14,700

So November has been calculated by examining the sales from October which are £17,000, and calculating 70 per cent of this. Therefore, £17,000 × (70/100) = £11,900.

Once the purchases have been calculated for each of the six months you need to determine how much cash will be paid out for cash transactions and credit transactions. Below are the values for each month:

Purchases	Jan £	Feb £	Mar £	Apr £	May £	Jun £
Cash purchases	6,440	4,480	7,000	7,280	6,160	5,880
Credit purchases	7,140	6,300	9,660	6,720	10,500	10,920

So if we examine the values for January again we can see that in cash £6,440 will leave the business for cash purchases and £7,140 will leave the business for credit purchases which will have been purchased two months earlier, in November. These are calculated as follows:

£6,440: In January you purchased a total of £16,100 worth of goods. 40 per cent of these were bought in cash which means £16,100 × (40/100) = £6,440 was given to the suppliers in cash.

£7,140: In November you purchases £11,900 worth of goods. 60 per cent of these were bought as credit transaction which means you received the good in November but you had two months to pay for them, this means you pay in January. This means £11,900 × (60/100) = £7,140 will leave the business in cash in January for those credit purchases.

Wages

Wages are straight forward as point 7 states you have to pay wages of £3,000 every month.

Sales commission

In point 8 of the questions it tells you that sales commission is paid one month in arrears, which means one month later and that it equates to 5 per cent of the sales. So if you examine the sales figures for December which are £23,000 and you calculate 5 per cent of this you will get £23,000 × (5/100) = £1,150. This is the value that appears in January for sales commission.

Rent

Rent is discussed in point 9, from February you will pay £3,000 every two months so the first payment will leave the company in February and the next will leave the company in April, two months later.

Heating and lighting

In point 10 you are told that your average monthly use of heat and lighting is £300 which is paid only every quarter which means every three months. The first payment is due in March. Therefore in March you will pay £300 × 3 = £900. The next payment will be three months later which is June.

Dividends

Company dividends have been announced to be 5p per share, see point 11. With the company holding 20,000 shares this means a cash payment will be paid to shareholders which amounts to 20,000 × 0.05 = £1,000 and this will be paid in June.

Tax

The final item refers to cash in point 13. You are provided with the tax bill which is £1,500 and you are told you will need to pay this in May.

● ● ● Recommended reading ● ● ● ● ● ● ● ● ● ● ● ● ● ● ● ● ● ●

- Armstrong, P. (2011) 'Budgetary bullying', *Critical Perspectives on Accounting*, 22(7), pp. 632–43.

  This article provides a view that budgeting and target setting can be a mechanism for bullying managers to maintain psychological ascendancy on the bullied workforce. Using case study based work, this paper challenges some of the traditional work carried out in bullying in the workforce.

- Fauré, B. and L. Rouleau (2011) 'The strategic competence of accountants and middle managers in budget making', *Accounting, Organizations and Society*, 36(3), pp. 167–82.

  Set in a large field study within the construction industry this paper examines how both accountants and middle managers use strategy to shape their budgeting preparation. Analysing the use of strategy to activate local projects, providing strategic relevance and legitimatization of numbers to external parties and to reconcile differences between local and global relations.

- Harradine, D., M. Prowle and G. Lowth (2011) 'A method for assessing the effectiveness of NHS budgeting and its application to a NHS Foundation Trust', *CIMA report*, 7(10).

  This report analyses the complex process and nature of budgeting within the NHS. The report investigate the appropriateness of the current budgeting system within the current political climate.

- Moll, J. and Z. Hoque (2011) 'Budgeting for legitimacy: the case of an Australian University', *Accounting, Organizations and Society*, 36(2), pp. 86–101.

Analysing the use of budgeting in the process of legitimation this paper examines budgeting within an Australian university. This papers follows the behaviour of lecturers when a new budgeting systems is established which is linked to external bodies. Focusing on the institutional demands and reaction of the internal members.

- Uyar, A. and N. Bilgin (2011) 'Budgeting practices in the Turkish hospitality industry: an exploratory survey in the Antalya region', *International Journal of Hospitality Management*, 30 pp. 398–408.

Analysing budgets within a tourist area of Turkey, this paper examines the process and use of budgeting within local hotels. They find the use of budgeting manuals and committees common practice and full participation in the negotiation process.

••• References ••••••••••••••••••••••••••

Baldvinsdottir, G., J. Burns, H. Norreklit and R. Scapens (2010) 'Risk manager or risqué manager? The new platform for the management accountant', CIMA report, 6(2).

CIMA (2009) 'Management accounting tools for today and tomorrow', www.cimaglobal.com/ma (accessed on 20 January 2012).

Harradine, D., M. Prowle and G. Lowth (2011) 'A method for assessing the effectiveness of NHS budgeting and its application to a NHS Foundation Trust', CIMA report, 7(10).

Hawkes, A. (2011) 'Household budgets hit by frozen pay and rising food prices', August, www.guardian.co.uk (accessed on 8 August 2011).

Jones, T. (2008) 'Changes in hotel industry budgetary practices', *International Journal of Hospitality Management*, 20(4), pp. 428–44.

Przybyla, H. and R. Rubin (2011) 'Budget-panel tasks will signal ability to find $1.5 trillion of US cuts', www.bloomberg.com (accessed on 8 August 2011).

Uyar, A. and N. Bilgin (2011) 'Budgeting practices in the Turkish hospitality industry: an exploratory survey in the Antalya region', *International Journal of Hospitality Management*, 30, pp. 398–408.

When you have read this chapter

Log on to the Online Learning Centre at **www.mcgraw-hill.co.uk/textbooks/burns** to explore chapter-by-chapter test questions, links and further online study tools for Management Accounting.

CHAPTER 9

STANDARD COSTING, FLEXIBLE BUDGETS AND VARIANCE ANALYSIS

Chapter outline

- Setting standards – and next steps

- Types of standards

- Flexible budgeting, variance analysis and sales variances

- Material variances

- Direct labour variances

- Variable overhead variances

- Fixed overhead variances (under variable costing)

- Standard absorption costing: allocation and variances

- When to investigate variances?

- Standard costing and variance analysis: now and the future

- Appendix 9A

Learning outcomes

On completion of this chapter, students will be able to:

LO1 Explain the usefulness of standard costing and variance analysis

LO2 Explain how to set standards

LO3 Calculate standard unit costs and margins

LO4 Calculate static and flexible budgets

LO5 Explain the usefulness of flexible budgets

LO6 Calculate variances

LO7 Make 'real-world' interpretations of variances

LO8 Decide on whether to investigate variances or not

LO9 Discuss criticisms to standard costing and variance analysis

Introduction

In Chapter 7 you explored planning and control and in Chapter 8 you learned about budgets, which provide a financial translation of adopted plans. In this chapter, you will learn about standard costing, flexible budgeting and variance analysis, which are common techniques used for planning, control, decision making and product costing. By connecting planning and control, these techniques address major managerial concerns, such as how well did we implement the plans, and why? What went right or wrong? Why didn't our expectations actually become reality? Based on this gained experience and knowledge, how can we improve?

Standards are performance benchmarks that allow comparisons against actual performance. But comparing organizational performance requires flexibility to adjust to changing circumstances. For example, costs may increase owing both to higher business volume and to poorer performance. So, how to distinguish between the two causes? *Flexible budgeting* is a simple, but powerful technique to improve comparability and support performance measurement, planning and decision making. At the end of a period, you can use variance analysis to uncover 'real-life' factors that did not meet, or exceeded, expectations. Thus variance analysis requires detailed standards, dividing (or 'drilling down') costs and revenues to find the precise causes and to support continuous improvements. For example, let us assume an airline has higher than expected costs. Through variance analysis, they may pinpoint problems as diverse as fuel consumption (for example, due to defective motor maintenance in certain planes), fuel prices (when oil market prices go up) or staff costs. Each scenario requires totally different managerial action. Importantly, variance analysis helps management by exception, directing attention to areas with more significant issues and greater potential for improvement.

Standard costing and variance analysis have been widely adopted for over a hundred years. Education and professional examinations keep these techniques as core topics, placing them increasing in commercial, business and strategic contexts. However, the applicability and usefulness of these techniques has been questioned owing to the speed of technological changes, new production processes such as lean production or mass customization, and limits in motivating continuous improvement. So, management accountants have to rethink the relevance of these techniques for today's environment and their particular organizations.

In this chapter, you will learn what standards, flexible budgeting and variance analysis are, their benefits and how to calculate them. First we introduce standards and outline their different types. Making meaningful comparisons is difficult, but you will see how flexible budgeting can support that. Then you will learn about the different variances which can be calculated. You will learn how to calculate variances and uncover 'real-life' factors underlying each variance, promoting organizational learning and improvement. Then you will learn how to decide when it is worthwhile to investigate variances. Finally, we will briefly contrast criticisms of standard costing and variance analysis with their persistently high adoption rates.

Setting standards – and next steps

What are standard costs and variance analysis?

Standard costs are expected costs under normal conditions, and refer to one unit of activity (for example, one unit of product or service). You can think of standard costs as the budget to produce one unit. Being defined on a per unit basis of activity makes standard costs different from *budgeted costs*, which are expected costs of the entire level of activity. Let us examine only direct costs for now. To estimate budgeted costs for a given product, you draw on the standard costs of each unit to estimate total expected costs for the total number of units at stake. For example, if the standard cost of producing one unit of a particular microwave is £50, the budgeted cost of an order of 100 microwaves is £5,000.

Then, **variance analysis** can be used to compare the expected cost with the actual cost of producing such an order (that is, to calculate the variances) and identify the 'real-life' factors causing the differences. When variances are unfavourable (for example, actual cost is higher than expected), you must identify and solve underlying problems. When variances are favourable, you should learn how to sustain that good performance, and even transfer that knowledge to other areas of the organization.

Keeping in mind the above airline company example, we may find two typical components of standards concerning direct costs: quantity and price.

- *Quantity standards* indicate how much of each input is expected to be used to obtain one unit of output. For example, some commercial planes have a standard consumption of 20 litres of jet fuel per travelled mile (using one travelled mile as an output unit).

- *Price standards* indicate the expected unit price of the inputs – for example, £5.00 per litre of jet fuel.

The fuel standard cost of travelling 1 mile is obtained by multiplying the quantity and price standards:

Standard cost = 20 litres of fuel per mile × £5.00 per litre of fuel = £100 per mile

A similar rationale is then repeated to define standard costs concerning other direct inputs (overheads are different and are discussed later).

Uses of standard costing and variance analysis

Standard costing and variance analysis have been popular given their multiple applications:

- *Decision making.* Standard costs provide a basis for decision making, since they provide readily available estimates of future costs. For instance, to decide on future transactions, estimates of future costs are more relevant than past costs, which may not be repeatable. Although pricing must evaluate far more than just cost issues, cost estimates are important in deciding whether to accept or reject orders at a given price, to bid and negotiate prices and when prices are defined on a cost-plus basis (for instance, in contracts with the government, particularly the military). Sometimes standards are very visible in business models; see in *Management Accounting in Practice 9.1* how Ford's car repairers use standards when charging customers. Variances may also suggest strategic changes. Suppose variances indicate that prices of a new product are falling below estimates. The product manager should question if market research failed to anticipate the value perceived by customers, and should call for product redesign; alternatively, competition may have become more intense and the market strategy may have to be adjusted.

- *Planning, motivation, performance evaluation and control.* Standards are objectives, or benchmarks, to be achieved. Unit level standards are essential in producing budgets, in particular *flexible budgets* – a popular planning and control tool to produce budgets for different activity levels and product mixes. Flexible budgets enable meaningful variances to be calculated, comparing actual costs with budgeted costs for the actual level of activity and product mix. *Variance analysis*, in a contextualized and critical way, can provide insights to control and assist performance evaluation. So, standards and variance analysis are important motivation tools, setting objectives and monitoring and rewarding performance.

- *Reporting.* Standard costs make calculating profits and valuing inventories simple. Exhibit 9.1 describes the usual approach in valuing both purchases and production at standard costs. So, cost of goods sold and end of period inventories are also valued at standard costs, in the income statement and in the statement of financial position, respectively. Variances between actual and standard costs are recorded separately and directly affect the income statement. Standard costs are a simple basis on which to value quantities and avoid the need to trace actual costs to individual products.

When can standard costing be applied?

Products such as yogurt, shoes or electric appliances are typically obtained in large quantities through mass production. Manufacturers of this type of goods usually have standards for both the production process and the product itself. Operations are repetitive and largely common to a wide range of products (for example, the various yogurt types, such as natural and with fruit).

9.1: Management Accounting in Practice

When standards are key in setting the price: the case of car repairers

Service companies can use standards as a basis for pricing. In such business models, standards increase transparency and impact upon firms' competitiveness and profitability. Such is the case of official repairers for car manufacturers that announce time standards for certain repair operations.

Car manufacturers such as Ford Motor Company define and announce the *standard quantity* of labour time for each operation for Ford's official repairers, such as replacing the front brakes of a Ford Fiesta. Importantly, time standards define how much time Ford's repairers can charge their customers. Each repairer also publishes the price charged for each hour of intervention, as previously agreed with Ford. So, when examining an estimate or a bill, a customer can confirm that the figures match the published standards. Published time standards increase the transparency of total repair costs and can help persuade customers not to use unofficial repairers, as it provides some reassurance against unpleasant surprises on the final repair bill – a risk well known to many car owners. Standards are also useful to deal with an important segment of the repair market: insurance companies.

Even if a Ford's official repairer does not actually have a costing system based on standards, his profitability is still strongly influenced by standards, since it can only bill customers according to standard times. Should a particular repair actually take longer, excess costs cannot be passed on to the customer and will compromise profitability.

Some multi-brand repairers use standards in a more aggregated and simplified way, by announcing the final price for the service pack, rather than separately announcing standard repair times and the hourly charge. Time standards become less visible but also underlie the final price. So, actually achieving standards remains important, since excess time cannot be charged to the customer.

Source: based on authors' own research at an official Ford repairer.

Exercises

1) What characteristics of official car repairers as Ford's make it possible to set time standards for the various operations?

2) Would it make sense for a traditional bicycle repairer to also set time standards?

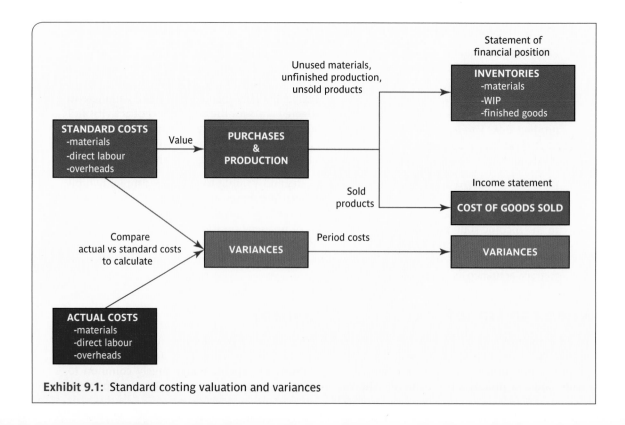

Exhibit 9.1: Standard costing valuation and variances

Inputs required to produce one unit of product (the output) are well established. Take strawberry yogurts as an example: the required quantities of milk, strawberries, sugar and other ingredients are standardized; the time in incubation machines, the energy those machines use, and so on, are also standardized. In turn, the products have consistent characteristics – all pots of strawberry-flavoured yogurts are homogenous. A standardized production setting, with repetitive and common operations and clearly defined input–output relations, is the context is which standard costing and variance analysis can best be applied. These techniques can also be applied to service organizations, provided that operations are also repetitive and input–output relations are clearly defined. Examples include regular flights by airline companies, daily door-to-door delivery of letters by postal companies, or car repairs.

Standard costing is not applicable when output units are heterogeneous or produced in varied, non-standardized ways. For example, it makes no sense to calculate the standard cost of a work of art like a marble sculpture, or of a unique piece of furniture exclusively designed and hand-made for one single customer. In mass customization and just-in-time (important alternatives to traditional, mass production models), standard costing and variance analysis have also been subject to criticism, as you will explore in the final section.

Information sources for setting standards

Management accountants may set standards based on various approaches: historical data analysis; engineering studies and interviews; external benchmarking.

Historical data analysis draws on input quantities and prices from previous periods. This is possible when an organization has experience in a stabilized production process. It is a relatively inexpensive approach, based on actual data, and provides a reference for future improvement. However, standard costs are future costs – so will past information provide reliable indications about future consumption and prices? Anticipated changes require adjusting past data to set revised standards. However, this approach has its problems. Past inefficiencies are included in past data and may be perpetuated through objectives that are too easy to achieve. Moreover, past cost data may become virtually irrelevant when changes to the production process are fundamental, and they do not even exist with regard to new products. Solving these problems requires an alternative approach: engineering studies.

Engineering studies estimate the input quantities that should be consumed, based on detailed technical analysis. Alternatively, *interviewing* operating personnel may provide informed estimates about efficient future consumption levels. Consumption and input prices estimates indicate what the product should cost. These approaches are future oriented, aiming to eliminate inefficiencies, and may reflect effects from expected changes, such as product redesign or a faster production process. However, they are typically more expensive and time-consuming than historical analysis. They require multidisciplinary teams, with production, human resources and sales staff combining their perspectives with a financial perspective. Involving the personnel performing the activities improves estimates reliability and increases commitment and motivation, but must take into consideration employees' incentive for biasing data, in order to set easy to achieve standards.

Finally, data about similar processes from companies perceived to be successful provides targets for *benchmarking* and may also be bases for standards. However, comparability and availability of such external data is often limited.

These various approaches can be combined for cross-checking or used selectively. For example, a company may use an engineering approach only on parts of the production process which have changed significantly with new machinery, and merely update historical cost standards of unchanged parts. In addition, it may also check how its past and future performances compare with that of competitors.

How ambitious should standards be?

Standards may be set at different levels of difficulty. Extremely low, very easy to achieve standards are unlikely to be adequate benchmarks. So, we will only discuss perfect standards (which have inconveniences) and normally attainable standards (usually adopted).

A *perfection (or ideal) standard* corresponds to performance in perfect conditions, including both production and purchasing operations. The problem with perfect standards is that perfect conditions are rarely or never actually achieved. So, adopting them risks damaging motivation and even encourages dysfunctional or unethical behaviour in attempts to lower actual costs. For example, employees may: neglect final product quality, hence putting customer satisfaction at risk; try to lower costs personally attributable to them, while causing increased costs attributable to others; or manipulate data to artificially report lower costs. Therefore, standards of perfection are unlikely to be adopted.

A *normally attainable standard* corresponds to performance under the usual conditions of operation, including normal interruptions and waste. These standards reflect practical efficiency, so they are realistic and achievable, although still demanding. This improves employees' motivation, particularly if they themselves were involved in setting the standards. So, these standards are the best benchmark with which to compare actual costs. When drawing on engineering studies to set standards costs, management accountants should ensure that these studies reflect normal conditions, rather than rigorous technical standards too unlikely to be achieved in practice.

Standards are expected to remain valid for a certain period, but technological or market changes can render them outdated. So, periodically and whenever necessary, we must ensure that standards remain valid estimates of normal conditions, adjusting them if necessary. One type of attainable standard is a *kaizen standard*. Kaizen standards reflect the Japanese philosophy of continuous improvement by small steps. They are dynamic, constantly changing standards, particularly those concerning cost reduction. This chapter analyses the more traditional types of standard, while Chapter 19 will discuss the kaizen approach.

Types of standards

Standards are usually concerned with costs, but they can also be associated with revenues. This chapter focuses on manufacturing costs: direct materials, direct labour, variable overheads and fixed overheads. Similar approaches apply to non-manufacturing costs, such as selling, general and administrative costs. In practice, each category must be broken down into many sub-categories, to provide detailed information for precise planning and variance analysis, and hence insightful managerial knowledge and action.

Introducing DrinkNat Ltd – and its standards

DrinkNat Ltd (a fictitious company) was recently established with the mission to produce natural and healthy fruit juice. DrinkNat considered that health concerns, which have recently supported an increasing demand for natural, organic, whole or probiotic foods, would continue to support the expansion of this market segment. DrinkNat initially launched a very popular type of fruit juice: a smoothie, made from blended oranges and mangos and labelled 'MangOrange'. After being washed and inspected, fruits are squeezed and the unusable bits removed. The resulting liquids are blended together and treated (pasteurized) to avoid the development of harmful micro-organisms. Finally, the smoothie is bottled.

To evaluate potential business profitability, DrinkNat analysed potential customers, competitors and distribution channels. For simplicity, let us assume one single product was launched: the 1-litre bottle of 'MangOrange' smoothie – the output unit. DrinkNat anticipated selling 100,000 units during the first year, at a unit price of £2.50 each. These are DrinkNat's revenues standards regarding sales quantity and price.

DrinkNat also estimated future production costs. Engineering and market studies allowed it to estimate the standard cost of producing a 1-litre 'MangOrange' unit – the standard cost per unit. A standard cost sheet details the various cost components making up the standard cost per unit. Table 9.1 contains the standard cost sheet and, based on the standard unit price, calculates standard margins per unit.

Note that fixed overheads are unitized only under absorption costing. In the following sections we will analyse standard variable costing, considering unit figures only up to the standard contribution margin. Towards the end of the chapter we will discuss standard absorption costing, which draws on unitized fixed overheads and the standard profit margin.

Table 9.1: DrinkNat's standard cost sheet and unit price and margins

	Standard quantity of input	Standard price of input	Standards (£) per unit of output
Direct materials:			
Oranges (50%)	0.6 Kgs	0.50 £/kg	£0.30
Mangos (50%)	0.6 Kgs	1.00 £/kg	0.60
Bottle	1 bottle	0.10 £/bottle	0.10
Total direct materials			**1.00**
Direct labour	0.02 DLH	10.00 £/DLH	0.20
	Standard quantity of allocation base per unit	Standard allocation rate	
Variable overhead	0.04 MH/unit	7.50 £/MH	**0.30**
Total standard variable costs			**1.50**
Standard selling price			**2.50**
Standard contribution margin			**1.00**
End of unitized calculations, under variable costing			
Under absorption costing, also include:			
	Standard quantity of allocation base per unit	Standard allocation rate	
Fixed overhead	0.04 MH/unit	5.00 £/MH	0.20
Standard profit margin			0.80

Direct material standards

The 'MangOrange' smoothie requires no other direct materials than mangos and oranges – and a bottle! Obtaining a 1-litre MangOrange unit should normally require 0.6 kilos of oranges – the standard quantity of this input per unit of output – and 0.6 kilos of mangos. Additionally, one customized bottle is required per unit of output. These standard quantities of materials are recorded on a bill of materials (BOM), as you learned in Chapter 4. Bills of materials are like culinary 'recipes', indicating the required quantities of each material for each product, without including the costs of each material. While an engineering perspective does not require this valuation, you need to define a value for each component in every BOM, to get a financial perspective over the whole production process.

Worked Example 9.1

Standard unit cost – direct materials

To estimate materials standard prices, DrinkNat surveyed fruit suppliers and estimated that 1 kilo of oranges should normally cost £0.50 during the next period. This standard price already includes the negotiated discount and additional costs normally incurred, such as fruits transportation costs. Standard quantities and prices determine the standard unit cost:

Standard unit cost = 0.6 kg × £0.50/kg = £0.30 per unit (concerning the orange input)

Likewise, the estimated standard price of £1.00 per kilo of mangos led to a standard unit cost of 0.6 kg × £1.00/kg = £0.60 per unit, concerning mangos. Surveying food containers suppliers indicated that a suitable customized bottle should cost £0.10. Adding up for all direct materials:

Standard unit cost = £0.30 + £0.50 + £0.10 = £1.00 per unit (including all direct materials)

Standards both influence and are influenced by many managerial options. Let us examine some practical marketing, technical, financial and risk options for DrinkNat. A smoothie can be produced from alternative fruit varieties, but DrinkNat considered that only sweet oranges were acceptable; a naturally high sugar level avoids having to add sugar, supporting DrinkNat's positioning in the healthy market segment. DrinkNat's technology involves throwing away outer and interior skins, so juicier oranges create less waste; however, they are more expensive. Mango varieties also have different prices and usable proportions, due in particular to the different seed sizes. So, choosing among fruit varieties requires both technical and financial trade-offs.

The standard quantity of 1.2 kilos of fruit (0.6 kilos of each) to obtain a 1-litre bottle of smoothie involves several factors. The type of production process and the technology adopted mean that several sources of waste normally exist. For example, skins and seeds are thrown away, occasional spilling may occur, and fruits may fail to pass inspection. Using unripe or overly mature fruits could ruin many litres of juice, causing a costly waste or, even worse, a poor customer experience; so, it is preferable to detect and remove unsuitable fruits before using them. Finally, slightly inaccurate bottling machines created the risk that some bottles could contain less than the advertised quantity. To avoid customer complaints and legal problems, DrinkNat sets machines to include slightly more than 1 litre per bottle. Therefore, the standard quantity of 1.2 kilos of fruit represents both normal waste and DrinkNat's managerial option to reduce business risk. In *Management Accounting in Practice 9.2*, we explore cost standards in the context of sustainable development concerns (see also Chapter 19).

Standards should reflect normal conditions, but these may change naturally during a particular period – for example, seasonality. During the winter, DrinkNat benefits from a greater supply of better quality oranges, with a higher juice content and higher yield, less damaged fruits, and at lower prices. Accordingly, DrinkNat has two alternatives for interim (for example, monthly) analyses. The first alternative is using different standards in each sub-period: 'winter-time' and 'summer-time' standards. Standards will better represent normal conditions in each particular period, but this will involve the additional complexity of changing standards more often. Alternatively, if it uses the same standards throughout the year, variances will also emerge reflecting the seasons, rather than just organizational performance. DrinkNat will then have to bear in mind this seasonal variation when analysing monthly variances, to avoid drawing the wrong conclusions about organizational performance.

9.2: Management Accounting in Practice

Options underlying standards: Innocent's sustainable development considerations

Companies in the fruit juices industry have been trying to reduce waste levels. Reducing the standard quantity of required direct materials is a straightforward economic reason, but it also addresses sustainability and ethical concerns. New techniques allow using 100 per cent of some types of fruits in the final product. These techniques decrease the standard quantity and therefore the standard unit cost – and benefits business and environmental sustainability.

Other concerns may, on the contrary, imply options that increase costs – at least in the short term. For example, Innocent Drinks states: 'We favour suppliers certified by independent environmental and social organizations (such as the Rainforest Alliance), and pay a premium for certified fruit.' This ethical option increases the fruit standard price, but addresses environmental and social responsibility concerns, and may ultimately benefit the company.

Management accountants may play an important role in measuring and comparing the various types of costs, such as economic, social and environmental costs, and contribute to decisions involving complex trade-offs. Developing insights on such diverse perspectives requires management accountants to move beyond the strictly financial domain, to be aware of broader business and societal issues and to keep up to date with emerging management accounting techniques to address these new concerns, as you will learn in Chapter 19.

Source: http://www.innocentdrinks.co.uk/us/ethics/sustainable_ingredients/ (accessed on 15 May 2012).

Exercise

Juices can be made from concentrate, rather than directly from fresh fruit. Concentrate is typically produced in the countries where fruits grow. Then, it is transported to regions nearer to the customer, where it is diluted and transformed into juice. Some people say that this production method uses less energy in transportation and leaves a smaller carbon footprint. Investigate and discuss how Innocent Drinks may counter this argument.

Direct labour standards

Direct labour standards follow the same basic logic as standards on direct materials and depend on:

1)   the standard quantity of labour time (for example, direct labour hours, DLH) required to produce one unit of output – the standard time;

2)   the standard price paid for one unit of labour time (for example, the wage rate for one DLH).

Let us assume DrinkNat carried out a time and motion study to determine the most efficient production method. According to this standardized production method, under normal conditions one average worker should need 72 seconds (that is, 1.2 minutes, or 0.02 hours) to obtain one bottle of smoothie. This standard quantity of labour includes delays inherent to the production process, such as normal time to switch between units and to carry out planned maintenance. In practice, this standard time must be broken down according to the various operations, such as washing and inspection, to allow for detailed analyses. Establishing the standard duration of particular operations is important in many industries. In *Management Accounting in Practice 9.1*, you found how standard times are key in the business model of auto repairers such as Ford Motor Company.

   DrinkNat's standard labour price (wage rate) amounts to £10 per hour, which includes the basic wage rate and additional costs (such as social security, health insurance and other benefits).

   On the basis of the above information from the production and the human resources departments, management accountants estimated:

Standard unit cost = 0.02 DLH × £10/DLH = £0.20 per unit (for direct labour; see again Table 9.1)

Overhead standards

Calculating manufacturing overhead rate standards follows the approach described in Chapter 5 to estimate predetermined overhead rates, distinguishing between variable and fixed costs and adopting an appropriate allocation base (see Chapter 4 for overhead allocation). Remember that overheads are typically highly diversified and are only indirectly related with particular products, which in turn may be also heterogeneous. Therefore, overhead rate standards, such as predetermined overhead rates, are useful to split overheads across products.

Variable overhead rate standards

To calculate variable overhead (VOH) rate standards, the allocation base should ideally capture what causes such costs. For example, companies may allocate energy costs based on the energy intensity of the various products. Alternatively, companies may use traditional, unit-level allocation criteria, like direct labour hours or machine hours – the alternative adopted in this chapter, for simplification purposes.

Worked Example 9.2

Standard variable overhead cost

DrinkNat budgeted £30,000 for VOH and chose machine hours (MH) as the allocation base because, we shall assume, almost all VOH is related to energy used by machines. Based on the standard machine time of 0.04 MH/unit and estimated production of 100,000 units, DrinkNat estimated needing the following machine hours:

Budgeted volume of the allocation base = 0.04 MH/unit × 100,000 units = 4,000 MH.

So:

Standard VOH rate = £30,000/4,000 MH = £7.50/MH

Since one unit should require 0.04 MH,

Standard VOH cost = 0.04 MH × £7.50/MH = £0.30/unit (one bottle of MangOrange).

Note that DrinkNat has only one product (the 'MangOrange' smoothie). So, overheads can also be allocated directly according to budgeted production:

Standard VOH cost = £30,000/100,000 units = £0.30/unit

However, companies usually produce multiple, heterogeneous products. In those cases, the budgeted volume of the allocation base (MH) must allow the manufacture of *all* products (not just one) and an allocation rate is indispensible to split costs across products.

Fixed overhead rate standards

Fixed overheads (FOH) are expected to remain the same within certain production intervals (the relevant range of each FOH level). The recording of FOH varies in standard variable or absorption costing, as you learned in Chapter 5.

Variable costing considers all FOH as a period cost, rather than allocating them to production. So, there is no need to calculate FOH unit costs or allocation rates. We merely budget the expected spending on FOH, as a single lump sum.

Worked Example 9.3

Standard fixed overhead cost (for absorption costing only)

Fixed overheads, such as rent, machines depreciation, wages of operational personnel not directly involved in production and other FOH, were budgeted at £20,000 and estimated to remain fixed as long as DrinkNat produced less than 150,000 units – the relevant range.

It was decided to allocate FOH according to budgeted capacity utilization of 4,000 machine hours (MH) to obtain 100,000 units, corresponding to a requirement of 0.04 MH/unit (see above). So:

Standard FOH rate = £20,000/4,000MH = £5.00/MH (on a MH basis)

or

Standard FOH cost = £5.00/MH × 0.04 MH/unit = £0.20/unit (on an output unit basis)

As commented about VOH, rates per allocation base unit are necessary for multi-product companies. However, in the single-product company, DrinkNat, the budgeted capacity utilization of 4,000MH is exclusively related to the budgeted 100,000 MangOrange units. So, you can readily obtain the same standard FOH cost of £0.20/unit by dividing £20,000/100,000 units.

Absorption costing allocates FOH to products (*see Worked Example 9.3*). Chapter 4 analysed alternative denominators to calculate predetermined rates. Alternatives include practical capacity, normal utilization of capacity (normal activity level) or budgeted utilization of capacity (budgeted activity level). Since a standard costing system attempts to capture normal operating conditions, adopting the normal utilization of capacity is a very suitable alternative. However, the budgeted utilization of capacity is a more common choice. Finally, it is necessary to define the measure of capacity – traditionally based on direct labour or machine time. Again, for simplification purposes, this chapter adopts these traditional unit-level hourly allocation bases, for fixed overheads.

Note that DrinkNat aggregates overheads into only two cost pools (variable and fixed overheads). However, remember that in real life overheads are typically highly diversified and meaningful analysis involves splitting each cost lump sum into detailed cost items.

Flexible budgeting, variance analysis and sales variances

Variance analysis: zooming in and zooming out

Variance analysis creates insights about 'what actually went right or wrong' across multiple areas of organizational performance, ranging from manufacturing and non-manufacturing costs, to revenues and profitability margins. To identify learning and action, variances have to be detailed to pinpoint precisely the areas requiring closer attention. We must break down cost categories into many sub-categories, for each product, operation and responsibility centre: that is, we must 'zoom in'. In addition, no variance should be interpreted 'on its own'. The interpretation of each variance should be integrated, examining insights suggested by other variances to construct a balanced and comprehensive conclusion': that is, we must also 'zoom out'. Throughout this chapter, exhibits titled 'A "real-world" interpretation' will alert you to potential causes underlying each particular variance.

A 'real-life' interpretation of variances usually requires a 'real-life', hands-on investigation, and discussing and learning about business operations. Providing qualitative, business-oriented interpretations for calculated variances is fundamental for management accountants, in particular since integrated information systems have increasingly replaced humans in purely mechanical calculation activities. Moreover, variances may play a significant role for control purposes even when they are not explicitly used for reporting (Dugdale et al., 2006). This usage of variances for control makes 'real-life' interpretations even more crucial, given the high economic and behavioural consequences of control.

To develop a distinctive, value-added contribution towards uncovering 'real-life' causes of variances, rather than merely calculating them, you should understand what each variance suggests about organizational performance, rather than merely memorizing formulae. This understanding will also tell you whether each variance figure is favourable or not, rather than merely relying on memory.

The quest for meaningful comparisons

In Chapter 8, you learned how to prepare a budget before a period starts. This is an initial, **static budget**, based on initial estimates about prices and quantities. Of course, predictions about organizational performance often do not become reality, as happened in DrinkNat's first year of activity. Table 9.2 displays DrinkNat's static budget and actual results, under variable costing. We assume there are no end of period inventories, so production equals sales. In the next sections, the terms 'production' and 'sales' are used interchangeably.

We must understand this mismatch between actual results and the initial estimates of the static budget. But not all comparisons are useful. Direct comparisons between actual figures and static budget figures, called **static budget variances**, are essentially meaningless, because they refer to different activity levels. An actual cost of mangos (£65,000) higher than budgeted (£60,000) may simply be due to higher actual sales (110,000 units, versus the budgeted 100,000 units). The consequences of different efficiency levels and different activity levels are mixed up. So we now turn to flexible budgeting to seek meaningful comparisons and insights.

Table 9.2: Static budget and actual results (under variable costing)

	STATIC BUDGET			ACTUAL RESULTS		
	Standard prices/rates	Budgeted quantity	Static budget	Actual price	Actual quantity	Actual figures
Sales	£2.50	100,000 units	250,000	£2.00	110,000 units	220,000
Direct materials						
Oranges	£0.50	60,000 kgs	30,000	£0.60	70,000 kgs	42,000
Mangos	£1.00	60,000 kgs	60,000	£1.00	65,000 kgs	65,000
Bottles	£0.10	100,000 bottles	10,000	£0.09	150,000 bottles	13,500
Total direct material costs			100,000			120,500
Direct labour costs	£10.00	2,000 DLH	20,000	£11.00	2,500 DLH	27,500
Variable overheads	£7.50	4,000 MH	30,000			31,000
Total variable costs			150,000			179,000
Contribution			100,000			41,000
Total fixed overheads			20,000			25,000
Operating profit			80,000			16,000

Flexible budgeting: a retrospective crystal ball and a tool for planning and decision making

In a **flexible budget**, we adjust, that is, *flex* the initial estimates to the actual volume of activity. A flexible budget is like a retrospective crystal ball: at the end of the period, we create the budget we would have prepared at the start of the period *if* we had correctly forecast the actual volume of activity. By adjusting the activity level, the quantities and costs of variable inputs are also adjusted.

In addition to the static budget (already shown in Table 9.2), Table 9.3 shows DrinkNat's flexible budget, based on:

- The actual activity volume of 110,000 units of 'MangOrange' – the only 'root' difference concerning the static budget

- The standard selling price and standard quantities and prices for variable inputs considered in the static budget; these standards are applied to the actual activity level, to obtain 'flexed' figures

- The same fixed costs considered in the static budget – do not forget that fixed costs remain at £20,000 within the relevant range between 0 and 150,000 units.

Calculate a flexible budget

Let us first calculate the flexed budget for mangos. For the actual 110,000 units sold, and given the standard quantity of 0.6 kg of mangos per unit, we could have anticipated to need:

Flexed quantity of mangos = £0.60/unit × 110,000 units = 66,000 kg

The expected cost of this flexed quantity would be:

Flexed budget of mangos = £1.00 × 66,000 kg = £66,000

Each line of revenues and costs is analysed below, as each variance is analysed.

Flexible budget costs represents costs recorded in a standard costing system: they are based on price and quantity standards (for direct materials, direct labour and overheads), applied to the actual activity level. This differs from other systems for product costing (Chapter 5), as summarized in Table 9.4. A *normal* costing system allocates overheads based on predetermined rates, but assigns direct inputs on the basis of actual costs; and an *actual* costing system bases product costing on actual costs of all three inputs.

Flexible budgeting is a simple, but powerful tool, that goes beyond the comparison between actual and expected figures. Flexible budgets allow us to simulate alternative scenarios, for different activity levels, and can help planning and decision making by providing estimates for revenues, costs and profits according to, for instance, different marketing strategies or different responses from competitors and other market shifts leading to different sales volumes. However, these estimates assume that variable costs vary in line with sales volume and that fixed costs do not change in the relevant range, as you learned in Chapter 3. Because these assumptions may not hold, you should view the results from flexible budgeting with caution.

You will now start exploring the various variances, starting with the sales margin volume variance.

Sales margin volume variance (under variable costing)

What does comparing the flexible and the static budgets tell us? It indicates the consequences of different sales volumes, in terms of cost, revenues and profit. This comparison leads to the sales margin volume variance.

Table 9.3: Static and flexible budgets – and the sales volume variance (under variable costing)

	STATIC BUDGET			FLEXIBLE BUDGET			Sales volume variance	
	Standard prices/ rates	Budgeted quantity	Static budget	Standard price/ rate	Flexed quantity	Flexible budget		
Sales	£2.50	100,000 units	250,000	£2.50	110,000 units	275,000	25,000	F
Direct materials								
Oranges	£0.50	60,000 kgs	30,000	£0.50	66,000 kgs	33,000	3,000	U
Mangos	£1.00	60,000 kgs	60,000	£1.00	66,000 kgs	66,000	6,000	U
Bottles	£0.10	100,000 bottles	10,000	£0.10	110,000 bottles	11,000	1,000	U
Total direct material costs			100,000			110,000	10,000	U
Direct labour costs	£10.00	2,000 DLH	20,000	£10.00	2,200 DLH	22,000	2,000	U
Variable overheads	£7.50	4,000 MH	30,000	£7.50	4,400 MH	33,000	3,000	U
Total variable costs			150,000			165,000	15,000	U
Contribution			100,000			110,000	10,000	F
Total fixed overheads			20,000			20,000	0	
Operating profit			80,000			90,000	10,000	F

Table 9.4: Comparison of the three costing systems

	Direct materials and direct labour	Overheads
Actual costing system	Actual	Actual
Normal costing system	Actual	Budgeted
Standard costing system	Standard	Standard

Worked Example 9.5

Calculate the sales margin volume variance

Actual volume was 110,000 units, 10,000 more than the 100,000 of the budgeted volume. What was the margin (profit) impact of selling these additional 10,000 units?

To measure exclusively the impact of the higher volume, you should use the standard contribution margin, based on the standard price and the standard variable costs:

$$£2.50/unit – £1.50/unit = £1.00/unit.$$

At the standard contribution margin of £1.00/unit, the additional 10,000 units were expected to produce an additional margin of £10,000 (hence, a favourable variance, indicated as £10,000F). This is the sales margin volume variance, in the bottom line of the last column of Table 9.3.

The **sales margin *volume* variance** is the difference between actual sales volume (AV) and budgeted sales volume (BV), valued at the standard contribution margin (*sm*):

$$(AV – BV) \times sm = (110,000 – 100,000) \text{ units} \times £1.00/unit$$
$$= 10,000 \times 1 = £10,000F$$

Note that changes in sales prices do not affect this variance, since the standard contribution margin is based on the standard price, not on the actual price.

A line-by-line view of Table 9.3 is also informative. You can also calculate each line by valuing the variation of each flexed quantity, based on standard prices and rates. Let us calculate for mangos: a cost increase of (66,000 kg – 60,000 kg) × £1.00/kg = £6,000 is expected exclusively due to the higher activity level which implies an additional 6,000 kg expected consumption of mangos. Finally, remember that fixed costs remain unchanged.

A reminder about standard variable versus absorption costing systems

Keep in mind that we are now considering a standard *variable* costing system, so fixed overheads are not charged to products. However, in standard absorption costing, fixed overheads are charged to products and affect unit margins – thus requiring a different approach to this sales margin volume variance, as you will learn towards the end of the chapter.

Using the above variance, that compares the static and flexible budgets, you have identified the financial impacts of different activity levels. Now, after a brief clarification of two formal issues, you will analyse the performance of various organizational areas, such as manufacturing and purchasing, through detailed analysis of flexible budget variances.

How to indicate variances and distinguish variables? A brief clarification

Note that variances are indicated in their absolute value, regardless of being favourable or unfavourable. **Favourable variances**, identified as 'F', mean an increase in profit, due to (1) actual revenues higher than budgeted, or (2) actual costs lower than budgeted. On the contrary, **unfavourable variances** ('U') mean a decrease in profit, either due to actual lower revenues or actual higher costs, when compared to the budget. To make formulas clearer, this chapter identifies:

- unit level variables in lower case (for example: '*sm*', standard contribution margin);
- total values in capital letters (for example: 'AV', actual sales volume).

Flexible budget variances: drilling-down on organizational performance

Comparing the flexible budget (from Table 9.3) with actual results (from Table 9.2) allows meaningful comparisons, since they both consider the actual activity level of 110,000 units. These comparisons are **flexible budget variances**, the last column of Table 9.5. They create insights about organizational performance at the various cost, revenue and profitability items, since comparisons are not biased by different activity levels.

However, even a line-by-line comparison between the flexible budget and actual results does not clarify why those variances happened. For example, was the £9,000 unfavourable variance on oranges due to higher than expected prices, quantities or both? Each variance needs more detailed analysis. First, you will analyse differences caused by the selling price (the sales price variance), complementing the variance on sales margin volume; the total sales margin variance then provides a global picture of revenues. Next, you will analyse each cost category in separate sections.

Sales price variance

In addition to sales volume, prices charged to customers influence sales revenues. So, in addition to the sales margin volume variance analysed above, we calculate the sales price variance. It tells us that charging the actual selling price of £2.00/unit, rather than the £2.50 standard price, in the actual sales volume (110,000 units) directly reduced profit in £55,000 (hence, an unfavourable variance). More generally:

Table 9.5: Flexible budget and actual results – and flexible budget variances

	FLEXIBLE BUDGET			ACTUAL RESULTS			Flexible budget variances	
	Standard price/rate	Flexed quantity	Flexible budget	Actual price	Actual quantity	Actual figures		
Sales	£2.50	110,000 units	275,000	£2.00	110,000 units	220,000	55,000	U
Direct materials								
Oranges	£0.50	66,000 kgs	33,000	£0.60	70,000 kgs	42,000	9,000	U
Mangos	£1.00	66,000 kgs	66,000	£1.00	65,000 kgs	65,000	1,000	F
Bottles	£0.10	110,000 bottles	11,000	£0.09	150,000 bottles	13,500	2,500	U
Total direct material costs			110,000			120,500	10,500	U
Direct labour costs	£10.00	2,200 DLH	22,000	£11.00	2,500 DLH	27,500	5,500	U
Variable overheads	£7.50	4,400 MH	33,000			31,000	2,000	F
Total variable costs			165,000			179,000	14,000	U
Contribution			110,000			41,000	69,000	U
Total fixed overheads			20,000			25,000	5,000	U
Operating profit			90,000			16,000	74,000	U

the **sales _price_ variance** is the difference between the actual price (ap) and the standard price (sp), applied to the actual sales volume (AV), that is,

$$(ap - sp) \times AV = (£2.00 - £2.50) \times 110,000 \text{ units}$$

$$= -0.5 \times 110,000 = £55,000U$$

Although this variance compares sales prices, it also compares margins. So, to calculate this variance you can also compare actual and standard contribution margins (am and sm), provided that the actual contribution margin 'am' (like the standard contribution margin 'sm') is also based on standard costs (sc). Then, we have:

$$am = ap - sc$$

$$sm = sp - sc$$

The following alternative formula, based on contribution margins, is directly comparable with the sales margin volume variance:

$$(am - sm) \times AV = (£0.50 - £1.00) \times 110,000 \text{ units}$$

$$= 0.5 \times 110,000 = £55,000U$$

Both formulas are based on standard costs, thus preventing the performance of the industrial area (concerning actually incurred costs) from influencing the evaluation of the sales area. However, since sales price and volume are typically inversely related, we should interpret the two sales variances in combination, as you can see next when you analyse the total sales variance.

Total sales margin variance

The total sales margins variance sums the two above variances to measure how changes in sales price and volume affected margins (Exhibit 9.2). In general:

the **total sales margin variance** is the difference between actual contribution (AC, based on standard costs) and budgeted contribution (BC), that is,

$$AC - BC.$$

Thus we can see the sales variances as follows:

- The *volume* effect is the final result in Table 9.3 (10,000F).

- The *price* effect is the first flexible budget variance in Table 9.5 (55,000U).

You may have noticed this total variance is not the difference between actual and budgeted sales of £220,000 – £250,000 = £30,000U. Why? Because the two sales variances measure the impact on margins, not on sales. This makes sense, since it is sales margin, not sales per se, that influences profit – and profitability should be the main focus when evaluating the sales function. Check again in Table 9.3 that higher volume impacts not only on revenues (£25,000F) but also on total variable costs (£15,000U); the impact on profitability is the increased contribution by £10,000, that is, the favourable sales margin volume variance. The following section explores a 'real-world' interpretation.

A 'real-world' interpretation: what do sales margin variances really mean?

In most products and services, increases in price usually reduce customers' purchases (that is, reduce the sellers' sales volume), and vice versa. This means that you should analyse the total sales margin variance and its two sub-variances in an integrated way.

Let us examine the £10,000 favourable sales margin *volume* variance. This can be due to customers' better acceptance of 'MangOrange' than anticipated by market research, or to poorer competitors' performance; both alternatives would lead to a larger than expected market share of DrinkNat. It can also be caused by an unexpected increase in the 'healthy food' market size – in such a case, sales volume increases even if the market share does not change. You can further explore variances about sales volumes (the sales mix, market share and market size variances) in Steven (2000).

However, an alternative explanation is related to the £55,000 unfavourable sales *price* variance. A price substantially below expectations (£0.50/unit, –20% of the initial estimate of £2.50/unit) may have fuelled the volume increase. But this price decrease may also be attributable to a general market price decrease – typical when more companies enter a recent, but maturing market. In this case, the 'MangOrange' price decrease would not lead to higher volume, unless the general market price reduction increased the market size. DrinkNat's sales and marketing managers may already have an explanation, but further market research may be needed.

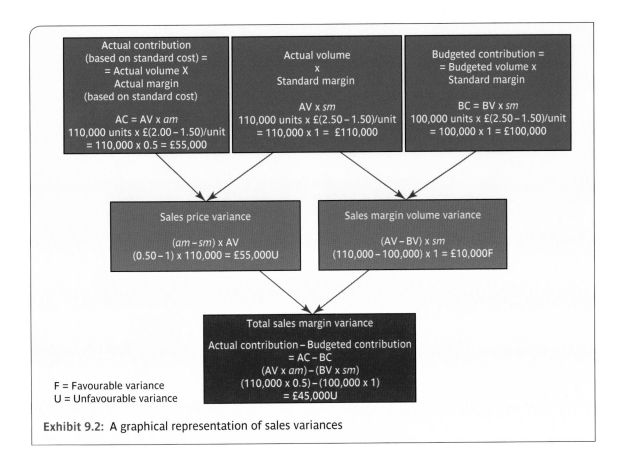

Exhibit 9.2: A graphical representation of sales variances

You have seen how a flexible budget and flexed figures contribute to meaningful comparisons and to understand 'real-life' factors underlying differences between actual and budgeted figures. Now that you have learned about sales variances, you will explore variances of the various cost categories in the following sections.

Material variances

Materials cost actually incurred may differ from expectations for two reasons: differences in prices and/or differences in quantities. Each difference is captured in the material *price* and *usage* variances, respectively (Exhibit 9.3).

Material price variance

Material price variances capture differences between actual and standard material prices (Table 9.5). In DrinkNat's case, oranges were actually more expensive than planned: the actual price was £0.60/kg, while the estimated standard price was only £0.50/kg. This unfavourable £0.10/kg price difference affected the actual quantity (AQ) of 70,000 kilos purchased. This led to total actual costs £7,000 higher than expected – the material price variance incurred in oranges. In general:

> the **material *price* variance** is the difference between the standard price (*sp*) and the actual price (*ap*) per unit of material, applied to the actual quantity (AQ) purchased, that is:

$$(sp - ap) \times AQ = (£0.50 - £0.60) \times 70,000 \text{ kg}$$

$$= £7,000U$$

You can also think about the material price variance as the difference between (1) what should have been paid if purchased materials had been bought at the standard price and (2) what was actually paid for them. So, an alternative formula is $(sp \times AQ) - (ap \times AQ)$.

A similar analysis applies to all materials. Mangos' actual price was in line with the standard, leading to a zero price variance. In the case of bottles, after the initial market research was conducted, DrinkNat switched to an alternative supplier charging a lower price (£0.09 per bottle)

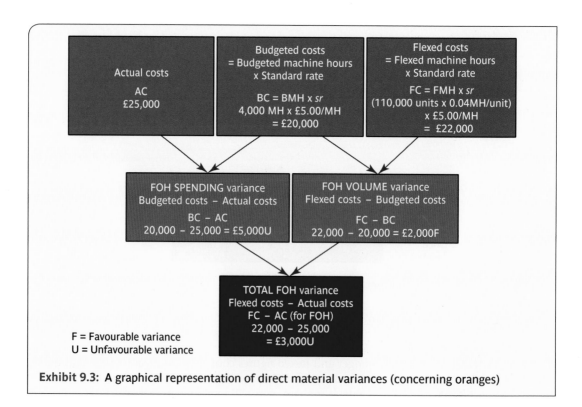

Exhibit 9.3: A graphical representation of direct material variances (concerning oranges)

than planned (£0.10) in 150,000 purchased bottles, allowing a favourable material price variance of (£0.10/bottle – £0.09/bottle) × 150,000 bottles = £1,500F.

Bear in mind that a variance only provides a preliminary perspective that needs to be integrated with insights from other variances and from wider business awareness. The section below explores a possible integrative, 'real-world' interpretation.

A 'real-world' interpretation: what do price variances really mean?

Let us examine DrinkNat's favourable price variance of purchased bottles you calculated. Obtaining a lower price by selecting a new supplier seems a sound managerial outcome. However, you must look beyond the unit price and analyse the global cost of purchasing activities, in line with activity-based costing insights. A lower global purchasing cost may be obtained through more efficient management of supply chain activities, such as placing, processing, receiving and controlling orders. On the contrary, materials returns and inefficient supplier administrative activities may increase the cost of the purchasing activity. In fact, an ABC approach may be useful to calculate the material standard price, as the unitized amount of the global purchase cost.

Another key area is materials quality. Are the cheaper bottles actually similar to the initial ones? Lower-quality bottles may cause operational problems and have to be thrown away, increasing waste and the quantity of bottles actually used. And if the problem is only detected during or after bottling, the smoothie may have to be thrown away, causing waste in all other inputs (oranges, mangos, labour and variable overheads).[1] This means that we must also look into the efficiency variances analysed next.

Packaging influences product identity, market positioning and customers' value perception. Might lower-quality bottles lead to lower sales quantities and/or prices (leading to unfavourable sales variances)? Furthermore, initial negative customer perceptions are often difficult to overcome – even after the problem is corrected. But long-term damages in future market positioning and performance are not captured by variances, which reflect past events and data. Clearly, management accountants must look beyond variances.

Finally, if DrinkNat continues to purchase from the new supplier, the price standard must be revised to meet the new normal purchasing conditions. In addition, should the new bottles also imply different normal production conditions, as speculated above, the production standards must also be revised.

We will assume that materials are recorded at standard costs immediately when purchased and that the price variance is also immediately calculated, based on purchased quantities. This is the most popular approach (rather than waiting until materials usage, as briefly discussed below), because managers can become aware of and address problems more quickly. However, managerial awareness and reaction should be even earlier, even before purchase, as *Management Accounting in Practice 9.3* illustrates.

9.3: Management Accounting in Practice

Action beating the variances

Airlines try to guarantee jet fuel prices in advance, to provide security for planning and, in particular, for setting ticket prices for trips that only happen months ahead. Failing that, airlines risk actual fuel prices rising significantly above those expected – creating an unfavourable fuel price variance, and putting at stake their profitability and competitiveness. Airlines protection is based on 'hedging' their position through sophisticated financial contracts on oil – although airlines buy jet fuel, not oil. The *Financial Times* reported that a problem recently arose for US airlines 'because of a rare divergence between the cost of jet fuel and the oil benchmark they traditionally use to insure against high energy costs. (. . .) US airlines hedge their exposure to energy costs mostly through the popular West Texas Intermediate (WTI) oil contract'. However, due to logistical problems, during the first two months of 2011, 'the cost of jet fuel in the US rose nearly 28%', while WTI prices rose less that 12 per cent. Airlines such as JetBlue Airways, Southwest Airlines and Virgin America expressed great concern with this divergence. In practice, this divergence 'means that US airlines are not insulated from rising fuel costs, prompting some to increase fares' to compensate for likely unfavourable fuel price variances.

Airline managers did not wait until more expensive jet fuel started being purchased, let alone being used. Both alternatives of calculating price variances, based on past data of either purchased or used materials, would be too late to prompt timely managerial action. However, the rationale underlying price variances remains invaluable, by proactively developing effective financial strategies to make actual future prices in line with standard prices and support profitable operations.

Source: 'US airlines rethink fuel hedging policy', Financial Times, 2 March 2011.

Exercises

1) How can companies adopt a similar rationale to protect them against increases in interest rates or unfavourable changes in exchange rates?

2) Discuss the limitations of ex post analyses as bases for managerial learning and action, in particular in today's volatile environment.

Material usage variance

The quantity of materials actually used in production may differ from the quantity that should have been used. In line with flexible budgeting, both quantities of material must refer to the same production volume. This means that we must compare the actual quantity with the flexed quantity, given actual production and the standard quantity of material per unit of product (see Table 9.5, and Exhibit 9.3). Since one unit of MangOrange should require 0.6 kg of oranges and 110,000 units were actually produced, we could expect using 66,000 kg of oranges. However, 70,000 kg were actually used, 4,000 kg more than expected (+6.7 per cent).

How do we financially value this higher consumption? Using the input standard price (£0.50/kg) (rather than the actual price) avoids distorting production staff evaluation due to higher or lower prices achieved by the purchasing department. This leads to a £2,000 unfavourable material usage variance for this input. More generally:

the **material *usage* variance** is the difference between the flexed quantity (FQ) of materials required and the actual quantity (AQ) of materials used, valued at the standard material price (*sp*), that is,

$$(FQ - AQ) \times sp = (110,000 \text{ units} \times 0.6 \text{ kg/unit} - 70,000 \text{ kg}) \times £0.50/\text{kg}$$

$$= -4,000 \text{ kg} \times £0.50/\text{kg} = 2,000U$$

Using the same approach, you can check, that mangos' actual usage fell below the quantity expected for the actual production level, leading to a favourable usage variance (£1,000F); and bottles usage variance was unfavourable (£4,000U).

You can further divide this variance to distinguish the financial impact of (1) changes in production efficiency and (2) changes in the combination of inputs with different prices (for example, increasing the percentage of oranges, which are cheaper than mangos). You can learn about these material *yield* and *mix* variances in the appendix to this chapter.

Unfavourable variances indicate that more costs were incurred than expected, and vice versa. But going beyond an accounting interpretation, what 'real-world' insights and lines of action can you get from such variances? Read the section below for clues.

A 'real-world' interpretation: what do material usage variances really mean?

Let us continue analysing DrinkNat's highly unfavourable bottles-usage variance – notice that, considering expected costs of $110,000 \times 0.10 = £11,000$, the £4,000 variance is a 36 per cent increase. A direct interpretation suggests a poor performance of the operational area, caused by problems such as defective bottling machines or careless storage and handling, requiring better machines maintenance or further training. But keep in mind that DrinkNat's favourable price variance may be related to buying lower-quality bottles, causing production problems and *bottles* waste. Might excessive usage have been caused by attempted savings in the purchasing area, rather than a poor performance of the industrial area?

Financially, the higher consumption of bottles outweighs their lower price – check the unfavourable total bottles variance of $1,500F + 4,000U = £2,500U$, analysed next. Moreover, production problems may imply a waste of other inputs – for example if bottles break after being full. Check Table 9.5. Actual consumption of oranges and mangos ($70,000 \text{ kg} + 65,000 \text{ kg} = 135,000 \text{ kg}$) exceeding flexed consumption ($66,000 \text{ kg} + 66,000 \text{ kg} = 132,000 \text{ kg}$) provides only limited support for this hypothesis, since the 3,000 kg (2.27 per cent) excess is far below the 36 per cent bottles usage variance. Finally, these problems may have required additional time from operational staff and more variable overheads.

Note that sometimes non-financial indicators are preferable to financial variances. For example, to test if production problems implied fruit waste, comparing quantities consumed (as above) is more appropriate than adding together the two fruit usage variances ($2,000U + 1,000F = £1,000U$), since this is influenced by their relative prices. However, financial variances are essential for measuring the financial consequences of different consumption volumes.

Alternatively, is the problem about DrinkNat's performance or its standards? A standard may have been set mistakenly and may need to be revised. DrinkNat set its standards through an engineering approach, before having actually started operations. Experience may now reveal that some technical or economic assumptions do not actually hold in reality. Take the standard unit consumption of precisely one bottle per output unit. Either management accountants forgot to consider the possibility of waste, or considered that waste should not occur in normal circumstances. They may now realize that, for example, rejecting 1 bottle per 100 approved reflects the usual waste in DrinkNat's normal conditions, rather than an unacceptable inefficiency. If so, standard quantity must be revised to 1.01 bottles per unit of output, to reflect normal waste.

Finally, might this unfavourable variance be due to workers' lack of experience during their first year of operations? Perhaps the expertise gained will help attain current standards in the future. Management accountants must gain a solid knowledge of the 'cruise speed' of this particular production process, performed by these particular workers (or others replacing them). If so, they must revise the standards to incorporate the anticipated learning effect and, in general, to reflect new 'normal conditions' standards resulting from technological, organizational or economic shifts.

Uncovering real-world business problems to correctly interpret variances often creates disputes, typically across different organizational functions. Therefore, the management accountant should have business knowledge and interpersonal skills to promote interfunctional dialogue, build consensus and promote organizational learning.

Total material variance

Summing up, total material variance is the aggregate effect of variations concerning materials price and usage, as shown in Exhibit 9.3. In other words:

> ***Total* material variance** is the difference between material flexed costs (FC)[2] and actual costs (AC), that is,

$$FC - AC \text{ [for direct materials]}$$

Considering the three direct materials, total material variance is 9,000U + 1,000F + 2,500U = 10,500U. Note that this variance compares the flexed budget with actual figures, as in Table 9.5, so it can also be calculated as $(FQ \times sp) - (AQ \times ap)$.

Note that the price variance in Exhibit 9.3 is based on materials used. However, we have previously opted for a more timely approach, calculating the price variance on the basis of purchased quantity, at the time of purchase. This chapter assumes purchased and used quantities are equal, for simplification purposes and also because new manufacturing approaches like just in time (JIT) tend to make this happen. But if they are different, price variances will also be different; in this case, the price variance (based on purchased quantities) and the usage variance do not add up to the total material variance.

Keep in mind that interpreting variances requires both 'zooming in' and 'zooming out'. We need to 'zoom in' on price and usage, both within and across the various materials. We also need to 'zoom out', uncovering relationships concerning the various inputs, revenues and even intangible aspects, with a long-term, business and strategic orientation. Going beyond individual variances and quantitative, short-term aspects is crucial for management accountants to create value in their organizations.

Direct labour variances

Variances about direct labour, like variances about direct materials, measure the consequences of variations in the input price (the wage rate) and usage, through (1) the *wage rate* variance and (2) the labour *efficiency* variance. You can use the graphical representation of material variances in Exhibit 9.3 as a guideline, given the similar rationale.

Wage rate variance

The wage rate variance compares the actual price paid for one hour of direct labour (actual wage rate) with its standard price (standard wage rate). DrinkNat's £11 actual wage rate per hour exceeded the £10 standard (see Table 9.5). This £1.00 unfavourable hourly excess (+10 per cent than expected) affected the 2,500 hours (DLH) actually worked, leading to an unfavourable wage rate variance of £2,500. In general:

> **Wage rate variance** is the difference between the standard wage rate (*sr*) and the actual rate (*ar*) per hour of direct labour, applied to the actual number of hours used (AH), that is,

$$(sr - ar) \times AH = (£10/DLH - £11/DLH) \times 2,500\,DLH$$

$$= -£1.00/DLH \times 2,500\,DLH = £2,500U$$

As in the material price variance, the input price difference is multiplied by the actual quantity. Note that you can also think about the wage rate variance as the difference between what was actually paid for used labour hours and what should have been paid if the standard wage rate had been applied, as in the equivalent formula $(sr \times AH) - (ar \times AH)$. The section below explores a 'real-world' interpretation.

A 'real-world' interpretation: what do wage rate variances really mean?

DrinkNat's unfavourable wage rate variance is related to a higher than expected wage level. This type of variance is typically beyond the control of lower-level managers, since wage levels are usually defined at a company level, and are affected by unions, legislation and pressures in the labour market. It may also have been caused by hiring more skilled staff. If so, we must investigate if higher skills allowed higher efficiency (captured in the next variance you will learn) or a better quality product (for example, potentially improving sales variances).

Labour efficiency variance

The labour efficiency variance compares hours actually used with hours expected to be needed: that is, the flexed quantity of the input, considering the actual production volume. See in Table 9.1 that DrinkNat estimated that a worker should need 0.02 DLH to obtain one bottle of smoothie. In general:

the **labour efficiency variance** is the difference between direct labour flexed hours (FH) and actual hours used (AH), valued at the standard wage rate (sr), that is,

$$(FH - AH) \times sr = (110,000 \text{ units} \times 0.02 \text{ DLH/unit} - 2,500 \text{ DLH}) \times £10.00/\text{DLH}$$
$$= -300 \text{ DLH} \times £10.00/\text{DLH}$$
$$= £3,000U$$

Note the absolute similarity with the material usage variance. In the appendix to this chapter, you can see how to gain further insights by splitting this variance into direct labour mix and yield variances. The section below gives a 'real-world' interpretation.

A 'real-world' interpretation: what do labour efficiency variances really mean?

The unfavourable £3,000 variance means that more hours were used than expected. The most direct interpretation suggests lower performance from operational staff. If this was the case, this may compromise the above hypothesis that the unfavourable wage rate was due to hiring more efficient staff, and may call for additional training or closer supervision.

However, there are other alternatives, involving both the industrial area and beyond. Remember that we hypothesized that purchased bottles might have been of lower quality; could this have caused lower labour efficiency? Poorly maintained machines may also have affected efficiency beyond the line workers' responsibility; this calls for better maintenance. The production method may actually be less efficient than expected; this requires a production method redesign. Finally, commercial staff may have accepted last-minute orders, disrupting production plans and methods, calls for more than expected labour hours; this increasing awareness resulting in on the part of commercial staff about these problems, and closer communication between the commercial and manufacturing areas.

Finally, remember that standards were set through an engineering approach, before operations started. As noted about material usage, standards may have been excessively demanding; if so, the time standard should be adjusted to the normal, predictable efficiency of DrinkNat's staff. Alternatively, perhaps staff were still gaining experience during the first year of DrinkNat's operations; if it is expected that in the next year staff will have reached higher experience and skill levels, then standards may already be appropriate.

Total labour variance

Total labour variance aggregates wage rate and labour efficiency variances, in a similar way to Exhibit 9.3 (on materials). So:

Total **labour variance** is the difference between labour flexed costs (FC) and actual costs (AC), that is:

FC – AC [for labour costs]

DrinkNat's total labour variance is 2,500U + 3,000U = 5,500U. Again, since total variance compares flexed and actual costs (the last column of Table 9.5), it can also be calculated as $(FH \times sr) - (AH \times ar)$.

Variable overhead variances

Variable overheads (VOH) are allocated to products based on the standard allocation rate and the allocation base volume (remember that DrinkNat choose machine hours – MH – as the allocation base). But which volume? Standard costing systems consider the flexed volume of MH.

Worked Example 9.6

Calculating allocated variable overheads

Based on:

- actual production volume (110,000 units of MangOrange)
- the standard quantity of MH (0.04 MH/unit),

DrinkNat could anticipate using 4,400 MH.

Using the standard allocation rate of £7.50/MH (Calculated in *Worked Example 9.2*, by dividing £30,000 budgeted VOH and 4,000 MH), you will allocate:

$$4,400 \text{ MH} \times £7.50/\text{MH} = £33,000 \text{ VOH}$$

Check that this figure is in DrinkNat's flexed budget (Table 9.5).

Remember from Table 9.4 that this way to allocate OH (based on the flexed volume of the allocation base) is different from normal costing systems, which allocate overheads according to the actual volume of the allocation base.

There are two VOH variances: (1) the VOH spending variance; and (2) the VOH efficiency variance. They are similar to price/wage rate and usage/efficiency variances of direct costs. The difference is that VOH variances focus on the allocation base (MH, in DrinkNat's case), rather than on the input (materials and DLH for the variances of direct costs). So, keep in mind that, in VOH variances, quantities and rates refer to the allocation base.

Variable overhead spending variance

The VOH spending variance is based on comparing standard and actual VOH rates.

Worked Example 9.7

Variable overhead spending variance

Check again that the standard VOH rate is £7.50/MH.

You can see in Table 9.5 that actual VOH spending is £31,000. Additionally, consider that 5,000 MH were used (this figure had not been provided before).

The actual VOH rate divides actual VOH spending by the actual allocation base volume, that is, £31,000/5,000 MH = £6.20/MH – lower than the standard.

The favourable difference is then applied to the allocation base actual volume.

In general:

the **variable overhead *spending* variance** is the difference between the standard rate (*sr*) and actual rate (*ar*) of variable overheads, applied to the actual volume of the allocation base (actual hours, AH), that is,

$$(sr - ar) \times AH = (£7.50/MH - £6.20/MH) \times 5,000 \text{ MH}$$

$$= £1.30/MH \times 5,000 \text{ MH} = £6,500F$$

The actual rate of £6.20/MH, below the standard rate (£7.50/MH) might seem unexpected, since actual VOH (£31,000) exceeded the static budget estimate (£30,000) by 3.3 per cent; however, at the same time, note that actual MH exceed the initial estimate by a far greater percentage (+25 per cent). The next section shows which 'real-world' factors may be behind this.

A 'real-world' interpretation: what do VOH spending variances really mean?

Keep in mind that in real life VOH are typically highly diversified, including energy and indirect materials and labour. So, only a detailed analysis may provide useful insights. However, let us continue to assume that in DrinkNat's case VOH refer almost exclusively to energy used by machines, measured in kilowatts per hour (kWh).

DrinkNat's favourable VOH spending variance may have been obtained by:

1) lower prices of VOH items (the kWh price) – for example, due to economic slowdown, electricity market prices may have fallen below initial expectations; and/or

2) greater efficiency in using VOH items (kWh) per unit of the allocation base (MH). In turn, this greater efficiency may result from: lower consumption of VOH items (kWh), and/or more MHs. To reduce energy consumption, operational staff may have lowered some machine settings – for example, temperatures applied to the juice. However, this operational saving might compromise final product quality. If any defective products are not detected and rejected by DrinkNat, it may create public health risks, with devastating marketing and financial consequences – and a serious ethical issue.

Note that the MH efficiency in producing MangOrange units does not directly impact this particular variance. Also note that adopting an allocation base which accurately drives VOH costs is important. Suppose that DrinkNat's selected allocation base was direct labour hours, DLH, rather than machine hours. This alternative allocation base would probably be quite unrelated to machine energy consumption. To reduce energy consumption, operational staff may have switched machines off during every idle moment, beyond technical recommendations; this would lower VOH and, since DLH would not be affected, would lead to a favourable VOH spending variance. However, do not forget that a favourable variance in one factor may actually represent added costs in other factors. For instance, turning machines on and off too frequently may degrade machine, condition and require greater maintenance costs in the medium term.

Variable overhead efficiency variance

Given actual production, DrinkNat's flexed volume of the allocation base was 4,400 MH (see above), lower than the 5,000 MH actual volume. This unfavourable difference of MH, valued at the standard VOH rate, leads to an unfavourable VOH efficiency variance. More generally:

the **variable overhead *efficiency* variance** is the difference between the allocation base flexed volume (flexed hours, FH) and actual volume (actual hours, AH), valued at the standard variable overhead rate (*sr*), that is,

$$(FH - AH) \times sr = (110,000 \text{ units} \times 0.40 \text{ MH/unit} - 5,000 \text{ MH}) \times £7.50/MH$$

$$= -600 \text{ MH} \times £7.50/MH = £4,500U$$

In spite of the calculation similarity, the efficiency variances regarding VOH and direct costs have different meanings. Do not forget that VOH variances focus on the allocation base, not on the input (kWh). So, DrinkNat's unfavourable VOH efficiency variance does not suggest waste of VOH items, such as electricity. Instead, the unfavourable variance is caused by the higher volume of the allocation base; it merely reflects the facts that 600 more machine hours were used than expected to produce 110,000 units. Of course, if VOH are mostly related to energy consumed by machines, then additional 600 MH should cause additional VOH. But should a 'cause-effect' relationship not really hold, then this variance would not capture differences in the consumption of the main input, energy. This would be the case of the above examples, of machines being adjusted to change energy consumption per hour, or of selecting a somewhat arbitrary allocation base as DLH, instead of MH.

Total variable overhead variance

Total VOH variance aggregates the two variances, as previously described for total variance of direct inputs (see Exhibit 9.3). In DrinkNat's case, this amounts to 6,500F + 4,500U = 2,000F. In general,

> *Total* **variable overhead variance** is the difference between flexed costs (*FC*) and actual costs (*AC*) for variable overhead items, that is:

$$FC - AC \text{ [for VOH]}$$

Note that, like for materials and direct labour, this variance compares flexed and actual costs (as in Table 9.5), that is, it is also equal to $(FH \times sr) - (AH \times ar)$.

Bear in mind that a standard costing system allocates VOH to production according to flexed hours, as in the flexed budget (£33,000). Since actual VOH were only £31,000, there was a £2,000 over-allocation of costs. So, recording this favourable £2,000 VOH variance lowers recorded costs, reconciling standard costing valuation (of production and sales) and actual results.

Fixed overhead variances (under variable costing)

Fixed overhead variances differ whether we are on a variable or an absorption standard costing system. Do not forget that we have been considering a variable costing system – a choice which so far has only been relevant to the sales margin volume variance. This section completes the analysis of standard variable costing by analysing fixed overhead variances. The next section will analyse standard absorption costing systems.

The fixed overhead spending variance

In a standard variable costing system, fixed overheads (FOH) are directly charged to the income statement as a period cost, without being allocated to products. So, there is one single FOH variance:

> The **fixed overhead *spending* variance** compares budgeted costs (BC) and actual costs (AC) in FOH items, that is:

$$BC - AC$$

DrinkNat budgeted for £20,000 but actual FOH amounted to £25,000, causing a £5,000 unfavourable variance, as in Table 9.5.

The existence of a spending variance of fixed costs is not illogical. It is true that fixed costs are affected mainly by long-term decisions and are not expected to change within their relevant range. That is why they are the same in DrinkNat's static and flexible budgets. However, prices and/or quantities of FOH items can vary, and so will final actual spending; for example, increases in salaries of manufacturing staff not directly involved in production or greater machine maintenance costs.

Again, remember that FOH are a lump sum of highly diversified items, so a detailed disaggregation across the various items is indispensible for meaningful analysis.

Unlike the other types of costs, there is no efficiency variance concerning FOH; only the spending variance exists. Why? Because fixed costs are associated with the creation and maintenance of a given capacity, not with the usage of that capacity. So, more or less efficient usage of capacity does not affect fixed costs. However, that does not mean that the capacity usage level is economically irrelevant; it *is* relevant, and underlies the FOH volume variance, under absorption costing, as you will learn in the next section.

Standard absorption costing: allocation and variances

Fixed overhead allocation under standard absorption costing

In a standard absorption costing system, we unitize FOH and calculate standard FOH allocation rates. Remember that DrinkNat chose machine hours (MH) as the allocation base, using budgeted capacity utilization of 4,000 MH as the denominator. Given the £20,000 budgeted FOH, the standard FOH allocation rate is £5.00/MH (see Table 9.1 and *Worked Example 9.3*).

Standard absorption costing treats FOH *as if* they were variable. It allocates FOH to products based on the flexed allocation base (or actual production) volume and on the standard allocation rate – similar to the approach for variable overheads. We already know that producing the actual volume should require 4,400 MH (the flexed allocation base volume for FOH is the same as for VOH, given the same allocation base, MH). Based on the £5.00/MH standard FOH rate, DrinkNat allocated £22,000. (Note that, in single-product DrinkNat, the same allocation can be calculated by multiplying actual production of 110,000 units by the £0.20/unit standard cost).

To summarize: the flexible budget now reflects allocated FOH, based on the flexed allocation base volume. This contrasts with a variable costing system, in which the flexed budget had the same FOH of the static budget.

The two following tables describe what changes in standard absorption costing.

● A revised sales margin volume variance (Table 9.6).

● A total FOH variance, divided into two variances (Table 9.7).

    – the same FOH spending variance as in variable costing

    – a new FOH volume variance.

These three variances are explained next.

All other variances (concerning the sales price and direct costs) remain as in standard variable costing.

Table 9.6 Static and flexible budgets – and the sales volume variance (under absorption costing) (compare with Table 9.3, under variable costing)

	STATIC BUDGET			FLEXIBLE BUDGET			Sales volume variance	
	Standard prices/rates	Budgeted quantity	Static budget	Standard price/rate	Flexed quantity	Flexible budget		
Sales	£2.50	100,000 units	250,000	£2.50	110,000 units	275,000	25,000	F
All variable costs	(...)	(...)	150,000	(...)	(...)	165,000	15,000	U
Contribution			100,000			110,000	10,000	F
Total fixed overheads			20,000	£5.00	4,400 MH	22,000	2,000	U
Operating profit			80,000			88,000	8,000	F

Table 9.7: Flexible budget, actual results and flexible budget variances (under absorption costing) (compare with Table 9.5, under variable costing)

	FLEXIBLE BUDGET			ACTUAL RESULTS			Flexible budget variances	
	Standard price/rate	Flexed quantity	Flexible budget	Actual price	Actual quantity	Actual figures		
Sales	£ 2.50	110,000 units	275,000	£2.00	110,000 units	220,000	55,000	U
All variable costs	(...)	(...)	165,000	(...)	(...)	179,000	14,000	U
Contribution			110,000			41,000	69,000	U
Total fixed overheads	£ 5.00	4,400 MH	22,000			25,000	3,000	U
Operating profit			88,000			16,000	72,000	U

Sales margin volume variance (in standard absorption costing)

Check again DrinkNat's standard cost sheet in Table 9.1. In absorption costing, a FOH cost of £0.20/unit is deducted to the £1.00/unit standard contribution margin, leading to a lower £0.80/unit standard profit margin and allocated FOH of (110,000 units × 0.04 MH/unit) × £5.00/MH = £22,000 (as you have seen, in DrinkNat's single product company, you can also calculate allocations directly from the output: 110,000 units × £0.20/unit). This lower margin is used to value differences between budgeted and actual volumes, hence reducing the sales margin volume variance. In general:

under absorption costing, the sales margin *volume* variance is the difference between actual sales volume (AV) and budgeted sales volume (BV), valued at the standard profit margin (*spm*), that is:

$$\text{Sales margin volume variance} = (AV - BV) \times spm$$

$$= (110,000 - 100,000) \text{ units} \times £0.80/\text{unit}$$

$$= 10,000 \text{ units} \times £0.80/\text{unit}$$

$$= £8,000F$$

The lower unit margin explains why this variance drops £2,000, from £10,000 F under variable costing. Another perspective also explains this. Since under absorption costing FOH are treated as if they were variable, the higher actual production increased FOH allocation to £22,000. This is £2,000 more than in the flexed budget under variable costing, which keeps the £20,000 FOH initially budgeted. Logically, more allocated FOH reduce the sales margin volume variance.

Fixed overhead spending variance

The fixed overhead *spending* variance is the same in both costing systems. It reconciles budgeted and actual FOH, that is, BC − AC = 5,000U, as you learned in the previous section about variable costing.

Fixed overhead volume variance

The FOH volume variance is related with actual volume having used more or less production capacity than budgeted. Since fixed costs do not vary according to capacity usage, leaving capacity unused means missing the opportunity to produce some units at zero (fixed) cost.

DrinkNat's higher than budgeted production volume was favourable because it meant better capacity utilization, but also led to higher FOH allocation (£22,000, £2,000 more than in the static budget). But since fixed costs are not affected by volume variations within their relevant range, from an economic point of view these £2,000 are not 'real' costs. There was an over-allocation of FOH. A favourable FHO volume variance 'offsets' these 'fictitious' costs, bringing recorded FOH back to £20,000 as budgeted. In general:

the **fixed overhead *volume* variance** is the difference between flexed capacity utilization (flexed MH, FH) and budgeted capacity utilization (budgeted MH, BH), valued at the standard FOH rate (*sr*), that is,

FOH volume variance = (FH − BH) × *sr*

$$= (110,000 \text{ units} \times 0.04 \text{ MH/unit} − 4,000 \text{ MH}) \times £5.00/\text{MH}$$

$$= 400 \text{ MH} \times £5.00/\text{MH} = £2,000 \text{ F}$$

Note that in single-product companies like DrinkNat, this variance can be calculated directly from actual and budgeted production, valued at the FOH standard unit cost: (110,000 − 100,000) units × £0.20/unit = 2,000F.

Because of these 10,000 extra MangOrange units, the volume variance is favourable by £2,000. However, note that the 'real' gain from the extra units is their contribution (10,000 units × £1.00/unit = £10,000, the sales volume variance), *not* the FOH volume variance. You can think of the FOH volume variance as the 'free lunch' of producing those extra 10,000 units, at no extra fixed costs.

For the sake of clarity, let us examine the opposite scenario of only 90,000 units actual production, 10,000 less than budgeted. Following the same steps above, less FOH would be allocated: 90,000 units × £0.02/unit = £18,000. Having £2,000 less FOH would increase profit in the flexible budget. However, capacity usage would be lower, while fixed costs would remain similar; this is an unfavourable situation. The unfavourable FOH volume variance of £2,000 would represent the (fixed) cost proportional to the 10,000 units that were not produced. This variance would add to £18,000 allocated FOH to total the same £20,000 as budgeted.

The FOH volume variance can be divided into FOH volume efficiency and volume capacity variances. However, this further division does not seem to be used much in practice (Dugdale et al., 2006) and it is not analysed here. A 'real-world' interpretation can be found in the section below.

A 'real-world' interpretation: what do FOH volume variances really mean?

We commented that DrinkNat's favourable FOH volume variance is advantageous because it obtained additional MangOrange units without incurring in additional (fixed) costs. The opposite applies to unfavourable FOH volume variances. This is true, but there is more to it – especially if you take behavioural implications into account.

Pressure to obtain 'favourable' results promotes production managers' efforts to achieve the highest possible capacity utilization. But this may be at the expense of other costs. If demand slows down, keeping high levels of production increases inventories – sometimes causing significant costs, such as inventories holding costs and potential devaluation. Inventory costs may be significant, even in industries typically operating with low inventories, as you will explore in *Management Accounting in Practice 20.4* on hardware manufacturers. Critics accuse standard costing (or, rather, its misguided application) of promoting behaviours at odds with modern production methods, like just in time, aiming at low or even zero inventory levels (see Chapter 20). In addition, trying to increase sales to meet budgeted volumes (and avoid an unfavourable FOH volume variance) may require lowering prices for the entire quantity produced, leading to a globally lower profit.

So, an unfavourable FOH volume variance, caused by reduced production levels, may actually be a consequence of an appropriate response to lower demand. This justifies one of the main criticisms to standard costing – not because of the technique itself, but because of the potential dysfunctional effects when avoiding unfavourable variances becomes a target per se, regardless of a wider organizational view.

Finally, an unfavourable FOH volume variance does necessarily mean that existing capacity is excessive. First, since DrinkNat's FOH allocation rates were based on budgeted capacity (rather than normal or practical capacity), this variance actually tells us nothing about existing capacity (see p. 207). Second, an unfavourable variance does not mean excessive capacity even when practical capacity underlies allocation rates. Defining practical capacity is a strategic decision that cannot be adjusted in the short term. A sudden surge of demand beyond current capacity cannot be satisfied, leading to lost contribution and even a permanent loss of customers. The alternatives of building inventories against unexpected demand spikes are also costly and risky. So, maintaining some excess capacity may make sense to ensure short-term flexibility and is indeed indispensible in modern just-in-time environments.

Total fixed overhead variance

You may have found strange adding (or subtracting) FOH variance to allocated FOH, always totalling £20,000 budgeted FOH. After all, we are supposed to head towards actual profit, not budgeted profit! Well, you must bring the £5,000U FOH spending variance into the picture. DrinkNat adds both FOH variances, totalling £5,000U + £2,000F = £3,000U – the total FOH variance in Table 9.7. This unfavourable variance increases reported costs, adding to the £22,000 FOH in the flexible budget (allocated to production in standard costing) to obtain the £25,000 actual FOH. Exhibit 9.4 depicts overall variances formation.

So, in general:

The ***total* fixed overhead variance** is the difference between flexed costs (FC) and actual costs (AC) for fixed overhead items, that is,

$$FC - AC \text{ [for FOH]}$$

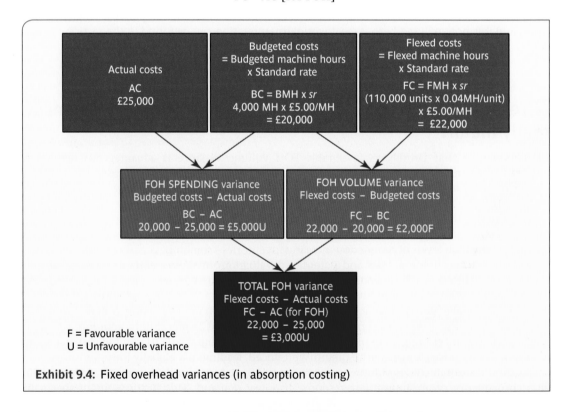

Exhibit 9.4: Fixed overhead variances (in absorption costing)

When to investigate variances?

Variances can orient management by exception, directing attention to areas with more significant issues and greater potential for improvement. Not all reported variances are worth the cost of investigating them. The significance, underlying causes and potential benefit of correction of each variance are different.

What is a 'significant' variance? Some popular rules of thumb define acceptable ranges for variation around each standard. They define upper and lower control limits, based on a certain absolute amount (for example, £2,500) and/or a certain percentage (for example, 10 per cent). If a variance is within the defined ranges, we may attribute it to random factors and consider the process still to be in control; in such case, no action would be taken. However, if a variance falls outside at least one of those ranges, then there may be a specific, non-random factor, requiring closer attention. For example, in Exhibit 9.3, the unfavourable usage variance of oranges was £2,000, that is, 6.06 per cent higher than the expected £33,000. This variance was within the absolute range (£2,500) but outside the relative range (5 per cent), hence recommending further investigation.

Different inputs should have specific acceptable ranges, to reflect differences in:

● inputs relevance. In an immaterial item, even a high relative variance may be irrelevant, and vice versa.

● inputs natural variability. Flexed wages are only £25,000 and wage rates typically do not vary widely; this suggests setting a tighter range (for example, £2,000 and 2 per cent). DrinkNat's unfavourable wage rate variance of £2,500, 10 per cent more than budgeted £25,000, falls outside both ranges and should be investigated.

Another aspect to consider is the 'real-life' factors that caused the variance. Reported variances may merely result from incorrect data entry, either by accountants or non-accountants. Pure human error in recording material or labour usage is common, especially when data entry is manual. The increasing adoption of integrated enterprise resource planning (ERP) systems have drastically reduced the number of data-entry operations and associated risks, but they are no automatic panacea, either. For example, often non-accountants enter operational data following non-accounting criteria and logic, or do not have the 'data discipline' required in accounting – and such data ripples through the integrated system directly into accounting calculations. This may create variances which do not represent operational performance issues (on this, see Chapter 21 and illuminating interview quotations in Dechow and Mouritsen (2005, pp. 712–13). Such problems may call for better integrated systems, more training or more sensitizing of non-accounting staff to accounting logics and rules.

When an unfavourable variance was indeed caused by to poor operational performance, we need to evaluate whether the underlying problem is likely to recur or not. If not, no action is needed. But if it is likely to recur, we need to establish: (1) if the problem can be solved, and (2) if the expected cost–benefit relationship of solving the problem is advantageous. Variance analysis may be extremely valuable to identify and evaluate improvement possibilities, but improving performance often has a price tag. If either of the two above answers is negative, then it may be preferable to simply adjust the standard.

Setting acceptable ranges for variations around each standard, whether absolute or relative, requires considerable business knowledge and even intuition, but it is quite subjective. Statistical methods allow greater objectivity, setting ranges based on the average (the standard) and standard deviation (δ) of past performance, assuming a normal distribution. Typically, a variance should be investigated when outside the control limits = mean ± 2 standard deviations, or when variances show a steady trend towards such limit even if it has not been reached yet.

Standard costing and variance analysis: now and the future

In line with budgets, analysed in the previous chapter, standard costs and variance analysis have been criticized. At this chapter outset, we noted that standard costing is not applicable in all production settings – in particular, when output units or production methods are not standardized, or drastically and frequently change. Throughout the chapter, we cautioned that the use (or misuse) of variance analysis can promote undesirable behavioural outcomes – for example, pursuing favourable material price variances and labour efficiency variances may result in neglecting quality, and pursuing favourable fixed overhead volume variances may lead to excessive production and inventories. This is the risk of myopia, when attaining standards – particularly through cost reduction – becomes the main goal per se, overlooking wider and more important organizational interests. These risks have fuelled criticisms of standard costing.

We also noted how insights from variances may be too late, and that timely and even anticipatory information is crucial for managers. There is also the risk of perpetuating the status quo, when employees are only expected to achieve – rather than outperform – standards. Today's increasingly changing business and technological conditions render standard costs obsolete faster, and if they are not quickly updated, variance analysis will be distorted. (Kaizen costing, the Japanese approach to standards, mentioned in this chapter and developed in Chapter 19, addresses this problem by constantly revising standards to reflect continuous attempts at improvement.) Finally, as products' life cycles become increasingly shorter, so do the validity of their standard costs.

However, research persistently reports the popularity of standard costing and variance analysis. In the latest CIMA survey (CIMA, 2009), variance analysis was in the fourth position among all management accounting techniques, with over 70 per cent of adopters. Among costing tools, variance analysis came first. Standard costing ranked third and approached a 50 per cent adoption rate. Flexible budgeting was only sixth among nine budgeting tools (around 30 per cent adoption). However, even if not very explicitly and autonomously reported, the flexible budgeting rationale underlies variance analysis (the most popular technique), and still outranks most 'modern' budgeting approaches discussed in the next chapter.

The Chartered Institute of Management Accountants' (CIMA's) results are consistent with research over the past 20 years, highlighting the continuing popularity of standard costing and variance analysis. Examples include Dugdale et al., 2006 (the UK), Hyvönen, 2005 (Finland), Joshi, 2001 (India), Chenhall and Langfield-Smith, 1998 (Australia), Guilding et al., 1998 (New Zealand and the UK) and Drury et al., 1993. In China, Wu et al. (2007) found that these techniques had a modest, mid-rank position with regard to perceived benefits and, in state-owned enterprises, a very low expected future emphasis. The authors attributed this low emphasis to expectations, in spite of significant reforms in these companies, that management accounting mostly supports inventory costing and cost budgeting, not decision making. Arguably, this is a radically different perspective on contemporary (or, at least, western) management accounting.

Note that companies use techniques in a selective and adapted way, to suit their particular business characteristics and managerial needs and to avoid adopting features not suitable to their particular case. Dugdale et al. (2006) noted that many companies calculated direct material and labour variances, but not overhead variances. In addition, for each variance, detail differed across companies. Some companies used simplified measures (for instance, not separating material price and usage variances). In contrast, other companies developed more sophisticated analyses, such as calculating an additional material exchange rate variance, to distinguish between exchange and 'non-exchange' rate impacts.

Persistently high adoption rates do not invalidate criticisms to standard costing and variance analysis. For example, Hyvönen's (2005) respondents anticipated a dramatic fall in future emphasis on these techniques and Dugdale et al. (2006) also confirmed criticisms and anticipated decline. In the next chapter (developing a critique and alternatives to budgeting, a technique often related with standards), Chapter 19 (focusing on value creation) and Chapter 20 (analysing quality and time) you can explore this debate further.

Chapter summary

This chapter focused on standard costing and variance analysis – traditional but widely used techniques. You learned various notions of standards and assumptions, objectives and processes of their calculation, linking them to relevant managerial issues. Then, you realized the difficulty of directly comparing initially budgeted and actual figures, and the solutions allowed by flexible budgeting and variance analysis. As you explored each variance throughout the chapter, you found 'real-world' interpretations of variances, to highlight their managerial usefulness, beyond strictly accounting objectives. You briefly explored criteria to investigate (or not) each variance and finalized by contrasting the persistent popularity and increasing criticisms around these techniques.

Key terms

Favourable variances Variances that mean an increase in profit, due to: (1) actual revenues higher than budgeted, or (2) actual costs lower than budgeted; identified as 'F' (p. 210)

Fixed overhead spending variance Difference between budgeted costs (BC) and actual costs (AC) in FOH items; valid in both variable and absorption standard costing (p. 222)

Fixed overhead volume variance (Only in absorption costing) difference between flexed capacity utilization and budgeted capacity utilization, valued at the standard fixed overhead rate (p. 225)

Flexible budget (or flexed budget) Budget produced after a period finishes, adjusting (flexing) the initial estimates to the actual volume of activity, in order to calculate flexed quantities, revenues and costs (p. 207)

Flexible budget variances Comparisons between actual results and the flexible budget; these comparisons are meaningful because both budgets consider the actual activity level (p. 211)

Labour efficiency variance Difference between direct labour flexed hours and actual hours used, valued at the standard wage rate (p. 219)

Material price variance Difference between the standard price and the actual price per unit of material, applied to the actual quantity purchased (p. 214)

Material usage variance Difference between the flexed quantity of materials required and the actual quantity of materials used, valued at the standard material price (p. 216)

Sales margin volume variance Under variable standard costing, it is the difference between actual sales volume and budgeted sales volume, valued at the standard contribution margin; under absorption standard costing, it is the same difference, valued at the standard profit margin (p. 210)

Sales price variance Difference between the actual price and the standard price, applied to the actual sales volume (p. 211)

Standard costs Expected costs of one unit of output, under normal conditions (p. 198)

Static budget Budget produced before a period starts, based on initial estimates (p. 207)

Static budget variances Comparisons between actual results and the static budget, typically meaningless because they refer to different activity levels (p. 207)

Total fixed overhead variance (Only in absorption costing) difference between flexed costs and actual costs for fixed overhead items (p. 226)

Total labour variance Difference between labour flexed costs and actual costs (p. 219)

Total material variance Difference between material flexed costs and actual costs (p. 217)

Total sales margin variance Difference between actual contribution (based on standard costs) and budgeted contribution (p. 212)

Total variable overhead variance Difference between flexed costs and actual costs for variable overhead items (p. 222)

Unfavourable variances Variances that mean a decrease in profit, due to (1) actual revenues lower than budgeted, or (2) actual costs higher than budgeted; identified as 'U' (p. 212)

Variable overhead efficiency variance Difference between the allocation base flexed volume and actual volume, valued at the standard variable overhead rate (p. 221)

Variable overhead spending variance Difference between the standard rate and actual rate of variable overheads, applied to the actual volume of the allocation base (p. 220)

Variance analysis Technique of calculating variances and identifying their 'real-life' causes (p. 198)

Wage rate variance Difference between the standard wage rate and the actual rate per hour of direct labour, applied to the actual number of hours used (p. 218)

● ● ● ● Review questions ● ● ● ● ● ● ● ● ● ● ● ● connect ● ● ●

Level of difficulty:	BASIC	INTERMEDIATE	ADVANCED

9.1 What may standard costs and variance analysis be used for? [LO1]

9.2 What are the main information sources for setting standards? [LO2]

9.3 Should standards reflect ideal performance? Why/why not? [LO2]

9.4 Which organizational characteristics make standard costing more applicable? [LO2]

9.5 Why is flexible budgeting necessary? [LO4]

9.6 How can variance analysis promote 'Management by exception'? [LO8]

9.7 How do you decide whether you should further investigate a given variance or not? [LO8]

9.8 What are the main criticisms directed towards standard costing and variance analysis? Are criticisms mostly directed towards technical characteristics or to behavioural dysfunctions? [LO9]

● ● ● Group discussion and activity questions ● ● ● ● ● ● ● ●

9.9 John and Peter are planning to create a business: selling fun T-shirts, after printing an amusing picture, typically designed by a design team. The users will examine and order the T-shirts through a website and the T-shirts will be shipped by a postal company. John argues that because they have no previous experience, they cannot draw upon historical costs to calculate standard costs. But Peter has a different opinion and suggests another approach. [LO1, LO2]

    a) What may Peter's opinion and suggestion be? Explore both lines of arguments.

    b) Discuss if standard costing is useful for this business.

9.10 'It is impossible to apply standard costing and variance analysis to services.' Discuss this sentence. [LO1, LO2]

9.11 Read *Management Accounting in Practice 9.2* again. Find examples of companies in other industries announcing ethical practices that increase operational costs, due to higher standard input quantities and/or prices. [LO1]

    a) Discuss possible reasons why those companies have decided to adopt such ethical practices.

    b) Discuss if the companies should separately account for these added costs in their standard cost system.

● ● ● Exercises ● ● ● ● ● ● ● ● ● ● ● ● ● ● ● ● ● connect ● ● ●

E9.1 **Calculation of standard unit cost and static budget [LO2, LO4]**

A company produces one single product, using mostly manual processes to assemble two materials – a metal material 'MM' and a wood material 'WM', both measured in kilograms. Managers are expecting to produce and sell 10,000 units next month. It adopts standard variable costing.

Required:

a) Considering that materials standard prices and used quantities per unit are:

  MM: £5.00/kg; 2 kgs/unit,
  WM: £3.00/kg; 4 kgs/unit,

  Calculate a static budget for materials, for the planned production volume.

b) Determine how much the company usually pays per direct labour hour, considering that operators usually need 2 hours to assemble one unit and that the direct labour cost in the static budget was £200,000.

c) The variable overhead rate is calculated based on budgeted direct labour hours. Calculate the VOH rate and the VOH unit cost, considering that budgeted costs were £100,000.

d) Fixed overheads were estimated to be £50,000. What is the figure for FOH in the static budget?

e) Calculate the standard unit cost.

f) The company plans to sell all its monthly production at a selling price of £60,00/unit. Considering all the above information, calculate the budgeted profit.

E9.2 **Calculation of flexible budget and variances [LO4, LO6]**

Consider the company and all data indicated in E9.1. The business activity conducted during the month led to the following information:

Sales: 11,000 units @ £62.00/unit
Purchased MM: 21,000 kg @ £5.00/kg
Purchased WM: 46,000 kg @ £2.50/kg
Direct labour: 21,000 hours @ £10.00/hour
Variable overheads: £110,000
Fixed overheads: £25,000

Required:

Calculate:

a) The actual monthly operating profit.

b) The flexible budget reflecting the actual activity of this month.

c) Sales variances.

d) Direct inputs variances (for materials and direct labour).

e) Overhead variances (for variable and fixed overheads).

E9.3 **Calculation of standard unit cost, flexible cost budget, variances; interpretation of variances [LO3, LO4, LO6, LO7]**

Plastic Co. manufactures a component for the construction industry, based on plastic which is then painted, through a relatively simple, labour intensive process. Based on historical data, the company calculated the following standards concerning direct inputs:

Plastic: 2 kg @ £15.00/kg
Paint: 0.1 litres @ £20.00/litre
Direct labour: 0.5hrs @ £10.00/hr

Plastic Co. recorded the following data regarding last month operations:

- Units produced: 10,000 units
- Plastic purchased: 21,000 kg @ £16.00/kg
- Paint purchased: 1,050 litres @ £18.00/litre
- Direct labour: 4,600 hrs @ £10.50/hr

There were no beginning or ending inventories.

Required:

a) Calculate the standard prime cost card of the product.

b) Calculate the flexible cost budget for the actual production level.

c) Calculate total, price and usage variances for direct materials.

d) Calculate total, wage rate and efficiency variances for direct labour.

e) Interpret reported variances, trying to identify possible 'real-life' factors and relations between them.

f) Who is the likely responsible for the variances, according to the possible causing factor you identified in the previous answer? What can Plastic Co. do to improve?

g) Discuss Plastic Co.'s risks of setting standards based on historic data.

E9.4   **Calculation of standard unit costs, flexible budget and variances [LO3, LO4, LO6, LO7]**

AB Systems assembles laptops and uses flexible budgeting and a standard costing system. Both variable and fixed overheads are allocated based on the number of material parts used. A performance report for June was produced as follows:

	Static budget (10,000 laptops)	**Actual results (11,000 laptops)**
Sales (£400 budget, £420 actual)	£4,000,000	£4,620,000
Manufacturing costs		
Materials (parts)	100,000	107,100
(cost £)	£1,000,000	£1,049,580
Labour (hours)	20,000	21,250
(cost £)	£280,000	£310,250
Variable manufacturing overhead (£4.00 per part budgeted, actual £4.10 per part)	£400,000	£439,110
Fixed manufacturing overhead (£)	£450,000	£465,000
Profit	£1,870,000	£2,356,060

Required:

Based on the above performance report:

a) Determine the standard cost of one laptop.

b) Prepare a flexed budget for June to support comparisons with actual results.

c) Calculate price and efficiency (usage) variances for materials and labour.

d) Calculate detailed variances for variable and fixed manufacturing overhead.

e) Calculate the sales margin variances.

f) Explain why AB Systems should calculate the sales margin volume variance based on the standard profit margin, rather than the standard contribution margin.

g) How may you confirm that the calculated variances are globally correct?

E9.5 **Standard costing and variance analysis: now and the future [LO6, LO7]**

Listed below are managers typically in the best position to influence variances related to revenues and direct costs:

a) Human Resource Manager
b) Line Operators Production Manager
c) Sales & Marketing Manager
d) Purchasing Manager

Required:

a) Match the following variances with the managers above, who are in the best position to influence that particular variance. (Note that the same manager might be responsible for more than one variance.)

Variance	Manager responsible
1) Sales margin variance	
2) Sales price variance	
3) Material price variance	
4) Material usage variance	
5) Wage rate variance	
6) Labour efficiency variance	

b) It is possible that the above variances may arise due to situations that are beyond the manager's control. Provide examples of circumstances where the manager typically considered responsible for each variance, may not actually be responsible.

E9.6 **Calculation and interpretation of variances [LO6, LO7]**

Riverside Products have produced the following standard cost card for their main product:

	Qty per unit	Cost	Unit cost £
Material A	3 kg	£6.00 per kg	£18.00
Material B	2 kg	£3.75 per Kg	£7.50
Skilled Labour	5 hours	£22.50 per hour	£112.50
Variable overhead	5 hours	£9.00 per hour	£45.00
Fixed overhead	See note 4 below		£37.50
Total standard cost			£220.50
Standard selling price			£255.00

During August 2012, the following actual details were recorded:

	Cost £
480,000 kg of material A purchased	2,887,500
320,000 kg of material B purchased	1,234,500
802,000 skilled labour hours worked	18,052,500
Variable overhead cost	7,296,000
Fixed overhead cost	6,037,500
Total expenses	35,508,000

Other information relevant to August 2012 is available as follows:

1) 160,000 units were produced. All of material A was used.

2) 2,000 kg of material B was not used.

3) 145,000 units were sold, generating revenue of £36,967,500.

4) Budgeted monthly fixed overheads are £6,000,000.

5) There were no opening or closing inventories of work in progress. Budgeted monthly fixed overheads are £6,000,000.

6) There were no opening inventories of finished goods.

7) Closing inventory of finished goods was 15,000 units.

8) All closing inventories are valued at standard cost.

9) All costs are paid by Riverside Products as incurred.

Required:

a) Calculate variances regarding revenues.

b) Calculate variances regarding direct costs.

c) Calculate variances regarding indirect costs.

d) Provide potential explanations for the usage variance of material B, also taking into account insights suggested by other variances.

E9.7 Calculation of static budget; calculation and interpretation of variances; direct materials yield and mix variances [LO4, LO6, LO7, LO9]

The 'Show' company is evaluating an entertainment site by the beach. Its 1,500 places are equally split among two physically separated areas: those more distant from the stage have cheaper tickets (standard price: £10); those closer to the stage have more expensive tickets (standard price: £20). At this time of crisis, managers estimate selling about 250 tickets for each area.

The business model is exclusively based on sold tickets, which include an unlimited number of free drinks at the bar (used by the audience from both areas). The bar offers Cheaper Drinks (CD, standard price: £0.50) and more Expensive Drinks (ED, standard price: £1). In previous years, an average spectator had one CD and two EDs. Among the costs incurred during the show, these are the only ones which depend on the number of spectators.

Estimated costs with artists, technicians and staff, and site and equipment rent, are £6,000 for each show. These costs are allocated according to estimated attendance, without distinguishing between the two areas.

Most of the audience are tourists. The shows promotion is mainly made by a commissioner who contacts the tourists. This makes the commissioner's performance crucial for the business success. The commissioner can either sell the tickets directly himself, or send the tourists to the ticket office. For the first time, the commissioner was allowed to cut down ticket prices, sold both by himself and at the ticket office. However, managers anticipated that price reductions would rarely be applied, so they did not even include them in their estimates. The commissioner gets £1 for each ticket, if at least 300 tickets are sold for a show.

One month after opening, the following data was calculated, per show:

	Tickets quantity/show	Average selling price
Cheap tickets	400	9
Expensive tickets	200	10

	Consumed quantity per person	Drinks cost (£/un.)
Cheap drinks (CD)	1	0.50
Expensive drinks (ED)	3	0.90

Commissions were paid according to agreed conditions. Staff and rental costs amounted to £6,000/show.

Managers expressed concern with obtained results.

Required:

a)   Compute the initial budget and actual results, per show.

b)   Propose a detailed variance analysis system to explain the situation, considering exclusively revenues and variable cost items. Compute suggested variances.

c)   Write a brief report (maximum 10 lines) with the insights obtained from reported variances.

d)   The manager in charge of drinks purchase and the manager of bar operations rejected responsibility for the worse than expected results. Comment (maximum 5 lines).

e)   The sales agent also rejected responsibilities, since he has succeeded in increasing sold tickets:

   i)   Comment (maximum: 5 lines).

   ii)   Relate your previous comment with the sales agent's incentive system. If adequate, propose possible alternatives to the incentive system.

f)   Now, include fixed costs in your analysis. Complement and/or change the system you previously suggested to also include fixed costs (opt for the most detailed analysis). Compute any new or changed variances.

E9.8   **Calculation and interpretation of variances [LO6, LO7]**

Chaff Co. processes and sells brown rice. It buys unprocessed rice seeds and then, using a relatively simple process, removes the outer husk of the rice to produce the brown rice. This means that there is substantial loss of weight in the process. The market for the purchase of seeds and the sales of brown rice has been, and is expected to be, stable.

   Chaff Co. uses a variance analysis system to monitor its performance.
There has been some concern about the interpretation of the variances that have been calculated in month 1.

1)   The purchasing manager is adamant, despite criticism from the production director, that he has purchased wisely and saved the company thousands of dollars in purchase costs by buying the required quantity of cheaper seeds from a new supplier.

2)   The production director is upset at being criticised for increasing the wage rates for month 1; he feels the decision was the right one, considering all the implications of the increase. Morale was poor and he felt he had to do something about it.

3)   The maintenance manager feels that saving £8,000 on fixed overhead has helped the profitability of the business. He argues that the machines' annual maintenance can wait for another month without a problem as the machines have been running well.

The variances for month 1 are as follows:

	£
Material price	48,000 (Fav)
Material usage	52,000 (Adv)
Labour rate	15,000 (Adv)
Labour efficiency	18,000 (Fav)
Labour idle time	12,000 (Fav)
Variable overhead expenditure	18,000 (Adv)
Variable overhead efficiency	30,000 (Fav)
Fixed overhead expenditure	8,000 (Fav)
Sales price	85,000 (Adv)
Sales volume	21,000 (Adv)

Note: Fav = Favourable, Adv = Adverse.

Chaff Co. uses labour hours to absorb the variable overhead.

Required:

a)   Comment on the performance of the purchasing manager, the production director and the maintenance manager using the variances and other information above and reach a conclusion as to whether or not they have each performed well.

In month 2 the following data apply:
Standard costs for 1 tonne of brown rice

- 1.4 tonnes of rice seeds are needed at a cost of £60 per tonne
- It takes 2 labour hours of work to produce 1 tonne of brown rice and labour is normally paid £18 per hour. Idle time is expected to be 10 per cent of hours paid; this is not reflected in the rate of £18 above.
- 2 hours of variable overhead at a cost of £30 per hour.
- The standard selling price is £240 per tonne.
- The standard contribution per tonne is £56 per tonne.

Budget information for month 2 is:

- Fixed costs were budgeted at £210,000 for the month.
- Budgeted production and sales were 8,400 tonnes.

The actual results for month 2 were as follows.

- Actual production and sales were 8,000 tonnes.
- 12,000 tonnes of rice seeds were bought and used, costing £660,000.
- 15,800 labour hours were paid for, costing £303,360.
- 15,000 labour hours were worked.
- Variable production overhead cost £480,000.
- Fixed costs were £200,000.
- Sales revenue achieved was £1,800,000.

b) Calculate the variances for month 2 in as much detail as the information allows and reconcile the budget profit to the actual profit using marginal costing principles. You are not required to comment on the performance of the business or its managers for their performance in month 2.

Source: adapted from Association of Chartered Accountants, Paper F5, Performance management.

E9.9   Sales volume variance [LO6, LO7]

A management accountant of a company using standard variable costing was called by top management to clarify doubts about an item of reported variances: a positive sales volume variance for fixed costs. In previous periods, this variance had a zero value, so top managers suspected of a calculation error.

Since no calculation error existed, can you help the management accountant justify what caused this variance to exist?

Case study problem • • • • • • • • • connect • • • •

C9.1   Standards in action in the health sector [LO1, LO2]

A key and contentious issue in the health sector has been defining systems to pay for the provision of health services. One of these payment systems is based on defining diagnosis-related groups (DRG) – called health-care resource groups (HRGs) in the UK. A payment system based on DRGs is based on a fixed payment per patient related to the patient's main diagnosis. For instance, a patient who had a stroke and needed a heart transplant is classified in the DRG of the corresponding transplant diagnosis. A DGR-based payment system defines standards for each DRG – the amount that will be paid to the health-care provider, by the government or other parties. The care provider will include this treatment when accounting for its total activity, in order to be reimbursed.

Systems vary significantly across countries and they have evolved throughout the decades. Boyle (2011) explains that before 2003 English hospitals were paid mainly on the basis of annual block contracts, defining a total payment based on activity estimates. So, hospitals were paid a fixed amount, regardless of the work actually carried out – that is, regardless of the actual activity level and the actual case mix.

In 2003–04, there was a major change in England, when a regulated tariff was introduced so that hospitals could be paid for the activity actually developed – that is, the actual activity level and the actual case mix. It was argued that this payment system would be an incentive to improve performance, since the same standard tariff would be applied to each treatment, regardless of the provider. This change has proved difficult to implement in England (Boyle, 2011). However, in other countries like Germany and Portugal it is widespread; for example, in Portugal DRGs have accounted for the entire in-patient budget of public hospitals since 2003, with 75–85 per cent coming from the National Health Service (NHS) and the remaining from third parties (Barros et al., 2011; Mateus, 2011; Tan et al., 2011).

Under the new regime, local commissioning reflects the volume, appropriateness and quality, but not price, since regional tariffs are used to reflect unavoidable differences in cost levels in different parts of the country. For example, it is natural that hospitals in the London area have higher costs because most inputs are more expensive in this area, for example wages of doctors and other practice staff, which may represent more than 50 per cent of total health costs. However, it is considered that drugs prices should be the same to all units. So, the standard tariffs are expected to reflect the providers' normal conditions of operation, after taking into account some regional specifics (Boyle, 2011).

This highlights the importance of the cost data underlying the defined payment tariffs at a national or regional level. Cost systems should be able to identify the costs generated by particular units of analysis – in this case, the costs of each DRG. As Tan et al. (2011) explain, considering imprecise cost data will lead to defining incorrect tariffs, which in turn will make hospitals to be overpaid or underpaid for specific DRGs. Overall, it might be argued that more profitable DRGs would compensate for less profitable DRGs, that is, there would be cross-subsidizing among DRGs. However, this creates dysfunctional incentives for hospitals. Excessive payments (induced by overestimated costs) for a specific DRG, such as strokes, reduce hospitals' incentive to improve cost performance in the area of stroke treatment. On the contrary, insufficient payments (caused by underestimated costs) for a specific DRG incentivize hospitals to reduce quality in order to lower actual costs and avoid losses. So, the correct definition of the standard cost of a particular DRG (in this example, a stroke) is crucial to provide the correct incentive for care providers, so that they achieve a balance between improving their effectiveness and providing quality care for each DRG.

Tan et al. argue that cost accounting systems facilitate comparing key performance indicators (KPIs) and benchmarking, promoting performance improvements by better managing and controlling processes. An example is hospitals using DRGs to estimate how changes in patients' volume and case mix could affect their budget, and to compare actual expenditure with expected levels. Cost accounting is also important for regulators to monitor unintended incentives that may result from a DRG-based system. Examples of unintended effects include focusing on 'profitable' patients (those to be treated for a condition in a DRG with excessive payment tariffs), up-coding of expensive DRGs to increase revenue (for example, classifying a patient has having a pneumonia, rather than a mere cold), cost minimization or shifting of treatment costs onto other parties, and reducing care quality.

So, Tan et al. conclude on a mutual implication and dependency between DRG systems and cost accounting. On one side, DRG systems require and benefit from accurate cost accounting. On the other side, cost accounting benefits since the DRG system provides a useful unit of analysis (the DRGs) and, in addition, the DRG system has given an external impetus and motivation towards developing more sophisticated cost accounting systems. The issue discussed here is both different and similar to what you have learned about standard costing and variance analysis. The discussion here is about calculating standard costs at a national/regional level, not at the level of particular organizations. However, these standard costs – and resulting standard tariffs – will provide benchmarks to be achieved by each organization and manager. Just as in the usual context described in this chapter, standards provide incentives, but in a different and potentially more effective way. These standards defined for the health sector are not mere internal targets to be achieved in order to avoid having an unfavourable variance reported in some internal report and, eventually, avoid the loss of a bonus (should compensation be tied to variances). On the contrary, these standards will directly influence the financial resources that each provider will receive. As such, the issue of calculating standards costs of each DRG has potentially far more fundamental repercussions than in most other types of organizations and industries.

Sources: Barros et al. (2011); Boyle (2011); Mateus (2011); Tan et al. (2011).

Required:

a) Are there any other examples in this chapter in which standards are used for a purpose similar to the one described in this case? Identify and discuss similarities and differences between the two examples.

b) Identify and discuss challenges of calculating standard costs for each DRG (Tan et al. offer guidance on this).

c) 'Since standard costs of DRGs are so important, we should always choose the most sophisticated cost accounting system.' Discuss.

d) Analyse the kind of system adopted for providers' reimbursements in your country (English students can explore Boyle's article in greater detail, as well as other sources. A link to the article is available online at www.mcgraw-hill.co.uk/textbooks/burns). If you have colleagues from other countries, compare the various systems.

e) Reimbursement systems based on DRGs are often controversial. Based on the above text and additional research, identify the pros and cons of such systems.

Appendix 9A: Unpacking direct inputs usage variance

You have calculated DrinkNat's material *usage* variances on page 216. Table 9.A1 shows the relevant data to calculate fruits usage variances, extracted from Table 9.5, p. 211.[3] Usage variances for oranges were £2,000U and for mangos were £1,000F, in a total of £1,000U. You will now learn how to split this usage variance, according to the mix and yield of these materials. Then, you will briefly explore the relevance of doing a similar analysis about direct labour.

Table 9A.1 Standard and actual data to calculate material mix and yield variances

	Flexible budget			Actual results			Flexible budget variances
	Standard price	Flexible quantity	Flexible budget	Actual price	Actual quantity	Actual figures	
Sales	(...)	110,000 units	(...)	(...)	110,000 units	(...)	(...)
Direct materials							
Oranges	£0.50	66,000 kgs			70,000 kgs		
Mangos	£1.00	66,000 kgs	–	–	65,000 kgs		
Total fruits		132,000 kgs			135,000 kgs		

Material mix variance

In some production processes and to limited extents, we can substitute one input for another without significantly, or at all, compromising the product existence and even its fundamental characteristics. Such is the case of fruit juice production: 'MangOrange' customers may not notice slight changes in the mix between oranges and mangos.

Check again the 'MangOrange' standard cost sheet (Table 9.1). DrinkNat's 'recipe' prescribed a 50/50 percentage mix between oranges and mangos. We assumed both fruits had the same waste level, and so obtaining one 'MangOrange' unit should require 0.6 kg + 0.6 kg = 1.2 kg of fruit.

Actual consumption of 70,000 kgs of oranges and 65,000 kgs of mangos did not respect the recipe, that is, the standard 50 per cent/50 per cent mix. The percentage of oranges increased to 70,000/135,000 = 51.85 per cent, making the actual material mix (51.85 per cent/48.15 per cent) different from the standard mix. And because materials standard prices were different, changing the mix changed total costs and created a material mix variance (Table 9.A2).

Table 9A.2: Calculating the material mix variance

	AQ (at standard mix)	(kg)	AQ (kg)	AQ(standard mix) – AQ (kg)	sp	Mix variance	
Oranges	50%	67,500	70,000	–2,500	£0.5	**(1,250)**	U
Mangos	50%	67,500	65,500	2,500	£1.0	**2,500**	F
		135,000	135,000	0		**1,250**	F

If DrinkNat had kept the standard 50 per cent/50 per cent mix, the actual consumption of 135,000 kg would consist of 67,500 kg of each fruit. However, the actual mix was different, increasing the consumption of the cheapest fruit (oranges) by 2,500 kg, matched by a (necessarily equal) decrease in the consumption of the most expensive fruit (mangos). Valuing these differences based on standard prices, we find that deviating from the standard mix lowered costs by £1,250 – a favourable material mix variance. In general:

the **material *mix* variance** is the difference, valued at the standard price, between: (1) the actual total quantity, in standard mix proportion, and (2) the actual quantity used.

Using standard prices to value this difference prevents price changes from affecting this variance – just like we did when calculating the usage variance now being split. Also note that this mix variance does not analyse the relation between inputs and outputs (the yield), since it always considers the actual quantity of materials. This yield analysis is provided by the next variance. Read the next section for a 'real-world' interpretation of what material mix variances may really mean.

A 'real-world' interpretation: what may material mix variances really mean?

We need to establish whether this shift in fruits mix was intentional or not. A common reason for intentionally changing the mix is responding to changes in material prices, increasing the percentage of materials which, during the period, became relatively cheaper when compared to others. This does not seem to be the case, since oranges actually became more expensive than expected (£0.60/kg versus £0.50/kg), while mangos price remained unchanged at £1.00/kg. But oranges were still cheaper than mangos, so we cannot rule out a possible temptation to use relatively more of the relatively cheaper fruit. If it was not intentional, then maybe the production process needs to be adjusted.

Perhaps more importantly: how favourable was this material mix really? Could this change have caused customers to like 'MangOrange' less than estimated in the initial market research, leading to a lower value perception and contributing to the dramatic drop in the selling price and margin? (Remember the huge £55,000U sales margin price variance.) If this happened, the small £1,250 cost saving has caused a marketing and financial disaster.

Material yield variance

The material yield variance measures the extent to which the inputs volume actually generated the expected output volume, based on the standard yield.

Actual yield (units)	Standard yield from actual consumption (units)	Actual – Standard yield (units)	Standard unit cost	Materials yield variance	
110,000	112,500	–2,500	£0.90	**(2,250)**	U

Producing one unit of 'MangOrange' unit should require 1.2 kg of fruits. So, the actual consumption of 135,000 kg of fruit should yield 135,000 kg/1.2 kg/unit = 112,500 units. However, only 110,000 units were obtained, 2,500 units less than expected.

Since the standard unit cost, concerning oranges and mangos, is 0.30 + 0.60 = £0.90/unit, the standard cost of the 2,500 lower yield was £2,250 – an unfavourable material yield variance. In general:

> The **material *yield* variance** is the difference between the actual yield and the standard yield, valued at standard unit costs.

Note that adding the material mix and yield variances, £1,250F + £2,250U = £1,000U leads to the fruits usage variance, calculated at the start. Read the section below for another 'real-world' interpretation of what material yield variances may really mean.

A 'real-world' interpretation: what may material yield variances really mean?

We must keep in mind that this was DrinkNat's first year of operations. It is likely that the standard yield, estimated through an engineering approach, has to be adjusted to DrinkNat's 'real' normal conditions of operation. Or maybe the unfavourable variance merely reflected some inexperience, already overcome during the second year; in this case, no action should be taken.

Unfavourable yield variances are often due to using lower quality fruits, with lower yield ratios, such as less juicy oranges. But an analysis of fruit prices does not support this hypothesis, since actual prices of both fruits are equal or greater than standards – unless, of course, prices went up only due to market pressures, and fruits indeed had lower quality and yield ratios.

Examine a final scenario in which used oranges are less juicy (that is, have a lower yield) but mangos have a higher yield than expected. Then, actual overall yield (aggregating the two fruits) may be in line with the standard yield, and material yield variance may be zero. Moreover, in this scenario, *if* we want to keep the 50 per cent/50 per cent standard mix in the final 'MangOrange' smoothie, we must increase the relative percentage of (less juicy) oranges used – and this could explain why the material mix changed. More research in the field would be needed to validate these hypotheses, emerging from 'zooming in' and 'zooming out' in variance analysis.

Direct labour mix and yield variances

Labour is a diversified and important cost component in many industries, both manufacturing and non-manufacturing. Think about large accountancy and professional services companies, like PwC and KPMG. Pay rates differ significantly from trainees up to partners. So, attributing tasks to more or less senior accountants makes a big difference in final costs. But if their work is included in one single labour cost category, with a single average wage rate, then labour efficiency variance misses important information.

So, similar to direct materials, we can split the direct labour efficiency variance into mix and yield variances. We start by differentiating labour categories (such as junior and senior) and their work hours and wage rates. Then, we can distinguish two cost impacts: the *direct labour mix variance* measures cost impacts of shifting work between junior and senior staff versus a standard mix, and the *direct labour yield variance* focuses on the relation between inputs and outputs (the yield). Variances formulas and interpretation are similar to those about direct materials, above.

Of course, final conclusions must include more than costs. For example, does the work performed by junior and senior staff have the same quality? Do clients' perceived value change when certain services are provided by more or less senior staff – even when both are equally technically capable of performing those services? Combining cost insights with market-focused business insights such as these is crucial for management accountants to provide value to their organizations.

Recommended reading ● ● ● ● ● ● ● ● ● ● ● ● ● ● ● ●

- Dugdale, D., C. Jones and S. Green (2006) Contemporary Management Accounting Practices in UK Manufacturing, London: CIMA.

The survey results and reflections provide insights on 'real-life' usage of standard costing and variance analysis (chapter 5, conclusions and recommendations) and also provides an interesting historical background (chapter 2).

- Steven, G. J. (2003) 'Ask a simple question', CIMA Insider, December/January: 20–1.

Short technical paper that further helps understanding the logic behind variances, solving exercises with data that does not 'fit' formulas and avoiding dependence on memorized formulas. Understanding these logics is a prerequisite to developing the 'real-world' interpretations emphasized in this chapter.

References ●

Barros, P., S. Machado and J. Simões (2011) 'Portugal: Health system review,' *Health Systems in Transition*, 13(4), pp. 1–156.

Boyle, S. (2011) 'United Kingdom (England): Health system review', *Health Systems in Transition*, 13(1), pp. 1–486.

Chenhall, R. H. and K. Langfield-Smith (1998) 'Adoption and benefits of management accounting practices: an Australian study', *Management Accounting Research*, 9(1), pp. 1–19.

CIMA (2009) Management accounting tools for today and tomorrow, http://www.cimaglobal.com/Thought-leadership/Research-topics/Management-accounting-in-different-sectors/Management-accounting-survey/ (accessed on 15 May 2012).

Dechow, N. and J. Mouritsen (2005) 'Enterprise resource planning systems, management control and the quest for integration', *Accounting, Organizations and Society,* 30(7–8), pp. 691–733.

Drury, C., S. Braund, P. Osborne and M. Tayles (1993) 'A survey of management accounting practices in UK manufacturing companies', ACCA Research Paper, Chartered Association of Certified Accountants.

Dugdale, D., C. Jones and S. Green (2006) *Contemporary management accounting practices in UK manufacturing,* London: CIMA.

Guilding, C., D. Lamminmaki and C. Drury (1998) 'Budgeting and standard costing practices in New Zealand and the United Kingdom', *The International Journal of Accounting,* 33(5), pp. 569–588.

Hyvönen, J. (2005) 'Adoption and benefits of management accounting systems: evidence from Finland and Australia', *Advances in International Accounting,* 18, pp. 97–120.

Joshi, P. L. (2001) 'The international diffusion of new management accounting practices: the case of India', *Journal of International Accounting, Auditing and Taxation,* 10(1), pp. 85–109.

Mateus, C. (2011) Portugal: Results of 25 years of experience with DRGs, *Diagnosis-Related Groups in Europe: Moving towards transparency, efficiency and quality in hospitals,* R. Busse, A. Geissler, W. Quentin and M. Wiley. Berkshire, McGraw-Hill: pp. 381–400.

Steven, G. J. (2000) 'Sales variances: time for the hard sell?' *CIMA Insider,* September, available at http://www1.cimaglobal.com/Documents/ImportedDocuments/CI_Sept_00_p23_24.pdf, (accessed on 7 July 2012).

Tan, S. S., L. Serdén, A. Geissler, M. van Ineveld, K. Redekop, M. Heurgren and L. Hakkaart-van Roijen (2011) 'DRGs and cost accounting: Which is driving which?' *Diagnosis-Related Groups in Europe: Moving towards transparency, efficiency and quality in hospitals,* R. Busse, A. Geissler, W. Quentin and M. Wiley. Berkshire, McGraw-Hill: pp. 59–74.

Wu, J., A. Boateng and C. Drury (2007) 'An analysis of the adoption, perceived benefits, and expected future emphasis of western management accounting practices in Chinese SOEs and JVs', *The International Journal of Accounting,* 42(2), pp. 171–185.

● ● ●   **Notes**   ●

1   See chapter 20 for additional costs due to quality failures. In particular, if defective bottles reach the customer, there is an external quality failure. Potential costs include product returns, legal costs, customer badwill, reputational costs and opportunity costs due to lost future sales. Typically, the later the problem is detected, the higher associated costs will be.

2   Note that the abbreviation for flexed costs, FC, is also commonly used for fixed costs. The expression 'flexed costs (FC)' is used in this chapter (rather than common alternatives such as 'standard costs') because it emphasizes that they are the costs that should have been incurred to obtain the actual production – that is, they have been flexed considering actual production.

3   Note that the flexible budget variances of fruits, in Table 9.5, include both the usage and the price variances (9,000U for oranges and 1,000F for mangos). Because we are now splitting the usage variance only, referring to Table 9.5 may be misleading.

When you have read this chapter

Log on to the Online Learning Centre at **www.mcgraw-hill.co.uk/textbooks/burns** to explore chapter-by-chapter test questions, links and further online study tools for Management Accounting.

CHAPTER 10

BEYOND TRADITIONAL BUDGETING

Chapter outline

- Traditional budgeting
- Beyond budgeting
- Alternative budgeting systems

Learning outcomes

On completion of this chapter, students will be able to:

LO1 Critically analyse the use of traditional budgets

LO2 Appreciate the role of alternative budgets in different industries and sectors

LO3 Illustrate the differences in the process of preparing rolling forecasts, kaizen budgets, zero-based budgets and activity-based budgets

LO4 Prepare a sales-based budget using activity-based budgeting

LO5 Discuss the nature of beyond budgeting

Introduction

In Chapter 8 we introduced traditional budgeting and discussed how a good budgeting system is used within an organization to plan, control, motivate, co-ordinate and communicate information. Chapter 9 extended your knowledge of budgets by examining the control aspect of budgeting, analysing standard costing to report the performance of the individuals or teams, within the organization. Although later in this book we will consider more sophisticated performance measurement systems (PMSs), such as the balance scorecard, you now understand that budgeting and target setting is a central focus of most organizations.

The budgeting processes detailed in Chapter 8 relates to traditional budgeting where a set future forecasts is produced and this is used to compare the actual outcomes of an event or accounting period. Within traditional budgeting there are set end dates where the comparison takes place. This chapter will present the argument against the use of traditional budgeting by examining the alternative systems. Budgeting systems such as **rolling forecasts**, **zero-based budgeting** (ZBB), **kaizen budgeting** and **activity-based budgeting** (ABB) will be explained. By examining these alternatives, you will be able to judge the advantages and disadvantages.

In addition to the alternative budgeting systems, this chapter will also consider a philosophy known as '**beyond budgeting**'. Beyond budgeting is a management way of thinking, not a system. It promotes good management thinking and innovation rather than restricting individuals to targets which are, more often than not, based on different circumstances than those the organizations are trying to adapt to. The financial crisis is a good example of how organizations have had to respond extremely quickly to maintain competitive advantage – can philosophies such as beyond budgeting provide a way of thinking that will help organizations break free from the constraints that traditional budgeting can create?

This chapter will not provide the answer as to which budgeting systems or philosophies are the best. As always, in management accounting, the role of the management accountant is to find the best fit for an individual organization, a system which will aid the strategic direction of the organization.

Traditional budgeting

In this chapter we are focusing on how budgets are prepared. Chapter 8 discussed yearly forecasts using line budgeting, which in many cases focus on volume. In many line budgets the yearly forecasts are incredibly detailed and use an incremental approach every year to update the figures within the budget. In other words they simply look at last year and add on an agreed percentage to cover inflation or an expected growth in production. Although the CIMA (2009) survey shows that yearly forecasts and incremental budgeting are still commonly used, they are renowned for the problems they can create.

Issues with traditional budgeting systems

One of the biggest problems with traditional budgeting systems is that there is a presumption that at the time the forecasts are set, the environment will remain the same for the time period in which they are used. By environment we are talking about the economy, the competitive environment, supply chain and customer preferences, for example. If a budget is set one year or three years in advance and any of these items change, such as the number of competitors in the market, your forecasts may become irrelevant because they do not meet the needs of the organization anymore.

Let us say the number of competitors in your market increases by 10 per cent, what can these competitors do that may affect your forecasts? New competitors can employ some of your current employees and this would result in you having to recruit new staff and train them to meet the needs of the jobs you are placing them in. In this case the learning-curve effect will be relevant; this is where the time taken to complete part of a process reduces the more it is completed (learning curves will be discussed in Chapter 12). The impact of training new staff will affect the training budget and may also impact on the labour budget. In addition to the impact on labour, new competitors may bring new products into the market which can make your products accelerate along the **product life cycle**, in other words your products may become outdated more quickly than you expected them to. Outdated products can place pressure on your research and design budgets because you will need to move your new product design ideas on, so you can compete at a quicker pace. These are only a couple of issues that may emerge is this circumstance.

The following two articles will give you an idea of how fast things can change in industry. Reeves and Deimler (2011) argue most traditional systems such as budgets assume that the world is predictable and relatively stable. However, as Frow et al. (2010) found, organizations are now facing economic uncertainty, new technologies, new business models and shorter product life cycles, all of which undermine the traditional budgeting systems. Considering these issues Reeves and Deimler (2011) suggest that companies, in order to remain competitive, can no longer rely on being known as excelling at something; instead they need to be really good at learning new things. To be able to respond to changes in the business environment an organization needs to provide their employees an opportunity to be creative which encourages innovation, and this means the budget or management philosophy needs to be flexible enough to deal with this.

Some chief executive officers (CEOs) have extreme views of the traditional budgeting system. For example, Jack Welch, former Chairman and CEO of General Electric is quoted as saying: 'The budgeting process at most companies has to be the most ineffective practice in management. It sucks the energy, time, fun and big dreams out of an organization. It hides opportunity and stunts growth'.[1] Jack Walsh is clearly against the use of budgets because he believes that they prevent a company from concentrating on what is important – innovation.

Some of the other general criticism of the traditional style of budgeting, using 12-month forecasts include game playing, as discussed in Chapter 8, and the issue of budgeting forecasts being very time-consuming which can distract the managers from adding value to the organization. The issue of traditional budgets focusing on costs rather than adding value to the shareholders of the organization has long been a criticism of traditional budgeting. Users of budgeting have complained that traditional budgets can be too time-consuming and therefore costly to produce. Spending time on preparing and following the budgets can prevent time being spent on improving the products or services. In addition to these criticisms, many complain that the budgets are not up to date because they are prepared infrequently and do not adjust with changes in the business environment. These criticisms are not an exhaustive list; many more will be examined by analysing the alternative methods and scrutinizing what they can overcome in terms of the problems with traditional budgeting.

Alternative budgeting systems

Alternative budgets offer organizations different ways of planning and managing their budgets, many of which overcome some of the criticisms of traditional budgeting. In this section, we will take a look at a few alternative budgets available to managers. They are called 'alternatives' because they offer a different way of preparing a budget, compared with the traditional incremental approach.

One of the roles of the management accountant is to find the most relevant systems to fit the organization they are working in, and this includes a budgeting system. It is important that all management accountants are aware of the different approaches available. CIMA (2011) reported that one of the most important roles of the management accountant is to provide up-to-date advice for planning and budgeting. This advice should fit with the strategic direction of the organization.

Rolling forecasts/budgets

With traditional budgeting being criticized for having fixed targets, often on a 12-month basis, rolling forecasts overcome this by offering continual reassessment of the environment within which the budget is set. Changes in the environment will result in changes to the forecast.

In a survey by CIMA (2009), rolling forecasts were used on average by 70 per cent of organizations questioned. This included organizations of all sizes and different geographical locations. The only area where rolling budgets were not so popular was in Africa where only around 40 per cent of the organizations surveyed currently used them.

Rolling budgets are popular within organizations because they are less detailed than traditional budgets. This results in managers having a clearer picture of what is important, rather than been confused by a level of detail that traditional budgets are often criticised for. In addition, rolling budgets do not have a set end date; managers are encouraged to continually think about the future. Using budgets which cover shorter periods, such as quarterly forecasts, while having predicted forecasts for the next six to eight quarters provides an opportunity for changes to be made, as and when they are required.

In practice if a company is working on a two-year rolling budget plan, with monthly revisions, and the budget period begins in January 2012, as soon as January 2012 is complete they will then forecast January 2014. There is always a two-year plan ahead; there is no fixed end date.

Rather than focusing on detailed fixed plans, rolling budgets analyse the drivers of the resources and focus on these issues within the budget. See Exhibit 10.1 for advantages and disadvantages of rolling budgets.

Advantages of rolling forecasts	Disadvantages of rolling forecasts
• There is a focus on the drivers of resources • Less detail • Can adapt to short-term changes in the market • Less manipulation because there are no fixed targets • Removes the 'spend it or lose it' mindset	• Not everyone understands the drivers of resources • Can demotivate employees as they are constantly working on the revision of budgets • Very time-consuming • Can create uncertainty with the budgets constantly changing

Exhibit 10.1: Advantages and disadvantages of rolling budgets

Zero-based budgeting

Zero-based budgeting (ZBB) is very distinctive; the past is not taken into consideration when setting new budgets. It is a technique that evolved in the 1960s. Every year a new budget is created which reflects the current environment to which they are working in. Zero-based budgeting is more popular with larger organizations than medium-sized ones. The CIMA (2009) survey demonstrated that around 45 per cent of large organizations are using ZBB but only around 35 per cent of medium-sized organizations use them. Around 40 per cent of very large and very small organizations used this type of budgeting.

The basic idea is that every year you start with a blank piece of paper and focus on what drives the resources. This type of budgeting is not as popular as rolling budgets because it is more relevant to organizations that do not have processes and businesses which are repeated on an annual basis. It is often associated with the public sector. This type of budgeting is easier to achieve with services or discretionary costs.

With traditional budgeting there is an incremental approach, the baseline is accepted from previous year and managers are only expected to justify any changes based on the predicted and the actual budget (as discussed in Chapter 9). With ZBB, variances on every item are required to be justified on a yearly basis. The concept is that resources will be allocated where they are needed.

10.1: Management Accounting in Practice

Zero-based budgeting in Tower Hamlets Council

Michael Portillo (a British MP) currently hosts a BBC documentary called *Power to the People*, which looks at ways more democracy can empower people. In a recent episode, Portillo describes what is in effect an example of zero-based budgeting (ZBB). What is ZBB? *ZBB is often associated with the public sector*. It is a technique used to create budgets which starts off with a figure of zero, and is often cited as being useful for discretionary type expenditure. From this, each item of expenditure must be analysed, discussed and ranked. Then, out of a limited pool of money, the highest ranking items get priority until all funds are used up. Sounds simple, but a lot of work is needed to discuss and rank expenditure items.

In the BBC documentary, Portillo visits a 'You Decide' session organized by the local council in Tower Hamlets, London. At this session, local people decide what is to be done with £250,000 of council money. They are given fully costed options under headings like health care, the elderly and local policing. The options in each category can be debated for a time, then all present 'vote' for their preferred option using an electronic voting system. This continues until all funds are used up. What in effect is happening here is that the local residents are undertaking the ranking and deciding part of ZBB. This, it could be argued, saves the council a bit of time and allocates resources to where residents want them most. Of course £250,000 is a long way off a council's full budget, but this is ZBB in action.

By the way, if you're in the UK you can watch this programme on BBC iPlayer.[2]

Source: http://martinjquinn.com/2010/03/22/locals-allocate-money-an-example-of-zero-base-budgeting/

Exercise

Can you think of any other examples of ZBB in practice?

Although *Management Accounting in Practice 10.1* provides an example of the public getting involved with the budgeting process, in general the process of using ZBB comprises three steps:

1)   All activities within the organization need to be identified. For each activity a report needs to be generated to analyse the costs, justify the reason for the activity to go ahead and to present all alternatives. At this stage appropriate targets should be identified as a performance tool. These activity reports are commonly referred to as 'decision packages'.

2)   Every activity report will then be given due consideration and they will be ranked in order of what is required for the forthcoming budget period.

3)   The final stage is the allocation of resources which is determined by the ranking performed in stage 2.

Advantages and disadvantages are listed in Exhibit 10.2.

Advantages of zero-based budgeting	Disadvantages of zero-based budgeting
• Based on current economic environment rather than what has happened in the past • Can motivate staff to be more innovative, finding better ways of functioning, using a bottom-up approach to budgeting • Drives communication and co-ordination throughout the organization • Encourages outsourcing opportunities to be examined • Encourages cost-effectiveness • Encourages elimination of outdated or unnecessary activities • There is a clear link between budgets and objectives	• Justification of each item can be difficult when no products are involved • Very time-consuming (more work than traditional budgeting) • Requires significant training for managers • Creates significant paperwork • The larger the organization, the harder the ranking due to the sheer number of activities involved • Once decision are made it creates problems throughout the year if the environment changes

Exhibit 10.2: Advantages and disadvantages of ZBB

Kaizen budgeting

Kaizen budgeting is part of the continuous improvement philosophy. This type of budgeting works within organizations that use quality systems working towards continuous improvement. An example of a company which implemented this type of system is Toyota. Any cost reductions, found through their drive to improve quality, would be accounted for on a continuous basis within their budgeting systems. Rather than maintaining one set of predetermined costs at the beginning of the budgeting period, the budget embeds a reduction in operational costs as they occur. Kaizen costing will be discussed in detail in Chapter 19. However, it is important to understand from a budgeting process, it can be very successful, especially in manufacturing organizations which are producing products on a daily basis. The process of Kaizen budgeting requires a manager to continually identify areas of improvement within the process of manufacturing. This is achieved by seeking small changes to every process within the production line.

Although the ultimate outcome is based on cost reductions, this is more within an accounting technique; Kaizen techniques are part of a cultural mindset. Everyone working with the environment should recognize that every process can achieve small improvements on a continuous basis. Therefore, for Kaizen budgeting to be successful it needs the full support of everyone working within this environment. See Exhibit 10.3 for Kaizen's advantages and disadvantages.

Advantages of kaizen budgeting	Disadvantages of kaizen budgeting
• Embeds detailed knowledge of products and processes into the managers' mind • Emphasis on operational employees who have the detailed knowledge of the system and products – motivation • Encourages teamwork • Removes the need for short-term targets	• Difficult to maintain continuous improvements to standard products • Can encourage managers to micro manage • Needs a long period to embed the culture that kaizen budgeting requires

Exhibit 10.3: Advantages and disadvantages of kaizen budgeting

Activity-based budgeting

In Chapter 6 we examined the technique of activity-based costing (ABC); activity-based budgeting (ABB) is an extended concept of this. In Chapter 8 we stated that traditional budgets are often created around functions, units or departments. Activity-based budgeting is based around activities; it centres on the information generated through the ABC system, focusing on the operations of the business within the value chain.

Activity-based budgeting is gaining significant use in very large organizations, the CIMA (2009) survey showing that just under 50 per cent of the respondents from this category using this method. Approximately 30 per cent of large and medium-sized organizations used ABB. However, within smaller organizations the use dropped to around 20 per cent. The process of creating ABB is as follows:

1) Analyse products and customers to be able to predict the production and sales demand.

2) Use the information from the ABC system to estimate the resources required to perform organizational activities.

3) With demand predicted, estimate the quantity of each resource that will be needed to meet the demand.

4) Allocate resources based on these predictions for each activity.

See the advantages and disadvantages of activity-based budgeting in Exhibit 10.4.

Advantages of activity-based budgeting	Disadvantages of activity-based budgeting
• Focuses on value-added activities • Elimination of non-value-added activities • Can help with investment decisions • Focuses on processes along the value chain creating new efficiencies	• Only works if the ABC system is up to date • If top management do not endorse activity-based management it can fail through lack of support • This is about change management which can create resistance

Exhibit 10.4: Advantages and disadvantages of activity-based budgeting

An example of how ABB can be used to predict a sales office budget can be seen below.

Worked Example 10.1

Preparing a sales budget using ABB

Twilight Inc. is an electronic component manufacturer. Based on predicted figures the forecast sales for the forthcoming year will be £10,000,000. The company is expecting to maintain the current customer base, with current customers placing an expected 50,000 orders. For existing customers the value per sales order is expected to be 5 per cent higher than the previous year.

A new base of potential customers has been identified, and including these new customers the budgeting sales forecast equals £10,785,000. The new customers are expected to produce an average sales value of £190.

Inflation is expected to be 3 per cent in the forthcoming budget period. The current sales manager suggests that the current year would produce costs of £250,000.

We are going to calculate the Sales office budget for the forthcoming period. There are several steps required to calculate this sales office budget:

1) Calculate the current budget cost per order.

2) Calculate the existing customers' sales budget.

3) Calculate the budgeted sales order for new customers.

4) Calculate the total sales orders – existing and new customers.

5) Calculate the new budget cost for the sales office.

Step 1 Calculate the current budget cost per order

Cost per sales order:

$$(£250,000/50,000) \times 1.03 = £5.15 \text{ per sales order}$$

In the above calculation we have taken the predicted sales budget of £250,000 and divided it by the expected number of sales orders, which is 50,000, to calculate the cost per sales order. However, as there is a predicted inflation increase of 3 per cent we have added 3 per cent to the predicted sales order cost, giving us £5.15 per sales order

Step 2 Calculate the existing customers' sales budget

This is based on predicted increased sales of existing customer:

$$£10,000,000 \times 1.05 = £10,500,000$$

The existing customers have a sales budget of £10,000,000 so we have adjusted this value to account for the expected increased sales value per order of 5 per cent.

Step 3 Calculate the budgeted sales order for new customers

$$(£10,785,000 – £10,500,000)/£190 = 1,500 \text{ orders}$$

If the budgeted sales forecasts for the forthcoming year is £10,785,000 and the existing customers are expected to account for £10,500,000 of these sales, then the incremental must belong to the new customers' sales. Therefore, by dividing the incremental by the anticipated sales value of new customers, £190, we can calculate the number of orders that belong to the new customers. In this case new customers are expected to produce 1,500 sales orders.

Step 4 Calculate the total sales orders – existing and new customers

$$50,000 + 1,500 = 51,500 \text{ orders}$$

With existing customers predicted to place 50,000 orders and new customers a further 1,500 orders, this means in total the company are expecting a total of 51,500 orders.

Step 5 Calculate the new budget cost for the sales office

$$£5.15 \times 51,500 \text{ orders} = £265,225$$

In step 1, we calculated the forecasted sales cost per order (including the inflation expected), which was £5.15. We need to take this value and multiply it by the number of expected sales (calculated in step 4). This means we have now calculated the sales office budget for the forthcoming year to be £265,225.

So far we have examined some of the alternative budgeting systems. However, as referred to in the introduction, there is now a movement that suggests using budgets in any form can result in innovation being stalled and full potential not being achieved. This is called beyond budgeting (BB).

Beyond budgeting

Many of the issues with traditional budgeting, such as setting targets based on fixed budgets rather than focusing on what was strategically important to the company, was the impetus for the beyond budgeting philosophy evolving. Hope and Fraser (2003) are often cited in this area; one of the articles brought the issue of 'who needs budgets?' to a wider audience. However, it must be noted that the discussion of beyond budgeting began much earlier than this, with companies such as Handelsbanken practising the principles of this philosophy since the 1970s. Handelsbanken is a Swedish Bank that for the second year running has been voted among the top 10 banks in the world by Bloomberg (Anon., 2012).

Hope and Fraser (2003, p. 108) began their argument with a very strong message: 'Budgeting, as most corporations practice it, should be abolished.' This was a very bold statement and resulted in budgeting in general being revisited, with academics questioning if companies need budgeting to be successful. Budgets, as discussed in Chapter 8, are argued to help organizations control, plan, motivate, communicate and co-ordinate. However, the beyond budgeting philosophy questioned whether traditional budgeting, in the way the majority of organizations were using them, actually achieved any of those things. Rather than improving existing budgeting systems, the beyond budgeting approach would be to abandon this type of budgeting altogether.

Hope and Fraser (2003) argued that many companies were introducing systems that supported strategic management accounting (SMA), such as process re-engineering and activity accounting. However, while introducing new strategic systems, they retained their old budgeting systems. The old budgeting systems were designed as 'control and command' and this prevented them focusing on the future strategy. Hope and Fraser (2003) stated that traditional budgeting distracted employees from what they should be doing by channelling attention to targets, based on irrelevant information.

Traditional budgeting produces a detailed document which emphasizes any deviations from what is expected. One of the examples highlighted by Hope and Fraser (2003) relates to sales figures. Rather than focusing on customer satisfaction, which will add value and bring in the sales, traditional budgeting focuses on the sales value. Focusing on the end sales value can create dysfunctional behaviour within the sales team. If the sales team are aware that their sales figures will be monitored closely, rather than engaging with the customers to improve the service and relationship they will focus on increasing the orders. Sales targets can encourage sales representatives to convince customers to make orders without considering if they may be returned after the budget period.

The argument behind the beyond budgeting philosophy is based on five issues, all identified as problems arising from using traditional budgeting:

1) Using fixed budgets to set targets will only ever achieve small improvements.

2) Setting incentives based on fixed targets can create fear, rather than encouraging innovation.

3) Fixed targets create a sense of compliance rather than adding value.

4) Allocating resources through traditional budgeting encourages managers to hoard resources rather than use them where they are needed.

5) Centralization ignores market reactions (Hope and Fraser 2003).

Following an increase in companies moving towards a beyond budgeting philosophy the Beyond Budgeting Round Table (BBRT) have developed 12 principles (see Table 10.1) for any company

Table 10.1: 12 Principles of beyond budgeting

Governance and transparency	
1. Values	Bind people to a common cause; not a central plan
2. Governance	Govern through shared values and sound judgement; not detailed rules and regulations
3. Transparency	Make information open and transparent; don't restrict and control it
Accountable teams	
4. Teams	Organize around a seamless network of accountable teams; not centralized functions
5. Trust	Trust teams to regulate their performance; do not micro-manage them
6. Accountability	Base accountability on holistic criteria and peer reviews; not on hierarchical relationships
Goals and rewards	
7. Goals	Encourage teams to set ambitious goals, don't turn goals into fixed contracts
8. Rewards	Base rewards on relative performance; not on fixed targets
Planning and controls	
9. Planning	Make planning a continuous and inclusive process; not a top-down annual event
10. Co-ordination	Co-ordinate interactions dynamically; not through annual budgets
11. Resources	Make resources available just in time, not just in case
12. Controls	Base controls on fast, frequent feedback; not budget variances

Source: adapted from www.bbrt.org (accessed on 14 May 2012).

wanting to adopt this management philosophy. The BBRT is an international shared learning network that consists of companies and academics. The member organizations have a shared interest in transforming their performance management models to enable sustained and superior performance.

From Table 10.1, you can see that the philosophy is based on four issues; governance and transparency, creating accountable teams, goals and rewards, and planning and control. What makes this philosophy different from using the traditional budgeting systems is that companies who follow these principles should be able to overcome the problems discussed earlier by:

1) Moving away from fixed targets, by using relative targets through benchmarking, will encourage employees to improve their own performance.

2) Using relative targets will encourage employees to be innovative and provide the confidence to take (positive) risks they would not have done before.

3) Continuously readdressing plans, employees are encouraged to think about value creation rather than achieving set numbers within the budget.

4) Using on demand allocation of resources rather than allocating for the year ahead reduces costs.

5) Using decentralization and passing the decision making to small local teams means market feedback is used within the process (Hope and Fraser, 2003).

Therefore, the central argument here is that organizations should move away from centralized hierarchical management and instead move towards a devolved network of teams who will be responsible for adding value and making the decisions necessary to achieve this. By providing authority to move resources where required, the system moves from a command and control system to a more adaptive management process. The concept of trust is central for this philosophy to work.

As mentioned previously, one company who has used all of the principles of beyond budgeting since the 1970s is Handelsbanken. Although all of the principles of beyond budgeting seem plausible and companies such as Handelsbanken have been incredible successful using them, the CIMA (2009) survey demonstrated that this was the least popular method currently used compared with other types of budgeting.

10.2: Management Accounting in Practice

The beyond budgeting philosophy at Apple Inc. and Netflix

Although Apple Inc. and Netflix do not specifically use the beyond budgeting philosophy, their approach to employees is similar. By using flat management structures and believing in your employee, by removing the office politics and by creating a culture of excellence and trust, you can actually reduce your cost of human capital. The principle is called 'talent density'. By securing and retaining one good employee you can save employing five additional staff that are just average at their jobs. The concept is that trust attracts excellent employees. However, one notable difference between Apple Inc. and the beyond budgeting approach is that they use a very strict line of command regarding the flat management structure.

Source: Reeves and Deimler (2011).

Exercise

Find other companies who use some of the beyond budgeting principles, which ones do they use and how?

10.3: Management Accounting in Practice

Handelsbanken – A world-class financial services model

Handelsbanken is a Swedish bank which has been consistently profitable for over 30 years. Throughout the financial crisis it maintained its profitability. The bank is not only profitable but it also maintains exceeding good customer ratings.

> High customer satisfaction ratings in Sweden and the UK, they have the lowest number of customer complaints. It is consistently one of the most cost efficient banks in the world with a cost-to-income ratio of around 40 per cent (compared with 60–80 percent for most of its rivals). Its profits even increased in 2008 when other banks were suffering huge falls and it has come through the credit crunch relatively unscathed (it was the only Swedish bank not to require Government support). (BBRT, 2012).

Handelsbanken follow the beyond budgeting philosophy and focus on continuous improvement rather than set targets. The improvement relates to performance and customer satisfaction. With beyond budgeting focusing on benchmarking rather than fixed targets, the bank chooses a few financial metrics which could be used to benchmark against the rest of their industry. With the banking industry commonly using return on-equity and cost/income ratio at group and regional levels and cost/income ratio and profit per employee at branch level, these were the chosen metrics.

The metrics were not used to set fixed targets within bank but were used to benchmark against the rest of the industry and to analyse performance improvement. The bank argues that the philosophy works because they trust their staff and the pressure of not letting the team down is the only incentive the employees need.

Each branch is effectively a profit centre, which means there is no centralized system of negotiation; each branch has full decision-making rights.

> Planning takes place at the branch level, usually at six-to-twelve week intervals according to the needs of the branch. Information is fast and open. Peer comparisons are used to spur improvement. Resources are made available through an internal market that enables branches to access them at any time. This approach drastically reduces waste and costs. (BBRT, 2012)

Source: adapted from www.bbrt.org (accessed on 14 May 2012).

Exercise

Identify the elements of the Handelsbanken practice which effect the Beyond Budgeting Philosophy. Go onto the Handelsbanken web page (www.handelsbanken.se) and research how they use the beyond budgeting principles as a marketing tool.

Why isn't everyone using the beyond budgeting philosophy?

Beyond budgeting works for many companies but imagine going to a bank for a loan to extend your business through a new project. The first item most banks will expect is a detailed business plan. It is the role of the management accountant to be able to analyse new projects and prepare both revenue predictions and costing information based on current economic conditions. It would be very difficult for most organizations to secure new funding without detailed long-term budgets.

The principles of the beyond budgeting philosophy are, in most people's minds, reasonable and good practice. However, sometimes maintaining these concepts is very difficult, especially when companies focus on new strategies and, in particular, growth strategies. Sometimes new strategies take priority over principles, and they can lose their vision.

Management Accounting Insight 10.1 argues that companies are taking budgeting very seriously and the beyond budgeting philosophy has not stormed the business world. However, Dugdale and Lyne (2010) did conclude that budgeting systems had advanced in the past five years.

10.1: Management Accounting Insight

Is the beyond budgeting philosophy turning traditional budgeting obsolete?

Although most individuals recognize the concepts of the beyond budgeting movement are sensible and logical, Dugdale and Lyne (2010) questioned whether this philosophy has resulted in companies abandoning budgeting. Within a field study based survey, Dugdale and Lyne examined eight large companies; sectors of these companies are provided in the table:

Business	Ownership	Structure
Aerospace	Part of aerospace multinational	Cost centre
Food ingredients manufacture	Irish group listed stock exchange	Corporate
Construction	Part of UK construction group	Profit centre
Frozen food manufacture	German private company	Profit centre
Food manufacture	Part of large UK food group	Profit centre
Plastic and glass product manufacture	Part of South African diversified group	Cost centre
Systems engineering	Private UK-based company	Profit centre
Wholesale, retail and leisure	Private UK-based company	Profit centre

This study found that 95 per cent of financial managers thought the budgeting process was important; they typically stated that budgeting was necessary for performance evaluation, control and planning. A small number of respondents criticized the budgeting process, and those who did argued the cause of the concerns were:

1) The 'top-down' nature of the process that could lead to lack of ownership.

2) A lack of accountability or involvement of operating managers.

3) The need for a better budgeting process.

From the survey, 55 per cent argued that in the past five years there had been improvements in the budgeting process, with junior management becoming more involved and the reports were now containing less detail. The result of their study demonstrated that the beyond budgeting movement had not influenced the use of traditional budgeting and, in fact, budgeting has become a more significant process of retaining financial control.

Source: adapted from Dugdale and Lyne (2010).

Exercise

Read the Dugdale and Lyne (2010) article and discuss their four field study findings regarding budgeting. *A link to the article is available online at www.mc-graw-hill.co.uk/textbooks/burns.co.uk.*

Organizations are organic in nature, and often take elements of different systems to address their own requirements and goals, and this has been seen within the budgeting process. One example of this relates to the case study on 'Astoria' by Frow et al. (2010), who examined a large multination company to identify how budgeting was used in practice.

As can be seen from *Management Accounting in Practice 10.4*, Astoria did not select one method of budgeting from a textbook and proceed to implement it. Organizations are always seeking to achieve competitive advantages; if they are profit-seeking organizations one technique/tool will never fit all. In the case of Astoria, they have used some of the elements of traditional budgeting in that they have 12-month goals and use variance analysis to identify any deviations from the plans, but they then incorporate an element of rolling budgets. Astoria continuously reassesses

10.4: Management Accounting in Practice

Evolving budgeting systems

Astoria is a large multinational organization which operates within the document technology and services market. Their budgeting system is based on yearly plans which are revised on a continuous monthly basis and analysed on a quarterly basis using variance analysis. The Variance report is based on key aspects of the business which are linked to strategically important goals. Individual targets are set which link to the vital key performance indicators (KPIs) which are identified through a performance monitoring system (PMS) called 'Performance Excellence Process' (PEP), which is strategy driven. However, the financial rewards are directly linked not to the KPIs of the individual but to the financial performance of the entire group.

The KPIs for individuals are negotiated through the PMS. Variance analysis is used to identify any deviations from the planned outcomes; however, the reaction to the deviations is not driven by the individual KPIs, but by the PEP. Responses to variances have to be supported by the strategically identified key objectives within the PEP rather than the individual targets, thereby creating strategically aligned action rather than dysfunctional behaviour.

This budgetary system has been designed to allow managers to respond to fast-changing circumstances within the market they operate.

Source: adapted from Frow et al. (2010).

Exercise

Explain how Astoria has avoided the dysfunctional behaviour that traditional budgeting can create.

---

the resources. So, they have fixed targets but with resource allocation that is based upon strategic alignment and not individual targets. Failure to meet individual targets was acceptable if they could demonstrate why they could not be met; acceptable reasons would evolve from the quality system, PEP. If Astoria required resources and attention to support something strategically important then this would take priority over the individual targets.

Although the beyond budgeting philosophy focuses on strategic alignment of system and provides principles and not rules, this philosophy has been criticized for a number of reasons. Frow et al. (2010) argue that some of the principles of beyond budgeting need more explanation, for example in relation to resource allocation, how would an organization deal with competing resources allocation requests? When the value of the requests is more than the supply of resources, who will arbitrate these requests?

In addition, Otley (2007) questions the use of relative targets within the beyond budgeting philosophy. He argues that while relative targets for senior managers can be useful to benchmark against competitors, when you are creating PMSs for lower-level managers the benchmarks can be very difficult to generate. Most companies keep this detailed information to themselves and therefore benchmarking can be very difficult in many industries.

Both CIMA (2009) and Dugdale and Lyne (2010) suggest that rather than abandoning traditional budgeting systems, organizations are focusing on improving the budgeting systems that they already have. Libby and Lindsey (2010) examined companies in America and Canada to analyse the views of budgets as the currently stand and improvements that the users wanted to see in the future, this can be seen in *Management Accounting Insight 10.2*.

Many of the findings in the Libby and Lindsey (2010) article show that organizations are in many cases wanting to achieve some of the ideas behind the beyond budgeting approach. However, the beyond budgeting philosophy is taking a 'leap of faith'; it is not simply replacing one system or adapting existing systems within an organization, but is an entire change to the way management think. Although there are concerns about whether some of the principles work in practice, the philosophy offers organizations an opportunity to create new business models, which for many organizations, have proven to be very successful.

10.2: Management Accounting Insight

Budgeting remains a core activity within organizations

A survey in America and Canada found that 80 per cent of Canadian respondents and 77 per cent of respondents from the USA continue to use budgets. Ninety-four per cent stated that they had no intention of abandoning their use of budgets as a control mechanism.

However, when asked if they planned to make changes to their budgeting systems within the next two years, 46 per cent answered that they did. The reasons behind the intended changes are the often recited disadvantages of using traditional budgeting, which include: taking too much time, lack of flexibility, manipulation, results not meaningful, removes the motivation to seek value-added improvements and the budgets are not in line with their strategies.

When asked what the companies wanted to achieve by seeking improvements in their existing budgeting systems, the responses included using a more bottom-up approach. Using rolling forecasts, aligning strategies with budgeting systems and to have a reporting system which has less detail but can be updated more regularly were also key areas of improvement.

Source: adapted from Libby and Lindsey (2010).

Exercise

Examine the improvements the respondents seek in the Libby and Lindsey (2010) article. How do they compare to the ideas behind the beyond budgeting approach?

Chapter summary

Although there are many issues and questions raised about the different approaches to budgeting, as discussed in this chapter the different styles offer the management accountant an opportunity to find one (or several concepts from various styles) to suit their own organization. The management accountant needs to find a budgeting system that aligns with the organization's strategy and operating style. The systems they choose must work within the pace of the changing environment, within which they compete. The system they choose must be able to adjust to changing information so that they can adapt their approach based on the signals they are receiving. Every market/industry is different and some industries change at a much quicker pace than others, therefore, as stated earlier, there is no single budgeting system that is suitable for everyone.

Key terms

Activity-based budgeting Budgeting based on activities rather than units, products, or departments. An extension of ABC (p. 244)

Beyond budgeting A philosophy which seeks the abandonment of budgets. Using relative target measure this approach seeks innovation and value-added activities to measure the success of a department, under a devolved process (p. 244)

Kaizen budgeting Budgeting based on a continuous improvement philosophy. Seeking small improvements in the operating processes which are recorded within the budget statement (p. 244)

Product life cycle Phases of a product life (p. 245)

Rolling forecasts An approach to budgeting that uses a continuous updating approach to forecasting, the time period of the budget remains constant (p. 244)

Traditional budgeting An approach to budgeting that has set targets within a set accounting period. Generally using a line approach to detailing all the information (p. 244)

Zero-based budgeting An approach to budgeting that starts with a blank piece of paper every accounting period. Resources are allocated on needs rather than past budgeted information (p. 244)

Review questions • • • • • • • • • • • • • • connect

Level of difficulty:	BASIC	INTERMEDIATE	ADVANCED

10.1 Provide four disadvantages of using traditional budgets. **[LO1]**

10.2 Describe the main differences of preparing a rolling forecast and a zero-based budget. **[LO3]**

10.3 Based on the studies within this chapter, what is the most popular budgeting system in industry? **[LO3]**

10.4 Discuss advantages and disadvantages of kaizen budgeting. **[LO3]**

10.5 Define Activity-based budgeting (ABB). **[LO3]**

10.6 List the principles of the beyond budgeting philosophy. **[LO5]**

Group discussion and activity questions • • • • • • • • •

10.7 Why have some organizations become disillusioned with traditional budgeting? **[LO1]**

10.8 Discuss some of the practical problems of using traditional budgets and how the users of traditional budgeting can manipulate the budget figures. **[LO1]**

10.9 Budgeting is no longer relevant to the rapidly changing economic environment that most organizations now operate within. Critically discuss. **[LO1, LO2, LO3, LO5]**

Exercises • • • • • • • • • • • • • • • • • connect

E10.1 Rolling budgets and zero-based budgeting **[LO3]**

a) Critically discuss the relevance of a rolling budget and state how a rolling budget could be applied. Explain its advantages and disadvantages.

b) Comment on the term 'zero-based budgeting'. Discuss why several managers are reluctant to introduce zero-based budgeting in their organizations.

E10.2 Traditional budgeting versus the beyond budgeting approach **[LO1, LO5]**

a) Traditional budgetary control systems have been employed in organizations for decades. Briefly outline the benefits of such systems.

b) The ongoing 'beyond budgeting' debate, argues for organizations to abandon traditional budgetary control systems. Describe the rationale for this argument and briefly outline the type of control system an organization might have without a traditional budgeting system.

E10.3 Zero-based budgeting **[LO3]**

Mr Mark Crehan, a Certified Public Accountant, is in the process of preparing the budget for Chicago Ltd for the forthcoming financial period. The company currently uses an incremental approach to budgeting but in the current economic environment Mr Crehan would like to investigate other budgeting systems, which may improve both the planning and control processes within the organization. One of Chicago Ltd's main competitors, Alaska Ltd, has recently introduced zero-based budgeting to their organization. Mr Crehan would like to develop a better understanding of zero-based budgeting before deciding on whether to recommend to the board of directors the adoption of this budgeting technique.

Required:

You are required to prepare a memorandum for Mr. Crehan outlining the following issues:

a) The stages involved in zero-based budgeting.

b) The advantages and disadvantages of adopting a system of zero-based budgeting.

c) The problems that Mr Crehan may face, from current employees, from changing the budgeting system to one based on zero-based budgeting principles.

Source: Institute of Certified Public Accountants in Ireland, Formation 2, Management Accounting.

E10.4 Incremental and zero-based budgeting [LO3]

Some commentators argue: 'With continuing pressure to control costs and maintain efficiency, the time has come for all public sector organizations to embrace zero-based budgeting. There is no longer a place for incremental budgeting in any organization, particularly public sector ones, where zero-based budgeting is far more suitable anyway.'

Required:

a) Discuss the particular difficulties encountered when budgeting in public-sector organizations compared with budgeting in private-sector organizations, drawing comparisons between the two types of organizations.

b) Explain the terms 'incremental budgeting' and 'zero-based budgeting'.

c) State the main stages involved in preparing zero-based budgets.

d) Discuss the view that 'there is no longer a place for incremental budgeting in any organization, particularly public sector ones', highlighting any drawbacks of zero-based budgeting that need to be considered.

Source: adapted from Association of Chartered Certified Accountants, Paper P5.

E10.5 Activity-based budgeting [LO4]

Plum Inc. is a mobile phone manufacturer. Based on predicted figures, the forecast sales for the forthcoming year will be £20,000,000 and the company is expecting to maintain the current customer base with existing customers placing an expected 2,000 orders. For the existing customers the value per sales order is expected to be 15 per cent higher than the previous year.

A new base of potential customers has been identified and including these new customers the budgeting sales forecast equals £24,000,000. The new customers are expected to produce an average sales value of £10,000.

Inflation is expected to be 4 per cent in the forthcoming budget period. The current sales manager suggests that the current year would produce costs of £200,000.

Required:

Calculate the sales office budget for the forthcoming period.

E10.6 Beyond budgeting [LO1, LO5]

For this question you will need to read the following article*: Otley, D. (2008) 'Did Kaplan and Johnson get it right?', *Accounting, Auditing and Accountability Journal* 21(2) pp. 229–39. The section on budgeting relates to this question.

Otley (2008, p. 234), on the subject of beyond budgeting said:

> A further threat to the role of the management accountant in practice comes from the arguments put forward by the beyond budgeting group. This group clearly points out the problems that traditional methods of budgetary control are encountering in contemporary organizations.

Required:

a) Describe the perceived problems with traditional budgeting as referred by Otley (2008).

b) Describe the approaches to budgeting as advocated by the beyond budgeting group.

A link to the article is available online at www.mcgraw-hill.co.uk/textbooks/burns.

E10.7 **ABC and beyond budgeting [LO5]**

(Note you may want to refer back to Chapter 6, ABC to help you with this question.)
Robust Laptops Co. (RL) make laptop computers for use in dangerous environments. The company's main customers are organizations such as oil companies and the military that require a laptop that can survive rough handling in transport to a site and can be made to their unique requirements.

The company started as a basic laptop manufacturer but its competitors grew much larger and RL had to find a niche market where its small size would not hinder its ability to compete. It is now considered one of the best quality producers in this sector.

For many years RL had the same finance director, who preferred to develop its systems organically. However, due to fall in profitability, a new chief executive officer (CEO) has been appointed who wishes to review RL's financial control systems in order to get better information with which to tackle the profit issue.

The CEO wants to begin by thinking about the pricing of the laptops to ensure that selling expensive products at the wrong price is not compromising profit margins. The laptops are individually specified by customers for each order, and pricing has been on a production cost plus basis with a mark-up of 45 per cent. The company uses an absorption costing system based on labour hours in order to calculate the production cost per unit.

The main control system used within the company is the annual budget. It is set before the start of the financial year and variances are monitored and acted upon by line managers. The CEO has been reading about major companies that have stopped using budgets and wants to know how such a radical move works and why a company might take such a step. He has been worried by moves by competitors into RL's market with impressive new products. This has created unrest among the staff at RL, with two experienced managers leaving the company.

Financial and other information for Robust Laptops Robust Laptops Data for the year ended 30 September 201X	
Volume (units)	23,800
	Total €000
Direct variable costs	
Material	40,650
Labour	3,879
Packaging and transport	2,118
Subtotal	46,647
Overhead costs	
Customer service	7,735
Purchasing and receiving	2,451
Inventory management	1,467
Administration of production	2,537
Subtotal	14,190
Total	60,837

Labour time per unit 3 hours

Data collected for the year:

No. of minutes on calls to customer 899,600

No. of purchase orders raised 21,400

No. of components used in production 618,800

Order 11784

Units ordered 16

Direct costs for this order:	€
Material	27,328
Labour	2,608
Packaging and transport	1,424

Other activities relating to this order:

No. of minutes on calls to customer 1,104
No. of purchase orders raised 64
No. of components used in production 512
Administration of production (absorbed as general overhead) 3 labour hrs per unit

Required:

Write a report to the CEO to include:

a)   An evaluation of the current method of costing against an activity-based costing system. You should provide illustrative calculations using the information provided on costs for 201X and Order 11784. Briefly state what action management might take in the light of your results with respect to this order.

b)   An explanation of the operation of a beyond budgeting approach and an evaluation of the potential of such a change at RL.

Source: adapted from Association of Chartered Certified Accountants, Paper P5.

● ● ●   **Case study problem**   ● ● ● ● ● ● ● ● ● ● ● ●   **connect** ● ●

C10.1 **Toyota – a world class manufacturing model [LO5]**

Following a disastrous year in 2010 for the Toyota brand, with litigation against them regarding deaths caused by unintended acceleration systems, in January 2011 they retained their position as the world's biggest car producer. Toyota is and has been renowned for being one of the most successful manufacturing companies in the world, and known for its management style, creating a culture of trust with its staff and installing core strategies of quality comes before anything else.

The Beyond Budgeting Round Table (BBRT) explains that Toyota follow many of the beyond budgeting principles:

Toyota Production System is legendary and spawned the lean manufacturing movement. The management focus is on continuously improving systems and meeting internal and external customers' needs. Everyone has a voice and is expected to contribute to the continuous improvement of their work. Medium-term operational goals aimed at best practice are set at every level. Planning takes place at the plant/team level and happens monthly within a clear strategic framework (12 month rolling forecasts support capacity planning). Knowledge about current performance is visual and immediate (e.g. throughput, downtime, inventory levels). Resources are made available just-in-time to meet each customer order. There are no fixed targets; no annual budget contracts and people are trusted with information to make the right decisions.

In addition, by comparison with industry standards the Toyota management team are paid very little.

Teams are expected to communicate with basic language so the whole team can understand and take responsibility, and any reports are simplified and usually one-page long. Using a kaizen system of continuous improvement they encourage staff to be innovative and to evolve.

However, following their growth strategy, it seems that quality may have taken second place. With reported recalls, following the deaths of a few of its customers, their principles were called into question. It was reported that within a typical Toyota car there used to be more than 30,000 parts and Toyota excelled at putting them together; however, following their drive for growth there are now 5,000 modules from many different suppliers. Their lean production processes in many cases were outsourced. Rapid growth resulted in production capacity expanding at a pace that can only be compared with the production process of the Ford group in the early 1900s.

If you would like to learn more about Toyota please refer to *Management Accounting in Practices 20.3* and *20.4* in Chapter 20.

Sources: based on www.bbrt.org (accessed on 14 May 2012); and KNC (2011); Takeuchi et al. (2008); Watenabe (2007).

Required:

a) Discuss how Toyota's growth strategy may have resulted in the management team moving away from following the main principles associated with beyond budgeting.

b) Critically analyse why Toyota's strive for growth did not work along their original strategy.

● ● ● Recommended reading ● ● ● ● ● ● ● ● ● ● ● ● ● ● ● ●

- Frow, N., D. Marginson, and S. Ogden (2010) '"Continuous" budgeting: reconciling budget flexibility with budgetary control', *Accounting, Organizations and Society*, 35, pp. 444–61.

Using a case study approach this paper considers the role of budgeting. Examining the existing tensions within an organization and pursuing the flexibility needed to achieve success this article provides an insightful example of how companies adapt their management accounting systems to suit their own needs.

- Hope, J. and R. Fraser (2003) 'Who needs budgets?' *Harvard Business Review*, 81(2), pp. 108–15.

Opening the discussion of the beyond budgeting approach to a wider arena, Hope and Fraser, consider whether budgets have a role to play within organizations. They question why many companies reject centralization yet retain the systems and processes which support it.

- Reeves, M. and M. Deimler (2011) 'Adaptability: the new competitive advantage', *Harvard Business Review*, 89(7/8), pp. 134–41.

This article considers, how in the current business climate, organizations can find the new competitive advantage. Moving away from the traditional view that the world is stable and predictable, they suggest that companies have to be good at learning new things rather than becoming good at one thing.

● ● ● References ●

Anon. (2012) One of the top ten strongest banks in the world, 3 May, http://www.handelsbanken.se (accessed on 12 May 2012).

CIMA (2009) 'Management accounting tools for today and tomorrow', www.cimaglobal.com/ma (accessed on 20 October 2011).

CIMA (2011) 'Developments in the global accountancy sector', www.cimaglobal.com/ma (accessed on 20 October 2011).

Dugdale, D. and S. Lyne (2010) 'Budgeting practice and organizational structure', CIMA Research Executive Summaries, 6(4).

Frow, N., D. Marginson and S. Ogden (2010) '"Continuous" budgeting: reconciling budget flexibility with budgetary control', *Accounting, Organizations and Society*, 35, pp. 444–61.

Hope, J. and R. Fraser (2003) 'Who needs budgets?', *Harvard Business Review*, 81(2), pp. 108–115.

KNC (2011) 'The strangest thing about Toyota's latest recall', *Economist*. 26 January, www.economist.com (accessed on 20 October 2011).

Libby, T. and R. Lindsey (2010) 'Beyond budgeting or budgeting reconsidered? A survey of North-American budgeting practice', *Management Accounting Research*, 21, pp. 56–75.

Otley, D. (2007) 'Did Kaplan and Johnson get it right?', *Accounting, Auditing and Accountability Journal*, 21(2), pp. 229–239.

Reeves, M. and M. Deimler (2011) 'Adaptability: the new competitive advantage', *Harvard Business Review*, 89(7/8), pp. 134–41.

Takeuchi, H., E. Osono and N. Shimizu (2008) 'The contradictions that drive Toyota's success', *Harvard Business Review*, 86(6), pp. 96–104.

Watanabe, K. (2007) 'Lessons from Toyota's long drive', *Harvard Business Review*, 85(7/8), pp. 74–83.

● ● ●   **Notes**   ●

1   http://www.apptio.com/products/budgeting-and-forecasting.php (accessed on 12 May 2012).

2   20 March 2012 BBC2, 21:00.

When you have read this chapter

Log on to the Online Learning Centre at **www.mcgraw-hill.co.uk/textbooks/burns** to explore chapter-by-chapter test questions, links and further online study tools for Management Accounting.

BUSINESS DECISION MAKING

11 Short-term decision making: cost-volume-profit analysis   265

12 Cost behaviour and estimation   290

13 Decision making: relevant costs and revenues   315

14 Pricing   349

15 Capital investment decisions   369

CHAPTER 11

SHORT-TERM DECISION MAKING: COST-VOLUME-PROFIT ANALYSIS

Chapter outline

- The economist's versus the management accountant's view

- Calculating break-even

- Multiple product analysis

- Graphical representations of CVP analysis

- Risk and uncertainty

Learning outcomes

On completion of this chapter, students will be able to:

LO1 Calculate the level of sales or business activity needed to break even or earn a desired profit

LO2 Determine the revenue required to break even or earn a desired profit

LO3 Apply cost-volume-profit analysis in a multi-product setting

LO4 Graphically depict the relationship between costs, volume and profits

LO5 Consider impacts of uncertainty and change in variables on cost-volume-profit analysis

Introduction

Cost-volume-profit (CVP) analysis is a very useful tool for managers, accountants and business owners in making short-term decisions. CVP analysis brings together the costs and revenues of a business and emphasizes the relationship with volumes. It helps to answer questions such as 'How much do I need to sell to cover my costs?' (see *Management Accounting in Practice 11.1*) or 'How will an increase in costs affect the sales level required to maintain current profit levels?' As a decision-making tool, it can be used to quickly identify problems. For example, in the highly competitive game console market, the Sony PS3 which launched at $599 in 2007 had made accumulated losses of $3.3 billion (Sony Annual Report, 2008). The price has continued to fall since its launch, squeezing profits further. Did Sony know this on launching the PS3 and why don't they do something about it? Yes they did, but their aim was to achieve market penetration against competitor consoles like the X-Box and at the same time reduce costs of producing the PS3. Sony will also generate profit from the sale of games and they have reported increased PS3 console and software sales alongside reduced manufacturing costs (Sony Annual Report, 2009).

CVP analysis is a modelling system which managers and accountants should be conversant with. Not only can it be used to answer questions such as those mentioned above. It can also be used to determine the sales level needed to make a certain profit, to assess the impact of price increase on profit and as a sensitivity tool to ascertain the effects of varying cost and price levels on profit and break-even levels. It is based on the short-term relationship (typically 12 months) between costs, revenues and profits. By confining its use to the short term, it constricts some of the variables and makes the analysis easier. For example, increases in production volumes take time and prices may have been agreed for a year ahead. On the other hand, resources such as labour and materials can be acquired in a much shorter time frame.

11.1: Management Accounting in Practice

Costs at a cheese producer

The West Cork region in Ireland has a number of cheese-makers who take advantage of lush pastures and high-quality dairy herds. Gubbeen Farmhouse Products, owned by the Ferguson family, is one such business. The family have worked the same land for six generations. One of the farm's products is Gubbeen Cheese, which was first produced in 1979. Then, and now, the cheese is produced from the farm's own 120-strong dairy herd.

In 1979, the liquid milk price paid to farmers was about €1.20 per gallon (approximately 25c per litre). One of the family had learned to make cheese as a child and they decided to exploit this expertise. Cheese-making added value to milk sales – the price per gallon obtained for cheese was (and is) about three times that of liquid milk. One of the first key decisions to be made was volume. Dairy farmers are only permitted to sell an agreed volume of milk – referred to as a milk quota. The Gubbeen farm spans 300 acres, which will sustain 120 dairy cows. This translates to approximately 158,000 gallons of milk (720,000 litres). The family originally had a quota of 83,000 gallons and have since increased this quota to 158,000 gallons. In terms of cheese output, this allows Gubbeen to produce up to 75 tons of cheese annually. In the early stages, production was less than this maximum, but the family at least had secured the quota for future expansion.

On the cost side, the business initially received grant aid to purchase the necessary equipment. As the farmhouse cheese sector developed across Europe, the European Union began to regulate the sector, which increased costs as strict production and hygiene standards had to be adhered to. According to the family, setting a selling price for the cheese was more 'instinctive' in the early days. Today, they scan the market and compare Gubbeen cheese with other comparable products. Additionally, distribution channels add a sizeable margin, meaning the business has to consider the impact on what they term 'the farm gate price'. Too low a price effects the longer-term sustainability of production, which the family estimate at about 35 per cent reduction in sales before making a loss.

Gubbeen Cheese has proved very successful and has been recognized internationally. It won awards and was named 'Best Irish Cheese' at the 2009 British Cheese Awards. The company employs 20 people and continues to increase sales despite tough economic conditions. The family are happy they can continue to grow the business and their brand in the future. See www.gubbeen.com for more information on the business.

Exercises

1) What do you think are the main variable and fixed costs at Gubbeen Cheese?

2) Having an ample milk quota determined the volume of cheese Gubbeen could produce. How important is obtaining sufficient sales volume to a business?

3) In the early days, pricing was based more on instinct. Could Gubbeen have been more technical in deriving a price? How?

The economist's versus the management accountant's view

The economist's model

The relationship between costs, prices and volumes was originally developed by economists as shown in Exhibit 11.1.

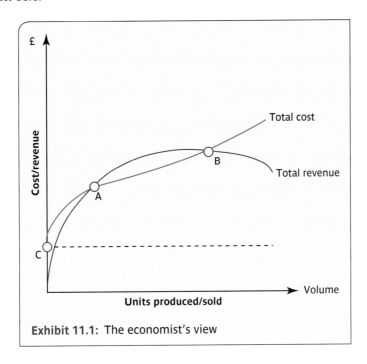

Exhibit 11.1: The economist's view

Exhibit 11.1 depicts production and sales volume on the horizontal (X) axis and costs/revenue on the vertical (Y) axis. The total revenue line is assumed by economists to be curvilinear. As production increases, the selling price will be reduced in order to attract buyers for the goods. This means that at higher output levels, total revenues do not increase or may decrease in proportion to total output. This can be seen in Exhibit 11.1 by the less steep slope of the total revenue line, which eventually becomes a downward slope. This is because prices have to be decreased to a lower level to achieve sales.

The total cost line depicts costs as rising fast at first as the output levels are lower. This typically occurs as a business needs to reach a certain output level to operate efficiently. Between points A and B, the total costs rise at a slower pace as efficiencies such as optimum use of plant capacity and labour appear. After point B, as output increases beyond what the organization can comfortably achieve, total costs begin to rise. This is because the operational facilities may become crammed with too much work, sales orders and people for the space in which it operates. In such circumstances, bottlenecks occur, for example as materials cannot be obtained fast enough to meet output or overworked equipment breaks down. The effect of such issues is to increase the total cost per unit of output. You can also see in Exhibit 11.1 that the total revenue and total cost lines intersect at points A and B. This implies that costs and revenues are equal at these two levels of output, in other words, the business would break even.

Any organization also has a basic cost of operating, or a fixed cost. This is depicted by the dashed line starting at point C in Exhibit 11.1. Fixed costs remain stable at all output levels. As total costs are fixed costs and variable costs, it is the latter that most influences the economists total cost function. Exhibit 11.2 shows the economists assumptions on variable costs. Economists assume that variable cost per unit initially declines. This assumption is based on, for example, an increasing division of labour (that is, more specialized and efficient labour) and bulk-buying discounts. Economists call this **increasing returns to scale**. The unit variable cost is higher at low output levels meaning that total costs rise steeply (Exhibit 11.1). Unit variables costs decline as output increases, but gradually begin to rise. In Exhibit 11.2, you can see that at output level V1, unit variable costs decrease beyond this level and then rise gradually; as at output level V2. As output increases beyond V2, costs rise sharply again. Between output levels V1 and V2, the organization is operating at its most efficient level. However, as mentioned already, when output exceeds capacity, then efficiencies creep in. The effect is that the variable cost per unit of output increases. Economists call this **decreasing returns to scale**.

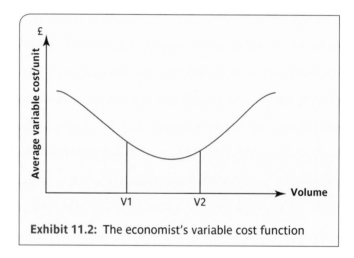

Exhibit 11.2: The economist's variable cost function

The accountant's model

Although based on the economist's model, a key difference with the accountant's approach to cost-volume-profit relationships is that it is viewed in the shorter term. Increasing efficiencies in a business are not realized overnight, nor are capacity-related inefficiencies. In the short term, output is likely to be relatively stable, or at least within a stable range. Exhibit 11.3 shows the cost-volume-profit relationships as used by management accountants.

The most noticeable difference in the accountant's model is that total revenues and costs are assumed to follow a linear pattern. Making this assumption is reasonable in the shorter term as the costs and revenues are likely to remain stable within a **relevant range** of output. This level of output is what has been planned by an organization in the short term and they are likely to have reasonable knowledge and experience of costs and revenues at this level. You can think of the accountant's model as a short-term slice of the economist's model. For short-term decision making, it is sufficient to assume that costs and revenues are linear within the relevant range. Outside this range, costs and revenues will need to be reassessed.

The fixed cost function is depicted as expected, at a constant amount regardless of output volume. This assumption is valid in the short term, but over the longer term fixed costs will rise in a typically step-like manner. Total costs, consisting of both fixed and variable costs, will steadily rise as output increases. Compared with the economist's model, the accountant's model does not assume cost will increase in an exponential fashion in the short term, hence the total cost line is linear. Total revenue, like total costs are also assumed to be linear in the short term, with prices assumed to remain stable and this increases total revenue as output increases.

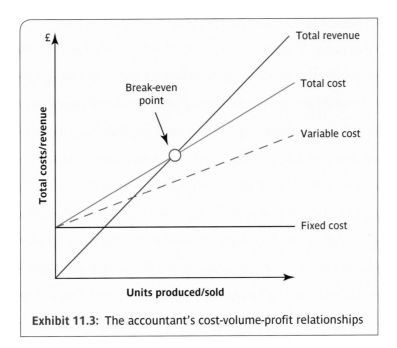

Exhibit 11.3: The accountant's cost-volume-profit relationships

As shown in Exhibit 11.3, the intersection between the total costs line and the total revenue line is called the **break-even point**. This is the output level at which neither profit nor loss is made. Output beyond this point yields increasing profits as fixed costs are spread over a larger volume – this can be seen by the widening gap between the total costs and total revenue line beyond the break-even point. Output below the break-even point implies an overall loss, with the total loss being greater at the lowest output levels.

Calculating break-even

Understanding the costs

As depicted in *Management Accounting in Practice 11.1*, costs are assumed to remain relatively stable in the short term. You know from Chapter 3, that fixed costs are costs incurred regardless of output, while variable costs increase as output increases. To use CVP analysis as a decision-making tool, these assumptions on cost are important, as without them it would not be possible to calculate a break-even point.

Both fixed and variable costs should be readily identifiable to a management accountant. They can be taken from budgets or be actual figures, preferably the latter, as CVP analysis is used to make short-term decisions. In reality, as already indicated in the economist's model, costs are not linear. Even in the short term, variable costs might be reduced due to volume purchasing discounts, or fixed costs might be reduced due to major cost-cutting efforts. Management accountants will of course know if and how costs are changing, and will update calculations of break-even accordingly. However, at any particular point in time, obtaining total costs for use in decisions under the assumption they remain stable is sufficient for short-term decisions.

Calculating the break-even output in units

Reflecting on Gubbeen Cheese (*Management Accounting in Practice 11.1*), this business had a general idea of its fixed costs and manufacturing (variable) costs, and thus could estimate the output level required to cover costs. As previously mentioned, the point where costs are covered and no profit is made is called the break-even point. To find the break-even point in units, we begin by first looking at the income generated from units sold.

The first decision for a business is to determine what it means by a unit of output. For example, Gubbeen Cheese (*Management Accounting in Practice 11.1*) might define a unit as 1 kg of cheese. Dell Computers might define a unit as a laptop or a desktop computer. In the service sector, the concept of a unit of output is more difficult to pin down. For example, Ryanair might define a unit as a one flight leg or Google might define a unit in terms of Google Ad clicks (or thousand of ad clicks).

The second decision involves the separation of costs into fixed and variable components. Fixed costs will include not just manufacturing costs, but fixed costs for the business as a whole. Likewise for variable costs, all costs that increase as output increases need to be identified. In both cases, it should be remembered that a short-term focus applies and thus cost increases envisaged or planned in the longer term are not considered.

If we think about an income statement, the profit of a business can be represented in an equation as below:

$$\textbf{Profit = Sales revenue – Variable costs – Fixed costs} \qquad \textbf{(11.1)}$$

Profit as show in equation (11.1) above is before taxes and any abnormal expenditure or income. This is because in CVP analysis we are concerned only with normal operations. The representation of profit in equation (11.1) can be expanded by expressing sales in terms of volumes and unit price, and variable costs in terms of volume and unit costs. This amends the equation as follows:

$$\textbf{Profit = (Sales price} \times \textbf{Units sold) – (Variable cost per unit} \times \textbf{Units sold) – Fixed costs} \qquad \textbf{(11.2)}$$

Considering equation 11.2, can you determine how many units need to be sold to earn zero profit, that is, break even? Let's use an example to answer this question. Whitely Ltd manufactures a standard desktop computer and their projected income statement for next month is as follows:

Sales (1,000 units @ £400)	£400,000
Variable costs	£325,000
Contribution	£75,000
Fixed costs	£45,000
Profit	£30,000

We can see that the selling price per computer is £400 and the variable costs are £325 (£325,000/1,000). If we take these figures together with the fixed costs of £45,000, we can fill in the equation as below and solve it. Remember that the profit is zero at break-even point and we don't know the number of computer (units) yet.

$$0 = (£400 \times \text{Units}) – (£325 \times \text{Units}) – £45,000$$
$$0 = (£75 \times \text{Units}) – £45,000$$
$$£75 \times \text{Units} = £45,000$$
$$\text{Units} = 45,000/75$$
$$\text{Units} = 600.$$

Thus, Whitely Ltd needs to sell 600 computers to cover all fixed and variable costs. We can check this by drafting an income statement:

Sales (600 units @ £400)	£240,000
Variable costs (600 units @ £325)	£195,000
Contribution	£45,000
Fixed costs	£45,000
Profit	£0

We do not need to solve these equations to calculate the break-even output/sales unit each time. Instead, we can focus on the contribution. Contribution (see also Chapter 3) is sales revenue less variable costs. In equation 11.2, contribution will be equal to fixed costs at the break-even output level.

Contribution can be substituted in equation 11.2 as follows:

$$\textbf{Profit = (Units sold} \times \textbf{Contribution per unit) – Fixed costs} \qquad \textbf{(11.3)}$$

Solving this equation we obtain the following formula for break-even:

$$\text{Break-even in units} = \frac{\text{Fixed costs}}{\text{Contribution per unit}}$$

Using the Whitely Ltd example, the break-even output can be calculated according to this formula, giving the same answer as above:

$$\text{Break-even in units} = \frac{£45,000}{(£400 - 325)} = 600 \text{ units}$$

To calculate the break-even in sales revenue in the Whitely Ltd example, we can simply multiply units by the selling price: 600 units × £400 = £240,000. This is the easiest way to calculate break-even in revenue terms, but only in single-products scenarios. Later, the method will be extended for multiple-product scenarios.

11.2: Management Accounting in Practice

Variable cost of an iTunes download

On average Apple Inc. charges about 99 pence/cent per music track downloaded from its iTunes store. While figures are not available, industry sources estimate variable costs at 70–90 per cent.[1] This means each track has a contribution of 10–30 pence/cent.

Exercise

What fixed costs would be incurred in operating a platform like iTunes?

Target profits

The break-even point is useful information for any business. In addition, the techniques just detailed are also used to determine how many units need to be sold to achieve a targeted profit. For example, a business might decide it wants profit to be 20 per cent of sales revenues or perhaps a fixed sum of £500,000. We can use the break-even formula to calculate the units required to achieve this desired profit. Using the Whitely Ltd example, let's see how to calculate the units required to attain the following target profit scenarios:

> Scenario 1: Obtain a profit of £60,000
>
> Scenario 2: Obtain a profit of 15 per cent of sales revenue
>
> Scenario 3: Obtain a profit after tax of £50,000, where the tax rate is 20 per cent.

Scenario 1

Using the break-even formula, we can simply add the target profit of £60,000 to the fixed costs, as follows:

$$\text{Units} = (£45,000 + £60,000)/ (£400 - £325)$$

$$= £105,000/£75$$

$$= 1,400 \text{ units}$$

As a check, here is the income statement if sales of 1,400 units are made.

Sales (1,400 units @ £400)	£560,000
Variable costs (1,400 units @ £325)	£455,000
Contribution	£105,000
Fixed costs	£45,000
Profit	£60,000

An income statement as above is not required to check the number of units required. We know the contribution is £75 per unit. Thus, for every unit sold above the break-even point £75 profit is generated. We can thus multiply the contribution per unit of £75 by the number of units above break-even, that is, £75 × 800 = £60,000.

Scenario 2

In this case, the targeted profit is 15 per cent of sales revenue and we can use equation 11.2 to calculate the answer. Here is equation 11.2 again:

Profit = (Sales price × Units sold) − (Variable cost per unit × Units sold) − Fixed costs

If profit is to be 15 per cent of sales revenue, the equation can be rewritten as follows based on the data from Whitely Ltd:

$$0.15(£400 × \text{Units}) = (£400 × \text{Units}) − (£325 × \text{Units}) − £45,000$$
$$£60 × \text{Units} = (£75 × \text{Units}) − £45,000$$
$$£15 × \text{Units} = £45,000$$
$$\text{Units} = 3,000$$

In a similar manner to Scenario 1, we can check this using the contribution per unit for units above the break-even point to calculate profit:

$$£75 × (3,000 − 600 \text{ units})$$
$$£75 × 2,400 \text{ units} = £180,000$$

Sales revenue will be £1 200,000 (3,000 units × £400), which means a profit of 15 per cent of revenue equals £180,000 as calculated above.

Scenario 3

In this case, we need work out the profit before tax first. This can be calculated as follows:

Profit after tax − (1 − tax rate)

Thus, profit before tax is:

$$£50,000 × (1 − 0.20) = £62,500$$

The break-even units can now be calculated.

$$\text{Units} = (£45,000 + £62,500)/(£75)$$
$$= £107,500/£75$$
$$= 1,433.33 \text{ units}$$

Again, we can perform a quick check. Units sold above break-even is 833.33 (1,433.33 − 600) × £75 contribution gives a profit of £62,500, less tax at 20 per cent of £12,500 (£62,500 × 20%) equals £50,000 profit.

These three scenarios are examples of how accountants and managers can use break-even techniques. The techniques can be applied to many other scenarios. As you can see from the above examples, the contribution per unit is a key figure which alone can be used to make business decisions. For example, in Whitely Ltd, if a new sales manager were appointed on a fixed salary of £75,000, we can quickly determine that an additional 1000 units (£75,000/£75 contribution per unit) must be sold to cover this increased fixed cost.

The contribution per unit can also be used to determine the **contribution margin ratio**. This ratio is the contribution as a proportion of sales. In the Whitely Ltd example, the contribution margin ratio is 0.1875 (£75/£400). As CVP analysis assumes costs and prices are constant in the short term, then the contribution margin ratio is also constant. Thus, it can be used in the break-even formula used previously.

Here is Equation 11.1 again:

$$\text{Profit} = \text{Sales revenue} - \text{Variable costs} - \text{Fixed costs}$$

We can insert the contribution margin ratio as follows:

$$\text{Profit} = (\text{Sales Revenue} \times \text{CM ratio}) - \text{Fixed costs}$$

At break-even, profit is nil so this equation can be solved as follows:

$$\text{Sales revenue} = \frac{\text{Fixed costs}}{\text{CM ratio}}$$

This is a useful formula to calculate the break-even point in sales revenues. For Whitely Ltd, we have previously calculated the sales revenue at break-even as £240,000. Using this formula, the result is the same:

$$\text{Sales revenue} = \frac{£45,000}{0.1875} = £240,000$$

Multiple product analysis

Thus far, the examples given have presented a single product scenario. In reality, most businesses will make and sell many products. CVP analysis can be used in multiple product scenarios. In this section, you will see how we can adapt the formulas used so far to multiple product scenarios. We will use and extend the Whitely Ltd example used previously.

Let us assume Whiteley Ltd manufactures a personal computer and a more powerful business computer. The following projected income statements have been prepared for the coming year:

	Personal computer	Business computer	Total
Sales price £	400	800	
Units	1,200	800	
	£	£	£
Sales	480,000	640,000	1,120,000
Variable costs	390,000	480,000	870,000
Contribution	90,000	160,000	250,000
Direct fixed costs	30,000	40,000	70,000
Profit per product	60,000	120,000	180,000
Common fixed costs			26,250
Operating profit			153,750

There are two types of fixed costs in the example above. The direct fixed costs are costs which can be traced to the product and would not be incurred if the product was not made. For example, there might be a quality inspector for each type of computer. The common fixed costs are those which are not traceable to either product, and would remain if either were discontinued.

It is possible to calculate a break-even point for each computer type separately. The contribution per unit for the personal computer is (£90,000/1,200 units) £75 and (£160,000/800 units) and £200 for the business computer. The break-even point in sales units is thus:

$$\text{Personal computer} \frac{£30,000}{£75} = 400 \text{ units}$$

$$\text{Business computer} \frac{£40,000}{£200} = 200 \text{ units.}$$

Therefore, we now know that 400 personal computers and 200 business computers must be sold to achieve a profit at the product level. But, we have not taken into account the common fixed costs, so this is not the break-even point for the business as a whole. Some method is needed to ensure all costs are included in our calculations. One method is to allocate all common fixed costs to each product line before calculating break-even. This may mean arbitrary allocation of costs to product lines. Another method is to convert a multiple product scenario to a single product one, which we will now examine in greater detail.

Sales mix and CVP analysis

Sales mix refers to the relative proportions of products sold. It can be measured in terms of units or sales revenue. For example, if Whitely Ltd believe they can sell 3,000 personal computers for every 1,000 business computers, then the sales mix is 3:1. Of course, a sales mix in units will typically not be the same as a sales mix in revenue as the prices of products are unlikely to be identical. Sales of 3,000 personal computers would yield £1,200,000 in revenue, 1,000 business computers £800,000. This gives a sales mix of 12:8, or 3:2. An estimate of the sales mix may be obtained from the sales or marketing staff, and may be used in CVP analysis to calculate the number of each product to be sold so that the business as a whole breaks even.

The example in the table below assumes the sales mix of Whitely Ltd is three personal computers to every two business computers. To begin, we need to calculate the contribution for each sales mix bundle as follows:

Product	Unit contribution	Mix	Bundle contribution
Personal computer	£75	3	£225 (3 × £75)
Business computer	£200	2	£400 (2 × £200)

As shown in the table, for every bundle of three personal computer and two business computers, a total contribution of £625 is made. We can equate this to the contribution per unit in the break-even formula we have used thus far. We can also now add the direct and common fixed costs and treat them as one cost. Thus, the number of bundles Whitely Ltd must sell to break even as a business can be calculated as follows:

$$\text{Break-even bundles} = \frac{£96,250}{£625} = 154$$

Thus, sales of 154 bundles will mean the business breaks even. This means that 462 (154 × 3) personal computers and 308 (154 × 2) business computers need to be sold. We can check this quickly as follows:

Contribution from personal computer (462 × £75)	£34,650
Contribution from business computer (308 × £200)	£61,600
Total contribution	£96,250
Less fixed costs	£96,250
Profit	Nil

As before, the break-even sales revenue can be calculated by using the sales price for each computer type and the number of units required to break even. Thus, break-even sales revenue will be (462 × £400) + (308 × £800), or £431,200.

The sales mix depicted above – two product types – may be relatively simple compared to some modern business. Businesses today typically produce or sell multiple complex products or services, and product mix can change significantly in the short term. However, the core concept of CVP analysis still applies to such complex scenarios. For example, the product mix of a business like Apple Inc.'s iTunes or AppStore may change on a daily basis, yet its underlying fixed-cost base is likely to remain relatively stable. Thus, effects of changes in product mix could be assessed to determine the effect on contribution, and with relatively stable fixed costs, the effects on profitability may be easily assessed also.

Graphical representations of CVP analysis

We have already seen the accountant's model of costs, revenues and volumes depicted in Exhibit 11.3. This model of costs can be used to graphically represent the relationships of costs, volumes and profit in more detail. The resulting graph (or chart) is termed a **cost-volume-profit graph.** Exhibit 11.4 shows the cost-volume-profit graph for Whitely Ltd based in the data we used earlier:

Sales (1,000 units @ £400)	£400,000
Variable costs	£325,000
Contribution	£75,000
Fixed costs	£45,000
Profit	£30,000

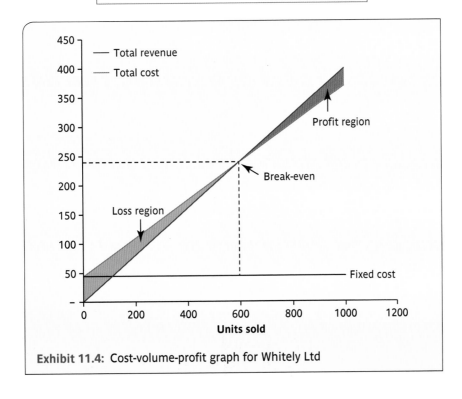

Exhibit 11.4: Cost-volume-profit graph for Whitely Ltd

Using this data, we can depict the relationships as follows. The fixed costs line is a constant value of £45,000 regardless of output. The revenue line can be drawn by taking any sales level (say 1,000 units × £400 = £400,000) and zero. The total costs line will start at a value of £45,000 when output is zero (that is, the fixed costs). As a second point on the total costs line, you can use the costs when sales are 1,000 units as above, that is, £370,000.

You can see the break-even point is depicted at 600 units or £240,000, as calculated previously. Any sales above the break-even point will generate a contribution towards profit. This is depicted by the shaded area where the revenue line is above the total cost line. Similarly, the other shaded area to the left of the break-even point depicts losses. Graphing the relationships of costs, revenues and volume as above can be used to quickly determine the costs and revenue at varying levels of output.

A variation of the graph shown in Exhibit 11.4 is called the **profit-volume graph** (PV). This shows the relationship between profit and sales volume and is depicted for Whitely Ltd in Exhibit 11.5.

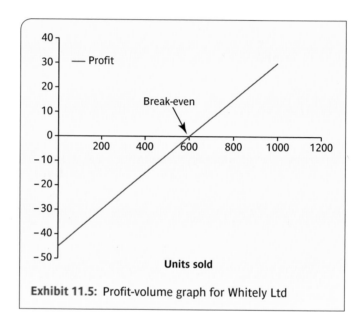

Exhibit 11.5: Profit-volume graph for Whitely Ltd

The profit-volume graph for Whitely Ltd is drawn by again choosing some known points. For example, we know that at zero output a loss equal to the fixed costs (£45,000) occurs. At break-even point the profit is zero, and as given, when output is 1,000 units profit is £30,000. A profit-volume graph can be used to access the profit or loss at any level of output, but it does not reflect the nature of costs, that is, fixed versus variable.

In multi-product scenarios, a profit-volume type chart is used to depict the profit and sales of each product. The chart typically starts with the product with the highest contribution to sales

11.3: Management Accounting in Practice

CVP graphs in practice – an example

The details of the company this example is based on are not revealed for confidentiality reasons, but the principles conveyed here have been researched by one of the authors. In a manufacturing company, as part of a drive to focus sales on more profitable customers, the management accountants used break-even techniques to produce a contribution per customer chart for sales managers each month. Exhibit 11.6 shows how this graph looked. Each month, fixed costs per ton of output were calculated from actual costs – shown as £250 in the graph. A contribution per ton for each of the top 50 customers was also calculated – based on standard costs divided by tons sold. Each customer was plotted as a point on a chart, with the fixed costs shown as a line intersecting the cost axis (that is, at £250 in the figure). Any point below this line suggested that the customer was performing poorly in terms of covering costs, points above the line suggested good contribution was achieved. This graph was used to refocus sales staff to maximize the number of customers above the line or more to the right hand side and remove or re-price those below the line. While not a perfect tool, it provided managers with a quick visual representation of where to focus attention. Incidentally, the underlying standard costs used were updated at least once a month and thus were quite reflective of actual costs.

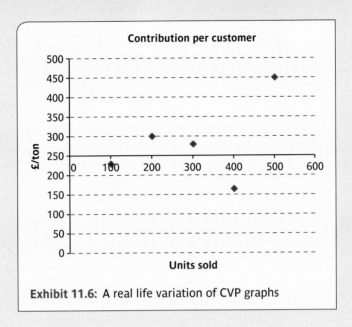

Exhibit 11.6: A real life variation of CVP graphs

Exercises

1) Can you find anything wrong with the assumptions underlying this graph?

2) How would the profile of a customer affect the ability of sales staff to take action based on data from this graph?

ratio and plots the cumulative sales and profit by adding each additional product. The point at which profit is zero is the highest sales level at which break-even occurs. An example is given in the exercises at the end of the chapter.

You might question why use a graphical method when the calculations can be done easily, as shown earlier in the chapter. Remember that one of the key roles of a management accountant is to provide information to managers for decision making. Information in a graphical format is quite common, and readily understood and accepted by managers. For example, the graph depicted in Exhibit 11.6 clearly conveys customers who are not generating sufficient contribution – a quick glance by a manager at such a graph may be easier than trawling through numbers.

Assumptions of cost-volume-profit analysis

As mentioned early in this chapter, the accountant's model on cost-volume- profit makes a number of assumptions, the main ones being:

1) Costs and revenues are linear functions of output.

2) It is assumed that costs and prices remain constant within a relevant range.

3) All units produced are sold.

4) In multiple product scenarios, sales mix is known and remains constant.

5) All prices and costs are known with certainty.

The first assumption can be seen in Exhibit 11.4. That is, as output increases, costs and sales increase in proportion. This is depicted by straight, evenly sloped lines for costs and revenues. In practice, this may not be so, as cost and revenues may increase or decrease as output varies. This takes us back to the economist's model depicted earlier. However, it is likely that costs and revenues do behave in a linear fashion in the short term and within a relevant range, suggesting the first two assumptions are reasonably valid. The third assumption is likely to be unrealistic, as some inventory is always possible. However, in the context of the decisions to be made using CVP analysis, we are looking to cover all costs of a particular period of time. Any inventories held from previous periods have already been embodied in previous costs. The fourth assumption is also likely to be unrealistic as sales mix will vary. In practice, changes in the sales mix may be examined using spreadsheets to determine the effects of changes in the mix on contribution. Or, the basic techniques might be applied in a different way (see Exhibit 11.6). Finally, while most businesses have a good knowledge of costs, it is unlikely that any business can be absolutely certain that its costs, and classification of costs (for example, fixed and variable) are correct. Again, tools such as spreadsheets might be used to build uncertainty into CVP analysis.

Despite the apparent limitations of CVP analysis stemming from its underlying assumptions, it is nonetheless a useful tool for any management accountant. The next section looks at ways to introduce uncertainties into the analysis, thereby overcoming some of the limitations.

Risk and uncertainty

As noted above, an important assumption of CVP analysis is that costs and revenues are known with certainty. This is unlikely to be the case in reality, but if managers and accountants have a good knowledge of underlying costs they can use this knowledge to (1) extend the concept of break-even to a band or range, (2) assess how risky the business or product cost structure is and, (3) conduct 'what if' or sensitivity analysis.

Margin of safety

The **margin of safety** is the number of units which are expected to be sold above break-even. For example, if the break-even output level is 10,000 units and a business currently sells 12,000 units, then the margin of safety is 2,000 units. It can also be expressed in terms of sales revenue. Let us look at an example using the data from Whitely Ltd and assume that they expect to sell 900 units. We know from our previous calculations that the break-even point is 600 units, or £240,000. If Whitely expects to sell 900 units for a total of £360,000, then the margin of safety is 300 units or £120,000. We can depict the margin of safety graphically, as shown in Exhibit 11.7 which is a reproduction of Exhibit 11.4 with the margin of safety added.

The margin of safety is often expressed as a percentage – 33.3 per cent in the case of Whitely Ltd. If you want to think of the margin of safety in an equation format, it can be represented as follows:

Margin of safety = Expected sales – Break-even sales

The sales figure can be expressed in units or monetary terms.

While it is a relatively crude measure, the margin of safety can be used by managers as a rule-of-thumb to ensure sales are not lost to the degree that the business fails to breakeven. If the margin of safety is quite high, then costs can increase or prices decrease considerably before remedial action might be required. If the margin of safety is quite low, then a greater emphasis might need to placed on keeping costs and prices under control. The ability of managers to adjust costs if required depends on the cost structure of the business, which is discussed in the next section.

Operating leverage

Operating leverage refers to relative amount of costs that are fixed and variable in the cost structure of a business. Some companies will have relatively high fixed costs compared with variable

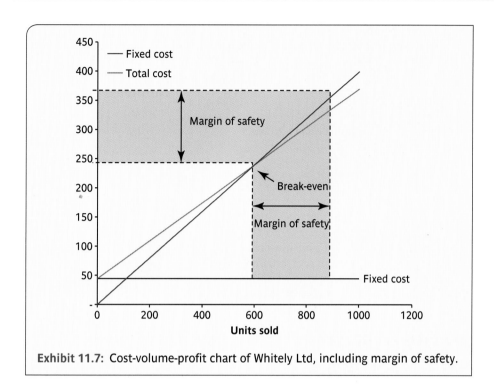

Exhibit 11.7: Cost-volume-profit chart of Whitely Ltd, including margin of safety.

costs and are said to have a high operating leverage. For example, pharmaceutical companies incur costs of up to $1 billon to develop new drugs over a 10 to 15 year period,[2] whereas the manufacture costs just pennies – just think of the price of a pack of paracetemol in your local pharmacy. Low operating leverage means variable costs are a relatively high proportion of total costs. Retailers like UK-based Tesco or Sainsbury have relatively low fixed costs and relatively high variable costs – the variable cost of each item sold (for example, the purchase price) is likely to be much higher than the associated fixed cost for that item.

The **degree of operating leverage** of a company can be used to assess its risk profile. Companies with high operating leverage are more vulnerable to decreasing sales, for example sharp economic and business cycle swings. Companies with a high level of costs tied up in machinery, plant and equipment cannot easily cut costs to adjust to a change in demand. So, if there is a downturn in the economy revenues and profits can plummet. On the other hand, companies with lower operating leverage can adapt their cost structure more rapidly as they have more variable costs.

The degree of operating leverage can be measured by taking the contribution in proportion to profit as follows (remember that contribution is sale minus variable costs):

$$\text{Degree of operating leverage} = \frac{\text{Contribution}}{\text{Profit}}$$

The following example illustrates this concept.

Assume a software company has invested £10 million into developing and marketing an application, which sells for £45 per copy. Each copy costs the company £5 to sell. Sales volume is expected to reach 1 million copies. The degree of operating leverage can be calculated as follows:

$$\frac{1,000,000 \times (£45 - £5)}{1,000,000 \times (£45 - £5) - £10,000,000}$$

$$\frac{£40,000,000}{£30,000,000}$$

Thus, the degree of operating leverage is 1.33. This means that, for example, a 25 per cent increase in sales volume would produce a 33 per cent (25% × 1.33) increase in profits – here are the figures to prove this:

	£million
Sales (1.25 m × £45)	56.25
Variable costs (1.25 × £5)	6.25
	50.00
Fixed costs	10.00
Profit	40.00

Conversely, if sales in the above example decreased by 25 per cent, profits would decline by 33 per cent.

What the operating leverage of a business teaches is that you should always be conscious of the risks associated with any changes in cost structure. As already noted, some sectors have high or low operating leverage. Nonetheless, having an appreciation of the degree of operating leverage assists managers in judging the effects of changes the relative proportion of fixed and variable costs.

Sensitivity analysis

Sensitivity analysis is used in many aspects of business and management accounting. It is in effect a 'what if' technique that examines effects of changes in underlying assumptions of a business scenario. Using spreadsheet software, it is relatively simple to input data on prices, costs and volumes, and then view effects of changes in any of the variables on the break-even point.

For example, Exhibit 11.8 shows two possible scenarios input in a spreadsheet for Whitely Ltd. The first shows the effects of an increasing sales price on profit, the second shows how increased fixed costs effect the number of units required to break even – the number increases to 800 units assuming all other variables remain constant. Any number of possible analyses could be quickly prepared in a spreadsheet, but remember that spreadsheets are only as useful as the data input to them. The management accountant will of course know and understand factors, such as a changing economic climate, which may impact costs and can incorporate such knowledge into sensitivity analyses.

Whitely Ltd – increasing sales price						
Sales price £	Expected sales units	Variable (cost) £	Contribution (per unit) £	Total (Contribution) £	Fixed cost £	Profit £
400	600	325	75	45,000	45,000	0
425	600	325	100	60,000	45,000	15,000
450	600	325	125	75,000	45,000	30,000
475	600	325	150	90,000	45,000	45,000
500	600	325	175	105,000	45,000	60 000
525	600	325	200	120,000	45,000	75,000
400	600	325	75	45,000	60,000	(15,000)
400	700	325	75	52,500	60,000	(7,500)

Exhibit 11.8: Example of sensitivity analysis for Whitely Ltd

Whitely Ltd – increasing fixed costs						
Sales price £	Expected sales units	Variable (cost) £	Contribution (per unit) £	Total (contribution) £	Fixed (cost) £	Profit £
400	800	325	75	60,000	60,000	0
400	900	325	75	67,500	60,000	7,500
400	1,000	325	75	75,000	60,000	15,000
400	1,100	325	75	82,500	60,000	22,500

Exhibit 11.8: (Continued)

Chapter summary

This chapter has detailed one set of techniques used by management accountants and business managers in general, namely CVP analysis. These techniques can be used in a number of practical ways:

Determine the output required to break even or achieve a target profit. In a single product setting, you learned that fixed cost divided by contribution per unit gives the number of units required to cover fixed and variables costs, that is, break to even.

Apply CVP analysis to a multiple-product setting. In multiple product scenarios, you have seen how an assumed sales mix can be utilized to effectively convert the scenario to a single product one. A break-even bundle of products can be calculated, but is should be remembered that the sales mix can change and this effects any previous calculations performed.

Prepare CVP and PV graphs. Several assumptions are made in CVP analysis. These assumptions are used when calculating break-even and also to graph the relationships between costs, revenues, volume and profit. The CVP graph can be used to quickly ascertain the effects of changes in volume on costs and revenues, while the PV graph relates output to profit. The assumptions used in CVP analysis and graphs include: (1) costs and revenues are linear; (2) prices and costs remain stable within a relevant range of output; (3) there are no inventories; (4) in multiple-product scenarios, a constant sales mix is assumed known; and, (5) all costs and prices are known and certain.

Risk and uncertainty. Measures of risk and uncertainty, such as the margin of safety, operating leverage and sensitivity analysis can be used to help managers gain more insight into the relationships of cost, volumes and profits. By incorporating risk and uncertainty, the effects of changes in underlying variables and assumptions can be seen.

Key terms

Break-even point The output/activity level at which neither a profit or loss is made (p. 269)
Contribution margin ratio Contribution as a proportion of sales (p. 273)
Cost-volume-profit The term used to describe the technique of analysing how costs and profits vary according to changing output volumes (p. 266)
Cost-volume-profit graph A graph which shows all costs (fixed, variable, total) in relation to output (p. 275)
Decreasing returns to scale A term used by economists to describe increasing variable costs as output increases beyond capacity and inefficiencies occur (p. 268)

> **Degree of operating leverage** A measure of the risk profile of a cost structure. Expressed as contribution divided by profit (p. 279)
> **Increasing returns to scale** A term used by economists to describe decreasing variable costs as output increases (p. 268)
> **Margin of safety** The sales volume (in units or monetary value) above break-even point (p. 278)
> **Operating leverage** Relative amount of costs that are fixed and variable in a business cost structure (p. 278)
>
> **Profit-volume graph** A variant of the CVP graph which reflects profits of varying levels of output (p. 276)
> **Relevant range** The range of output at which costs are assumed to be stable (p. 268)
> **Sales mix** The relative proportion of a product sales to total sales (p. 274)
> **Sensitivity analysis** A general term used in many business contexts to describe the analysis of how sensitive variables are to changes in conditions, for example, how fixed cost increases effect profits (p. 280)

Review questions

Level of difficulty:	**BASIC**	**INTERMEDIATE**	**ADVANCED**

11.1 How is CVP analysis used in short-term planning decisions? **[LO1]**

11.2 Define the term break-even point. **[LO1]**

11.3 Explain the difference between assumptions made by accountants on costs and revenues compared to economists. **[LO1]**

11.4 Explain what happens to the contribution once sales are made above the break-even point. **[LO1, LO2]**

11.5 Describe some of the main assumptions underlying CVP analysis. **[LO1, LO4]**

11.6 What is the margin of safety? **[LO1, LO5]**

11.7 In a business, if the contribution per unit of its product is £10 and the break-even point is 10,000 units, how much profit is made if 17,000 units are sold? **[LO2]**

11.8 What are the fixed costs associated with the business described in Review Question 11.7? **[LO2, LO3]**

11.9 Explain how CVP analysis can be extended to multiple product scenarios. **[LO3]**

11.10 The degree of operating leverage in a business is 1.75. If sales increase by 20,000 units, how much will profit increase by? **[LO3, LO5]**

11.11 What does operating leverage mean? **[LO5]**

Group discussion and activity questions

11.12 Do a web search of a product or service you are familiar with. Look at the any financial information available about the product/service. Perhaps use youtube.com to find videos about the product or service. Discuss the cost structure behind the product/service. **[LO1, LO2]**

11.13 Discuss the usefulness of CVP analysis in long-term decision making? **[LO1, LO2]**

11.14 Assume you are employed by a government organization which supports start-up businesses. Discuss whether or not you would advise start-ups on knowing the break-even point for their business. **[LO1, LO2]**

11.15 Assume you are a first time entrepreneur. You are seeking funds for your business for investors and government agencies. Discuss the usefulness of including CVP analysis in your business plans/proposals to potential lenders/investors. **[LO1, LO2]**

11.16 Do some research using the Internet on global hotel chains like Marriott and Hilton. Discuss whether such businesses have a high or low operating leverage. **[LO5]**

Exercises ●

E11.1 Price, costs and break-even [LO1, LO2]

A company is launching a new product. The variable cost of the product is £4.50 per unit and fixed costs total £21,000 per month. The initial selling price is to be set by adding a mark-up of 10 per cent to total unit cost based on estimated sales of 6,000 units per month.

Required:

(a) Calculate the initial selling price of the product.

After the initial launch phase:

1) The selling price is subsequently set at £9·50 per unit

2) Sales become 8,000 units per month

3) Costs are as set out above.

(b) Calculate, after the initial launch phase:

1) The expected profit per period.

2) The contribution to sales ratio (as a percentage).

3) The break-even sales units per period.

4) The total cost per unit.

Source: adapted from Association of Chartered Certified Accountants, Certified Accounting Technician, Paper T4.

E11.2 Break-even, margin of safety [LO1, LO2, LO5]

Elextra Ltd manufactures a single product, an electric motor for use in automatic door systems. The variable costs of the motor are as given below:

	£/motor
Material components	25
Labour cost	30
Variable overhead	20

The figure for fixed overheads is not readily available. However, it is known from last year's results that production of 50,000 units results in a loss of £1,500,000.

The selling price of the product is £125 and maximum sales are expected to be 100,000 units.

Required:

Calculate the following for Elextra Ltd:

a) The annual fixed costs.

b) The break-even point.

c) The margin of safety at maximum sales level.

d) The number of units, sales revenue, costs and profit or loss if 60,000 units are produced and sold.

E11.3 **Break-even, target profit [LO1, LO2, LO5]**

The following information relates to Yellow Ltd for the year to 30 June 2014:

Units sold	50,000
Selling price per unit	£40
Net profit per unit	£9
Contribution as percentage of sales	40%

During 2015, the company would like to increase its sales, but to do so would have to reduce price by 20 per cent. The variable cost per unit would not change, but due to increased activity, overhead will increase fixed costs by £30,000 per annum.

Required:

Calculate how many units the company will need to sell in 2015 in order to make the same level of profit as 2014.

E11.4 **Contribution to sales ratio [LO1]**

A company sells three different levels of television maintenance contracts to its customers: basic, standard and advanced. Selling prices, unit costs and monthly sales are as follows:

	Basic £	Standard £	Advanced £
Selling price	50	100	135
Variable cost	30	50	65
Monthly contracts sold	750	450	300

Required:

Calculate the average contribution to sales ratio of the company:

a) Based on the sales mix stated above

b) If the total number of monthly contracts sold remains the same, but equal numbers of each contract are sold.

Source: Chartered Institute of Management Accountants, Management Accounting Pillar, Paper P2.

E11.5 **Break-even, margin of safety, target profit chart [LO1, LO2, LO4]**

The following budget data relates to the business of Katharine Rader for the coming year:

Sales £	7,700,000
Variable costs £	3,200,000
Fixed costs £	1,700,000
Sales units	1,300,000

Required:

Based on the above data, calculate:

a)   The contribution per unit.

b)   The break-even point in sales units and value.

c)   The margin of safety as a monetary value.

d)   How many units must be sold to achieve a profit of £394,400.

e)   Prepare a graph showing all cost and revenue data and the break-even point.

E11.6 Budget and break-even [LO1, LO2, LO4, LO5]

You have been reviewing the internal management accounts of Diversions Ltd, prepared for the year ending 31 March 2015 as part of the annual budget review/preparation process. The company is organized into two divisions, wholesale and retail, each of which serves distinct markets. Each division has been adversely impacted by the economic downturn and the company overall has struggled to meet targets.

The following is the summarized management accounts for the year ended 31 March 2015:

	Note	Wholesale €	Retail €	Total €
Sales	1	350,000	200,000	550,000
Less:	2	240,000	80,000	320,000
Contribution		110,000	120,000	230,000
Less:				
Fixed costs	3	90,000	130,000	220,000
Net profit/loss		20,000	– 10,000	10,000

Notes:

1)   Sales in each division are categorized as either 'Full price sales' or 'Discounted price sales'. The following was the split of sales for each division by value and by unit volume in the year ended 31 March 2015:

	Wholesale division		Retail diviision	
	€	Unit volume [% of toal]	€	Unit volume [% of total]
Full price sales	70,000	5,000 items [12.5%]	140,000	4,000 items [40%]
Discounted price sales	280,000	35,000 items [87.5%]	60,000	6,000 items [60%]
	350,000	40,000 items [100%]	200,000	10,000 items [100%]

2)   The average variable cost of the items sold in each division during the year ended 31 March 2015 was €6 in the wholesale division (that is, €240,000/40,000 items sold) and €8 in the retail division (that is, €80,000/10,000 items sold). The additional amount of €2 per item in the retail division is accounted for by additional packaging and promotional expenditure.

3) Fixed costs in each division during the year ended 31 March 2015 were categorized as follows:

	Wholesale €	Retail €
Building and occupancy costs	40,000	70,000
Other administrative costs	35,000	20,000
Interest and financial costs	15,000	40,000
	90,000	130,000

The following changes are anticipated for the forthcoming budget for year ended 31 March 2016:

1) Unit volumes for each division: total unit volume in the wholesale division is not expected to change in the upcoming year. In the retail division, total unit volumes are expected to decline by 3 per cent.

2) Full price sales and discounted price sales: the split between 'Full price sales' and 'Discounted price sales' in each division is expected to be as follows in the forthcoming year:

	Wholesale	Retail
Full price sales	15% of division volume	50% of division volume
Discounted price sales	85% of division volume	50% of division volume

3) Selling prices in each division: the wholesale division's average selling prices are not expected to change for either 'Full price sales' or 'Discounted price sales'. However, due to pressures in the retail business, the average selling price under each category is expected to decline by €1 per item sold.

4) Variable costs in each division: no change in the average variable cost per item is expected in the wholesale division. In the retail division, a variable cost saving of €0.50 per item is projected by changing the packaging used for the items sold.

5) Fixed costs are expected to change as follows in each division:

	Wholesale	Retail
Building and occupancy costs	Increase by 2%	Decrease by 2%
Other administrative costs	Unchanged	Increase by 1%
Interest and financial costs	Increase by 1%	Increase by 1.5%

Required:

a) Using the values shown for the year end 31 March 2015, calculate separately the contribution to sales margin for the wholesale division, the retail division and the company overall.

b) Prepare the budgeted sales and costs for each division and the company overall for the year end 31 March 2016 using the same layout as shown for the year end 31 March 2015 and taking account of the anticipated changes outlined above.

c) Using the figures for the company overall which you have computed in the previous step, prepare a break-even chart, clearly identifying each of the following:

The revenue line

The variable costs line

The fixed costs line

The total costs line

The break-even point

The profit area

The margin of safety.

The activity axis should be in increments of 5,000 units and end at 55,000 units. The costs/revenues axis should be in increments of €50,000 and end at €600,000.

Source: adapted from The Institute of Certified Public Accountants in Ireland, Formation 2, Management Accounting.

E11.7 **Multi-product break-even [LO3]**

A company manufactures five products in one factory. The company uses a just-in-time production system. The company's budgeted fixed costs for the next year are £300,000. The table summarizes the budgeted sales and contribution details for the five products for the next year.

Product	A	B	C	D	E
Unit selling price (£)	40	15	40	30	20
Total sales (£000's)	400	180	1,400	900	200
Contribution/Sales ratio (%)	45	30	25	20	(10)

Exhibit 11.9 has been prepared to summarize the above budget figures in the table. The chart shows the cumulative profit and sales for products, starting with the product with the lowest contribution to sales ratio.

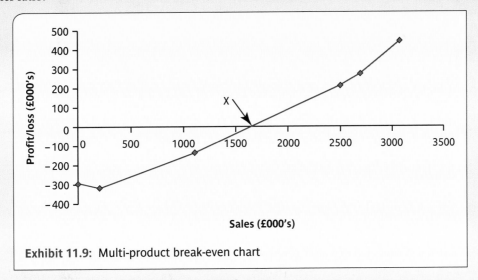

Exhibit 11.9: Multi-product break-even chart

After the diagram had been prepared, the Marketing Director has said that Products A and E are complementary products. The budget assumes that there are no sales of Product A without also selling Product E and no sales of Product E without selling Product A.

Required:

a) Explain two reasons why the chart does not provide a useful summary of the budget data provided.

b) Explain the meaning of point X on the chart.

c) Calculate the breakeven revenue for the next year using the budgeted sales mix.

Source: adapted from Chartered Institute of Management Accountants, Performance Pillar, P2 Performance Management.

● ● ● Case study problem ●

C11.1 Aidan Stone [LO1, LO2, LO3, LO5]

Aidan Stone set up an engineering business 18 months ago and operates as a sole trader. The business specializes in automated entry systems such as electric entrance gates for domestic houses or large automated entry gates/doors for business customers. The business does not manufacture or supply gates or doors, instead automating existing entrance gates/doors. This means Aidan typically holds a reasonable level of electronic components as inventory.

The business has grown rapidly. Within six months Aidan took on his first employee and currently has three employees. Each employee costs £30,000 annually, including all employer social insurance costs. Aidan's business has developed a good reputation and has seen an increasing volume of turnover in servicing existing automated entrances, that is, service or repair calls on entrance gates/doors not installed by the business. A typical week's turnover is as follows:

Sixteen service calls at minimum call out charge of £120.

Two new installations at average price of £2,200.

The average material cost associated with new installations is £500.

Aidan is not an accountant but, being an engineer, has a keen logical way of thinking and has a good ability to work with numbers. He has been trying to work out what he calls 'the minimum amount of work to keep afloat'. He is keen to develop such a rule-of-thumb measure as he would like to concentrate more on developing the business – currently most of his time is spent working on installations and service calls. To help him develop the business he plans to employ an apprentice engineer at a total cost of £20,000 per annum. Aidan is also conscious that the domestic market for his services may be weakening due to a general economic slowdown, hence a minimum work level measure would be quite useful for him. An extract from the most recent set of annual financial statements is given below – costs have remained relatively constant since then.

	£
Purchases of components	51,300
Employee and premises insurance	5,200
Repayments of leases on vehicles and equipment	10,500
Bank charges	500
Advertising	1,200
Salaries (of current staff)	90,000
Drawings (Aidan)	35,000

Required:

Aidan has asked you for some help to develop his rule of thumb. He would like a measure of how many service calls/installations he needs to do each week to 'keep afloat', assuming the business operates 50 weeks per annum. He also asked you to assume the apprentice engineer will be employed.

Based on the above information you should prepare a report for Aidan Stone which contains the following:

a) An explanation of a useful technique which you used to help develop a rule of thumb for Aidan.

b) An explanation of which costs are relevant to the technique you have chosen and any assumptions made in your analysis.

c) A 'minimum amount of work' rule of thumb for Aidan on a weekly basis and comments briefly on the result.

d) The limitations of the measure calculated and the analysis/information used.

Recommended reading

- http://entrepreneurs.about.com/od/businessplan/a/breakeven.htm (accessed on 27 June 2012).

This website provides a useful summary of break-even analysis from the view of an entrepreneur.

- Solomons, D. (1968) 'Breakeven analysis under absorption costing', *The Accounting Review*, 43(3), pp. 447–52.

This is a classic piece of literature on this topic.

- Powers, T. L. (1987) 'Breakeven analysis with semi-fixed costs', *Industrial Marketing Management*, 16(1), pp. 35–41.

A useful article on break-even analysis from a non-accounting perspective.

- Steven, G. (2005) 'Management Accounting fundamentals, CVP analysis – Paper C1, study notes', *Financial Management*, September, pp. 51–52 (also available at http://www1.cimaglobal.com/cps/rde/xbcr/SID-0AE7C4D1-7B4C0CEF/live/fm_sept05_p51-52.pdf, accessed on 27 June 2012).

This is a useful article from CIMA, which includes a worked example.

Notes

1 http://brainstormtech.blogs.fortune.cnn.com/2008/06/19/itunes-store-5-billion-songs-50000-movies-per-day/ (accessed on 30 November 2008).
2 http://www.washingtontimes.com/news/2009/mar/13/blocking-drug-development/(accessed on 4 December 2009).

When you have read this chapter

Log on to the Online Learning Centre at **www.mcgraw-hill.co.uk/textbooks/burns** to explore chapter-by-chapter test questions, links and further online study tools for Management Accounting.

CHAPTER 12

COST BEHAVIOUR AND ESTIMATION

Chapter outline

- Cost behaviour

- Effects of changes in activity on costs

- Cost estimation methods

Learning outcomes

On completion of this chapter, students will be able to:

LO1 Explain how changes in output/activity effects variable and fixed costs

LO2 Use a cost formula to predict costs when output/activity changes

LO3 Explain and analyse mixed costs using the high-low method, a scattergraph method and least-squares regression method

LO4 Understand multiple regression analysis and how spreadsheet software can be used for such analysis

LO5 Analyse the impact of learning curves on cost estimation

Introduction

In Chapter 3, you learned how costs can be classified according to how they behave when the level of production or business activity changes. The previous chapter showed how understanding the relationship between fixed and variable costs is very useful to managers making decisions on changes in cost structure or activity level. This chapter takes your knowledge of costs thus far, and extends it to show how an understanding of cost behaviour can help estimate and predict business costs. For example, if production output is to be increased by 30 per cent, a manager may know that fixed costs will step up to a higher level, causing total unit costs to increase. By being able to predict how costs behave in response to changing activity levels, managers should be able to avoid unsuspected cost increases and management accountants should be able to predict cost behaviour.

This chapter begins by briefly revising how costs behave in response to changes in business output or activity. Then, cost behaviour is examined in more detail for each cost type. The final part of the chapter presents some techniques used to estimate cost behaviour in mixed costs and how the learning curve effect impacts cost estimates.

Cost behaviour

From Chapter 3, you know the two main behavioural cost classifications are variable and fixed. Just to remind you, a variable cost varies (in total) according to the activity level of the business or organization; a fixed cost remains constant regardless of activity, within a relevant range. It is also possible for a cost to be a **mixed cost**, which means the cost portrays both fixed and variable elements as business activity increases. The make-up of an organization's costs is often termed its **cost structure**. For example, some industries have high fixed cost levels, while others have high variable cost levels. *Management Accounting in Practice 12.1* gives you some examples. The remainder of this section provides a more detailed analysis of cost behaviour, which is necessary before we look at some estimation methods.

12.1: Management Accounting in Practice

Some examples of cost structures

The following examples give some indication of the varying cost structures in real businesses.

iPhone/iPad apps

In early 2012, there were more than 300,000 apps available for the iPhone and iPad at the Apple app store. Some are free, some require payment. In 2010, the top-grossing paid app was a game called *Angry Birds.* This app can be downloaded for €0.79. The app is developed by a Finnish company called Rovio. This company is likely to have a high level of fixed costs in its cost structure. The costs of owning/running a premises are fixed, as is the cost of the information technology infrastructure used to develop the apps and the salaries of software developers. Arguably, the distribution costs on the app store are also fixed. Apple charge all app developers a $99 annual fee plus 30 per cent of all revenues. The variable costs per unit of an iPhone/iPad app are minimal, or even close to zero.

Mars Inc.

US-based Mars Inc. is a well-known global food and confectionary company. Its brands include Mars, Snickers, Uncle Ben's, Wrigley and Whiskas. Foods products such as those made by Mars are typically produced in a complex manufacturing process, the costs of which could be classified as a fixed cost over time (that is, depreciation). Other typical fixed costs like salaries, rent and insurance will also occur. However, at the product level, variable costs occur too. Thinking about a Snickers bar for example, the variable costs would include ingredients and process labour costs. Relative to the previous example, the cost structure of Mars Inc. is likely to have a relatively higher proportion of variable costs than the cost of a software development company.

Effects of changes in activity on costs

In Chapter 11, you learned how management accountants take some ideas from the economist's cost curve. In management accounting, it is typically assumed that costs follow a linear pattern within a relevant range of output or activity. Building on what you learned in Chapter 3, let us take a closer look at costs to see how they behave within this relevant range.

Variable costs

You know from Chapter 3 that a variable cost is one which varies in total with respect to changes in output or activity levels. For example, if output increased or decreased by 10 per cent, you would expect the total variable costs to also increase or decrease by 10 per cent. When we think of variable costs per unit of product or service delivered, then the variable cost per unit/service remains constant. Take a look at Exhibit 12.1, which depicts the costs of a doctors' surgery giving travel vaccinations.

No. of patients	Cost per vaccine £	Total cost £
20	50	1,000
40	50	2,000
50	50	2,500

Exhibit 12.1: Total cost example: vaccines at medical practice

As shown in Exhibit 12.1, the cost per vaccine remains constant at £50, with the total costs increasing as the number of vaccines given increases. This example also shows how total costs vary depending on the number of patients – which we can term the **activity/output base**. This activity/output base forms the relationship to the variable cost. There are likely to several activity/output bases in any organization which can cause variable costs to increase. The most obvious base is the output or activity level, but other examples might include the number of customer orders, the number of customer complaints, the number of deliveries, and so on. See Chapter 6, 'Activity-based costing' for more detail on what drives costs.

Looking again at Exhibit 12.1, if we chart costs against the number of patients, the chart would show a linear cost to output relationship as shown in Exhibit 12.2.

As already noted, the cost structure of a business determines the portion of fixed and variable costs. However, not all variable costs are likely to have a perfect linear pattern, or directly proportional variable cost as shown in Exhibit 12.2. Some variable costs follow a step-type pattern and can be termed **step-variable costs**. A step variable cost is depicted in Exhibit 12.3.

A good example of a step-variable cost is waste disposal costs. To encourage recycling, many local authorities increase the disposal cost per ton of waste as the volume of waste increases. A similar policy is applied to water supplies in some countries to encourage water conservation. Another example is support-type labour costs. As activity levels increase within the relevant range, more staff may be needed in maintenance or logistics departments. While it could be argued such costs are fixed, it could be equally argued they increase in steps in line with business activity/output.

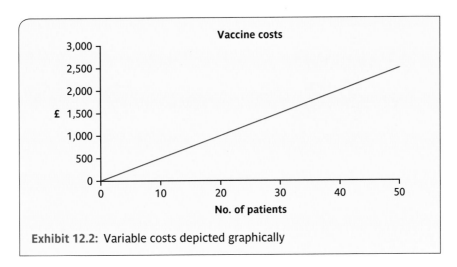

Exhibit 12.2: Variable costs depicted graphically

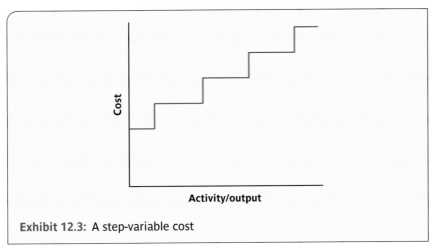

Exhibit 12.3: A step-variable cost

Fixed costs

From Chapter 3, you know that fixed costs remain constant in total regardless of the level of activity. Keeping with the example in Exhibit 12.1, let us now assume that a practice receptionist is employed at a cost of £400 per week. Even if no patients were vaccinated, this cost will be incurred; if 100 patients are vaccinated, the cost is still £400. However, the more patients vaccinated, the lower the fixed cost per vaccine. Exhibit 12.4 depicts the fixed cost in total and fixed costs per patient graphically. You can clearly see how the unit fixed cost decreases as the number of patients increase.

Fixed costs can be classified as either committed or discretionary. A **committed fixed cost** is one which is more longer term in nature and cannot be readily reduced or eliminated. For example, the costs of equipment, buildings or senior staff cannot be eliminated in the short run. Decisions to incur additional committed fixed costs are given careful consideration by managers due to the longer-term implications. A **discretionary fixed cost**, while constant regardless of output, has a shorter-term focus and can be eliminated or reduced. Typical examples are advertising costs and training costs. Discretionary fixed costs tend to be cut when business volumes drop, for example due to economic recession. Many organizations have experienced an increasing level of fixed costs in recent decades, often driven by increased automation. In turn, increased automation and information technology has increased demand for skilled knowledge workers. The salaries of these workers have increased the committed fixed costs in many organizations; typically such staff are retained due to their high skill levels.

Which costs are treated as fixed in an organization can vary. For example, some organizations treat labour as a fixed cost as they argue that labour is a cost which cannot be simply removed. Low-cost airlines like easyJet and Ryanair regard staff costs as fixed for two reasons. First, the staff cost remains

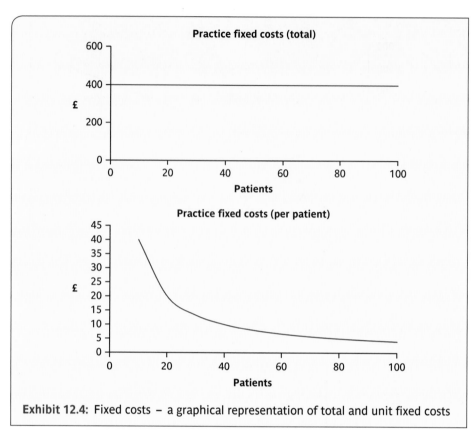

Exhibit 12.4: Fixed costs – a graphical representation of total and unit fixed costs

the same for a flight, day or week regardless of passenger numbers on a plane. Secondly, both airlines are based in Europe, where employment law protects workers, who cannot be just let go without pay.

As with variable costs, fixed costs too are likely to remain stable within a relevant range of output. Above or below the relevant range, fixed costs are likely to step up or down. Exhibit 12.5 depicts steps in fixed costs across all ranges of business output/activity.

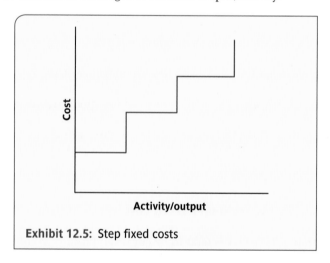

Exhibit 12.5: Step fixed costs

While steps in variable costs may occur within the normal relevant range, stepped fixed costs are more likely to occur as the relevant range changes. For example, the rent of a business premises is likely to stay stable from zero output up to the maximum capacity of the business. However, if the business needs to rent additional space, the additional rent cost will cause this fixed cost to step up. It will, however, remain at this new level until full capacity is reached again. The steps in fixed costs are thus much broader than a stepped variable cost, which can be seen in a comparison of Exhibits 12.2 and 12.5.

Mixed costs

A mixed cost is one which contains both fixed and variable elements. Mixed costs are also referred to as semi-variable costs. A simple example of a mixed cost is the running costs of a motor vehicle. Some costs are fixed – insurance, taxation and some depreciation – not varying regardless of how much the vehicle is used. Other costs – fuel, toll charges and some depreciation – increase the more the vehicle is used. Another example of a mixed cost is mobile telephone cost, as seen in *Management Accounting in Practice 12.2*.

12.2: Management Accounting in Practice

Mixed cost example – mobile data services

UK-based mobile telephone operators, such as O2, Orange and Vodafone, offer mobile voice and data services to personal and business users alike. Customers typically sign up to a contract with enough voice and data allowance to suit their needs – which implies a fixed monthly cost. However, if the voice or data allowance is exceeded, or calls outside the agreed package are made, then the cost takes on the qualities of a mixed cost. To give an example, in February 2011, O2 UK (www.o2.co.uk) provided a standard 0.5 GB data allowance to business customers. If data usage exceeds this allowance, then a charge per megabyte is payable.

In Chapter 11, you learned how to depict total costs graphically (see p. 275). The total cost line is in fact a mixed cost as it contains both fixed and variable elements. Exhibit 12.6 depicts a typical mixed cost, using the following data:

Fixed cost	£1,000
Variable cost	£2 per unit
Cost valid from 0 to 400 units output.	

As an exercise, work out the total costs for yourself before looking at the chart in Exhibit 12.6.

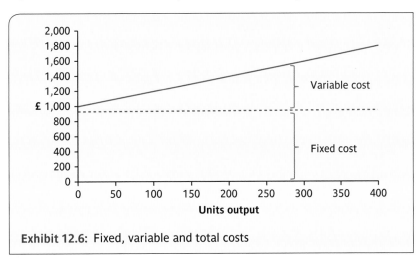

Exhibit 12.6: Fixed, variable and total costs

The cost line depicted in Exhibit 12.6 is similar to what you have already learned while depicting CVP charts in Chapter 11. From Chapter 11, you also know that costs within a relevant range of output are assumed to behave in a linear fashion. The total costs line shown in Exhibit 12.6 can be represented as a simple equation, which is a useful way to express the relationship between the fixed and variable elements of a mixed cost:

$$Y = a + bX$$

where:

    Y = Total cost

    a = Total fixed costs (which is £1,000 in Exhibit 12.6)

    b = The variable cost per unit, which in mathematical terms is the slope of the line (this is 2 in Exhibit 12.6)

    X = Output/activity level.

Using this equation and the cost information given in Exhibit 12.6, the equation would be:

$$Y = 1,000 + 2X$$

If we assume the costs used in Exhibit 12.6 would not change at an output of 500 units, the total costs at this level of output would be:

$$Y = 1,000 + 2(500)$$

$$Y = 2,000$$

You can easily work out this cost without using an equation, but we will build on this equation later in the chapter.

Cost estimation methods

As you have seen, mixed costs can be expressed in the form of an equation. Also, in Chapter 9, you learned how standards can be set for costs. These standards costs can be determined by conducting studies of tasks over time; for example, time studies of employees performing certain tasks may reveal an average task time, which is adopted as the standard. In other words, deriving standard costs is one method of estimating cost. While useful, setting standards is a time-consuming exercise. Standards also assume a physical and observable relationship between inputs and outputs, which may not always apply. Therefore, several computational and mathematical cost estimation techniques are often used by management accountants to analyse and estimate mixed costs. These are the subject of the remainder of this chapter.

High-low method

Looking at Exhibit 12.6, you can see the total costs at the lowest output level (that is, zero) and the highest output (that is, 400). Using costs at the highest and lowest levels of output is actually an estimation method used by management accountants to estimate costs. The **high-low method** uses two observed/recorded costs to estimate the behaviour of mixed costs at varying levels of output. Exhibit 12.7 shows some recorded costs paid for web-hosting by a fictional online retailer, WhiteKnight Online. WhiteKnight's web-hosting company charges it on a monthly basis depending on the bandwidth used (in terabytes, or TB) to process customer orders, customer payments and general customer browsing.

Month	Traffic in TB	Hosting costs £
Jan	6,500	9,210
Feb	6,600	9,310
Mar	6,000	9,000
Apr	8,500	10,060
May	14,750	11,425
Jun	15,000	12,000
Jul	13,250	10,975
Aug	10,400	10,120
Sep	11,300	11,520

Exhibit 12.7: WhiteKnight Online – cost data

The high-low method uses costs at the highest and lowest output/activity levels to estimate the variable and fixed cost components. In the case of the WhiteKnight example in Exhibit 12.7, the activity is the volume of data. The lowest month of activity is March, with June highest. Using this data, we can estimate the variable cost component as shown in Exhibit 12.8. The difference in activity level (that is, 9,000 TB) is compared with the change in cost as shown to derive the variable cost.

	Traffic in TB	Hosting costs £		
High activity	15,000	12,000		
Low activity	6,000	9,000		
Change	9,000	3,000		
Variable cost is thus	3,000 / 9,000		=	0.33 per TB

Exhibit 12.8: WhiteKnight Online – calculating variable cost

Having worked out the variable cost per TB used as £0.33, we can now work out the fixed cost component by taking either the high or low activity level. Using the low activity level, the fixed cost can be calculated as per Exhibit 12.9.

Fixed cost element	£
Total cost at low activity level	9,000
Variable cost (£0.33 × 6,000)	2,000
Fixed cost	7,000

Exhibit 12.9: WhiteKnight Online – calculating fixed cost

Now that we know the fixed and variable cost components, we can write cost equation as shown earlier. For WhiteKnight the equation would be:

$$Y = £7,000 + £0.33X$$

where Y is total cost and X is the TB of bandwidth used.

In terms of this equation, the total cost (Y) is known as the **dependent variable** as the total cost is dependent on the activity level – TB used in this case. The activity level itself is termed the **independent variable**, as it causes the increases of decreases in total cost.

We could also depict the hosting costs of WhiteKnight graphically using the high and low points and the fixed costs we have calculated, as shown in Exhibit 12.10. The graph uses the high and low cost and activity levels, but also extends the total cost line to the horizontal axis at the level of fixed costs (that is, £7,000).

The high-low method is simple to use, but it does suffer from a few problems. First, even if costs at many different activity levels over a reasonably long time frame are available, there is no way to know for sure that there is a direct relationship between the highest activity level and the highest cost, and the same for the lowest data. A further, and probably more critical issue, is that only two data observations (or points) are used to estimate costs within a range. This first assumes costs follow a linear relationship (as shown in Exhibit 12.10). Secondly, the high and low data points can themselves be distorted by irregular events, for example industrial action or clean-up after an industrial accident in a manufacturing company. There are some other methods, which are examined below, but a management accountant may use the high-low method as a quick estimation tool while being fully aware of its limitations.

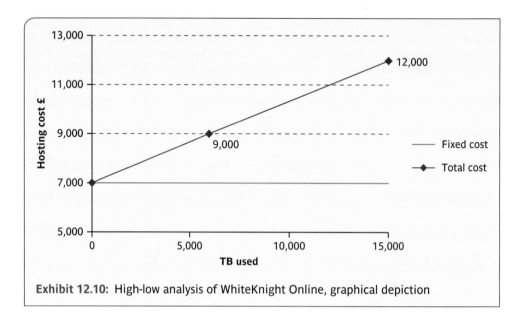

Exhibit 12.10: High-low analysis of WhiteKnight Online, graphical depiction

Scattergraph method

The scattergraph method, as its name suggests, uses a scattergraph to estimate costs. A scattergraph plots all observed data. The graph is very similar to the one shown in Exhibit 12.10, with the activity or output shown on the horizontal (X) axis, and costs and the vertical (Y) axis. To prepare a scattergraph manually, you plot each cost and activity level observed. Using the data for WhiteKnight from Exhibit 12.7, we can plot all the data points as shown in Exhibit 12.11.

The high and low data points can be seen in Exhibit 12.11 (in bold). Using the scattergraph method, the total costs line is estimated by drawing a line of best fit through the data points. The line should be drawn so that approximately equal number of the data points fall above and below the line. The line of best fit is termed a **regression line**, which in mathematical terms is a line of averages. As you might expect, the fixed cost can be determined by drawing the line to the

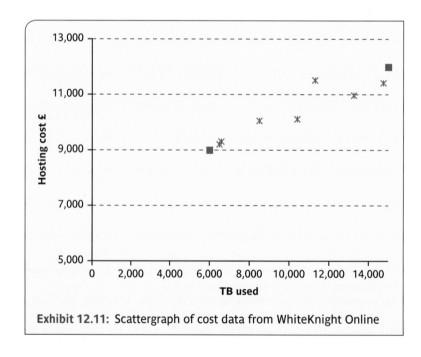

Exhibit 12.11: Scattergraph of cost data from WhiteKnight Online

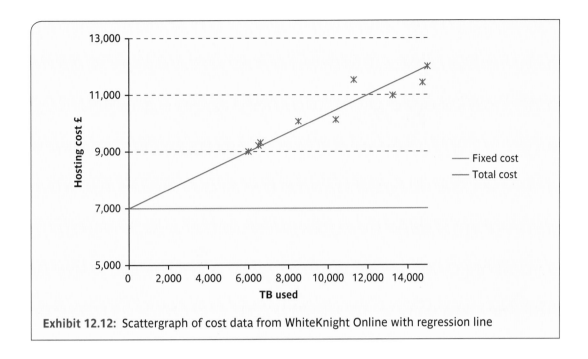

Exhibit 12.12: Scattergraph of cost data from WhiteKnight Online with regression line

vertical (cost) axis. Also the slope of the total cost line represents variable costs per unit of activity or output. A line of best fit based on the data for WhiteKnight Online (Exhibit 12.7) is shown in Exhibit 12.12. The fixed cost line is also shown.

The relevant range of activity based on the data provided for WhiteKnight Online is between 6,000 and 15,000 terabytes of hosting data. Within this range, the scattergraph in Exhibit 12.12 could be used to calculate the total costs at any particular level of activity. An advantage of the scattergraph method is that it uses all data points, and a skilled analyst or management accountant may even be able to exclude one-off instances where costs were higher or lower than normal due to extraordinary events. Using all data points is also an improvement on the high-low method, as is the visual depiction of costs which managers often find useful. A major disadvantage of the scattergraph method is that judgement is required to draw the regression line. It is quite likely that no two people will get the exact same solution using this method. Thankfully, there is a more mathematically sound approach called least squares regression, which we will explore below.

Least squares regression method

The concept of the **least squares regression method** is similar to the regression line used in the scattergraph method just discussed. However, using least squares regression a mathematical formula can be used to calculate and draw the regression line rather than visual inspection. This overcomes the major drawback of the scattergraph method.

A complex formula is used to calculate the regression line using the least squares method. The formula is given below, but we will use Microsoft Excel (a common spreadsheet program) to work out the regression line. The basic idea of least-squares regression can be seen graphically in Exhibit 12.13, which shows the data points and regression line for WhiteKnight Online. The distance between each data point and the regression line (shown by the vertical red lines) represent what are termed **regression errors**. The least square regression method computes the regression line which minimizes the sum of the regression errors.

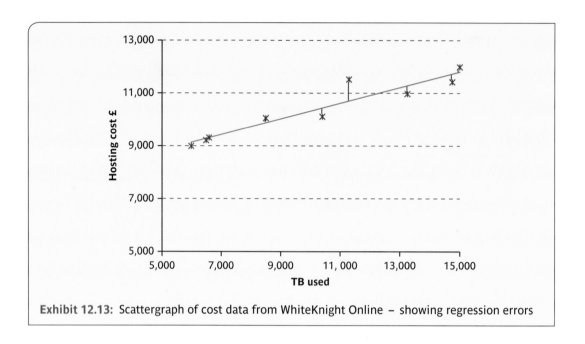

Exhibit 12.13: Scattergraph of cost data from WhiteKnight Online – showing regression errors

The formula for a regression line is $Y = a + bX$. Using the least squares regression method values for a and b can be determined as follows:

$$b = \frac{n(\Sigma XY) - (\Sigma X)(\Sigma Y)}{n(\Sigma X^2) - (\Sigma X)^2}$$

$$a = \frac{(\Sigma Y) - b(\Sigma X)}{n}$$

where:

X = the level of activity/output (the independent variable)

Y = the total cost (the dependent variable)

a = total fixed cost (vertical intercept)

b = total variable cost (slope of line)

n = number of observations

Σ = sum of variables across n observations.

You can see from the formula that a bit of work is required to work out the equation for the regression line if using the least squares regression method manually. One of the exercises for this chapter asks you to do it manually later. Fortunately Microsoft Excel can do the work very quickly. Before looking at an example using Microsoft Excel, one further point on least squares regression is necessary. If using Microsoft Excel (or some other software) to do least squares regression for you, the software can also provide a statistic called the **coefficient of variation** which is commonly referred to as r^2. The value of r^2 is a best fit measure, which indicates how well the values of the dependent variable (Y) are explained by the independent variable (X). The closer the value of r^2 to 1, the better the fit, or in other words, the more reliable the cost equation derived. Now let us see how we can do a least squares regression calculation in Microsoft Excel. The data used in the WhiteKnight Online is shown again here (Exhibit 12.14) for convenience, as it is used in the example shown in Exhibit 12.13.

Month	Traffic in TB	Hosting costs £
Jan	6,500	9,210
Feb	6,600	9,310
Mar	6,000	9,000
Apr	8,500	10,060
May	14,750	11,425
Jun	15,000	12,000
Jul	13,250	10,975
Aug	10,400	10,120
Sep	11,300	11,520

Exhibit 12.14: Hosting cost data for WhiteKnight Online

Exhibit 12.15 shows, and explains, how Microsoft Excel can be used to quickly determine a cost equation based on the least squares regression technique.

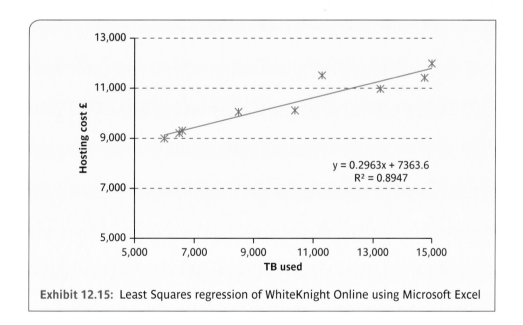

Exhibit 12.15: Least Squares regression of WhiteKnight Online using Microsoft Excel

Using Microsoft Excel, the graph in Exhibit 12.15 can be generated by first plotting the costs and terabytes of data used for WhiteKnight Online on an XY scatter chart (a particular type of chart of available in Microsoft Excel). This will generate a scattergraph just like the one shown in Exhibit 12.11. Next, an option to add a 'Trend line' can be selected – this the term used in Microsoft Excel for a regression line. When adding the trendline, options can be selected to show the equation and the r^2 value, which you can see in the graph above.

As you can see in Exhibit 12.15, Microsoft Excel provides the equation of the regression line (or trendline as it is called in the software), as well as the value for r^2. Earlier, when we estimated a cost equation using the high-low method, the result was $Y = £7,000 + £0.33X$. The cost equation given using the linear regression method above is $Y = £7,364 + £0.30X$ (rounded). This latter equation is more accurate as all data is used to derive the equation. Also, the r^2 value above is 0.89, which suggest that a relatively close relationship between costs and output in this example. Linear regression offers a number of advantages over all other methods we have used thus far to estimate costs. First, it is based on sound mathematical principles, for example all data points are used; the square of the regression errors are used, which give a greater weighting to values further from the regression line. Second, we can use tools like Microsoft Excel to do the calculations, which means we can use large volumes of data without too much trouble.

A limitation of linear regression as a technique is that it assumes costs are driven by one cause. This may not be the case and mixed costs may be driven by a number of factors. For example, management salary costs may be driven by factors such as age, years' experience, professional qualifications, and so on. **Multiple regression** techniques allow more factors to be included in the analysis of the dependent variable (cost). In such as a case, the equation for cost would look something like this:

$$Y = a + b_1X_1 + b_2X_2 + \dots b_nX_n$$

where n is the number of factors driving cost.

The mathematics behind multiple regression is complex and is not mentioned in detail here. However, Microsoft Excel can do multiple regression quite easily. Take a look at *Worked Example 12.1*, which gives an example using transport costs.

Worked Example 12.1

Multiple regression example

The following data relates to some observations of delivery costs for a company. The delivery costs are determined by the weight of the product and the distance to the customer's premises.

	X_1	X_2	Y
Delivery no.	Dist (km)	Weight (tons)	Cost £
1	498	31	500
2	380	9	280
3	394	30	450
4	234	8	250
5	238	12	300
6	205	23	440
7	440	19	500
8	556	7	335
9	526	10	400
10	173	14	340
11	285	7	280
12	557	17	530
13	156	8	230
14	375	31	440
15	364	9	280
16	318	18	435
17	388	9	380

As there are two independent variables in this example, distance and weight, the cost equation can be expressed as follows:

$$Y = a + b_1X_1 + b_2X_2$$

where X_1 is distance and X_2 is weight.

The full procedure for multiple regression analysis in Microsoft Excel can be seen in a video which accompanies this chapter – the video is available on this book's website www.mcgraw-hill.co.uk/textbooks/burns. An excerpt of the outcome of the analysis is shown in the table:

	Coefficients
Intercept	143.8161481
Dist (km)	0.324779747
Weight (tons)	7.435844138

The *intercept* in the table equals the value of a, and the values of b_1 and b_2 are also shown as 0.32 and 7.44 respectively. Thus the cost equation is:

$$Y = 143.8 + 0.32X_1 + 7.44X_2$$

So if the distance to a customer was 200 kilometres, and the weight of the delivery was 5 tons, the cost estimate would be:

$$Y = 143.8 + 0.32(200) + 7.44(5)$$

$$Y = £245$$

Microsoft Excel also provides an r^2 value, which is this case is 0.75, indicating a reasonably solid relationship between the dependent (transport cost) and independent variables (weight, distance).

In practice, any multiple regression calculations would benefit from a much larger number of cost observations than that shown in *Worked Example 12.1*. This can be quite easily managed by Microsoft Excel or other similar spreadsheet software.

Learning curve effects

One final concept which can be useful in cost estimating is the **learning curve effect**. This refers to a possible tendency for tasks to be performed quicker as employees learn them and become more efficient. Thus, over time, costs may decrease. The term **experience curve** is also used, but this term is used more to describe the relationship between cost and quality over time.

Typically, as employees learn a particular task, their efficiency improves at a high rate, but this tends to level off to a more steady state as less efficiency gains are possible. A learning curve can be depicted graphically as shown in Exhibit 12.16, which depicts a typical relationship between average time to produce a unit of a product and cumulative units produced.

The learning curve can be modelled mathematically. For example, if the time taken to complete a task is 10 hours, and each time the task is performed the time taken is reduced to 90 per cent of

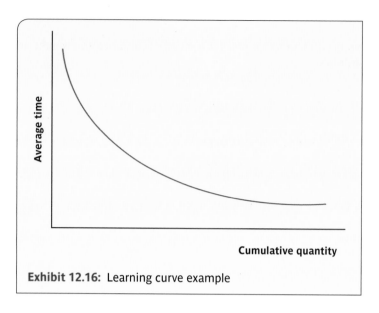

Exhibit 12.16: Learning curve example

the previous performance, the result would be as follows:

Time 1   10 hours

Time 2   9 hours (10 × 90 per cent)

Time 3   8.1 hours (9 × 90 per cent)

and so on.

The mathematical relationship for a learning curve effect is expressed as follows:

$$Yn = tX^l$$

Where:

   Yn = cumulative average time per unit of output for n units
   X = cumulative units output
   t = time taken for first unit
   l = rate of learning.

   The rate of learning, l, is derived as:

$$l = \frac{\ln(\text{learning rate})}{\ln(2)}$$

(Note: ln represents the natural logarithm of a number.)

Worked Example 12.2 provides an example of a learning curve chart prepared using a Microsoft Excel spreadsheet. This curve could be easily used by management accountants to estimate future costs of labour for example. This example assumes a known rate of learning of 90 per cent and you are likely to be given the figure in most examination settings. The spreadsheet used for this example can be found at this book's website www.mcgraw-hill.co.uk/textbook/burns.

Worked Example 12.2

Learning curve example

Assume the time taken to produce the first unit of a new product takes 55 minutes. The rate of learning has been calculated as 90 per cent. Using this data, let us use Microsoft Excel to do the calculations and draw a learning curve. Note that Microsoft

Excel does not have a built-in learning curve formula, so the formula above needs to be used. To draw a curve, we need some points to plot. We will calculate the cumulative average time for 5, 10, 15, 20, 50 and 100 units. The results are:

Units	Cumulative avg time/unit (in mins)
1 (Given)	55.00
5	43.06
10	38.76
15	36.44
20	34.88
50	30.35
100	27.31

Using these data points, we can plot the cumulative quantity in the horizontal (X) axis and the cumulative average time per unit on the vertical (Y) axis. Using the charting functions in Microsoft Excel, we can generate the graph in Exhibit 12.17.

Recent research, summarized in *Management Accounting Insight 12.1*, reports that the learning curve is used in practice, particularly when target costing methods are used.

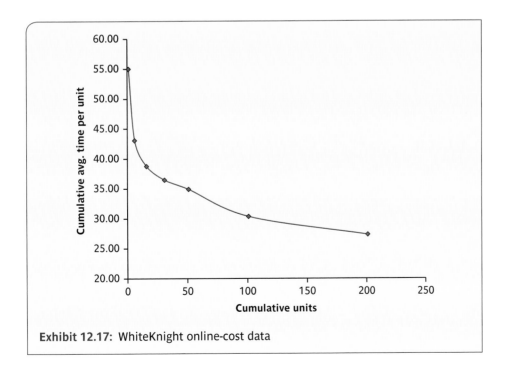

Exhibit 12.17: WhiteKnight online-cost data

12.1: Management Accounting Insight

Use of learning curve

Research undertaken by CIMA (2010) reports that learning curve techniques are used in practice for budgeting and planning, and in more recent times for target costing (see Chapter 19) – which accounts for about two-thirds of the respondent companies using the technique. The research found that learning curves are used in traditional assembly type industries, but also in the financial sector and government, for example. The research mentions how some manufacturing firms who were interviewed set initial product prices below cost as they anticipate a learning curve effect over time. While just over 5 per cent of respondent firms used learning curve techniques, one-third identified the tools as useful for their sector. Some key reasons for lack of use of the technique was a lack of knowledge on the part of managers/accountants and insufficient data.

Source: CIMA (2010).

Exercise

Do you think a learning curve effect is likely in service sector firms too? Can you think of an example?

Chapter summary

This chapter has developed what you have learned in Chapter 3, providing a more detailed account of cost behaviour in response to changes in output or activity of an organization. The chapter introduced several techniques used by management accountants to estimate mixed costs in particular. The most basic technique you learned was the high-low method, which uses two extreme observations of cost (the costs at the lowest and highest output) to estimate costs. A slightly more advanced method is the scattergraph method, which although using all data available on cost, requires some skill and judgement by management accountants in the drawing of a regression line. A more accurate and mathematically based approach is the least squares regression method, which you have seen can be easily done in spreadsheet software like Microsoft Excel. Least squares regression can be used when only one dependent variable exists which drives or influences costs. In the case of more than one dependent variable, multiple regression analysis can be adopted, and again this can be best done using spreadsheet software (as shown in *Worked Example 12.1*). Finally, cost estimation may be subject to a learning curve effect, which means that costs may decline sharply as efficiencies increase, but flatten out to a steady rate eventually.

Key terms

Activity/output base The output level used to estimate costs (p. 292)

Coefficient of variation A best fit measure, which indicates how well the values of the dependent variable are explained by the independent variable (p. 300)

Committed fixed cost A cost which is fixed and cannot be changed (p. 294)

Cost structure The relative amount of fixed and variable costs in a business (p. 291)

Dependent variable A variable (cost) whose change is dependent on other variables (p. 297)

Discretionary fixed cost A cost which is at the discretion of managers (p. 294)

Experience curve The ability to improve performance based on experience, represented by a downward sloping curve (p. 303)

High-low method A cost estimation method which use two extremities of output (high and low) (p. 296)

Independent variable A variable (output) which causes changes in the dependent variable (p. 297)

Learning curve effect See experience curve (p. 303)

Least squares regression method A mathematical formula that can be used to

calculate and draw a regression line rather than visual inspection or a scattergraph (p. 299)
Mixed cost A cost which has fixed and variable elements (p. 291)
Multiple regression A mathematical regression model with more than one independent variable (p. 302)

Regression errors The distance between a data point and the regression line (p. 299)
Regression line A line of best fit of multiple data points (p. 298)
Step-variable costs Variable costs which increase in steps beyond certain levels of output (p. 292)

● ● Review questions ● ● ● ● ● ● ● ● ● ● ● connect ● ● ●

Level of difficulty:	**BASIC**	**INTERMEDIATE**	**ADVANCED**

12.1 Distinguish between variable, fixed and mixed costs. **[LO1]**

12.2 Distinguish between committed and discretionary fixed costs. **[LO1]**

12.3 What is a stepped fixed cost? **[LO1]**

12.4 What is a stepped variable cost? **[LO1]**

12.5 Explain the high-low method as used to estimate costs. **[LO3]**

12.6 What is the main problem with the high-low method? **[LO3]**

12.7 Why is least squares regression superior to the high-low method? **[LO3]**

12.8 What is a 'regression' or 'trend' line? **[LO3, LO4]**

12.9 Explain the terms 'dependent variable' and 'independent variable'. **[LO3, LO4]**

12.10 What does a learning curve effect mean? **[LO5]**

● ● Group discussion and activity topics ● ● ● ● ● ● ● ● ● ●

12.11 Discuss sources of cost data that management accountants might use to estimate transport and haulage costs. **[LO1, LO2]**

12.12 Using the internet as a research tool, try to discuss the cost structure of the global hotel groups like Marriott and InterContinental. **[LO1, LO2]**

12.13 Identify and describe some instances when a learning curve effect may be present in a business or organization. **[LO5]**

12.14 Discuss how economic recessions might affect the cost structure of an organization. **[LO1, LO2]**

12.15 Discuss the relative merits of the high-low method of cost estimation versus least squares regression. **[LO3]**

12.16 Assume a business has seasonal sales patterns, for example winter clothing or ice-cream sales. What factors might be considered in a multiple regression model to determine sales levels? **[LO4]**

• • • • **Exercises** • • • • • • • • • • • • • • • • • **connect** • • •

E12.1 **Overhead using cost estimations [LO2, LO3]**

The following data has been extracted from the budget working papers of WR Limited:

Activity (machine hours)	Overhead cost £
10,000	13,468
12,000	14,162
16,000	15,549
18,000	16,242

In November 201X, the actual activity was 13,780 machine hours and the actual overhead cost incurred was £14,521.

Required:

Calculate the total overhead expenditure variance for November 201X. (Look back to Chapter 9 for the total overhead expenditure variance calculations if you need to.)

Source: adapted from Chartered Institute of Management Accountants, Paper P1, Performance Evaluation.

E12.2 **High-low methods [LO3]**

The following information for advertising and sales has been established over the past six months:

Month	Sales revenue £000's	Advertising expenditure £000's
1	155	3.0
2	125	2.5
3	200	6.0
4	175	5.5
5	150	4.5
6	225	6.5

Required:

Using the high-low method which of the following is the correct equation for linking advertising and sales based on the above data?

a)   Sales revenue = 62,500 + (25 × Advertising expenditure)

b)   Advertising expenditure = –2,500 + (0.04 × Sales revenue)

c)   Sales revenue = 95,000 + (20 × Advertising expenditure)

d)   Advertising expenditure = –4,750 + (0.05 × Sales revenue)

Source: adapted from Association of Chartered Certified Accountants, Paper 1.2, Financial Information for Managers.

E12.3 **Basic learning curve [LO5]**

A company is preparing a quotation for a new product. The time taken for the first unit of the product was 30 minutes and the company expects an 85 per cent learning curve. The quotation is to be based on the time taken for the final unit within the learning period which is expected to end after the company has produced 200 units.

Required:

Calculate the time per unit to be used for the quotation.

Note: The learning index for an 85 per cent learning curve is –0.2345.

Source: adapted from Chartered Institute of Management Accountants, Paper P1, Performance Evaluation.

E12.4 **High-low method [LO2, LO3]**

Amcor Limited, a manufacturing company, manufactures a single product, metal flywheels. One year ago, the company installed the first module of a new information system for accounting and product costing. This module has enabled the company to accurately record manufacturing information throughout the year. The management accountant at Amcor is anxious to proceed with a second module of the system, which will forecast costs using cost formulae.

During the first full year of data collection by the new system, the following information has been extracted.

	February	July
Units produced	7,500	11,250
Cost of goods manufactured	£210,000	£321,250
Work in progress – start of month	£11,250	£40,000
Work in progress – end of month	£18,750	£26,250
Material cost per unit	£7.50	£7.50
Labour cost per unit	£12.50	£12.50

The manufacturing overhead, not shown above, consists of both fixed and variable elements. To enable good quality data to be input into the second module of the system, the management accountant wants to determine how much manufacturing overhead varies with production levels.

Required:

a) Calculate, for both February and July, the total amount of manufacturing overhead. Assume all overhead has been absorbed.

b) Using the high-low method, derive a cost formula for manufacturing overhead, clearly showing the variable cost per unit.

c) If 8,750 units were produced during a month, calculate the total manufacturing costs, with an opening work in progress valued at £12,500 and closing work in progress valued at £15,500. You may assume all overhead is absorbed.

d) Outline the limitations of using the high low method as a cost estimation tool and mention another method which can yield better results.

Source: with thanks to Dr Barbara Flood, Dublin City University.

E12.5 **High-low method [LO3]**

Records from previous periods show the following relationship between machine hours and maintenance costs:

Machine hours	Maintenance costs
14,000	£26,800
9,800	£21,760
8,000	£19,600
15,400	£28,480

Required:

The estimated maintenance costs for 12,000 machine hours are:

a)   £22,200

b)   £23,000

d)   £24,400

d)   £26,600

Source: adapted from Chartered Institute of Management Accountants, Paper P1, Performance Evaluation.

E12.6 Learning curve [LO5]

PL is a manufacturing company that has just commenced and is now ready to begin full-scale production in July. It is hoped output volumes will gradually increase as the employees become more skilled at operating machines. The products are to be manufactured in batches of 100 units and the labour cost of the first batch is expected to be £200 at a labour rate of £20 per hour.

It is expected that there will be a 90 per cent learning curve effect on the direct labour cost for the first 64 batches. Thereafter the direct labour hours for each batch will be the same as that of the sixty-fourth batch until the total production equals 256 batches.

Required:

a)   Calculate the labour hours expected for the sixty-fourth batch.

b)   Calculate the total number of labour hours for the first 256 batches.

Note: The learning index for a 90 per cent learning curve is −0.152.

Source: adapted from Chartered Institute of Management Accountants, Paper P2, Decision Management.

E12.7 High-low method, regression [LO1, LO2, LO3, LO4]

Jack Robinson opened a small business six months ago. The business involves producing high-quality ready-to-eat meals on a subcontracting basis for restaurants which offer their customers a home delivery service. The following table indicates Jack's production levels and total costs in the months since he commenced business:

Month	1	2	3	4	5	6
Number of meals produced	50	100	200	370	270	340
Total costs £	990	1,470	2,520	4,030	3,180	3,900

In order to better understand the relationship between production levels and total cost, Jack carried out regression analysis on the above data (with 'number of meals produced' as the independent variable and 'total costs' as the dependent variable). The following is a summary of the results of this analysis:

R-squared	0.998
Slope (*b*)	£9.74
Intercept (*a*)	£522

Jack commented that, because of the very high R-squared statistic, an estimate of future costs based on the results of the regression analysis would be likely to be almost completely accurate.

The number of meals produced next month is expected to be 400.

Required:

a) Using the results of the regression analysis, calculate an estimate of total costs for next month.

b) Do you share Jack's confidence that the above estimate of next month's costs is likely to be almost completely accurate? Explain why or why not.

c) Develop an alternative estimate of next month's costs using the high-low method, and explain why this method is generally less reliable than regression analysis as a basis for cost estimation.

Source: adapted from The Institute of Certified Public Accountants in Ireland, Professional 1, Strategic Management Accounting.

E12.8 **Regression formula [LO3]**

Exhibit 12.7 in this chapter provided the following data for WhiteKnight Online:

Month	Traffic in TB	Hosting costs £
Jan	6,500	9,210
Feb	6,600	9,310
Mar	6,000	9,000
Apr	8,500	10,060
May	14,750	11,425
Jun	15,000	12,000
Jul	13,250	10,975
Aug	10,400	10,120
Sep	11,300	11,520

In Exhibit 12.15, you have seen how Microsoft Excel can be used to determine the equation for a regression line. The answer given in Exhibit 12.15 was $Y = £7,364 + £0.30X$, allowing for rounding.

Required:

Using the formulae given in this chapter (repeated below), manually work out the regression line equation based in the data for WhiteKnight Online. (Hint: Why not use a spreadsheet to do the calculations for you.)

$$b = \frac{n(\Sigma XY) - (\Sigma X)(\Sigma Y)}{n(\Sigma X^2) - (\Sigma X)^2}$$

$$a = \frac{(\Sigma Y) - b(\Sigma Y)}{n}$$

Where:

X = the level of activity/output (the independent variable)

Y = the total cost (the dependent variable)

a = total fixed cost (vertical intercept)

b = total variable cost (slope of line)

n = number of observations

Σ = sum of variables across n observations.

• • • Case study problem • • • • • • • • • • • connect™ • •

C12.1 **PRM Ltd [LO1, LO2, LO3, LO4]**

PRM Ltd is a manufacturing company based in the Midlands, England. They manufacture a range of industrial components for delivery throughout mainland UK. In the past, product costing was a simple rule-of-thumb exercise. However, in the past decade or so product costing has had to improve due to an increasing level of competitiveness from producers in Europe and China.

In recent months, a new product costing module has been added to the company's accounting system. The management accountant is very happy about this new module as it will replace a lot of existing spreadsheets and hopefully provide more accurate costs. After a few weeks investigating the functionality of the new software module, the management accountant is quite happy with it as basically he can manipulate data by providing cost data and cost relationships to the software. In some cases this is very simple; for example, each product will have the same number of labour or machine hours. However, in some cases the cost relationship is more complex. In particular, transport costs are proving difficult to estimate as the cost of transport to a customer's premises depends on the distance travelled, the weight of the products, whether tolled roads are used, and so on. The accountant also knows that multiple products may be delivered on the same truck to maximize load capacity (filling the truck as best possible), but he has decided to assume that one product shipment per truck is the only reasonable assumption he can start with.

In an effort to determine a cost relationship for transport costs, the following costs have been obtained from the dispatch department for last month, as well as the distance to the customer and the weight of the shipment. For convenience the distance has been rounded to the nearest 10 km.

Delivery no.	Dist (km)	Weight (tons)	Cost £
1	500	46.5	600
2	380	13.5	350
3	390	45.0	360
4	230	12.0	120
5	240	18.0	200
6	200	34.5	350
7	440	28.5	500
8	560	10.5	375
9	500	15.0	380
10	170	21.0	220
11	260	10.5	210
12	540	25.5	480
13	160	12.0	185
14	380	46.5	490
15	370	13.5	225
16	350	27.0	400
17	390	13.5	280
18	310	12.0	225

Delivery no.	Dist (km)	Weight (tons)	Cost £
19	390	18.0	360
20	350	34.5	490
21	120	28.5	340
22	180	10.5	225
23	380	15.0	400
24	110	21.0	275
25	260	10.5	320
26	260	25.5	440
27	250	12.0	320
28	270	12.0	320
29	300	18.0	320
30	290	34.5	440
31	240	28.5	250
32	230	10.5	320
33	380	15.0	390
34	500	21.0	500
35	510	10.5	395
36	320	25.5	350
37	120	12.0	240
38	170	21.0	400
39	240	23.0	425
40	310	25.0	490

Required:

a) Using the multiple regression tools available in Microsoft Excel, determine a cost equation for estimating delivery costs at PRM Ltd. A spreadsheet with the above data pre-loaded is available on the book's website at www.mcgraw-hill.co.uk/textbooks/burns. Note: you need only examine the r^2 value, as well as the values for the intercept and the dependent variables as given by Microsoft Excel for the purposes of this question.

b) Would you regard the cost equation in part (a) as being sufficient for the needs of the new product costing software module in (i) the short term and (ii) the longer term? Suggest remedies if any.

c) Further, to the analysis in part (a), the management accountant has had a chat with the dispatch manager about the load capacity of each truck. He has found out that all trucks travelling beyond 400 km are always fully utilized (that is, 100 per cent capacity), which the dispatch calls a load factor of 1. It also emerges that the average load factor on trucks travelling between 200 and 399 km is 0.80, with all others having a 0.70 load factor. The cost of each delivery is the same regardless of whether a truck is full or empty. Taking the load factors into account, re-analyse the data to derive a new cost equation for delivery costs. For convenience, retain the analysis as a two variable regression analysis, and adjust the cost according to the load factor. What comments would you give to the management accountant on the new equation?

d) Using the equation derived in part (a), calculate the cost of delivering a 16-tonne load to a customer 365 km from PRM Ltd.

● ● ● Recommended reading ● ● ● ● ● ● ● ● ● ● ● ● ● ● ● ● ● ●

This chapter has covered the basic details of linear regression and associated formulae, as well as multiple regression, using Microsoft Excel. For more detailed reading consult:

- Levine, D., M. Berenson, and T. Krehbiel (2007) *Statistics for Managers using Microsoft Excel*, Harlow: Prentice Hall.
- Swan, J. (2005) *Practical Financial Modelling*, London: CIMA.

Both of the above texts give more detailed on the use of the Microsoft Excel spreadsheet software in financial modelling scenarios.

● ● ● Reference ●

CIMA (2010) *The Learning Curve: The Key to Future Management*, Research Executive Summary Series, 6(12), London: CIMA, available at http://www.cimaglobal.com/Documents/Thought_leadership_docs/Learning_curve.pdf (accessed on 26 June 2012).

When you have read this chapter

Log on to the Online Learning Centre at **www.mcgraw-hill.co.uk/textbooks/burns** to explore chapter-by-chapter test questions, links and further online study tools for Management Accounting.

CHAPTER 13

DECISION MAKING: RELEVANT COSTS AND REVENUES

Chapter outline

- Short-term decision making
- Pricing decisions
- Product mix decisions
- Equipment replacement decisions

- Outsourcing decisions
- Discontinuation decisions
- Sell or process further decisions
- Relevant revenues

Learning outcomes

On completion of this chapter, students will be able to:

LO1 Identify and explain relevant costs and revenues for short-term decisions

LO2 Decide on special pricing decisions, including one-off special orders

LO3 Decide on the best short-term product mix given limited resources

LO4 Decide on whether or not to replace process equipment

LO5 Decide if a product or business activity should be discontinued

LO6 Decide, based on costs and revenues, if outsourcing is viable

LO7 Decide on whether a product should be sold or processed further

Introduction

In Chapter 3, we introduced the term relevant cost. We will revisit the topic in more detail in this chapter. As outlined in Chapter 3, information can be relevant to some decisions made on a daily basis by managers, and sometimes it is not relevant. For the more routine short-term decisions, such as what products to sell or which parts to make to or buy, managers have to filter out the relevant cost and revenue information to help them make the right decisions. This chapter will help you learn some of the skills applied by managers when faced with business decisions. This is achieved by illustrating how relevant costs and revenues can be determined in several typical decisions made by managers and accountants within and organization. The chapter will first refresh your memory on some basic cost concepts outlined in Chapter 3. Then, six different business decisions will be outlined in some detail.

Short-term decision making

A key element of making any decision is having the right information. With the right information to hand, the respective costs and benefits of various options can be compared and the most suitable option chosen. Not all costs are relevant to decisions. A **relevant cost** (see also Chapter 3) is one which differs between alternatives. A relevant cost typically has two main traits:

1) It is a future cost (incurred in the future), and

2) There must be a cost differential between decision alternatives.

Taking these two traits briefly, any costs incurred in the past (that is, sunk costs) are never relevant to decision making. Any sunk costs have been incurred already and cannot be undone. Secondly, if future costs differ, they are relevant; if they do not differ they are irrelevant. Chapter 3 has used the terms avoidable cost and unavoidable cost to distinguish costs which can differ between various decision scenarios. The former is a relevant cost; the latter, being unavoidable, does not differ with any chosen course of action and is thus irrelevant. *Worked Example 13.1* gives a brief example of distinguishing relevant from irrelevant costs. A **relevant revenue** is one which differs due to a particular course of action. In essence, it is the additional or differential revenues arising from making a decision. The relevant revenues are examined later in the chapter.

The only relevant cost in the example shown in *Worked Example 13.1* is the material cost, as it both differs and is a future cost if we assume the decision is made to use the higher-quality fabric. Labour cost remains the same regardless of any decision.

Of course, managers will also take into account non-financial information when making decisions. For example, as we will see later in the chapter, many firms outsource activities. In making the decision

---

Worked Example 13.1	**Identifying relevant costs**

A clothing manufacturer has a profitable business line making cashmere overcoats for corporate customers. The customers use the overcoats as gifts to retiring executives and their own customers. The garments use only high-quality cashmere which currently cost £80 per coat. Labour costs are £25 per coat. Several customers have recently requested that only fine Italian cashmere from a certain mill is used in their overcoats. Although small in number, these customers make up 80 per cent of the sales volume. Thus, the managers are considering using only the Italian cashmere for all overcoats. The Italian cashmere will cost £100 per coat.

The costs of the two options are set out below:

	Existing cashmere cost	Italian cashmere coat
Material cost £	80	100
Labour cost £	25	25
Total cost £	105	125

to outsource, the relevant costs will be things like cost savings from possible staff reductions and the cost of the outsourcing contract itself. The decision based on cost may be quite easy as typically specialized outsourcing companies can deliver services at lower costs. The final decision would also have to consider factors like the quality of service offered, knowledge of staff at the outsourcing company and loss of key staff. To give another example, many government authorities in the UK use solar-powered traffic warning signs at schools, for marine navigation and even for parking meters. The decision to invest in solar technologies must consider the amount of sunshine as a key relevant factor. Thus, in some areas mains or battery-powered back-up may be necessary; in others not.

For the most part of this chapter, we will adopt the relevant cost approach to analysing several business decisions. As shown in *Worked Example 13.1*, by isolating the relevant costs, a manager can quickly concentrate on the short-term effects of the decision being made, there is no need to analyse each and every cost. Using this approach, effects of decisions on profits can be easily assessed. As you progress through this chapter, keep the relevant cost concept in mind. You might also find it useful to revise Chapter 11, as we will separate fixed and variable costs for most of the decisions examined in this chapter, that is, use a contribution approach. The reason for separating fixed and variable costs is their very nature; fixed costs will tend to remain stable in the shorter term, and thus are typically not relevant to short-term decisions.

Finally, before delving into each of the decisions you may find it useful to consider the relevant cost of some cost elements, as follows:

- *Materials* – the relevant cost of materials is typically the current replacement cost if they have to be re-stocked. However, if materials are available and will not be replenished, the relevant cost will be the higher of their alternative use value and current resale value.

- *Plant and equipment* – the cash cost of purchasing new equipment is relevant, but any cost of existing equipment is not relevant. Depreciation is also irrelevant as it is an accounting entry. Any other incremental costs will be relevant.

- *Labour* – the cost of labour is usually not relevant unless any incremental labour cost is incurred as a result of taking a decision.

We will deal with the above costs and others in the decisions which follow, namely: pricing special orders, product mix decisions, equipment replacement, outsourcing, discontinuation of products/ services and further processing decisions. Finally, towards the end of the chapter a short discussion on relevant revenues is given.

13.1: Management Accounting in Practice

Fixed and variable costs in web-based firms

Web-based companies like Google, Facebook and Twitter are often seen as providers of 'free' services. Their business model is generally to accumulate as many users as possible through its targeted online adverts which accompany web searches. Facebook and Twitter as of yet have not realized ways to generate revenues in the same sense that Google has. However, these and similar web-based firms incur substantial costs each month – server farms, technical support, energy, bandwidth, and so on. Such running costs could easily be classified as fixed costs, and perhaps seen as irrelevant costs to many business decisions of these firms. Also in web-based business models, it is quite likely that revenues, as opposed to costs, will be more relevant to business decisions. For example, if Facebook currently has enough technical hardware and capacity to grow from its current 800 million or so users to 1 billion, then a large portion of the costs have been incurred and would be a sunk cost. There may be some variable costs as user volumes grow, for example, more technical support staff, but the likely focus will be on increasing revenues to cover the existing fixed costs. In summary, in web-based business models, revenues may be more relevant to decision making than costs.

Source: http://www.guardian.co.uk/technology/2011/nov/20/free-internet-twitter-google-facebook (accessed on 22 November 2011).

Exercise

Can you think of examples of costs relevant to decisions in the types of organization mentioned above?

Pricing decisions

Businesses will set prices based on the cost of the product or service they deliver and the profit margin they would like to achieve. Pricing is covered in detail in Chapter 14, but here we will explore the decision to accept or reject what is often called a special order. This means a one-time or infrequent customer order that has either lower/higher costs or a lower/higher selling price. The basic decision criteria for a special order is whether the additional revenues obtained exceed additional costs, that is, whether a profit is made. The decision also needs to take into account the available capacity of the organization to make or deliver the product/service in question. If capacity is available, then any special orders which yield a positive contribution would normally be accepted. If capacity is not available, then the contribution from any special order would have to be greater than the contribution forgone from existing orders. Of course, qualitative factors come into play too. For example, assuming capacity is not an issue, a high-value customer might ask for special orders at a lower one-off price. If we assume the contribution is negative, the order may still be accepted as opposed to losing existing sales volume.

Let us now look at some examples, one with spare capacity and one where capacity is fully utilized.

Worked Example 13.2

Spare capacity

AmsterDairy makes dairy products for the European market. It makes and sells its own brand butter to European markets and currently operates at 85 per cent capacity. It has been approached by a retailer to manufacture a high-quality butter under the retailer's own label. The order is a one-off order, as the butter is being used to mark the retailer's one hundred years in business. The current costs per 100 kg of butter are as follows:

	£
Ingredients – milk, colouring, and so on	80
Direct labour	25
Overhead	25
Cost per 100 kg	130

The overhead cost includes a fixed overhead allocation of £19. An additional ingredient would need to be added at a cost of £2 per 100 kg. AmsterDairy will also have to change the print on their packaging for the special order, at a one-off cost of £1,250. The retailer is offering a price of £150 per 100 kg for an order quantity of 12,000 kg. This is £10 less than the standard selling price.

To evaluate the special order from the retailer, we need only consider incremental costs and revenues, as set out below:

	£
Revenue (£150 × 120)	18,000
Less costs:	
Ingredients – normal (£80 × 120)	9,600
Ingredients – additional (£2 × 120)	240
Direct labour (£25 × 120)	3,000
Variable overhead ((£25 – £19)) × 120	720
Fixed overhead – print on packing	1,250
Total cost	14,810
Incremental profit	3,190

Note: An order of 12,000 kg is equal to 120 units of 100 kg each.

As you can see *Worked Example 13.2*, even though the selling price is £10 less than the normal price a profit can still be made on the special order and thus it should be accepted. This is because the company has spare capacity and there are no opportunity costs of production lost by making the special order. You will see in *Worked Example 13.3* how the analysis changes when capacity is fully utilized. Note too that only existing fixed costs (£19 per 100 kg) are not considered in the decision, as these costs will be incurred regardless of the decision.

Worked Example 13.3

Full capacity

Using the same cost data for standard butter production as in *Worked Example 13.2*, let us now assume that the butter processing plant is at full capacity. One of AmsterDairy's larger customers approaches them to produce a special order of the same price and quantity as given in *Worked Example 13.2*, that is, 12,000 kg at a price of £150. Additional ingredients will cost £1 per 100kg and there are no additional fixed costs.

As the plant is at full capacity, we need to consider the opportunity cost of lost sales. The incremental costs are revenues are as follows:

	£
Revenue (£150 × 120)	18,000
Less costs:	
Ingredients – normal (£80 × 120)	9,600
Ingredients – additional (£1 × 120)	120
Direct labour (£25 × 120)	3,000
Variable overhead ((£25 – £19)) × 120	720
Opportunity cost (see working)	5,880
Total cost	19,320
Incremental loss	1,320

Working:

The contribution from normal production is:
£160 – (£130 cost as given – £19 fixed overhead) = £160 –£111
= £49 per 100 kg,
Thus, the lost contribution is 120 × £49 = £5,880.

In *Worked Example 13.3*, AmsterDairy would lose money owing to the contribution forgone by relinquishing capacity to make the special order. Thus, on the basis of cost the decision would be to reject the special order request. However, we are told the order is from one of the largest customers, so AmsterDairy would need to carefully consider its options. For example, it may be able to subcontract some of the existing work, or the special order itself. We will examine this type of decision later in this chapter.

Product mix decisions

Basic product mix decisions

Most organizations make more than one product or deliver more than one type of service. They do their activities typically within certain constraints. These constraints may be the capacity of equipment/processes, a shortage of raw materials or a shortage of labour for example. While such constraints can be overcome in the longer term, in short-term decision making a manager needs to consider three factors:

1) Which constraint prevents the business from being able to meet demand for its products/ services?

2) Which products offer the best contribution towards profit?

3) Will selecting one product/service over another affect fixed costs?

Taking these three factors into account, a business should aim to maximize its profits by promoting products/services which yield the highest contribution per unit of the constrained resource. So, if a consulting practice has limited consulting hours to offer (for example, 40 hours per consultant per week), then ideally the consultant's time would be best spent working on clients who yield the highest contribution per hour. Note, too, that fixed costs normally do not change with product mix changes, at least in the short run.

Worked Example 13.4 shows an example in which labour hours are the constraining factor.

Worked Example 13.4

Product mix with scarce labour

Savvy Ltd makes two products which are used in the assembly of satellite navigation systems used in cars. The two variable costs of the two products are as follows:

	SM01 (£)	SM03 (£)
Material component costs	20	40
Direct labour (£30 per hour)	60	30
Variable overhead	20	20
	100	90

The sales price per unit is £200 for the SM01 unit and £150 for the SM03. During August the direct labour is limited to 8,000 hours. Sales demand in August is expected to be 3,000 units of the SM01 and 5,000 units of SM03. Fixed costs are £250,000 per month and are not affected by changes in product mix.

The decision to derive the profit maximizing product mix involves three steps.

Step 1

Confirm the constraint on output – you do not necessarily have to do this step for this exercise, but in practice it may be necessary.

	SM01	SM03	Total
Labour hours per unit	2 hours	1 hour	
Sales demand	3,000 units	5,000 units	
Hours needed	6,000 hours	5,000 hours	11,000 hours
Hours available			8,000 hours
Shortfall in hours			3,000 hours

Step 2

Calculate the contribution earned by each product per unit of scarce resource, which is labour hours in this example.

	SM01	SM03
Selling price £	200	150
Variable cost £	100	90
Contribution per unit £	100	60
Labour hours per unit	2	1
Contribution per hour £	50	60

As the SM03 unit has a contribution of £60 per labour hour, it should be produced in priority to the SM01 even though SM01 has a higher unit contribution.

Step 3

Determine the production/sales taking based on the contribution per unit of the constraint.

In this example, sufficient units of SM03 can be made to meet full sales demand, and the remaining labour hours available can be used to make units of SM01. The production and profits can be summarized as follows:

Product	Labour hours required	Labour hours used	Contribution £	
SM03	5,000	5,000	300,000	(5,000 hrs × £60)
SM01	6,000	3,000	150,000	(3,000 hrs × £50)
			450,000	
		Less fixed costs	250,000	
		Profit	200,000	

Worked Example 13.4 clearly shows that the using the unit contribution alone is not enough to make the correct decision. In fact, as we can see above if the decision was based on unit contribution, the SM01 would be produced in preference to SM03. Doing this would mean a loss of £10 per labour – SM03 yields a contribution of £60 per hour, whereas SM01 yields £50. We would also only produce SM01 and use up all available labour hours. If a company has limited capacity or labour, it could outsource some work and we will explore this decision later.

Complex product mix decisions

In the example shown in *Worked Example 13.4* there was a single factor constraining output, namely the availability of labour. There may be more than one constraining factor in business decisions and this means a more complex analysis is needed. For example, there may be a limit on materials, labour and overall production capacity. The goal of the organization may be to optimize its profits subject to such constraints. We will now explore a method which can be used to solve such optimization problems.

   Linear programming is a tool often used to resolve maximizing or minimizing of linear functions such as output or cost, where several variables affect the function. An alternative to linear programming is the **Simplex method**, which is a mathematical model to find an optimal solution. We will begin with the Simplex approach, depicting it graphically. Spreadsheet programs like Microsoft Excel can help too with optimizing problems, and we will explore how some tools offered by software providers can easily solve solutions to complex problems when more than one constraint exists. *Worked Example 13.5* shows how the simplex method works, including a graphical representation and *Worked Example 13.6* will use the same data to explore how Microsoft Excel can help.

Worked Example 13.5

Linear programming – Simplex method

Lemonella Ltd makes two products, Product A and Product B. Product A has a contribution of £17 and Product B £15. The resource usage of each product is as follows:

	Product A	Product B
Materials usage (kg)	5	8
Labour hours	1	4
Machine hours	3	2

For the next budget period, the availability of resources is as follows:

Materials (kg)	5,000
Labour hours	1,500
Machine hours	1,000

Lemonella Ltd needs to decide how much of each of Product A and B to produce in order to maximize its contribution. We can set out the above information is a series of linear functions (or equations):

First, we want to maximize contribution, which we can represent as follows, where A and B represent the output quantity of Product A and Product B respectively:

$$17A + 15B$$

This is known as the **objective function**, which is what we need to solve to maximize the contribution for Lemonella Ltd. The constraints can be represented as follows, again with A and B representing the output of Product A and Product B respectively:

$$\text{Material usage:} \quad 5A + 8B \leq 5,000$$
$$\text{Labour hours:} \quad 1A + 4B \leq 1,500$$
$$\text{Machine hours:} \quad 3A + 2B \leq 1,000$$

To find the optimal production of each product which will maximize contribution, we need to find values for A and B which will satisfy all constraints. The Simplex method helps solve this by graphing all constraints and determining an estimate of the product mix which will maximize contribution.

The first step using the Simplex method is to assume the output of each product is represented by an axis on a chart/graph. For Lemonella Ltd, we will plot Product A on the horizontal (X) axis and Product B on the vertical (Y) axis. We can then plot each of the above three constraints on the chart, as follows:

Material usage: $5A + 8B \leq 5,000$

If B = 0, then A = 1,000. Likewise, if A = 0, then B = 625. (These are our points to plot on the chart.)

Labour hours: $1A + 4B \leq 1,500$

If B = 0, then A = 1,500. Likewise, if A = 0, then B = 375.

Machine hours: $3A + 2B \leq 1,000$

If B = 0, then A = 333. Likewise, if A = 0, then B = 500.

Exhibit 13.1 depicts the three constraints using the data points above:

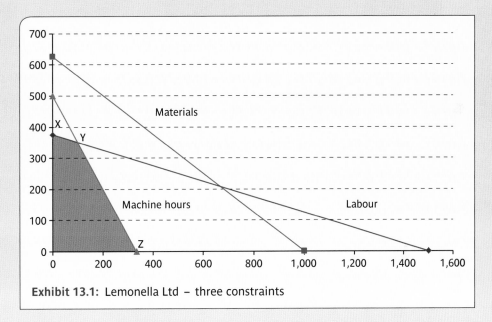

Exhibit 13.1: Lemonella Ltd – three constraints

The next stage is to find what is termed the **feasible region**. This is the area on the chart which satisfies all conditions. In Exhibit 13.1, the feasible region is the area within the origin (zero) and points X, Y and Z. Lemonella Ltd can produce any combination within this area. Once we know the feasible region, we can then draw an iso-contribution line, which is a representation of the objective function (*Note*: if we were maximizing profit, the line would be termed iso-profit, and similarly for other optimization problems, such as cost). The objective function is:

$$17A + 15B$$

To plot the iso-contribution line, we can determine some points by choosing a suitable contribution figure, for example (other figures are equally valid):

At a contribution of £1,020, Lemonella Ltd can produce as follows:

£5,100/£17 = 300 unit of A, thus our data point is (300,0)

£5,100/£15 = 340 units of B, thus our data point is (0,340)

The chart now looks like Exhibit 13.2, with the iso-contribution line added.

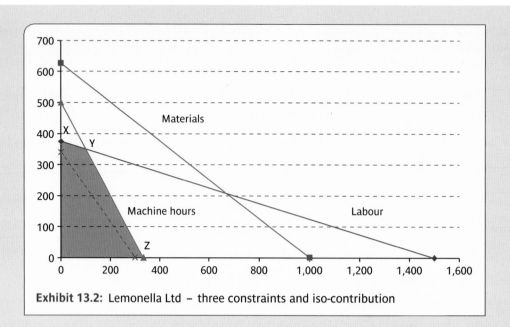

Exhibit 13.2: Lemonella Ltd – three constraints and iso-contribution

The dotted line in Exhibit 13.2 represents the iso-contribution line. To obtain the contribution maximizing solution, we can continue to draw iso-contribution lines parallel to the one shown until we reach the outermost extreme of the feasible region. Inspecting Exhibit 13.2, we can see that this will be point Y. This optimal solution is always a corner point and always furthest from the origin – we can prove this mathematically, but this is not necessary here.

Point Y is thus our optimal solution. It is the intersection of the machine hours and labour hours constraints, so we can use the earlier equations to work out the value of Y as follows:

Labour hours:	$1A + 4B \leq 1{,}500$	(1)
Machine hours:	$3A + 2B \leq 1{,}000$	(2)

Multiplying (1) by three we get:

Labour hours:	$3A + 12B \leq 4{,}500$
Machine hours:	$3A + 2B \leq 1{,}000$

Subtracting, we are left with:

$$10B = 3{,}500, \text{ thus } B = 350$$

And, substituting B in equation (1), we can determine A as follows:

$$1A + 1{,}400 = 1{,}500$$

$$\text{Thus, } A = 100.$$

Thus the output which will maximize contribution for Lemonella Ltd is to produce 100 units of Product A and 350 units of Product B. The total contribution will be $(100 \times £17) + (350 \times £15) = £6{,}950$.

In *Worked Example 13.5*, you can see quite a bit of work is required to work out the optimal product mix to maximize contribution. In the example, the objective was to maximize contribution, but this could equally be to maximize profit or to minimize costs. Microsoft Excel provides an add-on called Solver, which can be easily used to find solutions to optimization problems such as that portrayed above. *Worked Example 13.6* shows briefly how Solver can be used in the Lemonella Ltd example. A full video of the task completed in Exhibit 13.6 can be found on the website accompanying this textbook (www.mcgraw-hill.co.uk/textbooks/burns).

Worked Example 13.6

Linear programming using MS Excel

To use Solver to solve the contribution optimization problem for Lemonella Ltd, we need to set out the problem to solve and the constraints. In effect, we need to tell Microsoft Excel what the equations are, as used in *Worked Example 13.5*. The figure below shows the relevant data. Note that only a summary is shown in Exhibit 13.3 – go to the previously mentioned website to see the step-by-step video.

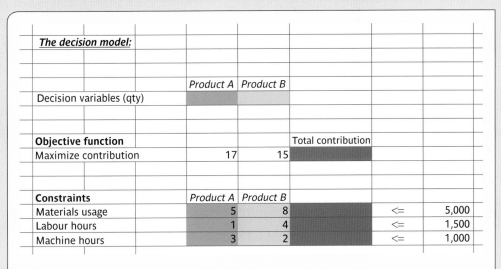

The decision model:				
	Product A	Product B		
Decision variables (qty)				
Objective function			Total contribution	
Maximize contribution	17	15		
Constraints	Product A	Product B		
Materials usage	5	8	<=	5,000
Labour hours	1	4	<=	1,500
Machine hours	3	2	<=	1,000

Exhibit 13.3: Decision model for Lemonella Ltd

The decision variables as shown above is the answer we need to solve. You can also see the contribution for each product, as well as the three constraints. The total contribution cell contains a formula, which is simply the sum of the contribution times the quantity of each product. Similarly, each constraint cell contains a formula to work out the quantity of each constraint used at any given output level. Solver needs the formulae to be able to fund a solution, as it works by continually putting in data to formulae until a solution is found. Now, all we need do is tell the Solver function in Microsoft Excel where the data for the optimization problem is. Solver is not by default shown on the Microsoft Excel menus, so you may have to install it. The Solver tool is normally under the Data Tab/menu. Once you click the Solver icon, you will see the screen shown in Exhibit 13.4:

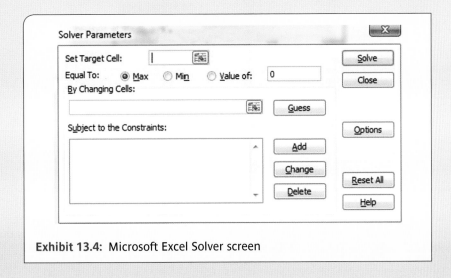

Exhibit 13.4: Microsoft Excel Solver screen

The target cell is what we want to optimize, in this case contribution. We also need to choose whether we want to minimize, maximize or achieve an exact value – maximize contribution in the Lemonella Ltd example. The 'By Changing Cells' box represents where we want the answer to be shown in the spreadsheet, which in this case is the two decision variables, that is, the quantity of Product A and B. We also need to set each constraint. In Exhibit 13.5 we see the various data boxes filled out.

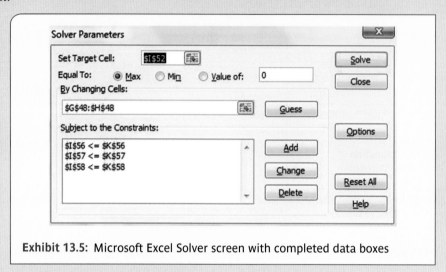

Exhibit 13.5: Microsoft Excel Solver screen with completed data boxes

Now simply click the 'Solve' button. The solution is shown in Exhibit 13.6.

The decision model:						
		Product A	Product B			
Decision variables (qty)		100	350			
Objective function				Total contribution		
Maximize contribution		17	15	6,950		
Constraints		Product A	Product B			
Materials usage		5	8	3,300	<=	5,000
Labour hours		1	4	1,500	<=	1,500
Machine hours		3	2	1,000	<=	1,000

Exhibit 13.6: Decision solution

As you can see, the answer is exactly as we worked out in *Worked Example 13.5*.

Tools like Solver in Microsoft Excel provide answers to some relatively complex product mix decisions, particularly when constraints exist. The solution can be obtained much faster than the manual process we have seen in *Worked Example 13.5*. Indeed, with a model like that in *Worked Example 13.6* set up in a spreadsheet, we can easily increase the number of products and/or constraints and run the tool as many times as necessary to help managers make a final decision.

Equipment replacement decisions

Businesses regularly invest in new equipment and often need to consider more than just the cost of the new equipment in the course of the replacement decision. Chapter 15 will give you much more detail on capital investment appraisal, but here we will briefly consider the relevant costs to the decision to replace equipment. We will use the data in *Worked Example 13.7* to explain the relevant costs.

Looking at *Worked Example 13.7*, we can see that the preferable option is to buy a new process machine as the cost savings are £30,000. If we look closely at the book value of the old machine, we can see that it is actually irrelevant – it is a past cost. If we keep the old machine for the rest of its useful life, the depreciation will be £150,000 for three years. If we buy the new machine now, the current book value of the machine (£450,000) will be written off as a lump sum. Note also that the depreciation charge of the new machine is also not relevant; as if the cost and depreciation were included the cost is double-counted. Given the irrelevance of the book value, we can simplify the decision to replace the process machine as shown in Table 13.1 to show only the differential costs of making the decision.

The data presented in *Worked Example 13.7* and Table 13.1 ignores the time value of money, but you will learn more about this in Chapter 15. While ignoring the time value of money is an over-simplification, it does allow us to focus on the relevant costs to help make a quick assessment of the course of action available. *Management Accounting in Practice 13.2* provides a useful real-life example of a business decision to refurbish old building facilities instead of replacing them.

Worked Example 13.7

Equipment replacement

A company has a large processing machine which it wishes to replace. The current book value of the machine is £450,000. A new machine costs £350,000. The new machine will lower variable costs per unit by £1 per unit and the company produces 180,000 units per annum. Variable unit costs are currently £3 per unit. The remaining useful life of the old machine is three years and the current sale value is £200,000.

Based on the above data, we can compare the costs of retaining the old process machine versus purchasing a new one.

	Keep old machine £	Buy new machine £
Variable operating costs		
180,000 × £3	540,000	
180,000 × £2		360,000
Depreciation – 3 years	450,000	
Lump-sum write off		450,000
Disposal value old machine		(200,000)
Purchase cost new machine		350,000
Total costs	990,000	960,000

Table 13.1: Differential costs of equipment replacement	
	£
Saving on variable operating costs	(180,000)
Sale proceeds of old machine	(200,000)
Purchase cost of new machine	350,000
Saving on purchase of new machine	(30,000)

13.2: Management Accounting in Practice

Replace or retrofit?

Reducing energy consumption and carbon emissions is a major goal for many organizations worldwide. In terms of buildings, high-rise buildings are frequently poor performers on energy consumption and carbon emissions. The Empire State Building in New York invested $13 million in 2010 to retrofit its 6,500 windows over a six-month period. The cost of a new window was in the order of $2,500 each, but instead each window was refurbished, cleaned and insulated at a cost of about $700. Alongside some other simple insulation measures, the retrofit would deliver a 38 per cent reduction in energy consumption – mainly from reduced heating costs. Similar savings have been realized at other high-rise building throughout the USA and other countries.

The relevant costs for the replacement versus retrofit decisions conveyed in this example are the differential costs incurred. The original cost of the windows at the Empire State Building or any subsequent maintenance cost, are not relevant to either decision. Savings in heating bills are of course relevant. We cannot be sure that the energy consumption savings from the two options are the same, but if they were then arguably the saving is irrelevant as there is no difference between the two courses of action.

Source: 'Greening the skyline: small fixes save big money', Time, 18 April 2011, available at http://www.time.com/time/magazine/article/0,9171,2063860,00.html.

Exercises

1) In decisions to replace old fixtures or refurbish a building, are costs such as the disposal of old building materials or fixtures relevant to the decision?

2) Can you think of other potential relevant costs in such a decision?

Outsourcing decisions

Any business which sells a manufactured or assembled product can choose to either (1) manufacture itself, or (2) buy the product or assembly services externally. This decision is more commonly referred to as a 'make or buy decision' or **outsourcing**. The key thinking behind an outsourcing decision is how to make the best use of an organization's resources. For example, it may be possible to outsource the manufacture of some less profitable products so that a company can use its resources like machines and labour to concentrate on more profitable products. The decision to outsource can be summarized as follows:

> *If incremental costs of making in-house exceed costs of outsourcing, then we should outsource.*

Let us now apply this decision rule to a basic outsource decision and also to an outsource decision when resources are scarce. We will first consider the example in *Worked Example 13.8*.

Worked Example 13.8

Oursourcing production

A company makes four industrial components A, B, C, and D for which costs in the forthcoming year are expected to be as follows.

	A	B	C	D
Unit production	4,000	6,000	8,000	10,000
Costs (£ per unit)				
Direct material	10	12	6	10
Direct labour	20	22	12	16
Variable overheads	6	4	4	6
Total cost	26	38	22	32

Directly attributable fixed costs for each component per annum are: A £4,000, B £14,000, C £14,000, D £18,000. Other fixed costs are £6,000. Units of A, B, C and D can be outsourced for £20, £46, £24 and £36 respectively. Which components should the company outsource or make in-house?

The relevant costs are the differential costs between making and outsourcing. If outsourced some fixed cost savings will occur, that is, those fixed costs directly attributable to each of the four components.

Below, we calculate the difference between the variable cost of making versus outsourcing and also consider the fixed cost savings.

	A	B	C	D
Variable cost to make (£)	26	38	22	32
Variable cost of outsourced units (£)	20	46	24	36
Unit cost/(saving) of outsourcing (£)	(6)	8	2	4
Units required	4,000	6,000	8,000	10,000
Cost/(saving) of outsourcing (£)	(24,000)	48,000	16,000	40,000
Fixed costs saved (£)	(4,000)	(14,000)	(14,000)	(18,000)
Total cost/(saving) of outsourcing (£)	(28,000)	34,000	2,000	22,000

The company would save £28,000 if it outsourced the production of component A.

Looking at the data presented in *Worked Example 13.8*, based on the lower variable costs per component and the fixed costs saved, the decision would be to outsource the production of component A. Component C may also be a consideration if the price of the outsourced supplier is reduced. What we see from the data on component A is that the variable costs of outsourcing are lower than the in-house costs, and fixed costs specific to component A will also be saved. These two relevant costs form the basis of the decision. Note that general fixed costs are typically not relevant to outsourcing decisions. For example, if the company in *Worked Example 13.8* absorbed general overhead to products, unless this general overhead is avoided by outsourcing, then it is not relevant.

However, in the scenario used in Exhibit 13.8 we are ignoring the productive capacity which has been freed up if the manufacture of component A is outsourced. Typically, some other use of the capacity would be found, which means there may be an opportunity cost of using capacity in one way versus another. *Worked Example 13.9* provides an example using the data on component D from *Worked Example 13.8*.

Worked Example 13.9

Free capacity and outsourcing

In *Worked Example 13.8*, component D is cheaper to manufacture by £22,000. If the capacity used to produce component D were available, the company's marketing manager could sell 15,000 units of a newly developed component E at a contribution of £4 per unit. Assume the specific fixed costs for component D (£18,000) will also be incurred if component E were produced.

The decision must now also consider the opportunity cost of been unable to produce component E. The relevant costs are set out below:

	Make in-house	Outsource
Variable cost (£)	32	36
Units required	10,000	10,000
Total cost (£)	320,000	360,000
Opportunity cost (£)	60,000	
Total cost (£)	380,000	360,000

If we take into account the opportunity cost of lost contribution from component E, we can now see from *Worked Example 13.9* that the company can save £20,000 by outsourcing the manufacture of component D. As you know from earlier chapters, an opportunity cost is not an actual cost or cash flow; rather they represent a benefit forgone by choosing one option over another. In the decision on component D above, to ignore the opportunity cost would lead to a poor decision for the company.

Outsourcing with scarce resources

Earlier in this chapter we examined how decisions are made when there are constraints (for example, material, labour) which affect the product mix that can be produced. When resources are constrained and it is not possible to produce sufficient output to meet demand, it may be possible to outsource the manufacture of some products. In this instance, the organization needs to minimize its total costs of outsourcing the manufacture. Any units of product outsourced should have the minimum extra variable cost of outsourcing per unit of scarce resource saved. *Worked Example 13.10* shows a worked example of this type of decision.

As you can see in the example portrayed in *Worked Example 13.10*, when there are constraints on the amount of product which can be produced internally, then if outsourcing is an option the product with the lowest variable cost per unit of scarce resource should be outsourced. Product B in *Worked Example 13.10* has the lowest cost per kilogram of raw material and is thus the best

Worked Example 13.10

Outsourcing – limited materials

A company manufactures two products A and B using the same raw material for each. The annual demand for Product A is 18,000 units, while demand for B is 16,000 units. The variable production cost of Product A is £22 and Product B has a variable production cost of £32. Product A requires 7 kg of raw material per unit, while Product B requires 16 kg of raw material per unit. Supply of raw material is limited to 180,000 kg per annum. An outsourcing company can supply both products and has quoted prices of £36 per unit for A and £52 unit for B. How many of each product should be manufactured in-house to maximize profit?

	Product A	Product B
Variable cost to make in-house	£22	£32
Variable cost of outsourcing	£36	£52
Additional cost of outsourcing	£14	£20
Raw material saved by outsourcing	7 kg	16 kg
Extra variable cost of outsourcing per kg raw material	£2	£1.25
Rank for internal manufacture	1	2

The production plan would be as follows:

Make Product A (18,000 × 7 kg)	126,000 kg
Make Product B	54,000 kg (balance)
	180,000 kg

54,000 kg/16 kg per unit of Product B means 3,375 units of the product should be made in-house. The remaining 12,625 units (16,000 – 3,375) of Product B should be outsourced to the external manufacturer.

option for outsourcing. Conversely, it is cheaper to manufacture as much of Product A as possible in-house. If we ignored the availability of raw materials on the decision in *Worked Example 13.10*, we would make an incorrect decision as seen in previous examples.

Other factors for outsourcing decisions

Both types of outsourcing decision detailed so far have been based solely on an analysis of relevant costs. There are a number of other relevant factors which should be considered before any outsourcing decision is taken. Before briefly mentioning some of these factors, read *Management Accounting in Practice 13.3*, which gives some examples of outsourcing in organizations.

Management Accounting in Practice 13.3 provides a brief insight into two differing cases of outsourcing. Both involve outsourcing of key aspects of the respective organizations. The Worcestershire Acute Hospital Trust's example differs from the US example in that the trust, although outsourcing a key feature of its organization, outsourced an activity that does not entail any non-standard knowledge. As the US example portrays, outsourcing high-skilled knowledge-type tasks may actually cost more in the long run as the outsourcing organization may not have the organization-specific knowledge to fulfil the task. This is one qualitative factor managers may need

13.3: Management Accounting in Practice

Outsourcing and non-cost factors

In the UK, Worcestershire Acute Hospitals Trust began to outsource the digital scanning of patient records in 2009. The trust predicts an annual saving of approximately £200,000 per annum. The savings materialize as the need to transport patient records is almost eliminated due to the centralization and digitization of the records. Time is also saved, and the trust reports a decrease in the number of internal forms from 1,500 to 300. The project was supported by staff and the trade unions involved. In contrast to the success at the Worcestershire trust, New York City took some previously outsourced activities back in-house to save money. A feature in the *New York Times* reports how rather than outsourcing commodity-type tasks like food-service and construction, some US municipal authorities have outsourced activities like information technology management, strategy development and personnel management systems. A reason cited for not outsourcing commodity-type activities is the lower pay available for highly skilled staff in the US public sector.

Sources: 'Is privatization a bad deal for cities and states', New York Times. 3 April 2011, available at http://www.nytimes.com/roomfordebate/2011/04/03/is-privatization-a-bad-deal-for-cities-and-states/outsourcing-the-wrong-jobs; 'Worcestershire predicts £2m savings by outsourcing patient records' Guardian Professional, 30 March 2011, available at http://www.guardian.co.uk/healthcare-network/2011/mar/30/worcestershire-2m-savings-outsourcing-patient-records?INTCMP=SRCH.

Exercise

In general, what kind of business activity do you think is suitable for outsourcing and what is not?

to consider before making the final outsourcing decision. Other qualitative factors might include loss of control, product/service quality, longer lead times to customers, disruption to supply and lack of direct customer support. Such qualitative factors may actually be more influential on the decision to outsource. An alternative to outsourcing which can save costs, but retain service activities in particular in-house, is the development of a **shared-services centre**. These are particularly common in organizational activities like human resources, information technology and finance. The concept is in effect an in-house outsourcing option. Services at individual organizational units are centralized at a suitable location. Costs are saved as the services at not replicated many times throughout the organization.

Discontinuation decisions

Businesses may need to make decisions on whether to continue or discontinue product lines, close business segments, store departments and so on. For example, Coca-Cola dropped its Cherry-Coke (now Coca-Cola Cherry) product in some European countries during the 1980s, and subsequently reintroduced the product in the 1990s. The Bank of Scotland closed its retail banking operations in the Republic of Ireland in 2010, despite investing more than £200 million in a branch network in 2005. And as shown in *Management Accounting in Practice 13.4*, businesses often have to close down facilities in response to drops in demand for their product or service. When managers are faced with decisions to discontinue some business operations, these are some of the typical questions posed which when answered will lead to the correct decision:

- Is a positive contribution generated by the product/sector/department?

- What fixed costs will remain if discontinued?

- What fixed costs are avoided if discontinued?

- Will the discontinuation affect other areas of the business?

- What can be done with any capacity freed up?

Answering each of these questions should allow a manager to determine the relevant costs for any discontinuation type decision. We will now work through an example, as shown in *Worked Example 13.11*.

13.4: Management Accounting in Practice

Closing mail centres

In June 2011, The Royal Mail – the leading postal service in the UK – announced job losses as its mail volumes continued to fall. The volume of mail has declined from approximately 80 million daily to 60 million items in the previous five years. Volumes are predicted to fall at a rate of 5 per cent per annum in future years. Royal Mail announced a loss of £120 million on its mail business for the year. Since 2002, Royal Mail has closed 12 mail centres and is planning to close another 16 in response to the falling volumes. The Chief Executive is quoted as saying 'we are going to be a smaller company in the future than we are today [and] we expect that around half of the mail centres could close by 2016/17'.

Exercise

Can you think of examples of costs that Royal Mail would save by closing a mail centre?

Source: 'More post jobs go after £120m loss', Guardian, 14 June 2011, available at http://www.guardian.co.uk/business/2011/jun/14/more-post-jobs-go-royal-mail-loss.

	Product X2 (£)	**Product Y1 (£)**	**Product BB (£)**	**Total**
Worked Example 13.11 — **Discontinuing a product**				

Oran Ltd is concerned about poor recent profit performance, and is considering whether or not to discontinue one of its products, product Y1. The market manager advises that selling prices cannot be raised without adversely affecting demand for product Y1, which would only make its performance worse. Of the fixed costs of producing Y1, £15,000 is direct fixed costs and these would be fully avoided if production ceased. All other fixed costs would remain the same if Y1 were discontinued. A summary of the overall company performance for the most recent financial year is given below:

	Product X2 (£)	**Product Y1 (£)**	**Product BB (£)**	**Total**
Sales	150,000	120,000	150,000	420,000
Variable costs	90,000	75,000	75,000	240,000
Contribution	60,000	45,000	75,000	180,000
Fixed costs	51,000	54,000	60,000	165,000
Profit/(loss)	9,000	(9,000)	15,000	15,000

To ascertain if Y1 should be discontinued, we need to reflect on the questions mentioned earlier. In this example, we are not given any information on what might happen the sales of the other two products or what can be done with the capacity available if Y1 is discontinued. Thus, we need only examine the affects of fixed costs saved as a result of the decision.

By discontinuing Y1, the consequences would be a £10,000 fall in overall profits as follows:

Loss of contribution	(£45,000)
Saving in fixed costs	£15,000
Incremental loss	(£30,000)

As the decision to discontinue would result in an overall loss of £30,000 it does not therefore seem a sound business decision to stop making product Y1.

The analysis in *Worked Example 13.11* focuses solely on the differential costs. The variable costs are of course irrelevant as they will no longer be incurred if product Y1 is discontinued. However, as Y1 makes a positive contribution, the loss of this contribution has to be included in the analysis. Similarly, the fixed costs totalling £15,000 saved if Y1 is discontinued are also relevant. The remained fixed costs of £39,000 (£54,000 – 15,000) allocated to product Y1 are not relevant as these cost will still be incurred regardless of the decision. Any such general fixed costs are irrelevant and will be allocated over remaining products. Remember too from earlier chapters that the allocation of any common or general fixed overhead may be subjective, regardless of whether activity-based or traditional overhead allocations methods are used.

Other factors to be considered in discontinuation decisions

Worked Example 13.11 provided a relatively simple scenario in which only some fixed costs would change as result of the decision to discontinue product Y1. One of the typical questions in discontinuation decisions posed earlier was what, if anything, can be done with any free capacity. It is possible that resources freed up could be used to provide more of an existing product or service. Looking back at the example in *Worked Example 13.11*, let us assume that if product Y1 is discontinued, the resources freed up (labour, equipment, and so on) can be used to sell an additional £100,000 of product BB. The additional sales do not affect the current variable or fixed costs of product BB. The section below shows how the decision will now change.

Discontinuation and increased revenues

Assuming the cost structure remains constant, an additional £100,000 in sales of product BB will yield additional contribution of £50,000 – the current contribution to sales ratio is 50 per cent (£75,000/£150,000).

Loss of contribution Y1	(£45,000)
Saving in fixed costs Y1	£15,000
Contribution gained BB	£50,000
Incremental gain	£20,000

The decision would be to discontinue product Y1 and divert the freed capacity to product BB – assuming no better use of the free capacity.

Finally, managers also need to consider the effects of discontinuing a product/sector in light of the overall business. In some business, products may be complementary to each other, so the discontinuation of one can have a knock-on effect on the sales of another product. In such a case, a best estimate of the contribution lost by reduced sales of the complementary product could be included in the cost analysis. Also, some businesses do sell products at a loss. Such **loss-leader** products are often used to entice customers to buy other profitable products. In such a case, the loss-leader is unlikely to be discontinued unless the contribution is minimal or becomes negative.

Sell or process further

In Chapter 4, the differences in costing a process compared to a job/order were highlighted. In a process environment, managers often need to decide at what point to sell the product(s)

13.5: Management Accounting in Practice

Google discontinues some services

While Google is known for developing new and innovative services to both enhance its web search core business and provide more information and data to users, even it sometimes discontinues products and services. Google's ongoing innovations may be due to the fact that staff are given 20 per cent 'free time' to work on new ideas and projects. Some of the Google services we take as standard – such as Gmail – evolved from free time of Google engineers. However, in September 2011, Google announced it was discontinuing a number of its products/services. One was FastFlip, which allowed news content to be browsed and read. Another was Google Desktop, which gave Google search capability to the searching of desktop computers. The reason for discontinuing these and other products was, according to Senior Vice President (VP) Alan Eustace, 'to devote more time to high impact products – the ones that improve the lives of billions of people' and allow Google to 'focus on building world-changing products'. According to Google's website, 'Google's mission is to organize the world's information and make it universally accessible and useful'. This mission ties in with reasons given by Eustace for discontinuing products. It would seem that products like FastFlip and Google Desktop are no longer in tandem with the firm's overall mission.

Sources: 'A fall spring clean', Alan Eustace, Senior VP, Google Inc., available at http://googleblog.blogspot. com/2011/09/fall-spring-clean.html; Google Company Information, available at http://www.google.com/about/corporate/company/.

Exercise

Although the Senior VP suggests Google wanted to spend more time on high-impact products, do you think costs and revenues were examined in the decision to drop certain products?

from the process. In many processes, common costs are incurred to a certain point (the **split-off point**) in the process – referred to as **joint costs**. If the process has more than one output product, then the common joint costs need to be allocated to the various products in some way. Methods to allocate costs are not covered here in detail but they include techniques such as allocating costs (1) based on a physical measurement of the final output (for example, weight), (2) based on a proportion of sales revenues of the final output and, (3) based on the net realizable value of products at the split-off point. The dairy produce sector is a good example of a business where joint costs are incurred and would need to be shared across multiple products. All milk needs to be pasteurized and homogenized, and this joint cost needs to be allocated in some way across multiple products – butter spreads, cheese, flavoured milk, yoghurt – which require further processing and have separable identifiable costs.

The decision as whether a product should be sold in its current state or processed further is our main concern here. Using the example of a dairy processor, managers may be faced with decisions such as whether to sell milk as is or process it further in flavoured milks. Using this example, any joint costs are irrelevant as they are sunk and are incurred regardless of the decision to sell the milk as normal or as a flavoured variety. Any additional costs of further processing and any additional revenues earned are relevant. *Worked Example 13.12* shows a worked example of such as decision.

| **Worked Example 13.12** | **Futher process decision** |

Glen Distilery is a farm-based cider and juice business. Currently, Glen processes 280,000 litres of juice per annum at a cost of £160,000. This input yields 160,000 litres of apple juice and 40,000 litres of cider when processed at the split-off point in the process. The apple juice currently sells at £8 for a 5-litre drum and the cider sells at £1 per litre.

Tom is considering processing the apple juice further into a gourmet type pressed juice. This will yield £10 for every 5-litre drum of juice and cost an additional £15,000 per annum to process half of the current juice output – the remaining half of the juice will not be processed further and can be sold at the prices mentioned above. He can also process the cider into a stronger apple brandy. Due to the nature of the technology involved, all existing cider output would have to be processed. The additional cost of processing the cider is £18,000 and it could be sold for £1.25 per litre.

Should Tom process the apple juice and cider further into pressed juice and apple brandy? These two decisions need to compare the additional revenues and costs after the split-off point only. The relevant costs and revenues are:

Process juice further	**£**
Additional revenue	32,000 (80,000 litres/5 × £2)
Further processing costs	15,000
Incremental profit/(loss)	17,000

As an incremental profit arises, the decision would be to process further into pressed apple juice.

Process cider further	**£**
Additional revenue	10,000 (40,000 × 0.25)
Further processing costs	18,000
Additional profit/(loss)	(8,000)

In this case, an incremental loss arises and the decision would be to not process the cider further into apple brandy.

As you can see in *Worked Example 13.12*, the decision to process a product further is relatively straightforward. If the incremental revenues from further processing exceed the additional costs, then the products should be processed further.

Relevant revenues

Thus far, the chapter has concentrated on relevant costs. Some of the decisions we have examined included some mention of relevant revenues. For example in 'the sell or process further' decision in the preceding section, it was noted that if additional revenues exceeded the cost of processing further, then the products should be processed. These additional revenues from further processing are the relevant revenues in this decision. Likewise, in a discontinuation decision, only those revenues which cease as a result of closing a division or ceasing a product are likely to be relevant. However, these examples are simplifying the analysis somewhat. The remainder of this section thus provides some brief discussion on relevant revenues.

As noted at the outset of this chapter, relevant revenues are those future revenues which arise from taking a particular decision. Consider the following simple example.

Relevant revenues

A business can generate sales revenue of £5,000 per week under normal circumstances. However, if it spends £500 on advertising, the sales revenue can be increased to £7,000 per week. Should the business advertise?

Incremental revenue	£2,000
Advertising cost	£500
Additional profit	£1,500

As an additional profit of £1,500 can be earned, the business should advertise.

In the example, the decision to advertise or not does not need to take into account the revenue earned without advertising, that is, £5,000. Thus, we can say that in most decisions, it is the differential revenues which are relevant. Existing revenues are less likely to be relevant. Earlier, in *Worked Examples 13.2* and *13.3* an example of a pricing decision was given, and in both examples only the additional revenues to be generated from additional orders were taken into consideration, that is, the differential revenues. However, as seen in *Worked Example 13.3*, when operations are at full capacity, the loss of existing revenues does become relevant, that is, it is an opportunity cost.

The emphasis on whether costs and/or revenues are relevant to a decision can depend on the type of business. For example, low-cost airlines like easyJet and Ryanair may consider all costs as fixed, in essence regarding the variable cost per passenger seat flown as nil. Thus revenues become a key decision factor. Low-cost carriers would likely argue that the only way fuel, staff and other costs can be avoided is to ground the aircraft. However, once an aircraft embarks on a flight, arguably all costs are fixed. This is why low-cost airlines have complex revenue management systems to ensure they obtain the best yields from flights. In simpler terms, revenues may be more relevant to the operational decision making in the case of low-cost airlines than costs. Kristandl and Quinn (2012) report that firms that operate in a cloud computing environment may similarly find revenues more relevant in day-to-day decision making – cloud computing refers to the provision of typical computing services across the Internet. According to their research, firms which provide cloud-based services – such as online accounting software – have a fixed cost base, or more precisely, a stepped-fixed cost base. This is because providers of computing power, infrastructure and disk storage typically offer services at various fixed levels. For example, Amazon Web Services (AWS) provide varying packages with levels of storage and other services suited to business needs. Kristandl and Quinn (2012) report that in one such cloud-based firm, all operational decisions are typically based on generating additional revenues only. For example, the owner of the firm regards all costs of providing their services as fixed and if a new staff member were to be employed, the decision is based on how much extra revenue is needed to cover this additional fixed cost.

In summary, revenues are as relevant to decision making as costs. In most cases, the differential (or incremental) revenues are relevant to the decision at hand; existing revenues are typically not, unless reduced in some way by the decision to be made. In some businesses however, revenues may be more relevant to decision making than costs, as shown by the example of low-cost airlines and cloud-based businesses.

Chapter summary

In this chapter you have learned how to isolate the relevant costs and revenues for a number of common business decisions. Relevant costs and revenues are the differential costs and revenues resulting from the particular decision. This means that only future costs are relevant to a decision, with past or sunk costs being irrelevant. In the chapter we have specifically examined special order pricing decisions, product mix decisions, equipment replacement decisions, outsourcing decisions, discontinuation decisions and further processing decisions. Each of these quite common business scenarios that used the principles of identifying the relevant costs and revenues to determine if an incremental profit or cost-saving would result from the decision. The chapter also introduced a relatively advanced optimization technique, linear programming, which can be used to help make decisions when multiple constraints exist, for example shortage of labour and materials. Finally, a brief discussion of the revenues relevant to decisions was given, which emphasized the importance of revenues in all decisions, as well as noting that revenues may be more relevant in some business sectors.

Key terms

Feasible region The area of a linear programming chart (Simplex method) which satisfies all constraints (p. 323)

Joint costs Common costs incurred before the split off point in a process (p. 335)

Linear programming A technique used to find optimum solutions when multiple constraints exist (p. 321)

Loss leader A product sold at a loss to encourage customers to buy (p. 334)

Objective function The function/equation to be solved (for example, maximize contribution) in a linear programming scenario (p. 322)

Outsourcing The transfer of an organizational activity/product/service to an external provider (p. 328)

Relevant cost A future cost affected by a decision (p. 316)

Relevant revenue A future revenue effect of a decision (p. 316)

Shared-services centre An internal centralized service provider to an organization (p. 332)

Simplex method A graphical approach to solving linear programming scenarios (p. 322)

Split-off point The point in a process when separate products become identifiable (p. 335)

Review questions ● ● ● ● ● ● ● ● ● ● ● ● ● connect ● ●

| Level of difficulty: | BASIC | INTERMEDIATE | ADVANCED |

13.1 What is a relevant cost? **[LO1]**

13.2 Are sunk costs relevant to short-term decision making? **[LO1]**

13.3 What revenue figures are relevant to sell or process further decisions? **[LO1, LO2]**

13.4 Are joint processing costs relevant to further processing decisions? Why or why not? **[LO1, LO2]**

13.5 Why is the level of capacity relevant to short-run pricing decisions? **[LO1, LO3]**

13.6 Are fixed costs relevant to decisions to discontinue products or business segments? **[LO1, LO5]**

13.7 Are variable costs relevant in decisions to discontinue products or business segments? **[LO2, LO5]**

13.8 What technique can be used to resolve optimization problems when there are multiple constraints on what can be produced? **[LO3]**

13.9 How does the optimization decision technique differ when only one constraint exists? **[LO3]**

13.10 Are qualitative factors relevant to outsourcing decisions? **[LO6]**

Group discussion and activity topics ● ● ● ● ● ● ● ● ●

13.11 A gourmet café is considering whether or not to expand its in-house bakery to include the baking of muffins. Currently, the café only bakes bread and bread rolls. Discuss what factors may be relevant in a decision to make or buy the muffins. **[LO1]**

13.12 Go to the websites of quality newspapers such as the *Financial Times*, the *Guardian* or the *New York Times* and search using the word 'outsource'. Find an article and discuss the article based on the following points **[LO6]**:

- What business area is being outsourced?
- What cost savings might be a result of the outsource decision?
- What qualitative factors may have been considered by the company making the outsourcing decision?

13.13 Think of a service organization you are familiar with. Discuss 'make or buy' decisions the organization might undertake. **[LO6]**

13.14 Multinational firms often discontinue manufacturing operations in one country and move to another. Discuss how you think they might arrive at the decision to discontinue. Try to think of cost and qualitative factors. **[LO5]**

Exercises ● ● ● ● ● ● ● ● ● ● ● ● ● ● ● ● connect ● ●

E13.1 Relevant costs **[LO1]**

X plc intends to use relevant costs as the basis of the selling price for a special order: the printing of a brochure. The brochure requires a particular type of paper that is not regularly used by X plc although a limited amount is in X plc's inventory which was left over from a previous job. The cost when X plc bought this paper last year was £15 per ream and there are 100 reams in inventory. The brochure requires 250 reams. The current market price of the paper is £26 per ream, and the resale value of the paper in inventory is £10 per ream.

Required:

Calculate the relevant costs of the paper to be used in the brochure.

Source: adapted from Chartered Institute of Management Accountants, Paper P2, Decision Management.

E13.2 Relevant costs [LO1]

A farmer grows potatoes for sale to wholesalers and to individual customers. The farmer currently harvests the potatoes and sells them in 20 kg sacks. He is considering a decision to make a change to this current approach. He thinks that washing the potatoes and packaging them in 2 kg cartons might be more attractive to some of his individual customers. Which of the following is relevant to his decision?

a)   The sales value of the harvested potatoes?

b)   The cost per kg of growing the potatoes?

c)   The cost of washing and packaging the potatoes?

d)   The sales value of the washed and packaged potatoes?

Source: adapted from Chartered Institute of Management Accountants, Paper P2, Decision Management.

E13.3 New customer order [LO1, LO2]

M Ltd manufactures advanced technical components for the computer hardware industry. The company has two divisions, U and D. U division manufactures a special sub-component at a variable cost of £70 per unit. The maximum monthly production capacity of the U division is 27,000 units, but its actual production each month is 25,000 units. Of this actual monthly production, 15,000 units are sold to external customers (at a price of £100 each) while the remaining 10,000 units are transferred to D division at the same price. The D division maximum production capacity is 13,500 units per month. However, market demand for the products of D division is only 10,000 units and therefore production is carried out at this level. In producing one unit of its product, D division uses one unit of the sub-component purchased from U Division and incurs additional variable costs of £90 per unit. The selling price of D divisions' product is £200 per unit. D division recently received an enquiry from a new customer, who has offered to purchase 3,000 units of their product each month at a price of £185 per unit.

Required:

Prepare calculations to indicate the increase in the monthly profits of M Ltd if the new customer offer is accepted.

Source: adapted from The Institute of Certified Public Accountants in Ireland, Professional 1, Strategic Management Accounting.

E13.4 Corporate incentive company, relevant costs [LO1, LO2]

Eventus, a corporate incentive company, which organizes corporate team-building special events and 'weekend-away' packages, has prepared a cost estimate for one of its clients, Carlson Group. The aim of the weekend team-building event would be to incentivize the performance of Carlson Group's line managers. The estimate was prepared by the marketing manager of Eventus and has been submitted to you, the management accountant, for approval:

Marketing manager's cost estimate for Carlson Group client

Note	Type of cost	£
(i)	Trainer fees	2,500
(ii)	Hotel accommodation costs	3,500
(iii)	Coach running costs	800
(iv)	Driver costs	600
(v)	Training brochures	1,500
(vi)	General overheads	1,300
	Total costs	10,200
	10% profit mark-up	1,020
	Selling price quote	11,220

To your mild irritation, the cost estimate has not been based on a relevant costing analysis, but the marketing manager insists he will give a fair price, to win the business from Carlson Group. You have requested more information about each of the costs (as shown below in notes (i) to (vi)) and are determined to come up with a correct costing and price, before the next management meeting.

i)   The company employs a specialist management trainer, who will have to be diverted from other work for a charitable organization, to which she had been assigned for the same weekend. This charity client which would have earned the company a contribution of £4,000 overall. The trainer's fee is a flat fee of £2,500 for three days of weekend work. Because of her specialist skills, it was felt that it was better to cancel the charity client rather than attempt to source another Eventus trainer or hire in a trainer from another competitor training company.

ii)   The hotel costs are the expected outlay costs of hiring the hotel rooms for the corporate team-building weekend.

iii)   The coach is owned by Eventus and the variable costs of fuel are £500 for the weekend, plus an amount of £300, which is an apportionment of the annual fixed costs of operating the coach. It is estimated that the only specific fixed costs that would be incurred for the Carlson Group weekend would be special insurance, costing £120.

iv)   The driver costs (of £600) represent the salary and related employment costs of hiring the driver for the three days of the weekend. The driver is thinking of retiring and has offered to do the work, only if the company pays a bonus of £500. This bonus is not included in the estimate. Should the company not pay the bonus, the replacement cost to the company of getting another driver would be £1,300.

v)   The general training brochures are already in stock and did cost £1,500 to produce and if not used for this client, because of a need to upgrade the content, have no other use and so would have to be scrapped, at a cost of £500 due to recycling requirements.

vi)   The general overheads are computed using an overhead absorption rate set annually at the beginning of the year. The only general overhead cost that will be specifically incurred for this client's weekend package is the administrative and marketing staff's time spent in preparing the quote and organizing the accommodation, trainer and events. This amounted to £600.

Required:

As the management accountant of Eventus, derive the cost estimate and selling price quote for the Carlson Group client, by using relevant cost principles. Show all workings and state all your assumptions clearly.

Source: with thanks to Dr Ruth Mattimoe, Dublin City University.

E13.5 **Product mix decision, maximize contribution [LO1, LO3]**

Elfina Ltd is a large clothing manufacturing company and its plant in Stoke-on-Trent produces two types of ladies coats. Due to shortages in some raw materials, the management team of the plant is having difficulty deciding on the optimum production schedule for the forthcoming period. You have been asked to analyse the situation and have been presented with the data which are set out below.

Production requirements	Coat 3 Per unit	Coat 4 Per unit
Direct materials:		
Material B (metres)	2.5	1.0
Direct labour:		
Type M (hours)	0.5	1.5
Type O (hours)	0.5	0.5
Variable overhead	£16	£15

The expected demand and selling prices for the four coats manufactured at the Longford plant are as follows:

	Selling price	Demand
Coat 3	£250	Unlimited
Coat 4	£170	8,000

The availability of the materials required for the manufacture of the coats is:

	Maximum availability	Price/rate
Material B	15,000 metres	£30 per metre
Type M labour	unlimited	£11 per hour
Type N labour	unlimited	£15 per hour
Type O labour	unlimited	£9 per hour

Required:

Advise the management team of the plant of the optimum product mix of Coat 3 and Coat 4, for the purposes of maximizing contribution earned in the forthcoming period.

Source: with thanks to Dr Barbara Flood, Dublin City University.

E13.6 **Product mix, maximize profit [LO1, LO3]**

Company C manufactures two products. The budgeted selling price and cost per unit are as follows:

Product	X £/Unit	Y £/Unit
Selling price	86	74
Direct labour (£8 per hour)	16	12
Direct material A (£3 per kg)	12	15
Direct material B (£4 per kg)	12	8
Other variable costs	20	15
Fixed overhead absorbed	12	12
Profit	14	12

Demand for the products is seasonal. In order to ensure that the production facilities are not idle at various times during the year the company has signed a contract with company D to supply them with the products as 'own label' goods.

Company D contract

The company is to supply company D with 500 units of product X and 300 units of product Y in November and December for £73 per unit respectively. If company C fails to honour this contract in full in each of these months then there is a significant financial penalty for each month of their failure.

November

The total number of direct labour hours available to produce products X and Y in November is limited to 4,000 hours, but all of the other production resources are readily available in November. In addition to the contract with company D, the demand for products X and Y in November is 1,000 units and 800 units respectively.

Required:

Prepare calculations to determine the production plan that will maximize the profit of company C in November.

Source: adapted from Chartered Institute of Management Accountants, Paper P2, Decision Management.

E13.7   Replace equipment [LO1, LO4]

Framanc Ltd purchased a new piece of equipment for £40,000 on 1 January – the first day of their accounting year. The annual running costs of the machine, before depreciation will be £28,000 per annum. The machine is expected to have a five-year useful life, with a nil residual value.

Less than a week later, the company is offered another new machine which can do the same work as the old machine, but costs £50,000. The running costs of this new machine are £20,000 per annum before depreciation. It also has the same useful life as the old machine, and a nil value is expected at the end of the useful life. The old machine can be sold for £20,000, less transport costs of £3,000.

Regardless of which machine is used, the turnover at Framanc will be £300,000 annually and total annual costs other than the machine operating costs mentioned will be £225,000.

Required:

a) Ignoring taxes, interest and the time value of money, prepare income statements for each of the four years under both alternatives and recommend the best option to Framanc Ltd.

b) How would you evaluation differ if you were asked to use cash flows instead?

E13.8   Stay Clean – discontinuation [LO1, LO5]

Stay Clean manufactures and sells a small range of kitchen equipment. Specifically the product range contains a dishwasher (DW), a washing machine (WM) and a tumble dryer (TD). The TD is of a rather old design and has for some time generated negative contribution. It is widely expected that in one year's time the market for this design of TD will cease, as people switch to a washing machine that can also dry clothes after the washing cycle has completed.

Stay Clean is trying to decide whether or not to cease the production of TD now or in 12 months' time when the new combined washing machine/drier will be ready. To help with this decision the following information has been provided:

1) The normal selling prices, annual sales volumes and total variable costs for the three products are as follows:

	DW	WM	TD
Selling price per unit	£200	£350	£80
Material cost per unit	£70	£100	£50
Labour cost per unit	£50	£80	£40
Contribution per unit	£80	£170	(£10)
Annual sales	5,000 units	6,000 units	1,200 units

2) It is thought that some of the customers that buy a TD also buy a DW and a WM. It is estimated that 5 per cent of the sales of WM and DW will be lost if the TD ceases to be produced.

3) All the direct labour force currently working on the TD will be made redundant immediately if TD is ceased now. This would cost £6,000 in redundancy payments. If Stay Clean waited for 12 months the existing labour force would be retained and retrained at a cost of £3,500 to enable them to produce the new washing/drying product. Recruitment and training costs of labour in 12 months' time would be £1,200 in the event that redundancy takes place now.

4) Stay Clean operates a just-in-time policy and so all material cost would be saved on the TD for 12 months if TD production ceased now. Equally, the material costs relating to the lost sales on the WM and the DW would also be saved. However, the material supplier has a volume based discount scheme in place as follows:

Total annual expenditure (£)	Discount
0–600,000	0%
600,001–800,000	1%
800,001–900,000	2%
900,001–960,000	3%
960,001 and above	5%

Stay Clean uses this supplier for all its materials for all the products it manufactures. The figures given above in the cost per unit table for material cost per unit are net of any discount Stay Clean already qualifies for.

5) The space in the factory currently used for the TD will be sublet for 12 months on a short-term lease contract if production of TD stops now. The income from that contract will be £12,000.

6) The supervisor (currently classed as an overhead) supervises the production of all three products spending approximately 20 per cent of his time on the TD production. He would continue to be fully employed if the TD ceases to be produced now.

Required:

Calculate whether or not it is worthwhile ceasing to produce the TD now rather than waiting 12 months (ignore any adjustment to allow for the time value of money)

Source: adapted from Association of Chartered Certified Accountants, Paper F5, Performance Management.

E13.9 **Sell or process further [LO1, LO7]**

The following details relate to ready meals that are prepared by a food processing company:

Ready meal	K	L	M
	£/meal	£/meal	£/meal
Selling price	5.00	4.00	3.00
Ingredients	2.00	1.00	1.30
Variable costs	1.60	0.80	1.85
Fixed costs	0.50	0.30	0.60
Profit	0.90	0.90	0.65
Oven time (minutes per ready meal)	10	4	8

Each meal is prepared using a series of processes, one of which involves cooking the ingredients in a large oven. The availability of cooking time in the oven is limited and, because each of the meals requires cooking at a different oven temperature, it is not possible to cook more than one of the meals in the oven at the same time. The fixed costs are general fixed costs that are not specific to any type of ready meal.

Required:

Show calculations to determine the most and least profitable use of the oven.

Source: adapted from Chartered Institute of Management Accountants, Paper P2, Decision Management.

E13.10 **Sunday opening [LO1, LO5]**

Bits and Pieces (B&P) operates a retail store selling spares and accessories for the car market. The store has previously only opened for six days per week for the 50 working weeks in the year, but B&P is now considering also opening on Sundays. The sales of the business on Monday through to Saturday averages at £10,000 per day with average gross profit of 70 per cent earned.

B&P expects that the gross profit percentage earned on a Sunday will be 20 percentage points lower than the average earned on the other days in the week. This is because they plan to offer substantial discounts and promotions on a Sunday to attract customers. Given the price reduction, Sunday sales revenues are expected to be 60 per cent *more than* the average daily sales revenues for the other days. These Sunday sales estimates are for new customers only, with no allowance being made for those customers that may transfer from other days.

B&P buys all its goods from one supplier. This supplier gives a 5 per cent discount on *all* purchases if annual spend exceeds £1,000,000.

It has been agreed to pay time and a half to sales assistants that work on Sundays. The normal hourly rate is £20 per hour. In total five sales assistants will be needed for the six hours that the store will be open on a Sunday. They will also be able to take a half-day off (four hours) during the week. Staffing levels will be allowed to reduce slightly during the week to avoid extra costs being incurred.

The staff will have to be supervised by a manager, currently employed by the company and paid an annual salary of £80,000. If he works on a Sunday he will take the equivalent time off during the week when the assistant manager is available to cover for him at no extra cost to B&P. He will also be paid a bonus of 1 per cent of the extra sales generated on the Sunday project.

The store will have to be lit at a cost of £30 per hour and heated at a cost of £45 per hour. The heating will come on two hours before the store opens in the 25 'winter' weeks to make sure it is warm enough for customers to come in at opening time. The store is not heated in the other weeks. The rent of the store amounts to £420,000 per annum.

Required:

Calculate whether the Sunday opening incremental revenue exceeds the incremental costs over a year (ignore inventory movements) and on this basis reach a conclusion as to whether Sunday opening is financially justifiable.

Source: adapted from Association of Chartered Certified Accountants, Paper F5, Performance Management.

E13.11 **Minimum price [LO1, LO2]**

A company producing electronic 'mother' boards for the computer industry has been offered a contract to supply 20,000 units of a customer designed board. The company is interested in this contract as it is currently operating below capacity and has not had any previous dealings with this customer. The customer has said that more regular business may follow if this contract is successful. The company has received the customer design specification and has gathered the following data relating to the contract.

Each board will require the following materials:

One, 0.2 m × 0.2 m C-type fitted architecture board

Two, AMD Z2 processors

Ten, R105 capacitors

- There are currently 12,000 C-architecture boards in stock that were purchased for £4 per board. This board has not been used recently and could be sold to an outside contractor for £4.50 per board. The replacement cost of these boards is now £6 per board.

- The AMD Z2 processors are currently used by all production lines. The stock on hand originally cost £50 and the replacement cost is currently £52 per unit.

- The ten R105 capacitors are an old model that has been replaced by the R106 model. Sufficient stock of the R105 is on hand to meet this contract. The book value is £1 per capacitor and if not used on this contract they will have to be disposed of at a cost of £2,000.

While the company is not currently operating at full capacity, it is expected that given the short timeline to fulfil this contract overtime may have to be worked. The production manager has estimated that the contract will take 8,000 direct labour hours. Of this total 3,000 hours will be overtime hours. The direct workers are highly skilled and paid for a standard 39 hours per week at £15 per hour. Overtime is paid at time and a half and the customer has agreed to pay for the extra cost to complete the order on time.

Manufacturing overhead is recovered as follows: variable manufacturing overhead, £2 per labour hour; fixed manufacturing overhead, £5 per labour hour

The production and design department has estimated that it has spent 20 hours on this contract. This department charges out its services at a fixed overhead rate of £50 per hour.

The company usually charges a profit margin of 25 per cent on all products.

Required:

a) Calculate, using relevant costing principles, the total minimum contract price and price per unit that the company should charge.

b) What non-financial factors might the company need to consider before pricing of this contract?

Source: adapted from Institute of Incorporated Public Accountants, Advanced Management Accounting.

E13.12 **Sell or process further, outsourcing [LO1, LO6, LO7]**

Sniff Co. manufactures and sells its standard perfume by blending a secret formula of aromatic oils with diluted alcohol. The oils are produced by another company following a lengthy process and are very expensive. The standard perfume is highly branded and successfully sold at a price of £39.98 per 100 millilitres (ml).

Sniff Co. is considering processing some of the perfume further by adding a hormone to appeal to members of the opposite sex. The hormone to be added will be different for the male and female perfumes. Adding hormones to perfumes is not universally accepted as a good idea as some people have health concerns. On the other hand, market research carried out suggests that a premium could be charged for perfume that can 'promise' the attraction of a suitor. The market research has cost £3,000.

Data has been prepared for the costs and revenues expected for the following month (a test month) assuming that a part of the company's output will be further processed by adding the hormones.

The output selected for further processing is 1,000 litres, about a tenth of the company's normal monthly output. Of this, 99 per cent is made up of diluted alcohol which costs £20 per litre. The rest is a blend of aromatic oils costing £18,000 per litre. The labour required to produce 1,000 litres of the basic perfume before any further processing is 2,000 hours at a cost of £15 per hour.

Of the output selected for further processing, 200 litres (20 per cent) will be for male customers and 2 litres of hormone costing £7,750 per litre will then be added. The remaining 800 litres (80 per cent) will be for female customers and 8 litres of hormone will be added, costing £12,000 per litre. In both cases the adding of the hormone adds to the overall volume of the product as there is no resulting processing loss.

Sniff Co. has sufficient existing machinery to carry out the test processing.

The new processes will be supervised by one of the more experienced supervisors currently employed by Sniff Co. His current annual salary is £35,000 and it is expected that he will spend 10 per cent of his time working on the hormone adding process during the test month. This will be split evenly between the male and female versions of the product.

Extra labour will be required to further process the perfume, with an extra 500 hours for the male version and 700 extra hours for the female version of the hormone-added product. Labour is currently fully employed, making the standard product. New labour with the required skills will not be available at short notice.

Sniff Co. allocates fixed overhead at the rate of £25 per labour hour to all products for the purposes of reporting profits. The sales prices that could be achieved as a one-off monthly promotion are:

- male version, £75.00 per 100 ml
- female version, £59.50 per 100 ml.

Required:

a) Outline the financial and other factors that Sniff Co. should consider when making a further processing decision.

b) Evaluate whether Sniff Co. should experiment with the hormone adding process using the data provided. Provide a separate assessment and conclusion for the male and the female versions of the product.

c) Calculate the selling price per 100 ml for the female version of the product that would ensure further processing would break even in the test month.

d) Sniff Co. is considering outsourcing the production of the standard perfume. Outline the main factors it should consider before making such a decision.

Source: adapted from Association of Chartered Certified Accountants, Paper F5, Performance Management.

● ● ● ● **Case study problem** ● ● ● ● ● ● ● ● ● ● ● **connect** ● ● ●

C13.1 **Happy Car Rentals [LO1, LO6]**

Happy Car Rentals are a global car rental company. They rent cars and vans to business customers, but their main market is tourist short-term rentals. The company has been in existence for more than 30 years and has operations in over 100 countries. In most countries, its operations are wholly owned, but a smaller number of countries are operating on a franchise basis.

The company has a central reservations system called Merlin. This system has been developed in-house over the past 20 years and is a highly complex, but yet robust and capable system. Regardless of the sales channel used (Internet, phone or walk-in to a branch), or regardless of whether a rental location is owned of franchised, the customer reservation will be made using the Merlin system. The majority of the information systems (IS) department's time is spent on this mission critical system.

However, over the past 10 years or so, more of the time of the IS department has been taken up installing and maintaining non-core software like email and desktop software applications (spreadsheets, email, and so on). The IS manager is quite adamant that this has to change, as her staff have less time to spend on developing many new features that customers and staff require from the Merlin system. To this end, the IS manager is considering putting a proposal to the finance director to outsource the hardware, software and maintenance of non-core software. She believes that recent advances in 'cloud' computing make this a viable option, which will not only save the time of IS staff, but also save the company money.

The IS manager seconded one of the management accounting staff for a few days and together, they have produced the following analysis of the existing costs of non-core software. The company currently pay a fee per user in their email address book, of which there are 23,000 approximately:

Variable costs	
Email licence	£1.50 per user per month
Desktop software	£3.00 per user per month
Virus protection software	£0.50 per user per month
Fixed costs	
Hardware costs	£45,000 per month
Salary costs – 4 IS staff with a salary cost of £5,000	£20,000 per month

The IS manager has done some research and has developed two possible outsourcing options:

Option A – this option involves outsourcing email only. An external email hosting company will provide the service of £1.80 per user per month including the licence fee. The hardware costs will remain as is, but one member of IS staff who is currently responsible for email will no longer be needed.

Option B – this option involves outsourcing email and desktop software. With this option, the number of IS staff needed will be reduced to one full time staff member and one part time, the latter working three days per week. The hardware costs will fall to £10,000 per month, no virus protection software fee will be paid and all email/software licence costs are incurred by the outsourcing company. The same external hosting company as mentioned in option A will provide this service for £7.00 per user per month.

Outsource training

In addition to option A and B above, the IS manager and the human resources (HR) manager are jointly considering outsourcing training on the Merlin reservations system. Currently, there are seven trainers employed by Happy Car Rentals to train new reservations and accounts receivable staff on the Merlin system. All seven trainers are former sales/accounts staff with many years experience. They all have at least 10 years' experience of working with the Merlin system and are capable of delivering training in at English at least one other language. Some trainers are fluent in three or four languages and deliver training in multiple locations. The HR manager has read about some other organizations outsourcing training to external providers and achieving substantial cost savings. While the HR manager is not under pressure to reduce costs, he is interested in at least considering the possibility of outsourcing.

To this end, a proposal has been received by the HR manager from SuperTrain as detailed below. The proposal is based on the training requirements for the past 12 months. Currently, the total annual salary of all seven trainers is £240,000. This figure includes all employer taxes, social insurance and the employer's share of pension contributions.

To provide training days per month as follows:

Proposal to Happy Car Rentals

Merlin systems training 10 days per month x 5 trainers

50 days x £200 per day	=	£15,000 per month
Annual fee		£180,000
Minimum contract term		5 years

Two of the current training staff would be retained by SuperTrain, meaning they would cease to be employees of Happy Car Rentals, but would not be entitled to a redundancy payment. The other five current training staff would be made redundant and each would receive a redundancy payment of £25,000 each.

Required:

a) Calculate the total monthly cost per user of the current set-up of non-core software at Happy Car Rentals.

b) Is option A a viable option? Support your answer with calculations and provide comments justifying you decision.

c) Is option B a viable option? Support your answer with calculations and provide comments justifying you decision.

d) Are there any other costs or factors (current or future) not mentioned in options A and B which would need to be considered before making a final decision?

e) Would you recommend the training for the Merlin system be outsourced to an external training company as suggested? Provide clear arguments for your recommendation.

● ● ● Recommended reading ● ● ● ● ● ● ● ● ● ● ● ● ● ● ● ● ● ●

- 'Shared service or outsourcing? Make the right choice', CIMA, 2006, available at http://www. cimaglobal.com/Thought-leadership/Newsletters/Insight-e-magazine/Insight-July-2006/Shared-service-or-outsourcing-Make-the-right-choice/ (accessed on 26 June 2012).

This is a useful article from CIMA on ensuring outsourcing is undertaken for the right reasons.

● ● ● Reference ●

Kristandl, G. and M. Quinn (2012) 'Old wine in new bottles? A preliminary exploration of management accounting in cloud business models', European Accounting Association, annual conference, Ljubljana, 9–11 May.

When you have read this chapter

Log on to the Online Learning Centre at **www.mcgraw-hill.co.uk/textbooks/burns** to explore chapter-by-chapter test questions, links and further online study tools for Management Accounting.

CHAPTER 14

PRICING

Chapter outline

- Why is pricing important?
- Economists' view on pricing
- Accountants' view on pricing
- Cost-plus pricing
- Pricing policies and strategies

Learning outcomes

On completion of this chapter, students will be able to:

LO1 Discuss the nature of pricing within an organizational setting

LO2 Analyse the impact of supply and demand curves on pricing

LO3 Describe the marketing strategies of pricing

LO4 Examine the strategic implication of strategies of company pricing polices

LO5 Match strategic pricing strategies to various business scenarios

LO6 Calculate cost plus pricing

Introduction

The **price** of a product or service is what is exchanged on receiving a product or service. In most cases the price of a product/service will have a value in currency, although in some cultures this can relate to exchanging other products and services rather than money. Within this chapter we will assume price has a currency value.

Pricing involves many different disciplines; you can examine pricing from economic theory, as a marketing tool, strategic focus and from a pure accounting perspective. Of course, in reality you need to be aware of all of these perspectives when engaged in pricing decisions. Throughout this book we have highlighted that management accountants are no longer the 'bean-counters' of an organization and are involved in many strategic decisions. Therefore, it is essential to cover the wider implications of pricing decisions in this chapter. Understanding just the basic calculations is not sufficient.

Throughout this chapter, in order to examine pricing from a wider perspective, we will analyse how companies such as Netflix and Procter & Gamble use **pricing strategies** to help them achieve new objectives. Pricing is not an easy task, and we will discuss some examples of companies that did not get their pricing policies right.

Companies know that it is fundamental to achieve the most appropriate pricing targets for their products and services, which is why they spend a lot of their time getting this right. To be able to get the pricing right regardless of the marketing tools and the strategies, the company must first understand their costing structure, which is why the earlier parts of this textbook focused on costing. We will be using some of the principles you learnt in earlier chapters when we look at some of the pricing calculations, so you may find it useful to refer back to Chapters 3 and 6.

In a 2009 CIMA survey it was recognized that some pricing techniques are used in larger organizations more than in smaller companies. In addition, they found that the main accounting techniques, such as **cost-plus pricing** and transfer pricing were more commonly used in the manufacturing sector than in the service sector. Although transfer pricing is a commonly used accounting tool it is not discussed in this chapter, but we will return to this topic in Chapter 18 in the context of multinational organizations.

Why is pricing important?

Pricing is not just a company decision. In many sectors and industries legislation and regulation which can impact on a pricing structure is imposed on companies to protect consumers from, for example, products becoming too expensive. Products which are considered necessary for a basic standard of living such as water, gas and electricity are heavily regulated in the UK and in many other countries. For example, in the UK in 2011, there were numerous debates about the six main suppliers of electricity increasing the price of electricity. Concerns were raised that prices may be increased to a level where a significant percentage of the population would not be able to afford to heat their homes throughout the winter. An investigation was undertaken by the regulators and they determined that high prices occurred in many cases because the pricing system offered to customers was simply too confusing to be able to determine the best deal. The result of the investigation in April 2012 was to begin a new structure of pricing to make it easier for consumers to understand the choices available to them.

More general products and services are not subject to such stringent regulation because the free market balances the pricing structure. Although the markets are generally left to determine the pricing framework, within industry there is legislation to protect consumers from anti-competitive practices. In the UK, the Competition Act 1998 prohibits any business activities that distort competition; in Europe this is legislated through Article 101 of the treaty on the functioning of the European Union.

To improve profits organizations sometimes try to 'set' prices within a particular industry, which means consumers pay more than is needed. Setting prices from an organizational perspective is aimed at maximizing shareholder wealth, which is important unless the organization's strategy is focused on increasing market share, in which case profit targets may be lowered. Companies are often tempted to try to set prices within an industry, however, this is strictly against anti-competitive legislation. Management accounting information on pricing is internal data and any pricing strategies devised from this information should not be disclosed to third parties. In 2011, in the UK, The Office of Fair Trading (OFT) declared that the Royal Bank of Scotland (RBS) and Barclays had engaged in practices, which were against the Competition Act 1988. It was found that RBS had disclosed future pricing strategies on their loan products for large professional firms to Barclays. This was considered an attempt to 'price set', which distorts competition and disadvantages consumers. Such malpractice is taken very seriously and RBS were fined £28.59 million.

Management accountants must understand the sensitive nature of pricing and have knowledge of the legal and regulatory aspects of pricing to ensure they work within these frameworks. They must also understand that small changes in pricing can make a significant impact on both revenues and profitability of an organization.

14.1: Management Accounting in Practice

Impact of regulation on companies seeking cost synergies, AT&T and T mobile

The recession has spurred companies to try to find ways to reduce costs, to combat their reducing profit margins. One industry which has highlighted the need to find new ways of increasing their margins is the telecommunications industry. Focusing on trying to compete through mergers and acquisitions to take advantage of cost synergies, many companies have tried to consolidate. However, although cost synergies would provide a way of improving profit margins, many have been blocked by the regulators. One example of this is in America where the US Department of Justice blocked AT&T acquiring T-Mobile as the £25 billion deal would have reduce competition from four down to three companies.

Source: Thomas (2011).

Exercises

Using the Internet as a research tool, find other examples of companies who have tried to either find cost synergies through mergers and acquisitions or set pricing strategies with other companies. What have been the outcomes of the cases that you have found?

Economists' view on pricing

Anyone who has studied economics will be familiar with the notion of the supply and demand and the elasticity of demand. Economic theory considers production from two perspectives: (1) scarcity of the product or service and (2) the opportunity cost.

In economic theory, when setting the price of a product or service, it should be priced on the **marginal cost** and the elasticity of the product or service, which incorporates relevant costing principles as discussed in Chapter 13. Economic theory measures elasticity of a product or service to determine the impact of price changes.

The **elasticity** of a product of service is simply analysing the unit sales change in relation to a change in the price. So, if a product or service has a price increase and the demand drops then it is said to be elastic and if there is no or little effect then it is known as inelastic. An example of product that is known to be elastic is petrol. When the price of petrol increases, people are more cautious in their consumption and when there is a drop in price, the demand increases over the short period of the price drop. In countries where the price of petrol is relatively low, consumers are not concerned with petrol consumption when purchasing cars. In countries where the cost of petrol is relatively high, you find that consumers are very aware of the changes in the price of the product and do factor this into their consumption of petrol and the cars they purchase. This of course is a little simplistic because consumers are also aware of environmental factors and tax implications.

The formula to calculate the elasticity of a product or service is as follows:

Elasticity = (percentage change in quantity/percentage change in price)

If the elasticity of a product is measured and the absolute value is less than 1 then it is said to be **inelastic** (obviously there are varying degree of inelasticity), if the value is above 1 then it is said to be **elastic**.

An example of a product which is inelastic would be cigarettes. The increase in price does not impact significantly on the demand of the consumer, or not at a level that makes a significant difference to the profit of the company selling the product. You must be very careful when talking about the elasticity of a product; what we have discussed so far relates to the elasticity of demand, not supply.

14.1: Management Accounting Insight

Price of tobacco – an Irish study

Cigarettes are traditionally the product everyone uses as an example when discussing inelastic products. Cigarettes are considered, in most studies, to have an elasticity value of between -0.5 and -1.0, which means they are relatively inelastic. However, in a study by the Office of Revenue Commissioners, Ireland, it was found that the elasticity of cigarettes had reached -3.6. Thus, suggesting that an increase in price of 1 per cent would result in a reduction of 3.6 per cent in consumption. Other studies have suggested that although price is considered the most significant factor in a reduction of consumption, other items such as the smoking ban in public buildings and income can contribute. However, none of these factors justified the -3.6 per cent finding within this study, which would mean cigarettes are more sensitive to price than DVDs and toothpicks which, considering the addictive nature of this product, did not make sense.

Upon further investigation it was found that the statistical results of this study were not reliable because the survey only counted legal consumption of cigarettes and not the illegal trade of the product, which had increased significantly following the price increases.

Sources: Reidy and Walsh (2011); Smith (2012).

Exercise

Why would the elasticity of cigarettes be of significant interest to governments?

The elasticity of demand of a product or service is driven by many factors, some of which were considered in *Management Accounting Insight 14.1*. In general elasticity of demand is considered to be influenced by the following factors:

1) *Disposable income* – how much extra cash consumers have to spend on non-essential items. The more disposable income individuals have, the less elastic some products become. The opportunity cost becomes less of an issue because the value of the disposable cash is reduced. Therefore, the nature of the product determines how much impact disposable income will have. Luxury products will be affected more by this factor.

2) *Availability of substitutes* – if there are many substitutes of a product available then a change in the price can impact on the demand of the product. The more substitutes, the more likely it is that price will impact on demand. The opportunity cost of individual brands will become a significant factor in the decision-making process to purchase the product. This links to the type of market you are working within, monopolies, oligopolies and full competition.

3) *The time factor* – time can be a significant factor in the elasticity of a product. Examining a product's elasticity over a longer period of time results in the consumer having more time to react to a change in the price. So products which are inelastic in the short term could become less inelastic in the longer term. This is due to the consumer having time to change their preferences and behaviour. The time factor can also relate to how long the price change will be around for.

It is important to remember that these factors can impact at the same time. For a pricing decision it is important to understand the price elasticity of demand. Companies often use the elasticity of a product to determine ways of improving their market share. So, if a product is relativity elastic, by lowering the price the sales volume would be expected to increase – but this is not always the case. Reducing prices might incentivize the consumers to buy more if no other competitors make changes. When one competitor changes their price and other competitors mimic those price cuts then only consumers win. Classic examples of this occurring can be observed in 'petrol price wars'. Many companies use price cuts because their business models include a differentiated product portfolio and if they can entice customers to buy one product then they can capture the attention of the consumer to buy other products. Consider supermarkets that sell petrol; they attract consumers with lower petrol prices and sell their other stock at the same time.

The more elastic the price demand is, the lower the mark-up of the product, because the consumers are more price sensitive and will lower their consumption as the price increases. The less elastic the price demand of a product of service, the higher the mark-up can be, because consumers are not put off with higher prices. The mark-up is simply how much you expect to gain as a margin over the cost structure of your product, in other words, the return on the product or service.

14.2: Management Accounting in Practice

Impact of the economic crisis and reputation on price

An example of product demand elasticity in practice comes from Song et al. (2011), who examined the demand elasticity of hotel rooms in Hong Kong. Through analysing different categories of priced hotels and consumers from different locations (in various parts of the world) they were able to conclude that hotel price elasticity is related to two factors: economic crises and word of mouth. The economic crisis is a factor because it affects the disposal income of both individuals and companies, and word of mouth because of the number of competitors and substitutes. By using data from Euro Monitor International and the International Monetary Fund (IMF) they identified that long-haul travellers were more income elastic in the highly priced hotels and the short/medium-haul travellers were more price elastic in medium-priced hotels and guesthouses. This kind of study helps the hotel industry to determine their pricing strategies for different groups of consumers. Pricing strategies will be discussed later in this chapter.

Source: Song et al. (2011).

Exercise

Consider the impact of the economic crisis and reputation on the hotel industry and find other examples of industries where the price of their product or service has been influenced by the economic crisis or how reputation has maintained their ability to maintain high prices.

Profit maximization when marginal cost meets marginal revenues

Economists argue that prices should be set using marginal costs because maximum profits are achieved when your production is set at a point where marginal cost equals marginal revenue. Assuming that price is the driver of demand and demand curves are known with certainty, optimum selling prices can be established by analysing **marginal revenues** and marginal costs. Marginal cost is the additional cost of producing one more unit and marginal revenue is the additional revenue when selling one more unit.

Economic theory establishes the idea that increasing prices does not generally maximize profits. Within an organization profit maximization can occur when cost reduction is achieved. By lowering the cost, the production volume needs to be adjusted to ensure that marginal cost and marginal revenues are equal; this is in a perfectly competitive market. In the short term, fixed costs are sunk and do not impact on the price of a product or service. Therefore, only the variable costs should be considered when setting prices under economic theory. Consider the example in Exhibit 14.1.

	A	B	C	D	E	F	G
1	Price	Sales demand/Output	Total revenue	Marginal Revenue	Total costs	Marginal costs	Profit
2	£	Units	TR £	MR £	TC £	MC £	£
3							
4	100	12	1,200		900		300
5	95	13	1,235	35	915	15	320
6	90	14	1,260	25	935	20	325
7	85	15	1,275	15	960	25	315
8	80	16	1,280	5	990	30	290
9	75	17	1,275	−5	1,025	35	250
10	70	18	1,260	−15	1,065	40	195
11	65	19	1,235	−25	1,110	45	125
12	60	20	1,200	−35	1,160	50	40
13	55	21	1,155	−45	1,215	55	−60

Exhibit 14.1: Pricing example

You can see in the scenario in Exhibit 14.1 the profit is maximized in cell G6, highlighted in yellow, this is when the price is £90. This is diagrammatically presented in the graph in Exhibit 14.2 with the point at which profit maximization is highlight by the bold red arrowed line.

The theory is that profit maximization happens when MC = MR, however this happens in between whole units being produced and sold. The graph in Exhibit 14.3 demonstrates the point at which MC = MR.

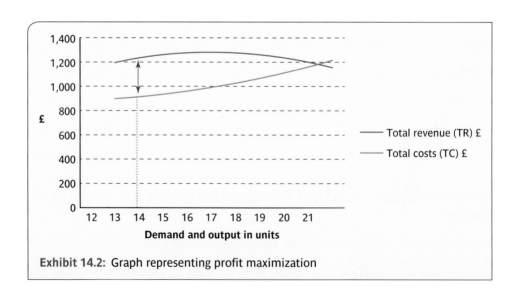

Exhibit 14.2: Graph representing profit maximization

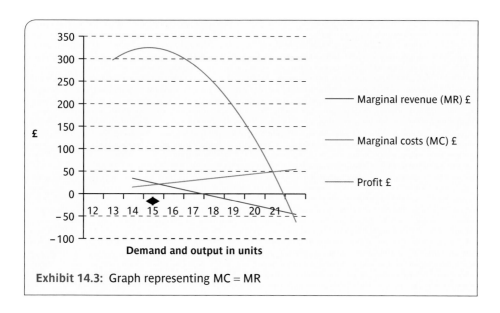

Exhibit 14.3: Graph representing MC = MR

You can see in the graph (Exhibit 14.3) that MC = MR between 14 and 15 units being sold, this is highlighted with a diamond shape on the horizontal axis. Earlier we mentioned that economic theory of pricing has two main assumptions: that demand is driven through pricing and that the demand curve can be calculated with certainty. Of course, these assumptions are the reason why many companies simply do not use this approach. Many companies believe that the price is only one factor in driving demand because there are many psychological factors which can inspire customers to go ahead with a purchase, some of these will be discussed within the marketing view on pricing, later in this chapter. The second factor which states that companies can predict accurate demand curves is an element of this theory which causes numerous problems. Although industry demand curves are widely available, when a company has a differentiated product it is very difficult to establish demand curves at an individual product level.

For products which are homogenous, which means a product cannot be distinguished from another product which is sold by a competitor, the economist model works well. An example of a commodity which works well in this model is electricity. In the generation sector of the electricity market, electricity is sold using marginal costs. Demand curves within the industry are known and the product is homogenous, therefore, it is easy for the companies to apply this theory within their pricing decisions.

Accountants' view on pricing

The major difference between the economists' view on pricing and the accountants' view on pricing is that accountants, use fixed costs in their pricing decisions. There are many ways in which the cost structure of a product or service can be established. We have considered many of these techniques in the earlier chapters of this book, for example absorption costing, in Chapter 5, and activity-based costing, in Chapter 6. Many companies do not use the MC = MR pricing strategy because they are concerned about ignoring their fixed costs. This is where the concept of full costing comes from.

Cost-plus pricing

In earlier chapters of this book we have examined costing very carefully. The general approach to pricing from the accountant's perspective is that all costs should be recovered and therefore included when calculating the price. However, to create a profit margin a mark-up will be added to the cost of the product or service. Recovering costs, both direct and indirect, and adding a mark-up is a long-term pricing strategy. It is worth noting that cost-plus pricing is also referred to as full-cost pricing. You may also be surprised to see that although the economists' view of pricing adopts the relevant costing principles you learned in the Chapter 13, the accountant's method ignores this concept.

Although the accountant's view on pricing is commonly used in creating pricing structures, the management accountant cannot ignore the product itself and the market within which it is selling. It is important to understand how the mark-up of a product can be established. There are many ways of adding value to a product to differentiate it other than examining the product itself. Marketing tools can help a company establish their pricing structures. By incorporating marketing principles the management accountant can overcome some of the criticisms of using long-term costing structure to determine prices within established markets.

Cooper (2011) argues that based upon a new global study, only 35 per cent of companies have the required power to achieve the price they want from their products or services. This study examined industries such as pharmaceuticals, construction and logistics. Cooper (2011) found that companies can achieve a higher pricing power by adding value through brand identity and product value. Pricing power is not the same in all industries and this study shows that construction and pharmaceuticals have the highest pricing power, with industries such as transport and logistics

---

Worked Example 14.1

Cost-plus pricing

Wearham Ltd produces and sells two products. The products are priced on a full-cost basis. The following table shows the production costs of the two products:

	Product X	Product Y
Demand	5,000 units	10,000 units
	£/unit	£/unit
Direct materials	15	20
Direct labour (£10 per hour)	20	30
Variable production costs	10	15
Fixed production costs per unit	6	9
Total production costs	51	74

The company's policy is to allocate 10 per cent of the total production costs for selling and administration overheads and a further 15 per cent mark-up for profit based on total cost.

Variable overheads are directly related to direct labour costs and fixed overheads are absorbed on the basis of labour hours.

Wearham Ltd are considering producing 10,000 units of product Z which will have material costs of £10 and will use 2 labour hours to produce per unit.

Required:

a) Calculate the selling price of product Z on a full cost basis. (You should work to two decimal places.) This question requires you to examine the current product portfolio, X and Y and analyse the changes product Z would have on the cost structure of the three products.

	Workings/notes	Product Z
Demand		10,000 units
		£/unit
Direct materials	a	10
Direct labour (£10 per hour)	b	20
Variable production costs	c	10
Fixed production costs	d	<u>4</u>
Total production costs	e	44.00
Selling and admin. overheads	f	4.40
Total cost	g	48.40
Profit margin	h	7.26
Selling price	i	55.66

Workings/notes:

a) The material costs are provided in the question.

b) In the cost structure of X and Y the question states that the cost per direct labour hour is £10 per hour, the questions states that product Z will require two hours in production. Therefore £10 × 2 hrs = £20.00.

c) The question states there is a direct relationship between variable cost and labour hours therefore the variable overhead cost is calculated as follows: Relationship is 20/10 = 2 (using data for X), test 30/15 = 2 (using data for Y).

The variable overhead cost for Z is 20/2 = 10.

d) Fixed overhead costs need more consideration. The question does not indicate that any additional fixed costs will be introduced due to the new product therefore the current fixed costs need to be allocated across the three products: X, Y and Z.

We need to first examine how many labour hours are used in total for X and Y because the questions states that fixed costs are absorbed on the basis of labour hours. Total labour hours when just X and Y are being produced:

$$X: 5,000 \times 2 = 10,000 \text{ hours}$$

$$Y: 10,000 \times 3 = 30,000 \text{ hours}$$

Which means the total labour hours = 40,000 hours (10,000 + 30,000).

The overhead rate at the moment is 6/2 = £3. This can be established by examining one of the current products such as X. Product X uses two labour hours for the production of one unit, you can calculate this by taking the labour cost and dividing it by the labour cost per hour £20/£10 per hour.

The total fixed overhead cost would be £3 × 40,000 hours = £120,000.

As fixed costs remain constant when producing Z the new overhead rate would be:

Labour hours for X and Y: (40,000 plus labour hours for Z: 2 × 10,000) = 60,000 hours.

New rate: £120,000/60,000 hours = £2 per labour hour.

Therefore fixed overhead rate for Z would be £2 × 2 hrs = £4.

e) Total production cost is simply the direct material, direct labour, variable cost and fixed cost.

f) In the question it states that the company has a policy to add 10 per cent of the total production cost to cover selling and administrations costs. Z would be £44.00 × 0.1 = £4.40.

g) Total cost is the production cost plus the selling and administration cost.

h) The question tells you that the company policy is to add 15 per cent on total cost as a mark-up. Z would require the total cost of £48.40 being multiplied by 15 per cent which is £48.40 × 0.15 = £7.26.

i) The selling price is the total cost plus the mark-up.

having the lowest power. It is the role of the management accountant to ensure that the accounting, in this case the pricing structure, is embedded within the strategy of the organization, which means they have to understand the value of the product as well as the cost.

Pricing policies and strategies

So far we have examined how pricing can be determined by analysing the cost structure, although this is not the only approach. From a marketing perspective this is not always the best way to approach pricing. It can be argued that of all the marketing tools available to organizations, pricing is one of the most valuable as it can make an instant impact on both the top and bottom lines of the income statement (Kohli and Suri, 2011). Kohli and Suri argue that on average a 1 per cent increase in price (assuming that the demand is not affected) can provide a 10 per cent increase in profit.

Kohli and Suri (2011) also argue that in many cases the cost of a product or service is irrelevant. One of the examples they use relates to the hospitality industry. Many of the ancillary services you receive in hotels do not reflect the real cost of the service or product. One example would be wireless technology such as wiFi. In many parts of the world they will charge very high prices for Internet access even though the cost of such a service is not high. However, because the customers are exposed to this high-level pricing on a continuous basis they perceive it as normal. It has to be remembered that pricing strategies are not easy to get right.

14.3: Management Accounting in Practice

Netflix and pricing strategies

Netflix is a large American company that hire DVDs to consumers through the post and also have an additional service of streamlining some films and television through the Internet. They have become extremely successful and in September 2011 had acquired 25 million subscribers to their service.

A strategic decision within the company to focus on streaming their films resulted in a new policy on pricing to complement the new strategic direction. Before the strategic change the pricing policy was a standard charge for consumers to be able to request DVDs to be sent through the post and to have the right to streaming of films, a charge of $9.99 was used. Following the strategic focus on streaming, the pricing policy changed to reflect that streaming would become their main method of delivery. Consumers would now have two options: (1) streaming services only for $7.99 and (2) for streaming and DVDs $15.98.

Consumers reacted badly to the new pricing strategy and following large complaints the CEO had to warn the investors that they faced losing large qualities of subscribers, making a significant impact of share price.

Source: Anon (2011).

Exercise

Why would NetFlix change their pricing policy? Find examples of others companies where there have been changes in pricing strategies, how did the consumers and stock market react to the changes – were they successful or not?

Consumers have different needs and these are based on their own preference, requirements and time frame. These factors can help to drive a marketing plan on pricing. There are specific pricing strategies that can be used to take advantage of consumer needs and also the market environment and these are known as pricing skimming and penetration pricing.

Price skimming is a marketing tool that can help organizations quickly recover many of their fixed costs when they have developed new products. This strategy takes advantage of consumers wanting to be one of the first people to get new products. When a new product, especially in the technology industry, appears on the market they are often priced very highly. They know that consumers want to be seen to be the first with the new products, for example with the game consoles such as the X-box. Technology has a very short life cycle and the manufacturer will push the price up as high as possible in the first phase, knowing that new competitors will enter the market very quickly to compete, which will drive the price down. Price skimming only works for products which have an inelastic demand curve.

Price penetration is the opposite of price skimming in terms of initial price. When a new product enters a market, where it is relatively unknown, or a new company enters a new market, by reducing the price of the service or product this can increase market share. The low price is a marketing tool to entice consumers to try it because they feel like they are getting a good deal. Once the consumer has tried the product and realized they like it, the price can be increased to reflect a more realistic price. This strategy is often used in the food industry. In a supermarket new products are often advertised on special prices. Penetration pricing works for products and services which have an elastic demand curve.

In addition to these basic marketing tools, strategically there are other ways in which organizations can take control of the pricing structure of their products and services rather than it being driven by costs, and this is through a process of 'de-commoditization'. Kholi and Suri (2011) state that 'de-commoditization' is where a company takes a product or service and differentiates it from alternatives, which can be direct competition or substitutes. Through differentiation a company then disentangles the pricing from the costing. They can add premiums to their prices because they have differentiated through service, quality or new additions (for example, new features). The example which Kholi and Suri (2011) use to explain this is Starbucks. Starbucks, managed to take a basic product like coffee and turn it into a brand. This is called value-based pricing and it examines the value a product or service can offer a consumer. Value creation will be examined in much more detail in Chapter 19, however, in this chapter we will examine some of the basic marketing ideas on how companies can establish pricing strategies by considering the value-added approach.

In a televised interview on BBC 4 in the UK, Cliff Burrows, the President of Starbucks, said 'We give a good experience' (24 December 2010). In other words their product is not just the 'coffee' they sell but also 'the experience' a customer gains when entering a Starbucks shop. That is not to say Starbucks no longer needs to consider the cost structure of coffee and can rely on 'the experience' the customer receives. Costs have to be analysed in every organization – even when they are not price sensitive. The change in the price of the coffee bean in 2011 affected the bottom line of Starbucks; their profits declined. The 'experience' which differentiates Starbucks from other companies competing in the same industry may protect them from price sensitivity but it does not protect them from reducing margins when the cost of raw materials increase.

In addition to using price strategies, companies also use marketing tools which provide an opportunity for companies to increase profit margins at various points by having different pricing structures. Companies use price bundling, price unbundling, discounting and versioning to create different pricing structures.

1) *Price bundling.* When a company offers more than one service or product they will often use their best selling product or service to entice customers to use or buy their other services or products. By offering one price to cover the cost of several services or products the company is working on the perceived value from the customer on their packaged deal. One example of a company using this kind of service is BSkyB. BSkyB is a well-known satellite television service provider. BSkyB use price bundling to offer different services. In addition to the basic package they also work on the principle of perceived value and offer packages at set prices. So not only do they offer their satellite television services but they also offer their customers a bundled price for adding their broadband services, for example. By taking more than one service the price is perceived to have more value by the customer. When selling the services BSkyB makes it very clear to the customer what it would cost as a separate service and what the price would be if purchased together.

2) *Price unbundling.* This marketing tool provides some companies with a way of advertising their products at a lower rate by offering a good price for the very basic service or product and then adding extra price structures for any additions or additional services that a customer may want. This can attract immediate attention from the consumer as they see what looks to be a very attractive offer. A good example of this is how the majority of low-cost airlines structure their prices and advertise. Companies such as easyJet and Aer Lingus often offer seats for incredibly low prices, however, when the customers then want to add luggage or choose to get to the front of the queue for a good seat, there is an extra charge. These additional services have been unbundled from the initial product or service. The Kindle sold by Amazon is also another example of price unbundling, the device is sold very cheaply with low profit margins but they then sell other services and content to add to their margins. Customers who buy a Kindle then use Amazon to download books onto the Kindle and the profit margin is created through the sale of books. This also locks customers into using Amazon to purchase future books.

3) *Discounting.* If companies want to attract customers they often use discounting to catch consumers' attention. Discounting sometimes means that profit margins are reduced significantly for a short period of time and then removed once the customer has signed up for a service and started using the product. Discounting can be used in new products; we have previously discussed penetration pricing. It can also be used for existing products or services, and can be used to try to encourage sales volume in periods when the company knows there is little call for their products or services. One industry that uses this on an annual basis is the travel industry. In the UK, in September and October, when most families are typically returning from their yearly holiday, companies in this industry try to attract customers by offering discounts if they book within a specific deadline for next year's holiday.

4) *Versioning.* This is a pricing structure which provides an opportunity for a company to offer their products or services at different ranges depending on the version of the product or service which the customer chooses. An example of a company who use this marketing ploy is Apple Inc. A classic and simple example is the iPhone, where customers can choose to buy the same model but with a choice of different memory sizes. Each version has a different price allocated to it. Rafi (2011) provides another example when Procter and Gamble used versioning during the recession; they offered their customers the opportunity to purchase a 'basic range'. Their products are known for quality but by offering one-ply tissue sheets the cost was reduced by 15–25 per cent.

Management accountants need to be aware of these marketing tools and although the costs are not always the driver in these tools, it is important to maintain close scrutiny on the costs. For example, although Starbucks have de-commoditized their product, which allows them to focus more on price than cost, the cost of the coffee bean is still important. When the cost of the coffee bean increased considerably it would have been easy to miss that a profitable product was becoming unprofitable. This is one of the key arguments used in trying to get management accountants to return back to some of the basic concepts within management accounting.

Although the strategic pricing policies and marketing tools are valuable to most companies, management accounting is very important to establish the profitability of individual customers. Not all customers will be profitable because the business models of different customers can vary. The way in which individual customers conduct their business can impact on the profitability of that customer, which brings us back to the essential nature of the management accountant – understanding the cost structures and activity-driven processes. This is when pricing and customer profitability analysis can work together (you learnt about CPA in Chapter 6). Analysing customers to drive profit rather than just pricing brings in the opportunity once again to consider outsourcing. By examining customer cost structure it may be appropriate at times to outsource some of the activities which are highlighted as resource intensive.

Chapter summary

Pricing is a very complicated area. It is not just a case of considering management accounting techniques. Every business is different and therefore each requires consideration of how the industry works, what the product actually is and how the customer reacts to psychological factors that can impact on the purchasing choice of the consumer. Therefore it is vital to have a knowledge of economics and marketing when considering the pricing strategy of any business.

Pricing will be considered further in terms of value-based pricing and transfer pricing in the strategic chapters, later in the book.

Key terms

Cost-plus pricing A method whereby the cost of a product is estimated and a mark-up is added for profit (p. 350)
Elastic Where the demand of a product or service changes in relation to a change in the price (p. 352)
Elasticity The sensitivity of one variable against another (p. 351)
Inelastic Where the demand of a product or service does not change with a change in price (p. 352)

Marginal costs The cost of increasing one unit of output (p. 351)
Marginal revenues The revenue gained in increasing one unit of output (p. 354)
Margins A measure of profitability (p. 351)
Price the value of a product or service that is used in the transaction process of selling to a consumer (p. 350)
Pricing strategies A portfolio of strategies that enable a company to target different markets or take advantage of the various stages of the life cycle of a product or service (p. 350)

Review questions ● ● ● ● ● ● ● ● ● ● ● ● connect ● ● ●

| Level of difficulty: | BASIC | INTERMEDIATE | ADVANCED |

14.1 Why is pricing important within a business? **[LO1]**
14.2 How does the demand curve impact on price setting? **[LO2]**

14.3 Give three examples of marketing tools used for price setting. **[LO3]**

14.4 Why should pricing link to the strategy of a company? **[LO4]**

14.5 What type of pricing strategy suits a highly technological/innovative focused company? **[LO5]**

14.6 If the variable cost of a product is £10 and the fixed cost per unit is £7, how much would the price of the product be if the company has a mark-up policy of 20 per cent using full-cost pricing? **[LO6]**

Group discussion and activity questions

14.7 Why are some companies reluctant to use the economic model for pricing? **[LO1, LO3, LO4]**

14.8 Is full-cost pricing suitable for short-term pricing decisions? **[LO6]**

14.9 Why are marketing strategies and tools used more for companies selling to the end consumer rather than intermediary buyers? **[LO3]**

14.10 How can companies determine their mark-up policies? **[LO6]**

Exercises   connect™

E14.1 **Target costing versus standard costing [LO6]**

HJ is a printing company that specializes in producing high-quality cards and calendars for sale as promotional gifts. Much of the work produced by HJ uses similar techniques and for a number of years HJ has successfully used a standard costing system to control its costs.

HJ is now planning to diversify into other promotional gifts such as plastic moulded items including key fobs, card holders and similar items. There is already a well-established market place for these items but HJ is confident that with its existing business contacts it can be successful if it controls its costs. Initially HJ will need to invest in machinery to mould the plastic, and it is likely that this machinery will have a life of five years. An initial appraisal of the proposed diversification based on low initial sales volumes and marginal cost-based product pricing for year 1, followed by increases in both volumes and selling prices in subsequent years, shows that the investment has a payback period of four years.

Required:

a) Explain the relationship between target costs and standard costs and how HJ can derive target costs from target prices

b) Discuss the conflict that will be faced by HJ when making pricing decisions based on marginal cost in the short term and the need for full recovery of all costs in the long term.

Source: Chartered Institute of Management Accountants, P2 specimen paper.

E14.2 **Pricing and ABC [LO6]**

You may wish to refer back to Chapter 6 to examine ABC principles before you attempt this question.

Brick by Brick (BBB) is a building business that provides a range of building services to the public. They have been asked to quote for garage conversions (GC) and extensions to properties (EX) and have found that they are winning fewer GC contracts than expected.

BBB has a policy to price all jobs at budgeted total cost plus 50 per cent. Overheads are currently absorbed on a labour hour basis. BBB thinks that a switch to activity-based costing (ABC) to absorb overheads would reduce the cost associated to GC and hence make them more competitive.

You are provided with the following data:

Overhead Annual	Activity driver	Total number category overheads	$ of activities per year
Supervisors	90,000	Site visits	500
Planners	70,000	Planning documents	250
Property related	240,000	Labour hours	40,000
Total	400,000		

A typical GC costs $3,500 in materials and takes 300 labour hours to complete. A GC requires only one site visit by a supervisor and needs only one planning document to be raised. The typical EX costs $8,000 in materials and takes 500 hours to complete. An EX requires six site visits and five planning documents. In all cases labour is paid $15 per hour.

Required:

a) Calculate the cost and quoted price of a GC and of an EX using labour hours to absorb the overheads.

b) Calculate the cost and the quoted price of a GC and of an EX using ABC to absorb the overheads.

c) Assuming that the cost of a GC falls by nearly 7 per cent and the price of an EX rises by about 2 per cent as a result of the change to ABC, suggest possible pricing strategies for the two products that BBB sells and suggest two reasons other than high prices for the current poor sales of the GC.

d) One BBB manager has suggested that only marginal cost should be included in budget cost calculations as this would avoid the need for arbitrary overhead allocations to products. Briefly discuss this point of view and comment on the implication for the amount of mark-up that would be applied to budget costs when producing quotes for jobs.

Source: Association of Chartered Certified Accountants, Paper F5.

E14.3 **Pricing strategies [LO4]**

a) Organizations use different strategies when determining how they should price their products. Explain how the use of target pricing could help the organization achieve the required rate of return in the first year.

b) Electricalprod Plc is producing a new electrical device to compete within the satellite navigation system industry. They normally use target pricing as a method of determining the price of a new product. They will compete with middle range models already on the market. From market research, they have identified that they should sell the new product for £170. At this price, it is predicted that they will sell on average 50,000 a year. To design, manufacture and sell these new products an initial capital of £6,000,000 will be needed. If the company wants to achieve a return on investment (ROI) of 12 per cent, what is the maximum cost that the new product can be?

c) Electricalprod Plc have an new innovative electrical product which is set to have a high demand when first released due to the fact that there is nothing else on the market that is like it. Discuss why this company may choose to use a different pricing policy in this situation and state what that may be.

d) Electicalprod Plc have been approached by a new company and they want to place a large order (which is still within the production capacity) of one of their products which is at the mature stage of the life cycle. The price offered is 5 per cent above the marginal price of the product but this remains at 3 per cent less than the targeted ROI. Discuss why Electricalprod Plc may accept this offer for this product.

Source: adapted from Association of Chartered Certified Accountants.

E14.4 **Pricing strategies [LO4]**

Mike Smith has told you that he is anxious for HCF (the company) to adopt a strategic approach to pricing. In the past, prices have often been set on a variety of ad hoc bases, such as charging full cost of production (plus a mark-up to cover distribution costs and profit) or charging the same price as competitors charge for similar products, but there has been little consistency across products or over time in the pricing bases adopted.

The proposed new strategic approach would not necessarily mean that the same basis of pricing would be adopted for all products, nor would it mean that a given product would necessarily be priced at the same level throughout its product life cycle. However, Mike is anxious that (at the beginning of each product's life cycle) there should be a strategy in place for pricing the product; such a strategy may include changing the price during the product life cycle.

Different strategies may be adopted for different products. Mike has given you the following examples of possible pricing strategies:

a) Permanently pricing a product at a level higher than competitors' comparable products.

b) Setting a high price for a product in the early months of its product life cycle, and then significantly reducing the price for the remainder of the product life cycle.

c) Charging a low price in the early months of a product's life cycle, and then significantly increasing the price for the remainder of the product life cycle.

d) Selling a product at a loss throughout its product life cycle.

e) 'Bundling' products, that is, selling some products only in combination with other products so that the price of any individual product is not apparent to the purchaser.

Required:

Draft a report to Mike Smith in which you (1) assess whether the ad hoc bases are appropriate for HCF's pricing decisions and (2) evaluate the extent to which each of the five examples of pricing strategies is likely to be appropriate for the company. In your answer, pay close attention to the nature of HCF's products and to the nature of existing and future competition.

Source: Institute of Certified Public Accountants in Ireland, Paper P2.

E14.5 **Pricing strategies [LO4, LO8]**

Stay Clean manufactures and sells a small range of kitchen equipment. Specifically the product range contains a dishwasher (DW), a washing machine (WM) and a tumble dryer (TD). The TD is of a rather old design and has for some time generated negative contribution. It is widely expected that in one year's time the market for this design of TD will cease, as people switch to a washing machine that can also dry clothes after the washing cycle has completed.

Stay Clean is trying to decide whether or not to cease the production of TD now or in 12 months' time when the new combined washing machine/drier will be ready. To help with this decision the following information has been provided:

1) The normal selling prices, annual sales volumes and total variable costs for the three products are as follows:

	DW	WM	TD
Selling price per unit	$200	$350	$80
Material cost per unit	$70	$100	$50
Labour cost per unit	$50	$80	$40
Contribution per unit	$80	$170	($10)
Annual sales	5,000 units	6,000 units	1,200 units

2) It is thought that some of the customers that buy a TD also buy a DW and a WM. It is estimated that 5 per cent of the sales of WM and DW will be lost if the TD ceases to be produced.

3) All the direct labour force currently working on the TD will be made redundant immediately if TD is ceased now. This would cost $6,000 in redundancy payments. If Stay Clean waited for 12 months the existing labour force would be retained and retrained at a cost of £3,500 to enable them to produce the new washing/drying product. Recruitment and training costs of labour in 12 months' time would be £1,200 in the event that redundancy takes place now.

4) Stay Clean operates a just-in-time policy and so all material cost would be saved on the TD for 12 months if TD production ceased now. Equally, the material costs relating to the lost sales on the WM and the DW would also be saved. However, the material supplier has a volume based discount scheme in place as follows:

Total annual expenditure ($)	Discount
0–600,000	0%
600,001–800,000	1%
800,001–900,000	2%
900,001–960,000	3%
960,001 and above	5%

Stay Clean uses this supplier for all its materials for all the products it manufactures. The figures given above in the cost per unit table for material cost per unit are net of any discount Stay Clean already qualifies for.

5) The space in the factory currently used for the TD will be sublet for 12 months on a short-term lease contract if production of TD stops now. The income from that contract will be £12,000.

6) The supervisor (currently classed as an overhead) supervises the production of all three products spending approximately 20 per cent of his time on the TD production. He would continue to be fully employed if the TD ceases to be produced now.

Required:

Note: part a of this exercise was used in Chapter 13.

a) Explain two pricing strategies that could be used to improve the financial position of the business in the next 12 months assuming that the TD continues to be made in that period.

b) Briefly describe three issues that Stay Clean should consider if it decides to outsource the manufacture of one of its future products.

Source: Association of Chartered Certified Accountants, Paper F5.

E14.6 Pricing policies [LO4, LO5]

Ogam Ltd intends to launch a commemorative product to mark the Olympic Games, one year before the start of the Games. The main objective of the company is profit maximization during the product's life cycle.

Required:

a) Explain the procedure in setting a selling price for the product, which is total cost plus profit mark-up.

Demand for the product is expected to be price dependent for the first six months after the launch date. After this time, competitors will enter the market: this will lead to an agreed market price. Thus, Ogam Ltd will obtain a fixed share of the market, which might be above or below its production capacity. Ogam Ltd however, intends to produce at maximum capacity for the first six months after launch.

b) Explain the impact of the following, when setting a launch price:

i) Price/demand relationship

ii) Market share

iii) Opportunity cost/shadow price of stock

After the Olympic Games have taken place, residual stocks will be sold.

c) Explain the relevant costs and revenues to be considered in the pricing of these stocks at this time.

Source: adapted from Association of Chartered Certified Management Accountants.

E14.7 **Pricing policies [LO4]**

This question will require research.

Pricing is a significant marketing tool. Critically discuss Apple Inc.'s general pricing strategies and discuss why some companies such as Amazon with their Kindle Touch chose to use very different pricing strategies.

E14.8 **Pricing policies [LO4]**

This question will require research

Read the following extract:

> *Apple's dominance in the tablet market is so entrenched now that rivals are resorting to aggressive pricing strategies to counter the iPad. Last week, Hewlett-Packard's TouchPad tablet went from commercial flop to instant hit when the company slashed the price to $99 from $399. Consumers flocked to grab these tablets prompting the company to do one more production run to keep customers happy despite losing money on those produced.*
>
> *Earlier this week, Forrester research suggested that Amazon could sell as many as 5 million tablets in Q4 this year by undercutting iPad's price drastically.*

a) Describe what you understand by the term 'cost plus pricing' and highlight any limitations this may have. How does this differ from 'target costing' pricing?

b) Describe the type of pricing policy being applied by Hewlett-Packard in regard to their TouchPad tablet.

c) Explain the pricing policy taken by Apple with regard to the tablet market.

d) With reference to all of the above companies 'pricing policies' explain how they relate to the product's life cycle and what risks they may face in the future.

Source: http://www.forbes.com 2 September 2011.

● ● ● Case study problem ● ● ● ● ● ● ● ● ● ● ● ● ● ● ● ● ●

C14.1 **Change in a pricing policy for Pitlochry Festival Theatre [LO3, LO5]**

The Pitlochry Festival Theatre (PFT) in Scotland has a theatre which holds 540 people. Their main source of income comes from two segments: local people and tourists. The theatre have marketed themselves using the line 'see six shows in six days' because during the period from May to October they run six shows on a continual basis.

In 2009 the PFT changed their range of performances and, rather than focusing on drama, they delivered a musical production. This change in production proved to be very successful and revenue increased by 16 per cent, bringing in over £1.1 million. Owing to the popularity of the musical, the theatre had to consider how to price its tickets for the following year's musical. The theatre was aware that typically in their industry the day, time and seats could be used for creating a pricing structure for their performances. A 'one-price policy' in theatre is not used because the day, time and seat differentiates the experience for different customers.

Based upon experience, the seats were categorized into three bands, with the best seats referred to as the top-band seats. It was found from past experience that the top-band seats always sold out before the other seats were taken and this was not affected by day or time. Based on this information the theatre decided that if the top-band seats always sold first, it was possible to market and increase the price. Top-banded seats could be identified as premium seats. Premium seats would be promoted as having the best views and more legroom. Through analysis it was possible to identify 6 per cent of the seating as 'premium seats'. Through further analysis, because the musical proved to be the most popular product the PFT decided to increase the cost of all seats for this one production.

This change in pricing policy in 2010 resulted in an increase in sales of 30 per cent for the musical production. At the beginning of the season the top-band seats sold very well but the premium seats did not sell out. Nor did the increased prices force customers to purchase cheaper seats. From previous analysis the PFT knew that from their customer base around 67 per cent of bookings would be pre-made, with the remaining seats purchased as last minute bookings, and customers buying last minute were often the customers prepared to purchase seats at a higher price based on better value seats. The PFT predicted correctly and by the end of the season the premium section of their seats allocation was sold out. In fact revenue increased by 9 per cent in 2010 compared with 2009 with no additional cost.

Required:

a) Discuss the advantages and disadvantages of using PFTs model of pricing; identify some of the pricing policies they use.

b) Are there any alternative marketing or pricing strategies that the theatre could consider?

c) Critically assess why it is important for a management accountant to understand the industry they are working within when setting prices. Use this case study as an example, and any others you can think of.

● ● Recommended reading ● ● ● ● ● ● ● ● ● ● ● ● ● ● ● ● ● ●

- Bertini, M. and L. Wathieu (2010) 'How to stop customers from fixating on price', *Harvard Business Review*, 88(5), pp. 84–91.

The article focuses on the so-called commoditized customer who is fixated on price instead of value when making a decision to buy, and four strategies for getting consumers' attention.

- Kohli, C. and R. Suri, (2011) 'The price is right? Guidelines for pricing to enhance profitability', *Business Horizons*, 54(6), pp. 563–73.

Kohli and Suri examine the relationship between pricing and enhanced profitability. They provide a discussion on the creative nature on pricing and offer a series of guidance on base pricing with suggestions of how to move from this position to achieve improved profitability.

- Lucas, M. and J. Rafferty, (2008) 'Cost analysis for pricing. Exploring the gap between theory and practice', *The British Accounting Review*, 40(2), pp. 148–60.

Using two case studies, Lucas and Rafferty seek to use old intuitional economic theory to examine the difference between the theory of pricing and the actual use in industry.

- Roslender, R. and S. Hart (2010) 'Taking the customer into account: transcending the construction of the customer through the promotion of self-accounting', *Critical Perspectives in Accounting*, 21, pp. 739–53.

Although organizations have in the past 30 years increasingly put the customer first, Roslender and Hart examine how accounting has failed to update its systems and techniques to match the level of commitment to the customer. While providing a critical review they also offer a good explanation of the various accounting approaches which seek to analyse customers.

References

Anon. (2011) 'Netflix messes up, the terror of the film and television business has become a lot less scary', *The Economist*, www.economist.com (accessed on 24 September 2011).

CIMA (2009) 'Management accounting tools for today and tomorrow', www.cimaglobal.com/ma, (accessed on 20 October 2011).

Cooper, T. (2011) 'Pricing power', *Financial Management*, www.fm-magazine.com (accessed on 16 October 2011).

Kohli, C. and Suri R. (2011) 'The price is right? Guidelines for pricing to enhance profitability', *Business Horizons*, 54(6), pp. 563–73.

Rafi. M. (2011) 'Ditch the discounts', *Harvard Business Review*, 89(1/2), pp. 23–5.

Reidy, P. and Walsh K. (2011) *Economics of Tobacco*, Office of the Revenue Commission, Research and Analytics Branch, www.revenue.ie (accessed in April 2012).

Song, H., S. Lin, S. Witt and Zhang X. (2011) 'Impact of financial /economic crisis on demand for hotel rooms in Hong Kong', *Tourism Management*, 32, pp. 172–86.

Smith, A. (2012) 'Laffer curve sighted in Ireland', Adam Smith Institute, http:/adamsmith.org (accessed in April 2012).

Thomas, D. (2011) 'Mobile operators push for mergers to survive', *Financial Times,* 20 September 2011.

When you have read this chapter

Log on to the Online Learning Centre at **www.mcgraw-hill.co.uk/textbooks/burns** to explore chapter-by-chapter test questions, links and further online study tools for Management Accounting.

CHAPTER 15

CAPITAL INVESTMENT DECISIONS

Chapter outline

- Accounting rate of return

- Payback

- Time value of money

- Net present value

- Internal rate of return

- Do all companies use capital budgeting techniques to determine their investments?

- Strategic investment decisions

- Real options

Learning outcomes

On completion of this chapter, students will be able to:

LO1 Calculate payback method

LO2 Analyse the time value of money

LO3 Calculate the accounting rate of return

LO4 Calculate the net present value method

LO5 Understand the difference between net present value and internal rate of return

LO6 Critically discuss capital budgeting techniques

LO7 Analyse the strategic nature of investments

LO8 Calculate and understand the nature of real options

Introduction

Companies frequently have to make decisions relating to investments. These investments can include decisions that question whether to buy new equipment; to purchase new property or to go ahead with the production of a new product. The life of these investments can vary enormously and different investments will have different risks attached to them. The management accountant needs to analyse the investments and offer sensible information within a business plan to allow the board of directors or manager to make an informed decision as to whether the **investment** will add value to their organization.

Pfeiffer and Schneider (2010, p. 1) propose that the process of capital budgeting 'defines a set of rules to govern the way in which managers at different levels of the hierarchy produce and share information about investment projects'. **Capital budgeting** provides not only a way of analysing a project/investment but also a shared language which can be used to explain the possible outcomes.

This chapter will analyse some of the traditional methods of analysing investment decisions; **payback** (PB), **accounting rate of return** (ARR), **internal rate of return** (IRR) and **net present value** (NPV). These techniques are known as capital budgeting or investment appraisal techniques. In addition to the basic concepts, this chapter will examine some of the more complex methods such as **real options** (RO). We will also examine the necessary calculations and highlight the use of Excel in this area. Although the technical nature of these techniques will be the main focus, the academic literature will also be examined to see 'what' and 'how' companies are using some of these calculations in their decision-making process.

As a focus of this book is to examine the changing nature of the management accountant; this chapter will continue to use examples of real companies to demonstrate how and why these techniques are fundamental in business decisions. We will also examine how these investments are not always decided by financial calculations; the strategic nature of the investment can be the driver of the decision. Throughout the book we have stressed the strategic nature of the management accountants' role within business and this chapter highlights this.

Stages of investment appraisal

When making investment decisions the management accountant or manager needs to go through a staged process to ensure they have gathered all the relevant information and performed the relevant financial calculations. The process will vary in different organizations but the general stages are shown in Exhibit 15.1.

Although the process, in Exhibit 15.1, looks linear and logical, it is in practice a web of complicated flows of information. The manager or management accountant will have to go backwards and forwards in gathering information, adjusting the model and re-submitting the proposal.

What techniques and tools are available to analyse capital investments?

There has been significant research conducted to find out what techniques are used in industry. A CIMA (2009) report found that the most popular technique in use was NPV. Net present value was used in around 60 per cent of the companies surveyed, followed by the payback method at around 55 per cent, IRR at around 43 per cent, ARR at around 18 per cent and real options being used by around 5 per cent. However, when analysing only the larger companies the use of all techniques increases.

Accounting rate of return

The accounting rate of return (ARR) is a financial ratio which uses 'profits after depreciation', in other words your operating profit, to calculate the return an investment provides. The formula is:

$$ARR = \frac{\text{Average profits}}{\text{Average investment}} \times 100\%$$

Indentify all investment possibilities and screen them

Before any analysis is performed the organization must start with their strategy, what do they want to achieve? From there they can search for opportunities that will add value to their organization and fit with the strategic direction of the company. Of course, not all investments will be strategy led because some investments will be required through legal or regulatory requirements.

Most organizations will not simply accept all projects, even when they are not mutually exclusive. Although the NPV or IRR analysis may suggest the investment should be accepted the company will have capital restrictions. A full screening analysis is required to filter those that have a strategic fit with the organization.

Gather all relevant information

Once all the future investments are identified the work now begins to gather all the relevant information, this includes relevant cash flows and the risks involved. This sounds much easier than it is in practice. Gathering information on prices and demand curves can be very difficult especially when you are analysing a project within a volatile market.

Performing a financial analysis of all appropriate investments

A full financial analysis will now take place to model all investments based upon the information gathered in the previous section; using techniques such as NPV, IRR, payback and ARR.

Present information into a business proposal

Most organizations require all models to be presented as part of a business proposal where the financial data will be presented along with strategic fit. The report will include a full risk analysis, feasibility test and acceptability test, and any additional benefits which cannot be quantified.

Selection and approval of business proposal

As will be discussed later in this chapter the financial models will not be the only factor in determining the outcomes of which investments are chosen. The board will examine the business proposal and determine which one(s) gain their approval.

Implementation of investment and post-audit

Following approval, the implementation process will follow requiring key performing indicators (KPIs) to be established and monitored. Following a relevant period of time the proposal should, in theory, be subject to audit.

Exhibit 15.1: Stages of the investment appraisal process

Worked Example 15.1

ARR example

You have a project which lasts three years and the expected annual operating profit (excluding depreciation) for the three years are £100,000, £150,000 and £200,000. The initial investment is £300,000 with a residual value of £60,000. Calculate the ARR.

Solution

Step 1: Calculate the average annual profit

$$\{(£100,000 + £150,000 + £200,000) - (£300,000 - £60,000)\}/3 = £70,000$$

In the first part of the calculation you simply calculate the operating profit for all three years before depreciation is accounted for. In the second part of the calculation you work out the total depreciation for the three years. Remember the depreciation must be the cost of investment less the **residual value**. Finally, when you subtract the deprecation from the profits you divide by three to work out the average operating profit over the life of the project.

Step 2: Calculate the average investment

$$(300,000 + 60,000)/2 = £180,000$$

If there is no residual value you simply take the cost of the initial investment and divide by two. One thing to watch out for here is that it is easy to presume you subtract the residual value from the initial investment. You should not do this; you must add the initial investment to the residual value.

Step 3: Divide the average investment into the average annual profit

$$(£70,000/£180,000) \times 100\% = 38.89\%$$

ARR can be problematic in that it is subject to accounting policies which will vary from one organization to another and can be subject to manipulation.

Payback

Companies always want to know how long it will take to recover the capital they investment in any project. When the economic climate is on a downturn this is even more important. Payback is a calculation which is measured in time. How many months or years will it take for the company to generate enough profit to pay the capital investment back?

Worked Example 15.2

Payback example

Company A is investigating whether to invest in a new piece of equipment at a cost of £60,000. It is estimated that the new equipment will create cost efficiencies of £20,000 a year. What is the Payback period of this project?

	Cost efficiencies	Payback calculation
Capital invested		£60,000
Year one	£20,000	(£20,000)
		£40,000
Year two	£20,000	(£20,000)
		£20,000
Year three	£20,000	(£20,000)
		0

In this simple example it is clear to see that the cost savings reduce the outstanding capital balance by £20,000 each year, and after three years the entire investment has been recovered. The payback for this investment is three years. The calculation in *Worked Example 15.2* was presented like this to illustrate how the capital invested is reduced on a yearly basis, however, it is much easier to perform a simply division as follows:

$$£60,000/£20,000 = 3 \text{ years}$$

Therefore, the formula for this calculation is:

Initial investment/Annual cash flow

If there are unequal cash flows throughout the project you would need to calculate the payback using the table approach in *Worked Example 15.2* because this formula would not work.

It is important to note that most investments will not have a payback period which is exactly on the year, so you need to consider whether you want to work out the payback in years or years and months.

Time value of money

Both the ARR and payback calculation, which we have just considered above, have one big criticism; they do not consider the time value of money. The time value of money relates to how the value of money reduces over a given period of time. To put this into perspective, consider someone offering you £1,000 today or £1,000 in one year's time. Let us assume you are not desperate for the money so this is not part of the decision. It is common sense that you would take the money today because you would have the opportunity to invest the £1,000 and increase the value of this gift over the following year.

Taking this concept one step further, if the £1,000 could be invested in a savings account which offers a 5 per cent yearly return then in one year's time the £1,000 will be worth £1,050:

$$£1,000 \times 1.05 = £1,050$$

This logic can be applied the other way around, if you are promised £1,050 in a year's time this means that its present value in today's money must be £1,000.

Now that we have the basic idea it is important to put this into a business context. Imagine you are a management accountant who is analysing a new project within your company; the project involves investing in the production of a new product. You will open your spreadsheet and forecast future cash flows relating to this project. Imagine the project is designed to last for the next 10 years. As the management accountant you will need to consider the value of this project. Now that you understand that money in the future is not worth the same as money today, the concept of the time value of money as discussed above, you can see it is difficult to simply produce a basic spreadsheet and gain any meaningful information from it.

What you need to do is calculate the value of the project in today's money which means you will need to discount the future cash flows. This will provide a value of the investment today. The discounting process uses the concept that we considered above, with the £1,050 future value equalling the same as £1,000 today. However, with business projects you need to consider the rate at which the cash flow should be discounted.

Most companies have set discounts which they use for this very purpose, although they may vary these rates depending on the nature of the project. However, in theory the **discount rate** should include:

1)   The risk-free rate of investing (the rate set for government bonds and so on)

2)   The risk of inflation

3)   The risk of other uncertainties.

It stands to reason that the more risks a project has, the higher the return you would expect from a project because you as the investor are taking on more risk. The more risk you take the higher the reward you would expect. If you have studied corporate finance, you will know it offers models such as the capital asset pricing model (CAPM) to calculate the '**rate of return**'. The CAPM model examines a company's performance against the stock market, the risk-free rate and the required additional return based upon the risks for the investment. The rate of return a company uses is also known as the '**cost of capital**'.

Once you have your rate of return you can calculate how much your cash flow needs to be discounted, this is known as the **present value** (PV) rate:

$$PV = 1/(1 + r)^n$$

Where:

r = cost of capital (this must always be placed into the formula as a decimal)

n = the number of compound years the cash flow is considering

Let us have a look at *Worked Example 15.3*.

Worked Example 15.3

Calculating discount rates and using them example

You invest in a project from which you will receive £200,000 in three years time, the cost of capital which is considered appropriate is 4 per cent. What is the present value of the £200,000?

Solution

The first thing you need to do is calculate the PV rate for three years at a cost of capital of 4 per cent:

$$PV = 1/(1 + 0.04)^3 = 0.8890$$

The second part of the calculation is to take the cash flow and multiply it by the PV rate:

$$£200,000 \times 0.8890 = £177,800$$

We have just calculated that the £200,000 cash flow that we will receive in three year's time is worth £177,800 today.

Using the discount tables

In Appendix A to this book you are provided with a present value discount rate table which has actually calculated all these values for you. Exhibit 15.2 provides an extract from the table.

When you use these tables, the year in which the cash flow is received is listed vertically, highlighted in blue. The cost of capital is listed along the top, horizontally, and this is highlighted in grey. If you are looking for the discount rate to use when you have a cash flow in year 3 when the company cost of capital is 4 per cent, the rate would be 0.8890, and this is highlighted in green.

Years	1%	2%	3%	4%	5%
1	0.9901	0.9804	0.9709	0.9615	0.9524
2	0.9803	0.9612	0.9426	0.9426	0.9070
3	0.9706	0.9423	0.9151	0.8890	0.8638
4	0.9610	0.9238	0.8885	0.8548	0.8227
5	0.9515	0.9057	0.8626	0.8219	0.7835

Exhibit 15.2: Discount table extract

Net present value

A technique which considers the cash flows of a project and incorporates the time value of money is called net present value (NPV). The basic concept behind this technique is to compare the investment of the project against the discounted annual cash flows. When you have calculated the NPV you must then examine the value (refer to Exhibit 15.3).

If the answer is **positive**	You accept the project because you have recovered your required rate of return, plus more.
If the answer is **zero**	You accept the project because you have recovered your required rate of return (remember your cost of capital included the additional return you want for the risk you are taking).
If the answer is **negative**	You typically do not go ahead with the project because you are receiving less than you are willing to accept for the risk you are taking on your investment. *Note this is using financial data only, there are often many other factors involved when making these decisions.*

Exhibit 15.3: Rules of NPV

Exhibit 15.3 provides guidance when the financial values are the only consideration when making a decision. In real business decisions it is not solely the financial status of a project that drives a decision, but we will examine this later in the chapter. You must also remember when applying this technique that you are assuming that the cash flows are received at the end of the year.

When analysing investments it is important to understand whether the investments you are analysing are mutually exclusive or not. Mutually exclusive means that the company will only invest in one of the options because the investments you are analysing cannot be taken at the same time.

Worked Example 15.4

Net present value

You are considering a project that lasts five years. You invest £1,000,000 at the beginning of the project and you are expecting to receive annual cash flows of £300,000. The company has a cost of capital of 7 per cent. Should you accept this project?

Solution

Year	Cash flow £	PV rate	PV £
0	(1,000,000)	1.0000	(1,000,000)
1	300,000	0.9346	280,380
2	300,000	0.8734	262,020
3	300,000	0.8163	244,890
4	300,000	0.7629	228,870
5	300,000	0.7130	213,900
			NPV = **230,060**

The table, on the previous page, presents the spreadsheet of information for a project. With the first column displaying the year in which the information relates to, the second column showing the cash flow for that year (with money leaving the project displayed in brackets), the third column lists the PV rates (using the tables in Appendix A, so no calculations were required) and the final column is the PV of the cash flows. The PV of the cash flows is calculated by multiplying the cash flows in the second column two by the PV rates in the third column. Once all PVs have been calculated you perform an addition of all the PVs, highlighted in blue. This NPV calculation is positive so using the theory of NPV this project is viable.

Using the concept of annuities

You may have noticed in this example that the cash flows are the same every year. When you have a project like this there is actually a much quicker way of calculating the NPV. Instead of calculating each individual year separately, as we have above, you can consider the use of an annuity calculation. In practice an annuity is an investment which provides you with a stable income every year for a set number of years. This is what we have in this project, every year you will receive £300,000 for five years. The annuity rate can be calculated just as the PV rates were calculated or you can use the table in Appendix B. The formula for calculating the annuity rate is:

$$PV(A) = \frac{A}{r}\left[1 - \frac{1}{(1 + r)^n}\right]$$

Where:

A = the yearly income

r = the cost of capital (in decimals)

n = the set number of years involved in the annuity

Worked Example 15.5

Using annuity discount rates

So if we relate this to our example:

$$PV(A) = \frac{300,000}{0.07}\left[1 - \frac{1}{(1 + 0.07)^5}\right] = 1,230,000$$

Now you simply subtract the initial investment from the value of the annuity:

$$1,230,000 - £1,000,000 = 230,000$$

Using the discount tables you would do the following:

Years 0 to:	1%	2%	3%	4%	5%	6%	7%
1	0.990	0.980	0.971	0.962	0.952	0.943	0.935
2	1.970	1.942	1.913	1.886	1.859	1.833	1.808
3	2.941	2.884	2.829	2.775	2.723	2.673	2.624
4	3.902	3.808	3.717	3.630	3.546	3.465	3.387
5	4.853	4.713	4.580	4.452	4.329	4.212	4.100
6	5.795	5.601	5.417	5.242	5.076	4.917	4.767
7	6.728	6.472	6.230	6.002	5.786	5.582	5.389

The above is an extract of the annuity discount table. In this case the annuity discount rate would be 4.100 as highlighted in green. So now you simply multiply this rate by the £300,000 yearly cash flow and subtract the initial investment:

$$£1,000,000 - (£300,000 \times 4.100) = £230,000$$

You will note some slight variations in these calculations due to rounding (to three decimal places).

Of course in practice the management accountant or manager would not sit in their office calculating their NPVs like this. They would use some form of software. Spreadsheets like Microsoft Excel already have functions within it to help provide quick calculations. Exhibit 15.4 is the calculation if it is performed in Excel, with the formatting set so there are no decimal places.

	A	B
1	7%	
2		£
3	Initial investment	−1,000,000
4	Cash-flow year 1	300,000
5	Cash-flow year 2	300,000
6	Cash-flow year 3	300,000
7	Cash-flow year 4	300,000
8	Cash-flow year 5	300,000
9		
10	NPV	230,059

Exhibit 15.4: Calculating NPV within Excel

Revealing the formula, in Exhibit 15.5, you can see that this has been modelled with the formula highlighted in blue. The cost of capital has been set in A1 because in practice you would probably use something like a dropdown list to provide the user with different rates so you could perform a scenario analysis.

	A	B
1	0.07	
2		£
3	Initial investment	−1,000,000
4	Cash-flow year 1	300,000
5	Cash-flow year 2	300,000
6	Cash-flow year 3	300,000
7	Cash-flow year 4	300,000
8	Cash-flow year 5	300,000
9		
10	NPV	=NPV(A1,B4:B8)+B3

Exhibit 15.5: Using formula in Excel to calculate NPV'

This section has demonstrated that the NPV calculation can be performed in many ways. However, you must remember the annuity method can *only* be used when the cash flows are the same every year.

When deciding what discount to use, follow the rule in *Exhibit 15.6*.

Rules:

1) Use the present value factor discount tables when the cash flows **are not the same** every year.

2) Use the cumulative present value factor discount tables when the cash flows **are the same** every year.

Exhibit 15.6: Deciding what discount tables to use

Cash flows

Present value calculations are performed using cash flows. This means you must not include any accounting concepts that are not cash flows. Common problems are as follows:

- Depreciation is not a cash flow it is an accounting concept to reduce the value of an asset.

- Working capital is considered an out-flow at the beginning of the project and an in-flow at the end of the project.

- Cash flows should be future incremental cash flows; you should not include any sunk costs or allocated fixed costs.

- Any costs that relate to financing of the project should not be included as they are already included in the cost of capital used in the NPV calculation.

Taxation issues

Although, as explained in the previous section, depreciation is not a cash flow and therefore cannot be used in your NPV calculation, the tax authorities often provide businesses with something called a **capital allowance** (this is the term used in the UK). A capital allowance is something offered to encourage investment in certain areas; it reduces the value of the asset on a yearly basis, and in turn reduces the amount of taxable profit. When you are calculating cash flows within your NPV calculations you cannot ignore taxation or the impact of capital allowances.

The impact of the capital allowances and calculation of taxable profits are usually performed before they are incorporated into your NPV model.

Worked Example 15.6

NPV with taxation

A company is considering buying a new piece of machinery at a cost of £100,000. The machine would generate net cash inflows of £40,000 (excluding taxation and capital allowances) a year, for four years. The residual value is £20,000.

The tax authority is currently allowing a 25 per cent **writing down allowance** (WDA) for all new machinery and the corporation tax rate for this company is 30 per cent.

Required:

Calculate the tax payable for each year. Every year you need to calculate what is known as writing down allowance.

Year	Workings	WDA (in bold) £
0		100,000.00
1	£100,000 × 0.25	**(25,000.00)**
		75,000.00
2	£75,000 × 0.25	**18,750.00**
		56,250.00
3	£56,250 × 0.25	**14,062.50**
		42,187.50
4	Subtract the residual value	(20,000.00)
		22,187.50

You will note this simple calculation is similar to calculating a depreciation charge using the reducing balancing method. The only part of the calculation you have to consider carefully is when a residual value is given. Residual value is simply the value that you can sell the asset for at the end of its useful life and then the remaining balance is your WDA for the final year.

Once you have calculated the WDAs you then need to calculate the tax payable.

	Year 1 £	Year 2 £	Year 3 £	Year 4 £
Net cash flows	40,000.00	40,000.00	40,000.00	40,000.00
WDA	(25,000.00)	(18,750.00)	(14,062.50)	(22,187.50)
Taxable profit	15,000.00	21,250.00	25,937.50	17,812.50
Taxation (30%)	4,500.00	6,375.00	7,781.25	5,343.75
Taxation payable in	2	3	4	5

In this NPV calculation it is assumed that there is a one year time lag in paying the taxation. So the taxation calculated at the end of year 1 would be paid in year 2. Once you have reached this stage you are ready to perform a normal NPV calculation with the taxation included.

Issues of multiple projects with different lifespans

In addition to the taxation you also have to remember that when considering projects, you often have more than one option. Unfortunately life is not perfect and when considering projects which do not run for the same time period, you need ways in which to analyse them over the same period of time so you can make a fair judgement on each case. The theory behind this is called replacement theory. To put this in it simplest form, it asks you to consider what you would replace the investment that has ended with while the other project is still running. So, if you had one project which ran for five years and another that ran for seven years, after the first five years what would you do for the remaining two years while the other project is still running? By analysing both projects for the same length of time you can make a fair assessment of the value of both projects.

There are two methods which can be used in this situation: lowest common multiply method and the equivalent annual cost method.

Common multiple method

The first method uses the lowest common multiple of the lives of the projects involved. When this is established you simply analyse the project for this period. This can be observed in the *Worked Example 15.7*.

Common multiple method example

You are considering two projects:

- Project 1 lasts three years and has an initial investment of £400,000 with an annual cash flow of £200,000.

- Project 2 lasts two years and has an initial investment of £300,000 with an annual cash flow of £180,000.

The company's cost of capital is 10 per cent.

Required:

Calculate the lowest common multiple of the two projects.

Solution:

Step 1: Project 1 lasts three years and projects 2 lasts two years. Therefore, the lowest whole number which both projects divide into is 6.

Step 2: Calculate the NPV of all projects for the time period calculated in step one, the lowest common multiple. This will mean you will repeat the investment until you reach the lowest common multiple.

Year	Project 1 cash flows £	Project 2 cash flows £	Discount factor 10%	PV of project 1 £	PV of project 2 £
Workings – columns multiplied				(2 × 4)	(3 × 4)
0	(400,0000)	(300,000)	1.0000	(400,000)	(300,000)
1	200,000	180,000	0.9091	181,820	163,638
2	200,000	180,000 + (300,000)	0.8264	165,280	(99,168)
3	200,000 + (400,000)	180,000	0.7513	(150,260)	135,234
4	200,000	180,000 + (300,000)	0.6830	136,600	(81,960)
5	200,000	180,000	0.6209	124,180	111,762
6	200,000	180,000	0.5645	112,900	101,610
NPV				**170,520**	**31,116**

Step 3: Compare NPV for each project over the same time period which is set by using the lowest common multiple.

In this case we can see that project 1 is the better project because it has a higher NPV.

You can see that by using this method the investment is assumed to keep repeating itself until it reaches the value of the lowest common multiple, in years. By doing this you ensure there is an equal time period by which the two projects are evaluated. You use a simple NPV calculation over the lowest common multiple period. The only item you must take care with is ensuring that you place the investment cost into the calculation at the end of each cycle. In other words, if you look at project 2, you are provided with information in the question which states that the project lasts two years. Therefore, after two years the project ends so you must reinvest the capital required to start the project. At the end of year 4 the project ends again so you must reinvest the initial capital once more. For both projects the reinvestment is highlighted in blue in the Worked Example table.

You are, of course, placing many assumptions into this model; you are presuming that the cash flows would remain the same over the time period you are examining. In practice, there would be many uncertainties surrounding the reinvestment of cash flows. You are also placing an assumption that the investments can be repeated which once again in practice may not be possible. Consider the technology industry, the industry thrives on innovation. Market share is gained by companies like Apple Inc by continually creating new versions of their key products like the iPhone and Ipad, new versions result in new cash flows.

There is a limitation to this method, in that, many large capital investment projects are long term. The project we considered in this project was short term so the lowest common multiple method is very low, therefore, the process of calculating the reinvestment was not time-consuming. However, imagine if you have two projects spanning across time periods of 10 and 15 years, the lowest common multiple here would be 30 years.

Equivalent annual cost method

To overcome the problem of analysing projects over very long time periods this next technique, equivalent annual cost method, continues to examine all projects over the same time period, however, instead of extending the investment time period it actually reduces it by examining all projects using the yearly annuity that would be received. The yearly annuity simply means the average annual cash flow that would be received from this project.

To observe how this method is calculated we will return to the example used in the lowest common multiple method where we had two projects, project 1 and project 2, *Worked Example 15.7*.

Worked Example 15.8

Equivalent annual cost method example
Solution

Step 1: Calculate the standard NPV for all projects, using the standard time period for each project.

Year	Project 1 Cash flows £	Project 2 Cash flows £	Discount factor 10%	PV of Project 1 £	PV of Project 2 £
Workings – columns multiplied				(2×4)	(3×4)
0	(400,000)	(300,000)	1.0000	(400,000)	(300,000)
1	200,000	180,000	0.9091	181,820	163,638
2	200,000	180,000	0.8264	165,280	148,752
3	200,000		0.7513	150,260	
NPV				**97,360**	**12,390**

Step 2: Divide the NPVs calculated in step number one by the annuity rate for the correct time period and cost of capital for each project.

Project 1: The time period is three years and the cost of capital is 10 per cent, therefore the annuity rate would be 2.487 (taken from the annuity table, see Appendix B).

$$£97,360/2.487 = £39,147.57$$

▶

Project 2: The time period is two years and the cost of capital is 10 per cent, therefore the annuity rate would be 1.736 (taken from the annuity table in Appendix B).

$$£12,390/1.736 = £7,137.10$$

This method shows you that project 1 provides a higher annual equivalent cash flow than project 2, therefore project 1 adds more value to the organization.

Internal rate of return

Although we have discussed the NPV in detail there is another measure which can be used, namely the internal rate of return (IRR). The IRR is a calculation that measures the efficiency or yield of a project, whereas, in contrast the NPV measures the value of the return. The NPV is measured in currency and the IRR is measured as a percentage. To calculate the IRR you are working out what the rate of the project would need to be for all cash flows in the NPV calculation to equal zero. The higher the IRR the better and if there are no restrictions in terms of mutual exclusivity or capital funds, all projects with an IRR higher than the cost of capital in theory should be taken. If funds are limited or the projects are mutually exclusive then you would rank the IRRs and take the highest.

Calculating the IRR can be a lengthy process, the following formula shows you what you are looking for:

$$NPV = \sum_{n=0}^{n} \frac{Cn}{(1+r)^n} = 0$$

Where:

   C = cash flows

   n = number of years

   r = cost of capital (in decimals)

So in this case you are looking for r, the unknown variable.

Calculating r is a process of testing different possibilities. Testing involves guess work and you need to keep testing different rates until you get to where the NPV equals zero. Alternatively you can use Excel to calculate this for you, if we return to the example used in the NPV calculation, using Excel, Exhibit 15.4, we can model this project as shown in Exhibit 15.7.

	A	B
1	**7%**	**£**
2	Initial investment	−1,000,000
3	Cash-flow year 1	300,000
4	Cash-flow year 2	300,000
5	Cash-flow year 3	300,000
6	Cash-flow year 4	300,000
7	Cash-flow year 5	300,000
8		
9	NPV	230,059
10	IRR	15%

Exhibit 15.7: Using Excel to calculate IRR 1

You can see that both projects have been modelled and the NPV and the IRR function with Excel have been calculated. In Exhibit 15.8 you can see the formulas that have been used.

	A	B
1	0.07	£
2	Initial investment	−1,000,000
3	Cash-flow year 1	300,000
4	Cash-flow year 2	300,000
5	Cash-flow year 3	300,000
6	Cash-flow year 4	300,000
7	Cash-flow year 5	300,000
8		
9		=NPV(A1,B3:B7)+B2
10	IRR	=IRR(B2:B7)

Exhibit 15.8: Using Excel to calculate IRR 2

The IRR calculation in Excel uses an iterative technique which works to accuracy of 0.0001 per cent. To test this, in Exhibit 15.9 we have played with the model to test if the IRR works by setting the cost of capital rate in cell A1 to the rate calculated for the IRR.

	A	B
1	15%	£
2	Initial investment	−1,000,000
3	Cash-flow year 1	300,000
4	Cash-flow year 2	300,000
5	Cash-flow year 3	300,000
6	Cash-flow year 4	300,000
7	Cash-flow year 5	300,000
8		
9	NPV	5,647
10	IRR	15%

Exhibit 15.9: Testing the IRR Excel function

The modelling, in Exhibit 15.9, shows that if we set the cost of capital to be 15 per cent the NPV value is reduced to £5,647. Therefore, 15 per cent is the lowest whole number which reduces the NPV value to as near as zero as it can get. If you set the rates at 14 per cent and 16 per cent, and compare, you can see that the process uses an approximation rate (Exhibit 15.10).

Cost of capital %	NPV £
14	29,924
15	5,647
16	−17,712

Exhibit 15.10: 'Comparison of different cost of capital rates'

Although IRR has many advantages – the main ones being that managers like percentages and everyone understands them – it has some disadvantages that you need to be aware of. If a project is being considered which is set within an uncertain market where conditions change regularly, this can create problems for the IRR technique. When a project has many positive and negative cash flows because the project has to be updated on a regular basis due to market conditions, this can lead to more than one possible IRR. However, the IRR technique cannot handle this type of scenario, it can only work on the basis that there is one IRR. The NPV calculation can accommodate changing discounts rates because each year can be discounted separately.

Do all companies use capital budgeting techniques to determine their investments?

Everything we have achieved so far in this chapter assumes that all companies are profit maximizers and the theory of the firm stands true, in other words, these financial calculations achieve profit maximization and should be followed without any other considerations. In practice the use of these techniques will be determined by a number of factors: the size of the organization, the size of the investment and expertise within a company. For example Ekanem (2007) argued that smaller firms will use intuition in their investment decisions – called the 'bootstrapping' techniques – where they use past experience to determine what is best for their companies.

In addition to Ekanem's observations, common sense tells you that organizations are complex entities and the interaction of the employees within the organizations can also be a factor in the decision-making process. Politics and lobbying can be a great source of power when decisions are made. There are also legal and regulation requirements which may mean that organizations have to invest to satisfy statutory objectives. Investments which are based on legal requirements often fail to achieve the company cost of capital. These kinds of investments may be related to health and safety requirements or environmental regulation.

The strategic use of capital budgeting techniques

Thus far we have considered how capital investment decisions need to use more than just capital budgeting evaluations; they need strategic considerations and in many cases managers will use intuition and business experience (Ekanem, 2007; Haka, 2007). It is also important to understand that companies also use capital budgeting techniques to strategically consider the future; they do not use them solely to provide financial evaluation of current investments.

Miller and O'Leary (2007) argue that capital budgeting techniques are more than financial evaluations and state that they are 'mediating instruments' that can help organizations manage and co-ordinate investments in both intra-organizational and interorganizational investment decisions. Miller and O'Leary (2007) found that capital budgeting instruments helped to shape the future of the technology industry. Further analysis by Warren (2012) found that capital budgeting techniques were also used as 'mediating instruments' within the UK generation electricity market. In her study she found that capital budgeting techniques were use as (1) an international language across different markets within the same sector, (2) a source of power by modelling current regulation to mobilizing resources which would create the need for consultation of the future of the market and (3) a legitimizing tool which could be used to justify a lack of investment, using real options theory (this will be discussed shortly).

Strategic investment decisions

Modelling the future involves strategy. Management accountants have many financial techniques that can help to determine suitable investments in addition to these tools, they also need to appreciate that not all projects are driven by financial considerations alone. The techniques we have considered so far highlight which projects offer economic value to the organization; however,

Coca-Cola and their strategic initiatives

Coca-Cola invest in their future through a strategic initiative called 'Live Positively'. This investment is a fund set up by Coca-Cola to protect their brand, thereby adding strategic value. The fund allows local communities, governmental organizations and non-government organizations (NGOs) to apply for funds that will help improve the environment, fitness or lifestyle of local communities. The investment has nothing to do with adding economic value to the organization; it is about adding and retaining strategic value by presenting the company as being socially responsible.

Source: www.thecoca-colacompany.com.

Exercise

Find other companies who have similar initiatives and consider why they offer these investments.

---

organizations are also interested in projects that add strategic value. Payback and the traditional capital budgeting techniques do not incorporate the strategy which the organizations are trying to achieve.

This example of Coca-Cola shows that organizations will invest to protect their brand status. Coca-Cola, in the past, have, often been criticized for wasting water in developing countries and for the bad impact in health that some of their products are said to contribute to. By investing in this type of initiative they are demonstrating that they take corporate social responsibility seriously, so the emphasis is not financial but strategic.

Real options

The standard capital budgeting techniques that we have considered so far in this chapter are embedded with the implicit assumption that once the project is accepted, the managers involved are passive, will follow the project through and will not make any changes. In reality, not all investments develop as expected and managers often need to adjust their plans. Standard capital budgeting techniques do not take this into account. Management accountants will adjust cash flows to respond to the fact that they know the cash flows are uncertain but this does not reflect the reality of uncertainty within these investments.

Increasingly, real options analysis (ROA) is used within investment analysis. This is a theory borrowed from corporate finance and embedded within the decision-making process. A financial option provides the investor the right (but does not obligate them) to sell or buy an asset in the future at a set price. When this is translated into the kind of decisions management accountants have to analyse, we are talking about an investment in a project which will lead to possibly expanding, delaying, abandoning or even outsourcing in the future. The company is making an initial investment with the knowledge that this offers the possibility to change direction in the future, but is not an obligation to do so. If a decision is taken later in the process, to expand for example, further capital will be deployed at this point.

In practice companies often choose to wait, to see how the market reacts to new policies or regulation that may affect the economic viability of a project.

Management Accounting in Practice 15.2 demonstrates how investments are often undertaken to ensure that companies are strategically placed if they choose to enter the market at a later stage. This can be determined by the market development, economics conditions or government policy. If companies do not start the process and invest in the initial consultation process or the research and development stage they can fall behind their competitors.

15.2: Management Accounting in Practice

Impact of regulation on making decisions

Europe is facing an energy crisis because of green-influenced legislation and regulation, and difficulty in obtaining planning approval for key projects, energy companies warned yesterday.

Europe needs to spend €2tn (£1.5tn) on upgrading power networks in the next 25 years but leading energy companies have cancelled investments in new power plants worth billions of Euros because of increased regulatory uncertainty, a senior executive claimed yesterday.

One of the reasons investments are not taking place is explained by Johannes Teyssen, chief operating officer at E.ON, Germany's biggest energy group. He blamed the European commission's plans to make companies pay for all their pollution permits from 2013, huge delays in approving planning applications and confusion among national regulators for the cancellations. (Gow and Woodward 2008)

Within the European Union high targets have been set to achieve a lower carbon environment which nuclear energy can help to achieve. Nuclear energy is part of the investment mix companies have, however, not all chose to invest in this area. Although many companies choose to set up projects which investigate the possibility of moving into nuclear investment, these are not followed through. In many cases the companies have placed an initial investment to investigate nuclear energy but many have chosen to abandon these investments. The investments are abandoned due to policy and regulation uncertainty emerging from local government.

Source: adapted from Harvey (2011).

Exercise

Discuss why real options theory is a useful concept in the electricity generation industry. Research other industries and companies where you can see examples of real options theory being used. You should look for examples where companies have started the initial research but then decided not to continue or where they have started small projects with the opportunity to expand in the future.

Worked Example 15.9

Real options

Imagine you are offered the opportunity to invest in a project where market research shows there is an equal chance of the investment being successful; if successful you will receive £10,000 in return and if unsuccessful you will lose £12,000. There is an option available to invest in this project and the price of this option is £1,000. Would you purchase this option?

Solution

Step 1: Assume there is no option:

$$(0.5 \times £10,000) - (0.5 \times £12,000) = £5,000 - £6,000 = -£1,000$$

Step 2: Calculate the value of the investment if the option is available:

$$[(0.5 \times £10,000) - (0.5 \times £0)] - £1,000 = £4,000$$

You can see that by investing in the option and waiting to see, the value of the project is much higher because you have the right to not complete the full investment.

Chapter summary

This chapter has introduced you to some of the financial techniques available when analysing capital investments. Although the techniques have being presented as a very important part of the investment appraisal process, we have also identified that numbers alone do not determine the final decision on whether a project will go ahead or not.

With the role of the management accountant becoming more strategically focused this has also emphasized the strategic nature of the investments becoming a significant factor in the decision-making process. Not all companies are focused just on adding economic value; they also consider the longer-term issues of strategic value-added activities.

Companies use capital budgeting in many ways. This chapter has provided you with a very detailed explanation of how capital budgeting can be used to provide a financial valuation of current projects, but it is important to remember that these techniques can also be used to strategically model the future. Modelling the future can help to shape the market by moving resources and co-ordinating projects to channel the strategic requirements of a company.

Key terms

Accounting rate of return A quick method of calculation the rate of return of a project – ignoring the time value of money (p. 370)

Capital allowance The rate set by the tax authorities to calculate the taxable profit of an investment (p. 378)

Capital budgeting A set of normative theories which examines the most appropriate investment to be undertaken based upon a company's financial requirements (p. 370)

Cost of capital The return that is required for an investment (p. 374)

Discount rate The rate which is used to reduce the value of money into the present value based upon the rate of return and the time period (p. 373)

Internal rate of return The rate of return which would produce an NPV of zero (p. 370)

Investment The purchase of an opportunity or physical asset (p. 370)

Net present value The sum of a time series of discounted cash inflows and outflows (p. 370)

Payback The length of time it takes to recover the initial investment of a project (p. 370)

Present value The current worth of a future stream of cash (p. 374)

Rate of return The return which is required for an investment (p. 374)

Real options An investment which incorporates an opportunity to change the course of the decision at some point in the future (p. 370)

Residual value The value of an investment at the end of its useful life (p. 372)

Writing down allowance A yearly allowance, calculated to reduce the cash flow to a taxable profit value (p. 378)

Review questions • • • • • • • • • • • • • • connect • • •

Level of difficulty:	BASIC	INTERMEDIATE	ADVANCED

15.1 The initial investment of a project is £20,000. Annual cash flows are predicted to be £4,000 a year, what is the payback? **[LO1]**

15.2 Explain the concept of the time value of money. **[LO2]**

15.3 You have a project which lasts three years and the expected annual operating profit (excluding depreciation) for the three years are £200,000, £300,000 and £200,000. The initial investment is £500,000. Calculate the ARR. **[LO3]**

15.4 The initial investment of a project is £50,000. Annual cash flows are predicted to be £10,000 a year with the length of the project being projected at nine years. The company cost of capital is 7 per cent. What is the NPV? **[LO4]**

15.5 Provide three examples of investment decision which would be appropriate to use real options theory. **[LO8]**

● ● ● Group discussions ● ● ● ● ● ● ● ● ● ● ● ● ● ● ● ● ●

15.6 Discuss the process of making investment decisions within an organization. **[LO6]**

15.7 If an NPV is positive a company should you invest in the project – critically discuss. **[LO4]**

15.8 NPV and IRR measure the same thing – discuss whether this statement is correct. **[LO4]**

15.9 Debate the nature of lobbying within the investment decision-making process; provide examples to support your claims. **[LO7]**

● ● ● Exercises ● ● ● ● ● ● ● ● ● ● ● ● ● ● ● ● ● connect ● ●

E15.1 **NPV and unequal lives [LO4]**

Jasmine PLC, an engineering company is appraising two capital investment decisions. The company needs to replace its machinery and the production manager is considering the following options:

● Machine W, which is more expensive and has an estimated life of 12 years, or
● Machine P, which has an expected life of six years. If machine P is selected, it will be replaced by another P type machine, at the end of six years.

The pattern of costs for each of the machines is detailed below:

	Machine W £	Machine P £
Purchase price	25,000	18,000
Trade-in value	3,000	3,000
Annual repair costs	2,200	2,000
Overhaul costs	5,000 (at year 8)	3,000 (at year 4)
Estimated financing costs averaged over machine life	10% each year	10% each year

Required:

a) Define and describe an appropriate method of comparing replacement proposals with unequal lives.

b) Recommend with supporting figures, which machine to purchase and state all assumptions.

In addition to the machine replacement, the directors of Jasmine plc wish to introduce a new product and there are two alternative methods of promoting the product:

Method 1 This would involve an immediate cash outflow of £200,000 for advertising costs, a predicted cash inflow at the end of year 1 of £360,000, followed by further advertising outflows of £150,000 at the end of two years.

Method 2 This would involve an immediate cash outflow of £100,000 for advertising costs, and net cash inflows of £67,000 at the end of years 2 and 3.

One of the directors, Mr Morrison commented as follows:

> *I prefer the payback method for choosing between alternative investment decisions . . . I am concerned about the delay in receiving cash inflows from method 2 and feel that this will reduce reported profit next year, as there are no net revenues from the sale of the product, until the end of year two.*

Required:

c) Calculate the net present values of the two methods of promotion, using Jasmine plc's cost of capital of 10 per cent per year.

d) Advise whether the two methods of promotion are financially viable.

e) Advise whether Mr Morrison's comments are valid.

E15.2 **NPV and payback [LO1, LO4]**

XYZ plc is considering manufacturing a new product to upgrade its range of cooking equipment. A proposal has been submitted by the departmental manager in conjunction with the finance manager. The information given below is necessary to evaluate the financial viability of the project:

- The initial cost of the project requires machinery costing £2,000,000.
- The machinery has a four-year lifespan and a residual value of £600,000.
- There will be initial working capital amounting to £250,000, which will be recovered in full by the end of year 4.
- Working capital does not qualify for any capital allowances and Revenue and Customs rules do not allow working capital to be included as an expense when calculating taxable profit.
- Profits before depreciation from the project will be £1,000,000 (year 1), £900,000 (year 2), £800,000 (year 3) and £800,000 (year 4).
- The initial cost of the project and initial working capital will be incurred at the beginning of the year; all profits will occur at the end of the year.
- Tax allowances on the machine are 25 per cent per year reducing balance.
- Tax is payable one year after the end of the accounting year in which it is based, at a rate of 30 per cent. The start of the project is also the start of the accounting year.
- The cost of capital is 12 per cent.

Required:

a) Explain the concept of net present value (NPV) and its role in appraising capital investment projects.

b) Evaluate the project by calculating the net present value, and state your recommendations.

c) The payback method for appraising capital investment projects is frequently used in practice. Explain the concept of payback, explain its limitations and justify why it is frequently used in practice.

E15.3 **NPV and sensitivity [LO4]**

SKC plc is a pharmaceutical company that is considering investing in a new project and has to select one location, either in Scotland or Malaysia. Both projects have a life of 10 years. The discount rate for the company is 6 per cent. The company wishes to test the sensitivity of the projects for all parameters. You are provided with the following information:

	Scotland	Malaysia
Investment	£10,000,000	£12,000,000
Sales volume	500,000 units	350,000 units
	Unit (£)	**Unit (£)**
Estimated selling price	26	35
Variable costs:		
Labour	8	17
Material	10	3
Variable overhead	2	6
Total unit variable costs	20	26
Fixed overhead per annum	£750,000	£245,000

Required:

a) Calculate the Net Present Value (NPV).

b) Calculate the sensitivity of the projects. You should use all variables to test the sensitivity.

c) What is the main benefit to the management in conducting a sensitivity analysis and comment in practice the types of software that companies use to conduct sensitivity analysis?

E15.4 NPV and changes in demand [LO4]

The directors of Advanced plc are currently considering an investment in new production machinery to replace existing machinery. The new machinery would produce goods more efficiently, leading to increased sales volume. The investment required will be £1,150,000 payable at the start of the project. The alternative course of action would be to continue using existing machinery for a further five years, at the end of which time it would be replaced. The following forecasts of sales and production volumes have been made:

Sales (units)		
Year	**Using existing machinery**	**Using new machinery**
1	400,000	560,000
2	450,000	630,000
3	500,000	700,000
4	600,000	840,000
5	750,000	1,050,000

Production (units)		
Year	**Using existing machinery**	**Using new machinery**
1	420,000	564,000
2	435,000	637,000
3	505,000	695,000
4	610,000	840,000
5	730,000	1,044,000

Further information:

1) The new machinery will reduce production costs from their present level of £7.50 per unit to £6.20 per unit. These production costs exclude depreciation.

2) The increased sales volume will be achieved by reducing unit selling prices from their present level of £10.00 per unit to £8.50 per unit.

3) The new machinery will have scrap value of £150,000 after five years.

4) The existing machinery will have a scrap value of £30,000 at the start of year 1. Its scrap value will be £20,000 at the end of year 5.

5) The cost of capital to the company, in money terms, is currently 12 per cent per annum.

Required:

a) Prepare a financial analysis to report whether the new machinery should be purchased.

b) When management are considering to purchase new machinery in circumstance such as these what non-financial factors should they consider?

Source: adapted from Chartered Institute of Management Accountants.

E15.5 **NPV with sales demand function [LO4]**

Quarefel plc is considering entering the market for a single product which has an estimated life cycle of three years. The following information has been gathered.

1) The total market size is estimated as follows: year 1,800,000 units; year 2, 1,200,000 units and year 3, 600,000 units.

2) Quarefel plc intends to use a flexible manufacturing system which will be able to produce up to 200,000 units per year. The equipment will cost €2,000,000 (payable in year 0) and will have an estimated residual value of €400,000 (receivable at the end of year 4).

3) An advertising campaign will be implemented by Quarefel plc on the following basis: year 0, €1,200,000; year 1, €1,000,000 and year 2, €800,000.

4) Quarefel plc has estimated its sales (Q) in 000 units and selling price per unit (P) for each year over the life of the product. This may be expressed in terms of the price/demand function $P = 70 - 0.15Q$.

5) The year 1 market share is crucial. Annual sales for Quarefel plc for years 2 and 3 are expected to increase or decrease from the year 1 level achieved in proportion to the change in the size of the overall market from one year to the next, in so much as the production capacity of Quarefel plc will allow. The prices set by Quarefel plc in each of years 2 and 3 will be set in accordance with the price/demand function estimate detailed above.

6) Variable cost is estimated at €25 per product unit.

7) Fixed costs directly attributable to the product (other than advertising) are estimated at €600,000 per year for each of the years 1 to 3.

8) Quarefel plc has an estimated cost of capital of 12 per cent for this type of proposal.

9) Ignore taxation and inflation.

Required:

a) Using the information above, calculate the net present value (NPV). You should use $60 per unit to be the launch price of the product in year 1.

b) Explain how target pricing could help this organization ensure they are successful in their first year.

Source: adapted from Chartered Institute of Management Accountants, Paper P2.

E15.6 **NPV and payback [LO1, LO4]**

Crossgates Ltd produces and sells electrical components to be used in various kitchen appliances. They are currently considering new projects. The manager of one of the departments has submitted a proposal to produce and sell a new enhanced motor to be used in juicing machines. He has provided you with a three-year financial plan, for the new motor:

	Year 1	Year 2	Year3
Sales	1,080,000	1,200,000	1,400,000
Direct material	150,000	180,000	210,000
Direct labour	200,000	240,000	280,000
Direct overheads	390,000	390,000	390,000
Depreciation	200,000	200,000	200,000
Profit before tax	140,000	190,000	320,000

The departmental manager has a limited understanding of accounting and you are provided with some additional information that will help in the evaluation of this new project:

1) The initial cost of the project is £1,000,000 (this is the cost of all new machinery needed).

2) The machinery bought for this project has a three-year lifespan with £400,000 residual value.

3) The working capital of the project will be £50,000 which will be recovered in full at the end of the three-year project.

4) Working capital does not qualify for any capital allowance and Inland Revenue rules do not allow working capital to be included as an expense when calculating taxable profit.

5) Both the initial cost of the project and the working capital requirements will be incurred at the beginning of the year. However, all expenses will occur at the end of each year.

6) The Inland Revenue capital allowance for all machinery is currently 25 per cent per year on a reducing balance basis. In the year of disposal, a balancing charge or allowance will arise being the difference between the disposal proceeds and the tax written-down value.

7) All tax is paid with a one year time lag at a rate of 30 per cent.

8) The companies cost of capital is 15 per cent.

Required:

a) Using all the information available calculate the net present value of this project and state your recommendation.

b) Management in the past have used the payback method to analyse new projects. Calculate the payback period and discuss the general problems of using this technique.

c) The organization has limited funds for new projects and this project will compete against others within the company – many of the other projects have different lifespans. Explain what technique can be employed to evaluate these projects fairly and why this is necessary

E15.7 **NPV with taxation [LO4]**

Katon Plc needs to replace one of their machines within their operations department. The manager of this department has found two suitable replacement machines and has provided you with the following information:

Machine X

The cost of this machine is £4,000,000 and has an expected life of three years. This machine is expected to have incremental cash flows of £2,000,000 for the next three years (no taxation has been taken into account for machine X).

- The writing-down balance of 25 per cent is applicable to machine X.
- Corporation taxation is 30 per cent.
- Taxation is paid one year in arrears.
- The residual value for the machine will be the written-down value as calculated for taxation purposes.

Machine Y

The cost will be £10,000,000 with an expected life of five years. The incremental cash flows for this machine have been calculated as follows (note that taxation charges and residual value have already been accounted for in the net incremental cash flows for machine Y):

Year	Net incremental cash flow
0	(10,000,000.00)
1	3,600,000.00
2	3,270,000.00
3	3,082,500.00
4	2,941,875.00
5	5,209,322.00
6	(842,695.32)
	7,261,001.70

The companies cost of capital is 10 per cent.

Required:

a) Calculate the incremental net cash flows for the full working life of machine X, incorporating taxation charges.

b) Calculate the net present value of the two new machines. Which machine would you recommend they purchase?

c) NPV provides you with numeric information to base your decisions on. However, what other considerations should you include in your decisions to buy assets?

E15.8 Real options [LO8]

The managers at Greenwich Inc. believe the current economic uncertainty is making it difficult to evaluate investments. The details for an investment in a new machine are as follows:

Cost of machine is £850 with a discount rate at 10 per cent.
Cash flows:

	Year 1 Cash flow	Year 1 Probability	Year 2 Cash flow	Year 2 Probability
Scenario 1	£500	0.7	£400	0.2
			£500	0.5
			£600	0.3
Scenario 2	£700	0.3	£620	0.7
			£700	0.2
			£850	0.1

Scenario 1 is a pessimistic forecast for year 1 and assumes that cash flows will be higher in year 2 which will be in the range of £400–£600. Scenario 2 assumes cash flows will be higher in year 1 and this will result in higher cash flows in year 2. For both of the scenarios the year 2 cash flows are therefore dependent on the year 1 cash flows.

The company does have the option to sell the machinery at the end of year 1 for £500.

Required:

a) Determine the value of the option to abandon for this investment and advise the managers whether or not the investment should be approved.

b) Identify and evaluate the problems of incorporating different types of real options into the analysis of an investment for a new product.

● ● ● ● Case study problem ● ● ● ● ● ● ● ● ● ● ● ● connect ●

C15.1 **UK electricity generation industry and regulatory uncertainty [LO7]**

The UK power sector has undergone significant changes in the past 25 years, with the industry being privatized in 1990 and changes in the market structure when selling electricity in 2001. In 2001 a system called the New Electricity Trading Arrangements (NETA, and this was updated in 2005 with a system called the British Electricity Transmission and Trading Arrangements, BETTA) was introduced which results in electricity being traded like any other commodity.

Following the change in the way electricity is sold, the industry has experienced a significant increase in regulation relating to environmental protection. Environmental policy within the UK, Europe and internationally has became a stronger initiative for many governments. Environmental policy has now started to shape the investment strategy within the sector, with governments imposing strict regulation to reduce pollution. Regulation was used in two ways: command and control, and incentives to encourage certain behaviour. Laws were put in place to force through investment in new technology which would reduce pollution; if the generator chose not to accept the new laws and not invest they would have to shut down their coal power stations within a certain deadlines.

At the same time the UK government began to motivate generators to invest in greener technology by offering financial incentives which were called Renewable Obligation Certificates (ROCs). The ROCs were designed to encourage investors (the generators) to invest in capital projects which would help to meet environmental targets, therefore investments in hydro, wind and technology which uses co-generation all attracted financial incentives. Most of the investments, using ROCs, focused on onshore and offshore wind technology.

Within the industry this influenced the technology that was invested in because of the certainty that the financial incentives gave the generators. However, while this was shaping the investment patterns in greener technology, other technologies which produce the majority of the electricity demand within the UK slowed down. A lack of strong policy from the government and changing environmental targets resulted in significant uncertainty emerging when analysing future investments within this sector. Although many capital budgeting calculations demonstrated positive NPVs, these investments have not been implemented because the risk associated with changing regulation was deemed to be too high.

Therefore, the ability of the industry to produce the future generation of electricity became worrying because the generators were not investing at the rate that the country required. The environmental regulation was closing power stations down before the natural end of the useful life of the power stations. In addition, investment requirement levels increased because greener technology, such as wind, requires additional investment. When investing in wind technology there is a need for additional investment in reliable technology for when the wind does not blow. These additional assets are known as stranded assets on the statement of financial position; they are present to fulfil the contractual requirements of future contracts when the greener technology can not satisfy demand. The final investment problem has emerged because generators were reducing investment owing to the sheer uncertainty which was due to the lack of solid policy in the energy sector within the UK.

The UK government began the process of reforming the UK power sector in October 2010. This was due to the recognition that £200 billion worth of investment was required to maintain the supply of demand. The UK government finally accepted that the sector was in desperate need of reform to provide more certainty, which would trigger the investment required. The UK was having to compete with other countries which were already responding to their own investment needs by offering the same generators fixed rates of return for investing within their countries, thereby reducing the risk of the these capital projects.

Required:

a) Discuss, using the energy sector within the UK as an example, why financial predictions and analysis are not sufficient to win the capital for investments.

b) Evaluate other factors which influence the decision-making process in relation to investment strategies.

c) Explain why capital rationing can create problems for countries, like the UK, when they are slow to respond to the needs of organizations when making investments.

Source: based on author's own research.

Recommended reading ● ● ● ● ● ● ● ● ● ● ● ● ● ● ● ● ●

● Alkaraan, F. and D. Northcott (2006) 'Strategic capital investment decision-making: a role for emergent analysis tools? A study of practice in large UK manufacturing companies', *The British Accounting Review*, 38, pp. 149–73.

This paper considers strategic capital investments in complex situations. An analysis is presented on the challenges that managers are faced with when evaluating these projects. Highlighting the over-reliance on financial appraisal tools and the resulting bias decision makers face against undertaking strategic projects that are crucial to the development of business capability and innovation. This paper examines the use of traditional financial analysis tools and selected emergent analysis approaches in the capital investment decision-making of large UK manufacturing companies.

● Carr, C., K. Kolehmainen and F. Mitchell (2010) 'Strategic investment decision making practices: a contextual approach', *Management Accounting Research*, 21, pp. 167–84.

Carr et al. (2010) find substantial strategic investment decision (SID) differences across four contextual categories of market creators, value creators, refocusers and re-structurers. This paper proposes a contextual approach to explaining differences in SID making practices. SIDs practices are explored through 14 case studies of UK, US and Japanese companies from both stable and dynamic business sectors.

● Ekanem, I. (2005) '"Bootstrapping": the investment decision-making process in small firms', *The British Accounting Review*, 37, pp. 299–318.

Offering a view of how capital budgeting is used in small companies, Ekanem (2005) presents findings from a study in the printing and clothing industries. The study uses 'insider accounts' which involves in-depth, semi-structured interviews and direct observation, conducted longitudinally in eight case study companies. The paper presents findings which suggest that owner-managers predominantly use 'bootstrapping' techniques for their investment appraisal rather than the more formal methods suggested in the financial management literature.

● Khamees, B., N. Al-Fayoumi and A. Thuneibat (2010) 'Capital budgeting practices in the Jordanian industrial corporations', *International Journal of Commerce and Management*, 20(1), pp. 49–63.

Khamess et al. (2010) provide an empirical paper based upon capital budgeting practices in an emerging economy, Jordan. The results of this study show that both discounted and undiscounted methods are used in industry with the profitability index being used the most frequently with payback following.

- Miller, P. and T. O'Leary (2007) 'Mediating instruments and making markets: Capital budgeting, science and the economy', *Accounting, Organizations and Society*, 32, pp. 701–34.

This paper provides an insightful view of capital budgeting techniques as 'mediating devices', offering the reader an opportunity to examine the way in which capital budgeting techniques are used in practice. It also provides rich explanations as to how the techniques are used to examine the future and develop markets.

- Pfeiffer, T. and G. Schneider (2010) 'Capital budgeting, information timing, and the value of abandonment options', *Management Accounting Research*, 21, pp. 238–50.

This paper, by Pfeiffer and Schneider investigates how an abandonment option influences the optimal timing of information in a sequential adverse selection capital budgeting model. The findings show that the abandonment option favours delayed information because under the timely information regime the value of the abandonment option is zero, whereas under the delayed information regime the value of the option is positive.

References

CIMA (2009) 'Management accounting tools for today and tomorrow', www.cimaglobal.com/ma (accessed on 20 October 2011).

Ekanem, I. (2007) '"Insider account": a qualitative research method for small firms', *Journal of Small Business and Economic Development,* 14(1), pp. 105–117.

Gow, D. and W. Woodward (2008) 'Green law and regulation risk energy crisis, say European energy companies', *Guardian*, 7 February.

Haka, S. (2007) 'A review of the literature on capital budgeting and investment appraisal: past, present and future musings', in *Handbook of Management Accounting Research*, C. Chapman, A. Hopwood and M. Shields (eds), Oxford: Elsevier.

Harvey, F. (2011) 'EU energy chief calls for new renewable energy targets', *Guardian*, 15 December.

Miller, P. and T. O'Leary (2007) 'Mediating instruments and making markets: Capital budgeting, science and the economy', *Accounting, Organizations and Society,* 32, pp. 701–34.

Pfeiffer, T. and G. Schneider (2010) 'Capital budgeting, information timing, and the value of abandonment options', *Management Accounting Research*, 21, pp. 238–50.

Warren, E. (2012) 'Can we keep the lights on? Investment, regulation & sustainability in the UK electricity industry', unpublished PhD, University of Southampton.

Online **LearningCentre**

When you have read this chapter

Log on to the Online Learning Centre at **www.mcgraw-hill.co.uk/textbooks/burns** to explore chapter-by-chapter test questions, links and further online study tools for Management Accounting.

PART **5**

PERFORMANCE MEASUREMENT

CHAPTER 16

PERFORMANCE MEASUREMENT AND MANAGEMENT: IDEAS, THEORIES AND PRINCIPLES

Chapter outline

- Performance measurement

- Performance management

- Roles of management accountants in performance management

Learning outcomes

On completion of this chapter, students will be able to:

LO1 Appreciate the complexities of performance measurement, and its distinction from the broader process of performance management

LO2 Describe and distinguish between the shareholder approach and the stakeholder approach to performance measurement

LO3 Explain the principles of responsibility accounting and describe the various types of responsibility centres that an organization might have

LO4 Explain the pros and cons of centralization and decentralization

LO5 Relate to how and why organizations might choose to align rewards systems to their performance measurement systems

LO6 Highlight some of the possible non-technical problems and challenges that an organization might face when designing and implementing new performance measurement systems

LO7 Discuss, in conceptual terms, some of the key features of a performance measurement system, and have some awareness of the key functional and contextual considerations for its design and implementation

LO8 Describe some of the roles for management accountants in the design, implementation and ongoing involvement with performance measurement systems

LO9 Define and explain performance management, explain its difference to (static) performance measurement

Introduction

In this book we have consistently highlighted how important management accounting information is for facilitating (1) planning, (2) control and (3) performance measurement. Chapters 7 to 10 of this textbook concentrated on some of the concepts, principles, tools and techniques which together comprise how management accounting can be used for facilitating organizational planning and control. This chapter, however, introduces some of the ideas and principles which underpin how management accounting facilitates performance measurement (and, as we will develop, performance management also). This chapter is a more general overview of performance measurement and performance management, exploring the topic from a rather more conceptual angle. Chapters 17 and 18 will subsequently and more deeply investigate some of the specific tools and techniques of performance measurement and performance management.

As mentioned in Chapter 7, although the respective themes of planning, control and performance measurement appear in different parts of this textbook, it is important that we keep in mind how these three dimensions are interconnected. In other words, although planning, control and performance measurement can each be presented as stand-alone themes, all three represent intertwined dimension(s) of an organization's decision-making process.

Performance measurement

Definition

Performance measurement is about 'seeing' how an organization is doing, in comparison to its aims and objectives. It is a way of gauging how well (or not) an organization is doing against its short- and long-term goals and targets. There are usually numerous types of performance measurement systems across different parts of different organizations; for example, it would not be surprising to find localized performance measurement systems within the production unit(s) of a dishwasher manufacturer, in the research and development department of a producer of high-technology digital radios, in the dispatch unit of an online retail company, or in the sales office of a large sports arena.

Traditionally, performance measurement constitutes a role that has taken up a significant part of a management accountant's time, but primarily: (1) involving the measurement of financial (or financially related) performance, (2) comprising comparison of actual performance measures against historic targets, and (3) encompassing more of a controllership and policing remit for accountants. In this chapter we will first describe some of the more common features of traditional performance measurement, from a management accounting perspective, not least because *some* of these aspects remain as relevant today as they did two decades and more ago.

Later in this chapter, we will focus more on fundamental changes that have occurred over the past 20 years or so, more specifically the increased adoption of **performance management** which involves not just measuring an organization's performance at a particular point in time but also a process of continually (re)designing, monitoring and acting upon such measures. Performance measurement is no less important nowadays, as we shall discover, and it promises to continue to be an important part of a management accountant's future role. However, extension into performance management in the future will involve management accountants dealing with an organization's performance as an ongoing and continual task, with a focus on producing information which is real time and of a feed-forward orientation. That is, although the snapshot of performance measures at any particular point in time will remain important, equal if not more important will be the need to measure into future time periods and contexts. We begin by introducing some of the more traditional and enduring principles underlying performance measurement.

Why do organizations need to measure performance?

Organizations measure performance because they need to gauge how they are doing, when set against their short- and long-term goals. Traditionally, organizations would tend to rely upon mainly historical and financial measures to gauge their performance, for example using such measures as 'return on investment' (ROI), and financially oriented performance measures still remain as popular as ever (see Chapter 18).

However, during the 1980s in particular such measures were on the wrong end of a considerable wave of criticism, most notably aimed at their ignorance of non-financial aspects of organizational activity (for example, customer satisfaction, service quality, innovation), as well as accusations that a predominant focus on financial measures fuelled a tendency for short-termism. The predominance of financial measures was also criticized by many on the grounds that when such measures underpinned managers' rewards (which they frequently did), this could have serious dysfunctional consequences whereby managers aimed to maximize their personal economic benefit at the expense of organizational benefits.

Subsequently, in the late 1980s and early 1990s, there was a rush of publications on 'new' performance measurement tools, both within the academic and the practitioner-oriented literature. There were two main strands of argument, the first representing calls for an increase in the use of non-financial performance measures and the second clamouring for new 'more modern' financial measures. Fitzgerald (2007) classified this wave of literature (or schools of thought) into two parts, which she called: (1) the shareholder approach, and (2) the stakeholder approach. We will adopt a similar classification here, summarized (briefly) below.

Shareholder approach

A **shareholder approach** argues that financial performance measurement remains the most important measurement within organizations, and that any perceived failure of traditional financial performance measures should not lead to its abandonment but, rather, its replacement with new and more sophisticated financial measures that better reflect the broader organizational and environmental context of the present day.

Underpinning the shareholder approach is an assumption that measuring (and rewarding) those activities which generate shareholder wealth will actually lead to shareholder wealth. A basic premise is that all measurement of profit should take into account the cost of capital employed to generate it. This is done by applying a **residual income** approach (or similar) to the key financial measures.

Residual income involves subtracting the cost of capital from accounting profit to ascertain how much of this profit remains to be able to reinvest or distribute as dividends to an organization's owners. Behind this is an argument that merely using traditional accounting profit to measure organizational performance will reflect only the cost of debt capital, whereas the use of residual income (or similar) also takes account of the cost of equity capital.

A residual income performance measurement system retains some popularity, especially in mainstream accounting academic circles, probably because it is grounded in economic theory, although most recent evidence suggests that its uptake in practice remains disappointingly low for its advocates. The main advantage of such an approach is that it ensures focus on a single financial objective, a focus that will drive all decisions and will avoid the trade-offs between multiple measures from a stakeholder viewpoint (see below). More recently, management consultants have developed alternative and highly publicized versions of the residual income approach, such as economic value management, discounted economic profits and economic value added (EVA®), the latter of which is a registered trademark of consultants Stern Stewart & Co. We will explore more of these tools in Chapter 18.

Stakeholder approach

A **stakeholder approach** advocates that organizations adopt sufficient non-financial performance measures to supplement any use of financial measures. Such non-financial performance measurement should be closely linked to, or integrated in, some way with the strategy of an organization.

From a stakeholder perspective the overriding view is that an organization's ability to compete in its relevant markets is an amalgam of various capabilities and achievements, not just financial performance. So, such an approach would emphasize the need to measure (non-)achievements in multiple business areas that ultimately feed through to an organization's level of competitive advantage, such as customer satisfaction, quality in products and/or services provided, employee well-being, training, investment, and more.

A main advantage of measuring performance with a wider stakeholder lens is that it forces senior managers to take a more holistic view of their business activities, and ultimately of their organization's ability to compete in the markets. To avoid overload, however, the usual approach is to concentrate on a reasonably small number of key performance measures in each main business activity.

Several multidimensional frameworks have been offered, which provide a way to capture and assess performance across a variety of organizational activities, including but not dominated by, financial performance. Examples are the performance prism (Neely and Adams, 2001) and the tableau de bord (Bourguignon, 2004). But probably the most popular of all broad performance measurement systems today is the balanced scorecard (Kaplan and Norton, 1992); we explore this particular tool in greater detail in Chapter 17.

The common thread running through all such multidimensional performance measurement systems is fourfold (Fitzgerald, 2007), namely:

1) Linking with an organization's strategy, over time.

2) Incorporating both external (for example, customer, suppliers) and internally derived measures.

3) Built around both financial *and* non-financial measures.

4) Highlighting and making explicit any trade-off between respective measures of performance.

Whether an organization follows the shareholder or the stakeholder approach, it is important for us to consider how performance measures are used in practice. Performance measures not only provide senior managers with a guide on how their organization is faring, but also provide management with a means to monitor if business units, organizational subgroups and individual employees are doing what they are assigned to do and they are able. To make this happen, organizations usually assign responsibility to particular individual units – for example, subsidiary divisions, operating units, departments and/or individual workers. The precise nature of the responsibilities handed out depends on the context of the organization in question but also the level of analysis at which the performance measurement is to be carried out. Very often, organizations will also assign rewards and compensation (for example, bonuses, promotion) against the achievement of particular objectives and targets, as expressed in the performance measures. We can now explore these aspects of performance measurement in more detail.

Responsibility

Establishing lines of responsibility, starting with the identification of duties that different organizational members or groups are expected to do, is a common feature in most organizations. This is an important aspect of organizational life because it formalizes 'who does what' and, by implication, creates (or *should* create) a template for whose performance can be measured, and for what. All organizations will have some form of organizational chart which sets out (hopefully clearly) who is responsible for which activities.

Most organizations are typically composed of subunits, which individually represent work groups and/or managers who hold specific responsibilities. The nature of such subunits can differ across organizations but examples might include where an organization is divided into different functional areas or departments for production, marketing, procurement, IT and human resources. Other organizations might design their structure, and subsequently their system of responsibility, around individual products or services. A university is often organized around a small number of colleges, each of which contains schools, and in them a further division among different academic departments. All through this hierarchical structure, and at different levels, there will be responsible managers with defined duties and accountability towards particular performance measures.

We can think of any organizational structure as starting at the highest level of authority, usually the owners, and then responsibility cascading down through the various organizational levels. We might also think of a typical situation whereby the owners of an organization assign ultimate strategic and operational responsibility to the chief executive (CE), but the owners will retain power to replace the CE and also to establish or change his/her salary. The more that responsibility is then passed downwards and outwards to other people, the more we say an organization is **decentralized**. Conversely, where responsibility remains largely with a small group of very senior people we would refer to this as a relatively **centralized** organization. Decentralization or centralization can particularly become a major issue for global organizations, including multinationals, which have subsidiaries in different countries all over the world. The question which the head office needs to ask is to what extent the subsidiary units should be handed local responsibility, and on which particular key measures.

Some organizations prioritize a decentralizing approach, delegating as much responsibility as possible away from central headquarters. The argument behind this process is that it passes authority on to local people who possess the necessary local knowledge to make key decisions. In turn, so the argument goes, this should feed through to a better connection between the organization and its customers' needs (for example). Another advantage would be that having responsible managers at local levels would mean speeding up the decision-making processes, assuming appropriate levels of local knowledge. Alternatively, in a more centralized structure where decisions need to be made, a requirement to always seek approval from some centralized headquarters could extend the time taken quite considerably and potentially too long so that it is detrimental to the business. The downside of empowerment, at whatever level, is the relinquishing of control from the more senior responsibility unit (for example, head office) to the subordinate unit (for example, a subsidiary organization). This is especially of concern where it might be possible for the people with local knowledge to use this advantage to their own personal benefit (for example, to maximize personal bonuses) to the detriment of broader organizational goals. Outsourcing activities to external organizations can also suffer from these kinds of concerns. Careful monitoring is needed in all such circumstances, but much will also depend significantly on the degree of trust.

The (re)design of an organization's structures, including reporting and responsibility lines, will also be a management accountant's task and requires continual review. **Responsibility accounting** is a process whereby the managers of subunits within an organization are assigned certain responsibility, and their performance against such responsibility, also possible rewards, are evaluated by their peers. Responsibility, supplemented and reinforced by a system of incentives and rewards represents a long-standing feature of most management accounting systems. At the centre of this model is an assumption that individual entities (for example, business units, segments, departments and individual managers) can be made responsible for their own performance. For instance, a business unit's most senior manager can be made responsible for the performance of that unit. Then, responsibility for the performance, say, within departments can be passed down to the relevant departmental managers, and then, other subordinate workers can be made responsible for performance in their particular part of a department, and so on.

Thus an organization can establish a mapping of performance responsibility which covers all of the different business activities, and through all hierarchical levels. Traditional management accounting models would assume that the performance of entities which are held responsible for a particular activity can be measured, and that incentive systems can also be aligned to such measurement systems. These incentive systems are usually linked to individual performance, and are very often financial (for example, bonuses). Traditionally, management accountants play a key role in monitoring and controlling through formal and responsibility-based mechanisms. They monitor the performance of each area of responsibility in an organization, and produce reports to pass up through the organizational hierarchy.

There are different types of responsibility centres, depending on the specific organization and its context. For many organizations, probably most except the smallest of firms, some form of responsibility structuring is essential. The complexity in which today's organizations operate makes it inevitable that most cannot be controlled entirely from a central headquarters. This particularly applies to large and complex organizations, including most multinational organizations, which usually comprise multiple divisions, business units, and so on. Given its predominance in today's business environment, we shall explore the larger organization in more detail, in Chapter 18.

While advances in information technology and real-time reporting have made communication between units, head office and other parties much easier than it once was, the sheer volume and pace of information flows will usually make it likely that an organization's top management decentralize some of the control. As mentioned already, decentralization describes the establishment of responsibility centres within an organization, where a responsibility centre represents an individual unit for which ultimately a manager is held responsible for its performance. There are usually four main types of responsibility centres: (1) cost or expense centres, (2) revenue centres, (3) profit centres and (4) investment centres. We can now consider each type, in more detail.

Cost or expense centres

In Chapter 3, we defined **cost (or expense) centres** as responsibility centres where the manager has accountability for the costs over which he or she has control. It is usually the type of centre where the manager has the least responsibility relative to other responsibility centre managers (see below). Cost centres are normally one of two possible types: (1) a **standard cost centre**, or (2) a **discretionary expense centre**. A standard cost centre describes where outputs of production are known and can be measured in financial terms, and the quantity of inputs necessary for producing one unit of output are also known. As part of its control procedures, an organization will regularly compare the expected cost of inputs per unit of output (that is, the standard costs) against the actual costs. Any difference between the standard and actual costs, respectively, is called a variance. Astute readers will recognize that these aspects of management accounting were covered in depth in Chapter 9.

The second type of cost centre, that is, discretionary expense centres, represent where outputs cannot be measured in financial terms, and where there is difficulty in pinning down any obvious relationship between inputs (that is, resource consumption) and outputs. A common type of discretionary expense centre is an organization's 'internal services', such as human resources, information technology (IT) and finance; other examples might include research and development (R&D) and advertising. Normally an organization would assign an agreed budget amount for a particular expense category, and the budget holder would exercise some discretion over expenditure allowed and ensuring that budgets were not exceeded, hence the term 'discretionary'. Assessing the worth and long-run payback of discretionary expenditure can be one of the most difficult aspects of an organization's attempt to control its activities – such decisions are extremely complex, their parameters can change over time, there is always a short-long run tension, and more.

Revenue centres

Revenue centres represent those responsibility centres where managers are accountable for the financial outputs associated with generating sales (or, more specifically, sales revenues). A simple example might be a divisional sales manager for a soft drinks distribution company in Italy, who will be responsible for sales revenues earned in that sales region. Technically, revenue centres may also be held accountable for some selling expenses – for instance, sales people salaries and bonuses. But, importantly, revenue centres will not be accountable for the cost of goods or services sold.

Profit centres

Where managers are responsible for both revenues and costs, we call this a **profit centre**. Such situations describe a manager who commands a great deal of autonomy over organizational affairs, So, for example, in a profit centre the manager will have authority to establish and change selling prices, choose the markets to target and the mix of products or services to prioritize, select the main suppliers, and more.

As an example, we can think of the manager of a hotel as heading up a profit centre; that is, being responsible for both hotel costs and pricing. Reporting to the manager, there may be several cost centre managers – for instance, the restaurant chef, the head cleaner, the operations manager, and so on. As profit centre manager, the head person in the hotel has responsibility for the pricing of hotel rooms, functions, conference suites, and more, and is also ultimately responsible for the mix of services being offered by the hotel.

Profit centres, like the hotel example above, will be measured at least partly by profit and profit-related performance measures, although increasingly alongside non-financial measures such as customer satisfaction and quality of service. Care is also needed to take into account any possible factors which might affect a hotel manager's profit-related performance but for which there was not much hope for the manager to avoid such impacts. For example, this could be due to an economic recession, or because there has been some high-profile adverse publicity for a sister hotel belonging to the same chain, which has had a generally negative effect on customers' opinions towards the hotel brand.

Investment centres

Managers in an **investment centre** have all the responsibility assigned to a profit centre (that is, sales revenues and costs) but also responsibility for working capital and capital investment decisions. In other words, the manager of an investment centre also has the right to expand or contract the size of operations, although there may still be a need to gain authority from someone of higher rank within the organization, especially when a potential investment decision involves significant expenditure. There are particular performance measurement techniques that assist managers to deal with such decisions, for instance 'return on investment' calculations and economic value added (see Chapter 18).

Investment centres will usually comprise numerous profit centres (and within them, various cost and revenue centres). For example, we can assume that a local branch from a national chain of bakeries in Ireland is treated as an individual profit centre, but the regional (or divisional) area is treated as an investment centre. So, the regional manager first has responsibility over all of the individual bakeries (profit centres) but, secondly, will also have responsibility over identifying new bakery locations or ceasing operations in others. As mentioned above, however, there is usually some centralized control over the financing of major decisions such as expansion or contraction of operations.

An investment centre represents the highest level of autonomy that management can behold. It is a level that normally covers an entire organization and through to its subsidiaries, divisions, business units and more, depending on the actual structure of a particular organization.

A *structure of responsibility centres* is an enduring and still popular technique within organizations, which facilitates the planning/control/performance measurement process, and which usefully offers a sense of organizational hierarchy and authority. Such a structure is, however, not an easy task; its design needs careful thought so as to identify the appropriate manager for each category. A key aspect to any design is ensuring that when assigning a particular manager to an area of responsibility, the manager chosen has appropriate knowledge of that area.

Design is also difficult because there can be some situations where the assignment of a particular manager to one particular responsibility centre is questionable. For example, a manufacturing manager would typically be a cost centre manager; however, there might be a reasonable argument in some organizations for saying that a manufacturing manager has at least part-influence on the quality of a product and the satisfaction of customers (via, say, impressive delivery options), hence this manager also maybe has some influence on sales (revenues).

Another aspect of responsibility accounting which demands great care is trying to integrate appropriate incentives and motivation; this is normally achieved, but again with potential difficulty, through rewards systems that are aligned to particular performance measures. We can now explore such rewards systems in more detail.

Rewards

Many organizations align their performance measurement systems to mechanisms through which employees are given **rewards**, including salaries, commission and bonuses. Therefore, since rewards are based on performance measures, it is highly likely (even natural!) that group and/or individuals' behaviour will to some extent be geared towards influencing the outcome of such performance measures. This clearly presents an organization with a potential problem if they fail to adopt appropriate incentivizing measures. Selecting inappropriate performance measures, especially when rewards are interlinked, can create conflict in an organization and/or work towards failure to reach organizational goals.

Rewards systems need to be designed with diligence, since it is quite easy to establish structures that, while beneficial to individual people, are not necessarily in the interests of the organization as a whole. For example, a sales manager might benefit significantly through commission and bonuses from an impressive round of product sales, in absolute terms. Yet the benefit might not be equally as great for the organization if they actually represent low-margin sales. Thought needs to be given to establishing performance measures that, if achieved, will be to the benefit of both the responsible person and the organization as a whole. Fitzgerald (2007) suggests three important attributes for a reward system:

1) *Clarity*: do those employees who are impacted by performance targets know and understand why this is so? This ultimately relates to understanding what the main strategic objectives of an organization are, and how the targets in question reflect the attainment (or not) of such objectives. As well as having full confidence in the strategic objectives as a way forward, and in the robustness of the assumed relationship between strategic objectives and the various targets, this also entails a need for good communication (up, down and across an organization's structure).

2) *Motivation*: It is generally accepted that many people will not go the extra mile for their employers, as reflected in challenging performance targets, if they are not motivated in some way to do so. Usually such motivation will be in the form of financial reward (for example, higher salary, bonuses) but they can also be non-financial in nature (for example, promotion, additional holidays, fringe benefits). The design of the rewards system in an organization is a difficult but extremely important task; if done poorly it could very quickly ruin any chance of attaining strategic goals and performance targets. The main thing is that employees generally accept the targets being imposed upon them, but equally that the rewards system primarily supports the attainment of benefits when targeted employee contributions are being made, rather than a rewards system that carries more negative and blameworthy tendencies when targets are not being met.

3) *Controllability*: when an organization establishes its rewards system it is important that responsible managers are only set targets for things which they have control over. It can be very demotivating for staff when they are being assessed on performance for some activity which they cannot easily influence or which is, for example, largely dictated by unpredictable external events.

Some criticisms of the traditional approach

The traditional 'responsibility and incentives' approach which mainly is what we have covered so far in this chapter has been adopted for many decades in many organizations; it can particularly assist managers in their planning and controlling endeavours. However some have criticized this approach for being grounded in too narrow an economic view of rationality and motivation (ter Bogt and Scapens, 2012). For instance, the assumptions underpinning such an approach conceal the potential for more subtle and intrinsic incentives and rewards that people value, such as personal development, community galvanizing and self-fulfilment. There has also been some criticism directed at the individualizing effect of the responsibility incentives model, whereby individual responsibility centres (including individual employees) are formally separated, and assumed to be in competition with each other. So, this might also be accompanied by management league tables, performance ladders and similar tools used for visualizing the results of competitions between individual responsibility centres. These sorts of tools carry a risk; they can lead to dysfunctional behaviour – for example, where one business unit out-manoeuvres another to gain competitive advantage in the corporate league tables, although overall this may have been a less favourable move for the whole organization, not to mention the potential that such formal competitive traits can have on the (de)motivation of poor achievers. The latter can be made worse when poor achievers (that is, those nearer to the foot of a league table) have reservations about the fairness and credibility of the tools which have been imposed upon them.

Another angle of criticism against traditional responsibility incentive models has been specifically aimed at the predominance of financial measures, and the potential nurturing of a 'financial mentality'. Such criticism formed part of what subsequently drove the emergence of more non-financial performance measures, in particular from the late 1980s onwards, as we discussed in Chapter 2.

Things to consider when choosing key performance measures

As has been described so far, it is a very complex and difficult task to design an organization's performance measurement systems, and every organization will have its own (changeable) requirements. A 'good' performance measure will unambiguously and fairly convey how well a responsible party has (or has not) performed their duties, and will motivate them to achieve the goals and targets they are set. As part of the information base of an organization, we would also argue that performance measures must possess the qualities and characteristics of 'good' information (as defined in Chapter 2) such as being accurate, timely, practical and flexible.

Performance measurement by itself has its limitations; to have any impact there need to be decisions and actions taken as consequence of such measures. One of the key contributions that performance measures *can* achieve is evaluation of how well (or badly) an organization is doing in relation to its strategic objectives or targets. Therefore, these strategic objectives and targets are absolutely necessary before any performance measures can really make any impact. Whatever its particular performance perspective (that is, a shareholder or a stakeholder approach, as explained above), an organization needs to translate its strategic aims into quantifiable objectives. Whether an organization adopts mainly financial metrics (a shareholder approach) or a mixture of financial and non-financial metrics (the stakeholder approach) will determine the 'dimension' of performance that an organization elects to monitor in its quest for achieving its strategic goals (Fitzgerald, 2007).

Consistent with our approach throughout this textbook, we do not subscribe to there being any 'best' way to measure performance in a particular organization; each case, we argue, is context specific. Nor would we suggest that 'good' performance measures are easy to identify. While performance measures aim to show and evaluate the actions of responsible parties, they can quite often be affected by outside factors which are out of the responsible party's control. With these possible external factors in mind, we now offer some discussion and pointers with regard to the design of an organization's performance measurement tools.

Fairness and achievability

Performance measures must be achievable and set at fair levels. A good example of where such issues might come to the fore is when bonuses are awarded to sales staff based on the amount of sales revenue their efforts generate. But there are numerous scenarios whereby a salesperson could do everything expected of them, yet not reach targets. For example, there might be a recession and economic downturn, or the unexpected entry of a major and highly resourced new competitor in the market. In such cases, the fairness and achievability of a salesperson's performance measures might be questionable, and could lead to demotivation.

Controllability

Since part of the aim of using performance measures is to reveal the behaviour of responsible persons, and their direct achievement (or not) of goals set, it is wise to avoid establishing measures which are out of the control or influence of that responsible unit. Uncontrollable measures will generally not reveal the actions of individual managers (groups and so on) and so rarely make for useful performance measures. For instance, the manager of a Canadian travel agent can be given responsibility and rewarded accordingly against holiday sales in the resort of Florida (USA). It would be hoped that her skills of persuasion can influence such sales, and therefore her behaviour will to some extent be reflected in the measurement of such sales over a particular period of time. But when sales take a huge dip due to a major hurricane that sweeps across the majority of Florida's landscape, inflicting major damage to the area, there can conceivably be a question as to whether the performance measurement system is still fair because the effect of the hurricane is something which is out of travel agent's control. Scenarios such as this can create a major challenge for the design of performance measures. Some organizations might, for example, choose in such a situation to measure the travel agent's performance in a portioned or percentage way that reflects the relative or proportionate degree of controllability, therefore isolating the effect on sales from the hurricane. As time goes on, an organization might also begin to find ways to integrate learning into their performance measurement systems – for example, after five continuous years of having hurricanes in Florida, this might be something that is formally reflected within the model.

16.1: Management Accounting in Practice

An operation manager's woe at a lack of controllability

An operations manager in a factory where pharmaceutical drugs are produced was very unhappy at the composition of his management accounts, as responsible manager for a cost centre. His costs comprised both direct and indirect categories. Direct costs, such as raw materials and skilled labour were very much under his control, and over the years he had worked very hard to economize on such costs via increased operational efficiencies. However, overall this manager's cost centre accounts were generally viewed by more senior managers to be conveying poor performance, because overall his costs were higher than expected. But it was indirect costs, overheads, which created this overall adverse situation, much to the operation manager's annoyance. The bulk of overheads that were allocated to his cost centre were for use of corporate shared services, for example, IT, personnel and finance. The operations manager had no control whatsoever over the services charge allocated to his cost centre; the amount was calculated and allocated on a simple average basis by the company accountants. But, importantly, in his opinion the charge got nowhere near to reflecting *actual* use of such services within his cost centre. He was, in his opinion, being charged far more than was warranted by his cost centre's use of such services, and he suspected that other cost centres were getting an 'easy ride' by being charged less than should be allocated to them. However, the approach taken was designed and controlled by the central accountants, and the operations manager had little choice but to continue with what to him seemed an unfair way of accounting.

Source: based on author's own research; the broader case study from which this particular issue is taken was published in Burns and Baldvinsdottir (2005).

Exercise

What could have been done to try to alleviate the problems and grievances which the operations manager had? Would what you are suggesting be an easy and complete solution, or would there be other issues and potential problems to address?

Alignment

As well as conveying how successfully (or not) a responsible party has performed against targets, performance measures should also be set in a way that they motivate those parties to act in the best interests of the organization as a whole. When performance measures are tied to rewards, it should probably not come as any surprise that responsible parties go about their work in ways that will hopefully maximize their personal reward. So, for this reason in particular, it is imperative that any performance measure is also intrinsically linked to the achievement of organizational goals. Without such provisions, there is always a possibility of dysfunctional behaviour which ultimately damages organization goals.

Groups

Some performance measures within organizations will focus on the results of group actions, rather than the action of individuals which can be more easily isolated. Where this is the case, organizations will need to put in place certain controls that the performance measures roughly reflect the average effort and input of all group members. What an organization should avoid most of all is the potential for certain group members to dodge their responsibilities within the team effort. Control mechanisms such as peer evaluation, as well as team ethic and/or peer pressure can sometimes help, but they will never guarantee a solution. This is an important and usually quite difficult aspect of designing performance measurement systems.

Culture

Differences in culture can have an impact on how particular performance measures can be effective. This is because people's behaviour and reactions to particular measures will differ according to their cultural background. Culture can comprise an amalgam of many things, such as religious beliefs, economic history and language. One illustration might be the much written about group orientation in Japan. That is, all other things being equal, one might expect that it would be less difficult or less confrontational to implement group-based performance measures in a Japanese organization than it might be in much of the western world where individualism tends to dominate. This type of conundrum can become a particularly challenging task for those designing a suite of performance measures in a multinational organization which has subsidiaries spread all over the world.

Performance management

What is performance management?

The more specific and narrower issue of performance measurement has received a considerable amount of attention over many decades, in both practice and among academic scholars, with focus being especially directed at: (1) measuring individuals' performance and rewards, and (2) concentrating on a wider set of performance measures (but with emphasis still on measurement per se). Some academic scholars have called for a broadening of this 'measurement' perspective to explicitly look at the broader issues underpinning the *management* of performance (Broadbent and Laughlin, 2009; Ferreira and Otley, 2009; Fitzgerald et al., 1991; Otley, 1999), which incorporates performance measurement but also a whole lot more.

In a seminal piece, Otley (1999) warned against what he viewed as being overemphasis on performance measurement in organizations at that time and stressed the more important focus to maintain is performance management. In a similar vein, Broadbent and Laughlin called for more research attention to be given to 'ex ante performance management as opposed to ex post performance measurement' (2009, p. 283). Performance management systems, they argued 'are concerned with defining, controlling and managing both the achievement of outcomes or ends *as well as* the means used to achieve these results at a societal and organizational, rather than individual, level' (ibid. original emphasis).

Elements of performance management

The building blocks of performance management can be centred on asking three questions relating to the strategic objectives of an organization (Fitzgerald, 2007, p. 228), as follows:

- What *dimensions* of performance does the organization seek to develop?
- How will appropriate *targets* be set?
- What *rewards* and/or penalties will be associated with achievement of performance standards?

Fundamentally the 'dimensions' aspect of the performance measurement tool will be shaped by whether an organization adopts a shareholder or a stakeholder approach, as discussed earlier, or possibly a combination of both. If the former, then dimension will focus on a relatively small number of financial-oriented performance measures. Whereas, if the latter, an organization's dimension will encompass a variety of key non-financial performance measures alongside the financials. This, however, is not intended to give the impression that establishing an organization's dimension is a simple process involving, say, a choice between two alternative extremes. Rather, the choice of dimension is organization and context specific, may involve a choice somewhere between the extremes, and might change over time in the same organization. It is likely to be a complex and difficult ongoing task that involves managers understanding and learning what aspects of business activities are particularly key for attaining strategic goals, how we might 'best' measure such activities.

Designing performance management systems

Once an organization has decided which measures are believed to be key for continuous monitoring of achievement against strategic objectives, it next has to establish appropriate targets for each of these key measures. Fitzgerald (2007) argues that establishing targets involves considering who sets the targets (that is, ownership), the level at which such targets should be set (that is, achievability) and whether the respective targets provide a means to make comparisons across different responsible units (that is, equity).

Ownership

When designing a performance management system, an important consideration to take into account is whether managers should impose targets on their subordinates, or whether those who are charged with delivering the performance should themselves participate in setting the targets. The assumed advantages of subject participation in target setting include more likely acceptance of the targets and standards set and a likely reduction in dysfunctional (self-interested) behaviour owing to a greater feeling of ownership of the targets. On the other hand, there needs to be caution against participants influencing targets which are set at too easy a standard, thus allowing for a slack and an 'easy life'. Continual review and feedback between targets and their delivery (or not) should reduce any such occurrences.

Achievability

A considerable challenge faced by managers is the level at which targets should be set; it is a case of trying to find a balance between (1) motivating and rewarding employees to achieve high levels of performance, and (2) demotivating employees through setting unrealistic and impossible-to-attain targets. In trying to reach a sensible (motivational, but not unrealistic) set of performance targets, managers might do worse than to look back at previous achievements, and also to benchmark against known performance metrics in similar organizations. For example, a large global organization can make comparisons across its different subsidiary units, albeit taking into account any significant local contextual differences. It is also quite common for competitors in the same industries to share such information as performance metrics.

Equity

Finally, in setting performance targets, an organization should consider comparability or equity across different responsible units, in particular to ensure that a particular target does not open up unfair advantages to some units compared with others. An obvious example might be to not impose the same revenues targets on an established subsidiary organization which operates in an established and vibrant market as a new subsidiary setting out in new markets. Such a scenario might be a situation where managers choose to supplement their financial measures with other non-financial measures, but also draw on subjective opinion and judgement.

Otley's framework of performance management

Recent decades have seen considerable progress made in terms of broadening our understanding of performance management in its wider organizational and social contexts. Otley's work, in particular, has been influential in this respect (Ferreira and Otley, 2005, 2009; Otley, 1999). In his 2005 paper (with Ferreira), Otley sets out a framework for conceptualizing performance management which is premised on 12 questions that should be asked in relation to the design and nature of a performance management system (see also Broadbent and Laughlin, 2009). Otley's main argument is that empirically discovering answers to these 12 questions will present pointers and insight for the design of a performance management system. His first eight questions relate to more functional or design-related matters and the last four relate more to cultural and contextual issues which are assumed to have an influence on the nature of a particular organization's performance management. Otley's 12 questions are reproduced in Exhibit 16.1.

1) What is the vision and mission of the organization and how is this brought to the attention of managers and employees?

2) What are the key factors that are believed to be central to the organization's overall future success?

3) What strategies and plans has the organization adopted and what are the processes and activities that it has decided will be required for it to ensure its success?

4) What is the organization structure and what impact does it have on the design and use of the performance management and control system? How does it influence, and is influenced by, the process of strategy implementation?

5) What are the organization's key performance measures deriving from its key objectives, key success factors, and strategies and plans? How does the organization go about assessing and measuring its success in achieving them?

6) What level of performance does the organization need to achieve in each of the areas defined in the above questions, and how does it go about setting appropriate performance targets for them?

7) What processes does the organization use for evaluating individual, group and organizational performance? How important is formal and informal information on these processes? What are the consequences of the performance evaluation processes used?

8) What rewards, both financial and non-financial, will managers and other employees gain by achieving performance targets? Or, conversely, what penalties will they suffer by failing to achieve them?

9) What specific feedback and feed-forward information flows has the organization devised for itself? What sort of information flows have been created for monitoring current performance and bringing about adaptation of current behaviour? What types of feedforward information flows (if any) have been formulated to enable the organization to learn from its experience, to generate new ideas and to recreate strategies and plans?

10) What type of use is given to feedback and feedforward information flows and to the various control mechanisms in place? Is use predominantly diagnostic, interactive, or a combination of both?

11) How has the performance management and control system changed in the light of the change dynamics of the organization and of its environment? What changes have occurred at the level of those systems in anticipation or response to such stimuli?

12) How strong and coherent are the links between the components of the performance management and control system (as denoted by the above 11 questions?

Exhibit 16.1: Twelve key questions to ask when designing a performance management system
Source: Ferreira and Otley (2009).

Roles of management accountants in performance management

It is not unreasonable to suggest that performance *management* (as opposed to just performance measurement) is one of the most, if not *the* most important aspects of tomorrow's roles for management accountants. This is because performance management gets to the heart of an organization's machinery. More specifically it aims to steer an organization (and all its interlinking activities, people, processes, and so on) in a direction which aligns to strategic objectives, but which is also subject to moveable contexts surrounding the organization and its people. As Broadbent and Laughlin (2009, p. 291) stated, 'the complexity of context plays a major part in [performance management systems] design', and they added that context will also impact how organizations will approach the matters highlighted in the more functional questions (1 to 8) of Exhibit 16.1.

Performance management encompasses many aspects of organizational life, and to work well it needs reliable information that can be communicated far and wide, and at various levels of seniority. It requires piecing together and connecting different parts of this organizational life – for example, how does the marketing process interlink with the production process, is the R&D department focusing on product development that is aligned to strategic objectives, and so on?

Performance management is much more than measurements per se. It is about making the measurements 'work'; they should inform decisions and actions which promise to improve organizational performance. This challenging task is something that tomorrow's management accountants need to be equipped for. But even that will not be enough because, as we have highlighted at several junctures already in this textbook, designing and implementing new performance management systems go far beyond the technical aspects. Indeed, any change implementation programme such as this will be rife with at least potential for behavioural and organizational difficulties, including challenges in terms of culture, the embedded present or legacy systems, and norm behavioural patterns.

Performance management promises to be an area of organizational activity that will remain important in future years, and it presents a significant opportunity for those management accountants who wish to engage in it. But there will be major challenges ahead. Apart from those already mentioned above, tomorrow's organizations will be subject to constant change and new circumstances, and tools and techniques will likely develop further (some may appear, some disappear, some reappear in new forms). Also, as has already been said, while on the face of it management accountants would seem to have a 'natural' leaning towards overseeing a performance management system, they will in some organizations probably face competition from other professionals (for example, human resources) who themselves claim 'ownership rights' in this area – see Exhibit 16.2.

The following is extracted from the web pages of the Chartered Institute of Personnel and Development (CIPD), a professional body for employees in human resource/personnel vocations. Connection to, and overlap with, our discussion in this chapter, in relation to performance management, should be fairly obvious:

What is performance management?

Fully realized, performance management is a holistic process bringing together many of the elements that make up the successful practice of people management including, in particular, learning and development. But for this very reason, it is complex and capable of being misunderstood.

[...] performance management should be:

- **Strategic** – it is about broad issues and long-term goals

- **Integrated** – it should link various aspects of the business, people management, individuals and teams

Performance management should incorporate:

- **Performance improvement** – throughout the organization, in respect of individual, team and organizational effectiveness

- **Development** – unless there is continuous development of individuals and teams, performance will not improve

- **Managing behaviour** – ensuring that individuals are encouraged to behave in a way that allows and fosters better working relationships

Exhibit 16.2: Human Resource's approach to performance management

Source: web pages of the Chartered Institute of Personnel and Development (CIPD).

There is little doubt that management accountants have potentially significant roles to play in an organization's performance management. They must however be alert to the fact that performance management – its concepts, tools and most of all its *language* – thrive in other parts of most organizations. And, to an extent, management accountants should be alert to the need to be involved in (and lead?) the performance management process. Ultimately, long-run financial performance is critical for any organization, whether this is making economic profit in commercial enterprises or maintaining a reasonable surplus or break-even in public sector organizations, and management accountants can be the overseers of ensuring that such aims are reached.

Notwithstanding that long-run financial achievement is likely the most important concern of all organizations, the performance management process of today's organizations reaches far and wide – for example, operational efficiency, research and development, social and environmental impact, employee well-being and personal development. The monitoring, (re-)evaluation and ongoing management of performance also occurs at different levels. For example, performance management can be at the level of individuals, groups, business units, and more. But it is their involvement and concern with long-term organizational economic performance which suggests that management accountants should be at the helm in performance management.

Chapter summary

Performance measurement, extended to performance management, is an essential tool – a philosophy even – for tomorrow's organizations. It is an aspect of organizational life that management accounting information, and management accountants, have much to contribute towards. Broadbent and Laughlin sum up its importance succinctly:

> *any (performance management system) is based on knowing whether its current strategies are achieving their intentions in organisations or parts of organisations. Constant, up-to-date accountability information, not necessarily through formal reports, is vital to allow this judgement to be made. This intelligence is essential to know whether (performance management systems) strategies are working or whether they need to be changed. (2009, p. 292)*

Key terms

Centralized Where responsibility rests mainly with senior management at the higher levels of an organization's hierarchical structure (p. 403)

Cost (or expense) centres Responsibility centres where the manager has accountability against the costs which he or she has control over (p. 404)

Decentralized Where responsibility and accountability to one's own actions and decisions is passed out, downwards and outwards, from senior management (p. 403)

Discretionary expense centre Where outputs cannot be measured in financial terms, and where there is difficulty in pinning down any obvious relationship between inputs (that is, resource consumption) and outputs (p. 404)

Investment centres Where the manager has all the responsibility assigned to a profit centre (that is, sales revenues and costs) but also responsibility for working capital and capital investment decisions (p. 405)

Performance management A process of not just measuring an organization's performance, but also continually (re)designing, monitoring and acting upon such measures (p. 400)

Performance measurement Seeing how an organization is doing, in comparison to its aims and targets (p. 400)

Profit centres Where managers are responsible for both revenues and costs (p. 404)

Residual income An approach to performance measurement which holds that all measures of profit or surplus should take into account the cost of capital employed to generate it (p. 401)

Responsibility accounting A process whereby the managers of subunits within an organization are assigned certain responsibility, and their performance against such responsibility (p. 403)

Revenue centres Responsibility centres where managers are accountable to the financial outputs associated with generating sales (or, more specifically, sales revenues) (p. 403)

Rewards Benefits which are aligned to performance, such as bonuses (p. 405)

Shareholder approach Argues that financial performance measurement remains the most important measurement within organizations (p. 401)

Stakeholder approach Advocates that organizations adopt sufficient non-financial performance measures to supplement any use of financial measures (p. 401)

Standard cost centre Where outputs of production are known and can be measured in financial terms, and the quantity of inputs necessary for producing one unit of output are also known (p. 404)

Review questions · · · · · · · · · · · · · connect · · ·

| Level of difficulty: | BASIC | INTERMEDIATE | ADVANCED |

16.1 What is performance measurement? [LO1]

16.2 Define a 'shareholder approach' to performance measurement. [LO2]

16.3 Define a 'stakeholder approach' to performance measurement. [LO2]

16.4 Explain and contrast the differences between centralization and decentralization. [LO4]

16.5 What is performance management? [LO9]

16.6 Define responsibility accounting and recite the four main responsibility centres that an organization might have. [LO3]

Group discussion and activity questions · · · · · · · ·

16.7 What is the purpose of performance measurement? [LO1, LO7]

16.8 Which is most appropriate for (which of) today's organizations – the shareholder or stakeholder approach? [LO1, LO2]

16.9 If you were CEO of a multinational electronics company, with many subsidiaries all over the world, would you opt for centralization or decentralization? Explain your choice. [LO4]

Exercises · · · · · · · · · · · · · · · · connect · · ·

E16.1 **Different approaches to performance measurement [LO2]**

Fill in the missing word:

The 'stakeholder approach' argues that _____ performance measurement remains the most important measurement within organizations.

E16.2 **Approaches towards performance measurement [LO2]**

Which of the following describes a performance measurement approach where all measures of profit or surplus should take into account the cost of capital employed to generate it?

A) Discounted value?

B) Net profit?

C) Residual income?

D) % Capital payback?

E16.3 **Centralization versus decentralization [LO4]**

Where responsibility remains largely with a small group of very senior people, we would refer to this as a relatively *decentralized* organization: true or false?

E16.4 **Performance measurement versus performance management [LO1, LO9]**

Describe the differences between performance measurement and performance management.

E16.5 **Decentralization [LO2, LO4, LO6]**

What are the relative advantages and disadvantages of decentralization?

E16.6 **Rewards [LO5]**

You are Chairman of a real estate business in Spain. What rewards system aside of an agreed minimum salary would you establish for your realtors, and why?

E16.7 **Accountants' roles [LO8]**

What do you think are the main roles (if any) of management accountants in the future with respect to performance measurement *and* management?

Case study problem ● ● ● ● ● ● ● ● ● connect ● ● ● ●

C16.1 **Traffic-light systems at Dundee University [LO1, LO2, LO6, LO7]**

In 2006, Dundee University implemented a traffic-lights system to plan, measure and monitor its performance in key organizational areas, mostly because at that time the university (and the Scottish higher education sector generally) was facing some extremely tough economic conditions, and the general management opinion was that this particular university needed to undertake a thorough investigation into its strategic goals.

The traffic-lights system was quite simple and fairly 'static', comprising less than 10 key performance indicators, measured across the 13 different academic schools. These measures included such things as research grant income, financial surplus, student employability and staff–student ratios. When a particular measure was of no concern to managers, it would be allocated a green traffic light in the management report. If a particular measure warranted some discussion and further monitoring, but no investigation, it was given an amber colour. And, if a particular measure caused concern and warranted some investigation and action, a red traffic light was given.

If desired, these measures could be broken down further in terms of their overall composition, for example across individual academic departments. But this did not happen, since the main purpose of the traffic-lights system was to alert senior university managers to business areas that were potentially problematic. The traffic-lights system soon became an inherent feature of senior management meetings and began to inform multiple key decisions, including staffing decisions and investment in new buildings. Thus, the traffic-lights system was an extremely powerful management accounting tool that went beyond performance measurement per se. It provided a new way of seeing the organization, illuminating aspects that may previously have been suspected but were now quantified, and most of all it was a significant driver of change in an environment that was normally characterized by stability and inertia. It helped ignite and facilitate some key alterations in the way the university was managed and structured. Interestingly, the university accountants had minimal connection to this powerful tool; the traffic-lights system was designed by a professor of engineering!

Source: based on author's own research.

Required:

Think of the university/college where you are studying and/or your workplace, and answer the following:

a) If you were asked to identify 10 key measures which need to be monitored, what would they be, and why?

b) What is the problem with simply measuring key performance targets in a rather static (say, annual) way such as in the example above, particularly for fast-moving organizations which are exposed to significant external change?

c) Identify five key performance measures for universities in the next five years, and explain your choice?

Recommended reading

- Broadbent, J. and R. Laughlin (2009) 'Performance management systems: a conceptual model', *Management Accounting Research*, 20, pp. 283–95.

This paper presents a conceptual framework for the design of performance management systems (PMS). It challenges the underlying philosophical assumptions of traditional and dominant PMS design, and offers alternative design principles which are underpinned by assumptions of a more encompassing and highly communicative approach to design.

- CIMA/CGMA (2012) 'Strategic performance management in the public sector', a research report by CIMA/CGMA, January.

An interesting summary of the varied performance management-related challenges facing public sector organizations.

- CIMA/CGMA (2012) 'Performance measurement and management control in non-profit organizations', a research report by CIMA/CGMA, May.

An insightful discussion of challenges for non-profit organizations, in relation to the design and implementation of performance measurement and management control systems.

- Ferreira, A. and Otley, D. (2009) 'The design and use of management control systems: an extended framework for analysis', *Management Accounting Research*, 20, pp. 263–82.

Building on an earlier paper in 2005, this is an extended framework for conceptualizing and informing the design of management control systems.

- Fitzgerald, L. (2007) 'Performance measurement', in T. Hopper, D. Northcott and R. Scapens (eds), *Issues in Management Accounting*, 3rd edn, Harrow: FT/Prentice Hall.

An interesting overview of the two main approaches to performance measurement, shareholder and stakeholder approaches respectively, since the move away from a purely historical financial performance measurement approach in the late 1980s.

References

ter Bogt, H. J. and R. W. Scapens (2012) 'Performance management in universities: effects of the transition to more quantitative measurement systems', *European Accounting Review*, 21(3), pp. 451–97.

Bourguignon, A. (2004) 'The American balanced scorecard versus the French tableau de bord: the ideological dimension', *Management Accounting Research*, 15(2), pp. 107–34.

Broadbent, J. and R. Laughlin (2009) 'Performance management systems: a conceptual model', *Management Accounting Research*, 20, pp. 283–95.

Burns, J. and G. Baldvinsdottir (2005) 'An institutional perspective of accountants' new roles – the interplay of contradictions and praxis', *European Accounting Review*, 14(4), pp. 725–57.

Ferreira, A. and D. Otley (2005) 'The design and use of management control systems: an extended framework for analysis', AAA Management Accounting Section 2006 meeting paper. Available at SSRN: http://ssrn.com/abstract=682984 (NB. A later but changed version of this paper was published in *Management Accounting Research*, 2009, 20(4), pp. 263–82).

Ferreira, A. and Otley, D. (2009) 'The design and use of management control systems: an extended framework for analysis', *Management Accounting Research*, 20(4), pp. 263–82.

Fitzgerald, L. (2007) 'Performance measurement', in T. Hopper, D. Northcott and R. Scapens (eds), *Issues in Management Accounting*, 3rd edn, Harrow: FT/Prentice Hall.

Fitzgerald, L., R. Johnston, T. J. Brignall, R. Sivestro and C. Coss (1991) *Performance Measurement in Service Businesses*, London: CIMA.

Kaplan, R. S. and D. P. Norton (1992) 'The balanced scorecard – measures that drive performance', *Harvard Business Review*, 70, pp. 71–9.

Neely, A. and C. Adams (2001) 'The performance prism perspective', *Journal of Cost Management*, 15, pp. 7–15.

Otley, D. (1999) 'Performance management: a framework for management control systems research', *Management Accounting Research*, 10(4), pp. 363–82.

Online
LearningCentre

When you have read this chapter

Log on to the Online Learning Centre at **www.mcgraw-hill.co.uk/textbooks/burns** to explore chapter-by-chapter test questions, links and further online study tools for Management Accounting.

CHAPTER 17

ACCOUNTING FOR STRATEGIC MANAGEMENT

Chapter outline

- Organizational strategy

- Strategic management accounting

- The balanced scorecard

- Roles of management accountants in accounting for strategic management

Learning outcomes

On completion of this chapter, students will be able to:

LO1 Appreciate the organizational necessity, and difficulty, in being 'strategic'

LO2 Explain how strategizing involves a holistic, integrated and feed-forward orientation

LO3 Describe some of the key components (tools and techniques) comprising 'strategic management accounting'

LO4 Describe the core elements of a balanced scorecard

LO5 Describe the roles for management accountants in accounting for strategic management

LO6 Critically appraise the balanced scorecard in its aims and achievements

Introduction

Much of the prior content of this textbook has described various tools and techniques of management accounting which assist an organization to undertake short-term planning, and monitor and control its activities in a fairly static manner. But, nowadays organizations need to be strategic, and in this chapter we will consider the role(s) of management accounting in assisting an organization to maintain alignment between its operational activities and daily decision-making processes, on the one hand, and long-term strategic goals, on the other. The chapter begins with a brief exploration of what we mean by 'strategy' and what we mean by being 'strategic'. Next, we describe what constitutes so-called strategic management accounting, a collection of tools and techniques which some have claimed together represent management accounting's main contribution to the organizational endeavour of aligning decisions and actions with strategic goals. The remainder of this chapter is then to a large extent devoted to critical consideration of probably the most enduring of strategy-facing management accounting tools, the balanced scorecard.

Organizational strategy

What is strategy?

A **strategy** is some form of grand scheme or plan which sets out a vision or aim for where an organization wants to be in the longer term. Being **strategic** is the ongoing process of endeavouring to achieve an organization's strategy. Managers in all organizations must be strategic, when faced with the complex, fast-moving, often volatile and unpredictable environments in which they operate. We say that they engage in a complex process of **strategic management**, and management accounting is one of the important sources, though by no means the only source, of information produced and used by managers to make decisions and subsequently steer their organization in preferred directions.

Being strategic in an organization is about establishing the aims and goals of an organization, planning and making decisions on how to achieve such aims, monitor performance against the aims along the way and take action when necessary to ensure realignment to these aims. A useful management (accounting or other) tool for steering an organization in its strategic direction might offer the following:

- A tool or technique for when an organization appears to be on course to achieve its strategic aims, that information can be trusted as reliable and accurate, things can be learned from the past experiences and pointers can be gleaned as to areas which might need some attention, to ensure that such achievements are reached.

- A tool or technique for when an organization appears to be 'off course' in respect of its strategic goals, that things can again be learned so as to make better and more informed decisions in the future, but also that pointers will be available to guide managers towards decisions that will reinstate strategic aims.

In so doing, managers will be taking into account significant alterations to both internal (organization-specific) and external factors which impact the context in which organizational goals have been established. This process of ongoing monitoring and realignment is nowadays cumulative and open-ended for most organizations. Being strategic, that is, engaging in strategic management and all that this entails in terms of gathering and using management information, is not a static phenomena but rather a movable process, necessarily changeable and adaptable so as to accommodate the fast- and frequent-changing environment in which organizations operate.

All organizations need to be strategic – not just commercial and profit-seeking entities. There are many reasons why organizations might need to make changes to bring things back in line with strategic goals. For example, a local government will likely need to take a close look at its committed services to the local community when it has been hit with a worse-than-expected winter during which there has been far greater than planned expenditure on such things as salt for melting ice and snow on the roads.

17.1: Management Accounting in Practice

Football after the Bosman ruling

In 1995, football underwent a revolutionary change when the European Court of Justice made a decision concerning the freedom of workers in the region, which effectively meant that restrictions had to be lifted for the transfer of football players between European teams. The ruling also meant that professional footballers in the European Union were allowed to move freely to another football club at the end of the term of contract with their present club. The *Bosman ruling* changed the face of the football industry immediately; all football clubs became governed by the new ruling, and there was no chance to resist or reverse the decision. As a consequence, *all football clubs were forced to rethink their strategies*, with massive ramifications for many, but especially the larger clubs in Europe. The context within which all football clubs' strategies had been devised, was completely overhauled by a new ruling imposed upon the game. New strategic aims would surface (some no doubt were better than others), and management accounting would need to be adapted to provide the business and sports managers at a football club with useful information for decision making.

Examples of the types of changes that arose from the Bosman ruling (and, by implication, the types of impact these changes had on the required managerial information set, hence on management accounting) include:

●   The players' market in the European football industry opened up significantly – the pool from which clubs could seek and acquire the skills of new football talent had increased markedly. So, for example, this then ignited expansion (and increased costs) of the scouting systems, changes in the cultural backgrounds of players in squads (again, with corresponding increase in costs of additional support for such players).

●   Footballers' agents were now much more influential and powerful, since they negotiate new or extended contracts on behalf of the footballers. Clubs would need to plan for increased costs in relation to new contracts, player-transfers, and so on, due to the frequently excessive fees which these agents would demand.

Source: adapted from http://www.bosmanruling.co.uk/.

Exercise

The above described a situation where significant external changes caused a whole raft of revolutionary changes to an entire industry (football), with inevitable consequences to ways of working and a need to adapt the information available to business managers. Consider how the following scenarios might impact the strategic direction of an organization, and the potential impact that such strategic change might have on management accounting and the role of management accountants:

1)   A state-run postal service is deregulated, and the industry is opened up to private-sector providers who now compete with the national provider.

2)   A famous Japanese baseball club has a disastrous season, both on and off the pitch. As a result there has been a sharp drop in attendances, and the main sponsor has not renewed its contract for next season.

3)   UK low-fare airlines have a shock when airport authorities impose a significant hike on their airport landing fees, but also the government raises flight taxes, so much so that the label 'low fare' is starting to lose its validity and credibility.

4)   As the owner of a small bakery shop in a village in the suburbs of Gothenburg (Sweden), you are worried that a large supermarket chain which has its own bakery is building a new store just 1 km away from your shop.

5)   You are an executive manager for a global charity. A starvation crisis has worsened in a country within the African continent. You are tasked with exploring the reasonableness to send aid, but your biggest problems are the remoteness of the worst-hit areas and a very severe war which is under way across the whole country.

Equally, there are many examples where, because of shifts in internal and/or external factors, an organization changes its strategic goals and aims (rather than changing its core actions to try to achieve the same goals). For example, commercial organizations will possibly downgrade their profitability goals when a global recession takes hold; some organizations might choose to continue in more or less the same (operational) way, doing 'what they do', but just on a smaller scale and expecting less profit than was planned before the recession began.

Cumulative strategy (strategizing)

When thinking about an organization being strategic it is important to think in a cumulative or processual way. Traditionally, many organizations would design a strategy (for example, a three- five- or 10-year strategy) and this would influence the 'strategy tool' for managers over the particular period adopted. Importantly, for many organizations in the past, such strategies would not change or be changed in the relevant period, and it is therefore not surprising that by the end of their term such strategies frequently bore only a sketchy resemblance to the real organizational situation.

Nowadays, static strategies are of limited use in most organizational settings, especially because the landscape for many organizations changes so quickly. In some cases the change is so radical and fast that a static strategy would become dated in a very short period of time. Thus, many of today's organizations will adopt a more fluid, adaptable and cumulative notion of strategy; indeed, managers nowadays will tend to be *strategic* rather than be designers of a strategy per se.

Being strategic is about continuously attempting to align an organization's internal capabilities with its external circumstances, such as customer/market opportunities, technological advance, economic conditions. In so doing, management accounting offers various tools and techniques that can assist managers to implement and monitor behaviour which is intended to work for the organizational goals. Internal capabilities in this respect means, for example, an organization's control systems, business processes and performance measurement systems.

Strategic management accounting

Strategic management accounting (SMA) is a term that has been assigned previously by some commentators to describe an amalgam of management accounting tools and techniques which, both individually and collectively, inform management decisions and assist managers to design, manage and steer their organization in the direction of **strategic intent**. The notion of 'strategic intent' in this respect is not a strategy per se. Rather, it represents a notion of cumulative strategizing in today's society (as described above); an organization's strategy nowadays can be continually recast, fluid and changeable over time (Hopwood, 2009).

Strategic management accounting emerged especially from calls in the 1980s and early 1990s for the creation of tools and techniques that were more suited to providing useful management information in the business environment of the time. Among the first in-print mentions of SMA were the seminal works of Michael Bromwich in the UK (Bromwich, 1990; Bromwich and Bhimani, 1994) and by advocates of so-called strategic cost management in the USA (Shank, 1989). **Strategic cost management** is the application of cost management tools and techniques which simultaneously aims to improve an organization's strategic position and reduce its costs.

To date there remains no overall framework for SMA; and there is no universally agreed definition (Langfield-Smith, 2008). Tools and techniques comprising SMA are labelled as such because they are viewed by their advocates as providing information about the design, implementation and ongoing management of organizational strategy. However, SMA is not a uniform concept – that is, its composition will differ across, and within, organizations. It will also likely differ and change over time for the same organization, driven by both internal and external factors. There is no one-size-fits-all template of SMA for organizations.

Past literature would suggest that SMA comprises tools and techniques that would offer the following to an organization:

- Information about an organization's main competitors
- Aligning accounting emphases with an organization's strategic positioning
- Exploiting cost-reduction opportunities across the value chain
- Cost driver and competitive advantage analysis
- Customer/marketing information.

Thus, specific management accounting tools and techniques that have been associated with SMA, and which have been discussed, or will be discussed, in more detail in this textbook, include: activity-based costing (see Chapter 6), the balanced scorecard (see below), target costing (see chapter 19) and life cycle costing (see chapter 19).

What is SMA becoming?

Much of what constitutes original SMA, at least in terms of individual tools and techniques, still exists in some of today's organizations, though in general its broader adoption seems to have been far less than its advocates had hoped for (see Langfield-Smith, 2008). Moreover, since the early days of SMA's inception, things have moved on, both within and outside organizations. However, despite its apparent lack of success in terms of adoption, there are definitely some more enduring aspects, in particular the balanced scorecard (see below). Strategic management accounting concerns information that assists in (re)inventing, (re)modelling, monitoring and managing the interplay between an organization's strategic intent and its actual performance. The discrepancy between intended (strategic aims) and actual (performance) over time is very real – the organizational environment is a fluid and dynamic scenario, not static. Moreover, this scenario of discrepancy between the intended and actual performance has potential to be opened up and managed, via internal and external forces. Some scholars have recently claimed that SMA should take its lead from strategic management (Nixon and Burns, 2012), whereby scholars and practitioners in the strategic management field continue to seek to bridge the strategy implementation 'gap', and SMA tools and techniques can remain one of the key pillars of support to foster this.

17.1: Management Accounting Insight

Strategizing for new product design and development – tensions and conflict

An important area for strategic management accounting is new product design and development (NPD&D), since such activity is paramount for mobilizing strategic intent over time. For many organizations today, NPD&D lies at the centre of an organization's ongoing battle against changing business landscapes and the continual strategizing that this entails.

An article by Nixon et al. (2012) describes the innovative approach which a premium-car manufacturer adopts in trying to manage the tension between the immediate and short-term costs and the eventual benefits of NPD&D. Without NPD&D such a business would soon fall behind its competitors (innovation in the car industry is rife at present, particularly with the race to design eco-cars). But, NPD&D is incredibly expensive, and must be managed by strict (financial and other) controls. The management accountant has a significant role to play in managing this conflict between creativity and a necessity to maintain short-run feasibility (including cash flow) and the achievement of *long-term* net value. Management accounting activities, it is argued play a significant role as a 'language' which binds all the constituent participants in the NPD&D process, including the car manufacturer, its customers and its suppliers.

Source: Nixon et al. (2012).

Exercise

Read the article* Nixon et al. (2012): 'Profitable new product design and development' (Technical Notes), *Financial Management* (CIMA), April, pp. 50–53.

a) What aspects (tools and techniques) of management accounting do you see being utilized in the NPD&D process?

b) Describe the roles which management accountants play in the NPD&D process?

c) How would you go about managing NPD&D in a premium-car manufacturer; can you think of different initiatives that might be worth considering?

A link to the article is available online at www.mcgraw-hill.co.uk/textbooks/burns.

The balanced scorecard

Its origins and purpose

As mentioned above, one particularly enduring management accounting tool that claims to assist managers to map out and achieve their strategic goals is the balanced scorecard. Given such impressive endurance, we shall now explore this tool in more detail.

As an integrated and holistic performance measurement system, a **balanced scorecard** is intended to communicate and steer an organization's journey through time. In so doing, it integrates financial measures with non-financial measures. Although financial measurement (profit, surplus, cost, cash) remains essential to all organizations in the long run, many would argue that an overemphasis on financials at the expense of non-financial performance measures can be detrimental. Frequently, though not always, improvement in non-financial aspects of organizational activity – for example, customer satisfaction, and product quality – can eventually lead to improvement in financial measures.

Elements and characteristics of a balanced scorecard

The origins of the balanced scorecard date back just over 20 years ago, grounded in the ideas of Robert Kaplan and David Norton (Kaplan and Norton, 1992, 1996). Partly related to calls around the early 1980s for a loosening of the domination of *financial* performance measurement within organizations at the time, as well as the short-termism which attached to such an approach, the balanced scorecard was launched as a holistic and integrated performance measurement tool which could assist managers to plan and conduct their business in a manner which aligns with an organization's strategic aims.

Being **holistic** we mean that a balanced scorecard adopts a broad perspective of business activity, across multiple functions and through different levels of organizational hierarchy. Traditionally, many organizations would plan, put into operation and monitor their performance, in strategic terms, via predominantly financially oriented measures. In recent times, organizations have increasingly focused on non-financial performance measures, alongside their financial indicators.

When we say that a balanced scorecard (BSC) is an **integrated** tool this means that any one particular perspective of organizational activity (for example, financial performance) is not to be viewed independently of alternative aspects of organizational activity (for example, customer related or impact on the environment). The future mindset in organizations is likely to embrace management tools that inform connecting decisions, rather than decision making for silos, such that all parts of an organization can be simultaneously planned for and monitored, and all moving in the same direction. This notion of enhanced communication and greater collective understanding of the workings of an organization, both within and across different business activities, all knitted together in a common strategic direction, is a key and distinguishing and conceptual feature of tools such as the balanced scorecard. However, such ambition in practice presents an incredible challenge that is not always achievable.

Designing a balanced scorecard

The BSC philosophy creates strategic focus by translating an organization's vision into operational objectives and performance measures covering four perspectives: (1) the financial perspective, (2) the customer perspective, (3) the internal business perspective and (4) the learning and growth perspective. The BSC is a strategic management technique for communicating and continually (re)assessing performance against strategic aims.

For each of the four perspectives, an organization is encouraged to identify the main *objectives* (not too many), then associated performance *measures*, *targets* and *initiatives* which aim to increase the chances of reaching such objectives, measures and targets. Exhibit 17.1 conveys, in diagrammatic form, what the balanced scorecard entails and how each of the perspectives (including objectives, measures, targets and initiatives) are connected to each other.

A 'perspective' in the balanced scorecard is usually designated more than one objective, and multiple performance measures are possible for each objective. However, it is usual for an

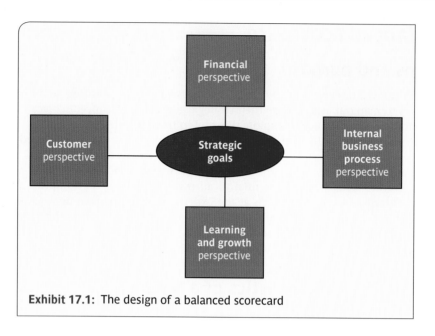

Exhibit 17.1: The design of a balanced scorecard

organization to limit the number of objectives and measures to a manageable number, prioritizing those which are believed to be most critical for strategic attainment, otherwise it could create a situation of informational paralysis.

Managers would normally prefer to have sight of a performance measurement system that has a reasonably small number of *key* objectives and measures for each perspective, and which at any point in time will (together) provide a useful spot check of their organization and its direction. Importantly though, the chosen 'critical' objectives and measures at any point in time can be changed to reflect external- and/or internal-driven strategic changes. We can now examine each of the four perspectives in more detail, all of which are summarized in Exhibit 17.2.

The financial perspective

The **financial perspective** of a BSC conveys the financial performance objectives of an organization, resulting from its strategy; it also conveys any financial impact from expected outcomes in the three other perspectives – a barometer of financial success. In the financial perspective, objectives might include such things as: (1) increased shareholder wealth, (2) lower costs of production and (3) growth. Then, performance measures need to be assigned to each of these objectives, for instance (and in relation to the objectives above): (1) percentage return on assets, (2) percentage cost per unit of production and (3) percentage increase in turnover. Respective targets could be: (1) 30 per cent return on assets, (2) 10 per cent decrease in unit costs of production and (3) 40 per cent rise in turnover. Finally, associated initiatives to promote achievement of the targets might include: (1) shifting emphasis away from loss-making and towards profit-making and high profit-margin products, (2) place restrictions on overtime hours worked and (3) invest in new online sales facilities.

The customer perspective

The **customer perspective** of a balanced scorecard focuses an organization on its markets and customers. There will an assumed link, hence 'integration', between elements of this perspective and any revenues-related elements of the financial perspective (above). That is, there is a built-in assumption that the achievement of customer perspective objectives would mean that an organization will reach its revenues (that is, part of the financial perspective) targets and objectives.

Objectives within the customer perspective might include: (1) increase in market share, (2) increase in customer satisfaction and (3) improved quality of customer-related services. Corresponding

Perspectives	Objectives	Measures	Targets	Initiatives
Financial	• Increased shareholder wealth • Lower costs of production • Growth	• % return on assets • % cost per unit of production • % increase in turnover	• 30% return on assets • 10% decrease in unit costs of production • 40% rise in turnover	• Emphasis shift from loss-making to high margin products • Restriction on overtime hours • Invest in new online sales facilities
Customer	• Increase in market share • Increase in customer satisfaction • Improved quality in customer services	• % market share • % customers in a survey who claim to be 100% satisfied • % product returns	• 20% increase in a particular market share • 99% of customers who claim to be 'fully satisfied' • < 5 products returned out of every 1000 sold	• Increase in advertising • Improved after-sales services • More personal one-to-one service
Internal business	• Increase in process efficiency • Decrease in process costs	• Decrease in throughput time • Decrease in average product costs	• 20% decrease in throughput time • 5% fall in average product costs	• Investigation into non-value-adding activities • Switch to cheaper raw materials
Learning and Growth	• Reduction in employee turnover • Improvements to the information systems	• % annual turnover of staff • Increase in total systems-literate staff	• 10% decrease in annual staff turnover • 30% increase in systems-literate staff	• New profit-related bonus scheme • New IT/systems training courses for staff

Exhibit 17.2: Illustrations of the detail in a balanced scorecard

performance measures to be assigned to these objectives could include, respectively: (1) percentage market share, (2) percentage of customers in a survey who claim to be '100 per cent satisfied' with an organization's product or service, and (3) percentage of product returns from customers. Targets could include: (1) a 20 per cent increase in a particular market share, (2) 99 per cent of customers who claim to be 'fully satisfied' and (3) less than five products returned out of every 1,000 products sold. Finally, possible initiatives associated with the customer perspective might be: (1) an increase in advertising, (2) better after-sales services and (3) more personal one-to-one service.

The internal business perspective

The **internal business perspective** captures the things which an organization must do well internally if it is to attain its strategic goals. In deciding which aspects to incorporate into the balanced scorecard, an organization should try to identify those internal processes which will improve the opportunity for positive results being reflected in the customer and financial perspectives. This, again, is another example of the *integration* philosophy which underpins the balanced scorecard.

In Kaplan and Norton's original works, they subdivide an organization's internal business process into three parts: (1) the innovation process, (2) the operations process, and (3) the post-sales service process. Together these three elements comprise what Kaplan and Norton called a **process value chain**.

The innovation process refers to how organizations identify: (1) new products or services to engage with, or (2) new markets and customers to attract. Therefore, the innovation element has a clear linkage to both the financial and customer perspectives. Typical performance measures for the innovation process could be: (1) percentage of total sales accounted for by newly launched products, and (2) percentage of total sales from a major new customer. The related targets could easily be based on a percentage increase in the performance measure, while possible initiatives could include: (1) bonus schemes for successful researchers and innovation teams, and (2) discounts on bulk-buying with the new customer.

The operations process refers to that part of the value chain which entails producing and delivering goods and services to an organization's customers. Again, there is an assumption here of linkage to both the financial and the customer perspectives. Objectives for this part of the internal business process perspective might include: (1) increase in process efficiency, and (2) decrease in process costs. Respective measures could be: (1) a decrease in throughput time, in other words the time taken for the conversion of raw materials into saleable products, and (2) a decrease in average product costs. The respective targets might be, for example: (1) a 20 per cent decrease in throughput time, and (2) a 5 per cent fall in average product costs. Finally, possible initiatives might include: (1) a thorough investigation into non-value-adding activities, and (2) switching to cheaper supplies of key raw materials.

The third and final sub-element of the internal business process perspective is the post-sales process, which highlights an organization's performance in relation to dealings with customers after products or services have been traded. Again, there is an assumed link here to the financial and customer perspectives of a balanced scorecard. Post-sales services include things like warranties and product repairs, defects and returns, and refunds. Setting objectives, as well as identifying measures, targets and initiatives for the post-sales process is similar to the operations process (above) in that such things generally revolve around increasing efficiency and/or decreasing costs in later stages of the value chain.

The learning and growth perspective

The final perspective of the balanced scorecard is the **learning and growth perspective**, which focuses an organization and its employees on continual learning and its resource capabilities. The main thrust of this particular perspective is ensuring that organizations continue to invest in their infrastructure (that is, people, systems and procedures) so as to nurture and maintain its ability to reach the objectives of the three other perspectives.

Objectives for the learning and growth perspective might include: (1) a reduction in employee turnover, and (2) improvement to the information systems. Related measures and targets could be: (1) percentage annual turnover of full-time staff (for example, 10 per cent decrease), and (2) an absolute increase in the number of employees who are information systems-literate. Respective initiatives might involve: (1) the introduction of new profit-related bonuses, and (2) the launching of IT/systems training courses for staff.

Features of a balanced scorecard

In this section we explore some of the underpinning assumptions and underlying mechanisms of a balanced scorecard, thereby illuminating some of its unique and defining characteristics.

Cause-and-effect relationships

Underpinning the balanced scorecard concept is a particularly key assumption that cause-and-effect relationships exist through and between the four different perspectives, ultimately impacting on the financial perspective. A cause-and-effect relationship defines where a particular outcome has occurred due to some other happenings. So, for example, if you were to prick a balloon with a pin, the balloon would pop. The cause-and-effect relationship flows from pricking with a pin (action) to the popping of the balloon (outcome). More relevant, organizations endeavour to identify cause-and-effect relationships between things that the organization can do, and beneficial outcomes as a result of such actions. It is important for an organization to recognize and incorporate such cause-and-effect relationships when designing a balanced scorecard; such endeavours will also strengthen the integrative nature of the tool which is designed.

A hypothetical example of cause-and-effect relationships could be as follows: organization XYZ invested in new information systems as well as staff training in these systems (that is, the learning and growth perspective), which considerably improved performance in respect of on-time deliveries to key customers (that is, the internal business process perspective). This improvement was positively received by existing customers, whose loyalty grew, became more widely known and brought in additional new customers (that is, the customer perspective). In turn, and over time, the increase in customer loyalty and the acquisition of new customers fed through to the achievement of significantly more sales and higher profitability (that is, the financial perspective).

By mapping out an organization's cause-and-effect relationships across the different perspectives, it has potential to make clearer some of the possible ways that managers might eventually influence financial outcomes. Moreover, in so doing, such an exercise highlights and particularly exposes which non-financial activities might (or might not) stand a reasonable chance of facilitating a positive financial effect. However, we stress that the recognition and establishment of valid and stable cause-and-effect relationships is an arduous task in any organization, and has been criticized by some notable commentators (for example, Nørreklit, 2000) as being risky and potentially misleading for decision making (see 'critiques' section, below).

Lag and lead indicators

Well designed balanced scorecards will comprise a mixture of both *outcome* measures (otherwise known as **lag indicators**) and *performance drivers* (otherwise known as **lead indicators**). An example of a lag indicator in the 'learning and growth' perspective for a firm of chartered accountants might be the number of newly qualified employees in a particular year, whereas a lead indicator for the same organization and in the same perspective might be the number of new graduates beginning their professional training in that same year.

Lag and lead indicators should be designed into all of a balanced scorecard's perspectives, thereby creating two-way cause-and-effect relationships within a particular perspective. But at the same time lag and lead indicators will also be connected vertically through and between different perspectives (as outlined above). In other words, the lag indicator in one perspective (for example, customer satisfaction in the customer perspective) can at the same time be assumed to represent a lead indicator for another perspective (for example, the financial perspective). This horizontal *and* vertical mix of connectedness among key performance indicators, if achievable, can be a very powerful tool for organizations.

Common attributes of balanced scorecards

There is, we contend, no perfect balanced scorecard, but there are some attributes that can be useful in some organizational situations (see below). One way to approach this situation is to begin with the balanced scorecard as just a concept, a platform of ideas on how to view your organizational activity, but be willing then to (re)adapt this model in a case-by-case manner and as changing circumstances demand for the same organization. However, as a useful 'starter kit' for designing a balanced scorecard, in any given organizational setting, it might be useful to check that:

- The BSC 'tells the story' of an organization's strategic intent by attempting to articulate a complexity of cause-and-effect relationships (but, see the 'critique' section below).

- A scorecard is changeable over time, and adaptable to shifting internal and external circumstances. Static performance measurement systems will over time lose their validity and usefulness, as the organizational and environmental contexts in which they operate will inevitably change, frequently at rapid pace.

- It provides a comprehensive framework for translating strategic goals into a coherent set of performance measures, while limiting such measures to a manageable number. As stated at several junctures already, it is important also to arrive at reliable interconnections between such measures and their underpinning assumptions.

- It brings together a focus on performance-versus-goals in different areas of activity in one holistic report that not only serves as communication to various external stakeholders but also provides invaluable information and knowledge for managerial decision making.

A range of possibilities

We have focused here on the original concept of a balanced scorecard as set out in Kaplan and Norton's early writings. But it is important to appreciate that in practice many organizations will choose to develop their bespoke version of an integrated holistic performance measurement tool. In so doing, the tools in some organizations might convey quite different characteristics to those described in this subsection of the book. For instance, whereas it would possibly be fair to treat the model (above) as one that aligns more to a profit-seeking organization, it would be quite reasonable to expect a balanced scorecard of noticeable difference in a public-sector organization, whose primary objective is to break even or achieve a capped level of surplus.

Other organizations have also extended the make-up of an original balanced scorecard, beyond the four perspectives described above. For example, Tesco plc (a large UK retail organization) employs a **corporate steering wheel** which has a fifth perspective for social and environmental-related performance (see Case Study Problem C17.1). Another potential perspective might be a focus on business risk, and its management over time. However, there is always a danger of over-complicating an organization's balanced scorecard, for instance with too many perspectives or too many objectives or measures.

Positive aspects of a balanced scorecard

A potential mistake is assuming that a *balanced* performance management tool can be captured simply by supplementing traditional financial measures with non-financials relating to performance in such areas as customer satisfaction, product quality and staff training. This is not so, however; the impact of a balanced scorecard, conceptually at least, is that cause-and-effect relationships between performance outcomes and their drivers are brought to life. A mapping is established that allows managers to 'see' what business areas need to be done particularly well (improved, and so on) in order to reach organizational goals (for example, financial success) in the future. For this reason in particular, some scholars have claimed that a balanced scorecard constitutes a feed-forward control system (de Haas and Kleingeld, 1999).

The design of a balanced scorecard is such that it aims to highlight the drivers of long-range achievement for an organization. It translates organizational strategy into meaningful measures which further augment communication of strategy among managers and workers.

A balanced scorecard potentially brings together different aspects of what makes an organization tick, and what might help an organization achieve its goals, into just one summary report. Multiple dimensions that can assist an organization to reach its goals will normally feature somewhere in its balanced scorecard – for example, it is common to see objectives and measures that relate to new product development, customer satisfaction, employee well-being and increased production efficiency. Before the balanced scorecard concept emerged, such aspects of organizational activity (plus others) would have likely been analysed, reported and acted upon in many organizations, but possibly independently of each other. The benefit of a balanced scorecard is that it captures all such aspects in one place and, importantly, it illuminates the interconnections and potential knock-on effects of such different aspects, as part of the epic but ongoing journey towards strategic goals.

Another potential benefit of a balanced scorecard is that it avoids organizational strategy becoming merely a *manager's dream*. Through its interconnecting of different perspectives and focus for each perspective on objectives, measures, targets and initiatives, the balanced scorecard is a tool that guides managers from strategic aims into real practice (that is, monitoring, measuring, analysing, changing, and so on). The same visible interconnectedness in just one tool, or one report, also enhances the communication of the strategic goals across an organization.

Why has the balanced scorecard stood the test of time?

We began this chapter with a discussion of strategy and strategic management, and then moved on to describe some of the early forms of management accounting in this field. The concept of strategic management accounting emerged as an amalgam of particular tools and techniques, at least part of which reflected actual practices at the time. However, we suggested that an apparent failure in the endurance of SMA as a lead concept in organizations is that its advocates have yet to further develop SMA in a way that reflects subsequent and cumulative changes in practice. Indeed, several academic writers claim that over the past two decades there have been too many questionnaire surveys of the uptake of various tools and techniques associated with SMA, rather than more useful studies of why, how and with what consequences particular organizations actually implemented such tools (Langfield-Smith, 2008).

On the contrary, the tool known as a balanced scorecard has seemingly stood the test of time, and we should ask why this is so? Why has the balanced scorecard remained so popular (if not always in a positive way!), in both business practice and among academic researchers over the past two decades, when so many other 'strategic' management accounting tools have conveyed more fad-like qualities?

One reason has to be the significant machinery behind the balanced scorecard cause – for example, a continual upgrading and additional features, and promotion, via a stream of newsletters for the BSC Consortium and the Balanced Scorecard Institute, articles in the *Harvard Business Review* and new books every three or four years written by Kaplan and colleagues. So, the advocates and main proponents of the balanced scorecard have continually updated their original concept of the tool, to reflect changes in organizational practices which, in turn, tend to be responsive to changes in an organization's external environment. However, despite such ongoing development, the fundamental underpinnings of the original balanced scorecard remain intact, and these underpinnings have been on the receiving end of criticism. We will now explore this criticism.

Critique of the balanced scorecard

The balanced scorecard concept, to align organizational activity and information used for strategic goals, is an improvement on primarily short-term, financially oriented performance measurement practices that were once dominant. However, as we stated at the beginning of this chapter, there are also some health warnings that should come with a balanced scorecard (Nørreklit, 2000; Nørreklit et al., 2008), as we now explain in more detail.

Cause-and-effect relationships

The usefulness of a balanced scorecard comes especially from its potential to predict future financial performance via the measurement of key non-financial performance indicators. However, for this to be so, we must identify and then place *trust* in the various cause-and-effect relationships which an organization builds into its tool as representing the flow and connectivity of core activities which ultimately generate economic profits (or losses). Put another way, a fundamental but implicit assumption of the balanced scorecard concept is that financial performance measures can convey something about an organization's past performance, whereas non-financial performance measures represent the drivers of performance in the future (Kaplan and Norton, 1996).

However, an assumed relationship can sometimes be misleading, and as such can actually encourage poor decision making. For example, consider the customer perspective, for which we might think of customer satisfaction as being a lead indicator for financial success. But, customer satisfaction is only really a lead indicator for financial success if it relates to satisfied customers who are profitable, and who will remain as customers in the long term. A survey can convey impressive levels of satisfaction from customers who have been offered and accept price discounts or 'extras', meaning that overall the revenues generated from these customers are not as high as they would be under normal trading circumstances, and made worse when such customers blatantly intend a 'quick grab' at such opportunities but have no intention of remaining customers in the long term. In such situations we are likely to see happy customers but declining profitability. Conversely, customers who pay high prices, and who generate impressive profit margins, may for several reasons choose to remain as customers in the long run because, for example, they are contractually locked in over a particular period or they simply value the quality of the products. However, purely on grounds of the high prices they pay, such customers may indicate in a questionnaire survey that they are dissatisfied.

In summary, an organization needs to be extra careful when establishing its assumed cause-and-effect relationships; otherwise a balanced scorecard's ability to predict financial outcomes from different activities becomes seriously compromised, and thus the tool can become misleading and potentially damaging in strategic decision making.

Balancing the balance

It has been suggested already that to be manageable, particularly at the higher levels of an organization where it is used as a tool for strategic decision making, a balanced scorecard should not include too many performance indicators. However, those performance indicators that 'are' included in the scorecard likely command differences in their respective levels of importance. Furthermore, such relative differences can change over time.

So, for instance, one would expect that in more difficult economic times financial performance measures are likely to be regarded as relatively more important than in more comfortable economic times. In a similar fashion, we might reasonably expect (though not necessarily so!) that in financially 'flush' times, investment in learning and growth (for example, staff training, R&D) is assumed to be relatively more important and of higher priority than in difficult times.

The main point here is that there will inevitably be a need to appropriately communicate the relative importance of different key performance indicators, and which can change over time. In practice such decisions will shape and direct organizational focus and behaviour more towards certain aspects of its activities at the expense of primary focus on others. It is highly unlikely that at any one point in time a particular organization devotes equal levels of importance to its different perspectives. There are inevitably going to be trade-offs between the various perspectives (and associated objectives, measures, and so on).

Timelessness

Another reason to heed caution with a balanced scorecard is that there is an absence of any time dimension within the model. This becomes an issue when there are differences in the timing of the effects of various lead measures. In other words, lead outcomes will not occur at the same point in time. Timescales inherent to different perspectives will usually differ significantly; for example, initiatives relating to staff training (that is, the learning and growth perspective) might be possible to enact quite quickly, however their impact on financial improvements will take much longer.

Moreover, because measures in the financial perspective are assumed to be affected by a multitude of other measures, which in turn are likely to all differ in respect of timings, it might prove difficult in practice for managers to decipher the extent to which a particular non-financial performance lead indicator has 'had' an impact on financial performance, as distinct from the impact of other lead indicators.

Level confusion

Implicated within the balanced scorecard is a complex set of financial and non-financial performance measures which spread over multiple levels of an organizational hierarchy. That is, all balanced scorecards will comprise measures (also objectives, targets and initiatives) that are focused at the higher strategic decision-making level. Yet their 'connected' measures can rest primarily at lower operational levels of organizational activity, and these respective measures will not always be in synch or aligned. Senior strategic-level managers of an organization may become distanced and remote from the reality of day-to-day organizational activity, representing a potentially adverse gap in knowledge for when strategic-level measures are devised, implemented and monitored.

The balanced scorecard concept is about connecting all aspects of organizational activity, across functions but also journeying through different levels of the organizational hierarchy. It is important therefore that its designers and users are continually in touch with each others' levels of activities, preferably connected and communicated through the balanced scorecard mechanism itself. Such connectedness up and down the organizational hierarchy will also militate against distrust in someone else's measures and targets, as well as maintain a degree of sensibility and common sense in the constituent elements of the balanced scorecard being used.

Design problems

As has been argued already in this chapter, there is no 'best' or template way to design or implement a balanced scorecard or similar strategic performance measurement tools in an organization. Balanced scorecards are usually easier to conceptualize and design than to actually implement and use in practice.

There are examples, for instance, where organizations have genuine difficulty in attaining useful, accurate and timely information for some (especially non-financial) performance measures (see *Management Accounting in Practice 17.2*). As described above, organizations frequently experience difficulty in establishing precise, clear and useful cause-and-effect relationships. This, in turn, can undermine the aim to capture a representative and all-encompassing perspective of the range of organizational activities, as well as their interconnectedness.

17.2: Management Accounting in Practice

Using a balanced scorecard to promote responsible sourcing

An increasing number of organizations today attempt to be more responsible (that is, sustainable) in its sourcing of raw materials. A trip to any major supermarket, for example, could highlight the ways in which they attempt to show customers how they care for the way in which their products were made. One example would be how some leading supermarkets source tuna fish only from suppliers which adopt dolphin-friendly practice – a contentious issue that attracts league tables from the likes of Greenpeace (see http://www.greenpeace.org.uk/tunaleaguetable).

The expansion of free-range dairy products and fairtrade products such as coffee would also be examples of how lead supermarkets increasingly convey that they accept responsibility for how and where their supplies are produced.

Some organizations, including Novo-Nordisk (NN), a Danish pharmaceuticals company, use a balanced scorecard to promote responsible sourcing. Different suppliers are measured and graded in relation to each other according to this balanced scorecard, and Novo Nordisk's procurement personnel are assessed in respect of their performance in relation to suppliers they deal with. They also get bonuses depending on their ability to reach performance targets in the 'sourcing balanced scorecard'. The process of using a balanced scorecard tool for improving (responsible) sourcing has not been easy, however. One major problem has been obtaining the appropriate information from suppliers to then feed into the balanced scorecard. And, even when supplier information is received, it could be in a non-friendly format, untimely and needs to be trusted.

Source: author's own research and the corporate website http://novonordisk.com/sustainability/Responsible-business-practices/responsible-sourcing.asp.

Exercise

Can you think of other (probably less obvious) aspects of organizational activity where a balanced scorecard can be used to measure, incentivize and improve performance? For each aspect, suggest also where the organization might face problems (like the example above of obtaining appropriate information from outside parties) and how these problems might be overcome.

There is no doubt that organizations should attempt to design a performance measurement system that is (intended to be) strategic, integrated and holistic, and that a balanced scorecard as set out by Kaplan et al. is a good start for such purposes. However, in most cases off-the-shelf balanced scorecards will likely not be tailored for individual organizations – and will undoubtedly be very expensive!

It is unlikely that any generic balanced scorecards will neatly 'fit' any organization; organizations, and particularly the process of managing organizations, are far too complex for that to be so. We cite Nørreklit et al. to illustrate the complexities at play here, and in so doing again highlight the imperative needs for caution when (re)designing a balanced scorecard:

> *Kaplan and Norton (1996) liken its operation to a pilot flying a jet. The BSC provides a control panel that pilots can observe to make midcourse adjustments that affect the journey. But this does not do justice to the corporate manager's role. If only achieving good corporate results were as easy as 'pressing buttons' and 'pulling levers'. To achieve a planned result may require a circuitous route. To build a business, for example, it may be best to sell at low prices at first in order to gain market share and a favourable image. Raising prices to get better financial results may not be possible until later. In short, the BSC model does not fit all business circumstances. (2008, p. 66)*

While external parties such as consultants and other external advisers can provide useful guidance and assistance, strategic and holistic performance measurement systems can be mostly developed in-house by people who live and breathe an organization, and its (re)design and implementation should be an ongoing process. We sympathize with the views of Nørreklit et al. (2008) that a strategic performance measurement system should be treated as 'an explorative and iterative learning approach for management rather than the mechanical learning system that the BSC assumes' (p. 67). By this we are not necessarily criticizing the balanced scorecard per se, in fact we argue that conceptually it is a very powerful starting point for any organization to build its own strategic performance measurement system. But we are stressing the need to be alert to some of the potential shortcomings of a generic off-the-shelf package.

A useful balanced scorecard can be (re)designed partly, if not mostly, by local organizational participants who have maintained close proximity to the activities which are to be measured and who over time have developed a feel for how different activities are interlinked with each other, including less obvious or surprising relationships and their change over time. Managers build up beliefs about 'what makes the business tick' (Nørreklit et al., 2008, p. 67) and how different activities relate to each other to achieve potential outcomes across different perspectives. This accumulation of organizational knowledge and learning takes time, but is the most valuable attribute that any balanced scorecard can have if it is to accurately capture the organizational story.

Also, once designed, the designers and users of a balanced scorecard must continually review, and adjust where necessary, its make-up to reflect any changes that have occurred. For example, there may be reason to question the continued validity of a particular cause-and-effect relationship, or there may be reasons to revisit the trade-off and prioritization among the different perspectives.

Roles of management accountants in accounting for strategic management

In tomorrow's organizational environment, being strategic is a given, an essential part of both routine *and* ad hoc activity. With the intensification of global competition and exponential technological capacity, in particular, being strategic will increase in importance. Management accounting has, in recent decades, contributed towards this organizational need – it has offered various tools and techniques that extend the information kit and thereby assist managers to plan, monitor and (re) adjust its actions so that strategic goals will be met. In this respect the balanced scorecard, a tool which appeals to managers because it captures the notion of holistic and integrated management, with a forward-oriented perspective, is the most enduring.

Until now, management accountants have generally been the leaders and drivers behind such developments. Their primary role is, after all, to provide useful information for managers. The balanced scorecard concept emerged from leading management accounting scholars in Harvard (USA), and has been especially promoted via academic and professional course books and textbooks of management accounting. A management tool such as a balanced scorecard can become an overriding 'control centre' for tomorrow's organizations and, with that, potentially becomes an incredible source of power. Given its holistic and integrated nature and more specifically its 'connected' oversight of an organization's various activities, a balanced scorecard can reasonably assume a leadership role in terms of strategic planning, measurement of performance against various targets and goals, and rewards or punitive actions based on such performance. Given such power, it would not be surprising to see different organizational actors vying for ownership of an organization's balanced scorecard, or similar steering tools.

The balanced scorecard, and accounting for strategic management in general, can and probably will remain a key part of the remit of management accountants who, to ensure this, should continue to advance our understanding of the actual workings, including reasons for success and failure, of balanced scorecards in different real organizational settings. However, there is equally no obvious reason why the balanced scorecard could not be designed, owned and managed by non-accountants. Already there is at least anecdotal evidence that holistic, integrative management tools are being driven and ultimately managed by other professional disciplines such as human resources or engineering (Langfield-Smith, 2008). This will represent a key challenge for tomorrow's management accountants, especially in terms of their traditionally assumed role of being the main provider of useful information for managerial decision-making.

The above highlights the potential power embedded in a tool such as the balanced scorecard, for organizations which adopt them. If embraced by an organization, the balanced scorecard can, and usually will, be the 'king-pin' for multiple interrelated aspects of organizational management – including planning, control, measurement and strategizing. It will establish and visualize, ultimately through objectives and targets, where an organization needs to go. It will determine what aspects of organizational activity will be measured and given priority, and influence who and how people might (or might not) get rewarded for their work. This is a scenario of considerable potential power resting with the balanced scorecard and its owners; and, thus, it should not come as any surprise that other professionals within an organization attempt to be at the helm of and 'own' the balanced scorecard (rather than the accountants).

Chapter summary

This chapter has explored contemporary ways in which managers have attempted to align organizational behaviour and decision-making with strategic goals. We briefly explored a raft of tools and techniques which together have been dubbed by some as strategic management accounting. But, in particular, we have explored the most enduring of all strategic-facing management accounting tools, namely the balanced scorecard. For some organizations, the balanced scorecard is a powerful mechanism for steering an organization in its desired strategic direction, but also offers a control aspect to organizational activity. However, it has not been without its criticism, particularly of off-the-shelf packages which many consultancy firms offer (at extortionate prices) and often with insufficient consideration given to the specific organizational context in which any such design and implementation takes place.

Key terms

Balanced scorecard A tool that uses financial and non-financial information, in an integrated and holistic way, to assist managers to map out and aim for strategic goals (p. 423)

Corporate steering wheel An alternative version of the balanced scorecard but with similar and overlapping features (p. 428)

Customer perspective Objectives, measures, targets and initiatives which focus on an organization's markets and customers (p. 424)

Financial perspective Conveys the financial performance objectives of an organization, plus associated measures, targets and initiatives (p. 424)

Holistic Adopting a broad perspective of business activity, across multiple functions and through different levels of organizational hierarchy (p. 423)

Integrated Where any particular perspective of organizational activity (for example, financial performance) is not to be viewed independently of alternative aspects of organizational activity (for example, customer-related or impact on the environment) (p. 423)

Internal business perspective Objectives, measures, targets and initiatives which an organization must do well internally in order to attain its strategic goals (p. 425)

Lag indicators Outcome measures, indicators of achievement in a particular perspective (p. 427)

Lead indicators Performance drivers, activities which aim to assist the achievement of objectives in particular perspectives (p. 427)

Learning and growth perspective Objectives, measures, targets and initiatives which focus an organization and its employees on continual learning and its resource capabilities (p. 426)

Process value chain Another way of viewing the internal business process, comprising: (1) the innovation process, (2) the operations process and (3) the post-sales service process (p. 426)

Strategic Is the ongoing process of endeavouring to achieve an organization's strategy. Being strategic gives some degree of fluidity and an underpinning notion of ongoing process to a strategy (p. 426)

Strategic cost management Is the application of cost management tools and techniques which simultaneously aims to improve an organization's strategic position and reduce its costs (p. 421)

Strategic intent Is the notion of cumulative strategising, ongoing (re)formulation of organizational strategy in the context of changing external and internal conditions (p. 421)

Strategic management Is the process through which usually an organization's executive managers will devise plans, establish controls, monitor and use various tools and techniques to fulfil their organizational aims (p. 419)

Strategic management accounting (SMA) Is an amalgam of management accounting tools and techniques which assist managers to steer their organization in the direction of strategic intent (p. 421)

Strategy Some form of grand scheme or plan which sets out a vision or aim for where an organization wants to be in the longer term (p. 419)

● ● ● Review questions ● ● ● ● ● ● ● ● ● ● ● connect ● ● ●

Level of difficulty:	BASIC	INTERMEDIATE	ADVANCED

17.1 Define strategy, and explain what it means to suggest that the concept is too static for tomorrow's organization. **[LO1, LO2]**

17.2 What does it mean to say that an organization is being strategic? **[LO1, LO2]**

17.3 Describe the main components and features of tools and techniques associated with strategic management accounting. **[LO3]**

17.4 Describe the purpose, and the key characteristics, of a balanced scorecard. **[LO4]**

17.5 Explain what you understand by the four different perspectives of a balanced scorecard. **[LO4]**

17.6 Suggest why (it is claimed) the balanced scorecard has been enduring over time, yet strategic management accounting has not. **[LO1, LO3]**

17.7 Explain the cause-and-effect assumption of the balanced scorecard, and discuss what challenges this poses for management accountants. **[LO4, LO5]**

17.8 Define lag and lead indicators in a balanced scorecard. **[LO4]**

17.9 Explain some of the common attributes of a balanced scorecard-type tool. **[LO2, LO4]**

17.10 Describe some of the main roles for management accountants in relation to the balanced scorecard. **[LO4, LO5]**

● ● Group discussion and activity questions ● ● ● ● ● ● ● ● ●

17.11 Do some research, and prepare to discuss why it is important for tomorrow's organizations to be strategic, and explain (using real-world examples) what this means. **[LO1, LO2]**

17.12 As a management consultant, you have been asked to design a 'scorecard' performance measurement system for four new clients. One client is a world-leading pharmaceuticals organization (with its headquarters in the USA), the second client is a well-known German bank, the third is an Italian football club and the final client is a well-known Australian university. For each new client (or one client per group, as advised by your teacher) you are required to write a report to the respective chief executive outlining your reasoning behind, and suggestions for, the scorecard being put forward. You are particularly encouraged to include diagrams, tables and other images to help assist your arguments, and it would be acceptable to include some (sensible) hypothetical numbers. In so doing, you are advised to particularly concentrate on the following aspects: **[LO1, LO3, LO4, LO5]**

1) The potential benefits of a scorecard for this particular organization

2) The main stakeholders of your client (around whom the scorecard should be largely designed)

3) The likely objectives and strategic goals of your client

4) The possible measures that your client may focus on

5) Some targets that your client should consider including within the scorecard

6) Initiatives that your client might consider implementing as motivation to achieve the relevant targets.

17.3 Discuss, and enhance through research via the Internet and/or articles, what you think should comprise the key strategic objectives for the following organizations: **[LO1, LO3, LO4, LO5]**

1) A police force in an Italian city, faced with significant cuts in government funds.

2) A charity for heart research, which has experienced substantial recent decline in public donations due mainly to the fall-out of the global economic recession and the shift towards funding charities (indirectly) via lotteries.

3) A Swedish ice-hockey team, in the top division but lacking much success in recent times, and facing a dramatic decrease in crowd attendances.

4) A manufacturer of speedboats, located in Zurich and catering mostly for the higher/expensive end of its market.

5) A high-class restaurant in Paris, with worrying signs of falling revenues from what has previously been a fairly reliable and extremely affluent client base.

● ● ● **Exercises** ● ● ● ● ● ● ● ● ● ● ● ● ● ● ● ● ● connect ● ●

E17.1 **Strategic management accounting [LO3]**

Which of the following would *not* normally be associated with strategic management accounting (SMA) tools and techniques?

a) Information about an organization's main competitors

b) Cost driver and competitive advantage analysis

c) Analysis of performance via variances against standards

d) Customer/marketing information

E17.2 **Strategic performance management tools [LO4]**

Lag indicators are performance drivers which aim to assist the achievement of objectives in particular perspectives: true or false?

E17.3 **The balanced scorecard [LO4]**

Fill in the missing words:

The four main perspectives of the balanced scorecard designed by Kaplan and Norton are: (1) financial, (2) customer, (3) learning and growth, and (4) _____ _____.

E17.4 **The internal business perspective [LO4]**

The internal business perspective of a balance scorecard can be divided into three subparts – (1) the innovation process, (2) the operations process and (3) the post-sales service process.

Required:

Identify the internal business perspective that each one of these measures relate to.

1) Providing regular security updates to customers

2) Decrease in throughput time

3) Percentage of total sales from new product launched

4) Decrease in average product costs

5) Increase in total sales from a major new customer

6) Reducing the time taken to process the refunds for defective goods.

E17.5 **The appeal of a balanced scorecard [LO1, LO2, LO4]**

What do you think makes the balanced scorecard so intuitively appealing to business managers?

E17.6 **The future of the balanced scorecard [LO1, LO2, LO4, LO5, LO6]**

Do you think the balanced scorecard will be more, less or about equally as popular in ten years time? Will the balanced scorecard become yet another management 'fad', to be replaced by 'the next best thing'; or will it evolve (and be adapted) into new and extended forms over time? Improve your arguments with some research, particularly critical academic articles.

E17.7 **The balanced scorecard and the management accountant [LO1, LO2, LO5]**

Do you think that management accountants will or will not oversee and lead the (re)design and (re)development of an organization's balanced scorecard, or similar strategic performance management tool, in five years time? Explain your reasoning.

E17.8 **The balanced scorecard [LO4]**

Search on the Internet for a well-known organization which adopts the balanced scorecard tool. How do they describe their tool, and the way that they use it? Are there differences between this organization's use and design of its balanced scorecard and the original model of Kaplan and Norton?

E17.9 **Core elements of a balanced scorecard [LO4]**

Mycra is a large consultancy services company. Below are some of the objectives of the company in its balance scorecard.

Objectives	Financial	Customer	Internal business	Learning and Growth
1) Increasing employee productivity				
2) Improving post-sales services				
3) Increase in systems-literate staff				
4) Increasing return on assets				
5) Increasing revenue				
6) Increasing shareholder wealth				
7) New product development				

Required:

For each of these objectives, identify the balance scorecard perspective that the objective best fits into.

E17.10 **Perspectives in a balanced scorecard [LO1, LO2, LO4, LO6]**

Are the four perspectives in Kaplan and Norton's balanced scorecard sufficient for all organizations, over time? Can you think of other perspectives that might be useful to incorporate within the (holistic, integrated) performance management system of some organizations?

E17.11 **Using the balanced scorecard in operational areas of an organization [LO1, LO2, LO4]**

The balanced scorecard has to date probably been presented mostly as a tool for executives to (performance) manage their organizations. Can you think of ways and situations through which the balanced scorecard can be used at lower and more operational levels of an organization?

E17.12 **Priority in the respective perspectives [LO2, LO4]**

Do you think that all organizations give (roughly) equal ranking to each of the four perspectives in a balanced scorecard, or do you think there might be trade-offs and compromises between respective perspectives over time (and why)? Give real illustrations and scenarios to back up your suggestions.

E17.13 **Strategic management accounting [LO3, LO4, LO5]**

Fill in the blanks with the appropriate terms given below:

Balanced scorecard	Lag indicator
Corporate steering wheel	Process value chain
Learning and growth	Lead indicator

1) A _____ comprises of the innovation process, the operations process and the post-sales service process.

2) A _____ is alternative version of the balanced scorecard having similar and overlapping features.

3) A _____ is a performance driver which aims to assist the achievement of objectives in a particular perspective.

4) A reduction in employee turnover will be included in _____ perspective of the balance scorecard.

5) A _____ is a strategic management accounting tool developed by Robert Kaplan and David Norton.

6) A _____ is a measure of results that shows the achievement of an objective in a particular perspective.

E17.14 **Critique of the balanced scorecard [LO1, LO2, LO4, LO6]**

Describe and critically assess some of Nørreklit's views on the balanced scorecard. Is her work highly critical of the balanced scorecard as a concept, or more a cautionary tale?

E17.15 **Radical events causing strategic change [LO1, LO4, LO5]**

The example earlier of the ramifications of the 'Bosman ruling' showed how the entire landscape of an industry changed suddenly, requiring organizations to implement considerable change to its strategic plans. Can you think of other revolutionary/shock events in the past five years which likely caused organizations to have to undertake a significant review of its strategic direction? Can you research what specific strategic changes actually took place in these organizations?

E17.16 **Strategic management accounting [LO3]**

After reading the articles* by Langfield-Smith (2008) and Nixon and Burns (2012), describe why you think SMA has failed to establish its popularity as much as its early advocates would have liked.

*Links to the articles are available online at www.mcgraw-hill.co.uk/textbooks/burns.

E17.17 **Lag and lead indicators [LO4]**

Doreen Cosmetics Ltd. is a manufacturer of cosmetics and pharmaceutical products.

Required:

a) The financial perspective of the balance scorecard of Doreen Cosmetics shows 'Increasing shareholder wealth' as an objective. Identify each of these indicators as a *lead* indicator or *lag* indicator of this objective.

	Lead indicator	Lag indicator
1) Return on equity		
2) Advertising expense		
3) Vertical integration		
4) Revenue growth		
5) Product mix		
6) Customer satisfaction		

b) The customer perspective of the balance scorecard shows "Increasing customers' loyalty" as an objective. Identify each of these indicators as a *lead* indicator or *lag* indicator of this objective.

	Lead indicator	Lag indicator
1) Quality of post-sales services		
2) Level of customer satisfaction		
3) Number of customers retained		
4) Average order processing time		
5) Market share		
6) Customer relationship		

• • Case study problem • • • • • • • • • • connect™ • • • •

C17.1 **Tesco PLC – the corporate steering wheel [LO1, LO2, LO4, LO5]**

Tesco, the UK-based retail organization, adopts a corporate steering wheel (see Exhibit 17.3) to measure and monitor its strategic performance. This tool bears much resemblance to the original balanced scorecard concept (that is, the four 'segments' of finance, customer, operations and

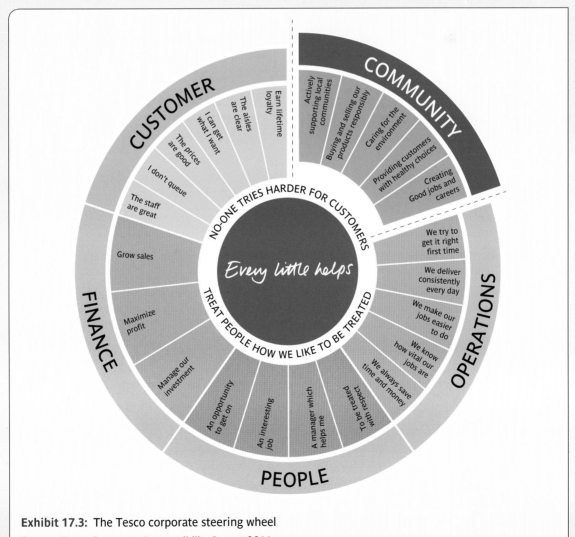

Exhibit 17.3: The Tesco corporate steering wheel

Source: Tesco Corporate Responsibility Report 2011

people resonate closely with the four perspectives of the original balanced scorecard); however, the principal difference is the addition of one further perspective, community.

The community segment integrates objectives and measures for Tesco's performance in relation to acting responsibly in the communities in which they operate, as well as fulfilling particular commitments to their communities. In some organizations, such concern for their communities is expressed as 'corporate social responsibility' or 'sustainability policy'. Thus, Tesco's corporate steering wheel aims to see that concern for its communities is not a specialist function, but a feature of day-to-day activity.

The objectives for each of Tesco's segments are as follows:

Finance

- Grow sales
- Maximize profit
- Manage our investment

Customer

- Earn lifetime loyalty
- The aisles are clear
- I can get what I want
- The prices are good
- I don't queue
- The staff are great

Operations

- We try to get it right first time
- We deliver consistently every day
- We make our jobs easier to do

- We know how vital our jobs are
- We always save time and money

People

- An opportunity to get on
- An interesting job
- A manager which helps me
- To be treated with respect

Community

- Actively supporting local communities
- Buying and selling our products responsibly
- Caring for the environment
- Providing customers with healthy choices
- Creating good jobs and careers

Required:

a) List three (each) possible measures, targets and initiatives for all five segments.

b) Critically appraise possible assumptions for cause-and-effect relationships that might exist in a retail organization such as Tesco.

c) Discuss some broader (external or internal) developments or scenarios that might point to the need for close inspection of Tesco's corporate steering wheel, and suggest possible changes that might be made in each (new) circumstance.

● ● ● **Recommended reading** ● ● ● ● ● ● ● ● ● ● ● ● ● ● ● ● ● ● ●

- Langfield-Smith. K. (2008) 'Strategic management accounting: how far have we come in 25 years?', *Accounting, Auditing & Accountability Journal*, 21(2), pp. 204–28.

This paper presents a 'review of reviews' of both professional and academic literature on SMA since its inception, plus analysis of its (non-)achievements and possible ways forward.

- Kaplan, R. S. and D. P. Norton (1992) 'The balanced scorecard as a strategic management system', *Harvard Business Review*, January–February, pp. 61–6.

The original seminal piece on the balanced scorecard, by Kaplan and Norton; students should also try to read other subsequent articles and books by the same author(s).

- Nørreklit, H., M. Jacobsen and F. Mitchell (2008) 'Pitfalls in using the balanced scorecard', *The Journal of Corporate Accounting & Finance*, September–October, pp. 65–8.

This is a useful (brief and easy-to-read) summary of the potential shortcomings with a balanced scorecard, and suggests ways to avoid such shortcomings.

References

Bromwich, M. (1990) 'The case for strategic management accounting: the role of accounting information for strategy in competitive markets', *Accounting, Organizations & Society*, 13(1/2), pp. 27–46.

Bromwich, M. and A. Bhimani (1994) *Management Accounting: Pathways to Progress*, Oxford: Elsevier/CIMA.

De Haas, M. and A. Kleingeld (1999) 'Multi-level design of performance measurement systems: enhancing strategic dialogue throughout the organization', *Management Accounting Research*, 10, pp. 233–61.

Hopwood, A. (2009) 'The economic crisis and accounting: implications for the research community', *Accounting, Organizations & Society*, 34, pp. 797–802.

Kaplan, R. S. and D. P. Norton (1992) 'The balanced scorecard as a strategic management system', *Harvard Business Review*, January–February, pp. 61–6.

Kaplan, R. S. and D. P. Norton (1996) 'Linking the balanced scorecard to strategy', *California Management Review*, Fall, 4, 53–79.

Langfield-Smith. K. (2008) 'Strategic management accounting: how far have we come in 25 years?', *Accounting, Auditing & Accountability Journal*, 21(2), pp. 204–28.

Nixon, B. and J. Burns (2012) 'The paradox of strategic management accounting', *Management Accounting Research*, 23(4).

Nixon, B., J. Burns and M. Jazayeri (2012) 'Profitable new product design and development' (Technical notes), *Financial Management* (CIMA), April, pp. 50–53.

Nørreklit, H. (2000) 'The balance on the balanced scorecard – a critical analysis of some of its assumptions', *Management Accounting Research*, 11, pp. 65–88.

Nørreklit, H., M. Jacobsen and F. Mitchell (2008) 'Pitfalls in using the balanced scorecard', *The Journal of Corporate Accounting & Finance*, September–October, pp. 65–8.

Shank, J. K. (1989) 'Strategic cost management: new wine, or just new bottles?', *Journal of Management Accounting Research*, 14(3), pp. 255–79.

Tesco Corporate Responsibility Report 2011, available at http://www.tescoplc.com/media/60113/tesco_cr_report_2011_final.pdf.

When you have read this chapter

Log on to the Online Learning Centre at **www.mcgraw-hill.co.uk/textbooks/burns** to explore chapter-by-chapter test questions, links and further online study tools for Management Accounting.

CHAPTER 18

FINANCIAL PERFORMANCE MEASUREMENT AND TRANSFER PRICING

Chapter outline

- Divisionalized financial performance measures

- Transfer pricing

Learning outcomes

On completion of this chapter, you will be able to:

LO1 Compare and evaluate market and accounting financial performance measures

LO2 Use and evaluate the return on investment (ROI) measure

LO3 Use and evaluate the residual income (RI) measure

LO4 Describe the economic value added (EVA®) measure

LO5 Describe the purpose and mechanisms of transfer prices

LO6 Characterize and discuss the advantages and limitations of transfer prices based on market prices, costs or negotiations

LO7 Discuss the tax specificities of transfer pricing in multinationals

LO8 Discuss the impacts of adopting tax-compliant transfer prices for internal purposes

Introduction

In this chapter, you will learn about financial performance in large, divisionalized organizations and explore the specific features of multinational organizations. The previous chapter made a broad, conceptual approach to performance measurement and management, with a particular focus on the balanced scorecard (BSC) and its multiple perspectives on performance. While non-financial perspectives are recognized as increasingly important, as highlighted by the BSC, financial performance remains as the ultimate objective in the BSC when applied to private sector firms. In this chapter, you will take a closer look on how to measure financial performance within large, decentralized organizations, such as those organized by divisional financial responsibility centres, analysing various measures of performance and exploring the importance of the transfer prices applied in intra-group transactions.

Divisional managers of profit or investment centres have substantial autonomy to make decisions. So, a first challenge is to create measures that may orient their autonomous, self-interested decisions towards outcomes that also benefit the organization as a whole – that is, to create goal congruence between divisional and organization-wide interests. A second challenge is to create measures that adequately capture and support the evaluation of performance at a divisional level. In this chapter, you will explore these challenges.

To achieve these performance measurement purposes, particularly in vertically integrated groups, we need to measure intra-group flows of goods, services, intangibles and capital. This is a major challenge for global companies. Their industrial and commercial operations, as well as research and development (R&D) and support activities, are scattered across subsidiaries around the world. Flows across these entities are massive. Examples include materials, goods to be further processed or ready to be sold to external customers, consulting services, administrative services provided by shared services centres, intellectual property, loans provided by larger companies to small companies which do not have access to bank loans, and so on.

The financial valuation of these intra-group flows is made through transfer prices. These intra-group exchanges typically differ substantially from market exchanges between unrelated companies. The terms and conditions (among which, price) set in intra-group exchanges may be defined through hierarchic imposition by headquarters and they may be totally unrelated with conditions emerging from bargaining processes. You will see that it is virtually impossible to define a transfer price meeting all possible goals. There are three main goals: create goal congruence, support the evaluation of divisions' performance and minimize tax-related costs. You will explore the trade-offs of the various solutions for transfer pricing. These difficulties of financial performance measurement in large, divisionalized organizations make this a challenging and exciting area of management accounting and control.

In this chapter, you will first explore divisionalized financial performance measures. Then, you will learn about transfer prices and explore the various available methods to define them. Finally, you will read about multinationals' specificities on transfer pricing, in particular concerning tax issues, and potential impacts on management control systems.

Divisionalized financial performance measures

You have seen in the previous chapter that performance measurement requires both financial and non-financial measures. In spite of their limitations, financial measures remain a fundamental component for management control and performance measurement. In the BSC framework applicable to the private sector, they remain as the ultimate perspective to which the other perspectives should contribute. In large organizations, in particular those adopting a decentralized structure in which managers of investment and profit centres have significant autonomy, financial measures are particularly useful, since they provide a summary measure of performance.

This section focuses on financial performance measures at the divisional level. After a brief comparison between market-based and accounting-based measures, you will study three popular accounting measures: return on investment (ROI), residual income (RI) and economic value added (EVA®). This is followed by some considerations on calculating these measures. Finally we highlight that real-life situations often place management accountants in 'murky waters', leading to difficult questions and requiring careful judgement combining accounting, business and political skills.

Market versus accounting measures

Measuring performance in financial terms may be based on (financial) market measures or accounting measures. Market measures include firm market value or return to shareholders. Market measures have the appeal of being theoretically aligned with the objective to maximize shareholder value – as suggested by BSC proponents with regard to the private sector. However, their applicability has some limits and disadvantages. First, market measures are only available for listed companies. They are not available for non-listed companies, not-for-profit organizations or company subunits, such as divisions – our section focus. Second, market measures may suffer from fluctuations largely beyond the control of managers. For example, during financial markets crises such as those experienced in recent years, the market value of virtually all companies suffered a significant decline – without necessarily signalling a poor performance by the companies' managers. Third, market prices largely reflect investors' expectations about future financial performance of the firms, rather than an evaluation of the actual (past) performance of the managers. Fourth, investors may not be fully informed of or may not correctly evaluate existing information. Finally, in large organizations the performance of most employees, when considered individually, is likely to have a negligible impact on the overall firm market value. So, at best, only the performance of top managers making far-reaching decisions could eventually be measured by market measures.

Accounting measures have been widely adopted alternatives to market measures. Accounting systems are usually pervasive in all types of organizations, although with varying degrees of sophistication. Therefore, it is usually possible to obtain accounting measures not only at the highest level of listed companies, but also in non-listed companies, not-for-profit organizations and in organizational subunits. Accounting measures are also less subject to market fluctuations beyond managers' control and less dependent on the expectations and evaluations of market participants. So, when compared with market measures, accounting measures capture more directly the consequences of past performance, both at higher and lower responsibility levels.

To understand better the advantages of accounting measures versus market measures, consider the examples of a manager at a small Nokia mobile phone store or a small Co-operative Food store (the community food retailer of the UK-based Co-operative Group; the group is owned by over 6 million consumers and focuses on serving members and building a better society, not on profitability). The managers' performance may have a clear impact on accounting measures in their store; however, it is virtually irrelevant to the Nokia stock price, and the Co-operative Group does not even have a market value. In both cases, market measures are inadequate.

But what accounting measures should you adopt to measure performance at a lower level and when market measures are inadequate? It depends on the manager's responsibility areas and, therefore, on the type of responsibility centre at stake (see Chapter 17). Given our chapter focus on divisions (or other organizational levels defined as investment centres, such as subsidiaries), we now analyse three accounting measures for performance measurement at a divisional level: ROI, RI, and EVA®.

Return on investment

Return on investment (ROI) is widely used to measure the financial performance of divisions. In a generic formula, ROI divides divisional profit by the assets used by the division:

$$\text{ROI} = \frac{\text{Profit}}{\text{Investment}}$$

There are countless variations for this generic formula, for both the numerator and denominator. For divisions, profitability is typically measured by divisional operational profit, that is, profit before interest and income taxes. Investment typically includes assets such as land, buildings, equipment, inventories, receivables and cash. Note that you can use different measures to define profit and investment, depending on your purpose for measuring performance as you will see below.

ROI-type measures have numerous advantages that explain their widespread use. These measures combine revenues, costs and investments, thereby encouraging managers to simultaneously evaluate the interactions and trade-offs between these three major variables. By expressing profit as a percentage of assets, rather than an absolute figure, ROI enables the profitability of divisions of different size to be compared. More generally, since ROI is a percentage, it is also often used to compare the financial performance of divisions in different industries, competitors and different types of investments. Finally, there is an important non-technical advantage which is very significant: ROI has been so widely used for so long (see *Management Accounting Insight 18.1*), that most managers recognize it, are familiar with what it means and know how they can take decisions to improve it.

A particularly useful comparison at a higher, corporate level is to check if divisional ROI exceeds the opportunity cost of the capital invested in each division. If ROI lags behind the cost of capital, then the invested capital would gain a greater return if invested in an alternative use, inside or even outside the company. Look at the upper part of Table 18.1. Although division A has lower absolute profits than division B (£300 million versus £600 million), it has a better ROI than division B (30 per cent versus 10 per cent), and it is above the company opportunity cost of capital (20 per cent). So, division A would be evaluated favourably, unlike division B.

Table 18.1: The bias risk of ROI-based divisional decisions

	Division A	Division B
Cost of capital	20 %	20 %
Profit (£, m)	300	600
Assets (£, m)	1,000	6,000
ROI	**30 %**	**10 %**
Potential investment (£m)	200	200
Potential contribution (£m)	50	30
Return on new investment	25 %	15 %
Investment impact on company profitability	25 % > 20 % ⇒ improves profitability	15 % < 20 % ⇒ worsens profitability
Division manager's perspective and incentive	Worsens divisional ROI ⇒ do not make investment ⇒ biased incentive	Investment improves divisional ROI ⇒ make investment ⇒ biased incentive

However, usage of ROI has its problems. Using ROI to evaluate managers and determine their bonuses may lead divisional managers to adopt decisions that improve the ROI of their division (and their bonuses) but make the company globally worse off, and vice versa. The lower part of Table 18.1 explores this problem by comparing the investment and return of projects of two divisions. The 25 per cent ROI of the division A project would worsen the division ROI (currently 30 per cent). So, the divisional manager will tend not to invest – although the project return exceeds the opportunity cost of capital of the company (20 per cent) and would benefit the company as a whole. In contrast, the 15 per cent ROI of the division B project will improve the division ROI (currently 10 per cent). This is an incentive for the divisional manager to pursue with the investment – although this is against the company financial interests, since the investment ROI is lower than the opportunity cost of capital. Overall, using ROI at divisional level to evaluate projects tends to favour projects of divisions currently less profitable (as measured by ROI) and tends to play against projects of divisions with higher ROI – an undesirable bias from a strictly financial, corporate-level perspective.

The second problem is that ROI's usage of accounting profit may promote myopic, short-term behaviour. The previous chapter has already discussed the myopia risk when using traditional accounting measures such as profit. To improve profit in the short run, managers often resort to cost reduction on discretionary items like R&D, advertising, training or maintenance, although this may actually compromise long-term competitiveness and profitability.

Given ROI's limitations as a measure of divisional performance, we now turn to other accounting measures: residual income and economic value added – although ROI, along with profit, remains clearly ahead, as you can see in *Management Accounting Insight 18.1*.

18.1: Management Accounting Insight

Research by CIMA (2009) confirms previous studies indicating the continuing popularity of traditional performance measures. Although adoption rates vary across sectors, relative preferences are consistent across all sectors, including manufacturing, services and public and education. Profit before tax is particularly dominant, with over 80 per cent adoption across sectors – in fact, it is the second most widely used management accounting tool across the entire survey, only surpassed by financial year forecasting. Return on capital employed (ROCE) and cash flow return on investment (CFROI), both ROI-type measures, are also included in the top 20. By contrast, adoption rates of RI and EVA® are quite low – usually below 20 per cent (see Exhibit 18.1).

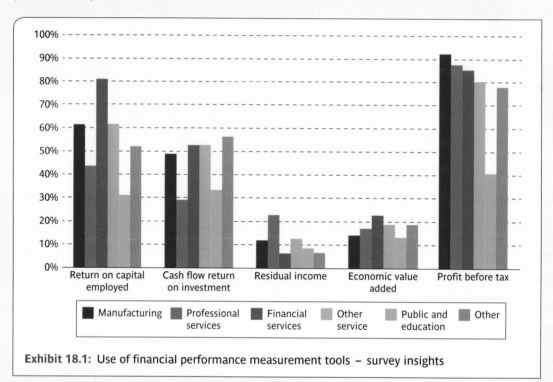

Exhibit 18.1: Use of financial performance measurement tools – survey insights

Surveys characterizing adopters of performance measures sometimes provide puzzling results. For instance, it could be expected that firms with higher R&D spending (measured as R&D/sales) would adopt EVA more, since EVA capitalization of R&D expenses would benefit their measured performance. However, Lovata and Costingan (2002) found the opposite: firms with higher R&D spending adopted EVA less than firms with lower R&D spending. Why? The authors suggested that the future success of more innovative firms is less dependent on current earnings than that of less innovative ones. So, these firms are more likely to adopt a range of performance measures, including non-financial ones, such as new product developments, time to market and customer satisfaction. It is possible that they perceive that EVA insights are not relevant and its complexity is not worth the effort. As the authors concluded: 'Identifying optimal incentives for managers appears to be more complex than inferred by proponents of EVA' (Lovata and Costingan, 2002, p. 226).

Sources: CIMA (2009) and Lovata and Costingan (2002).

Exercises

1) How do public and education organizations typically rank in the adoption of the above measures? Discuss possible reasons for this.

2) Draw on the strategic insights from Chapter 17 to further discuss the suggestions by Lovata and Costingan.

Residual income

Residual income (RI), unlike ROI, includes the cost of capital tied up in the division. Residual income subtracts from profit a cost of capital charge for the investment:

$$RI = Profit - (Required\ rate\ of\ return \times Investment)$$

Although investment was already considered in ROI, the cost of capital of such investment was not visible – it was only visible when ROI was compared with the company cost of capital. Return on investment may make capital seem almost free for divisions, promoting excessive investments (creating huge inventories 'just in case' or building excessively sophisticated offices are recurrent real-life examples). Residual income addresses this problem by placing a major emphasis on the cost of capital.

As with ROI, you will analyse different measures to define profit and investment. The required rate of return should reflect the weighted average cost of capital (WACC), taking into account debt and equity costs.[1] You will see below that this rate may be adjusted to reflect the specific risk of each investment, by incorporating a premium for riskier investments – a differentiation not possible when using ROI.

Table 18.2 calculates the residual income of the two projects introduced in Table 18.1. Assume that the WACC is 20 per cent and that both projects have similar risk levels. The residual income of each project is its contribution minus its cost of capital charge. The project of division A is expected to provide a contribution (£50 million) that exceeds its cost of capital charge (£40 million). Division A's positive RI (£10 million) provides an incentive for its manager to make the investment. By contrast, the negative RI (£10 million) of the division B project provides an incentive for its manager not to make the investment. Note that both decisions are aligned with company-wide interests, since managers only have incentive to pursue projects whose contribution exceeds the cost of capital – regardless of the divisions' current performance.

Now, suppose that the project of division A was considerably risky and its risk-adjusted required rate of return increases to 27 per cent. After adjusted for the higher risk, the cost of capital charge of the division A project would increase to £54 million. Since the RI of the division A project would now be negative (–£4 million), it would provide an incentive for its manager not to make the investment.

Despite its advantages, RI has not been popular among companies, as you can see in *Management Accounting Insight 18.1*. In addition, RI's usage has two limitations).[2] First, RI is an absolute measure of performance and hence limited when comparing divisions of different size. There are two ways to mitigate this limitation: (1) calculate the additional measure of RI as a percentage of investment – this percentage is comparable across divisions; (2) calculate the percentage change in RI, from

Table 18.2: RI promoting unbiased divisional decisions

	Division A	Division B
Potential investment (£, m)	200	200
Potential contribution (£, m)	50	30
Required rate of return (WACC; investments have equal risk)	20 %	20 %
Cost of capital charge (required rate of return × investment) (£, m)	40	40
Residual income (£, m)	10	– 10
Investment impact on company profitability	Positive RI ⇒ improves profitability	Negative RI ⇒ worsens profitability
Division manager's perspective and incentive	Positive RI ⇒ make investment ⇒ Unbiased incentive	Negative RI ⇒ do not make investment ⇒ Unbiased incentive

year to year. This second approach may allow comparisons across divisions, although it may stop being meaningful when RI is negative or is positive, but very small (with very small RI, percentage changes tend to be very large). The second limitation is that RI does not address the myopia problem of ROI: managers are still encouraged to cut discretionary expenses to improve short-term profit, potentially sacrificing long-term success. To lessen the myopia problem, we now turn to the third accounting performance measure: economic value added.

Economic value added

Economic value added (EVA®) is a variation of RI, developed and registered as a trademark by Stern Stewart & Co. Economic value added has a strong presence within the academic and professional media, which have announced its adoption by several major global firms. However, academic research has consistently reported relatively modest adoption rates (see again *Management Accounting Insight 18.1*). We consider EVA as after-tax operating profit minus after-tax cost of capital employed, plus/minus accounting adjustments, that is:

$$\text{EVA} = \text{After-tax operating profit} - [\text{after-tax WACC} \times (\text{total assets} - \text{current liabilities})]$$
$$\pm \text{ accounting adjustments}$$

Major differences between EVA and RI concern EVA's adoption of after-tax measures (regarding profit and the cost of capital charge) and numerous adjustments to accounting figures (of profit and assets) to convert them into economic profit and assets. Typically, these adjustments aim to correct economic measurement distortions that Generally Accepted Accounting Principles (GAAP) introduce in accounting figures. Stewart proposed over 100 adjustments, although for many companies fewer than 10 adjustments may suffice to provide a satisfying result. Typical major adjustments include the capitalization of expenses in intangibles, such as R&D, training, advertising and restructuring, which may not be recognized as assets under GAAP. So, for EVA calculation, these intangibles should be added to the invested capital. On the other hand, and consequently, EVA calculations will amortize, on a periodical basis, these now to be considered assets. So, EVA will include this amortization, reducing after-tax operating profit.

The advantages of EVA include those of RI (in particular, making capital cost very clear to divisional managers) and those from the economic perspective of the company. The accounting adjustments may reduce the managerial myopia risk of ROI and RI. Expenditures that are in intangible items that as important for long-term success no longer hit the performance measure under EVA. So, managers are not as likely to cut them as when accounting profit is used in indicators as ROI and RI.

As with all measures, EVA also has its limitations. First, it shares the RI characteristic of being an absolute value (rather than a percentage), so it is not suitable for comparing divisions of different size. Second, EVA's accounting adjustments cannot totally create an economic measure reflecting estimates of future cash flows, since EVA is still grounded on accounting information primarily reflecting past events. Economic value added does not eliminate the myopia bias completely. Managers may still, for example, cut short-term costs by lowering quality standards; this may allow improvements in short-term profit but risks undermining customer satisfaction and hence longer-term profitability. Third, as illustrated in the case study problem at the end of the chapter, many managers find EVA difficult to understand. It may also be expensive to implement. Dozens of accounting adjustments may sound challenging for accountants producing the information, so hiring consultants is often necessary. Adjustments may also sound daunting for managers using the information, so training is essential. These difficulties (and additional costs) contrast with the ease-of-use and familiarity of measures like ROI and contribute to EVA's relatively low adoption rates.

Recent studies have produced mixed results about EVA's superiority to other financial measures, including traditional accounting measures, to explain companies' market performance. Recently, Kumar and Sharma (2011) reviewed such mixed results and provided further results against EVA adequacy. Some of these studies have led to developments of the original EVA measure. For example, Warr (2005) found that EVA, as a nominal measure, is distorted by inflation even in low-inflation periods; so, they proposed real EVA, adjusting the measure for inflation. Before that, Bacidore et al. (1997) had proposed refined EVA (REVA), using the market value of assets, rather than their book value. Refined EVA® was found to be superior to EVA in later studies (for example, Lee and Kim, 2009, on the hospitality industry) but was rejected by other authors (for example, Ferguson and Leistikow, 1998). While the debate is not closed, it is often suggested that non-financial measures may provide important contributions to assess the value of a firm. *Management Accounting Insight 18.1*, based on survey studies, concludes with similar suggestions.

Detailed choices regarding financial measures

So far, you have learned the broad concepts underlying ROI, RI and EVA. However, there are various alternatives to operationalize them. Now, you will explore the main issues concerning (1) the adopted time horizon and (2) the definition and measurement of profit and investment.

Shorter or longer time horizons?

Adopting shorter or longer time horizons for calculating the measures has an impact on the consequences of their usage. While shorter periods (for example, one year or less) have the intuitive appeal of allowing faster evaluation, motivation and correction, they may also exacerbate myopia risk by encouraging managers to sacrifice long-term success to meet short-term objectives. This risk is particularly relevant when using ROI and RI. In contrast, longer periods provide the time and opportunity for strategies for long-term success to develop and produce their results – although requiring other approaches to measure, evaluate, reward and correct performance in sub-periods.

How to define and measure profit and investment?

You have already been alerted to the fact that the definition and measurement of profit and investment is open to alternative approaches. In fact, their correct definition depends on whether the objective is to evaluate the performance of the division manager or to evaluate the economic performance of the division. Before exploring each alternative, be aware that divisional profit may not actually be a good measure of profitability; instead, contribution-type measures will be preferred for both objectives.

For the first objective – evaluating divisional managers – only the manager's controllable contribution and controllable (net) assets should be included. To calculate the controllable contribution, you should exclude costs directly attributable to the division but that the manager does not control, such as costs of headquarters' staff providing services exclusively to particular divisions. You should also exclude costs incurred at headquarter level which are indirect and are merely allocated among divisions (for example, general administration costs). To calculate controllable assets, you should exclude assets beyond the responsibility of the divisional manager. In addition, when the divisional manager is also responsible for liabilities, you should use the concept of net assets (that is, assets minus liabilities).

Alternatively, if the objective is to evaluate the economic performance of the division (rather than the performance of the division manager), profit and investment should be defined differently. It makes sense to consider profit as the divisional contribution – that is, the controllable contribution minus non-controllable costs that could be avoided by closing the division. The first example above (costs of headquarters' staff fully dedicated to the division at stake) would now be included, thus reducing the performance measure. The second example (general administration headquarters' costs) would remain excluded, because these would not be avoided by closing down the division. A similar logic applies to the definition of investment. All the (net) assets supporting the division's operations should be included, even if they are not managed or controllable by the division, and even if they are owned by headquarters and are merely allocated to divisions. Why? Because all these (net) assets are being used to attain the division economic performance. Unused assets (because, for instance, they are kept as a reserve to support future growth) may be disregarded.

Note that divisional profit (before taxes) has not been adopted for either objective. Why? Because to measure both types of performance you should exclude indirect costs merely allocated among divisions (the second example provided). Because this allocation is often arbitrary and these costs would not disappear by closing down the division, excluding these costs is preferable. This makes divisional profit (before taxes) unsuitable for either objective (an exception may be using it to compare a division with other companies in the same industry, whose performance also reflected these types of costs).

Finally, note that variations are possible to measure investment. Measures may be based on current or historical costs of the assets. It is theoretically preferable to adopt current costs, based on assets' economic value or replacement cost, although this requires more complex estimates. If historical figures are adopted, then you still have to decide whether adopting assets' net book value or their gross cost. Net book value is often preferred because it allows consistency with the figures in the statement of financial position and with the way profitability was calculated (that is, taking into account depreciation). However, Table 18.3 shows that adopting net book value has two problems, regardless of using ROI, RI or EVA®. The exhibit includes data for a company that used the same equipment in years 1–4 and in year 5 replaced it for a new one with the same purchase cost.

The first problem of adopting net book value is that it will tend to make performance measures improve in time, simply because net book value decreases as depreciations accumulate, as in years 1–4. This happens in ROI, RI and EVA results. Second, it discourages replacing old, highly depreciated equipment, because the higher net book value of new equipment will worsen performance measures. This is very visible in year 5. Even though this investment increases profitability (from £100,000 to £160,000), ROI falls dramatically from 50 per cent to 17.5 per cent and RI/EVA also drops from £80,000 to £60,000. These problems may influence managers' decisions towards keeping old, less competitive equipment and greatly compromise the company's competitiveness. In contrast, if you adopt gross cost, performance measures remain stable in years 1–4 and, importantly, they increase (rather than decrease) in year 5. This encourages managers to replace the equipment, hence promoting competitiveness. As a final remark, note that as international reporting standards (increasingly promoting the adoption of fair value, a notion completely unrelated to historical costs and potentially closer to current value) are increasingly used, this distinction between current and historical costs gradually becomes less relevant.

Table 18.3: Impacts on ROI, RI and EVA of using assets' net book value or gross cost

	Year 1	Year 2	Year 3	Year 4	Year 5 (equipment replaced)
Assets (equipment) Gross cost	1,000,000	1,000,000	1,000,000	1,000,000	1,000,000
– accumulated depreciation (20 per cent)	– 200,000	– 400,000	– 600,000	– 800,000	– 200,000
Net book value	800,000	600,000	400,000	200,000	800,000
Profitability measure	100,000	100,000	100,000	100,000	140,000
Adopting assets net book value					
ROI	12.5 %	16.67 %	25 %	50 %	17.5 %
Charge of capital (10 per cent of assets net book value)	80,000	60,000	40,000	20,000	80,000
RI or EVA (based on assets net book value)	20,000	40,000	60,000	80,000	60,000
Adopting assets gross cost					
ROI	10 %	10 %	10 %	10 %	14 %
Charge of capital (10 per cent of assets gross cost)	100,000	100,000	100,000	100,000	100,000
RI or EVA	0	0	0	0	40,000

Real-life situations present many controversial areas to management accountants, requiring an evaluation beyond typical textbook examples. We have already depicted some situations which are not clear-cut or may need varied approaches. We now leave a short, sensitizing note about 'murky situations' of real life.

A word of caution: the murky situations of real life

Bear in mind that organizations differ in their ways to define their responsibility areas and even in the labels they attribute to each option or variable. In addition, distinguishing between controllable and non-controllable items is typically difficult. Management accountants are likely to be confronted with situations not clearly matching textbook definitions and approaches, and with many 'grey' areas which practitioners may not understand or may interpret differently among themselves.

Here is an example about costs controllability. Many large global groups create a shared services centre (SSC) to carry out activities like payroll processing or routine financial accounting tasks for all companies in the group, in exchange for a fee (this fee is a transfer price, as you will learn in the next section). Typically, the group's companies do not have the choice of hiring external service providers and have to pay to the SSC fees defined by headquarters; divisional managers typically cannot control the price of those services. If those fees are determined in a somewhat arbitrary basis (if for example, they are based on the percentage of divisional sales within total group sales), then they are basically not controllable by the divisional manager – it is most unlikely that a manager would intentionally reduce sales in order to reduce SSC fees! But what if fees are determined on a pay-per-use basis, for example dependent on the number of processed documents originated from each division? Then, in line with insights from activity-based costing and management (Chapters 6 and 19), divisional managers may try to 'generate' fewer documents by, for instance, aggregating sales to each customer into fewer invoices, hence incurring lower SSC fees. So, to determine controllable contribution, we may consider that the divisional manager can (only partially) control the quantity of services used, but not the price paid for them.

Let us now turn to assets controllability. For example, if divisions are fully responsible for sales payment conditions and daily management, then accounts receivable should be considered as controllable assets. However, if the policy concerning customers' credit limits is defined by headquarters but it is up to divisional staff to keep outstanding debts within those limits, it may make sense to distinguish between accounts receivable within and beyond the credit limits. This flexibility is likely to create difficulties both in technical and fairness terms. Let us briefly discuss the fairness problem. Divisions may have pressured headquarters to approve more generous sales conditions; such approval has improved division competitiveness, sales and profitability. Who will be held responsible: the entity approving the conditions or the entity pushing for their approval and directly benefiting from them?

Questions like these – and others more complex encountered in real-life situations – are unlikely to have universal solutions, and require management accountants to combine technical accounting knowledge with detailed business knowledge and social and political skills. This combination is important to design management control systems that may be accepted and implemented from both technical and political perspectives, matching the context of each particular organization.

Conclusion on divisional performance: financial measures and beyond

This section discussed return on investment, residual income and economic value added, popular accounting tools to measure performance in divisionalized organizations in a financial perspective. However, they all have limitations and their usage may encourage possible dysfunctional behaviour – as for all performance measures. For example, all three analysed accounting measures (even EVA®) suffer from short-term myopia. The combination of financial measures may lessen these problems, but it remains restricted to a financial view of performance.

As you know from Chapter 17, non-financial performance measures are increasingly adopted across organizations to supplement this financial perspective. The balanced scorecard is perhaps the most prominent example of this novel, holistic approach that combines the flexibility and long-term focus of multiple non-financial measures with the ultimate focus on financial performance, and that can be used as a tool for performance management, rather than merely measurement. The two following chapters further discuss financial and, in particular, non-financial approaches to measuring, understanding and managing crucial dimensions for organizations' success.

Keeping our chapter focus on the financial aspect of divisionalized and multinational organizations, a major issue concerns how to account for the multiple transactions occurring *within* these large organizations. The financial valuation of these flows of goods, intangibles, services and capital has an impact on the financial performance measures of the individual divisions and subsidiaries and, potentially, of the entire group. This financial valuation is based on the transfer prices defined for these flows, for which see the next section.

Transfer pricing

Transfer prices are used to define the financial value of flows of goods, intangibles, services and capital between subunits of organizations. Transfer pricing is a major issue in large organizations and multinationals, in particular when these are highly vertically integrated. Think about car or electric appliance producers. Typically, they design products in one location, manufacture parts in another location, assemble them in yet another location and then send finished products to commercial subsidiaries worldwide. Each of these intra-group transfers is valued based on transfer prices. We label as *intermediate products* those goods transferred within the group – even if they are already finished products from a physical perspective, such as in the last stage of intra-group commercial distribution. Our discussion may be extended to include intangibles, services and capital traded within the group as 'intermediate products'. In *Management Accounting in Practice*

18.1: Management Accounting in Practice

The automotive industry and the transfer pricing challenge

Major car makers have their value chain scattered among multiple organizations, both within and outside the group. The consultancy firm PWC (2008) demonstrates that the automotive industry is a high-value, consumer product business and therefore has characteristics that make transfer pricing particularly important. Examples include:

● Massive, upfront investments to develop products, in spite of their short lifespans (four to five years)

● Constant technological improvements to meet customers' and regulators' requirements

● Constant innovation in branding to ensure continuing competitiveness.

Fundamental decisions about group structure and location must consider these industry characteristics and transfer pricing implications. We need to define the legal entity getting the residual profit of the value chain, that is, the profit after routine functions such as assembling or distribution have been paid for. This central entity acts as the 'spider in the web', with significant operational responsibility and the required capital and key assets such as patents and know-how (PWC, 2010a). The location and co-ordination of activities will determine intra-group flows, to be valued according to transfer prices. These decisions include:

● 'whether to centralize research and development and intellectual property ownership;

● where to locate manufacturing and how to manage capacity; and

● determining the extent of cooperation with suppliers and even with other manufacturers.' (PWC, 2008, p. 1)

Thorny issues arise with regard to intellectual property flows. Areas with significant intangible value include product technology and designs, process development know-how and marketing intangibles such as trademarks and brands. Indeed, the automotive industry is a major contributor to worldwide expenditure on R&D and marketing. Therefore, the financial evaluation of these massive intellectual property flows, based on transfer prices, also has massive economic consequences.

Finally, there are extensive collaborations and partnerships between producers and suppliers. For example, the Jaguar X-type is built on the Mondeo platform and Toyota and Peugeot Citroën use the same line to produce three cars with different brands. The technology sharing implied by these agreements require significant reflection on strategic, financial and legal perspectives, in which transfer prices cannot be ignored.

Source: PWC (2008, 2010a).

Exercise

Identify another industry with highly integrated and dispersed value chains and business processes and discuss if the challenges posed to that industry are different (and in what ways) from those in the automotive industry.

18.1 you can explore why transfer pricing is so important in one of the largest industries in the world, the automotive industry.

If you are the manager responsible for the group as a whole, you might think that intra-group transfers do not matter for your group-wide level of responsibility. You might think that all that matters at a group-wide level are purchases and sales to entities external to the group. However, transfer prices do matter and should be carefully designed, for several reasons. First, transfer prices strongly influence divisional profitability, across all financial performance measures. If these measures are used for divisional evaluation, they influence motivation and decisions taken by divisional managers. Motivational impacts alone are sufficient to justify paying attention to the issue, but also remember that divisionalized managers can make selling, buying or production decisions. Second, there is the risk that these divisional decisions may not be in the best interests of the group and lead to suboptimal group profitability. Ideally, transfer prices should create goal congruence between divisional and group-wide interests. Finally, for multinationals, with subsidiaries in different regions subject to different tax regimes, transfer prices adopted for external purposes (and hence tax purposes) have important tax consequences, including shifting taxable profits across locations.

Next, you will learn to define transfer pricing and identify its purposes. Then, you will explore various methods to define transfer prices. A discussion about transfer pricing in multinationals closes the section.

Definition and purposes of transfer pricing

Transfer prices are the prices of flows of economic goods between divisions[3] of the same organization. Transfer prices influence the revenues of the selling division (the supplier) and the costs of the buying division (the receiver). Although from a corporate perspective this intra-organizational exchange might seem irrelevant at first sight, transfer prices do clearly influence the profitability of each division. Higher transfer prices increase suppliers' revenues and profits, at the expense of increasing buyers' costs and decreasing their profits. So, when organizations are decentralized, transfer prices influence divisional managers' decision about buying from (and selling to) inside or outside the organization. These decisions may lead to different production quantities and have a substantial impact on organization-wide profitability.

Transfer prices have three main purposes:

1) *To motivate divisional managers to make good economic decisions* from an organization-wide perspective. This happens when transfer prices ensure goal congruence between divisional and

organization-wide interests. With adequate transfer prices, managers may focus exclusively on improving their divisional performance and ignore organization-wide impacts, because their division-oriented decisions will also improve organization-wide performance.

2) *To evaluate managerial and economic performance at divisional level.* Transfer prices should allow correct performance measurement and fair evaluation of both supplier and buyer divisions. Inadequate transfer prices will overstate the performance of one division at the expense of the other. This creates motivational problems in both divisions – even the one whose performance was overstated, since its members will have fewer incentives to improve divisional performance.

3) *To shift profits across locations*, for tax and other purposes. Divisions in different locations and, in particular, in different countries may be subject to different tax laws. In those cases, shifting profits from divisions in high-tax locations to divisions in low-tax locations allows minimizing taxation at a group-wide level. However, legislators around the world have been producing increasingly strict tax laws to limit such tax-saving possibilities. Shifting profits across locations may also be intended to circumvent national restrictions to repatriate local units' profits to headquarters; although such restrictions may sound unrealistic in the context of today's developed economies, they still exist in some less developed economies. To achieve that objective, transfer pricing policy should reduce the profits generated in those countries. Profit distribution among units also has an impact on their financial health and their financing options. For example, transfer prices promoting higher profits for a unit struggling with limited credit access is a way to strengthen its statement of financial position and lessen its financing problems.

Other goals may also exist. First, groups may wish to minimize taxes, duties and tariffs charged on intra-group transactions, particularly imports. This objective is always achieved through minimizing the transfer price, rather than adjusting transfer prices upwards or downwards as appropriate to shift profits to lower-tax locations. Second, in bargaining processes with local governments, companies may commit to generate a minimum percentage of products' total value in local subsidiaries; defined transfer prices will affect these measures. Also, the increasingly serious consequences of failing to comply with tax regulations has sometimes made tax-compliance a goal in itself (rather than a mere constraint) when setting transfer prices. This objective has motivated many multinationals to adopt **tax-compliant transfer prices** even for their internal reporting, with significant consequences on their management control system (Cools and Emmanuel, 2007), as you will read later in this section.

Such varied goals are unlikely to be met by any single transfer price. For example, a transfer price suitable to evaluate divisional managers may lead to unsatisfactory economic decision making, and only by chance will it also minimize organization-wide taxation. You will now analyse the main bases for setting transfer prices: market prices, costs (marginal costs, full costs or 'costs plus a mark-up') and negotiation between the parties. Two other method variations, attempting to overcome problems with previous methods, are then discussed: transfer pricing at 'marginal costs plus a fixed lump-sum fee' and transfer pricing at dual rates.

Main transfer pricing methods

Exhibit 18.2 summarizes the various types of transfer prices.

The five main types of transfer prices are:

- *Market-based* transfer prices – based on: (1) the price of a similar or identical item in a publicly available list (e.g., oil prices in the stock market); (2) a competitor's price; (3) the supplier division's selling price to external customers (potentially adjusted to account for lower transaction costs in intra-group exchanges).

- Three alternatives of cost-based transfer prices:

  - *Marginal cost* transfer prices – in accounting, marginal cost is usually represented by variable costs, both direct and indirect.

  - *Full-cost* transfer prices – include both variable and fixed costs of all resources committed in the long-run to produce a good or service.

  - *Cost plus a mark-up* transfer prices – to allow supplier divisions to be profitable.

- *Negotiated* transfer prices – result from a bargaining process between both parties, potentially (but not necessarily) oriented by market price and cost information.

There are two additional methods, analysed later, which attempt to overcome limitations of the above methods:

- Transfer pricing at 'marginal costs plus a fixed lump-sum fee'

- Transfer pricing at dual rates.

Exhibit 18.2: A summary of the multiple alternatives to define transfer prices

The following example will assist our discussion of the various transfer price methods. GroupCo, a vertically integrated group operating in the electric appliances industry, holds multiple divisions. Exhibit 18.3 describes essential information about GroupCo's divisions. Table 18.4 summarizes costs and revenues for both divisions.

GroupCo holds multiple divisions, among which:

- *ManCo*, a manufacturing division

  ManCo buys raw materials to produce plastic parts and sells this *intermediate product* to AssembCo. For simplicity, let's consider that: ManCo has significant excess capacity; ManCo produces a single type of plastic part; one plastic part is needed for each electric appliance; all figures are on a unit basis.

  The market price of raw materials required to produce a plastic part is £10. In production and shipping activities, ManCo incurs in other variable costs of £2 and fixed costs of £3 per unit.

  We initially assume that the intermediate product is undifferentiated and is also traded by external units in competitive markets, currently at a market price of £20.

- *AssembCo*, an assembling division

  AssembCo buys the plastic parts from ManCo. AssembCo incurs in additional variable costs of £4 and fixed costs of £1 per unit.

  AssembCo sells the final product to external customers, where a market price of £30 currently prevails.

In the ensuing discussion, we will introduce alternative assumptions as convenient to explain the various transfer prices methods.

Exhibit 18.3: Presenting GroupCo's divisions

Market-based transfer prices

Market-based transfer prices are ideal for both decision-making and managerial evaluation purposes. However, this is only valid in perfectly (or at least highly) competitive markets. In competitive

Table 18.4: Unit costs and market prices for the manufacturing and the assembling divisions

	£
ManCo	
Market price raw materials	10
Other variable production and shipping costs	2
Fixed costs	3
Full costs	15
Intermediate product (plastic part) market price	20
AssembCo	
Other variable production and shipping costs	4
Fixed costs	1
Finished product (electric appliance) market price	30

Note: The transfer price of the intermediate product is missing, since it will depend on the adopted transfer price method.

markets, no product differentiation exists and the market price does not depend on any individual seller or buyer. However, as you know, such competitive markets are the exception, rather than the rule.

Transfer prices based on competitive market prices encourage managers of both divisions to exchange within the group, since they do not provide any advantage for either division to buy or sell plastic parts in the external market. Let us see why:

- The minimum transfer price accepted by the selling division ManCo is the market price, £20; should it be lower, ManCo would prefer to sell only in the external market, to non-group assembling units, and no intra-group exchanges would occur.

- The maximum transfer price accepted by the buying division AssembCo is also the market price, £20; should it be higher, AssembCo would prefer to buy only in the external market, from non-group manufacturers.

Market-based transfer prices lead to divisional profits similar to those generated by independent divisions, correctly expressing the contribution of each division to group-wide profits and allowing comparisons with similar companies in the industry. This is consistent with the autonomy characterizing profit and investment centres. Remember that, in competitive markets, potential shortage or excess capacity problems can be solved by resorting to external entities, buying or selling the products at the same market price, when profitable (if not profitable and without improvement possibilities, closure of divisions should be considered). So, in competitive markets both divisions can make their decisions and operate independently.

Intra-group transfers often allow lower transaction costs, such as lower selling, collecting or warranty expenses by the supplying division. This improves the profitability of intra-group transfers for the group – remember that obtaining lower transaction costs is a common justification to create vertically integrated groups. So, to motivate the buying division to buy within the group (and to keep the supplying division indifferent), market-based transfer prices may be adjusted, including a discount to reflect the typically lower expenses in intra-group sales.

Adjustments to market prices in distressed markets

Markets sometimes undergo periods of industry-wide excess capacity and particularly low prices – called distress market prices. If the (temporarily) low market prices make the supplying division currently unprofitable, setting the transfer price at such low level would promote closing down the supplier division – or, in divisions with multiple lines of products, to reallocate resources to more profitable product lines. Without an intra-group provider, the buying division would purchase from external suppliers. However, divestiture decisions based on short-term indicators may be damaging in the long term, in the case of future market recovery; rebuilding the capacity to return to a previously abandoned market is typically lengthy and costly – in production, commercial and organizational terms.

To avoid this problem, transfer prices may be set at the long-run average market price (higher than the temporarily depressed level). This temporary method of transfer pricing better evaluates the long-run viability of the supplier and justifies keeping its operations, waiting for market recovery.

This approach has some problems. The buying division would obviously have to be obliged to purchase within the group, although this imposition would hurt its short-term performance and undermine its autonomy. Therefore, transfer prices would no longer support accurate divisional performance evaluation. Moreover, it is often difficult to distinguish between temporary and definitive market trends. Many companies have mistakenly interpreted adverse market trends as being temporary and insisted continuing in the business although losing money, only to later realize that the market decline was definitive. In this case, transfer prices not reflecting distressed market prices may contribute to wrong economic decisions.

Marginal cost transfer prices

Marginal cost transfer prices (like the other types of transfer prices analysed below) are valuable when the intermediate product market prices are difficult or impossible to get, in particular when the market for the intermediate product does not exist at all. That may be the case for our example if (and we are now changing the initial scenario for the three cost-based transfer prices) ManCo is using patented technology to obtain a unique part, especially designed to provide a competitive advantage for AssembCo's finished products. So, ManCo is not allowed to sell externally and AssembCo's cannot buy that unique part except from the group manufacturer.

The economic concept of marginal cost (the incremental cost of producing one additional unit) is often interpreted, for management accounting purposes and in a short-term perspective, as short-term variable cost, constant within the relevant range and including both direct and indirect costs. In brief, this approach considers that:

$$\text{Marginal cost transfer price} = \textbf{Supplier division's variable unit costs}$$
$$\textbf{(Raw materials + Other variable inputs)}$$
$$= 10 + 2 = £12$$

In the absence of perfectly competitive markets, economic theory (see, for example, Morgan et al., 2009) tells us that setting the transfer price at the supplier's marginal cost motivates the buying division to purchase within the group the quantity that maximizes group profitability. Why? In short, because the supplier's marginal cost is also the group's marginal cost for the intermediate product. Should transfer prices be higher, the buying division would reduce purchases, leading to lower group profitability. Setting transfer prices at marginal cost would promote goal congruence and hence good economic decisions.

Setting transfer prices at marginal (or variable) cost has not been popular among companies. A major problem of this method is not supporting the evaluation of either division. The supplying division has no chance to be profitable on intra-group transfers. If ManCo transfers the parts at the £12 variable costs, its contribution will be zero and it will have negative profitability. Conversely, the buying division's profits will be highly benefited by the low transfer price. Additionally, marginal costs are often difficult to accurately estimate for two reasons: marginal costs are not in general constant, that is, they vary with the level of output due to, for example, economies of scale, and it is often difficult to identify and allocate variable indirect costs. The allocation problem may be severe in traditional methods and an ABC approach may only lessen it, but not eliminate it (see Chapter 6). Third, the short-term perspective underlying this method is limited, since it totally ignores fixed costs – which should also be included in longer-term decisions. To address this last problem, the following method includes fixed costs in the transfer price.

Full-cost transfer prices

Full-cost transfer prices include not only the supplier division's unit variable costs, but also fixed costs. This approach better conveys the long-term perspective in which fixed costs can be avoided, and lessens the evaluation bias of the previous method. In this method, ManCo would charge the following transfer price:

$$\text{Full-cost transfer price} = \text{Supplier division's variable} + \text{Fixed unit costs}$$
$$= (10 + 2) + 3 = £15$$

However, this approach has three problems. First, it does not ensure goal congruence. By increasing the transfer price above the supplier division's marginal cost, it promotes decisions by the buying division which reduce group-wide profitability. In particular, it has a major problem. From AssembCo's perspective, the transfer price of £15 is considered a variable cost – although, from a group economic perspective, producing parts at ManCo only implies variable costs of £12. Why did this happen? Because the supplier's fixed costs of £3 became included in the transfer price and are now viewed as variable by the buyer. This distorts analysis, from a group-level perspective.

Second, defining transfer prices based on full costs increases the problem, already present in the previous method, potentially caused by inaccurate allocation of indirect costs, because now both variable and fixed costs are at stake.

Third, because the supplier division's profit margin is still not included in the transfer price, this method still does not fully solve the evaluation bias problem of the previous method; it stills introduces a bias against the seller and in favour of the buyer. The following method attempts to address this last problem.

'Cost plus a mark-up' transfer prices

This method sets transfer prices by adding a mark-up to the supplier division's costs in order to allow it to make a profit and approximate market prices. This makes transfer prices more adequate for divisional evaluation than previous cost-based alternatives. This method is particularly useful if there is no competitive market price. If this method uses full costs data, then the mark-up should only reflect the profit margin; alternatively, if it uses marginal costs, then the mark-up should reflect both fixed costs and the profit margin. Given ManCo's full costs and a 20 per cent profit margin, we obtain:

$$\text{Cost plus a mark-up transfer price} = \big(\text{Supplier division's variable} + \text{Fixed unit costs}\big)$$
$$\times \big(1 + \text{Supplier division's profit margin}\big)$$
$$= (10 + 2 + 3) \times (1 + 20\%) = £18$$

However, note that this method does not completely and permanently proxy the market price. Market prices may change quickly and at any time, but these transfer prices are based on internal data and are only revised occasionally. In addition, the goal congruence problem is even worse in this method than in the full cost-based method, because the transfer price is even higher.

A note on cost-based methods: standard or actual costs?

In all three cost-based methods, the supplier division's standard costs should be used, rather than actual costs. Why? Because if there is no competitive market price, using actual costs would allow inefficiencies of the supplier division to be passed along to the buying division through a higher transfer price. The supplier's performance would be protected from inefficiencies, providing no incentive to the supplier to keep costs under control. Instead, using standard costs keeps the supplier focused on controlling its costs, since its potential unfavourable variances cannot be compensated through a higher transfer price.

Negotiated transfer prices

When there are imperfect external markets, there may be a case for setting negotiated transfer prices through a bargaining process between the two parties. In not perfectly competitive markets, slight differentiation possibilities, based on product characteristics or on other sales terms, or the power of particular market participants, may allow multiple prices to coexist. Market price and cost information may be used in this bargaining process, but note that such information may also be ignored.

An essential requirement of this method is that both parties have actual and equal bargaining capacity. This is the first problem of this method. Bargaining outcomes (and therefore profit sharing) may be influenced by different bargaining skills of divisional managers. Bargaining outcomes may also be influenced by different divisional economic circumstances. The division most dependent on intra-group transactions (because, for example, group-specific products or services represent a higher share of the divisional activity) will have a bargaining disadvantage. On the contrary, the party less dependent on these intra-group transactions can more easily reject proposed conditions and exchange in external markets (or credibly threaten to do so), giving it a powerful bargaining argument. In the extreme, if both parties have full access to perfect markets, then this method is also not adequate, since the transfer price should be the market price and there is no room for negotiation. So, this method may be applied when imperfect markets exist, although bargaining outcomes may lead to biased economic divisions and unfair evaluations of divisional performance.

Bargaining processes may divert managerial time and focus away from activities generating company-wide benefits. In addition, although politics and conflicts are an inevitable feature of organizations, bargaining among divisions may create divisiveness and lack of co-operation which may damage company-wide performance. When such problems are kept at low levels, corporate managers may accept them as a necessary (and not measurable) cost for having the benefits of a decentralized organization. However, if problems escalate, corporate-level intervention may be required – an intervention which would likely undermine divisions' autonomy and compromise decentralization benefits.

Politics and roles of management accountants in transfer-pricing negotiations

Management accountants are often at the hub of potentially difficult bargaining processes. The negotiation of transfer prices is an example that makes the political dimension of organizations – and of its participants, management accountants included – particularly visible. However, this dimension of the roles of management accountants is often overlooked. At a theoretical level, management accountants are usually prescribed a supposedly neutral role – a role that, in practical terms, is presented as one endorsing the perspective of the organization as a whole.

However, in practice, negotiation of transfer prices often makes clear the political nature of the activities of management accountants – as for any other organizational member. In practice, divisional management accountants are likely to endorse a divisional perspective. Endorsing the perspective of the organizational area to which the individual is committed – due to hierarchical, social or psychological pressures, wanting to reinforce its membership to a particular organizational domain or network – is a common feature of real people in real organizations. And it is likely that members of a particular division develop a lot of 'membership work' directed to that division. 'Taking sides' does not only exist with regard to taking the side of one particular division, but equally applies to corporate-level management accountants – they are taking the side of the organization as a whole and, indirectly, the side of those that benefit from organization-wide performance.

How may 'taking sides' affect the activities of management accountants? Suppose that the reward mechanism in place makes divisional bonuses depend on a particular divisional performance measure. Divisional management accountants may provide financial arguments to their divisional managers in order to justify transfer prices favouring their division evaluation, hence increasing their bonuses – even if they are detrimental to the company as a whole. For example, management accountants are often the experts of cost classifications and costs allocations. As you have seen, alternatives to classify or to allocate costs are often subject to controversy. It is often possible to present equally plausible arguments to support (or contest) different alternatives. Divisional management accountants are likely to be crucial to provide plausible and convincing technical arguments supporting alternatives that favour divisionalized objectives.

This political dimension is typically overlooked. However, ignoring it implies ignoring (intentionally or not) the inevitable political nature of organizational activities, and it limits future management accountants' awareness of the real-world situations they will be part of in their professional life.

Method variations to overcome limitations

As you have seen in the previous section, only prices from competitive markets can lead to transfer prices that are adequate both for decision-making (ensuring alignment between divisional and group-wide interests) and for performance evaluation. Even so, you may have noticed that we excluded from our discussion the remaining transfer prices goals indicated at the start, such as profit shifting across locations for group-level tax optimization. Of course, only by chance would market-based transfer prices, or any of the other alternatives, also simultaneously ensure all additional goals.

Now, you will learn two variations of previous methods that may improve transfer prices outcomes when there are no perfectly competitive markets: setting prices at 'marginal costs plus a fixed lump-sum fee'; using dual-rate transfer prices. As you will see, both methods are adequate both for decision-making and for performance evaluation.

Transfer pricing at 'marginal costs plus a fixed lump-sum fee'

Transfer pricing at 'marginal costs plus a fixed lump-sum fee' intends to join the benefits of two systems. Each intra-group exchange is charged according to the marginal cost transfer price method; this ensures the goal alignment benefit of this method. However, remember that charging at marginal costs does not provide any profit to the supplying division. To prevent such a problem, this method variation adds a fixed lump-sum fee to be paid to the supplying division, independent of individual transactions, to cover its fixed costs and a profit margin. Adding this fee intends to achieve the goal of supporting divisional evaluation, as well. This fee is calculated at the start of each period, based on the supplying division's capacity expected to be used (and therefore reserved) to meet the buying divisions' estimated orders.

If actual orders (and hence actual capacity usage) differ from estimates, the paid fee will be incorrect. Two solutions may solve this problem. The first can be applied when there are multiple intra-group buying divisions involved. Divisions may be allowed to shift a portion of their reserved capacity (and a proportional part of the fee) among themselves. This flexible allocation improves group-wide capacity usage and performance. The second solution is recalculating the fee at the end of the period to reflect the actual capacity used by the supplying division. Remember that the fee will include a part of fixed costs (now based on actual capacity usage) plus a profit margin. So, this solution will lead to similar results to the 'cost plus a mark-up' method. Overall, although this variation for defining transfer prices may provide good results, it also has some challenges which may explain its low popularity in practice.

Transfer pricing at dual rates

Transfer pricing at dual rates allows divisions to record distinct transfer prices for each exchange. Typically, the supplying division records transactions at market or 'cost-plus a profit margin' transfer prices; this supports the performance evaluation goal. However, the buying division records transactions at the supplying division's marginal cost; this promotes good economic decisions. These dual-recording criteria will lead to double count profits, requiring an accounting adjustment at corporate level.

Adopting dual rates motivates both divisions to trade among themselves: the supplier will get a 'fair' price and the buyer may well get 'a bargain' (only paying for the marginal cost, probably quite below market prices). However, faced with such an appealing deal, the buyer will virtually always purchase from the intra-group supplying division – hence protecting the supplier from external competition and reducing its incentives to be cost-efficient. Moreover, double counting profits and later cancelling them at corporate level may raise tax inspectors' and auditors' suspicions, and it is also confusing for managers. Owing to such problems, this method is not very popular in practice either.

Transfer pricing in multinationals: taxation and management issues

This section ends by discussing the specific transfer pricing difficulties of multinationals. Multinationals have all the transfer prices challenges of divisionalized organizations, plus additional issues such as being located in multiple countries, with likely different tax regimes. Differences across tax jurisdictions open up room for income tax planning at group level, shifting profits across locations in order to lower group-wide taxes. Income tax optimization involves reducing the profits of units in higher-tax locations (by adopting transfer prices that reduce their revenues and/or increase their expenses). In turn, the corresponding profit increase (due to increased revenues and/or reduced expenses) of units in lower-tax locations will be subject to lower tax rates. Overall, total taxes at group-wide level will be reduced.

Note that other charges such as taxes, duties and tariffs may apply to cross-border, intra-group transfers. Higher transfer prices always imply higher charges. This always promotes lower transfer prices. The ensuing discussion focuses exclusively on income taxation issues rather than these other charges.

Empiric evidence confirms that multinationals' tax planning includes using transfer prices to shift profits, typically from higher-tax, industrialized countries towards lower-taxes locations, in particular 'tax havens' (Bartelsman and Beetsma, 2003). However, national governments have been increasingly setting tighter regulations to limit tax optimization in multinationals, by limiting opportunities to shift profits to other countries. National tax authorities may punish tax-compliance failures by making tax adjustments and applying fines. These adjustments and fines may be very significant and may lead to double taxation if the same profit is taxed in two countries. Finally, note that multinationals' tax planning may also include a shift of real activities and resulting profits to lower-tax countries (Bartelsman and Beetsma, 2003); however, this shift is not related, at least not directly, to the transfer prices issue.

To assist both tax authorities and multinationals, international bodies like the Organization for Economic Co-operation and Development (OECD) have been issuing and revising guidelines for decades. The knowledge, interpretation and application of these guidelines and relevant national tax regulations is a complex arena which requires consulting a detailed and updated publication (such as PWC, 2010b, regularly updated on the website) and possibly seeking tax consultancy services. Next, you will briefly overview the main OECD guidelines and recommended methods for transfer pricing, to create awareness about this issue and identify potential roles for management accountants. In the next section, you will read further about possible implications for management control from pursuing tax-compliance objectives when setting transfer prices.

An overview of OECD guidelines

The OECD (OECD, 2010) elects the **arm's-length principle** as the fairest and most reliable basis for defining where profits should be taxed. Under this principle, intra-group transactions should be charged at the price that would be defined between unrelated entities, keeping all other aspects of the relationship. Clearly, this principle is similar to the recommendation of market-based transfer prices. However, this market referent may not exist or may not be directly available. So, the OECD recommends comparing the conditions of a controlled (intra-group) transaction and the conditions of independent transactions, even if those comparisons are inexact. These conditions include (PWC, 2010b, pp. 35–6):

- 'The specific characteristics of the property or services;

- The functions that each enterprise performs, including the assets used and, most importantly, the risks undertaken;

- The contractual terms', such as price, payment conditions and warranties;

- 'The economic circumstances of different markets, for example differences in geographic markets, or differences in the level of the market such as wholesale vs. retail; and

- Business strategies, for example market penetration schemes when a price is temporarily lowered.'

PWC (2010b) indicates and illustrates the various methods to determine an arm's-length price:

- 'Traditional' transaction-based methods:

  - *Comparable uncontrolled price (CUP)* method – the most direct and preferred by the OECD. It compares the price charged in controlled versus comparable uncontrolled transactions. Comparable uncontrolled price may suffer adjustments if the differences between the two transactions are minor and can be easily valued.

  - *Resale price* method – the actual resale price minus a discount for the reseller's activities. The discount is the reseller's gross margin in an uncontrolled environment and may also be adjusted for differences between the two transactions.

  - *Cost-plus* method – the cost plus a mark-up (the manufacturer's gross margin in an uncontrolled environment).

  - *Cost-plus* method, *adjusting for capacity usage*.

- Profit-based methods:

  - *Profit split* method *(PSM)* – the multinational's profit is divided in the same way that independent enterprises, in a joint-venture relationship, could be expected to divide.

  - *Transactional net margin* method – analyses the operating profit relative to an appropriate base (such as costs, sales or assets) from a particular intra-group transaction (or group of transactions), compared to independent companies.

This summary, expanded and illustrated in PWC (2010b), suggests that management accountants are likely to play important roles in establishing tax-compliant transfer prices. For instance, in the resale price method and the cost-plus method, comparing gross margins requires ensuring that expenses have been categorized (for example, as industrial, commercial or administrative costs, or as capitalized costs) using similar criteria in the companies being compared. While this may be a relatively straightforward task regarding the management accountant's own company, evaluating third-party information may be challenging. The profit split method entails even more complicated challenges: the scarcity of public information often requires judgement to determine a formula to split the profit among parties. Determining such a formula to reflect each party's relative contribution of tangible and intangible assets requires careful user judgement and in-depth business knowledge, in addition to accounting knowledge. The transfer pricing challenges identified in

18.2: Management Accounting in Practice

Transfer pricing challenges in the digital media industry

The consultancy firm KPMG recently highlighted specific transfer pricing challenges in the digital media industry. In this industry, groups are often highly vertically integrated, with very significant intra-group transfers and, in particular, intellectual property transfers – typically, the most complex for transfer pricing. This industry has expanded from traditional media companies (such as broadcasters, recorded music and films, advertising, publishers and theatres) to include content creation, aggregation and distribution, even stretching to mobile applications. Internet and mobile wireless technology (smart phones, tablets and so on) have revolutionized media content distribution and consumption. New business models placed new transfer pricing challenges, as illustrated next:

1) Creation of content may occur in one country and distribution may happen in worldwide television networks. How to define this local content transfer price, across the entire value chain, often involving affiliated networks? The overall value of the distribution network must be split across all participants of the value chain, and local content typically only represents a small part of it. In addition, affiliated networks may transfer bundles of several programs (rather than one single program) or may exchange programs among themselves, making the definition of the transfer price for a particular program even more difficult.

2) Media content aggregators (like iTunes, Google, Yahoo or YouTube) are new players in this business value chain and affect how the industry profit is shared among participants. What is the importance and value of (a) the content, (b) the distribution intangibles (the network and marketing intellectual property) or (c) the aggregator's intellectual property (its brand and technology)? This question is important to define transfer prices and, hence, profit allocation.

3) Digital video recorders allow consumers, when viewing recorded television shows, to fast forward past advertisements – hence reducing the value of advertisements. Advertisers have found alternative ways, such as strategically embedding their products in the content. For instance, you may remember James Bond driving cars of particular brands, in various films. In this case, we need to split value and revenues between content and advertising.

4) Websites such as YouTube or Google have substantial revenues from selling advertising space. Adequate transfer prices for transactions regarding advertising sales are necessary to allocate the resulting revenues and profits to the various elements of the value chain, including the content creator, distributor and/or aggregator.

KPMG notes that the value chain and associated transfer prices should be defined when designing or redesigning business models. For that, it is essential to 'identify the key value drivers and apply transfer pricing methodology to the key functions, risks and assets used' (2011, p. 17). As argued throughout this book (and particularly in the next chapter), management accountants clearly have an important potential role in identifying and measuring value drivers.

Source: KPMG, 2011.

Exercise

Compare the challenges faced by the media industry and the automotive industry (analysed in *Management Accounting in Practice 18.1*). Identify and discuss the areas you believe to be the most problematic for transfer pricing, in each industry.

Management Accounting in Practice 18.2 about the rapidly changing digital media industry clearly illustrate these new requirements for a strong business orientation. You may also like to reread *Management Accounting in Practice 18.1* and read PWC (2008, 2010a) to explore similar transfer pricing challenges in the automotive industry.

The risk of adopting tax-compliant transfer prices for management control

Cools and Emmanuel (2007) suggest that multinationals may now be led to prioritize tax compliance in transfer pricing and hence adopt tax-compliant methods for internal purposes as well. Why? To reduce the risk of being investigated by increasingly aggressive tax authorities, potentially imposing large transfer prices adjustments and heavy penalties in case of non-compliance with tax legislation. They argue that, as a safeguard, multinationals may choose to comply with the most demanding tax authorities, currently the US Internal Revenue Service (IRS), in a 'highest-common-denominator-effect' (p. 573). The problem is that tax-compliant transfer prices may not support other important transfer pricing goals, such as supporting divisional decision making and economic and managerial evaluation.

Cools and Emmanuel (2007) suggest several likely consequences of such tax compliance focus for the management control system. First, internal tax units and external fiscal consultants are likely to become more influential and involved in operational matters. They will be important in maintaining and updating transfer price analyses, and in developing the functional analysis and the databases of comparables that justify adopted transfer prices. The role of the internal audit function may also expand to ensure compliance with the detailed rules supporting transfer prices. Second, the strong motivation to adopt a detailed and universal transfer pricing policy requires centralization and uniformity, further empowering the internal tax and audit functions.

Third this trend is likely to severely constrain divisions' discretion by failing to support divisional decision-making and financial performance measurement. Fourth, using tax-compliant transfer prices for divisional targets or budgets may cause highly perverse effects. High-performing divisions greatly outperforming their target may risk attracting the attention of tax authorities. This risk severely undermines their incentive to outperform targets. In addition, budgets reflect unchanging tax-approved transfer prices. Transfer prices are unlikely to change quickly to match quick market changes, given the demanding functional analysis and extensive documentation needed to justify changes to tax-compliant transfer prices. Obviously, targets no longer reflecting divisional current conditions will severely compromise the motivation to improve performance.

Fifth, given the above problems, financial measures may become inadequate to motivate divisional managers. This opens up room for the manipulation of reported financial information or for the adoption of alternative, non-financial measures. However, the divisional specificity of many non-financial measures complicates their linkage with corporate level reward strategy. As a conclusion, Cools and Emmanuel (2007) suggest that for learning and motivation the limitations of using tax-compliant transfer prices for internal purposes may indeed cause multinationals to ossify. This is a serious risk to long-term success, and should make designers of management control systems pause to consider if the advantages to be gained from lessening tax-compliance problems justify taking such risk.

Conclusion on transfer pricing

In this section you learned the merits and limitations of the various bases to define transfer prices: market prices; costs (marginal costs, full costs or full costs plus a mark-up) and negotiation between the parties. Market prices ensure: (1) goal congruence between divisional and group-wide interests, hence promoting good economic decisions and (2) provide good information for divisional performance evaluation. However, this method requires markets to be perfectly competitive, and that is not often the case. Cost-based and negotiation-based methods may be limited in achieving one or both goals above. Two proposed improvements (using 'marginal costs plus a fixed lump-sum fee' and using a dual-rates method) have not been widely used. Then, you read about the increasingly important tax dimension of transfer prices, its mechanisms, objectives, the basics of its regulations (in particular, OECD guidelines) and how this may create potential roles for management accountants. Finally, you explored the potential consequences – and risks – for management control systems in multinationals that adopt tax-compliance transfer prices for internal purposes.

Chapter summary

In this chapter, you explored financial performance in large, divisionalized organizations, and explored specificities of multinational organizations. First, you studied divisionalized financial performance measures: return on investment (ROI); residual income (RI); and economic value added (EVA®). Then, you studied transfer prices as a fundamental cornerstone for measuring financial performance in vertically integrated organizations, explored the various available methods and learned about multinationals' specificities. While financial performance measures and transfer pricing are both traditional topics in management accounting, this chapter has highlighted that both place exciting and relevant challenges that management accountants must address by mobilizing a diversified set of technical, business and political skills.

Key terms

Arm's-length principle The OECD's preferred approach to transfer pricing, based on the price that would be defined between unrelated entities, keeping all other aspects of the relationship (p. 461)

Economic value added (EVA®) A type of residual income, adopting after-tax measures and adjusting several accounting measures of profit and assets to avoid distortions caused by Generally Accepted Accounting Principles (GAAP). These adjustments aim at approximating accounting measures to economic measures (p. 488)

Residual income (RI) Operating profit minus a cost of capital charge on investment (profit and investment may be defined differently, depending on the purpose of the analysis) (p. 447)

Return on investment (ROI) Profit divided by investment (profit and investment may be defined differently, depending on the purpose of the analysis) (p. 444)

Tax-compliant transfer price Transfer price that complies with applicable tax legislation (p. 454)

Transfer price Price charged for flows of goods, intangibles, services or capital within an organization (p. 452)

Review questions ● ● ● ● ● ● ● ● ● ● ● connect ● ● ●

Level of difficulty:	BASIC	INTERMEDIATE	ADVANCED

18.1 Why are accounting measures often preferable to market measures to evaluate divisionalized financial performance? **[LO1]**

18.2 How does the residual income (RI) measure the cost of capital? **[LO3]**

18.3 What kind of intra-group exchanges must be valued at transfer prices? **[LO5]**

18.4 Why are transfer prices important in an organization-wide perspective? **[LO5]**

18.5 How can multinationals reduce company-wide taxation (and other similar costs) through transfer pricing policies? **[LO7]**

18.6 What are the dangers of using ROI for divisional performance measurement? **[LO2]**

18.7 What are the major differences between accounting profit and economic value added? **[LO4]**

18.8 If a market for the intermediate product exists and is perfectly competitive, would you recommend using cost-based transfer prices? Why? If not, what alternative would you suggest? **[LO6]**

18.9 What is gained and lost if we replace marginal cost transfer prices with 'cost-plus a mark-up' transfer prices? **[LO6]**

18.10 Why do some multinationals adopt tax-compliant transfer prices for internal control purposes? What is the risk of this option? **[LO8]**

● ● ● Group discussion and activity questions ● ● ● ● ● ● ● ● ●

18.11 'The limitations of both market and accounting measures of performance are well known. They are evidence for the fact that investors should abandon financial measures and adopt frameworks like the balanced scorecard.' Discuss these claims. **[LO1]**

18.12 'If designers of performance measurement systems are competent, they should always be capable of designing a transfer pricing mechanism that enables all potential objectives of transfer prices to be achieved simultaneously.' Discuss. **[LO5, LO6]**

18.13 'Much research has shown that management accounting is not subservient to financial accounting. This means that it is not reasonable to think that multinationals may consider adopting tax-compliant transfer prices for internal purposes.' Discuss. **[LO1]**

18.14 'Return on investment is a performance measure which encourages investments in the worst divisions. That is totally wrong.' Discuss. **[LO2]**

● ● ● Exercises ● ● ● ● ● ● ● ● ● ● ● ● ● ● ● connect™ ● ● ●

E18.1 Calculation of ROI & RI [LO2, LO3]

The manufacturing company IndCo has reported the following information:

- Operating profit: £40 million
- Investments: £400 million
- Required rate of return: 12 per cent.

Required:

a) Calculate IndCo's return on investment.

b) Calculate IndCo's residual income and interpret the result.

c) To compare IndCo's performance with another company in the same industry but 10 times smaller, which performance measure would you choose? Why?

E18.2 Calculation of ROI & RI [LO2, LO3]

A global consumer goods manufacturer has three divisions which operate in different businesses. The financial information for each division is as follows:

	Division A	Division B	Division C
Cost of capital	10 per cent	8 per cent	6 per cent
Operating profit (£ m)	900	1,500	600
Investment (£ m)	5,000	10,000	6,000

Required:

a) Calculate the return on investment for each division. Which divisions have a better and worse performance, according to the ROI measure?

b) Indicate possible reasons why the divisions have different costs of capital.

c) Calculate the residual income of each division. Which divisions have a better and worse performance, according to the RI measure?

d) Are the divisions' rankings different between the first and third question? Why/why not?

E18.3 **Usage of ROI and RI information: effects on investments decision [LO2, LO3]**

Consider the same global consumer goods company described in Exercise E18.2. A new technology applicable to the three divisions has become available, yielding a 13 per cent rate of return to any division making the £150m investment.

Required:

a) If ROI is used to measure divisions, what would each division decide about making the investment? Why? Is this decision aligned with corporate-wide interests?

b) What if residual income is used instead? What will the decision be, why, and is it aligned with corporate-wide interests?

E18.4 **ROI calculation and manipulation [LO2]**

Pace Company (PC) runs a large number of wholesale stores and is increasing the number of these stores all the time. It measures the performance of each store on the basis of a target return on investment of 15 per cent. Store managers get a bonus of 10 per cent of their salary if their store's annual ROI meets the target each year. Once a store is built there is very little further capital expenditure until a full four years have passed.

PC has a store (store W) in the west of the country. Store W has historic financial data as follows over the past four years:

	2009	2010	2011	2012
Sales (€000's)	200	200	180	170
Gross profit (€000's)	80	70	63	51
Net profit (€000's)	13	14	10	8
Net assets at start of year (€000's)	100	80	60	40

The market in which PC operates has been growing steadily. Typically, PC's stores generate a 40 per cent gross profit margin.

Required:

a) Discuss the past financial performance of store W using ROI and any other measure you feel appropriate and, using your findings, discuss whether the ROI correctly reflects Store W's actual performance. (8 marks)

b) Explain how a manager in store W might have been able to manipulate the results so as to gain bonuses more frequently. (4 marks)

Source: adapted from Association of Chartered Certified Management Accountants, Paper F2.

E18.5 **Transfer prices [LO5, LO6]**

Kick and Rush plc produces footballs for various amateur leagues in South-East England. They consist of two divisions, the leather division which cuts and waterproofs the leather, and the stitching division, which sews the leather together, inserts an air bladder, and sells the footballs to the various leagues.

The leather division prepares the leather in the correct size per football, and charges a transfer price of £17 per unit to the stitching division. This price is based on the current market price for very large wholesale orders less selling and distribution costs which are not applicable in the case of internal transfers. These costs are variable and amount to £3 per unit. The leather division also has access to the external market, where it sells their prepared leather for £20 per (equivalent) unit. These external sales, however, only account for 20 per cent of their total sales volume of 12,000 units per year.

The summarized financial details for the leather division for the last year are as follows:

Leather division – combined internal and external sales	
Sales	216,000
Variable costs (£15 external, £12 internal)	151,200
Contribution	**64,800**
Fixed cost	35,000
Net profit (loss)	**29,800**

Recently, the English branch of a German leather processing company, Wildleder plc, has approached the stitching division with a leather product similar in quality for £15 per unit. The director of the stitching division, Charles Valiant-Tailor, now wants to stop all internal purchases and to obtain the required leather from Wildleder plc. The division manager of the leather division Linda Shagreen however, states that this price is not feasible for her division to match and that they would not be able to recover more than 33 per cent of the lost internal sales externally. The performance of both divisions is measured on the basis of profit generated and neither director is willing to give way on this issue. Headquarters need to step in and resolve the situation.

Required:

a) Appraise the situation after the offer of Wildleder plc, taking into account the changes in profit and costs, and consider the financial impact on the company.

b) Headquarters suggest using the same transfer price as the price offered by Wildleder plc. Analyse the outcomes of this suggestion, and decide if they are better off compared to the initial scenario and the scenario where the leather division would lose their internal sales. Consider the financial impact on Kick and Rush plc if they go forward with this suggestion.

c) Critically interpret the results.

Source: with thanks to Gerhard Kristandl, University of Greenwich (adapted).

E18.6 **Transfer prices and taxation: overhead allocation [LO7, LO8]**

The Frod Company has its headquarters in country Middle, with a corporate tax of 25 per cent, and fully owns subsidiaries in two countries: country Low, with a corporate tax rate of 20 per cent; country High, with a corporate tax rate of 30 per cent.

For next year, the subsidiary in country Low expects to sell to the subsidiary in country High 1 million units of product X. Last year, the transfer price was equal to £10/unit, the prevalent price in the market of this rather undifferentiated product. Country High applies an import tariff of 5 per cent. The country Low subsidiary has total costs of £7 million. The country High subsidiary has £2 million in other costs (in addition to those specified above) and a selling price of £15/unit.

Required:

a) A new director of Frod is determined to increase group level profitability and is contemplating changing the transfer price, in a limit of 20 per cent upwards or downwards. Indicate the price change that would contribute the most towards the director's objective and the resulting after-tax profit increase.

b) Currently, the subsidiary in country High has problems accessing bank credit. Discuss how the change suggested in the previous question might affect this financing problem. What could Frod's headquarters do to lessen this problem?

c) Frod's headquarters provides back-office services to the two subsidiaries, in particular processing documents in their behalf. In exchange for these services, headquarters charge £100,000 in fees. Currently, these fees are allocated among the two subsidiaries according to their sales volume. The new director is now examining two alternatives:

i)   Alternative 1: allocate fees according to the number of subsidiary documents that headquarters process. Currently, 80 per cent of the processed documents are related to the subsidiary in country High.

ii) Alternative 2: allocate fees according to the country markets' total size. The markets of countries Low and High are valued at £20 million and £80 million, respectively.

Indicate the alternative (including keeping the current criterion) that the director would choose to achieve his objective to minimize taxes.

d) Discuss whether tax authorities may object to the alternatives selected in questions 1 and 3.

e) Discuss potential problems of adopting a transfer price different from the current one (the market price) for internal purposes.

Case study problem ● ● ● ● ● ● ● ● ● connect ● ● ●

C18.1 **Challenges in introducing measurement tools – insights from a case study [LO1, LO4]**

In the mid-1990s, a large UK retailer, RetailCo, had successfully overcome a long financial profitability crisis and by 1996 it had significantly improved its profits. However, it attracted negative publicity by being poorly ranked in a league table published in the press, based on its negative EVA®. So, RetailCo's board decided to introduce a new performance evaluation system based on EVA.

Before introducing EVA, RetailCo had measured performance based on sales and margins. Since the performance system ignored the cost of capital, treating it as a cost-free resource, it encouraged high inventory levels and investments hardly covering the cost of capital. EVA was expected to bring discipline in resource use. A major consultancy firm was hired to internally 'sell' the EVA concept and its benefits. Accountants explained EVA calculations and produced a detailed manual and a spreadsheet. In addition, RetailCo organized a 'road show' and created a help team to assist managers with specific local problems.

However, managers of stores and from purchasing and merchandising believed that sales and margins were the fundamentals of retailing. They had become highly familiar with management reports (and performance measurement) based on those sales and margins. In spite of the efforts from consultants and accountants, EVA calculation was problematic and not fully understood by many managers, who did not see the need of EVA. In addition, EVA calculations included charges regarding assets about which managers had no control or information of. To make things worse, EVA was used to calculate bonuses – which dropped against previous periods. Managers became distrustful of EVA in general and accountants in particular.

Two contrary views emerged. Managers argued that EVA introduction was misguided, irrational and motivated by accountants' self-interest to improve their corporate esteem. On the contrary, accountants argued that managers' resistance was also misguided, irrational and motivated by their self-interest.

Six months later, the process was suspended. Although the justification was a pending demerger, the process was never resumed in either of the demerged companies. This suspension was in line with the interests of managers (purchasing and merchandising managers were powerful players in RetailCo) and against the position of accountants. For accountants, the suspension of EVA® was a lost opportunity.

What went wrong? In addition to the problems identified above, Burns et al. (2003) highlighted that EVA information had not become a part of managers' daily practices. Existing routines and underlying taken-for-granted beliefs (that is, prevalent institutions) among these managers were based on sales and margins, and remained unchanged. Implementation efforts focused on 'technical' aspects (the new system), but neglected that these were incompatible with prevailing institutions among stores managers, buyers and merchandizers. Hence, resistance and conflict emerged, leading to the failure of EVA implementation at RetailCo.

Source: Burns et al. (2003).

Required:

a) Which characteristics of EVA does this case illustrate?

b) Synthesize the reasons for the failure of EVA implementation at RetailCo.

c) How may the introduction of EVA negatively interfere with 'the fundamentals of retailing' (in line with the managers' arguments)?

d) Suppose that accountants suggested the implementation of an information system that performed all EVA calculations with no need of managers' intervention. Furthermore, to avoid the discussion about how calculations were performed, accountants suggested that the system should only provide the final EVA score of each unit, rather than the detailed calculations. Do you think this is a good idea? Discuss its benefits and problems.

e) Discuss if the accountants' position should be considered as rational and neutral.

● ● ● Recommended reading ● ● ● ● ● ● ● ● ● ● ● ● ● ● ●

- Busco, C., E. Giovannoni and R. Scapens (2008) 'Managing the tensions in integrating global organizations: the role of performance management systems', *Management Accounting Research*, 19(2), pp. 103–125.

This papers draws on a case study of Nestlé Waters to explore the role of performance management systems in integrating global organizations. The diverse entities within a global organization can be coordinated and integrated in multiple ways to achieve a global unity of effort. However, it is also possible to leave space for local adaptation, differentiation and flexibility. The paper sets performance measurement and management in a broader context, going beyond the mainly technical approach of this chapter.

- PWC (2010b) *International Transfer Pricing*, http://www.pwc.com/en_GX/gx/international-transfer-pricing/assets/itp-2011.pdf (accessed on 19 November 2012).

This over 800 pages free publication of a leading consultancy firm, regularly updated on the website, provides detailed explanation of transfer pricing tax compliance principles and regulations, with examples of varying difficulty. It also includes practical advices on transfer pricing tax compliance and country-specific issues.

● ● ● References ●

Bacidore, J. M., J. A. Boquist, T. T. Milbourn and A. V. Thakor (1997) 'The search for the best financial performance measure', *Financial Analysts Journal*, 53(3), pp. 11–20.

Bartelsman, E. J. and R. M. W. J. Beetsma (2003) 'Why pay more? Corporate tax avoidance through transfer pricing in OECD countries', *Journal of Public Economics*, (87), pp. 2225–52.

Burns, J., M. Ezzamel, and R. Scapens (2003) *The Challenge of Change in Management Accounting: Emphasising the Behavioural and Cultural Aspects of Change Management*, London: Elsevier/CIMA.

CIMA (2009) *Management Accounting Tools for Today and tomorrow*, London: CIMA.

Cools, M. and C. Emmanuel (2007) 'Transfer pricing: the implications of fiscal compliance', in C. S. Chapman, A. G. Hopwood and M. D. Shield (eds), *Handbook of Management Accounting Research*, Amsterdam: Elsevier, Vol. 2, pp. 573–85.

Ferguson, R. and D. Leistikow (1998) 'Search for the best financial performance measure: basics are better', *Financial Analysts Journal*, 54(1), pp. 81–5.

Hillier, D., S. Ross, R. Westerfield, J. Jaffe and B. Jordan (2010) *Corporate Finance*, European Edition, Maidenhead: McGraw-Hill.

KPMG (2011) 'Transfer pricing: issues and solutions for digital media 2011 http://www.kpmg.com/global/en/issuesandinsights/articlespublications/pages/transfer-pricing-digital-media-2011.aspx (accessed on 12 May 2012).

Kumar, S. and A. K. Sharma (2011) 'Further evidence on relative and incremental information content of EVA and traditional performance measures from select Indian companies', *Journal of Financial Reporting and Accounting*, 9(2), pp. 104–18.

Lee, S. and W. G. Kim (2009) 'EVA, refined EVA, MVA, or traditional performance measures for the hospitality industry?' *International Journal of Hospitality Management*, 28(3), pp. 439–45.

Lovata, L. M. and M. L. Costigan (2002) 'Empirical analysis of adopters of economic value added', *Management Accounting Research*, 13(2), pp. 215–28.

Morgan, W., M. Katz and H. Rosen (2009) *Microeconomics*, 2nd European Edition, Maidenhead: McGraw-Hill.

PWC (2008) 'Intellectual property in the automotive industry: transfer pricing aspects', http://www.pwc.com/gx/en/automotive/transfer-pricing/intellectual-property-transfer-pricing-aspects.jhtml (accessed on 12 May 2012).

PWC (2010a) 'Global automotive perspectives: preparing to compete', http://www.pwc.com/gx/en/automotive/issues-trends/global-auto-perspectives-2010-issue1.jhtml (accessed on 12 May 2012).

PWC (2010b) 'International Transfer Pricing', http://www.pwc.com/en_GX/gx/international-transfer-pricing/assets/itp-2011.pdf (accessed on 12 May 2012).

Warr, R. S. (2005) 'An empirical study of inflation distortions to EVA', *Journal of Economics and Business*, 57(2), pp. 119–37.

Notes

1   The WACC is the weighted average of the cost of each capital component: equity and dept. The equation weights each cost by the proportional weight of each component of market value. It also adjusts debt costs to account for the possibility of their tax deduction.

$$\text{WACC} = (E/V) \times R_e + (D/V) \times R_d \times (1 - T_c)$$

where:

R_e = cost of equity
R_d = cost of debt
E = market value of the firm's equity
D = market value of the firm's debt
$V = E + D$
E/V = percentage of financing that is equity
D/V = percentage of financing that is debt
T_c = corporate tax rate

Source: Hillier et al. (2010).

2   RI has an inconvenience that comes from a wider issue in financial analysis: the difficulty and even subjectivity of calculating the required rate of return – a component of the weighted average cost of capital. The RI measure is quite sensitive to this variable and different assumptions may lead to significantly different results and evaluations.

3   The term 'division' is here used to refer to any organizational subunits, such as departments, operations, subsidiaries of a multinational, and companies within a group.

When you have read this chapter

Log on to the Online Learning Centre at **www.mcgraw-hill.co.uk/textbooks/burns** to explore chapter-by-chapter test questions, links and further online study tools for Management Accounting.

PART **6**

STRATEGIC MANAGEMENT ACCOUNTING

CHAPTER 19

COST MANAGEMENT, VALUE CREATION AND SUSTAINABLE DEVELOPMENT

Chapter outline

- Views on costs and value

- Activity-based management (ABM): exploring and extending ABC

- Life cycle costing

- Continuous improvement and kaizen cost management (or kaizen costing)

- Target costing (or target cost management)

- Business process re-engineering (BPR) and management (BPM)

- Sustainable development and accounting

Learning outcomes

On completion of this chapter, you will be able to:

LO1 Explain the relevance of value and the value chain

LO2 Uncover managerial insights from activity-based information

LO3 Identify the advantages of product life cycle analysis

LO4 Describe the potential of kaizen cost management

LO5 Describe the potential of target cost management

LO6 Describe the stages of target cost management

LO7 Describe the advantages and difficulties of business process re-engineering

LO8 Distinguish between business-focused and enlightened perspectives of sustainability

LO9 Describe techniques for sustainability-oriented reporting and decision making

LO10 Identify management accountants' roles in implementing value-oriented techniques

Introduction

This chapter explores a strategic, value-enhancing perspective to management accounting. In previous chapters, you learned various cost and management accounting techniques. But these chapters have already pointed out that a single-minded focus on costs may actually harm companies' profitability, both in the short term and in the long term.

The traditional focus on costs usually means attempts to reduce costs. However, cost management is more than just cost reduction and, in particular, more than just cost minimization. Cost management must also evaluate the value produced by the organization and by each of its activities. Cost management is about trade-offs between costs incurred and value produced. Reducing costs without considering impacts on value is a short-sighted approach and risks compromising competitiveness. 'Reducing costs' cannot mean 'reducing costs at all cost'!

This chapter explores managing and balancing costs and value – with a particular emphasis on creating value and on how management accountants can contribute towards this fundamental managerial concern. A future orientation is crucial. More than calculating past costs, we need to estimate future costs. Even more importantly, we need guidance to take appropriate decisions and actions to ensure that future costs will be supported by generated value. We need a time horizon longer than the typically short reporting periods. Cost management can be performed as activities unfold, but the greatest impact is obtained when cost management is performed in advance, designing processes and products guided by cost and value concerns. Finally, we must also consider the future from a fundamentally different perspective: sustainable development. It is now clear that environmental and social sustainability cannot be taken for granted – at the level of particular products, organizations, industries or the entire planet. In consequence, various proposals have emerged to support reporting and decision making with a sustainable development perspective.

The next section briefly discusses the need to go beyond costs and to develop techniques that consider value; the classic value chain concept is also discussed. The following section discusses activity-based management (ABM), a management-oriented approach exploring activity-based insights, including ABC cost information; an example supports practical advice on exploring ABM information. Next, life cycle costing is discussed, widening the typically reduced time horizons of management accounting. The chapter also analyses two Japanese contributions to management accounting: kaizen and target cost management (or costing), improving cost and value during and before the manufacturing stage, respectively. The radical proposals of business process re-engineering are then presented. A final section discusses the increasingly important issue of sustainable development, its relevance for businesses and society, and various reporting and decision-making techniques aligned with, and promoting, sustainability concerns.

Views on costs and value

Beyond costs and exploring value and sustainable development

The traditional management and management accounting focus on costs usually meant attempts to reduce costs. Lower costs may benefit profitability, either directly through higher margins or indirectly by allowing aggressive pricing strategies to increase volume. Reducing costs is still high in companies' agenda and may even be a key competitive variable, and even more critical in periods of crisis – when demand slows down, competition increases and short-term survival becomes crucial. Around the world, large and small companies alike have reduced costs through, for example, layingoff workers, reducing management bonuses, cutting advertising or closing down operations. Nokia, Philips, Bank of Scotland and Bank of America are some examples, and you can probably add to the list a few small businesses near you.

However, the notion of 'value' has long entered the language of business and academia – and every one of us. The well-known saying of 'knowing the cost of everything and the value of nothing' has been often directed towards accountants, due to accountants' traditional focus on cost. Techniques like variable, absorption, standard and activity-based costing (ABC) deal with costs, not value, even when they are more sophisticated (for example, ABC). To analyse profitability, we need to determine externally the prices charged to customers, and then compare them with information from costing systems. In addition, the price paid and the value perceived by customers are two different concepts (see Chapter 14 on pricing strategies).

Costing systems do not have an external focus, so they cannot provide indications about the value of products, services or processes. Therefore, a strategic management tool to improve profitability, considering companies' competitiveness through their value proposition, needs to supplement insights on costs (for example, from ABC) with insights about customers' perceptions – in particular, customers' perceptions of value.

Fortunately, the need to go beyond costs and the importance of value has long become established in management accounting. The International Federation of Accountants identified four stages in management accounting focus (IFAC, 1998):

- **Stage 1** – Before 1950: *cost determination and financial control*, through budget and cost accounting

- **Stage 2** – By 1965: assist *planning and control*, through decision analysis and responsibility accounting

- **Stage 3** – By 1985: *waste reduction*, through process analysis and cost management

- **Stage 4** – By 1995: generation of *value* through the effective use of resources, examining the drivers of customer value, shareholder value, and organizational innovation.

Each new stage has an increasingly greater focus and scope, encompassing and extending the characteristics and techniques of the previous stages, as represented in Exhibit 19.1. During the last few decades, creating value became the main challenge for management accounting. However, a fifth stage might have emerged: a stage focused on *sustainable development*. This stage, added to the original IFAC framework, does not ignore previous notions and concerns about value, but widens the scope to include additional stakeholders and adopts a particular focus on environmental and social impacts. You will explore, in the final section, various techniques to support sustainable development.

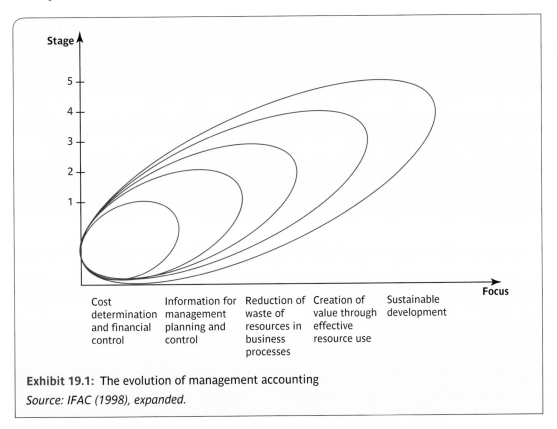

Exhibit 19.1: The evolution of management accounting

Source: IFAC (1998), expanded.

Value-added and non-value-added activities

The notion of value adopted at this stage is based on the customers' perspective. From a customer perspective, and using ABC's focus on activities, a value-added activity increases the worth of a company's products and services if it increases customers' willingness to pay a higher price and/or buy greater quantities. In contrast a non-value-added activity does not directly affect customers and the value they perceive. So, strictly from a customer perspective, these activities could be eliminated.

However, a simple dichotomy between value-added and non-value-added activities is limited. First, there are different levels of customers' perceived value, ranging between completely non-value-added and the highest value-added activities. Second, activities perceived as non-value-added by customers may be essential for the company existence – for instance, paying employees and suppliers, or any other activities currently required for technological, organizational or regulatory reasons. Finally, other activities invisible to customers (and so not directly adding to customer value) may be important for long-term success. Activities supporting family and work conciliation (for example, a nursing facility), team-building initiatives (for example, a day out with radical activities requiring joint efforts of employees across hierarchical levels and functional areas) and other employee-oriented activities (for example, sport facilities) may be significant in attracting, retaining and motivating key individuals and promoting collective work, relations and trust.

Activities should be rated in a scale of value (for example, from 1 to 5), rather than using a non-value-added versus value-added dichotomy. Activities which clearly do not add value are rated 1 and become a main target for elimination – for example, manufacturing defective products, or products not meeting customers' expectations and that will not get sold. The highest valued activities are rated 5 – for instance, operations supporting on-time delivery of products meeting customers' quality expectations. Improvements in these high-value activities may also include cost reduction, but with an utmost care to preserve or even improve customer-perceived value.

Finally, activities necessary for company operations or considered important for success, but not perceived as valuable by customers, can be rated as 3. The emphasis should be on reviewing their underlying objectives and how these objectives can be attained in an efficient and effective way. Reasons valid in the past may no longer hold: for example, new technologies may eliminate most activities regarding payments, eliminate the production of defective units or more effectively comply with regulations; regulations themselves may have changed. Since those activities do not directly add to customer-perceived value, they should be scrutinized more closely, to avoid unnecessary waste of resources.

Value: for whom?

We have so far evaluated value from the perspective of customers and, in particular, of external customers, who purchase the company products and services. There are also internal customers – those individuals or parts of the company that use products and services provided by other parts of the company. For example, each employee is an internal customer benefiting from payroll services provided by the human resources (HR) department or a shared services centre.

Value for shareholders is an alternative perspective for value. Finance is based heavily on shareholder value and in the previous chapter you explored various financial measures which, in varying degrees, are aligned with this perspective. While this chapter will typically focus on customer value rather than shareholder value, it is plausible that companies successfully delivering customer value may be rewarded with significant revenues from satisfied customers and hence ultimately may deliver shareholder value. Although this link is far from deterministic and customer value may not lead to shareholder value, a customer-value focus is likely to be adequate to orient operational and business decisions and is hence the major focus of this chapter.

In a radically different way, value can be seen from an environmental and social perspective. The increasingly relevant accountability for corporate impacts on environment and society takes the notion of value beyond customers' and shareholders' perspectives and includes other direct and even indirect stakeholders. Managers increasingly realize that ensuring sustainable development is a crucial requirement. This and ensuing sections predominantly discuss value from a customer perspective, given its more direct impact on the organization and to simplify the discussion. However, wider considerations on value, including those in the sustainability perspective analysed in the last section, should permeate all analyses and decisions, rather than standing as an isolated thought or the exclusive responsibility of a specific department.

Value: where does it come from? A value chain perspective

Management accounting usually focuses on a particular company – its products and services, its activities, its profitability, its value added, and so on. But the activities of a company are preceded by activities carried out by suppliers and are typically followed by activities carried out by other entities, such as distributors and retailers, before reaching the final customer.

It is now accepted that value created and costs incurred outside a company are crucial to its own success. Take the example of a producer of consumer goods. Suppliers that fail to deliver on agreed quality and time compromise the company's capacity to meet its own promises. Distributors that mishandle or incorrectly deliver the company products, or retailers who provide inadequate customer service, are compromising the sales, the image and success of the producer. Exhibit 19.2 depicts this **value chain** perspective, expanding Porter's (1985) seminal conceptualization of the company value chain – the traditional focus of management accounting – to include both upstream and downstream stages of the value chain, right to the final customer.

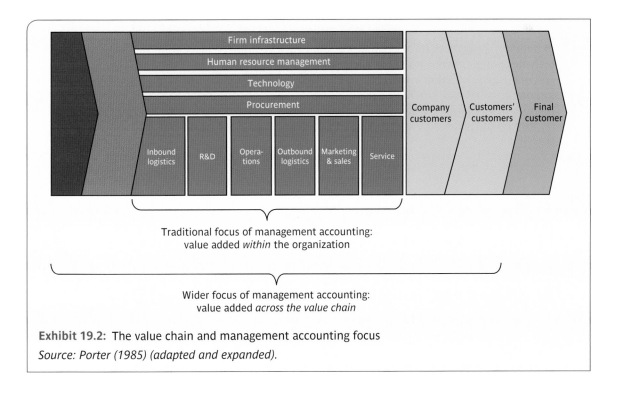

Exhibit 19.2: The value chain and management accounting focus

Source: Porter (1985) (adapted and expanded).

Successful value chains are those that are able to deliver the best value/cost relationship – considering the entire value chain. No company, no matter how efficient, can succeed in the long term if it is included in an ineffective value chain, when compared to competing value chains.

To understand the industry value chain and evaluate its performance, both globally and for each of its components, management accountants must separate the linked strategic activities contributing to the satisfaction of the final customer, and identify their costs, revenues and assets. This requires an external focus and places challenging problems of estimating figures for suppliers, customers and competitors – and competitors' suppliers and customers. Even if only rough estimates are possible, the process of strategic reflection to identify value chain activities and estimate their value contribution and costs is, in itself, useful.

Activity-based management (ABM): exploring and extending ABC

Operational and strategic ABM

In Chapter 6 you learned about activity-based costing (ABC), a costing approach proposed to overcome the shortcomings of traditional costing systems. Here we will extend the concepts of ABC to the management of the organization. **Activity-based management** supplements ABC, combining ABC insights on costs with value considerations, to better orient managerial action. Customers' perceptions are the key criteria to assess value in ABM approaches.

Activity-based management can be used for operational and for strategic purposes. Operational ABM aims to 'do things right', based on measuring activity costs and understanding what drives those costs; it has a particular focus on operations. Strategic ABM aims to 'do the right things', such as selling the right products, to the right clients, in the right mix, at the right prices. Often, this strategic analysis also leads to operational adjustments.

For operational ABM, only the first three stages of ABC are required:

1) Identify the major activities, which become the cost pools.

2) Assign costs for each activity cost pool.

3) Select a cost driver for each activity and calculate the cost rate of each cost driver.

In addition, operational ABM requires attributing a customers' perception of value to the various activities, ranging from no value added to high value added. Such rating is important to orient cost management efforts, in particular towards reducing costs and improving processes, both internal and external – including relations with customers. For instance, if you find that customers highly value obtaining a first-class customer service, this activity is rated as high value added; so, improvements plans should first ensure that potential cost-saving measures do not put to risk this crucial positive perception.

Strategic ABM requires all the above, plus the last stage of ABC, product costing:

4) Assign activity costs to products (or other cost objects) according to the usage of activities by each product (or cost object).

Finally, we can compare revenues with ABC cost information to conduct profitability analysis, essential for strategic decisions, such as products and customers mix and pricing. Changes in relationship management may also be suggested at this stage.

Extending ABC calculation to become ABM action

Let us retrieve the example from Chapter 6, when ABC was discussed. Elviso Ltd manufactures two parts for medical equipment, Alpha and Beta, and sells both for £60 per unit. Elviso's previous costing system allocated overhead across the two products according to the number of units produced, leading to the cost and profitability data shown in *Worked Example 6.1* (p. 128), included again in the comparative Table 19.3. By adopting ABC, Elviso identified five activities and allocated their overhead costs to products according to various cost drivers. Table 19.1 summarizes this information and calculates the cost of each cost driver unit (as in *Worked Example 6.1*). In addition, it also includes a 1–5 rating to express customers' perception about the value of each activity, reflecting ABM's concern on value.

According to Elviso's market research conducted through a multidisciplinary team of marketing and operational staff, 'Production', 'Quality enhancing and inspection' and 'Delivery' reap the highest value rating of 5. 'Materials handling' ranks lowest, with a rating of 2, since customers do not value Elviso's efforts to handle materials – an activity that can often be substantially improved with better materials and warehouse management, without negatively impacting customer value. Finally, 'Product returns management' was rated 3 due to opposing evaluation perspectives: on the positive side, it addresses a clear customer need; on the negative side, it results from a previous

Table 19.1: Elviso's activities, cost drivers and costs

Activity	Annual cost	Cost driver		Cost per cost driver unit	Customer value perception (1–5 scale)
	£		Volume	£	
Production	180,000	Machine hours	4,500	40 per hour	5
Material handling	78,000	Number of orders executed	260	300 per order	1
Quality enhancing and inspection	130,000	Number of production runs	130	1000 per run	5
Delivery	26,000	Number of shipments	65	400 per shipment	5
Product returns management	52,000	Number of returned products	130	400 per return	3
Total overheads	**466,000**				

failure by Elviso to meet customer expectations and should have been avoided in the first place. It is an important activity but ideally its need should be eliminated by addressing the original source of customer lack of satisfaction, as you will learn in Chapter 20.

As in Chapter 6, for each activity and cost driver, Elviso's ABC system allocated overheads across the two products based on: (1) the cost driver unit cost and (2) the cost driver usage by each product. Table 19.2 shows this overheads allocation, both in pounds (as in *Worked Example 6.1* and as a percentage). Table 19.3 then compares Alpha's and Beta's cost and profitability data based on ABC and on the traditional costing system.

Exploring ABM information – a practical guide

You can extract from the above calculations insights for two purposes: for operational ABM and for strategic ABM. Next, you will find some hints on exploring ABM information, but bear in mind that the analysis of each organization may provide unique challenges, findings and opportunities.

Operational ABM: directing attention to activities and costs drivers, improving processes and reducing costs

By dividing overheads across five activities, managers can have a better idea about why costs are incurred; this improves information richness when compared to using a single overhead figure, as in the traditional costing example. In particular, after choosing adequate cost drivers, their volume indicates the output of each activity, thus showing what drives the cost and at which rate – the cost rate of each cost driver. The costs of each activity and of each cost driver should then be evaluated on the basis of value perceptions by customers and based on the value rating of Table 19.1.

Which activities should you focus on, at least to start with? Several criteria are possible:

- *Activities with the largest costs.* These may provide the largest-scale savings. However, bear in mind that if they are high value added, utmost care must be taken not to diminish that perceived value, or at least to attain a clearly beneficial relation between value and cost reduction. In addition, note that a costly activity may already be extremely efficient at the present time, in which case further improvements are likely to be minor and difficult to achieve.

Table 19.2: Assignment of activity costs to products (in £ and as a percentage)

	Alpha		Beta		Total
	£	%	£	%	£
Production					
Alpha: 40 × 2100 machine hours	84,000	46.7%			
Beta: 40 × 2400 machine hours			96,000	53.3%	180,000
Material handling					
Alpha: 300 × 150 orders	45,000	57.7%			
Beta: 300 × 110 orders			33,000	42.3%	78,000
Quality improvement and product inspection					
Alpha: 1000 × 90 production runs	90,000	69.2%			
Beta: 1000 × 40 production runs			40,000	30.8%	130,000
Delivery					
Alpha: 400 × 50 per shipment	20,000	76.9%			
Beta: 400 × 15 per shipment			6,000	23.1%	26,000
Product returns management					
Alpha: 400 × 90 product returns	36,000	69.2%			
Beta: 400 × 40 product returns			16,000	30.8%	52,000
Total overhead	**275,000**	**59.0%**	**191,000**	**41.0%**	**466,000**
Number of units	12,000	46.2%	14,000	53.8%	
Overhead per unit	**22.92**		**13.64**		

- *Activities with no or little value added.* These activities, identified with the lowest value ratings adopted above, are primary targets for reduction or even elimination, since they have little or no impact on customers' value perceptions and even on company essential operations. However, if non-value added activities have very little costs, or if they are already extremely efficient and cannot be eliminated entirely, potential savings will not be significant;

- *Activities currently highly inefficient.* These may provide the best targets for reaping 'low-hanging fruit', that is, to achieve savings without major efforts. Kaplan and Cooper (1998) suggested another 1–5 scale to identify activities ranging from the lowest opportunities for improvement (< 5 per cent, already highly efficient, getting a rating of 1) to the greatest opportunities (50–100 per cent, currently highly inefficient and main targets for elimination, getting a 5 rating). Reaping 'low-hanging fruit' is particularly important at the start of ABM projects. Remember that ABC projects tend to be lengthy and costly, so getting some quick results is essential to strengthen internal legitimacy, support and give impetus to additional ABM steps.

- *Combinations of the above criteria.* For example, all activities with the lowest value ratings (1 and 2) may be initially selected, and then start improving those activities with the largest costs.

You can find in *Worked Example 19.1* possible interpretations about the above data to guide operational ABM decisions. They should be used with caution, as mere orientations for analysis. Keep in mind that each case may suggest unique relationships and explanations.

Table 19.3: Products cost, sale price and profit, under traditional costing and ABC

| | Traditional costing | | | | ABC | | | |
| | Alpha | | Beta | | Alpha | | Beta | |
	Total (£)	£/unit	Total (£)	£/unit	Total (£)	£/unit	Total (£)	£/unit
Direct material	240,000	20.00	350,000	25.00	240,000	20.00	350,000	25.00
Direct labour	168,000	14.00	147,000	10.50	168,000	14.00	147,000	10.50
Overheads								
• Production					84,000	7.00	96,000	6.86
• Material handling					45,000	3.75	33,000	2.36
• Quality improvement and product inspection					90,000	7.50	40,000	2.86
• Delivery					20,000	1.67	6,000	0.43
• Product returns management					36,000	3.00	16,000	1.14
Total overheads	215,040	17.92	250,880	17.92	275,000	22.92	191,000	13.64
Total cost	**623,040**	51.92	**747,880**	53.42	**683,000**	56.92	**688,000**	49.14
Sale price		60.00		60.00		60.00		60.00
Profit		8.08		6.58		3.08		10.86
Profit (% of sale price)		13.47%		10.97%		5.14%		18.10%
Profit change (% vs traditional system)						**−61.8%**		**+65.0%**

<table>
</table>

Worked Example 19.1

Operational ABM in Elviso

Let us focus on the *costliest activities* first. More than half of Elviso's overheads are incurred in 'Production' (£180,000) and 'Quality enhancing and product inspection' (£120,000) activities. Both are rated as high value added, so caution is required when trying to reduce costs in these activities. Since 'Production' is the costliest, it becomes a primary target for attention.

The nature of the 'Quality improvement and product inspection' activity requires further attention. Parts for medical equipment require a high quality level, justifying the high value added rating (5) attributed to this activity. However, note that this activity actually encompasses two sub-activities: 'quality improvement' (to 'build-in' quality into the product) and 'product inspection' (looking for defects). As you will see in Chapter 20, preventively 'building-in' quality is typically preferable to searching for defects. In fact, the 5 value rating is more applicable to quality building than product inspection: doing things right, the first time, every time (the goal of total quality management) drastically reduces the need of further inspection activities. For ABM, it might be worthwhile to separate these two sub-activities and their costs (we have no data to do it). For example, if most costs concern 'product inspection' and only a minority concern 'quality improvement' efforts, then cost and value improvements might be possible by redirecting efforts from the former to the latter.

The usefulness of disaggregating this activity illustrates a distinctive characteristic of ABM, when compared to ABC. ABM requires a more detailed breakdown of activities, leading to many activity cost pools and cost drivers. This is necessary for effective cost management, based on an in-depth understanding of the value and of what causes costs in those activities. On the contrary, for costing purposes in ABC you may not require such detailed analysis. In a trade-off between accuracy and simplicity, it may not pay off to obtain higher cost allocation accuracy from disaggregating activities using more specific and appropriate cost drivers. For example, for ABM it may be crucial to question whether inspection costs are actually driven by the number of production runs – the current cost driver. It is possible that this is not correct, and you may examine alternatives such as the number of units inspected – a transactional cost driver – or inspection time – a duration cost driver. However, for ABC aggregating cost pools with similar cost drivers may be a still satisfactory option.

The *cost rate of cost drivers* can also provide important insights. The £400 cost per returned product is amazingly high, especially when compared with the £60 sale price. As already stated, managing product returns is a necessary activity to address the needs of unsatisfied customers. However, it is mandatory to investigate why those returns happen, how can customer satisfaction be strengthened to avoid future returns (hence reducing future demand for this activity), and why does each return lead to such high costs.

The 'Product returns management' activity also recalls that an activity-based approach enhances cost visibility, by aggregating costs of activities spanning across different functional areas and departments. Customer service activities may use resources from customer service, engineering, shop floor, public relations, legal and finance departments. It may well be that because traditional costing systems kept these costs in separate department accounts, managers were until now unaware of the actual costs incurred across the company anytime a product was returned. It may also well be that an ABM project uncovers significant *inefficiency* in this activity (the third criterion to investigate activities) due to, for example, lack of integration across the various departments, leading to task duplication, unnecessary search for information and processing errors. Business process management (BPM), analysed later in this chapter, may allow integrating inter-functional process flows, leading not only to lower costs but also to faster, more accurate response and increased customer satisfaction.

Strategic ABM

Profitability analysis of cost objects (products, in this case, but also others like customers and markets) based on ABC information may provide important insights about product and customer mix and pricing. It can also suggest more detailed, product- or customer-specific operational changes.

Product profitability substantially changed under ABC. Remember that the sale price was £60 for both products. Under traditional costing, Alpha was slightly cheaper and more profitable than Beta (with a profit of £8.08/unit and £6.58/unit, respectively). However, due to different overhead allocation in ABC, profitability of both products changed, in inverse directions, by over 60 per cent (remember that direct costs – materials and direct labour – do not change in ABC). Alpha costs rose and profitability dropped to £3.08/unit, or 5.14 per cent of sale price, while Beta costs decreased and profitability increased to £10.86/unit, or 18.10 per cent of sale price. Alpha's low profitability is worrying. Do not forget that additional costs, not included in this ABC analysis, are likely to exist and need to be covered from the contribution obtained from the various products.

Why were these costs incurred and what courses of action can be suggested for management? *Worked Example 19.2* 'Managing products usage of activities', *Worked Example 19.3* 'Changing sale prices' and *Worked Example 19.4* 'Changing relationships with customers and "menu-based pricing"' explore tentative suggestions that are often relevant in strategic ABM.

Worked Example 19.2

Strategic ABM in Elviso: managing products usage of activities

By reassigning overhead, we have discovered that Alpha is costlier than we initially thought, and costlier than Beta. The next stage is to know why. A useful heuristic approach is:

- *Compare the percentage of overheads assigned to each product* under ABC – in Table 19.2. Alpha uses a larger percentage than Beta of almost all activities. Although in the costliest activity, 'Production', that does not happen (only 46.7 per cent), the aggregated effect of Alpha's greater usage of all other activities explains why Alpha's *total* overheads are greater than Beta's.

However, you should use benchmarks against which to compare these percentages, as suggested next.

- *Compare these percentages* (of overheads assigned to each product) *with the percentage of each product output.* Considering a total volume of 12,000 + 14,000 = 26,000 units, Alpha accounts for 46.2 per cent and Beta accounts for 53.8 per cent of total volume. You can see that overheads of all activities were assigned to Alpha in a percentage greater than 46.2 per cent. So, Alpha's *unit* overheads became greater than Beta's.

- *Compare these percentages* (of overheads assigned to each product) *under ABC* (Alpha: 59 per cent; Beta: 41 per cent) *with the percentages under the traditional costing system* (Alpha: 46.2 per cent; Beta: 53.8 per cent) (calculations based on assigned overheads in Table 19.3). What does that mean?

In ABC, overheads of all activities assigned to Alpha are greater than in traditional costing (46.2 per cent), so Alpha's cost increased in ABC (remember that Elsivo's traditional costing system allocated overheads according to volume; that's why this comparison and the previous draw on the same percentage, 46.2 per cent).

In ABC, overheads assigned to Alpha in individual activities are greater than at an aggregated level (59 per cent) in the following activities:

- Quality improvement and product inspection: 69.2 per cent of costs and cost driver volume

- Product returns management: 69.2 per cent of costs and cost driver volume

- Delivery: 76.9 per cent of costs and cost driver volume.

Investigating these activities may help you to understand if Alpha's above average usage of these activities is justifiable or if it can be improved. You should also keep in mind the magnitude of the costs of each activity: if they are insignificant, even large efficiency improvements will yield small cost savings.

Let us analyse each one of these three activities:

1) Alpha is charged with 69.2 per cent of 'Quality improvement and product inspection' costs because Alpha is responsible for 69.2 per cent of production runs (the selected cost driver). By merely reducing the number of Alpha production runs, assigned overheads would decrease. If this cost driver really captures quality-related costs caused by each product[1] then organizing Alpha production into fewer production runs would reduce this important cost component of Alpha (£90,000/12,000 units = £7.50/unit, almost a third of total £22.92/unit overhead cost).

2) The 69.2 per cent of 'Product returns management' costs assigned to Alpha deserves attention. Why are so many Alpha products returned? Should it be due to quality issues, then the greater quality efforts devoted to Alpha (as measured in the previous activity) are apparently not successful. Since this activity may correspond to a quality failure that should not happen in the first place, and since it has a significant impact on Alpha's cost structure (£36,000/12,000 units = £3.00/unit), improvements should be sought in this activity and, particularly, by eliminating the source of the activity costs: product returns.

3) 'Delivery', the activity whose costs are more concentrated in Alpha (76.9 per cent), comes third and last. Why? Because activity costs are smaller and costs assigned to Alpha are only £20,000, or £1.67 per unit. Even significant improvements in this activity may yield only small savings. In addition, delivery is a high-value-added activity. If frequent deliveries, in small shipments, is key to customer satisfaction and even an important competitive advantage, then reducing the number of shipments to reduce costs might actually destroy Alpha's value proposition.

Note that these 'heuristics' do not automatically signal problems. A higher percentage of assigned overhead to a product, in a given activity, only means that the product consumes a larger share of that activity when compared with other benchmarks; in turn, this indirectly represents a higher consumption of resources, that is, costs by that product. A business-grounded interpretation is always necessary to make a correct diagnosis and decide appropriate action.

Worked Example 19.3

Strategic ABM in Elviso: Changing sale prices

The sale price of both products was the same, £60, perhaps because the traditional cost system indicated very similar product costs. Elviso might practise a cost plus pricing policy, common to both products. Sold quantities (Alpha: 12,000 units; Beta: 14,000 units) reflected the market reaction to that price. With ABC information and market research, the company may revise its pricing (see Chapter 14). Since Alpha profit dropped and Beta profit increased, Elviso may increase Alpha price to avoid a near loss in this product; Elviso may also use the higher margin in Beta to reduce its price and become more price-competitive in this product.

As you learned in Chapter 14, market research is fundamental to gauge pricing, including short-term and long-term strategic analysis. Short-term analysis may include estimating changes in demanded quantities due to price changes and estimating profitability impacts – for example, by how much would Beta sales increase if price is reduced by, say, 5 per cent? Would Beta profitability increase or decrease? Long-term, strategic analysis may include how price changes affect the product market positioning, as well as competitors' reaction.

Do not forget that ABC analysis does not automatically identify the most adequate policy changes. A business-oriented analysis is always required to decide on these sensitive and crucial issues. Elviso may decide not to reduce Beta's sale price and instead keep the higher margin, because reducing the price might send the wrong message to the market, suggesting that Beta has less quality. A price reduction could also be perceived by competitors as a price war, triggering a similar move from them, reducing their market price. This reaction from competitors might thus offset the market-share increase that could result from Beta's price reduction.

Worked Example 19.4

Strategic ABM in Elviso: changing relationships with customers and 'menu-based pricing'

You have found out that delivery costs are mostly due to Alpha, which is delivered in smaller shipments. A possible managerial action would be to start charging a fee for small deliveries, or even a fixed fee for every shipment of Alpha (this would hit smaller deliveries the most, on a unit basis). Introducing this fee would discourage customers from requesting many, but small deliveries, hence reducing the cost driver volume; and, even if it did not reduce, it would generate revenues to compensate the additional costs. This 'menu-based pricing' is common in online retailers like Amazon.com, that charge a fixed fee per shipment, but which may be waived for higher-value shipments.

However, again, keep in mind the high value added of the delivery activity and even the competitive advantage that may be associated with frequent, smaller shipments. Charging such a fee may turn out to be extremely negative – in particularly if we take into account that delivery costs are relatively insignificant. So, again, market research is indispensible to this pricing decision.

In this section, you explored how activity-based insights may affect operational and strategic decisions. Once again, remember that your analysis should depend on the characteristics of each case, based on calculated figures, the nature of activities and the business itself. So, the suggested questions, comparisons and analyses may yield useful insights, but you should not view them as a definitive road map for ABM analysis. In the next section, you will widen your perspective beyond the typically short time frames adopted for reporting and cost analyses, and will focus on the entire life of a product, by exploring life cycle costing.

Life cycle costing

Why is life cycle costing important?

When deciding about the introduction of a new product (or service), managers need to estimate all revenues and costs arising during that product life cycle – typically, extending beyond a particular year. A product generates revenues during the period it is sold to customers – its market life cycle. In turn, costs start arising before the product is launched due to, for instance, product development and marketing activities. And costs extend until after it is withdrawn from the market owing to, for example, product warranties or ecologically responsible disposal. **Life cycle costing** supports the life cycle profitability analysis: the evaluation of products profitability in this extended time horizon – the entire product life cycle – rather than the yearly or monthly segments usually used in common costing and profitability analysis. The following analysis focuses on products, but the fundamental ideas also apply to services. For an environmental perspective on products and, life cycle, see p. 503 later in this chapter.

When car manufacturers plan the launch of a new model, they need to estimate total revenues during the model *market* life cycle – typically a few years. With regard to costs, calculations are more complex and span a larger period. The development of a new model is complex, costly and takes several years *prior* to market introduction. Production and sales costs are incurred during the market life cycle. The manufacturer is still committed to incur additional costs, such as those related with warranty commitments, for several years *after* each car is sold – even after the model is withdrawn from the market and replaced by another one. Some car manufacturers have generous warranty policies – extending for long periods, such as five years of basic warranty or a 12-year warranty against corrosion. On occasions, they may even offer indefinite warranty against certain damages, limited only by mileage. This actually extends the product life cycle indefinitely – with regard to costs.

Prospective life cycle costing is also important because it supports a financial perspective at a time when few things in the product are yet committed. As you will see later in the target costing section, at an early R&D stage almost no life cycle costs are yet committed. So, it is the perfect time to evaluate alternative products and production processes and how life cycle costs and revenues change.

Products often have a four-stage market life cycle, as in Exhibit 19.3. Sales are low when products are first introduced, they grow until they reach their peak and then stabilize. Finally, sales decline when customer preference dwindles, until the product is removed from the market. Increasingly, products have shorter market life cycles, due to faster technology advances and increasingly shifting customer preferences towards new products. In addition, some products do not have a typical market life cycle. For example, Harry Potters' books and Apple's new versions of iPhone, iPod and iPad have massive sales on their release day and they can even be reserved in advance with sellers like Amazon. Also, cars and technological products are often removed from the market before their sales start declining and they are replaced with new versions, to prevent market share loss to competitors.

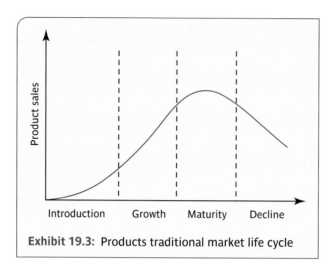

Exhibit 19.3: Products traditional market life cycle

19.1: Management Accounting in Practice

Comparing Microsoft's Windows operating systems life cycle

Even a very superficial comparison of the life cycle stages of two operating systems from Microsoft, Windows Vista and XP, provides some interesting insights. Windows Vista, launched in January 2007, had a market life cycle of only about 4.5 years: final sales, through pre-installation in PCs, ended in October 2011 (sales through retailers ended a year earlier). This was substantially lower than the total market life cycle of the previous system, Windows XP, which lasted almost nine years.

However, Windows Vista's pre-launch stage was clearly longer than XP's: Windows Vista was developed in 5.5 years, against only 1.5 years taken to develop Windows XP. Windows Vista's after-sale stage was also longer than XP's. The after-sale stages are not so different. The end of mainstream support, when Microsoft stops providing automatic fixes, updates or online technical assistance for the general public, happened in April 2012 for Windows Vista, that is, half a year after end of sales. For Windows XP, mainstream support ended in April 2009 – even before sales through PC pre-installation ended and about a year after the end of retail sales. For both products, Microsoft provides extended support – at a cost – to commercial customers for an additional period.

Comparing the life cycle of the two systems, Windows Vista's shorter market lifetime and longer development stage suggests worse financial results – although, of course, any conclusion is impossible without knowing all revenues and costs. Allocating development costs to particular products is not straightforward. Fundamental technical developments, such as IT architecture, may be used in several products. Microsoft's following operating system, Windows 7, was developed in only one year, but benefited from developments incorporated in Windows Vista – often described as mostly an intermediate version between Windows XP and Windows 7.

Sources: http://windows.microsoft.com/en-us/windows/products/lifecycle;
http://en.wikipedia.org/wiki/Development_of_Windows_Vista;
http://en.wikipedia.org/wiki/Development_of_Windows_XP;
http://en.wikipedia.org/wiki/Development_of_Windows_7 (accessed on 15 May 2012).

Exercises

1) Suppose a financial analyst argued that Windows Vista was prematurely withdrawn from the market because its short market life cycle damaged its financial return. Discuss this opinion.

2) Identify alternative ways to allocate development costs benefiting various generations of product releases, and discuss advantages and disadvantages of each alternative.

The product pre-launch stage

Pre-launch costs may be very significant and extend for a long time, due to R&D, marketing, certification and business development activities. In the pharmaceutical industry, R&D costs and length are particularly high and uncertain. Drugs may take decades to be developed, tested in a laboratory environment, tested in human patients in clinical trials and certified by health regulators (typically, in every country), before they can be introduced in the various markets. Estimating pre-launch costs of future products is also critical because they are incurred when there are still no revenues generated by the yet-to-be-launched product.

Companies need to evaluate their capacity to support those upfront expenses, using resources previously accumulated or generated on an ongoing basis by other products already on the market. The famous BCG matrix, developed by the Boston Consulting Group in the 1960s, is still a useful framework to think about a company portfolio of products or business units, and about balancing the needs and generation of resources from the various areas – although we should bear in mind that the life cycle of many products is now substantially different from the typical life cycle some decades ago.

The product production and sale stages

This is the most traditional focus of accounting systems. Unfortunately, sometimes information systems can only analyse one period at a time. However, keep in mind that a life cycle perspective typically encompasses multiple financial periods, so suitable information systems must be able to aggregate multiple-period data.

The product after-sale stage

After a unit is sold, and even after a product is removed from the market, further costs may arise from the need for to customer service and support and, increasingly, for environmental and sustainability responsibilities.

Producers of batteries and tyres are responsible for the proper disposal of their products after use by clients, and mining companies have to rehabilitate the sites when they end extracting activities. Product warranties are one or two years for most electric appliances and longer for cars and real estate, depending on legislation and sellers' policy. Software manufacturers provide support for several years after ending sales. This commitment to customers may be an important component of the value offer, since it protects customers' investment. See *Management Accounting in Practice 19.1* regarding Microsoft, followed by the life cycle costing *Worked Example 19.5*.

Continuous improvement and kaizen cost management (or kaizen costing)

The continuous improvement/kaizen approach

Ranging from the proverb 'Slowly but surely' to successful business stories of brands like Tide (a major laundry detergent brand from Procter & Gamble in the USA and many other countries) and companies like Toyota, many examples demonstrate the importance of a permanent, long-term commitment towards improvements. Procter & Gamble has been continuously introducing innovations in the Tide brand and product, such as better cleaning power and energy efficiency, reduced packaging and lower manufacturing and distribution costs. This continuous stream of incremental innovations to improve customer value and lower costs – at an impressive pace of one innovation per year, for over 60 years – has allowed a remarkable history of growth and profitability (Barwise and Meehan, 2010). When Toyota set out to identify and write down its

> **Worked Example 19.5**
>
> ## A life cycle costing example
>
> Company 'ElectriCo' is planning to develop a new small electric appliance with a two-year warranty. To estimate product profitability, ElectriCo built the following product life cycle budget (see Table 19.4), including:
>
> - Costs of product development (pre-launch): £200,000
>
> - Costs of warranty repairs: £10 per repair, in 5 per cent of units, one year after sales (that is, occurring both during and beyond the product market lifetime)
>
> - Costs of end-of-product-life responsibilities due to ecologically responsible product disposal: £2 per unit, two years after sales (that is, occurring both during and beyond the product market lifetime)
>
> - Selling price: £40 per unit in year 1 and reduction of £8 each year during market life, as the product becomes no longer a novelty and competition intensifies
>
> - Variable cost: £18 per unit in year 1 and reduction of £2 each year, as individuals gain experience; this is a simplified application of the 'learning curve' effect – see Chapter 12.
>
> This product life cycle budget, estimating a modest £2,500 profit, allows several important insights:
>
> - The importance of development costs: managers may forget development costs and only include costs during the production and sale stages – even when development is still to happen. Since ElectriCo has still not started and is not yet committed to product development, forgetting its estimated £200,000 future development costs would report a misleading estimated £197,500 profit. To protect long-term profitability and even company survival, revenues must be able to cover all costs of the product's entire life cycle.
>
> - The importance of costs beyond the product sale stage: cutting-off the analysis at this point and ignoring the £52,500 warranty and product disposal costs of years 4 and 5, or their entire £87,500 amount between years 2 and 5, would also misleadingly suggest higher profitability. These costs are locked in by previous commitments with customers and cannot be avoided without breaching that commitment, with potentially high reputation and legal costs.
>
> - A life cycle analysis is also useful for a year-by-year analysis. Although year 3 contribution margin is still positive (£50,000), high fixed costs of £100,000 lead to a loss. Since the product is expected to be discontinued at the end of that year, anticipating such decision to year 2 may be preferable, depending on the amount of fixed costs reduction.[2] Note that anticipating product withdrawal does not avoid after-sale costs related with sales from previous years 1 and 2, but it does avoid after-sale costs related with (cancelled) year 3 sales, of £12,500 (2,500 + 10,000). So, ElectriCo should withdraw the product in year 2 if:
>
> Year 3 fixed costs reduction > *Lost contribution margin (£50,000) – Avoided after-sales costs (£12,500)*
>
> Which is:
>
> Year 3 fixed costs reduction > £32,500
>
> - Strategic analysis of product portfolio: withdrawing the product earlier, in year 2, may also make sense from a strategic point of view, if ElectriCo is able to replace it with a new version in year 3. Predicted sales decline in year 3 is significant, both in volume (–75 per cent) and particularly in value (–81.25 per cent), reflecting a clear reduction in market acceptance and allowing competitors to gain market share. That is why many car and electronic equipment manufacturers replace their current products while demand is still strong.

Table 19.4: Product life cycle budget

	Year 0	Year 1	Year 2	Year 3	Year 4	Year 5	Life cycle
Volume (units)	0	10,000	20,000	5,000			
Price (£/unit)		40	32	24			
Sales (£)		400,000	640,000	120,000			1,160,000
Variable costs (per unit) (£)		18	16	14			
Total variable costs (£)		180,000	320,000	70,000			570,000
Contribution margin (£)		**220,000**	**320,000**	**50,000**			590,000
Development costs (£)	200,000						200,000
Fixed costs (£)		100,000	100,000	100,000			300,000
Repair costs under warranty (1 year after sale) (£)			5,000	10,000	2,500		17,500
End-of-life costs (total) (2 years after sale) (£)				20,000	40,000	10 000	70,000
Total profit (£)	**−200,000**	**120,000**	**215,000**	**−80,000**	**−42,500**	**−10 000**	**2,500**

Note: *For simplicity, the time value of money is ignored. See Chapter 15 for how to adjust financial flows occurring in different periods.*

founders' wisdom and core values, until then transmitted orally, their senior executives identified continuous improvement as a key pillar of 'The Toyota Way' (Takeuchi et al., 2008).

Continuous improvement is a company-wide approach of never-ending improvement. It is an important concept of the wider total quality management and just-in-time philosophies (see Chapter 20), developed by Toyota in Japan and now adopted worldwide, by large and also smaller companies. Continuous improvement (or kaizen, in Japanese) stresses that no company can rest on past success and stop improving. It proposes an alternative way of seeking improvements, which is not based on large yet discontinuous objectives. Instead, continuous improvement stresses ongoing efforts, to gradually obtain small, incremental improvements – but which in the long run may produce significant and long-lasting impacts. For example, rather than a one-off major effort to improve quality or reduce costs, the continuous improvement approach calls for a permanent, integrated, company-wide effort towards always shifting goals – replaced by new ones as soon as they are achieved.

As a company-wide approach, continuous improvement extends beyond the manufacturing domain and encompasses all functional areas and hierarchical levels, including management. Improvement is a permanent responsibility and goal of each and every individual. The scope of continuous improvement goes even beyond the organization. This includes improvements in both internal and external resources (for example, improving the skills of the staff of both the company and its suppliers) and relationships between the company and external entities such as suppliers.

Applying kaizen principles to cost management

When applied to costs, a continuous improvement (kaizen) management approach leads to **kaizen costing**, more appropriately called kaizen cost management. As part of ongoing efforts to reduce costs, companies set kaizen goals of cost reduction for their products, processes, parts of processes or parts of their cost structure – particular direct materials, labour, or any particular area considered crucial to achieve and maintain competitiveness. Continuous improvement efforts are then targeted to lower costs through higher efficiency and waste reduction. When those goals are attained, the improved performance level becomes the starting point to new, more ambitious goals.

Incorporating kaizen principles in cost management and accounting techniques allows to overcome some of the limitations pointed towards traditional accounting practices, such as budgeting (Chapter 8) and standard costing (Chapter 9). First, both practices have been accused of quickly becoming obsolete if circumstances change after the start of the period. As you learned in Chapter 10, kaizen budgeting incorporates the ongoing progresses and search for cost improvements within the budgeting process. So, the budget will embed cost improvements and estimates for cost reductions on a continuous basis, rather than keeping initial budget costs.

Second, budgeting has been accused of limiting incentives to improve, since incentives tend to focus on attaining the budget – but not exceeding it. At this point, the cultural component of continuous improvement is crucial, based as it is on a socially embedded, collective continuous commitment towards improvement. The importance of these cultural traits, typical of the Japanese context where these techniques emerged, has justified concerns about whether Japanese-originated techniques can easily be adopted by organizations in very different cultural contexts.

Gains from continuous improvement differ substantially from the learning curve effect discussed in Chapter 12. Both concepts anticipate that costs may be reduced during the manufacturing stage. However, the learning curve concept seems to assume that cost reduction will happen in a somewhat automatic and 'natural' way: as cumulative quantity increases and as individuals learn and gain experience with their task, they first obtain high efficiency gains, which then level off to a more steady state as less efficiency gains are possible. Although the learning curve concept actually requires active efforts for this improvement to occur, its formula suggests that a greater accumulated volume will make this gain emerge. This suggestion is at odds with the continuous improvement approach, for two reasons. First, the continuous improvement approach does not take improvements for granted or as natural. Instead, improvements will only happen if actively sought after by everyone, all the time; production volume, in itself, plays little or no role. Second, the continuous improvement approach believes that improvements, albeit small, are always possible and, importantly, will add up to very significant accumulated gains in the long run. This belief contrasts with the insignificant gains suggested by the learning curve effect at high levels of cumulative production, which discourage a major commitment towards improvement when those stages are reached.

Next, we will explore another Japanese cost management technique, which is centred on an earlier stage of the product life cycle: target costing, focused on the development stage.

Target costing (or target cost management)

What is target costing and why is it important?

The continuous improvement/kaizen approach may yield significant gains over time, but it has a key limitation: it is only applied in a late stage of the product life cycle, the manufacturing stage. The problem is that most future costs of the product life cycle become committed, or 'locked in', when a product (or service) and its production process are designed. Product design and technological choices at the R&D stage largely shape costs of future activities such as production, distribution and customer support, throughout the product life cycle. After production starts, the possibility of cost improvements becomes more limited.

The R&D stage is the best time for cost management. First, because the improvement potential is greater: companies may make choices influencing future costs without the constraints of an already designed product and production process. Second, because only R&D costs have been incurred so far. So, obtained savings will apply to the entire volume of the product life cycle. Finally, if the company realizes the proposed product to be incapable of delivering the desired profitability, the project never passes that initial stage, hence avoiding additional costs.

Target costing explores the greater potential for cost management at the R&D stage. More appropriately described as a target cost management system, target costing is a proactive, future-oriented costing approach, at the R&D stage, orienting design options to develop new products that attain a desired future profitability level. For that purpose, target costing estimates expected costs, as well as revenues and profits, throughout the entire product life cycle. Target costing was also developed by the Japanese at Toyota in the 1960s, with some underlying ideas stretching back to Ford's principles in the early 1900s, and is now a widespread practice.

Target costing is important because many R&D efforts fail to deliver products which are both marketable and profitable. Frequently, R&D efforts fail because developers are too focused on technical aspects per se, without considering the extent to which customers will value the product's technical characteristics. At other times, R&D efforts, although oriented by market research, fail to seriously examine cost issues until the product is ready to leave the laboratory – or, even worse, accurate cost estimates are only made after the product has entered the manufacturing stage. At that stage, significant resources and time have already been spent and, in addition, a large percentage of future product life cycle costs may have already become locked in.

Integrating the marketing, engineering and costing perspectives

By ultimately concentrating on profitability, target costing focuses on more than just costs. In fact, its starting point is the market and customers' perceptions of value, as stated early in this chapter. Insights from employees with closer contact with customers and market research are essential to determine those customers' value perceptions which influence their willingness to pay. In particular, companies need to perform **attribute pricing**, based on estimates of customers' willingness to pay for different attributes (such as different functionalities, performance and reliability levels), both individually and when integrated within particular product configurations. The ultimate objective is to determine the alternative product designs and market prices that support the company's strategic competitive position.

In addition, customers' perceptions of value and willingness to pay only translate into sales and revenues within a particular market context, with both current and potential competitors. The target costing approach must also examine competitors, their products, their overall value proposition and prices, and customers' value perception of competitors' offer. This requires further marketing and technical insights, including the use of **reverse engineering**, a practice included in the wider value engineering approach. Reverse engineering involves disassembling competitors' products to obtain detailed insights about their design features, materials and production techniques.

Target costing typically involves various cycles of the following stages, as described in Exhibit 19.4.

1) *Market research* and *target pricing*: market insights about customers and competitors are fundamental and the starting point for target costing. Attribute pricing evaluates customers' willingness to pay for particular attributes, both in isolation and in the context of alternative configurations of the final product. Through examining the company's strategic objectives for sales, market share, image and overall profitability, as well as information about competitors' offers, companies estimate target prices. Typically, at this stage, various alternative product configurations are examined. As you learned in Chapter 14, pricing practices should support strategic and financial objectives, something which often does not lead to simply maximizing short-term profitability, and requires a product life cycle perspective.

2) Set *target margins* and *target costs*: based on the target price, a target margin is calculated to meet corporate profitability objectives. This desired margin on sales may be common to all products or may be product-specific to reflect the perceived risk of the particular product. The **target cost** is the target price minus the target margin, for the selected product or the various alternative configurations under evaluation. This is a distinctive feature of target cost management: keeping every R&D member focused on both value and costs objectives, right from the start of the ensuing design cycle.

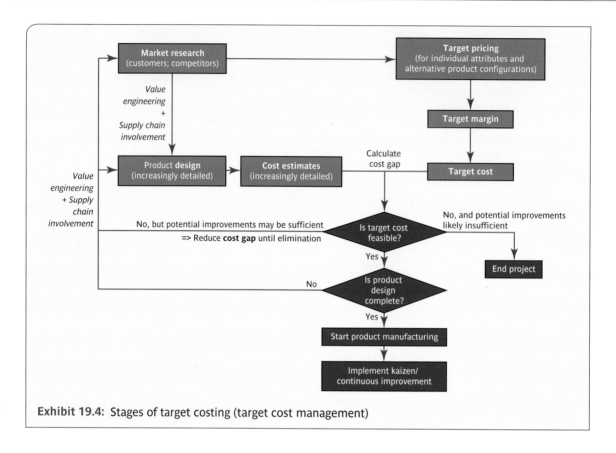

Exhibit 19.4: Stages of target costing (target cost management)

3) *Iterative product design cycle, focused on customer value and costs*: development of product and process design alternatives is permanently guided by insights about customers' perceptions of value. **Value engineering** is key from an early conceptual design stage and throughout the entire R&D process. It aims to avoid spending resources on technical features with little or no customer value. It distinguishes a continuum between high value added and non-value added product attributes and company activities, as you learned at the start of the chapter. Non-value added attributes and activities are priority targets for elimination. For instance, activities related to quality failures, such as disposal of scrap or rework, are non-value added and their costs can be eliminated if quality can be built into the process to prevent failures (see Chapter 20). Reverse engineering of competitors' products, described above, may also be an important source of ideas for improvements. Importantly, the entire value chain has to be examined for cost-reduction and value-enhancement opportunities. In particular, suppliers are typically involved in the process and they may even be essential to identify and develop improvement opportunities, both within and outside the organization.

You can then estimate expected costs on the basis of early conceptual design. Initial cost estimates may not be very detailed, but they should be as encompassing as possible and include the product entire life cycle, and both variable and fixed future costs.

4) Now, you can calculate a *cost gap* between expected costs and the target cost. Initially expected costs typically exceed the target cost, requiring further rounds of value engineering to reduce the cost gap. Only when improvements at initial stages make the target cost seem feasible, does the R&D move to more detailed stages of product development.

Target cost management is an iterative, multidisciplinary process. Value engineering typically involves making trade-offs between perceived value and costs – rather than taking customer value as unchangeable and focusing entirely on cost reduction. **Attribute costing**, associated with attribute pricing, is a fundamental component of value engineering to obtain 'value-efficient' products. Attribute costing involves estimating the likely costs of offering individual attributes in a product. In a doll, what are the cost and value (price) implications of having three or four colours, the ability to cry or make bubbles or the doll reliability? How do cost savings from using components common to other dolls compare with a potential loss of value through lower differentiation? How do alternative features interact? For example, might more sophisticated functionalities require fragile components and hence compromise the doll's reliability and result in additional customer service costs?

This iterative process may take us back to the starting point: market research. As new product alternatives emerge during the process, there may be the need to obtain new market information about customers' perceptions and competitors' offers. For these new alternatives, new target prices, margins and costs are calculated; new costs are estimated and compared with the new target costs, and the new cost gap is analysed.

So, there are ongoing value engineering efforts at each R&D stage from conceptual design to final design options. Throughout these R&D cycles, the expected cost and the target cost are compared to calculate the cost gap, leading to one of the following results:

a) The cost gap has been eliminated. In this case, the R&D process moves on to a more detailed stage or, if product design is completed, manufacturing may start; alternatively,

b) The company concludes that the cost gap cannot be eliminated and abandons the project. Abandoning a R&D project, in particular before incurring in huge costs, should not be necessarily seen as a failure, since this is preferable to developing and manufacturing a product that either fails to please the market or to provide the desired profitability.

5) When manufacturing starts, with the selected product and process design, the goal becomes not only to control and ensure that costs estimated during the R&D stage are actually achieved, but also to continuously improve – the kaizen approach described before. Again, both cost reduction and value improvements are sought, now at the manufacturing stage, on a continual basis.

Note that the R&D process may be reopened when it becomes apparent that more fundamental changes are possible and are required – thus restarting target cost management. Even more fundamentally, R&D processes are typically never ending: when a product enters the manufacturing stage, R&D efforts are then directed to further improve it or to develop its future successor. For instance, in the automotive industry, given the long stages of conceptualization, development and production, manufacturers are often producing one model, finalizing the design of the next model and conceptualizing the successor of the next model – all at the same time.

Conclusion about kaizen and target costing/cost management

Both target costing and kaizen costing are not actually costing techniques, but rather prospective, future-oriented cost management systems. This system requires the involvement of members of marketing, engineering and production in multifunctional teams. Management accountants can play a key, direct role as a team member highlighting the financial orientation that underlies this cost management system and by providing cost estimates suitable for the various stages of target cost management.

Business process re-engineering (BPR) and management (BPM)

Business process re-engineering (BPR) aims to design and implement radically different processes to conduct business. Business processes are linked sets of activities that organizations perform to attain their objectives, potentially involving multiple functional areas within organizations, in line with what you learned about ABC/ABM. For example, a customer service process may be triggered by a customer complaint to the call centre and then involve the shop floor (to investigate a potential problem and carry out repairs), the legal department (to avoid or settle a dispute) and the financial department (to issue a refund or other payments).

Business process re-engineering goes beyond mere process improvement and aims to fundamentally question the way processes are performed at a given time, redesigning them in significantly, even radically, different ways. For instance, consumer product manufacturers like

Unilever or Procter & Gamble have complex logistical processes involving their packaging suppliers. Logoplaste, a Portuguese-based producer of packaging solutions, was a pioneer in its industry by offering its multinational clients a radically different approach: rather than merely improving traditional logistic processes, Logoplaste started building its own plants inside customers' plants across the world. This re-engineers business processes both inside the customer organization and in its relationships with external parties. It eliminates transportation of goods between the packaging supplier and the customer and it fosters closer co-operation between them (see the case study at the end of the chapter).

Business process re-engineering became popular in the 1990s through management gurus like Michael Hammer and Thomas Davenport. Hammer (1990) (see also Hammer, 2007) identified non-value activities within long-established business processes as main causes of competitive difficulties. So, he urged managers to fundamentally question the assumptions and beliefs underlying those activities and processes. Hammer further argued that information systems were not providing needed improvements because they were only mechanizing old, obsolete business processes. In other words, information systems were not triggering fundamental organizational change. So, BPR gurus urged managers not to automate (old) processes, but rather to obliterate them, through radical re-engineering.

Business process re-engineering was implemented by many companies. However, the disruption implied (and indeed recommended) by BPR also caused some BPR initiatives to fail. As much research points out, history matters in organization and much change is path-dependent – what we can do and change now is dependent on previous choices, actions and beliefs. 'Starting from scratch', as sometimes implicitly suggested by BPR, is not a realistic option, since all change implementation is situated, that is, carried out in particular organizations, with a particular history and characteristics (see Chapter 22).

Furthermore, BPR also became associated with drastic cost reductions, in particular through massive layoffs, promoting organizational resistance, decreasing morale and causing the loss of key staff and organizational knowledge. Davenport (1995) reflected on severe problems with BPR development and implementation, and explained how this huge management fad of the 1990s was fuelled by converging powerful interests of top managers, major management consultancies and major IT vendors.

The failure of many BPR implementations and the criticisms BPR received promoted the emergence of less radical approaches towards business process improvements. In particular, business process management (BPM) has emerged as a major concept, with a less radical approach than BPR, and has been endorsed and promoted by major consultancies and IT vendors, such as IBM and SAP. Business process management's less radical approach may potentially yield smaller-scale improvements when compared with BPR; however, less organizational disruption and fewer managerial challenges have fuelled BPM's popularity, as well as easier integration with other managerial tools such as continuous improvement (analysed in this chapter) and total quality management (analysed in Chapter 20). Hammer (2007) also proposed the 'process and enterprise maturity model' (PEMM), explored in the *Management Accounting Insight 19.1* – a less radical proposal than BPR.

19.1: Management Accounting Insight

BPR is calling for a 'mature' management accounting discipline!

Hammer (2007) recognized that BPR is 'terribly tough to manage' and reflected on why companies often achieve little improvement through BPR initiatives. As a less radical alternative, he recently proposed the 'Process and Enterprise Maturity Model' (PEMM) for companies to deliver higher performance over time, by making their processes more mature.

The PEMM distinguishes between process enablers and enterprise capabilities. The five process enablers are related to individual processes and include: design; performers; owner; infrastructure and metrics. Process enablers are all necessary and mutually interdependent, but they are not sufficient. Enterprise capabilities, related with the entire organization, are crucial to allow process enablers and the redesigned processes to take root and become sustained practices – that is, to become institutionalized (see Chapter 22 on institutionalization). The four enterprise capabilities are leadership, culture, expertise and governance.

While management accounting is absent from Hammer's analysis, his model (PEMM) provides insights on how management accounting and accountants can fit and support fundamental changes in organizational processes. Drawing from Hammer's characterization of four levels of increasing maturity, you can see how management accounting processes and professionals may – and must – become more mature, across various process enablers and enterprise capabilities.

Process enablers

Metrics is a traditional area of management accountants. To improve the maturity of processes, they must develop the following cumulative metrics, from the most basic to the most mature level:

1) Some basic cost and quality metrics

2) End-to-end process metrics derived from customer requirements

3) Individual and cross-process metrics based on the organizational strategic goals

4) Metrics based on inter-organizational goals.

This requires management accountants to move beyond the traditional domain of cost accounting and adopt metrics with a wider scope, including customer-relevant metrics, strategy-oriented metrics and inter-organizational metrics (see Chapters 17, 19, 20 and 22).

Infrastructure is also often an intervention area of management accountants, when they become involved in designing and implementing information systems, in particular integrated information systems (Chapter 21), or become involved in performance measurement and evaluation processes.

Enterprise capabilities

Management accountants must also contribute to enterprise capabilities. They should develop a *culture* based on customer focus, teamwork, personal accountability and willingness to change. Finally, they should improve BPR *governance* by developing mechanisms that support managing complex projects and change initiatives.

Source: Hammer (2007).

Exercises

1) Make a list of the first five management accounting techniques (concerning metrics) that come to your mind. Considering the four items listed above, what maturity level does each technique have?

2) What does your previous answer reveal about your management accounting background? If more 'mature' metrics were missing, did you also learn about them but did not 'come first thing to your mind'? Why/why not?

Sustainable development and accounting

The sustainable development movement

Sustainable development (SD) has increasingly become a major concern for organizations and society. There is an increasing awareness that environmental resources are limited, with potentially serious consequences for individual companies, business models and society. Social factors related to the well-being of employees, local communities and society at large have also emerged as relevant ethical and business issues. Both environmental and social factors influence the sustainable development of companies, business models and the society. A generally accepted definition of sustainable development is 'an approach to progress which meets the needs of the present without compromising the ability of future generations to meet their own needs' (World Commission on Environment and Development, 1987, p. 8). As proponents argue, 'sustainable development is the only conceptual game in town' (Bebbington, 2009) and it is now a hot topic in academic and professional journals and the media in general.

A very narrow view of sustainable development can be found in financial evaluation techniques adopting a long-term perspective. For example, calculating the net present value (NPV) of an investment in a new plant requires financial estimates for a long period of time, hence requiring estimating financial flows over the relevant (long) period. But this concern on the sustainability of financial flows (in particular, inflows) typically ignores whether the continuous usage of indispensable social and environmental inputs is, itself, sustainable. Increasing awareness of limits to resources usage led to two types of concerns. The first concern is how those limits can affect the sustainability of business models – an extension of the traditional, financially oriented view of sustainability. The second concern is to measure, manage and protect those environmental and social resources themselves with an ultimate objective to protect Earth's multiple stakeholders, including humans, animals and plants. Together, both concerns promote the increasingly acknowledged requirement to have business models which themselves promote the various dimensions of sustainable development. As you will see in the remainder of the chapter, accountants may support the design, implementation and running of sustainable business models by deploying various techniques, both in management accounting and financial reporting. These techniques and practices are commonly referred to as sustainability accounting.[3]

A business case for sustainable business models – the role for management accountants

Does it pay off to develop sustainable business models? Critics point out the sometimes substantial design and implementation upfront costs. On the other hand, sustainability proponents argue that not only is sustainability free (by its benefits matching its costs), but it can even improve performance.

Golicic et al. (2010) discuss incentives leading major companies to increasingly pursue sustainability, by focusing on the supply chain and, in particular, on transportation. Only 44 among the Fortune 500 companies address environmental impacts of transportation, with varying levels of detail; almost all acknowledge them, most report changing practices and only a minority reports achieved reductions. The authors acknowledge that profitability pressures may still play against more widespread adoption of sustainable practices. However, they recommend starting with projects targeted at 'low-hanging fruit', that is, easier to implement, likely to have measured success and visible to key stakeholders.

Other accounts are more positive. Haanaes et al. (2011) report the findings of a survey from MIT Sloan Management Review/Boston Consulting Group, indicating that 69 per cent of surveyed companies are planning to increase their investment in sustainability. Interviewed top executives shared the idea of integrating sustainability in the fabric, rather than as a layer, of the business. And a recent report from Accenture and CIMA indicate numerous examples of business gains from sustainability (see *Management Accounting in Practice 19.2*).

Researchers and practitioners converge on one aspect: metrics of both costs and results are essential for a business justification of sustainable development. And metrics are a traditional expertise area of the finance and management accounting function. As highlighted in the recent Accenture and CIMA (2011) survey, the finance function has three main roles in assisting sustainable development: investment analysis (including making the business case), tracking key performance indicators (KPIs) and reporting metrics to meet business and customer needs (see Exhibit 19.5). Overall, identified roles contribute towards the three main business drivers for sustainable development – efficiency, compliance and supporting revenue generation. This is in line with many examples given in *Management Accounting in Practice 19.2*, with benefits in both top and bottom line improvements and a stronger statement of financial position.

19.2: Management Accounting in Practice

Business benefits from sustainability

An Accenture and CIMA report illustrates how leading companies benefited from sustainability, by increasing revenues, controlling costs, building trust, managing risks and exploring opportunities across the entire organizational value chain.

Company value chain		Revenue generation	Cost control	Building trust	Risk management
Procurement and logistics	• Supply chain • Warehousing • Equipment • Inbound logistics	The **Co-operative** switched its own-label chocolate to Fairtrade suppliers in 2002, resulting in a 50% sales volume uplift in the following 12 months	**Walmart** substantially exceeded a target of 25% improvement in fleet efficiency against 2005 baseline within one year	**Walmart's** ethical standards programme for sourcing merchandise is recognized as one of the 'gold standards' in the industry	In July 2009, energy drink manufacturer **Red Bull** was ordered to pay over £270,000 in fines and costs for breaking recycling laws
Operations	• Products • Services • Operations • Buildings • Manufacturing	**Philips** earns 38% of total revenue from 'green product' sales (up from 31% in 2009). **M&S's** 'Plan A' generated £50 million profit from new products – such as M&S Energy which provides insulation and solar panels for 300,000 customers – and reduced costs in only the third year of its operation in 2009–10	**IKEA** saved £1 million by removing plastic bags from checkouts in the UK in 30 months. Its stores are 9% more energy efficient compared to 2005. Japanese pharmaceutical firm **Tanabe Seiyaku** hit annual savings of ¥33m with new environmental accounting techniques	**GE's** brand value increased by 17% after the launch of 'Ecomagination', a business initiative to meet customer demand for more energy-efficient products	**Taylerson's Malmesbury Syrup** realized that sales of their products were linked to cold weather and would decline within the next 20 years as winters become milder. The product range was reviewed and they now provide syrups to be used with ice creams and cold frappes
Marketing, sales and service	• Marketing • Sales • CRM • Retail • Customer service • Outbound logistics	**Vodafone's** 'Carbon Connections' report demonstrates a potential for 113Mt reduction in CO2e and €43 billion in cost reductions through 1 billion new mobile connections	**M&S's** 'Marks and Start' programme (work experience for disadvantaged adults) has lower attrition rates than comparable schemes for new employees	77% of consumers have, in the past year, refused to buy products/services from companies they do not trust. Trust must be built or sales are put at risk	The **Co-operative Bank** showed the risk associated with a loss of trust, citing the 'flight to trust' after the banking crisis as one of the key drivers of a 38% increase in their own current account sales in 2009
Support activities	• Finance • Technology • R&D • HR • Legal • Firm infrastructure	**Novo Nordisk** bring products to market faster by including environmental, social and economic impacts in new drug applications	**Fife Council** have identified additional cost avoidance opportunities of £75 million that can be achieved by improving its carbon reductions by a further 3% per annum between 2007 and 2021	Graduating MBAs from leading North American and European business schools are willing to forgo financial benefits to work for a more ethical employer	**Ribena** noticed that local weather patterns have been changing, affecting their blackcurrant harvests. They have been developing new varieties of blackcurrants that will thrive in a changing climate

The vice-president of brand and global corporate responsibility at Unilever, Santiago Gowland, clearly describes the business perspective of sustainability: 'The only way to continue growing and continue being a successful business [is] to treat sustainability as a key business lever in the same way that you treat marketing, finance, culture, HR or supply chain. So really [it's] core to the ability of the business to grow.'

Sources: Accenture and CIMA (2011) (the report fully references each example); Haanaes et al. (2011).

Exercise

Inspired by these examples, propose, justify and discuss improvements towards sustainable development that may be applicable in your university or in a local business in your area.

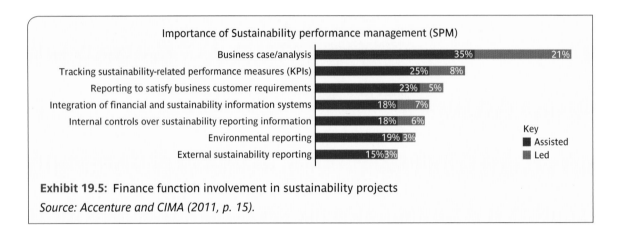

Exhibit 19.5: Finance function involvement in sustainability projects
Source: Accenture and CIMA (2011, p. 15).

Enlightened management for sustainable development – the role for management accountants

Sustainable development proponents such as Dillard (Dillard et al., 2005) stress the need to increasingly adopt a more 'enlightened' management approach (see Table 19.5). This goes beyond seeking relatively short-term benefits, only focused on searching legitimacy or competitive advantage through improved operations and market relations. Instead, this 'enlightened' approach is concerned with society-at-large, rather than only the organization and its shareholders. Therefore, it places a particular emphasis on social and environmental impacts (rather than only on complying with regulations and maximising shareholder value) and on indirect stakeholders (rather than only internal agents and stakeholders with direct, stronger impact). Enlightened management does not see sustainability as an impediment or means to obtain financial gains. Instead, sustainable development is seen as an end in itself. Table 19.5 compares the various logics, views, foci and strategic questions considered relevant in each stage of approaching sustainable development.

The enlightened perspective does not rule out traditional accounting measures, but requires extending or supplementing them to measure environmental and societal impacts without assuming a single focus on the organization itself. This paradigm shift will require that management accounting professionals add new skills and foci to their traditional ones. Supporting SD is both a challenge and an opportunity for accounting, management accounting and their professionals. We will now analyse some SD-supporting solutions for reporting and decision-making purposes.

Reporting on sustainable development

Organizations increasingly report on their commitments and efforts towards SD. Oriented by guidelines such as those set by International Standards Organization (ISO) or the Global Reporting Initiative (GRI), organizations increasingly produce reports on their social, environmental,

Table 19.5: Stages of approaching and managing sustainable development

Stages	Logics	View of sustainability	Focus	Strategic questions
Past	Legitimacy	An impediment to achieve economic ends	Organization (Compliance/legal; operations)	1. What are the minimum requirements? 2. How do I accomplish it in the most economical way?
Present	Competitive advantage	A means to achieve economic ends	Market (economic)	1. What is the most economically beneficial alternative? 2. How do I accomplish it in the most responsible way?
Future	Enlightened management	An end in itself	Society (social, environmental)	1. What is the most responsible/sustainable alternative? 2. How do I accomplish it in the most economical way?

Source: Dillard (2009) and Dillard et al. (2005), (adapted)

sustainable development and corporate social responsibility (CSR) performance. The triple bottom line, measuring economic, environmental and social perspectives, has long been proposed and underlies many recent advances (see various chapters in Henriques and Richardson, 2004). Now you will explore recent proposals from two organizations, the ISO and the IIRC.

The International Organization for Standardization (ISO)

The ISO is the largest issuer of international standards: over 19,000 by the end of 2011. A recent addition was ISO 26000, with guidance on social responsibility and SD. This standard intends to encourage organizations to go beyond legal compliance and to promote a shared understanding of social responsibility. Guidance covers the following topics, concerning social responsibility:

- Concepts, background, trends and characteristics
- Principles, core issues and practices
- Socially responsible behaviour within and beyond the organization
- Stakeholder identification and engagement
- Reporting commitments, performance and other information.

Another family of standards, ISO 14000, aims to minimize environmental impacts of organizations' activities. There were over 200,000 ISO 14001 issued certifications in 2010. ISO 14001 defines an environmental management system (EMS) taking into account both legal requirements and voluntary commitments, as well as relevant environmental information. There are several related standards, such as ISO 14006, on eco-design, and ISO 14005, on phased implementations towards ISO 14001. A phased adoption of an EMS is particularly relevant for small and medium enterprises and has several advantages, such as a quick evaluation of the cost reductions and overall return of the EMS, and better stakeholder relations and satisfaction. Other recent related standards include ISO 14064 and ISO 14065 for greenhouse gas accounting, verification and emissions trading.

The International Integrated Reporting Committee (IIRC)

The International Integrated Reporting Committee has launched a discussion paper on the future of integrated reporting, calling for a new and more ambitious approach to organizational disclosure.

> *Integrated reporting brings together material information about an organization's strategy, governance, performance and prospects in a way that reflects the commercial, social and environmental context within which it operates. It provides a clear and concise representation of how an organization demonstrates stewardship and how it creates and sustains value. (IIRC, 2011, p. 2).*

Therefore, the concept of value is placed in a wider context, rather than merely seen through the perspective of customers and share-holders, as traditionally suggested.

The IIRC (2011) envisions the creation of an integrated report: a single report replacing, rather than adding to, existing requirements and separate reports. It is envisioned to become the primary report on the most relevant issues to the organization's long-term success. Exhibit 19.6 compares today's scarce articulation between corporate reports (financial statements as the main report, supplemented by the management commentary, sustainability reporting and governance and remuneration), with tomorrow's coherent narrative ambitioned by integrated reporting. Integrated reporting is an ongoing project and will continue to evolve over the coming years.

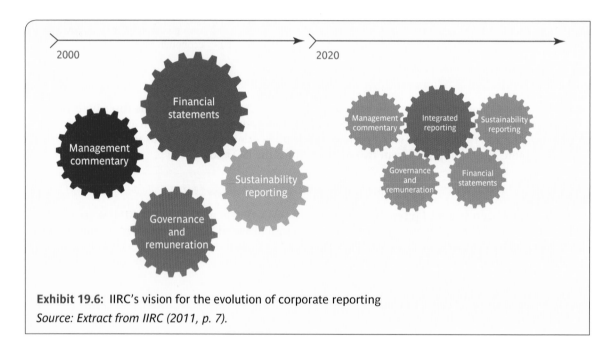

Exhibit 19.6: IIRC's vision for the evolution of corporate reporting
Source: Extract from IIRC (2011, p. 7).

'Integrated reporting' may address shortcomings currently felt by companies like Novo Nordisk, as reported by Accenture and CIMA (2011). Novo Nordisk integrated sustainability information into its annual report, oriented by principles of triple bottom line reporting. Without internationally recognized standards in sustainability reporting, they had to explore with the external audit and assurance teams to expand the boundaries of auditing and assurance to include a sustainability framework. The goal is to move towards an integrated management system oriented towards sustainability and shared among internal and external stakeholders. See Chapter 22, and *Management Accounting in Practice 22.2* in particular, for further discussion and examples of integrated reporting.

Decision-making techniques for sustainable development

In addition to reporting, Bebbington (2007) and Riccaboni and Leone (2010) argue that the goal to achieve SD should also be reflected in organizational decision-making. So, new challenges arise for accounting, to support and orient decision-making processes towards SD, in instances such as planning processes, capital allocation and performance evaluation. Sustainable development-oriented capital allocation is particularly critical, since it plans and shapes how operational activities will be performed at a later stage. You will now explore two proposals: full cost accounting and the sustainability assessment model.

Full-cost accounting

Full-cost accounting (FCA) is an alternative, SD-oriented valuation technique that incorporates the use of environmental and social resources in the full cost of production. Full-cost accounting goes beyond the economic costs traditionally considered, based on the usage of economic resources such as the cost of used materials, labour, utilities and machines. Full-cost accounting promotes identifying and accounting for externalities of an organization's activities, in particular negative environmental and social externalities, such as pollution and unfair employment practices (Bebbington and Gray, 2001; Bent, 2004). By becoming explicitly included in the product's (full) cost, managers are more likely to try to minimize them by adopting practices with less environmental and social impacts.

The sustainability assessment model

Bebbington (2007) presents the **sustainability assessment model (SAM)**, developed by the oil company BP to orient project evaluation towards SD, by modelling and accounting for SD performance and raising awareness to SD among employees. The SAM builds on FCA, so it encompasses not only economic costs but also environmental and social costs. The SAM is applicable both to the capital allocation stage and to retrospective evaluation. To apply the SAM, you must:

1) Define the cost objective (for example, a particular investment project).

2) Specify the scope of analysis: the SAM should include the full life cycle of the project. This includes not only the activities of the project itself, but also all upstream and downstream activities related with the project. This is closely related with life cycle costing discussed above in this chapter, but now taking an environmental and social perspective. For example, disposal of batteries used by electronic equipment should be considered at the R&D stage, to evaluate and lessen the total environmental impacts of the equipment, 'from cradle to grave'.

3) Identify impacts of the cost objective, concerning:

   a) Economics, as measured in traditional accounting terms over the project life, based on historical or estimated future economic flows

   b) Resource use, in the part that exceeds economic flows, in particular to reflect resource depletion and its future unavailability for alternative, potentially more valuable uses; these negative externalities may be offset, partially or in full, by positive externalities (for example, the development of individuals' intellectual capabilities)

   c) Environmental flows, such as: emissions; noise, odour and visual impact; land occupation and waste

   d) Social flows, concerning: employment creation, contribution to a sustainable society, and social impacts from products based on the project. These externalities can be positive or negative and are typically the most difficult to measure, in particular in financial terms – the SAM's final stage.

4) Monetizes the impacts, to allow comparing the different impacts. Applying the SAM to a oil and gas field development, Bebbington (2007, p. 50) drew a typical SAM signature, as in Exhibit 19.7

The SAM, a model still under going development, can be applied to other types of settings, such as the construction and energy generation industries (Bebbington, 2007). A related development is Procter & Gamble's 'product sustainability assessment tool' (PSAT) (Riccaboni and Leone, 2010), summarized in *Management Accounting in Practice 19.3*. The PSAT and the SAM share important similarities, since both aim to integrate the sustainability rationale in everyday operations (although PSAT is particularly focused on new product development) and adopt a product life cycle approach. However, the two approaches also have differences. First, the PSAT does not monetize the different impacts (the fourth and final stage of the SAM). The lack of monetization prevents reaching a single measure of project 'sustainable value', thus requiring complex trade-offs between financial, social and environmental perspectives and leading to ambiguity in some decisions. However, by avoiding monetization, the PSAT also avoids the criticisms addressed to this step of the SAM, as recognized by Bebbington (2007).

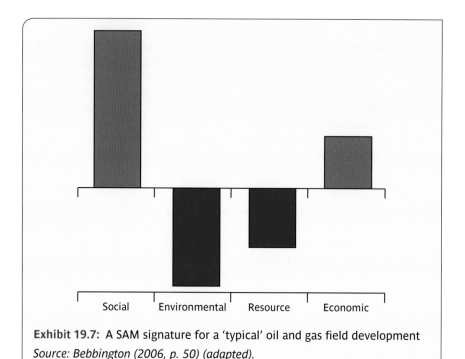

Exhibit 19.7: A SAM signature for a 'typical' oil and gas field development
Source: Bebbington (2006, p. 50) (adapted).

19.3: Management Accounting in Practice

Assessing product sustainability at Procter & Gamble

Procter & Gamble developed a tool to integrate the sustainability rational in everyday actions: the 'product sustainability assessment tool' (PSAT). PSAT applied particularly to R&D activities, evaluating innovation proposals in line with the triple bottom line perspective: financial, environmental and social. Analyses were developed by a multidisciplinary team:

1) 'a person responsible for Finance provides financial analysis of the product's profitability through traditional capital budgeting criteria, such as the net present value;

2) a person responsible for Health Safety and Environment provides an environmental assessment, through the life cycle assessment (LCA), measuring the overall environmental footprint of the new product from the provision of raw materials to the disposal; and

3) a person responsible for External Relations (sometimes supported by the consumer market knowledge) provides an assessment of the new product, analysing the stakeholders' point of view through techniques such as "stakeholder management" (Riccaboni and Leone, 2010, p. 138).

Proposals were rated between 1 and 10 in each perspective. No aggregation of the three ratings was attempted, and managers had to make difficult trade-offs between the three perspectives.

Source: Riccaboni and Leone (2010).

Exercise

Could it be argued that, because the person from Finance only performed the financial analyses through traditional capital budgeting techniques, there was no need to get involved in the other perspectives?

Chapter summary

This chapter, after recognizing the persistent importance of cost reduction and control, went beyond costs and costing systems and analysed cost management with a value enhancing perspective. It expanded the scope beyond the organization to include the entire value chain. It combined activity-based information on cost and value to obtain managerial insights through operational and strategic ABM. It expanded the usually short time horizon to encompass the entire product life cycle, in life cycle costing. It discussed how cost and value can be improved during and before the manufacturing stage, through kaizen costing and target costing, respectively. It discussed the radical challenge of business process re-engineering and its difficulties, as well as the less radical proposal of business process management. The chapter finalized by discussing the increasingly important issue of sustainable development and how management accounting can contribute towards it.

Key terms

Activity-based management (ABM) The use of ABC information to identify operational and strategic improvement possibilities (p. 480)

Attribute costing Estimation of expected costs of offering individual attributes in a product (p. 494)

Attribute pricing Estimation of customers' willingness to pay for different product attributes, both individually and when integrated within particular product configurations (p. 493)

Business Process Re-engineering (BPR) A radical approach to organizational change, fundamentally questioning and re-engineering business processes, rather than merely improving them (p. 495)

Continuous improvement (kaizen, in Japanese) A company-wide approach of never-ending pursuit of improvements, typically small and incremental but adding up to significant cumulative improvements (p. 491)

Full-cost accounting (FCA) A costing technique that includes the use of environmental and social resources in the full cost of production, in order to support management decisions promoting sustainable development (p. 503)

Kaizen costing Cost management technique to reduce costs during the production stage, in a kaizen/continuous improvement approach to increase efficiency and reduce waste (p. 491)

Life cycle costing Analyses costs throughout the entire life cycle of a product, from development to after-sales stages; an input for life cycle profitability analysis (p. 487)

Reverse engineering Engineering practice of disassembling competitors' products to obtain detailed insights about their design features, materials and production techniques (p. 493)

Sustainability assessment model (SAM) A project evaluation technique to support decisions that promote sustainable development, based on full-cost accounting (p. 503)

Sustainable development (SD) 'An approach to progress which meets the needs of the present without compromising the ability of future generations to meet their own needs' (WCED, 1987, p. 8) (p. 497)

Target cost Target price (based on market research) minus the target margin (based on corporate profitability objectives) (p. 493)

Target costing (or target cost management) A cost management technique for the product development stage, to determine the maximum allowable product cost, based on customers' willingness to pay and corporate profitability objectives, and to design a product that can be sold at such maximum target cost (p. 493)

Value chain The major activities that add customer value; it may be analysed at an organizational level or at an industry-wide level, from suppliers of basic raw materials through to the end customer (p. 494)

Value engineering A technique for product development oriented by customers' perceptions of value and expected costs of each product attribute (p. 494)

Review questions • • • • • • • • • • • • connect • •

Level of difficulty:	BASIC	INTERMEDIATE	ADVANCED

19.1 Describe the industry value chain concept. **[LO1]**

19.2 Identify and characterize the two uses of activity-based management. **[LO2]**

19.3 Describe the importance of life cycle costing. **[LO3]**

19.4 Discuss the applicability and importance of kaizen costing. **[LO4]**

19.5 Discuss the applicability and importance of target costing. **[LO5, LO6]**

19.6 What are the key messages of business process re-engineering? **[LO7]**

19.7 Distinguish between business-focused and enlightened perspectives of sustainable development. **[LO8]**

19.8 Describe the process of target cost management. **[LO5, LO6]**

19.9 Describe techniques for reporting and decision-making that promote sustainable development. **[LO9]**

Group discussion and activity questions • • • • • • • • •

19.10 Measuring the multiple contributions towards the value added throughout an entire value chain may be challenging. Select a particular value chain, identify its most relevant participants and place yourself as a management accountant of an organization participating in an intermediate stage of that value chain. Discuss the ways and the difficulties of measuring the value added: **[LO1]**

a) By your organization.

b) By other participants, both upstream and downstream in the value chain.

19.11 Identify a product which was withdrawn from the market in an expectedly short time after its launch due to either market non-acceptance or insufficient profitability. Investigate in more detail the reasons behind its withdrawal. Discuss how kaizen costing and/or target costing techniques could have prevented this failure. **[LO3]**

19.12 Based on the improvement proposals you suggested in *Management Accounting in Practice 19.2*, discuss how you, as a management accountant, could contribute towards those improvements. **[LO8, LO9, LO10]**

Exercises • • • • • • • • • • • • • • • • connect • •

E19.1 **Select target activities for improvement initiatives; activities classifications; benchmark and 'make-or-buy' decision [LO2]**

Company DAI produces and distributes dairy products and has recently implemented an activity-based costing system. As DAI's controller, you were requested to propose a cost reduction plan for the next quarter. A key business process to sustain DAI's competitiveness was introducing new products in the market. You were aware that cost reductions in this business process should not compromise the process success. So, you extracted the costs of the various activities, their cost drivers and the volume of each cost driver in the last quarter. A manager classified each activity according to its value added and opportunity for improvement, as in the following table:

Business process: Introducing products						
Dept.	**Activity**	**Activity cost (£)**	**Cost driver**	**Quantity**	**Value added**	**Opportunity for improvement**
Marketing	Perform marketing actions	30,000	No. of hours of actions	2,500	2	High
	Save photos to museum	20,000	No. of hours spent	2,000	5	High
Production	Milk	70,000	No. of minutes	35,000	5	Low
	Feed animals	50,000	No. of kg food	2,500	2	Low
	Give medication to animals	21,000	No. of doses	700	4	Average
Laboratory	Prepare samples	3,000	No. of hours preparations	100	2	High
	Analyse samples	26,000	No. of samples	400	3	High
	Total	220,000				

Required:

a) Given the importance of this business process, you wish to start improvement efforts only on activities classified as low added value (1–2 rating) and as offering high opportunities for improvement. Calculate total cost savings if efforts in these activities yield cost savings of: (i) 25 per cent; (ii) 50 per cent.

b) A manager argued that one of the activities classified as 'high-value added' does not actually add value. Identify and reclassify that activity. Considering the new classification of the activities, recalculate the two scenarios of the previous question. Explain why the total cost savings in questions (a) and (b) are different.

c) Another manager argued that improving one of the activities selected in the first question is useless. Do you agree? Why/why not?

d) A company from the animal health industry proposed carrying out three activities:

   i)   'Give medication to animals', charging £20 for each dose.

   ii) 'Prepare samples', charging £35 for each hour of preparation.

   iii) 'Analyse samples', charging £65 for each sample.

Should DAI accept the proposals, hence ceasing to internally perform those activities? What aspects should DAI evaluate before taking these decisions?

Source: with thanks to Raul Dores, University of Minho.

E19.2 Kaizen costing [LO4]

The controller of an accounting firm has decided to adopt a kaizen costing approach to reduce office costs, perceived to be excessive. A benchmarking exercise against data from two other firms suggested aiming at a 4 per cent reduction in the next quarter. A staff brainstorming exercise allowed identifying four areas where changes in practices could generate savings.

	Costs in last quarter, in (£)	Expected costs with kaizen changes, in (£)
1. **Communication costs:** eliminate calls to customers' mobile phones unless in urgent cases; rely mainly on VoIP-based phone calls	1,500	1,000
2. **Electricity costs:** reduce time for computers to enter in stand by mode from 10 minutes to 1 minute	2,000	1,950
3. **Paper costs:** set '2-sided printing' as default print option	100	80
4. **Labour costs:** reduce staff symbolic bonus usually granted each quarter	30,000	29,000
Other office costs	50,000	50,000

Required:

a) Are all suggested changes (1–4) in line with a kaizen costing approach?

b) Do the suggested changes achieve the kaizen costing goal? What are the reasons for the firm achieving/failing to achieve such a goal?

c) What problems might arise due to the suggested changes? How serious do you think they might be?

E19.3 Activity-based management, evaluation of product profitability [LO2]

The Ornamental Company (TOC) makes and sells a range of ornamental products in Baseland. TOC employs experienced sculptors who have an excellent reputation for producing high-quality products. TOC has been approached by the Superior Garden Group (SGG) and asked to make two products. The two products are a water fountain known as 'The Fountain' and a large garden gnome known as 'The Goblin'.

The management accountant of TOC has estimated the variable costs per unit of The Fountain and The Goblin as being £622.50 and £103.75 respectively. She based her calculations on the following information:

1) Product data:

	The Fountain	The Goblin	Other products
Production/sales (units)	2,000	4,000	16,000
	£000's	£000's	£000's
Total direct material costs	450	150	1,200
Total direct labour cost	300	100	1,200

2) Total variable overheads for TOC will amount to £2,400,000 of which 30 per cent relates to the procurement, warehousing and use of direct materials. All other variable overheads are direct labour related.

3) TOC currently absorbs variable overheads into product units using company-wide percentages on total direct material cost and total direct labour cost.

4) SGG is willing to purchase The Fountain at £750 per unit and The Goblin at £150 per unit.

5) TOC will not undertake any work which does not yield an estimated contribution to sales ratio of 28 per cent.

6) The directors of TOC are considering switching to an activity-based costing system and recently appointed a firm of management consultants to undertake a detailed review of existing operations. As part of that review, the management consultants concluded that estimated relevant cost drivers for material and labour related overhead costs attributable to The Fountain and The Goblin are as follows:

	The Fountain	The Goblin	Other products
Direct material related overheads:			
The cost driver is the volume of raw materials held to facilitate production of each product.			
Material proportions per product unit:	4	7	4
Direct labour related overheads:			
The cost driver is the number of labour operations performed.			
Labour operations per product unit:	6	5	4

Required:

a) Calculate the variable cost per unit of both products using an activity-based costing approach.

b) Using the unit cost information available and your calculations in (a), prepare a financial analysis of the decision strategy which TOC may implement with regard to the manufacture of each product.

c) Critically discuss the adoption of activity-based management in companies such as TOC.

Source: adapted from Association of Chartered Certified Accountants.

E19.4 Life cycle costing, standard costing [LO3]

Wargrin designs, develops and sells many PC games. Games have a short life cycle lasting around three years. Performance of the games is measured by reference to the profits made in each of the expected three years of popularity. Wargrin accepts a net profit of 35 per cent of turnover as reasonable. A rate of contribution (sales price less variable cost) of 75 per cent is also considered acceptable.

Wargrin has a large centralized development department which carries out all the design work before it passes the completed game to the sales and distribution department to market and distribute the product.

Wargrin has developed a brand new game called Stealth and this has the following budgeted performance figures:

● The selling price of Stealth will be a constant £30 per game.

● Analysis of the costs show that at a volume of 10,000 units a total cost of £130,000 is expected. However at a volume of 14,000 units a total cost of £150,000 is expected.

● If volumes exceed 15,000 units the fixed costs will increase by 50 per cent.

Stealth's budgeted volumes are as follows:

	Year 1	Year 2	Year 3
Sales volume	8,000 units	16,000 units	4,000 units

In addition, marketing costs for Stealth will be £60,000 in year one and £40,000 in year two. Design and development costs are all incurred before the game is launched and has cost £300,000 for Stealth. These costs are written off to the income statement as incurred (that is, before year 1 above).

Required:

a) Explain the principles behind life cycle costing and briefly state why Wargrin in particular should consider these life cycle principles.

b) Produce the budgeted results for the game 'Stealth' and briefly assess the game's expected performance, taking into account the whole life cycle of the game.

c) Discuss the extent to which a meaningful standard cost can be set for games produced by Wargrin. You should consider each of the cost classifications mentioned above.

Source: adapted from Association of Chartered Certified Accountants.

> **E19.5** **Target costing [LO5, 6]**

Edward Co assembles and sells many types of radio. It is considering extending its product range to include digital radios. These radios produce a better sound quality than traditional radios and have a large number of potential additional features not possible with the previous technologies (station scanning, more choice, one-touch tuning, station identification text and song identification text, and so on).

A radio is produced by workers assembling a variety of components. Production overheads are currently absorbed into product costs on an assembly labour hour basis. Edward Co is considering a target costing approach for its new digital radio product.

Required:

a) Briefly describe the target costing process that Edward Co should undertake.

b) Explain the benefits to Edward Co of adopting a target costing approach at such an early stage in the product development process.

c) Assuming a cost gap was identified in the process, outline possible steps Edward Co could take to reduce this gap.

A selling price of £44 has been set in order to compete with a similar radio on the market that has comparable features to Edward Co's intended product. The board have agreed that the acceptable margin (after allowing for all production costs) should be 20 per cent.

Cost information for the new radio is as follows:

Component 1 (Circuit board) – these are bought in and cost £4.10 each. They are bought in batches of 4,000 and additional delivery costs are £2,400 per batch.

Component 2 (Wiring) – in an ideal situation 25 cm of wiring is needed for each completed radio. However, there is some waste involved in the process as wire is occasionally cut to the wrong length or is damaged in the assembly process. Edward Co estimates that 2 per cent of the purchased wire is lost in the assembly process. Wire costs £0.50 per metre to buy.

Other material – other materials cost £8.10 per radio.

Assembly labour – these are skilled people who are difficult to recruit and retain. Edward Co has more staff of this type than needed but is prepared to carry this extra cost in return for the security it gives the business. It takes 30 minutes to assemble a radio and the assembly workers are paid £12.60 per hour. It is estimated that 10 per cent of hours paid to the assembly workers is for idle time.

Production overheads – recent historic cost analysis has revealed the following production overhead data:

	Total production overhead	Total assembly labour hours
	£	
Month 1	620,000	19,000
Month 2	700,000	23,000

Fixed production overheads are absorbed on an assembly hour basis based on normal annual activity levels. In a typical year 240,000 assembly hours will be worked by Edward Co.

Required:

d)   Calculate the expected cost per unit for the radio and identify any cost gap that might exist.

Source: adapted from Association of Chartered Certified Accountants.

E19.6   **The strategic assessment model (SAM) [LO9]**

A mining company is evaluating a new extraction project. Based on geologists' estimates, the finance director calculated that the project has a net present value of £10 million for the company. However, the general manager is aware of the importance of contemplating other impacts beyond those considered in the financial director's calculations. He commissioned an expert to evaluate the environmental costs associated with the project.

Required:

a)   What kind of environmental costs is the expert likely to consider?

b)   Is the commissioned evaluation scope sufficient?

c)   Discuss the advantages and disadvantages of monetizing different perspectives, as recommended by the strategic assessment model (SAM).

• • • Case study problem • • • • • • • • • • • connect • • •

C19.1   **Innovation and sustainable development through a value-chain focus [LO1, LO5, LO7, LO8, LO9, LO10]**

Logoplaste is a world player in the rigid plastic packaging industry. It was founded in Portugal and now owns over 60 factories across 18 countries, while still keeping its headquarters in Portugal. It provides integrated solutions for some of the world's most reputable companies, in the sectors of food and beverage, personal care, household care and oil and lubricants, such as Procter & Gamble, Unilever, Nestlé, Coca-Cola or Danone.

Logoplaste was an industry pioneer through developing the 'hole in the wall' concept: manufacturing the packages inside or right next to their customers' factories. At the time, competitors had central factories manufacturing for different customers, requiring the empty packages to be transported to the customer's factory. However, the 'hole in the wall' concept allowed Logoplaste the competitive advantage of delivering the packages 'just in time' and without transportation costs, which are often a major part of the total cost. 'Empty packages don't travel well' is a common expression in the industry (Morgado, 2008, p. 1416). Other competitors later adopted the same concept, although Logoplaste may still be enjoying 'first-mover' advantages, as illustrated by the final example of this case.

Logoplaste is fully integrated in the customers' logistic and value chains. Logoplaste customers traditionally considered packaging a non-core step of the value chain, and its outsourcing was a way of obtaining cost savings from a specialized company. However, packaging has become increasingly important, beyond its traditional functions of containing, protecting and preserving the product and informing consumers. Packaging has become a major marketing variable, strongly impacting on consumers' perceptions. This increases the value added by the packaging step of the value chain. Logoplaste has explored packaging's increasing importance by expanding its role in the value chain: instead of being a mere packaging producer, it offers a complete, integrated solution, with services ranging from the package initial concept to its production and quality control.

Logoplaste has developed the capacity to design packages that create innovation and value in customers' products. For example, packaging played a big part in the huge success of Procter & Gamble's Sunny Delight. The drink was placed in the refrigerated display (although preservatives actually made this not necessary) and packaging suggested similarities to real 100 per cent fruit juices. This positioning allowed a considerable price premium (Morgado, 2008).

Packaging importance for customers' perceptions and customer value led to joint development of packages, by a team of staff from Logoplaste and its customers. In addition, customers' attention 'mostly focused on developing new container functions and designs at an acceptable price point' (Alcacer and Leitão, 2010, p. 2). The design teams of Logoplaste and Heinz, the food company famous for its ketchup, establish close collaboration at very early stages. This allows them to explore in detail the best design concepts, with each side bringing its expertise to optimize the final production solution. The final objective is 'to enable the team to choose the best cost/performance solution' (Logoplaste website).

To encourage deeper collaboration with customers, the Logoplaste Innovation Lab was created to develop new products and package design, from early conceptualization to production. This technological centre 'offers an integrated and complete packaging development solution that goes from early marketing and design research and strategy definition, to engineering, manufacturing and implementation' (Logoplaste website), including activities such as rapid 3D prototyping, making moulds and trials. 'The organized sequence of these activities is the foundation for the Logoplaste 360° concept which assures the partner, not only integration of the above tasks through a single supplier, but also reduction of times and costs, thus optimising the whole development process for a new package' (Morgado, 2008, p. 1418).

Logoplaste also performs product development jointly with suppliers. The supplier Repsol Chemical, a part of the oil and gas Repsol company, also has a technological centre and shares technical support with Logoplaste to develop the next generation of materials and product applications. 'Both [companies] share their commitment with their clients. "Logoplaste focuses on product design and innovation by testing the new developments in their in-house pilot plant. These are the type of things we have in common"' says a Repsol manager (Batey, 2010, p. 66). Likewise, the innovation laboratory also co-operates closely with various equipment manufacturers.

Logoplaste's customers are usually under price pressure, so they typically require continuous cost reduction from Logoplaste. Actually, this goes beyond a bargaining practice: the long-term contracts actually include 'efficiency-gain clauses, which established a price reduction schedule in line with anticipated improvements in efficiency' (Alcacer and Leitão, 2010, pp. 3–4). Cost (and price) reduction are actually intertwined with the Innovation Laboratory's research, that continuously tries to reduce costs and so offer new solutions for customers. For example, Logoplaste's partnership with Arla Foods UK, a company originated in Scandinavia, has allowed Arla to win two 'Food Manufacture' excellence awards and extends to design and innovation. 'Continuous development in packaging technology and manufacturing capabilities has seen the Logoplaste designed bottles give significant material reductions, making them the lightest in the industry' (Logoplaste website).

This last example leads to an additional strength: Logoplaste's contribution to sustainable development. Eliminating transportation to customers' factories significantly reduces the carbon footprint. GlaxoSmithKline (GSK), maker of Lucozade, Lucozade Sport, Ribena and other drinks and pharmaceutical products,

wanted to be more environmentally responsible and stop shipping bottles to the drinks plant from a production site located more than a 3-hour drive away. GSK asked for bids from companies that could make the bottles on-site at the plant in Coleford, England, and Logoplaste's long experience gave it the edge over the supplier at the time, which had also bid on the project. (Logoplaste website)

So, a more sustainable business model has also been a source of competitive advantage to Logoplaste.

Sources: Alcacer and Leitão (2010); Batey (2010); Morgado (2008); www.logoplaste.com.

Required:

a) 'The success of any company is dependent of the value chain in which it participates.' Discuss if this sentence is particularly applicable to Logoplaste or not.

b) Discuss the development of Logoplaste's 'hole in the wall' model as business process re-engineering.

c) Analyse Logoplaste's practices related with target costing, describing instances of the various stages of this technique.

d) Analyse Logoplaste's practices related with kaizen costing. Are kaizen costing and target costing related in this case study?

e) Discuss factors with a potentially positive or negative impact on components of the sustainability assessment model (SAM) for Logoplaste.

● ● Recommended reading ● ● ● ● ● ● ● ● ● ● ● ● ● ● ● ●

- Accenture and CIMA (2011) 'Sustainability performance management: how CFOs can unlock value', CIMA, Oxford.

This report provides numerous insights (beyond the extract mentioned in Management Accounting in Practice 19.2) on the potential contribution, and also necessity, of management accountants to support sustainability oriented practices in their organizations.

- Bragg, S. M. (2010) *Cost Reduction Analysis: Tools and Strategies*, Hoboken NJ: John Wiley & Sons.

This practice-oriented book shows than even when cost reduction is a primary objective, value concerns should permanently orient decision making and organizational change.

- Henriques, A. and J. Richardson (eds) (2004) *The Triple Bottom Line: Does It All Add Up?* London: Earthscan.

This book contains multiple contributions offering a comprehensive review of the classic 'triple bottom line' concept. It discusses achievements, failures and challenges to be solved and aims at assessing the sustainability of business and corporate social responsibility (CSR). It offers an academic perspective on sustainable development.

- *MIT Sloan Management Review*, Fall 2009, Summer 2010, Winter 2011.

These three issues include several articles about sustainability, its business opportunities, metrics difficulties, many examples and cases, and the 2009 and 2011 surveys on sustainability. It offers a recent and rich empirical and practitioners' perspective on sustainable development.

● ● ● References ●

Accenture and CIMA (2011) 'Sustainability performance management: how CFOs can unlock value', CIMA, Oxford.

Alcacer, J. and J. Leitão (2010) 'Logoplaste: global growing challenges', *Harvard Business School Cases*, December, pp. 1–20.

Barwise, P. and S. N. Meehan (2010) 'Is your company as customer-focused as you think?', *MIT Sloan Management Review*, 51(3), pp. 63–8.

Batey, E.-J. (2010) 'Message in a bottle', *Packaging Europe*, 4.4 (December), pp. 58–69.

Baxter, T., J. Bebbington and D. Cutteridge (2004) 'Sustainability assessment model: modelling economic, resource, environmental and social flows of a project', in A. Henriques and J. Richardson (eds), *The Triple Bottom Line: Does It All Add Up?*, London: Earthscan, pp. 113–20.

Bebbington, J. (2007) *Accounting for Sustainable Development Performance*, Oxford: CIMA.

Bebbington, J. (2009) 'Organisations, policy, economic context and sustainable development', 7th ENROAC International Management Control Research Conference, Dundee.

Bebbington, J. and R. Gray (2001) 'An account of sustainability: failure, success and a reconceptualization', *Critical Perspectives on Accounting*, 12(5), pp. 557–88.

Bent, D. (2004) 'Towards a monetized triple bottom line for an alcohol producer', Sustainability Accounting and Reporting proceedings, Environmental Management Accounting Network (EMAN).

Davenport, T. H. (1995) 'The fad that forgot people', http://www.fastcompany.com/magazine/01/reengin.html (accessed on 10 October 2011).

Dillard, J. (2009) 'An ethic of accountability for sustainable organizations', 7th ENROAC International Management Control Research Conference, Dundee.

Dillard, J., D. Brown and R.S. Marshall (2005) 'An environmentally enlightened accounting', *Accounting Forum*, 29(1), pp. 77–101.

Golicic, S. K., C. N. Boerstler and L. M. Ellram (2010) '"Greening" transportation in the supply chain', *MIT Sloan Management Review*, 51(2), pp. 47–55.

Haanaes, K., B. Balagopal, M. T. Kong, I. Velken, D. Arthar, M. S. Hopkis and N. Vischuitz (2011) 'New sustainability study: the "Embracers" seize advantage', *MIT Sloan Management Review*, 52(3), pp. 23–35.

Hammer, M. (1990) 'Reengineering work: don't automate, obliterate', *Harvard Business Review*, 68(4), pp. 104–12.

Hammer, M. (2007) 'The process audit', *Harvard Business Review*, 85(4), pp. 111–23.

Henriques, A. and J. Richardson, Eds. (2004). *The Triple Bottom Line: Does it all add up?* London, Earthscan.

IFAC (1998) *International Management Accounting Practice Statement: Management Accounting Concepts*, New York: IFAC.

IIRC (2011) 'Towards integrated reporting: communicating value in the 21st century', International Integrated Reporting Committee, http://theiirc.org/wp-content/uploads/2011/09/IR-Discussion-Paper-2011_spreads.pdf (accessed on 15 May 2012)

Jollands, S. E. (2011) 'Management control systems and sustainability', unpublished PhD thesis, University of Auckland.

Kaplan, R. S. and R. Cooper (1988) *Cost & Effect: Using Integrated Cost Systems to Drive Profitability and Performance*, Boston, MA: Harvard Business School Press.

Morgado, A. (2008) 'Logoplaste: innovation in the global market: from packaging to solution', *Management Decision*, 46(9), pp. 1414–36.

Porter, M. E. (1985) *Competitive Advantage*, New York: Free Press.

Riccaboni, A. and E. L. Leone (2010) 'Implementing strategies through management control systems: the case of sustainability', *International Journal of Productivity and Performance Management*, 59(2), pp. 130–44.

Takeuchi, H., E. Osono and N. Shimizu (2008) 'The contradictions that drive Toyota's success', *Harvard Business Review*, 86(6), pp. 96–104.

World Commission on Environment and Development (WCED) (1987) *Tokyo Declaration*, Tokyo: WCED.

• • • Notes •

1 Remember from page 485 doubts about the adequacy of this cost driver with regard to the 'product inspection' sub-activity.

2 Remember that some costs typically classified as fixed may indeed change, particularly if activities cease entirely, as considered for year 3, since assets or contracts creating fixed costs may be totally or partially eliminated.

3 Drawing from Jollands (2011), sustainability can be seen as a dichotomous state (being sustainable or not) while sustainable development can be seen as a continuous, never-ending process towards achieving that state. In practice, these terms are often used interchangeably.

When you have read this chapter

Log on to the Online Learning Centre at **www.mcgraw-hill.co.uk/textbooks/burns** to explore chapter-by-chapter test questions, links and further online study tools for Management Accounting.

CHAPTER 20

MANAGING QUALITY AND TIME

Chapter outline

- Quality, time and the management accountant's role

- Managing quality to create value

- Managing time to create value

- Total quality management and just-in-time

- Management accounting techniques

Learning outcomes

On completion of this chapter, you will be able to:

LO1 Explain the strategic importance of quality and time

LO2 Characterize various dimensions of quality

LO3 Characterize management accountants' contributions to quality and time initiatives

LO4 Identify quality financial indicators (costs of quality) and non-financial indicators

LO5 Set quality targets and detect poor quality

LO6 Identify operational measures of time

LO7 Characterize total quality management and its benefits and difficulties

LO8 Characterize just-in-time and its benefits and difficulties

LO9 Relate throughput accounting with previously studied techniques

LO10 Use backflush costing

Introduction

In this chapter, you will learn two important creators of value: quality and time. In Chapter 19, you analysed various drivers of value in contemporary organizations, going beyond mere cost reduction and exploring insights and techniques to support companies' competitive position. Mastering quality and time, the focus of this chapter, is increasingly indispensible to actually achieve this objective.

We all have an intuitive notion about what quality is. We tend to think we recognize quality when we see it – or, at least, recognize when quality is missing. But quality is multidimensional: try writing down what *you* think quality is and you will probably end up with a fairly long and diversified list of quality dimensions. If you compare your list with that of a colleague, you will probably find both similarities and differences. That is because quality has different meanings for different people. Companies too must manage quality in a customer-centred, flexible way. In this chapter, you will find insights to help you think about quality and techniques to manage it in an effective way.

Time is important in multiple ways. Bob Dylan sang, in the 1960s, that 'Times they are a-changing' and throughout this book you have realized how companies have to be able to adapt quickly to a fast-changing environment. While Chapters 1 and 22 address time (and change) from a high-level perspective, this chapter focuses on time 'in itself' – on the time organizations take to perform and respond to customers. And you will start questioning the popular proverb 'Haste makes waste', and realize that speed and quality are indeed two faces of the same coin, rather than opposing features.

The next section emphasizes the importance of quality and time, discusses the contentious relation between these concepts and highlights how management accountants can contribute and create value in these key areas. In the subsequent section, you will learn four perspectives to manage quality, including financial and non-financial measures, and how to set and monitor quality targets. Then, you will find operational measures of time and realize how the just-in-time approach contributed to remarkable competitive improvements around the world. The next section describes two approaches to quality and time (total quality management and just-in-time) that the Japanese developed and that have been adopted around the world. A final section discusses the management accounting techniques of throughput accounting (which aims to improve performance by better management of constrained resources and where time is key) and backflush costing (a simplified costing technique for a just-in-time environment).

Quality, time and the management accountant's role

Introducing quality

Let us examine the hotel industry and the many ways it measures and signals quality. Hotels are classified by official agencies according to a rating system between 1 and 5 stars – sometimes reaching 6 or even 7 stars, in exceptionally luxurious sites. Marketing information services companies, such as J. D. Power and Associates, survey thousands of hotel customers to assess their satisfaction and announce results in their website. In recent years, Internet-based social networks opened up new possibilities to assess satisfaction. A company exhibiting many 'Like's in Facebook provides an indication of satisfaction – but in a very simplistic, non-informative way. How much did people really like it and why? Did those Facebook users and 'friends' actually experience the service or product, or did they only 'Like' it to enter a contest or get some other benefit? How many users would have clicked a 'Dislike' button, should it exist in Facebook? These are usually unanswered questions. So, let's look at more informative alternatives to evaluate quality.

These examples point out an important criterion to assess quality: the customers' perspective. Traditional views of quality focused on objective, production-centred criteria to assess quality – for example, compliance with production norms. However, it is now widely accepted that customer-focused quality is crucial for capturing customers' subjective perceptions of quality and identifying the underlying key factors so that they can be managed (and potentially improved) in a customer-relevant way.

So, what *is* quality? A leading professional body on quality, the American Society for Quality (ASQ), acknowledges that the concept of quality is subjective and may mean different things to different people or industries. Instead of providing a single definition, they provide two.[1] First, quality may refer to 'a product or service free of deficiencies' – that is, a definition focused on the product and compliance with specifications. Second, quality may also refer to 'the characteristics of a product or service that bear on its ability to satisfy stated or implied needs' – that is, a customer-focused definition.

Dimensions of quality

To manage quality, we need to identify and measure key quality dimensions. First, we distinguish between: (1) *design quality* and (2) *conformance quality*. Then, each of these aspects can be divided into: (a) *product or service attributes* and (b) *customer service*.

Design quality and conformance quality

Design quality evaluates the extent to which the designed specifications of a product or service address clients' expectations. In the service industry, a hotel targeted towards business professionals must design all aspects of its offering very differently to a holiday resort, since expectations of each group differ vastly. A central location with good accesses, efficient customer services and room wi-fi are important requirements for business travellers, while a relaxed atmosphere and romantic or children-oriented perks are more appreciated by holiday makers. If a particular hotel fails to design its offering to meet the specific expectations of its target customers, it has a design quality failure. The same applies to products. For example, some professionals require high laptop reliability (one of the dimensions of quality, as you will see below). With this in mind, Toshiba designed a range of laptops (Tecra and Portégé) to specifically meet those needs. For example, these laptops have a spill-resistant keyboard, allowing users three minutes to save their data before shutting down.[2] The emphasis on reliability is so well justified that, in some countries, the marketing campaign is based on a promise: 'Toshiba does not break down.' Toshiba offers other product lines with less stringent specifications with regard to this dimension, but which addresses other specific needs better.

In turn, **conformance quality** evaluates the extent to which the actual characteristics of the product or service match their design specifications. Some retailers promise to provide an additional cashier whenever more than two customers are waiting in line to pay; if they fail to do it, they have a conformance quality failure. If a Toshiba Tecra client spills his coffee over the keyboard and the laptop fails to resist the fluid for atleast three minutes, as it was designed to do, then there is a conformance quality failure.

So, first, companies must have a customer focus to design quality into their offerings, to meet clients' expectations. Then, they must perform and deliver according to the designed specifications, in order to achieve conformance quality. Failure in either of the above two types of quality compromises clients' satisfaction, incurring in losses or lost revenues, as you can see in Exhibit 20.1.

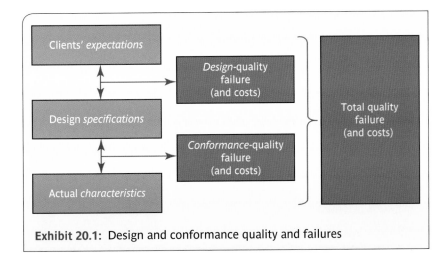

Exhibit 20.1: Design and conformance quality and failures

Product/service attributes and customer service

Attributes of products or services provided refer to tangible or intangible features that characterize them. Let us examine a hotel setting again and see *Management Accounting in Practice 20.1*. Tangible attributes include aspects like performance (the wi-fi connection speed) and functionality (whether gym machines are working or not). Intangible attributes may be crucial in some industries and for some clients. Think about the importance some customers may attribute to staying in hotels with such diversified intangible attributes as: a sense of ultimate luxury through a particularly ostensive hotel lobby; a relaxed, 'zen' ambiance through music and natural construction materials; a sense of belonging to an exclusive community of royalty, presidents or movie stars who have stayed at the same hotel; or the reputation of having near 10/10 in Booking.com's score or boasting a 6 or 7 stars ranking. Another example is a catchphrase in the computing community, during the decades when IBM dominated with a superior reputation for quality: 'Nobody ever got fired for buying IBM.'

Customer service refers to the services provided to customers throughout the entire relationship – before, during and after the purchase. From a marketing perspective, customer service may be merely considered as another component, or attribute, of the overall value proposition. However, it is often considered a separate category from the other attributes thanks to its importance and distinctiveness; in particular, it may be totally unrelated to the product itself and it extends beyond the period in which the purchase happens or the core service is provided. Customer service quality is often necessary both to start commercial relations and promote clients' loyalty. Quick and accurate information before reservations, courteous treatment from arrival to check-out, quick and effective follow-up of complaints during or after the stay, or a follow-up call or email after the stay, may strongly increase customers' *perception* of quality – the ultimate criterion for assessing quality.

Time

Time is increasingly a fundamental part of strategy. This is obvious for transportation companies. Ryanair complemented its main slogan 'the low fares airline' with 'the on-time airline' and emphasizes its high percentage of on-time flights. Arriving on time does not rely on flight

---

20.1: Management Accounting in Practice

Customers' satisfaction at Booking.com and the crucial role of quality

A useful example is the rating system of Booking.com, an online hotel reservations agency. Clients are requested to rate the hotel they stayed in according to their perceptions of six areas. The first four areas are cleanliness, comfort, location and services, representing *attributes* of the service. The fifth area is staff, mostly assessing *customer service*. The sixth is value for money and measures the *quality/price relation*. The site reports scores for each area and then a final average score for the hotel, based on the ratings of all clients or segmenting for particular groups (for example, young or mature couples, solo travellers or groups of friends). Finally, reviewers can also leave positive and negative comments, providing a qualitative insight to complement their quantitative assessment.

Attributes (of services or products) and customer service are the two main dimensions of quality, and constitute 5 out of the 6 areas surveyed by Booking.com. The sixth, value for money, incorporate the important issue of price, but only in the perspective of its relation with quality. Clearly, obtaining the 'Exceptional' category in Booking.com, for scores equal or above 9.5 out of 10, requires hotel managers to pay utmost attention to perceived quality. Even hotels in mid-scale or economy segments cannot neglect quality and rely exclusively on low prices to get a reasonable overall score, because quality underlies all surveyed areas – even 'value for money'.

Exercises

1)   Select another site providing hotel rankings and identify the underlying criteria.

2)   To what extent may a low perceived price compensate for lower-quality perceptions, under such rating criteria?

speed only. It requires well-coordinated and efficient operations, both on land and air, such as moving customers from terminals to their seats, refuelling, maintenance and catering operations. Coordinated timing of multiple activities is increasingly a fundamental requirement to compete in today's globalized environment – both to Ryanair and to companies around the world.

Large retailers are at the bottom end of a complex supply chain. Out-of-stocks is a big problem for all parties and time is at the core of it. Supplier deliveries are planned at utmost detail. If a truck does not meet its scheduled delivery time – its time slot – due to transportation or production problems, it may not be able to unload the cargo. Production has long been focused on time, ever since Taylor introduced the first techniques of 'scientific management' at the start of the twentieth century and Ford implemented them in his car plants. By analysing production flows and carrying out time and motion studies, Taylor aimed at improving efficiency and labour productivity. Since then, the organizational scope for analysing time has expanded enormously, going beyond the individual organization to expand the entire supply chain. In Chapter 19, you were made aware of the importance of the entire value chain in order to achieve sustainable competitiveness. The usage and co-ordination of time across all parties of the entire value chain is, increasingly, an important component of that competitiveness.

Later in the chapter, you will learn how to measure and manage time. You will also see how the just-in-time technique (coupled with total quality management) improves time and reduces waste in companies, by only producing the products which are required, when required and in the quantity required (that is, in the perfect timing). For now, let us analyse the controversial relation between quality and time.

Quality and time: mutually necessary and reinforcing, in the short and the long term

Popular wisdom created the proverb 'Haste makes waste'. Why? Because quality and speed are (too) often regarded as being almost mutually exclusive or, at best, creating tensions difficult to overcome. Academics and consultants often endorse this common-sense view. You have learned that in performance measurement and incentive systems (Chapters 16 and 17), evaluation criteria should not be contradictory. A typical common-sense example is to avoid defining 'fast service' and 'quality service' as simultaneous objectives. In variance analysis (Chapter 9), when you analysed direct labour efficiency, you were alerted that favourable variances (workers taking fewer hours than expected) may come at the cost of neglecting quality. Unfortunately, some notorious disasters had underlying causes related to time pressures that encouraged the neglect of quality issues (see *Management Accounting Insight 20.1* in the next subsection).

However, in this chapter, we question this widespread assumption that a tension exists, almost amounting to opposition between quality and time. On the contrary, an effective approach to quality and time both requires and allows that *both* improve simultaneously.

First, let us analyse how time both requires and improves quality. Succeeding with regard to time *requires* quality, because the company has to get the delivery right the first time, every time. This is particularly the case for companies operating on a just-in-time basis, with minimal or zero inventories. Having little or no inventories means that the company has no slack to accommodate defects or operational problems. It has no inventories of finished goods to satisfy customers if production is delayed. One single problem can shut down the entire production process. This quality requirement to achieve success with regard to time extends across a tightly coordinated supply chain. As the above example about retailers illustrated, on-time delivery of defect-free products is essential – any defective products will be returned, creating again an out-of-stock problem. In addition, succeeding with regard to time *improves* customer-relevant quality. For example, when a retailer reduces the time required for customers to pay for their shopping (for example, by offering self-service checkouts) and when a postal company succeeds in delivering a parcel at the agreed time, they are building a potentially relevant customer perspective of quality.

Now, let us analyse the inverse relation: quality both *requires* and *improves* successful time management. A customer's perception of quality may be compromised if an otherwise 'perfect' product was delivered with significant delay. In turn, quality improves time performance. For example, fewer defects and production problems decrease manufacturing cycle time to obtain a given output. More intuitive, user-friendly Internet portals allow more precise, error-free and faster ordering, reducing order-receipt time and order-waiting time (check these concepts in Exhibit 20.4).

Finally, note that you must measure, control and manage quality and time in varied time horizons. To support quick reaction, you should typically produce short-term, interim reports – monthly, weekly, daily or even more frequently, depending on the type of measure. For example, very short-term, even online information is needed for some operational measures, but not for organizational learning about quality (see next section). In addition, longer-term reports are also important to detect trends, ranging from multi-period reports (for example, several months) to really long-term reports (for example, several years). Longer-term reports allow monitoring and shaping strategies on quality and time, and are extremely useful whenever companies can compare them against key competitors' or industry performance.

Management accountants' contributions to quality and time improvement initiatives

Why should management accountants be interested, or at all involved, in issues of quality and time? Some may think that quality and customer satisfaction should be the realm of production staff and marketeers alone, or that time concerns are satisfactorily addressed by operations staff alone. However, involving management accountants in quality and time issues is a win-win situation for both management accountants and their organizations.

The involvement of management accountants in quality and time issues is beneficial to management accountants because it allows them to contribute to crucial operational and strategic issues in their organizations. A deep understanding and involvement in these issues raises management accountants' relevance within their organization and develops specific and transferable skills which are highly appreciated in the job market. Few people would disagree with this. So, the crucial question is: do management accountants have enough competitive advantage to provide such value-added contribution?

Any approach to quality – like any other business aspect – must have an underlying assessment of its benefits. As you will see in the next section, there are multiple perspectives to measure quality – or, from the opposite perspective, lack of quality. One of these perspectives is the financial assessment of quality (or lack of quality). Alternatives to improve customer-focused satisfaction should be subject to a cost–benefit analysis. Consider a project to replace an old machine with a new one, allowing production with fewer defects. What is the direct financial impact of replacing those assets? What is the expected increase of customer satisfaction and, in turn, of revenues, through higher selling prices or volumes? What is the expected decrease of costs related to defects waste, rework, and so on? In stringent quality projects (like in the six sigma approach, discussed in the next section), data-based justifications – including costs and benefits – are essential, and mere intuitions are not accepted.

Often, engineers and marketers design and estimate operations and business improvements mostly oriented by their functional expertise alone. However, they may lack the sensitivity, technical expertise and/or data to assess their *financial* benefits. Identifying and estimating relevant costs and benefits to evaluate alternatives may well depend on the management accountant. It may also be the case that multiple financially worthwhile improvement opportunities may be detected, but resources may be insufficient to implement them all, at least simultaneously. The management accountant can contribute in deciding which initiatives should be adopted or prioritized, using a strategically informed financial evaluation. Even considering the diffusion of financial awareness among non-accounting people (see Chapter 2, on the decentring of accounting knowledge), management accountants must insist that financial information is indeed being understood and used correctly.

Gaining insights into quality and time may require new, or at least changed, information systems. Management accountants may have to set up new accounting systems to gather relevant information about quality costs – which, as you will see next, is often not available and not easy to obtain. This information must be accurate, timely and in particular relevant, so designing these information systems requires a deep understanding of actual business processes and challenges. In addition, new information systems to obtain *non-financial* data may also be required. Management accountants involved in quality and time issues are familiar with both financial and non-financial perspectives and, in addition, often possess skills in information systems design. This promotes management accountants' involvement in developing both financial and non-financial systems on quality.

20.2: Management Accounting in Practice

Management accountants' contributions to improvement programmes

'Restricting management accountants' contribution solely to 'blessing the numbers' in improvement programs is a poor decision', say Rudisill and Clary (2004). Instead, they should take principal roles as 'intricate members'. The following examples refer to six sigma projects (analysed in the next section), but could apply to any improvement programme. Proactive management accountants are in privileged positions to detect excessive costs, waste and errors – when they develop 'real-world' interpretations of variances (as emphasized in Chapter 9). In a paper-cup plant, a cost clerk was intrigued by recurring reports of 'negative' paper waste – given paper consumption, it should not be possible to produce so many cups. An investigation revealed that methods to predict waste and production had not been updated when equipment was replaced, causing wrong pricing decisions for at least two years. In a foam rubber company, an order entry clerk, involved in a project to improve an unfriendly ordering process, discovered that sales associates had been using wrong pricing information which led to lost revenue. Both problems, uncovered by proactive management accountants, were corrected.

Measuring the bottom-line impact of improvement projects is a key area for management accountants. In a textile plant, experts had found ways to speed up machine changeovers. However, the financial analyst estimated that neither would produce bottom-line savings. So, improvement efforts were redirected to more rewarding projects.

Management accountants can contribute to focus efforts only on truly valuable projects, by making realist estimates and preventing companies' tendency to overestimate potential savings and underestimate required resources. Finally, actual process improvements may not produce cost savings immediately, but only in later periods. Making that clear has the enormous merit of avoiding disappointment by poor short-term results and further justifies and legitimates top managers' commitment to improvement initiatives.

Source: Rudisill and Clary (2004).

Exercise

In addition to individual characteristics of the management accountant, what organizational characteristics may be required for 'real-world interpretations' of variances to be actually proposed and ultimately produce results? What organizational characteristics may prevent this from happening?.

Management accountants can contribute to quality and time improvement efforts by providing relevant financial information, by diffusing financial awareness and by developing new financial and non-financial information systems. And they can become 'intricate members' of initiatives to improve quality, time and profitability, in line with recent trends of including management accountants as members of operational teams (Burns and Baldvinsdottir, 2005). The following *Management Accounting in Practice 20.2* example illustrates this new and value-added role.

All these contributions – even financially oriented ones – require that management accounting professionals and systems deal with both financial and non-financial information, originated from within and outside the organization. It requires competencies gained in various courses in their higher education degrees, ranging from operations management and statistics to marketing and change management. In addition, management accountants must become a recognized pivotal member of the cross-functional teams – even encompassing members from the entire value chain – analysing quality and time.

Now that you have explored linkages between quality and time, the two following sections provide more detailed insights about how to manage quality and time to create value.

Managing quality to create value

Contemporary approaches to value recognize the need to adopt both financial and non-financial perspectives. So, you will start by analysing the financial perspective of quality, including the estimation of costs of quality. Then, you will analyse three non-financial perspectives of quality, related to customers, internal processes, and learning and growth. Of course, you may have recognized these four perspectives from the balanced scorecard – an appropriate tool to provide multidimensional perspectives about such a multidimensional aspect as quality.

The financial perspective and costs of quality

The financial perspective of quality provides insights about how quality affects revenues and costs, and is expressed as **costs of quality (COQ)**. In management accounting and operations management, the term 'costs of quality' does not have the common-sense meaning of, for example, the additional costs of using a higher grade of leather to produce a better-looking wallet. Briefly here, costs of quality refer to costs incurred to achieve high quality and hence avoid defects, as well as the financial consequences of poor quality that caused defects to occur.

Traditionally, the financial impacts of quality included in COQ calculations were limited to costs recorded in the financial statements. In addition, these costs were scattered across financial statements accounts, such as manufacturing costs (for example, testing and inspection activities, spoilage costs), commercial costs (for example, addressing customers' complaints) or general costs (for example, product returns, which reduce revenues). In addition, other relevant financial impacts of lack of quality are never recorded in financial statements, such as opportunity costs due to lost sales, as you will see next. This limited visibility over costs of quality substantially complicated and constrained a financially oriented understanding and management of quality.

Identifying relevant costs and revenues can be challenging. 'Out-of-pocket' costs, reported in financial accounts, are easier to identify – once we manage to track them down in the cost accounts. In fact, tracking them may turn out to be a difficult task without an adequate costing system in place. As mentioned above, opportunity costs (for example, the contribution lost due to poor customer perception of quality) are not recorded in financial accounts and have to be estimated. Often, opportunity costs are difficult to estimate and have a significant importance within overall costs of quality. This is why some companies prefer to report opportunity costs separately from 'more objective', out-of-pocket costs. However, in practice estimates are required in more than only opportunity costs – in particular when we are estimating impacts of alternative, future courses of action. So we are including both types of costs in a single costs of quality report (see Table 20.1).[3]

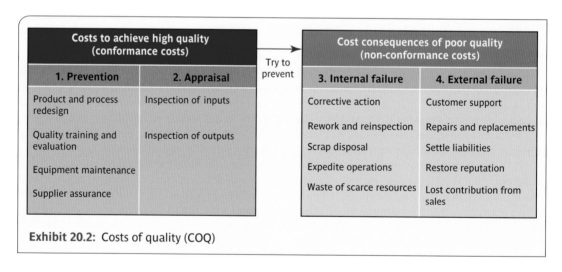

Exhibit 20.2: Costs of quality (COQ)

Exhibit 20.2 identifies the two major categories of costs of quality. The first category refers to conformance costs, which aim to achieve high quality, through *prevention* and *appraisal*. The second category refers to non-conformance costs as consequences of poor quality emerge in *internal failures* and *external failures*. In fact, the costs of trying to achieve quality (the first category of COQ, and in particular prevention costs) can be seen as an investment to prevent failure costs, as expressed by the proverb 'prevention is better than cure'. In fact, COQ tend to increase when quality problems emerge later in the value chain, closer to the customer.

The following list describes each type of COQ:

Table 20.1: A Costs of Quality (COQ) report

	Design	Purchasing	Production	Sales & Distrib.	Account. & Finance	Other	Total	% of COQ	% of sales
Prevention costs									
Training							80,000	20.0%	0.80%
Quality planning							26,000	6.5%	0.26%
(…)							10,000	0	0.10%
Other							24,000	6.0%	0.24%
Total prevention costs							**140,000**	**35.0%**	**1.40%**
Appraisal costs									
Inspecting products									
(…)									
Total appraisal costs							80 000	20.0%	0.80%
Internal failure costs									
Reworks									
(…)									
Total internal failure costs							60 000	15.0%	0.60%
External failure costs									
Warranty repairs									
(…)									
Total external failure costs							**120,000**	**30.0%**	**1.20%**
Total costs of quality	120,000	40,000	140,000	20,000	60,000	20,000	**400,000**	**100.00%**	**4.00%**
% of costs of quality	30.0%	10.0%	35.0%	5.0%	15.0%	5.0%	1.00%		
% of sales	1.20%	0.40%	1.40%	0.20%	0.60%	0.20%	4.00%		

1) *Prevention costs*: costs of activities to prevent poor quality from occurring, including:

- Product and process redesign, to reduce manufacturing problems.

- Quality training and evaluation, to improve employees' capabilities and motivation to enhance quality. Training programmes can be internal or external.

- Equipment maintenance.

- Supplier assurance, to promote receiving only materials, components and services suitable to achieve high quality. This goal may require supplier training, to improve up-stream quality in the value chain.

2) *Appraisal costs*: costs of inspection activities to uncover defects, that is, detect individual units not conforming to specifications. These activities include:

- Inspection of materials, machines and the overall production process.

- Inspection of work-in-process and finished goods.

   Inspection can include all or only a sample of units. Finished goods can be tested for their attributes or for their performance, according to how customers use them, either through simulation or field testing (analysing actual usage by customers at their location).

3) *Internal failure costs*: costs of activities related with defects in processes, product and services, detected in appraisal activities *before* delivery to customers. Some examples are:

- Corrective action to identify and solve the cause of failure.

- Rework to solve the defect and subsequent reinspection.

- Scrap disposal, if rework is unfeasible or not advantageous. Costs include all variable costs incurred in its production, plus additional disposal costs (deducted of potential scrap value).

- Expedite operations to compensate for lost time and secure timely delivery, at higher costs than normal. Examples include a more expensive delivery service (for example, next-day, rather than economy delivery) or manufacturing changes causing higher costs or compromising other production processes (this may involve both actual and opportunity costs).

- Waste of limited resources. Whenever defects have used scarce resources, recovery in those particular operations is not possible. Total output decreases and leads to lost contribution – an opportunity cost.

4) *External failure costs*: cost of activities to compensate for defects, *after* they have affected external stakeholders – typically customers, but also any entity affected by poor quality, even society at large. *Management Accounting in Practice 20.3* presents two well-known cases of extreme external failures: Toyota's faulty accelerator pedals in 2009 and BP's oil spill in 2010. Typical examples are:

- Above-normal customer support, resulting from defects.

- Warranty repairs and replacements.

- Settling liability claims due to poor quality affecting stakeholders. This includes liabilities arising from product usage and any other liabilities towards stakeholders.

- Restore reputation, in particular marketing activities in the aftermath of a well-publicized external failure.

- Lost contribution on lost sales (including cancelled orders) and future sales made at a lower price to compensate for poor quality. These are opportunity costs and can extend significantly into the future if customer badwill is not effectively and quickly overcome.

20.3: Management Accounting in Practice

Infamous external failures and their huge costs

Toyota

For decades, Toyota had a remarkable reputation for quality and was a case study worldwide. In 2008, Takeuchi et al. in the *Harvard Business Review* praised Toyota's success to quickly design and produce the world's best cars at the lowest cost. However, just a year later in the USA, one family died after the accelerator pedal got stuck, increasing vehicle speed to more than 120 miles per hour. The case had enormous media coverage. Official bodies got involved, with a House Oversight Committee secretary thus summing up customers' fears: 'Will I be next?' Toyota recalled more than 6 million vehicles and production and sales of eight models were suspended. Toyota estimated a $2 billion loss in North American sales alone. Worldwide, reputation losses are beyond calculation.

British Petroleum (BP)

In 2010, a gas blowout occurred in a BP oil rig off the Gulf of Mexico during a cementing operation, in which quality failures played an important role. Eleven workers died, almost 5 million barrels of oil spilled into the ocean and compromised animal and plant life and various economic activities, such as fishing. The case had worldwide media coverage for months. BP endured tough political pressures and enormous financial costs related to repair attempts and legal claims, related with loss of earnings from affected businesses or bereavement by families of the killed workers.

By April 2011, BP had incurred $17.7 billion costs, but more will occur. BP took a $40.9 billion pre-tax charge in 2010 due to the spill. BP's damaged reputation, like that of Toyota, is beyond calculation, stock prices collapsed and BP's survival was even questioned. Legal disputes may extend for many years. Disputes include BP's suits for contribution against contractors due to their alleged culpability – but which may play against BP attempts to recover reputation, if taken to court.

These extreme external quality failures had tremendous financial, human, social and environmental consequences. You will read in *Management Accounting in Practice 20.4* how non-financial quality indicators could have contributed to avoid them.

Sources: Takeuchi et al. (2008); Tinsley et al. (2011); http://www.ft.com/cms/s/0/23b5dc24-6d09-11e0-83fe-00144feab49a.html#ixzz1Y2GFWII2; http://www.youtube.com/watch?v=QQDLZ7Y15LQ (min 2 :20) (both accessed on 15 May 2012).

Exercise

From your memories or from a quick Internet search, what do you believe to have been the relative importance, attributed by each of these companies, to the financial, human, social, environmental or legal consequences of these accidents?

Categories of quality activities are often quite related and in ways difficult to estimate. Think about a hotel customer survey that detected a problem in a recent stay of a customer who did not complain at the time. The survey may trigger prevention activities to avoid those problems from reccurring. Now, suppose that the hotel decides to compensate the customer by offering the next stay. This influences external failure costs in complex ways. If the customer would return anyway, this offer would reduce future contribution (a short-term opportunity cost); if the customer would otherwise not return and still remain unsatisfied, his free stay will merely create additional costs. However, the offer may reduce customer badwill, avoiding losing the customer forever and having that customer tell every one about the poor experience – hence reducing longer-term opportunity costs. Note that opportunity costs can have different time horizons and that the difficulty in estimating them will also differ enormously.

The four categories of activities have a sequence. Mastering an earlier activity avoids costs in the following ones: detecting an internal failure prevents an external failure, and so on. In addition, detecting defects closer to the end of the process – in particular, the customer – tends to mean higher costs. So, typically, companies should invest in prevention activities. The focus on prevention activities is a particular feature of the total quality management approach, as you will learn later. Total quality management aims to do everything right, the first time, every time; this would allow zero defects to occur, eliminating later – and potentially higher – quality costs. However, it may be argued that avoiding any kind of errors from happening at all might be prohibitively expensive. Such concern represents the return-on-quality perspective, which you will also learn about later, which claims that is, it may be preferable (and more profitable) to allow some errors to happen, and incur some costs in appraisal and internal failure activities (in this order). Because external failures may be so expensive and may even have ethical consequences (in particular in extreme cases, as illustrated in *Management Accounting in Practice 20.3*), preventing them should be a major concern.

A COQ report must support managerial action, so it must be easily understood by managers and other users – not just by accountants. So, a COQ report must be tailored to adopt language – especially, cost categories – that is relevant and understood by users of each specific company. In addition, segmenting costs across products, processes, departments, plants or other relevant criteria helps pinpoint their root cause. Cost of quality reports can take a matrix format, combining rows for each cost category and columns for each department (or other segmenting criterion). Finally, to quickly highlight the relevance of each figure, reports should also include COQ as percentages (of total COQ, total operating costs, sales or another significant variable). To allow a dynamic view and identify trends, another COQ report can compare different periods. Table 20.1 shows a COQ report, to be customized according to specific company needs, omitting detailed figures for each cost category and organizational function and focusing on totals alone.

Table 20.1 reveals some key figures, based on sales of £10 million. You will see that prevention costs are the most important COQ category (35 per cent), as typically desirable. However, they are still a minority against the remaining 65 per cent that do not add value to the customer. In particular, 30 per cent of COQ caused by external failures may suggest vast room for quality improvement, and their weight of 1.2 per cent of sales may represent a huge percentage of total profit. Note that, admitting that this report only includes opportunity costs from lost sales during the present period, an alternative multiple-period COQ report will report substantially higher figures if customer badwill is not quickly overcome. Turning now to a functional analysis, the largest percentages of the design and production functions may be reasonable. However, the smaller 15 per cent of COQ (0.6 per cent of sales) traced to accounting and finance may deserve further investigation, given the non-core nature of these functions.

Costs of quality are essential to evaluate the financial effectiveness of quality initiatives. Within an external, financial perspective, we need to compare current COQ and the costs of implementing quality initiatives, to decide if a particular initiative should be pursued or not, or to select among alternative initiatives. Making this comparison basically involves identifying, for each alternative, the relevant revenues and costs, as you learned in Chapter 13.

Quality initiatives typically require incremental costs to implement them. In turn, we expect to obtain incremental gains from the expected quality improvement, through revenue increases (by higher selling prices and/or volumes) and/or costs reductions (such as in waste or rework). Remember that relevant costs do not include merely allocated costs, but only incremental costs, incurred specifically due to each particular course of action. Carefully estimating the impacts across the four types of COQ is crucial. However, keep in mind that opportunity costs of external failures (lost contribution from sales) may be very high and particularly difficult to estimate. Therefore, analysing various scenarios under alternative assumptions is particularly appropriate for assessing the sensitivity of the analysis to the alternative estimates.

Finally, you should note that a comprehensive financial analysis of quality should go beyond the organizational level and include the entire value chain. Some of the above measures focus on initiatives regarding external organizations, such as training suppliers to try to ensure the purchasing of only defect-free materials. Evaluating financial trade-offs of quality costs and savings incurred throughout the entire chain may be difficult. In addition to estimating internal costs of quality, you need to estimate costs (both 'out-of-pocket' and opportunity costs) of other parties of the value chain, such as suppliers or customers. In fact, costs are likely to be transmitted along the value chain, affecting the position of each party and the competitiveness of the entire value chain. Estimating external costs requires a high degree of trust among parties, so that they disclose sensitive operational and cost information. Of course, the difficulty may be even greater in estimating the impacts of quality initiatives yet to be implemented.

In addition to financial measures such as COQ, non-financial indicators are essential. Quality costs, including the usually significant opportunity costs from lost sales and other external failure costs, are often preceded by problems in customer relations, in internal business processes and in learning how to manage quality. Being quickly aware of those early signs is critical and requires incorporating **non-financial quality indicators** in our quality management information system, as you will see next.

Non-financial quality indicators

External, customer focused quality indicators

Indicators of quality as perceived by customers should focus on the two dimensions of quality analysed in the previous section: design quality and conformance quality. Indicators for particular organizations should suit their business and strategy, but common indicators focus on:

- *Market research*, through surveys or focus groups, to evaluate: (1) preferences, and (2) perceptions of, and satisfaction with, particular product/service attributes and customer service; these should include both the company and its competitors' offers.

- *Market share*, as percentages referring to total market value and market volume. A reduction of the value market share while the volume market share increases or remains stable signals a reduction of relative prices, to be investigated (for example, it may reflect a deteriorating perception of the company value proposition relative to competitors' propositions).

- *Repeat business*, as a percentage of total business and structured according to number of repetitions (for example, 2–4 purchases; 5–10; more than 10, depending on the type of business). It measures the importance of business resulting from customers who, after having bought the product once, remain satisfied with the product's overall value proposition (including their subjective perception of quality) and repeat the purchase.

- *Customer complaints*, in particular as a percentage of the number of transactions.

- *Products with early or repeated failures.*

- *Percentage of defective units* shipped.

- *Delivery performance*, such as on-time delivery rates, order-to-delivery (OTD) time and delivery delays (see the next section).

These indicators of customer satisfaction – as all others – should be monitored in time to detect trends. But, with regard to satisfaction, the importance of time extends to the indicator itself. Cumulative satisfaction (resulting from multiple purchases in time) is more important than transaction-specific satisfaction (that is, regarding the last purchase) to explain customers' willingness to pay more – an important driver of profitability (Homburg et al., 2005). Marketing insights such as this are useful for management accountants when designing quality management systems in multidisciplinary teams, promoting the adoption of more reliable indicators to predict future financial impacts.

These indicators are essential in evaluating the marketing effectiveness of quality initiatives. Some indicators concern results (for example, market share), while others are leading indicators (for example, a lower percentage of defects may anticipate future market growth, given greater expected customer satisfaction). In addition, and reflecting the balanced scorecard (BSC) causal structure, customer-based indicators allow better understanding what drives the financial effectiveness and results (for example, in-depth data about customers' complaints and returns help in understanding what actually caused repair, rework and warranty costs).

Internal business processes quality indicators

Indicators about the company's business processes should evaluate the internal dimensions of quality required to achieve customer-relevant quality and avoid failures. As you have seen, 'building-in' quality is typically preferable to inspecting it later to look for defects. So, indicators should focus on achieving quality at the first time and include:

- *Defective units produced* or *reworked* (in parts per thousand or parts per million).

- *Number of quality-driven changes* to products and processes.

- *Development time* of new products or services.

- *Order-to-delivery time*, in particular when separately analysing its individual components, about three business processes: order-receipt time; manufacturing cycle time; delivery time.

- *On-time performance*, i.e., the capacity to meet agreed timings.

- *Productivity and efficiency measures.*

20.4: Management Accounting in Practice

Tracing external failures to failures across non-financial BSC perspectives

Management Accounting in Practice 20.3 analysed the external failures (see again Exhibit 20.2, on costs of quality) of the Toyota faulty accelerator pedal and the BP Gulf oil spill. Tinsley et al. (2011) identified a pattern in dozens of disasters and business crises: they were preceded by 'near misses', similar situations of extreme risk that did not materialize in disasters mostly due to luck. Most of these 'near misses' were ignored and misread, instead of being taken as instructive failures. However, external failures (and their extraordinary financial and non-financial costs) might have been avoided if companies had considered existing indicators signalling root causes, across the three non-financial balanced scorecard perspectives.

Customer complaints about similar accelerator problems are common to all auto-makers and are usually a driver's excuse for speeding. However, after Toyota introduced a new accelerator design in 2001, complaints rose sharply. Regrettably, Toyota downplayed complaints, rather than considering their increase as signs of 'near misses' that should trigger an investigation. The *customer* quality perspective was overlooked.

Dozens of minor blowouts had occurred in Gulf of Mexico oil wells – but chance factors had always prevented an explosion. In addition, a history of technical problems in this BP Gulf oil rig made crew members call it 'the well from hell' (Tinsley et al., 2011, p. 90). However, according to Tinsley et al., BP and the rig owner's staff (executives, rig managers and drilling crew) overlooked warning signs from an *internal business processes* quality perspective, failing to recognize them as 'near misses' to be seriously addressed. In September 2011, the extensive US Federal Report also criticized other parties, and quoted employees of the oil rig owner admitting they had 'screwed up by not catching' a similar warning sign, just few weeks before.

Tinsley et al. considered that blindness to 'near-misses' is due to two cognitive biases. The first bias is 'normalization of deviance', when organizations accept that risky anomalies are normal. The second is 'outcome bias'. When outcomes are successful, people tend to focus on the results and neglect the process leading to them – even if it was highly risky. So, organizations need to detect and learn from near misses, implementing strategies to avoid those individual and collective cognitive biases. For example, organizations should reward individuals for exposing near misses they caused, rather than punishing them. By addressing organizations' *learning and growth* perspective, they will be better prepared to improve internal and external quality performance and avoid external failures with such extreme financial, social and environmental costs.

Source: Tinsley et al. (2011); 'Report on the causes of the April 20, 2010 Macondo well blowout', http://t.co/AqtAbDE; http://www.guardian.co.uk/environment/2011/sep/14/bp-blamed-deepwater-horizon-report (both accessed on 15 May 2012).

Exercises

1) Try to remember instances in which you were in a 'near-miss' situation, without serious actual consequences. Did that somehow change your attitudes or behaviours?

2) Discuss how the traditional accounting focus on historical costs may promote neglecting organizational learning from 'near misses'. How may such a situation be changed?

Learning and growth quality indicators

Quality indicators should also focus on the more intangible aspects related to organizational learning and growth – the ultimate driver of organizational performance in the balanced scorecard approach. Key drivers to be monitored include:

- *Training on quality, of company employees and from external parties.* For example, partnerships with suppliers to ensure quality inputs, or with distributors to ensure adequate end-customer support, may require the company to train their employees, in particular to meet company-specific quality requirements.

- *Employee satisfaction* and *turnover.*

- *Employee empowerment*, with regard to employees' possibility to make autonomous decisions; in particular, in total quality management any worker can halt the production process after detecting a problem.

The BSC on quality: a key component of the risk BSC

In Chapter 19, we discussed Kaplan's proposal of a balanced scorecard to manage strategic risk (Kaplan et al., 2009), addressing an increasingly growing concern for today's organizations. In this chapter, you have already realized the strategic importance of quality. In addition, risks are often associated with *lack* of quality. Lack of quality may not only erode firms' performance in their operations, but it may also cause costly external failures and even put the enterprise's future at stake.

The BSC framework to manage quality, laid out in this section, should be a component of a BSC to assess and manage enterprise risk. Naturally, since there are sources of risk other than quality, the wider risk scorecard should integrate only a few selected quality indicators – those with the largest or most likely disruption potential. Nevertheless, omitting the quality component would leave a glaring hole in the risk scorecard.

Setting quality targets

You have already understood the relevance of quality in creating value and its various dimensions. Now, you will learn bases to set quality targets, and techniques to monitor performance against those targets. Contemporary quality targets go beyond internal business processes and extend across the multiple dimensions and areas of quality. Companies can set those targets to be based on external and internal sources.

External quality targets

External benchmarks may be based on other companies in the same industry or on the industry average. Consultancy firms or industry, national and international associations may provide such external benchmarks. Regional and worldwide associations issue standards with wide recognition, such as the American Society for Quality and the International Standards Organization (ISO). In the previous chapter you have read about ISO and the ISO 14000 family of standards on environmental issues. Particular standards of this family address, for example, combating oil-spill disasters, to prevent accidents as the one we discussed of BP. Now, you will read about the ISO 9000 family of standards on quality.

ISO benchmarks

ISO 9000 is a widely known family of standards that deals with quality management in all businesses and industries. ISO 9000 specifies what organizations should do to meet customers' quality and regulatory requirements, aiming to enhance customer satisfaction and continuously improve performance towards these objectives.

ISO 9001 specifies the requirements of a quality management system. ISO 9001-certified companies passed the 1 million mark in 2009. Why this huge interest? Certified companies benefit from the operational benefits of quality improvement and gain legitimacy and reputation, allowing market benefits. Finally, public- and private-sector tenders increasingly require certification. So, for some companies certification becomes a necessity, not an option. Whether ISO 9001 pays off is somewhat controversial. Corbett et al. (2005) and Sharma (2005) report financial performance improvements and Sharma (2005) highlights that improvement is mostly driven by operational efficiencies and by a genuine interest in improving quality. However, Heras et al. (2002) reject the causing role of certification; instead, they attribute certified firms' better performance to the tendency of better performing firms to pursue certification.

Internal quality targets

Internal quality targets can result from past performance or from internal benchmarking, when companies have similar operations in multiple locations. Seeking and identifying best practices within the company can provide performance benchmarks to be used as quality targets for other parts of the company. The frequently updated standards of kaizen costing (Chapters 9 and 19) reflect the small, incremental improvements expected from continuous improvement efforts. Whenever these improvements refer to quality, they include internal quality targets. A particular attention is now devoted to the six sigma approach, thanks to its relevance in dramatically improving quality, mostly to internally set quality targets.

The six sigma approach to quality

The **six sigma** approach aims to improve business processes to achieve an extraordinarily high-conformance quality level, near perfection.[4] It aims to reduce process variability that causes defects and undermines customer satisfaction. Average performance is not enough; performance level must also be consistent, without variation. Customers tend to remember the extremes (for example, an extremely long waiting time), not the average. In addition, performance variability can also cause domino effects in processes within and across the organization: a delay in one process can disrupt other related processes and ultimate customer delivery and satisfaction.

Six sigma statistics only really make sense in extremely large production volumes (of millions of units), in mostly repetitive processes. However, six sigma approaches have been applied across multiple areas and manufacturing and services industries, far beyond their typical application environment. For instance, Furterer's (2009) case studies on six sigma improvement in services are as varied as financial services in a city government, managing inventories and assets in a college, and the discipline process in a high school. An earlier example, *Management Accounting in Practice 20.2*, provides examples of this in a manufacturing setting.

Six sigma projects adopt five 'DMAIC' steps, illustrated in Exhibit 20.3:

1) *Define* the project with a strong business-case, defining the problem and the objective.

2) *Measure* current performance, using reliable data.

3) *Analyse* the root problems, identifying cause–effect relationships and critical factors with maximum leverage.

4) *Improve* the process through generating and implementing solutions targeted at the critical factors.

5) *Control* the process to ensure sustainable performance – and avoid the common 'post-project dip'.

The six sigma approach brings opportunities and challenges for management accountants for each of these steps, as demonstrated in *Management Accounting in Practice 20.2*. Cost and profit implications are a main concern and management accountants can make an indispensible contribution both in six sigma and other related techniques. *Management Accounting in Practice 20.5* discusses taking a diagnostic 'X-ray' to the organization before starting a six sigma project, highlighting the crucial need of a financial perspective.

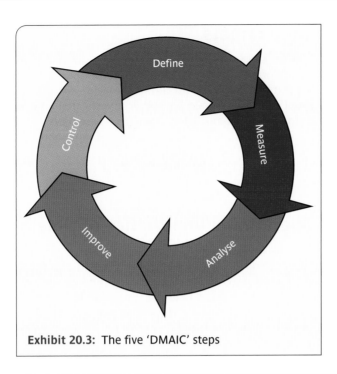

Exhibit 20.3: The five 'DMAIC' steps

20.5: Management Accounting in Practice

An X-ray vision to guide six sigma – and management accountants' roles

Neuhaus and Guarraia (2007) praise six sigma for solving relatively obvious problems, but suggest difficulties in identifying the most significant and hidden improvement possibilities. So, they recommend that the six sigma DMAIC steps are preceded by a 'diagnostic X-ray', made by a small team, to identify issues with the largest potential to be addressed later. We argue that management accountants may also contribute to this preliminary diagnostic.

This 'X-ray' starts by *value stream mapping*, identifying processes with the biggest cost cutting opportunities through waste reduction. Second, *benchmarking* of processes allows estimating gaps and setting improvement goals. Third, *prioritizing* aims to start by projects offering the greatest opportunities.

ConsumerCo, a large consumer products manufacturer, needed to increase capacity at two plants and reduce operating costs. The 'X-ray' team first mapped the value stream by breaking down reasons for performance gaps and waste – stopped or slow operating equipment due to breakdowns, changeovers or lack of materials. The plant finance group had a crucial contribution in allocating costs to each step, since some of those costs were not available (for example, materials wasted at each step) and required detailed, ad hoc investigation. Then, in addition to external benchmarking, cost experts compared costs at the two plants against other plants. This internal benchmarking confirmed suspicions of excessive costs and provided reasonable improvement targets.

Only the six initiatives with the greatest output increase at the lowest cost and time frame were prioritized. Only then did CompanyCo create six Six Sigma teams, to pursue the benefits identified by the 'X-ray' team. By focusing on the most promising initiatives, the six sigma teams uncovered detailed problems, unsuspected at the start but that actually had the largest impact. As a result, unit costs decreased 15 per cent and efficiency increased.

Financial awareness, guidance and competencies to flexibly create required insights were indispensable. The authors recommend regularly assessing progress and asking the key question: 'Are the generated savings manifesting to the bottom line?' (Neuhaus and Guarraia 2007, p. 5). We argue that management accountants are, and should be, key actors to answer that.

Source: Neuhaus and Guarraia (2007).

Exercise

The authors suggested that this 'X-ray' team should be small. As a management accountant, how would you argue that this restricted team should include you, rather than being exclusively composed of a few operational members?

Monitoring quality targets

After quality targets have been set, various methods allow the identifying and analysing of quality issues as operations unfold. Control charts plot observations of operations, at regular intervals, to evaluate whether the observations fall within an allowed range of variation. If not, the process may be out of control. Potential problems should be further investigated by diagnostic tools, such as histograms, Pareto diagrams and cause-and-effect diagrams. These tools were developed within the operations management science discipline, and you can learn more about them in the respective courses and textbooks (for example, Paton et al., 2011).

Managing time to create value

Strategic and operational importance of time

At the start of this chapter, we argued that time is closely related to quality and, indeed, they are mutually necessary and reinforcing. But the importance of time extends beyond that. An increasing pace of time is a key characteristic of contemporary society and business. Peter Drucker and other management gurus on innovation stressed that fast times require fast-changing companies and strategies. Davis et al. (2010) argued that even the few strategies which are successfully executed are nonetheless considered 'slow'. So, they called for achieving 'strategic speed', mobilizing people in order to accelerate execution.

So what do companies need to be faster at? On occasions – but increasingly frequently – they need to be fast at changing themselves, at implementing organizational (including accounting) changes in order to keep up within an increasingly fast-changing competitive environment. You have read about these deeper, structural changes in Chapter 1 and the final chapter of this textbook will resume this topic. In Chapter 6, you analysed how time is at the core of a recent development to 'traditional' activity-based costing: time-driven activity-based costing (TD-ABC). The latter allocates costs based on estimates about time (or, if adequate, other units of analysis). In addition, TD-ABC developed mainly out of a main criticism of 'traditional' ABC: implementing and maintaining ABC systems took too much time and, therefore, money.

This section focuses on time 'itself' and particularly from an operational perspective, rather than merely as a background variable or an accounting criterion. You will analyse time in two critical customer-relevant activities: developing new products and services, and responding to customers. However, note that improving these operational measures may require deep and structural organizational changes.

Operational measures of time

New product (or service) development time

Increasingly fast changes in customer preferences require companies to quickly catch up, even anticipate, those changes. Thus, decreasing the time to develop new products or services is crucial, from the moment they start being conceived until they are on the market. Japanese companies have been particularly successfully in developing and rolling out new products. Think of Sony's history, for example. It is about achieving design quality (that is, designing products that meet clients' expectations) and doing it fast. Find in *Management Accounting in Practice 20.6* US-based Procter & Gamble's strategy to start resorting to external entities, in order to reduce product development time (p. 533).

It is often difficult to define precisely when a new product development (NPD) process starts, as it is often preceded by a research stage, during which no precise product is considered, ranging from the fuzzy front end (FFE) of innovation to more directed efforts. However, determining when research becomes product development is also often unclear (International Accounting Standards 38, on intangible assets, sets guidelines to distinguish between them, but only for financial accounting purposes). Furthermore, as you read in *Management Accounting in Practice 18.1* in Chapter 18, industries like the automotive industry increasingly rely on using common platforms as a basis for developing several new models; so development processes of various models actually overlap and reinforce each other.

20.6: Management Accounting in Practice

Procter & Gamble's revolution in research to speed up innovation and growth

Procter & Gamble, a leading worldwide producer of consumer goods, gained worldwide recognition for excellent management for decades. But by the late 1990s, product development rate had decreased and more new, billion-dollar brands were needed – and fast. So during the following decade, Procter & Gamble accelerated research and development (R&D) activities and subsequent roll-outs, resorting to external entities to bring in ideas or expertise, instead of relying almost exclusively in internal development. Time pressures were at odds with the company tradition of playing safe, and a revolutionary change unfolded throughout the company.

Source: Huston and Sakkab (2006).

Exercises

1) What was the company's concern regarding time: operational or strategic?

2) What risks made the new approach potentially at odds with the 'company tradition of playing safe'?

Order-to-delivery (customer response) time

Order-to-delivery (OTD) time measures the time to respond to a customer order. OTD time has an internal perspective, since it focuses only on the stages between the customer placing an order and actual delivery. So, it is useful to plan internal processes. However, to adopt a customer perspective, you should widen the scope to include pre-order and post-delivery stages, as illustrated in Exhibit 20.4. Overall, the key message is: less time required will increase customer satisfaction.

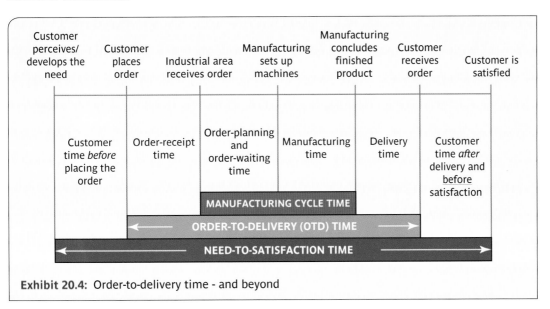

Exhibit 20.4: Order-to-delivery time - and beyond

For now, we restrict our analysing to OTD time components, that is, from the moment when the customer places an order until delivery. Let us start by analysing order-receipt time. With information systems integrated across the supply chain, orders created in the customer's information system feed directly into the supplier's system – just as when individuals order a product using an online shop. An incoming order may suffer additional delays before it reaches the factory. For instance, a controller may need to check that the order does not cause the client's credit limit to be exceeded, unless rules are introduced in the system and automatically enacted upon each in-coming order.[5]

Further time is required before production actually starts. One example is order-planning time, related to production planning activities that aim to optimize processes and resource usage, but which themselves take time. There may also be order-waiting time, if there is no available capacity. Capacity bottlenecks, creating constraints in production processes, will be briefly analysed in the discussion of throughput accounting, at the end of this chapter. Manufacturing time is the traditional focus of attention, concerning the actual manufacturing process, and will be further explored below. Finally, delivery-time can be minimized in various ways. An express delivery service can be announced as a competitive advantage in different ways: it can be included as a standard, emphasizing speed, or it may be optionally chosen (and explicitly paid in separate) by customers, as in Amazon.com, placing the emphasis on flexibly meeting the needs of speed of each customer. Delivery-time for book stores has now been reduced to virtually zero through e-books, read on ordinary computers or on e-readers like Amazon's Kindle.

Analysing OTD time is crucial for internal optimization of company resources and to provide fast delivery and satisfaction to the customer. However, from a customer perspective, what is really relevant is the time between when the perception of the customer need emerged, and when that customer need was satisfied. This lengthier period extends beyond OTD time, as Exhibit 20.4 represents, and we labelled it 'Need-to-satisfaction' time.

With regard to customer time *before* placing the order, transactions between companies typically involve information requests to clarify needs, product specifications and suitability, conditions, and so on; time for these activities is spent by both sides before an order exists, and should be minimized. Also, searching for pre-order information on a website or filling in an online order may be difficult and time-consuming. Although this time is spent by the prospective customer – not the company – the company should also try to reduce it. Even in the successful outcome that the customer is not put off and still makes the order, the company is still be penalized because the lost time has reduced customer satisfaction. Notice that some sites (for example, Amazon.com) announce '1-click ordering', enabling to quickly complete the order with just a few clicks.

In addition, you should also consider the required customer time *after* delivery and *before* the need is satisfied. Customers of the furniture producer Ikea know that – probably very well. After picking a flat pack with a disassembled wardrobe from Ikea's shelves and paying at the checkout, the customer knows that potentially lengthy and difficult tasks of transporting the pack and assembling the wardrobe still lie ahead, before the need to decorate the house is satisfied. Even though the time of Ikea staff is no longer at stake, Ikea carefully addresses that source of potential customer dissatisfaction. Customers can borrow car rooftop racks for free, rent a van, purchase home delivery (this actually delays the moment of final delivery, but spares the customer from transporting the products) and purchase assembly service. In addition, Ikea assembly manuals are extremely precise to ease installation by customers and all required tools are included. Ikea knows that only when the wardrobe is finally assembled, correctly and – hopefully! – without having caused any injury, will the customer be fully satisfied.

On-time performance

On-time performance refers to delivering the product or service on the *agreed* timing and is often measured as a percentage of deliveries. However, note that 'on-time' may not always mean delivery at or before the scheduled time, as it is often assumed. For example, a plane reaching the arrival gate less than 15 minutes after scheduled time is still considered as punctual, according to international regulations. Being ontime may also be different from being early. An earlier than scheduled delivery is not necessarily good. Remember the example early in this chapter (p. 519) about suppliers' need to meet the delivery schedules at major retailers. If a supplier arrives earlier than scheduled, it may not be able to deliver because it may not have an available delivery slot.

Total quality management and just-in-time

This section focuses on two complementary approaches to quality and time: total quality management and just-in-time. These techniques were successfully developed, refined and deployed in Japan in the 1970s, although they can be seen as international in two ways. First, some underlying seminal thoughts can be traced to Henry Ford and his early implementation of Taylor's ideas in the automotive industry. Second, both TQM and JIT are now widespread in leading organizations around the world; in fact, in industries like the automotive and electronics ones, the major players have, in various degrees, typically adopted TQM and JIT approaches, in turn promoting its adoption among other entities in their value chain.

Total quality management

Total quality management (TQM) is both a philosophy and a practical managerial approach. Developed to build and sustain competitive advantage in a global economy, TQM is about a permanent and integrated effort across the entire organization to excel in all customer-relevant quality dimensions of products and services. Each member, in each area of the organization must permanently examine all activities to identify improvement opportunities and set more ambitious targets. So, a TQM organization relentlessly seeks additional quality improvements.

An important tool to implement TQM is the **plan-do-check-act (PDCA) cycle**, illustrated in Exhibit 20.5. The PDCA cycle is a systematic, interactive approach to continuous improvement and problem solving, based on facts and on the scientific method. In the 'plan' stage, a team examines facts to find what is causing the problem and suggests a solution. The 'do' stage consists in making an experiment, whose results are examined in the 'check' stage (also called the 'study' stage). The final 'act' stage is about implementing the suggested solution if the experiment results are positive or, if not, returning to the initial stage again.

Total quality management assumes that costs of improving quality are more than compensated by cost reductions from efficiency improvements and by revenue increases from customers' reward for quality – buying larger quantities and/or paying a quality premium price (i.e., reducing lost contribution opportunity costs, an external failure COQ). So, the belief is not that higher quality is free; instead, the belief is that higher quality pays off, because globally it allows higher profits. Customer satisfaction is TQM's departure point, its main focus and pervading 'obsession'. Total quality management cannot ignore design quality, that is, designing the product or service to address customer expectations. However, TQM is equally focused on designing quality into the product and processes in order to prevent waste. It focuses on preventing defects, rather than detecting them. The Japanese engineer Genichi Taguchi emphasized that quality improvements at the product design stage are easier and cheaper to achieve than later at the production stage. Taguchi proposed *robust design*, an approach that aims to design products that succeed in performing according to specifications even in varied environmental circumstances, since these

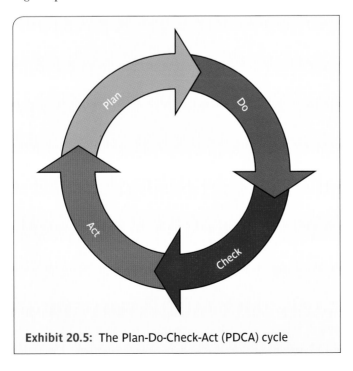

Exhibit 20.5: The Plan-Do-Check-Act (PDCA) cycle

are often impossible to control. Among the various costs of quality you have learned in this chapter, TQM emphasizes prevention costs, viewing them as an investment to avoid all other costs of quality, and particularly non-conformance costs caused by quality failures. So, TQM's concern about design quality takes on an overarching nature, designing products and services which address customer expectations *and* avoid non-conformance costs.

Note that TQM's assumption that higher quality pays off should still be validated for each quality improvement possibility. This relentless search for improvements assumes that it is always possible to improve quality. However, the financial impact of each improvement possibility should still be evaluated before implementing it. Notorious financial failures of companies heavily committed to quality led Rust et al. (1995) to coin the term 'Return on Quality' (ROQ), emphasizing the need to financially evaluate quality initiatives. The rationale is that costs of implementing particular quality improvement initiatives, or costs of improving quality beyond a certain level, may be excessive when confronted with expected benefits – from savings in other costs and from revenue increases. So, in a ROQ approach, a certain (albeit small) level of lack of quality may actually produce the highest return.

The financial cautiousness suggested by the ROQ approach requires each expected quality impact to be scrutinized. For example, are satisfied customers really willing to pay more – to the extent that the price premium compensates for the higher quality costs? Homburg et al. (2005) found that marginal pay-offs increased for very high satisfaction levels – apparently supporting a TQM approach. However, they also emphasized the significant costs to achieve such high satisfaction levels. So, in line with a cost–benefit ROQ perspective, they suggested striving for very high satisfaction levels only among highly valued, profitable customers – but settling for less satisfaction with regard to less valued, less profitable customers.

Let us now analyse the volume effect from higher quality and satisfaction. Will satisfied customers really buy more, through repeated purchases? Seiders et al. (2005) confirmed that satisfaction strongly increased customers' repurchase intentions – in line with the TQM belief. However, they also confirmed a common suspicion: behaviour is indeed different from intentions! In fact, with regard to actual behaviour (rather than intentions), the satisfaction–repurchase relationship was affected by several other factors, such as habit, convenience and task simplification. So, in line with a ROQ perspective, we should not take for granted that greater satisfaction from higher quality will always lead to higher sales volumes, revenues and profits.

Remember target costing, analysed in Chapter 19, originally a characteristic of Japanese companies. Its focus and starting point is to evaluate customers' perceptions of value of alternative product designs and their corresponding willingness to pay. Using these revenue estimates and desired profit margins, multidisciplinary teams research, in various iterative cycles, if and how those alternative product designs can be manufactured at the target cost – the cost that allows the desired financial return. So, you can see that target costing is a fundamental tool for any financially aware TQM company.

This financial awareness should obviously not place quality in the back seat. The word 'total' in TQM becomes particularly relevant when we analyse the just-in-time approach, next. As you will see, TQM and just-in-time are mutually required and supportive – in line with our initial argument about the bidirectional relationship between quality and time.

Just-in-time

Just-in-time (JIT) is a managerial approach that integrates activities to obtain high-volume production, while minimizing inventories of raw materials, work-in-progress and finished goods. Just-in-time takes customers' orders as the starting point, which creates the need for production. Nothing is purchased or produced until needed. A customer order is the trigger, demanding the activity of the last production stage (for example, assembly), which in turn will demand upstream activities, up to materials requisition and purchase from external suppliers.

Just-in-time is a 'pull' process, driven by customers and their actual demand. This is a significant difference with regard to the traditional 'push' system: on the basis of sales forecasts for a given period, companies order materials and other inputs and they schedule and execute production. So, finished goods inventories accumulate, waiting until units actually get sold (or forever, if actual sales lag behind forecasts). The traditional 'push' system also leads to producing higher lots of each item, and larger than immediate needs: for example, in day 1, a lot is produced to meet forecast demand for one entire week or month, inevitably leading to inventories. Just-in-time takes the opposite starting point, the actual customer order, producing only the number of units of those products already ordered. So, lots are typically small and inventories are avoided.

The JIT approach creates important contrasts with traditional techniques. The JIT 'pull' approach contrasts with the traditional 'push' approach that underlies the materials requirement planning (MRP) technique, which is widely adopted in western organizations to plan production activities. Enterprise resource planning (ERP) systems, enterprise-wide information systems that you will learn about in the next chapter, include MRP in their production module. The JIT 'pull' approach and waste elimination focus also avoids a dysfunctional problem typically criticized in standard costing (Chapter 9): production managers may be encouraged to produce as much as possible to avoid an unfavourable fixed overhead volume variance – even if those products are not required at the time by customers, leading to inventory build-up. The costs of inventories may be substantial and are often underestimated by conventional accounting measures, in particular when we encompass the entire value chain, as *Management Accounting in Practice 20.7* illustrates.

In JIT, reducing waste is a priority – hence JIT's other name of lean production. Waste is anything that does not add value. We have mentioned inventories, but back-up equipment (to replace equipment failing due to lack of maintenance), machine and human time, energy and space that do not add value are also considered waste. If taken to encompass all organizational activities (such as commercial or accounting activities), a lean approach aims to create a lean enterprise.

20.7: Management Accounting in Practice

High and hidden inventory costs in HP – and a staggering comparison with JIT competitor Dell

The hardware industry is characterized by very short product life cycles. Technological change is permanent and makes today's popular and high-priced innovative products soon become almost undifferentiated commodities fighting with competitors on price and narrow margins. Moreover, it creates the significant risk of product inventories becoming obsolete and having to be written-off at the end of a short life cycle.

Hewlett-Packard (HP), a leading hardware manufacturer, realized that inventory costs were prohibitively high and strongly eroded profit margins. Calculating some types of costs was simple, such as the holding cost of inventory, including its capital costs and physical costs (for example, warehouse costs, insurance and spoilage). However, more significant costs were hidden. A major cost component was devaluation, when market prices of inventory items decrease. And there were also obsolescence costs, when goods were retired from the market and had to be written-down.

Other costs were related to the supply chain, due to agreements to protect distributors against devaluation and ultimate obsolescence of inventories they held. So, addressing these costs required the involvement of supply-chain partners.

Hilton et al. (2008) compared HP (classified as a relatively traditional manufacturer) and Dell (a competitor with a JIT approach). At the time of Hilton et al.'s research, the difference in production and supply process efficiency was staggering: Dell's inventory turnover ratio (calculated as cost of goods sold divided by inventory) was almost 88.8, against only 7.5 in HP; more than 11 times higher! In their 2011 reports, a continuous rise in Dell's inventory significantly reduced the ratio gap: 28.3 for Dell, compared with 8.7 for HP. But this is still more than a three times difference.

Sources: Callioni et al. (2005); Hilton et al. (2008); annual reports of HP and Dell.

Exercises

1) Suppose a plant director reduced production of items with sluggish demand and was later criticized due to unfavourable fixed overheads variances. How might this criticism change the plant director's action for the ensuing period? What consequences may arise for the company?

2) Discuss situations in which a favourable fixed overhead variance indeed represents a beneficial outcome for the company.

The virtual absence of inventories to function as 'safety buffers' has important consequences. It requires absolute quality within and beyond the organization. Any production activity, at any stage, is only made to address a downstream need; so, any failure at any stage will compromise subsequent stages and ultimate customer satisfaction. This quality requirement extends across the value chain – especially upstream. You grasped in Chapter 19 the crucial importance of the performance of the overall value chain for the success of any business – and in JIT this is just too obvious, since JIT purchasing is typically associated with JIT production. For example, in September 2011 numerous PSA Peugeot-Citroën plants across Europe slowed down or halted production because an Italian supplier of screws and bolts had logistic problems, and Peugeot-Citroën did not have those screws in stock. Only two plants continued to operate normally thanks to deliveries by helicopter and taxi – an expedited delivery at very high costs.[6]

To promote suppliers reliability, JIT needs to establishing long-term partnerships, to achieve and improve coordination and trust – both indispensible when success requires that no actor misses his part. But these long-term partnerships also involve mutual lock-in and specific risks. For example, Peugeot-Citroën could not readily buy those much needed screws from alternative suppliers, because they were designed specifically to meet their strict standards (explore the discussion question 20.14 on Dell's and HP's reports for further insights).

So, the supply chain must be tightly integrated to quickly respond to the downstream demand. This worked particularly well in Japan, where JIT originated in the 1970s, given the tight linkages among companies and industries, typically under the supervision and coordination of a major company. Indeed, Toyota invented JIT, and the Toyota Production System became the benchmark for lean manufacturing, adopted and adapted by many other leading manufacturing companies – GE and Dell are widely cited examples. In addition, many smaller-scale industries, as well as services, operate under near JIT principles. For instance, local pharmacies have a huge variety of medicines, but typically keep very low inventories for each item. They operate near JIT purchasing, and wholesale dealers have to make frequent trips to local pharmacies – often more than once a day – to prevent out-of-stocks, delivering small lots of required items.

Just-in-time has far-reaching implications in organizations. For example, adopting JIT requires changing factory layouts. Traditionally, factory layouts put together similar types of operations and the various products move across the plant from one production stage to the following, whereas JIT adopts cell manufacturing, grouping different operations and equipments together – in a 'cell' – to manufacture a family of products with similar processing requirements. For example, one work cell produces luxury purses and performs all required operations (such as entirely manual assembling of delicate materials to ensure the desired visual result and aesthetically focused quality control); another work cell produces bags for rough professional use and performs all required operations (such as assembling of rough materials assisted by powerful knitting machines and resistance-focused quality control). Cell manufacturing reduces handling of materials and work-in-progress and reduces manufacturing cycle time, thereby improving flexibility and efficiency. Because each cell produces similar items, set-up times are low, further promoting flexibility and small lot sizes. All these features contribute to reduce inventories.

JIT philosophy = JIT manufacturing + TQM + Respect for people

As you have probably realized by know, achieving the encompassing JIT philosophy requires, not only JIT manufacturing, but also TQM across the entire organization and even across the value chain. Lack of quality is considered a waste and should therefore be eliminated. As we argued at the start, quality and time must (and should) not be considered as opposing objectives; rather, they are mutually necessary and reinforcing. In addition, a third element is essential to JIT philosophy: respect for people. Everyone is equally involved and responsible, bringing together functional areas to meet customer needs and involving managers in operations. Extensive training and empowerment is key, with individuals and self-managed teams being encouraged and expected to take autonomous decisions. In exchange, job security and quality rewards are characteristics of JIT companies, as Toyota.

Details about JIT are beyond the scope of this book and can be found in any operations management textbook (for example, Paton et al. 2011). You will now explore two relevant issues from a management accounting perspective: the financial perspective of JIT impacts and the adoption of management accounting techniques for a JIT environment.

How to financially evaluate JIT?

A financial evaluation of JIT is challenging. Multiple relevant costs and benefits must be included. As a major organizational change, implementing JIT implies significant and organization-wide costs. However, financial benefits are also significant and have multiple origins. The drastic reduction of inventories in a JIT organization (and value chain) offers substantial cost savings, which are sometimes hidden (as shown in *Management Accounting in Practice 20.7*). Just-in-time challenges and tries to improve existing processes and costs structures, while traditional approaches to manage inventories accept existing conditions and merely try to optimize results within those conditions. One traditional approach is the economic order size model, which determines the optimal order size by considering inventories holding costs and ordering costs, taking existing processes, costs and risks as a given (see discussion and calculations in Scarlett, 2010).

Since JIT should be associated with improved quality, we may expect reduced costs of quality (COQ), in particular non-conformance costs due to internal failure (for example, rework and scrap) and external failure (for example, repairs and replacements, restore reputation and lost contribution from sales). Finally, shorter manufacturing cycles improve efficiency and customer responsiveness, and capacity utilization is also improved, with likely significant financial benefits.

Particular JIT initiatives can be evaluated by adopting relatively short time horizons. However, JIT is a long-term commitment, so a complete financial evaluation of JIT should encompass a lengthy period. In addition, since JIT so thoroughly changes companies, it is often difficult to disentangle impacts of JIT from impacts driven by other factors. Estimating relevant costs and revenues may not be an easy task for management accountants, but they are in a privileged position to succeed in doing it.

Management accounting techniques

Throughput accounting

Chapter 5 introduced the concepts of throughput and throughput accounting (TA), based on the theory of constraints (TOC) proposed by Goldratt in the 1980s. Theory of constraints is a production scheduling methodology to manage production bottlenecks which constrain the entire system throughput – the output delivered during a given period, expressed in financial or non-financial terms.

From a production scheduling perspective, constraints are physical. For example, the slowest machine becomes the production bottleneck, constraining the output of the entire system. By increasing the throughput of this machine, overall output and profit are increased. However, going beyond the original scheduling perspective, Corbett (2006) noted that companies' constrains do not necessarily have to be physical. For instance, they can be a marketing constraint, when demand falls below production capacity; in this case, increasing production after removing physical constraints would merely build up inventories (and associated costs), rather than improve profitability.

Within an industrial context, TOC steps are the following:

1) Identify the relevant scarce resource which is the bottleneck for the entire system – thus limiting throughput contribution.

2) Keep the bottleneck resource fully used, subordinating all other decisions (for example, product mix decisions or scheduling non-bottleneck activities) to this objective. This maximizes the throughput contribution of the entire system.

3) Find ways to remove the constraint (for instance, buying a faster machine or redesigning products to reduce the need for the bottleneck resource).

4) Resume step 1, identifying the new bottleneck.

In Chapter 5, you learned key financial measures supporting TOC: throughput contribution (sales minus totally variable costs), other operating expenses (all operating costs except totally variable costs) and investments. This 'totally variable costing' is most appropriate for short-term decision making and, fundamentally, leads to the framework discussed in Chapter 13 to maximize profitability, by focusing on the contribution margin per unit of the scarce (or bottleneck) resource. Accepting this view (see Corbett, 2006, for an alternative perspective), TOC may complement activity-based costing, which adopts a longer-run, strategic perspective, viewing all resources as variable and privileging absorption costing. However, TOC popularity has declined in the fields of operations management and management accounting. As a management accounting technique, throughput accounting is little used, with an adoption rate of only 5 per cent in CIMA's (2009) survey.

Backflush costing – simplified costing for a JIT environment

Differences between JIT and traditional production approaches pave the way for adopting an alternative costing technique: backflush costing. The paradigm in traditional costing systems is to sequentially track the costs of the various physical flows: (1) inputs purchase; (2) inputs usage in production; (3) obtaining finished products, and (4) sale. Each physical flow 'triggers' a synchronous journal entry in the costing system. The existence of initial and ending inventories requires techniques to determine cost flows and value inventory (for example, first in first out (FIFO), last in first out (LIFO) or weighted-average, variable or absorption costing, as you learned in Chapter 4).

Backflush costing is an alternative costing technique that suits the JIT environment, simplifying procedures but with no significant information loss. In JIT, the start and end of a process – purchasing, production and sales – are close together. In addition, inventories (of materials, work-in-progress and finished goods) ideally do not exist. From a costing perspective, this allows adopting simpler and cheaper systems. If there are no initial or ending inventories, all manufacturing costs are incorporated into the cost of goods sold during the period. So, why bother about FIFO or LIFO, or about variable and absorption costing? Why bother to record the flows in and out of the production account, or in and out of the finished goods account, if they are the same?

Backflush costing flexibly proposes various alternatives, omitting journal entries of one or several stages before sales costs are recorded. In other words, some flows no longer 'trigger' journal entries. Given the reduced manufacturing cycle time and work-in-progress (WIP) inventories in JIT, a frequent option entails eliminating the production (or WIP) account (as in option A in Exhibit 20.6).

Table 20.2 includes information about company XPTO, which operates a near JIT approach, with very low inventories.

We first analyse a backflush costing system with no production (WIP) account (option A). *Worked Example 20.1* explains the system and calculations and Exhibit 20.6 shows the ledger accounts. Option A is suitable for companies with near zero WIP inventories, because nearly all manufacturing costs will have been incorporated in cost of goods sold – COGS – (rather than differed as closing inventory). Note that the raw materials account also includes any potential WIP closing inventory.

The company may still track the physical flows in and out of the production process for operational or other purposes; however, these flows are unaccounted for in this model of backflushing. Any variances between standard and actual costs are treated as in traditional standard costing systems.

Table 20.2: Company XPTO operational and financial information for a given period	
Purchase of raw materials	£430,000
Conversion costs incurred	£220,000
Finished goods completed	10,000 units
Sales	9,800 units
Opening inventories (of raw materials, WIP and finished goods)	0
Standard and actual unit costs (with regard to materials)	£40
Standard and actual unit costs (with regard to conversion costs)	£20

> **Worked Example 20.1**
>
> ## A backflush costing system with three trigger points (purchase, completion of finished goods and sales) for company XPTO, step-by-step: Option A
>
> Used materials and allocated conversion costs directly determine the cost of finished goods, based on standard or normal unit costs. So, the flow of inputs into production no longer triggers a journal entry from materials and conversion costs to a production account, as usual. A journal entry is only triggered when finished goods are completed, reaching back to the materials and conversion costs accounts to pull ('flush out') the costs from these accounts. So, 10,000 units of finished goods are valued at £40 + £20 each, totalling 400,000 + 200,000 = £600,000, in entry number 3. The number attributed to this entry is 3, because in fact there are two previous flows to be recorded, as analysed next. You will note, however, that both previous and subsequent entries (1, 2, 4 and 5) are identical to traditional systems.
>
> - The initial steps of purchasing materials and incurring in conversion costs trigger the first entries (1 and 2):
>
>   **£430,000 and £220,000, respectively**
>
> - Completing the finished goods triggers entry 3, as explained above:
>
>   **10,000 units × (£40 + £20) = 400,000 + 200,000 = £600,000**
>
> - Selling the goods triggers entry 4, recording the cost of goods sold based on the standard or normal unit costs:
>
>   **9,800 units × £60 = £588,000**
>
> - At the end of the period, we need to record under-allocated or over-allocated conversion costs (entry 5). Under-allocated or over-allocated conversion costs are typically disposed to COGS (or, alternatively, treated as period costs), because the usually low inventories of finished goods and WIP make proration immaterial:
>
>   **220,000 – 200,000 = £20,000 under-allocated costs**
>
> Considering both entries, the final COGS is 588,000 + 20,000 = £608,000.

Option B further simplifies the system, omitting not only the production (WIP) account but also the finished goods account. In this option, there are only two trigger points: purchase and sales. Otherwise, the rationale of the two options is similar:

- Record materials purchased and conversion costs incurred: (1 and 2): £430,000 and £220,000, respectively.

- Used materials and allocated conversion costs directly determine the cost of goods sold (rather than finished goods, as in option A). Only sales trigger a journal entry (3), reaching back to the materials and conversion costs accounts to pull the costs, based on the triggering flow (sales). In this option, COGS is: 9,800 × (40 + 20) = 392,000 + 196,000 = £588,000.

- Dispose underallocated overheads (220,000 – 196,000 = £24,000) to COGS, increasing them to £612,000.

Option B is suitable to companies with near zero inventories of both WIP *and* finished products. Note that the two options lead to only slightly different valuations for closing inventories (option A: 30,000 + 12,000 = £42,000 versus option B: £38,000) and COGS (£608,000 versus £612,000, respectively).

There are other alternative backflush costing systems, omitting different sets of accounts preceding COGS. The simplest variant admits only one trigger: sales. Again, do not forget that different alternatives provide different figures for closing inventories and COGS. However, if the company operates with low inventories as prescribed by JIT, or if inventories are stable across periods, differences across alternatives may be immaterial – even when compared with traditional costing approaches. If

Option A: Three trigger points: Purchase, obtaining finished goods and sales

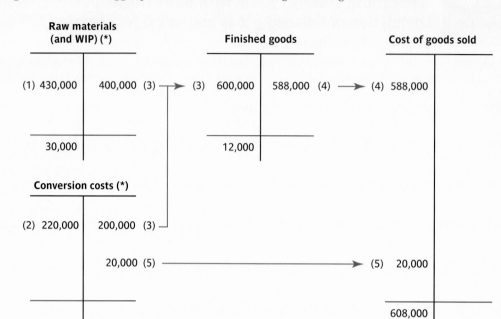

Option B: Two trigger points: purchase and sales

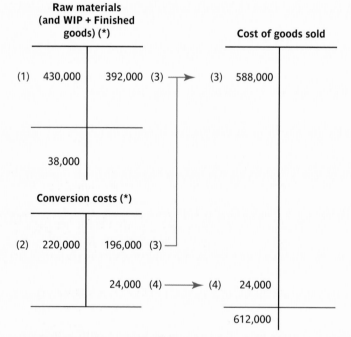

Notes:

(*) For simplicity:

The conversion costs control account and the conversion costs allocated account were merged into a single account 'conversion costs'.

The payables control account has been omitted (for entries 1 and 2).

Exhibit 20.6: Ledger accounts in Backflush costing

differences are immaterial when compared to traditional approaches in line with Generally Accepted Accounting Principles (GAAP), then backflush costing may be acceptable for financial reporting, even though it is not strictly GAAP compliant (for instance, backflush costing does not recognize certain closing inventories, in particular of WIP, even if they do exist in a particular period).

Finally, the advantage of backflush costing of being a simpler and cheaper costing system may be reduced in companies with integrated information systems, such as enterprise resource planning systems (see the next chapter). The integration of production and financial systems largely simplifies obtaining fast and reliable cost information about the operational flows throughout the organization – that is, the sequential tracking of costs required by traditional costing systems. So, integrated systems make backflush costing (which always implies some information loss) less appealing.

Chapter summary

In this chapter, you explored two increasingly essential characteristics to compete in today's competitive markets: quality and time. You are now aware that quality and time are mutually necessary and reinforcing, contrary to the popular belief that they tend to be mutually exclusive. Through financial and non-financial perspectives, you studied both financial and non-financial indicators of quality. Then, you explored the strategic importance of time and several operational measures. Quality and time concerns come together in the Japanese-originated techniques of total quality management and just-in-time, whose benefits and difficulties you explored, including in a financial perspective. Finally, you studied two management accounting techniques paying a particular attention to time, in order to improve performance (throughput accounting) or to simplify costing in a just-in-time environment (backflush costing). Throughout the chapter, numerous examples made clear that management accountants can play a relevant role by becoming involved in measuring and managing quality and time, hence creating value for their organizations.

Key terms

Attributes of a product or service Tangible or intangible features that characterize the product or service (p. 518)

Backflush costing A simplified costing technique for a JIT environment, with little or no inventories, without accounting for some flows in stages prior to recording goods sold (in particular, flows in and out of the work-in-progress account) (p. 540)

Conformance quality The extent to which the actual characteristics of a product or service match its design specifications (p. 517)

Costs of quality (COQ) Costs to achieve high quality and avoid failures, through prevention and appraisal activities, and cost consequences of poor quality, due to internal and external failures (p. 522)

Customer service Services provided to customers throughout the entire relationship – before, during and after the purchase (p. 518)

Design quality The extent to which the designed characteristics of a product or service address clients' expectations (p. 517)

Just-in-time (JIT) (or lean production) A system that only purchases or produces when needed to address a customer order, in order to minimize waste (inventories and anything that does not add value). Just-in-time philosophy requires JIT manufacturing + TQM + respect for people (p. 536)

Non-financial quality indicators Indicators on customers, internal business processes and learning and growth that anticipate and drive the financial consequences of quality (p. 527)

Plan-do-check-act (PDCA) cycle A systematic, interactive approach to continuous improvement and problem solving, and a key tool in total quality management (p. 535)

Six sigma A strategy to achieve an extraordinarily high conformance quality level, by reducing process variability that causes defects and undermines customer satisfaction (p. 530)

Total quality management (TQM) Permanent and integrated effort across the entire organization to excel in all customer-relevant quality dimensions of products and services (p. 535)

Review questions ● ● ● ● ● ● ● ● ● ● ● connect ● ●

| Level of difficulty: | BASIC | INTERMEDIATE | ADVANCED |

20.1 Discuss the importance of quality in today's business environment. **[LO1]**

20.2 Identify and discuss the main dimensions of quality. **[LO2]**

20.3 Discuss the importance of time in today's business environment. **[LO1]**

20.4 Identify potential roles for management accountants in quality and time improvement initiatives. **[LO3]**

20.5 Describe and provide examples of the types of non-financial quality indicators and discuss how they are related. **[LO4]**

20.6 Indicate the main objectives and characteristics of total quality management. **[LO7]**

20.7 Indicate the main objectives and characteristics of just-in-time. **[LO8]**

20.8 Discuss whether quality and time are incompatible objectives. **[LO1]**

20.9 Describe and provide examples of the types of costs of quality and discuss how they are related. **[LO4]**

20.10 Indicate the purpose of backflush costing and describe alternatives to design such a system. **[LO10]**

Group discussion and activity questions ● ● ● ● ● ● ● ●

20.11 Discuss the sentence: 'Risks of quality failures like a large scale oil leak are so small, and the costs to prevent all kinds of possible problems are so high, that a certain risk level has to be accepted.' **[LO4]**

20.12 Organize the class into proponents of a return on quality approach and proponents of a total quality management approach. Try to persuade the other party about the merits of your approach, but strive to find points of convergence between the two approaches. **[LO3, LO7]**

20.13 Discuss the following sentence, drawn from quality gurus W. Edwards Deming and Harold F. Dodge: 'you can't inspect quality into a product, you have to build it in.' **[LO2, LO4, LO7]**

20.14 Re-read the *Management Accounting in Practice 20.7* example and download Dell's and HP's annual reports (available on the companies' websites). Based on the 'risk factors' section of each report, find and compare the acknowledged risk factors due to low inventories, reliance on long-term relationships with suppliers and single sourcing – all JIT characteristics. Discuss which company seems to acknowledge greater risks. **[LO8]**

20.15 Examine why the economic and demographic context of Japan may have been a key reason why JIT first developed there rather than in western countries, and why JIT is now adopted internationally. **[LO8]**

Exercises ● ● ● ● ● ● ● ● ● ● ● ● ● ● ● connect ● ●

E20.1 **Costs of quality [LO4]**

A company has incurred the following costs:

- Materials inspection: £40,000
- Quality training of personnel: £80,000
- Quality training of suppliers' personnel: £30,000
- Complaints: £20,000
- Rework: £100,000
- Scrap: £200,000
- Quality laboratory: £50,000
- Warranty repairs: £10,000

Required:

a) Classify these quality costs.

b) Evaluate whether the company seems to be having the 'right' costs of quality.

c) Which type of cost is missing from the above list and which is usually the most difficult to estimate?

E20.2 **Non-financial quality indicators [LO2, LO4]**

The Health and Fitness Group (HFG), which is privately owned, operates various centres. Each centre offers dietary plans and fitness programmes to clients under the supervision of dieticians and fitness trainers. Residential accommodation is also available at each centre.

A marketing director stated at a recent board meeting: 'Our company's success depends on the quality of service provided to our clients. In my opinion, we need only to concern ourselves with the number of complaints received from clients during each period as this is the most important performance measure for our business. As long as the number of complaints received from clients is not increasing from period to period, then we can be confident about our future prospects.'

Required:

Comment on this statement. In particular, highlight limitations of this performance measure of service quality and suggest alternative measures, tailored to a health centre. What does the statement suggest about the marketing director's attitude towards quality?

Source: adapted from Association of Chartered Certified Accountants, Paper P5.

E20.3 **Costs of quality [LO4]**

CAL manufactures and sells solar panels for garden lights. Components are bought in and assembled into metal frames that are machine manufactured by CAL. There are a number of alternative suppliers of these solar panels. Some of CAL's competitors charge a lower price, but supply lower quality panels; whereas others supply higher quality panels than CAL but for a much higher price.

CAL is preparing its budgets for the coming year and has estimated that the market demand for its type of solar panels will be 100,000 units and that its share will be 20,000 units (that is, 20 per cent of the available market). The standards for each solar panel are as follows:

	£ per unit	£ per unit
Selling price		60
Bought-in components (1 set)	15	
Assembly & machining cost	25	
Delivery cost	5	45
Contribution		15

An analysis of CAL's recent performance revealed that 2 per cent of the solar panels supplied to customers were returned for free replacement, because the customer found that they were faulty. Investigation of these returned items shows that the components had been damaged when they had been assembled into the metal frame. These returned panels cannot be repaired and have no scrap value. If the supply of faulty solar panels to customers could be eliminated then, due to improved customer perception, CAL's market share would increase to 25 per cent.

Required:

a) Explain, with reference to CAL, quality conformance costs and quality non-conformance costs and the relationship between them.

b) Assuming that CAL continues with its present systems and that the percentage of quality failings is as stated above:

   i) Calculate, based on the budgeted figures and sales returns rate, the total relevant costs of quality for the coming year.

   ii) Calculate the maximum saving that could be made by implementing an inspection process for the solar panels, immediately before the goods are delivered.

Source: Chartered Institute of Management Accountants, Paper P2.

E20.4 **Operational measures of time, JIT and TQM [LO6, LO7, LO8]**

QW is a company that manufactures machine parts from sheet metal to specific customer orders for industrial customers. QW is considering diversification into the production of metal ornaments. The ornaments would be produced at a constant rate throughout the year. It then plans to sell these ornaments from inventory through wholesalers and via direct mail to consumers.

Currently, each of the machine parts is specific to a customer's order. Consequently, the company does not hold an inventory of finished items but it does hold the equivalent of one day's production of sheet metal so as to reduce the risk of being unable to produce goods demanded by customers at short notice. There is a one-day lead time for delivery of sheet metal to QW from its main supplier though additional supplies could be obtained at less competitive prices.

Demand for these industrial goods is such that delivery is required almost immediately after the receipt of the customer order. QW is aware that if it is unable to meet an order immediately the industrial customer would seek an alternative supplier, despite QW having a reputation for high-quality machine parts.

The management of QW is not aware of the implications of the diversification for its production and inventory policies.

Required:

a) Compare and contrast QW's present production and inventory policy and practices with a traditional production system that uses constant production levels and holds inventory to meet peaks of demand.

b) Discuss the importance of a total quality management system in a just-in-time environment. Use QW to illustrate your discussion.

Source: Chartered Institute of Management Accountants, Paper P2.

E20.5 **Backflush costing [LO10]**

A company reported the following operational and financial information:

Purchase of raw materials	£1,000,000
Conversion costs incurred	£7,000,000
Finished goods completed	£100,000
Sales	£80,000
Opening inventories (of raw materials, WIP and finished goods)	£0
Standard and actual unit costs (with regard to materials)	£80
Standard and actual unit costs (with regard to conversion costs)	£50

The finance director is considering the adoption of backflush costing to reduce complexity and costs of administrative processes.

Required:

a) A production manager became highly concerned when he heard rumours about the possibility of adopting a 'new system' that would ignore some internal physical flows. He was worried that he might stop having information he needed for managing production flows. Are his concerns justified?

b) Depict the general-ledger transactions of a backflush costing system:

    i) with no production (WIP) account;

    ii) with no production (WIP) and no finished goods accounts.

c) Do you think backflush costing is appropriate for this company? Why/why not?

E20.6 **Costs of quality [LO4]**

Telecoms At Work (TAW) manufactures and markets office communications systems. During the year ended 31 May 201X TAW made an operating profit of £30 million on sales of £360 million. However, the directors are concerned that products do not conform to the required level of quality and TAW is therefore not fulfilling its full potential in terms of turnover and profits achieved.

    The following information is available in respect of the year ended 31 May 201X:

Production data:	
Units manufactured and sold	18,000
Units requiring rework	2,100
Units requiring warranty repair service	2,700
Design engineering hours	48,000
Process engineering hours	54,000
Inspection hours (manufacturing)	288,000

Cost data:	
Design engineering per hour	96
Process engineering per hour	70
Inspection per hour (manufacturing)	50
Rework per communication system reworked (manufacturing)	4,800
Customer support per repaired unit (marketing)	240
Transportation costs per repaired unit (distribution)	280
Warranty repairs per repaired unit (customer service)	4,600

1) Staff training costs amounted to £180,000 and additional product testing costs of £72,000.

2) The marketing director has estimated that sales of 1,800 units were lost as a result of public knowledge of poor quality at TAW. The average contribution per communication system is estimated at £7,200.

Required:

a) Prepare a cost analysis which shows actual prevention costs, appraisal costs, internal failure costs, and external failure costs for the year ended 31 May 201X. Your statement should show each cost heading as a percentage of turnover and clearly show the total cost of quality. Comment briefly on the inclusion of opportunity costs in such an analysis.

b)   A detailed analysis has revealed that the casings in which the communications systems are housed are often subject to mishandling in transit to TAW's manufacturing premises. The directors are considering two alternative solutions proposed by the design engineering team which are aimed at reducing the quality problems that are currently being experienced. These are as follows:

Option 1 – Increase the number of immediate physical inspections of the casings when they are received from the supplier. This will require an additional 10,000 inspection hours.

Option 2 – Redesign and strengthen the casings and the containers used to transport them to better withstand mishandling during transportation. Redesign will require an additional 2,000 hours of design engineering and an additional 5,000 hours of process engineering.

Internal failure costs of rework for each reworked communication system are as follows:

	£
Variable costs (including direct materials, direct labour rework and supplies)	1,920
Allocated fixed costs (equipment, space and allocated overhead)	2,880
Total costs (as per note 2 on cost data)	4,800

The directors of TAW believe that, even if it is able to achieve improvements in quality, it will be unable to save any of the fixed costs of internal and external failure.

If TAW chooses to inspect the casings more carefully, it expects to eliminate rework on 720 communication systems, whereas if it redesigns the casings it expects to eliminate rework on 960 communication systems.

If incoming casings are inspected more carefully, TAW estimates that 600 fewer communication systems will require warranty repair and that it will be able to sell an additional 300 communication systems. If the casing is redesigned, the directors estimate that 840 fewer communication systems will require warranty repair and that an additional 360 communication systems will be sold.

External failure costs of repair for each repaired communication system are as follows:

	Variable costs £	Fixed costs £	Total costs £
Customer support costs	96	144	240
Transportation costs	210	70	280
Warranty repair costs	1,700	2,900	4,600

Required:

Prepare an estimate of the financial consequences of each option and advise the directors of TAW which option should be chosen.

Source: adapted from Association of Chartered Certified Accountants.

E20.7 **Costs of quality, measures of time [LO4, LO6]**

The Better Electricals Group (BEG) manufactures a range of high-quality electrical appliances such as kettles, toasters and steam irons for domestic use.

The directors considered that the existing product range could be extended to include industrial-sized products such as high-volume water boilers, high-volume toasters and large steam irons for the hotel and catering industry, in spite of significant competition.

The marketing director proposed applying to gain 'platinum status' quality certification in respect of their industrial products from the Hotel and Catering Institute of Voltland in order to gain a strong competitive position. He then stressed the need to focus on increasing the effectiveness of all operations from product design to the provision of after-sales services.

Table 20.3 contains financial and non-financial data relating to the application for 'platinum status' for each of the years 2013, 2014 and 2015.

The managing director requested a statement of total estimated costs for the application for platinum status for each of the years 2013, 2014 and 2015, detailing manufacturing cost estimates and costs of quality. The management accountant produced the following statement:

	2013	2014	2015
	Forecast	**Forecast**	**Forecast**
	£000's	**£000's**	**£000's**
Variable manufacturing costs	8,400	10,500	12,600
Fixed manufacturing costs	3,000	3,400	3,400
Prevention costs	4,200	2,100	1,320
Appraisal costs	800	700	700
Internal failure costs	2,500	1,800	1,200
External failure costs	3,100	2,000	980
Total costs	22,000	20,500	20,200

Required:

a) Explain how this statement could be of assistance to BEG with regard to their application for platinum status. Your answer must include commentary on the nature of the items contained in the statement.

b) Assess the forecasted performance of BEG for the period 2013 to 2015 with reference to the application for 'platinum status' quality certification under the following headings:

  i)   Financial performance and marketing.

  ii) External effectiveness, analysing how quality and delivery are expected to affect customer satisfaction and hence product marketing.

  iii) Internal efficiency, analysing how cycle time and waste are expected to affect productivity and flexibility and hence the financial evaluation of the application.

Table 20.3: 'Platinum status' quality certification application – Relevant statistics

	2013	2014	2015
	Forecast	**Forecast**	**Forecast**
Total market size (£m)	300	320	340
BEG – sales (£m)	24	30	36
BEG – total costs (£m)	22	20.5	20.2
BEG – sundry statistics:			
% of products achieving design quality standards and accepted without further rectification	92	95	99
Rectification claims from customers (£m)	0.96	0.75	0.1
Cost of after sales rectification service (£m)	1.8	1.05	0.8
% of sales meeting planned delivery dates	88.5	95.5	99.5
Average cycle time: customer enquiry to product delivery (days)	49	45	40
Product enquiries not taken up by customers (% of enquiries)	10.5	6	3
Idle capacity of manufacturing staff (%)	12	6	1.5

Source: adapted from Association of Chartered Certified Accountants.

• • • Case study problem •

C20.1   'Design thinking' in health care – Improving quality and time at Kaiser Permanente to address patients', practitioners' and financial objectives [LO1, LO2, LO3, LO4]

Kaiser Permanente is a leading health care organization in the USA, with 35 hospitals and over 450 medical offices, 15,000 physicians, 8 million members and $40 billion in operating revenue. Its mission is to 'to provide quality care for our members and their families, and to contribute to the well-being of our communities', as stated on Kaiser's website.

Brown (2008) reported that Kaiser Permanente wanted to improve quality of both patients' and medical practitioners' experiences. This is why it hired IDEO, Brown's innovation and design firm, to teach staff about 'design thinking' techniques, hoping to inspire them to generate new ideas.

The problem

One of the projects aims to re-engineer nursing-staff shift changes at four hospitals. Shift changes are a big challenge to the continuity of patient care, requiring a crucial exchange of information and duties to ensure safety, quality of care and efficiency. A multidisciplinary project team was created, including IDEO designers, one Kaiser Permanente expert from each area – strategy (a former nurse), organizational development, technology and process design – and a union representative.

The team worked with nurses to identify problems. Debriefing the in-coming shift about patients' conditions took up the first 45 minutes of each shift. Debriefing was done at the nurses' station. Each hospital and even each nurse had their own way to prioritize and communicate information – for example, recorded dictation or face-to-face conversations. The ways to record that information to later assist patients' care also varied and they were rather questionable – for example, by quickly scrawling on any available paper scrap.

Overall effectiveness was poor: although a lot of time was put into this process, nurses often missed information that was most relevant to patients. Missed information ranged from more emotional aspects, such as family visits, to technical knowledge about administered tests or therapies. For example, dispensing medication correctly 'means giving the right prescribed drug in the right dose to the right patient at the right time. The consequences of medication error can be catastrophic for the patient and very costly for both the institution's reputation and its bottom line' (McCreary, 2010, p. 95). While information losses in nurses' shifts changes are not the main cause for medication errors, they do create such risk. And, from a human-centric perspective, many patients felt 'a hole in their care' in each shift change (Brown, 2008, p. 87).

Solution design

The team redesigned the debriefing process, relocating it from the nurses' station to the patient's bedside and encouraging patients to participate. The team also designed new procedures and simple software for nurses to read and add notes about each shift. Information input could be done throughout a shift, avoiding a last minute, inefficient rush.

Solution results

The solution reduced required time and allowed better knowledge transfer. Arriving nurses' time to first contact with patients reduced by more than 50 per cent, significantly increasing total time available to actual nursing activities. It reduced errors in exchanging information and increased patient confidence. Finally, it improved the quality of nurses' work experience, as these comments illustrate: 'I'm an hour ahead, and I've only been here 45 minutes'; '[This is the] first time I've ever made it out of here at the end of my shift' (Brown, 2008, pp. 87–8).

A small process innovation had huge benefits on both patients' experience and nurses' job satisfaction and productivity, and it was later rolled out across Kaiser units. The new software to record patient information was also integrated into a company-wide IT project.

Brown (2008, p. 88) questioned '[w]hat might happen at Kaiser if every nurse, doctor, and administrator in every hospital felt empowered to tackle problems the way this group did?'. So, Kaiser created the Garfield Innovation Centre to institutionalize the organizational learning about 'design thinking' from this project and to continuously create and share tools and best practices. It acts as an internal consultant, is run by the same core team and contains a prototyping space and a full-scale clinic. Its mission is customer focused: 'to pursue innovation that enhances the patient experience and, more broadly, to envision Kaiser's "hospital of the future" (Brown, 2008, p. 88). As a result, the Institute of Healthcare Improvement recognized Kaiser Permanente as 'best practice' in health care.

A financial perspective

Kaiser Permanente launched other projects following this approach, with clear benefits – including financial ones. The MedRite project aims to reduce medication errors. According to McCreary (2010), development costs were $470,000 and avoided $965,000 in costs for treating consequences of medication errors. The ongoing roll-out across the organization requires little additional investment, so benefits are likely to increase further. MedRite also allowed intangible benefits, like increasing employee satisfaction and patient trust – hard to measure, but crucial benefits for a health care organization.

McCreary argues that Kaiser Permanente's emphasis on improving design has aimed to improve quality of care. But there are also financial savings, which address a concern about cost control. For instance, some redesign initiatives allowed transferring some duties from expensive clinicians to lower-paid staff. 'Kaiser is not without critics who question some of its motives and practices – sometimes alleging that its emphasis on cost control crosses the line into rationed care' (McCreary, 2010, p. 97).

Sources: Brown (2008); McCreary (2010); www.kaiserpermanente.org; http://www.ideo.com/work/nurse-knowledge-exchange; http://www.forbes.com/2010/01/14/tim-brown-ideo-leadership-managing-design.html (all accessed on 15 May 2012).

Required:

a) Provide examples of indicators that could have signalled problems in nurses' shifts changes.

b) Draw on this case to illustrate how quality and time can be mutually required and reinforcing.

c) Management accountants were not included in the innovation team and are not mentioned in either of the two articles. Discuss ways in which management accountants:

   i) Could have contributed to the described innovation.

   ii) Might contribute to Garfield Innovation Centre consulting activities at Kaiser Permanente. Reflect on how these contributions may fit with the missions of these two organizations, and discuss the criticisms at the end of the text.

● ● Recommended reading ● ● ● ● ● ● ● ● ● ● ● ● ● ● ● ● ●

- Rust, R. T., A. J. Zahorik, and T. L. Keiningham (1995) 'Return on quality (ROQ): making service quality financially accountable', *Journal of Marketing*, 59(2), pp. 58–70.

A seminal paper on the return on quality (ROQ) perspective. Authors argue that all quality investments must be financially accountable, that they are not all equally valid and that some may be excessive.

- Paton, S., B. Clegg, J. Hsuan and A. Pilkington (2011) *Operations Management*, Maidenhead: McGraw-Hill.

An operations management textbook, developing topics such as techniques to monitor quality targets and the wider approaches of six sigma, TQM and JIT.

- Takeuchi, H., E. Osonon and N. Shimizu (2008) 'The contradictions that drive Toyota's success', *Harvard Business Review*, 86(6), pp. 96–104.

Analyses how combining 'hard' techniques (as JIT) and 'soft' techniques (related to organizational culture characteristics and the focus on people) were influential in shaping Toyota's success.

- Hoque, Z. and M. Alam (1999) 'TQM adoption, institutionalism and changes in management accounting systems: a case study', *Accounting & Business Research*, 29(3), pp. 199–210.

Suggests that TQM initiatives may be driven by objectives of promoting 'institutional' and 'quality' culture, rather than 'hard' technical reasons, and that TQM may promote changes in management accounting and reporting.

References

Brown, T. (2008) 'Design Thinking', *Harvard Business Review*, 86(6), pp. 84–92.

Burns, J. and G. Baldvinsdottir (2005) 'An institutional perspective of accountants new roles – the interplay of contradictions and praxis', *European Accounting Review*, 14(4), pp. 725–57.

Callioni, G., X. de Montgros, R. Slagmulder, Luk N. Van Wassenhove and L. Wright (2005) 'Inventory-driven costs', *Harvard Business Review*, 83(3), pp. 135–41.

CIMA (2009) 'Management accounting tools for today and tomorrow', http://www/cimaglobal.com/Though-leadership/Research-topics/Management-accounting-in-different-sectors/Management-accounting-survey/ (accessed on 15 May 2012).

Corbett, C. J., M. J. Montes-Sancho and D. A. Kirsch (2005) 'The financial impact of ISO 9000 certification in the United States: an empirical analysis', *Management Science*, 51(7), pp. 1046–59.

Corbett, T. (2006) 'Three-questions accounting', *Strategic Finance*, 87(10), pp. 48–55.

Davis, J. R., H. M. Frechette and E. H. Boswell (2010) *Strategic Speed: Mobilize People, Accelerate Execution*, Boston, MA: Harvard Business Press Books.

Furterer, S. (ed.) (2009) *Lean Six Sigma in Service: Applications and Case Studies*, New York: CRC Press.

Heras, I., G. P. M. Dick and M. Casadesús (2002) 'ISO 9000 registration's impact on sales and profitability: a longitudinal analysis of performance before and after accreditation', *International Journal of Quality & Reliability Management*, 9(6), pp. 774–91.

Hilton, R., M. Maher and F. Selto (2008) *Cost Management: Strategies for Business Decisions*, 4th edn, New York: McGraw-Hill.

Homburg, C., N. Koschate and W. D. Hoyer (2005), 'Do satisfied customers really pay more? A study of the relationship between customer satisfaction and willingness to pay', *The Journal of Marketing*, 69(2), pp. 84–96.

Huston, L. and N. Sakkab (2006), 'Connect and develop: inside Procter & Gamble's new model for innovation', *Harvard Business Review*, 84(3), pp. 58–66.

Kaplan, R. S., A. Mikes, R. Simons, P. Tufano and M. Hofmann (2009) 'Managing risk in the New World', *Harvard Business Review*, 87(10), pp. 68–75.

McCreary, L. (2010) 'Kaiser Permanente's innovation on the front lines', *Harvard Business Review*, 88(9), pp. 92–127.

Neuhaus, K. and P. Guarraia (2007) 'Want more from lean six sigma?', *Harvard Management Update*, December.

Paton, S., B. Clegg, J. Hsuan and A. Pilkington (2011) *Operations Management*, Maidenhead: McGraw Hill.

Rudisill, F. and Clary, D. (2004), 'The management accountant's role in six sigma,' Institute of Management Accountants.

Rust, R. T., A. J. Zahorik and T. L. Keiningham (1995) 'Return on quality (ROQ): making service quality financially accountable', *Journal of Marketing*, 59, pp. 58–70.

Scarlett, B. (2010) 'Performance operations', *Financial Management*, April, pp. 44–5.

Seiders, C., G. B. Voss, D. Grewal and A. L. Godfre (2005) 'Do satisfied customers buy more? Examining moderating influences in a retailing context', *The Journal of Marketing*, 69(4), pp. 26–43.

Sharma, D. S. (2005) 'The association between ISO 9000 certification and financial performance', *The International Journal of Accounting*, 40(2), pp. 151–72.

Takeuchi, H., E. Osono and N. Shimizu (2008) 'The contradictions that drive Toyota's success', *Harvard Business Review*, 86(6), pp. 96–104.

Tinsley, C. H., R. L. Dillon and P. M. Madsen (2011) 'How to avoid catastrophe', *Harvard Business Review*, 89(4), pp. 90–7.

Notes

1 http://asq.org/glossary/q.html (accessed on 15 May 2012).

2 http://eu.press.toshiba.eu/en/articles/press/pr_professional_tecra_laptops (accessed on 15 May 2012).

3 The alternative option of reporting *opportunity* costs in a separate COQ report may not be sufficient to adequately deal with their higher uncertainty. In particular, some potential quality failures may cause catastrophic financial costs, but they are highly unlikely to occur. Referring to such rare but extreme failures as 'Black Swan' events, Kaplan claimed that quantifying their risks is not worthwhile. Instead, he recommended doing a scenario analysis to evaluate if the company could survive to such catastrophic events (Kaplan et al., 2009) – that is, including the calculation of those extreme costs of quality within a wider, strategic-oriented evaluation.

4 In statistics, *sigma* (σ) represents a population standard deviation (a measure of variation). Assuming a normal distribution, if performance stays within the limits defined by the distribution average plus and minus six standard deviations (six sigma), then virtually no items exceed the specification limits – in fact, only 3.4 or fewer defects per million are expected.

5 See in chapter 21 the related notions of information systems integration and coupling.

6 http://www.globalauto.biz/2011/09/screw-shortage-hits-psa-production and http://industryweek.com/articles/peugeot_factories_in_neutral_over_lack_of_screws_25539.aspx (both accessed on 15 May 2012).

When you have read this chapter

Log on to the Online Learning Centre at **www.mcgraw-hill.co.uk/textbooks/burns** to explore chapter-by-chapter test questions, links and further online study tools for Management Accounting.

CHAPTER 21

INFORMATION SYSTEMS AND MANAGEMENT ACCOUNTING

Chapter outline

- Background to information systems

- Basic terms and concepts in information systems

- Dilemmas and solutions in information systems

- Roles of management accountants in a changing information systems context

Learning outcomes

On completion of this chapter, students will be able to:

LO1 Provide examples of how information technology has changed business operations, costs and revenues

LO2 Be aware of 'big data' analytical challenges and opportunities

LO3 Define systems (de)coupling

LO4 Identify types of information systems software and architecture and discuss their implementation in organizations

LO5 Identify the advantages and disadvantages of integrated systems

LO6 Describe what cloud computing is and its impacts for management accounting

LO7 Identify how today's information systems might change the role of the management accountant.

Introduction

This chapter discusses how information systems (IS) are relevant for today – and tomorrow's – management accountants. Information systems have dramatically changed almost everything around the world – everyday life, the business environment and workplaces. Literacy on information technology (IT) is now important for almost everyone and is essential in an increasing range of professions – including the accounting profession. Professional accounting bodies outline IT roles for future accountants, ranging from IS users to designers, managers or evaluators – or a combination of these roles (IFAC, 2007). Information systems are an important pillar for the evolution of management accounting and its professionals. For example, IS promote the hybridization of management accounting. Management accountants start doing typical IT tasks (for example, designing reports using report writing software tools) or managerial tasks (for example, analysing market or operational information) and non-accountants embrace traditional management accounting tasks (for example, analysing variances).

This chapter provides an introduction to what a management accountant needs to know about information systems and technology. This is achieved by reviewing some major trends in information systems and technology in recent years. Finally, by reflecting on new roles for management accountants, it reviews management accounting concepts and trends discussed throughout the book, placing them in today's technological context.

The next section sets the historical context of IS and provides examples of how developments in technology and software have changed not only how business is done, but also how businesses develop and may be analysed. The following section briefly reviews basic terms and concepts from the IS arena. These two sections provide the basis and context for the remainder of the chapter.

The following section discusses major issues in IS, in particular from a management accounting perspective. It starts by discussing the challenge to achieve IT/organizational alignment and the dilemma of (de)coupling systems. Then, it analyses major types of information systems: stand-alone systems (including spreadsheets and best-of-breed systems) and integrated systems. In particular, the major shift towards integrated, enterprise-wide IS (enterprise resource planning systems – ERPs) during the last couple of decades has created major expectations and pressures for change in management accounting. The section concludes by examining the recent trend towards cloud computing. The final section discusses trends in professional roles in management accounting, with a focus on declining and emerging trends in activities carried out by management accountants and other professional groups. It also provides some examples of management accounting concepts and activities in the context of system design.

Background to information systems

Information systems (IS) refer to a set of connected technologies and resources that collects, transforms and disseminates information. Information systems have become pervasive in the vast majority of modern organizations and are now essential for virtually all staff at all levels to conduct business, make decisions and report. In management accounting, we often refer to the management information system (MIS). A management information system can be defined as a computerized IS which has been designed to support the activities of an organization and support management decision making and reporting. Understanding the rapid development of the computing equipment which forms the core of almost all IS serves as a useful starting point to understand how the role of information systems in management accounting has developed and changed over time.

The origins of the first programmable computer are not detailed here, except to say that the Second World War period resulted in the development of computers performing more than a single task. In the 1950s, large organizations started automating mundane tasks which could be easily programmed into computing logic – for example, General Electric automated their payroll systems in 1953. It was the time of 'mainframes', machines which were expensive to run, complex to operate and not available for use by wider organizational users. By the late 1970s, Apple introduced the first mass-produced personal computer, and were quickly followed by IBM. The change from mainframes to personal (or desktop) computers was crucial for the development of software useful to management accountants. For example, the first spreadsheet program, Visicalc, was released in 1979. Spreadsheets brought computing power to management accountants and saved hours of work given their in-built ability to instantly recalculate every cell in the sheet.

By the mid-1980s personal computers could be networked together. This meant that information could be shared among users over organizational networks. The ability to share data and resources (such as printers and larger computers) was the first step towards today's tools of managers and management accountants. Networking of computers also led to the growth of email and other methods of electronic communication. It was the advent of the Internet – a combination of programming languages and protocols – in 1993 which really opened up networking to the global business and personal community. The Internet not only changed how businesses could communicate – businesses could now be connected to one another at a relatively low cost regardless of location – but also changed how business is done.

21.1: Management Accounting in Practice

How the Internet has been changing businesses

Amazon.com was the first major online business, established in 1994, and in 2011 it processed more than $131 million in sales each day, almost doubling their 2009 sales (Amazon.com, 2011). Online business shook many industries of products and services, such as books, recorded music and airlines as it effectively changed how business was done in those sectors. As more and more organizations joined the World Wide Web, the primary problem became one of finding relevant information. Web search providers such as Google provided the answer and now businesses and consumers have quick access to vast amounts of information on any topic imaginable. Add to this the growth of organizations which seemingly do not offer a product/service in the traditional sense – Facebook, Twitter or Wikipedia, for example – and the picture from a management accounting stance is one of ongoing change in the business environment.

Exercise

Identify and briefly discuss how an online retailer and a traditional retailer differ in their business operations and how such differences are likely to affect management accounting figures.

Although there is little academic research on companies such as those mentioned above, it is not hard to imagine how the focus of management accounting may have changed. For example, there is likely to have been a shift to more fixed costs in many online businesses, as well as a greater focus on forecasting and analysing revenues – rather than costs. In addition, the power and spread of computing has improved exponentially with the recent ubiquitous use of devices such as tablet computers. Next, *Management Accounting in Practice 21.2* provides brief examples of how technology has changed the operations and even the structures of many organizations and *Management Accounting in Practice 21.3* explores costs and revenues of Web 2.0-based Wikipedia.

In summary, an ever-evolving information technology landscape has not only connected businesses and people, but has changed the way business is done and the way we lead our daily lives. This has had an impact both on management accounting practices and on the very role of management accounting and accountants, as analysed in the remainder of this chapter.

21.2: Management Accounting in Practice

Information systems transforming organizations

The US-based company Airstrip Technologies have developed a mobile medical software solution which uses smartphones to receive live cardiology information on patients in the field. For example, a patient can be monitored while in transit to a hospital. A consultant can receive the information anywhere, on or off site and provide treatment guidance. According to the company, aside from obvious medical benefits, this technological advance can deliver cost benefits, increased workflow efficiency, improved and accurate communication, mitigation of risk and reduced resource waste.

Companies are increasingly exploring Internet-supported social technologies, such as social networking (for example, Facebook), video sharing (for example, YouTube), blogs and micro-blogs (for example, Twitter). According to Bughin et al. (2011), from McKinsey, these social technologies are extending the organization, creating an emergent type of networked organization: internally networked, towards employees; externally networked, towards customers, suppliers and partners; and fully networked, both internally and externally. When adopting such technologies at scale and embedding them in their organizational processes, these organizations have reported improvements in financial performance and market share. Major benefits include increased marketing effectiveness and customer satisfaction, as well as lower communication and marketing costs.

Measuring, explaining and driving improvements in this shifting environment must be an increasing concern of management accountants. Bughin et al. (2011) stress that gains from social technologies sometimes do not persist. These authors suggest that this may be due to the difficulty of achieving benefits at scale. Should management accountants contribute to identify and explain the drivers of these gains, both financial and non-financial, they will be having a priceless contribution.

Sources: Bughin et al. (2011); www.airstriptech.com (accessed on 15 May 2012).

Exercises

1) Identify companies operating in traditional industries whose business model was successfully modified by innovations in information technology. Identify and discuss the key success drivers.

2) Discuss how management accountants may contribute to identify and manage those success drivers.

21.3: Management Accounting in Practice

Rethinking costs and revenues in the Internet age: the case of Wikipedia

Wikipedia's founder, Jimmy Wales, regularly appeals for users' donations. Wikipedia rejects publicity funding. 'Commerce is fine. Advertising is not evil. But it doesn't belong here. Not in Wikipedia. Wikipedia is something special. (. . .) I could have made it into a for-profit company with advertising banners, but I decided to do something different. We've worked hard (. . .) to keep it lean and tight.'

What does 'lean and tight' mean with regard to costs? Jimmy Wales details:
'Where your donation goes:

- Technology: Servers, bandwidth, maintenance, development. Wikipedia is the #5 website in the world, and it runs on a fraction of what other top websites spend.

- People: The other top 10 websites have thousands of employees. We have fewer than 100, making your donation a great investment in a highly efficient not-for-profit organization.'

None of the above cost items are strictly variable with the volume of accesses – a measure of the consumption of Wikipedia's output. Those costs are mostly fixed, at least under traditional IT architecture (later in this chapter you will read how the emerging cloud computing model changes the IT architecture and transforms some fixed costs into variable costs). Only bandwidth costs increase, whenever additional bandwidth capacity is bought; they are fixed within relatively narrow relevant ranges, that is, semi-fixed costs (see Chapters 3 and 11). With regard to Wikipedia's 'production' (for example, the number of articles), server costs are also semi-fixed (as additional servers are bought to increase storage capacity) and the others tend to be fixed.

Anyone can voluntarily contribute to Wikipedia articles. Resorting to the 'wisdom of the masses', with no financial remuneration, Wikipedia avoids massive costs, should experts have to be hired to write.

Finally, all costs are independent from the sole revenue source: voluntary donations. Hence Wikipedia's concern on generating that revenue, by appealing to users' sense of social responsibility.

Wikipedia's not-for-profit 'business' model is entirely based on Web 2.0 technologies to generate its 'product' (the Wikipedia contents), to eliminate costs (through voluntary contributions) and to provide funding (through voluntary donations). This makes Wikipedia a particularly successful case of 'crowdsourcing' and 'crowd funding'.

Source: http://wikimediafoundation.org/wiki/Fundraising (accessed on 15 May 2012).

Exercises

1) Wikipedia is a not-for-profit organization. Should it be concerned with cost effectiveness and revenues? Why/why not?

2) Discuss the financial and strategic aspects of the following suggestion: 'Wikipedia should start accepting advertisements to boost its revenues.'

3) Discuss ways in which you, as a management accountant, might provide useful insights for Wikipedia's management. Reflect both on structural decisions (for example, the 'business model') and operational decisions.

Basic terms and concepts in information systems

You may have already studied an IS module and have an appreciation of the concepts covered here. The purpose of this section is to briefly introduce or revise terms commonly used in IS circles and used throughout the remainder of the chapter. The material here can be supplemented by an accounting information systems textbook such as Boczko (2007). Not many management accountants will become IS experts. However, even as mere IS user, a solid knowledge of basic terms and concepts is extremely helpful when working with IS experts and understanding how IS operate and how they may impact on management accounting.

Information systems components

We now briefly introduce some key terms used within the information systems realm. Any computerized IS is composed of hardware and software. Hardware is the physical equipment and software refers to the programs which run on the hardware. Nowadays, hardware ranges from large servers to hand-held devices such as smartphones/tablet computers. Software can be subdivided into system software and application software. The former controls hardware (Windows, UNIX, Linux, iOS), while the latter refers to programs (or applications) that need an operating system to run. Familiar applications are software for word processing, graphic design or accounting.

With advances to mobile hardware technologies in recent years, application software once confined to desktop computers is increasingly available to users in any time or place. For instance, SAP, the world's number one provider of enterprise resource planning systems launched various iPad applications recently, such as SAP Business Objects Mobile to access business intelligence reports and metrics, and SAP Payment Approvals to approve payments anywhere and anytime.[1] Applications such as these allow vast amounts of business information to be viewed portably. In addition to the increasing power of hardware and software, the advent of the Internet, wireless networks and mobile data communications means that information is available to managers (and management accountants) seamlessly, regardless of their location or the location of the business operations. From a management accounting point of view, components like hardware and software are less important than how the IS itself is designed and how data is stored. This is discussed next.

Information systems architecture

The term information systems architecture refers to typically formal definitions of how technology is used, how data is stored, how business processes are mapped, how data is connected and the functions of software within an organization. In larger organizations, architecture will likely be documented, including details such as:

- An inventory of all hardware and software, the function of each piece and interfaces between pieces

- A flow-diagram detailing the system or parts thereof

- What and where data is stored

- Networking and security features

- A maintenance plan for hardware and software up-grading.

From a management accounting perspective, the most important component of an organization's IS architecture is to understand how and where data is stored. As you learned in Chapter 1, a major concern of management accounting is providing decision-making information. Thus, in the current technological environment, management accountants need to have an appreciation of how they can transform vast quantities of captured data into intelligible and useful information, to support the creation of knowledge for decision-making. To undertake this role, an understanding of some key terms and concepts is useful.

Typically all organizational data is stored in some form of database. A database is a comprehensive set of data which is organized in a logical manner and can be used for several purposes. For example, a database of customers' details may be used to invoice customers as well as for marketing purposes. Databases typically reflect elements or processes of a business, such as customers, sales invoices, suppliers, inventories movements, cash received and product costs. A key aim of databases is to create relationships between tables (sets of data elements) which share common attributes, to avoid duplication of data. For example, a customer table may identify each customer using a unique customer code. This same table may store details such as the customer's name, address, email and phone. When an invoice is raised to a customer, only the customer code needs be stored and this can be related to the same code in the customer table – allowing the address information to be used in the invoice. Almost all business information systems will use a database structure of some form.

Even if a software solution includes many built-in reports, no software can ever provide management accountants with *all* information. Therefore, a common task of management accountants today is to use additional software tools to extract information from various databases. Knowledge of what data is stored, where it is stored (that is, the physical computer location) and how data is related is a must of this task. The architecture documents mentioned above may be a useful tool for management accountants in this regard, too.

Finally, data location and IS architecture may actually be beyond the control of some organizations, at least to an extent. In the emergent business model of cloud computing, analysed in the next section, the main IS components (hardware, software or both) are not located within or operated by the organization. These resources are located 'in the cloud' and are owned by an external party, who then provides them as a service to companies and individuals. Cloud computing changes key IT aspects and may have significant consequences on businesses and management accounting. For example, CIMA (2010) suggests cloud computing may allow substantial cost savings and create a more adaptive finance function, as the speed and scale of application development can be increased.

Data versus information versus knowledge

Data, information and knowledge are sometimes used as synonyms, but they actually refer to rather different concepts. **Data** are mere records of raw facts, without being organized or arranged to be meaningful for humans. **Information** is data organized or modified in a way to become understandable and usable, and for a particular purpose. For example, a management accounting system may contain millions of records (data), but such data only becomes information when it is organized and aggregated so that people can use it. By applying management accounting criteria, we obtain reports with usefully structured information. Examples are: costs of inputs, individually or aggregating them as materials, labour and overheads, or as variable and fixed; costs and customer value of organizational activities and processes (as emphasized by ABM – see Chapter 19); costs and profitability by customers or groups of customers; yearly, monthly or daily information, and even at a finer detail, and so on.

Having information is essential, but not sufficient. Information must be transformed into knowledge to guide managers towards the right decisions. Managers must draw on structured information from the management accounting system, as well as from other formal and informal information sources, to develop in-depth knowledge about markets, clients, products, production and business processes, and many other areas. Relevant, accurate and up-to-date knowledge – not just information – is increasingly important for competitive advantage, in today's 'knowledge economy.'

To achieve success in a 'knowledge economy', valuable knowledge has to be disseminated across the organization or even across inter-organizational networks, rather than concentrated in a single individual or location. So, organizational knowledge and learning are increasingly important concerns. Knowledge management systems have been developed during the last few decades to support the creation, dissemination and management of organizational knowledge. In recent years, Web 2.0 technologies have been key to achieving this objective in novel ways.

What is the relevance of the rising importance of organizational knowledge to management accounting and control? As Nixon and Burns (2005, p. 264) note, 'knowledge management and control of Intellectual Capital are very different from financial management and control of tangible assets'. This means that management accountants must embrace new concerns, new foci of attention, new theoretical frameworks and new types of IS, to continue providing value to their organizations. As Nixon and Burns (2005) further note, intellectual capital and knowledge are less controllable than financial and tangible assets – and lack of control is quite the opposite of the traditional objectives of management accounting and control (see Elias and Wright, 2006).

The 'big data' concept

In recent years the concept of 'big data' has emerged in the field of information systems. **Big data** is data beyond the processing capacity of conventional systems. Its importance lies in the valuable patterns and information hidden in huge, unstructured data increasingly available. Today's society produces unprecedented volumes of data with multiple origins, such as social media sites, pictures, videos, banking transactions, purchase transaction records or financial markets – potentially generating continuous streams of data. The challenge lies in exploring this raw data in its totality – without making preliminary synthesis or aggregations to reduce the volume to be analysed, always at the cost of some content loss (IBM, 2012).

IBM (2012) provides a brief description of the three Vs characterizing big data: volume, velocity and variety. Big data can represent terabytes or even petabytes (millions of gigabytes) of information, a huge *volume* that creates analytical challenges. Big data high *velocity* means that analysis often cannot be periodic, running predetermined reports as traditionally done, and may even have to be online. For example, to detect fraud, credit card or insurance companies need to permanently analyse incoming data on transactions or claims to detect and deter fraud attempts in a timely way. Wall Street and Dow Jones daily produce thousands of documents, requiring finance professionals to use new ways to quickly analyse this big data and continually detect and anticipate opportunities and risks. Finally, big data has high *variety*. It includes structured and unstructured data, such as text (ranging from 'traditional' documents to posts in social media sites or tweets), audio, video and users' mouse clicks. Traditional relational databases, described above, cannot process such varied data. Finally, given the significant potential value from exploring big data (IBM, 2010a), a fourth 'V' (for *value*) could be added to characterize big data, in addition to the three Vs mentioned above.

Exhibit 21.1 describes the continuous growth in the volume and variety of potentially available data and relates them with different types of information systems analysed in this chapter. Enterprise resource planning systems already dealt with and created huge amounts of data, when compared to the pre-ERP stage. Customer relationship management (CRM) systems further expanded available

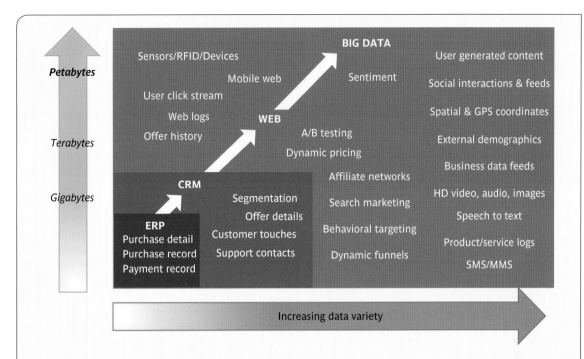

Exhibit 21.1: The growth of data volume and variety: from ERPs to Big Data

Source: adapted from http://hortonworks.com/blog/7-key-drivers-for-the-big-data-market/ (accessed on 6 July 2012).

data by collecting detailed information regarding customers. Big data includes all that data and much more, as the numerous examples of data sources make clear.

The analytical approach and tools to explore big data is different from analysing conventional data. This is a significant change when compared to the kind of analyses that management accountants are used to. However, big data has potentially significant financial repercussions that are relevant for management accounting. For example, IBM's (2010a) survey highlights the fact that analytics is a key value driver. When compared with respondents from lower-performing firms, respondents from top-performing firms had a greater usage of analytics to guide future strategies. They also had a stronger belief that their use of business information and analytics differentiated them from competition. IBM's survey also confirmed that the finance area clearly leads the tendency to apply analytics. So, management accountants' traditionally strong analytical skills may be leveraged to explore this new driver of value. In addition, suitable software and hardware are increasingly less restricted to organizations with big budgets; cloud computing, analysed in the next section, is a major facilitator of this expansion. So, increasing numbers of management accountants will have the opportunity – or be required – to explore big data in their organizations.

Dilemmas and solutions in information systems

Information systems and the organization: alignment and adaptation

The start of the design on an IS is mostly a managerial task, not a technical one. The organization and its IS must be aligned, so that these can support organizational members effectively. Failure in achieving this alignment will lead to the development of information systems which are irrelevant (in the 'less bad' case scenario) or indeed damaging for the organization. Organizational alignment is required in all types of information systems; however, it is a particularly crucial issue in large, company-wide enterprise resource planning (ERP) systems, discussed below.

Traditionally, in the 1970s and 1980s, organizations tended to develop their own information systems internally or to hire a software vendor to write 'bespoke software', designed specifically for that organization. These development approaches have relatively few external constraints in designing information systems to fit the existing organization (with regard to, for example, its structure, business model, policies or techniques) or to design these systems to promote desired organizational changes. However, organizations are increasingly adopting commercially available software packages, such as enterprise solutions from SAP and Oracle, rather than developing them themselves. This trend was fuelled by these commercial solutions becoming increasingly sophisticated, flexible and relatively affordable, as well as the difficulty and costs for an individual company to keep up within the rapidly changing software industry. While resorting to commercially available software is now a widespread option, there is also a downside: its adopters are inevitably confronted with software 'designed to fit everyone but not actually fitting anyone', as often described among the IT community. That is why commercial packages are more suitable when the processes and requirements of the company are reasonably standard. For example, an organization's requirements in the financial accounting area are probably quite common to other companies and can be reasonably satisfied by commercial software packages. Requirements for management accounting may be more company-specific if detailed information is requested for specific business processes or characteristics, or even for individual-level preferences about information for decision making and control. At the other extreme, very specific, even unique operational and business characteristics may not be adequately dealt with by standard commercial packages – although this is increasingly less the case with today's sophisticated and flexible solutions.

Implementing a commercially available software package always involves its configuration to meet organizational requirements. Configuration involves selecting among the alternatives already included in the software package. However, configuration alternatives are often insufficient to achieve alignment between the software and the organization. In those cases, implementation requires multiple trade-offs between:

- *customizing the software*, by changing the software package code to fit the organization, and

- *adapting the organization* to fit the built-in choices of the software package.

Customizing the generic package requires highly skilled programmers; it is typically very costly and may raise difficulties in future software upgrades. Organizations that customize their ERP system to extreme levels risk that the vendor stops supporting them (O'Mahony and Doran, 2008). So, a decision to customize software should be carefully justified, making clear that the advantages exceed costs and risks.

Customizing the software and adapting the organization are neither absolute nor mutually exclusive options and they can be used selectively. A company is likely to accept changing an existing organizational practice to better fit the software and save IT efforts, provided that such practice does not create a competitive advantage and can be changed relatively easily. However, if an existing practice is important for success but the standard software solution does not allow it, the company is likely to change the software (that is, customize it) in order to support that practice. The best solution often involves mutual adaptations – of both the organization and the software – to facilitate alignment and better outcomes.

Although configuration is less profound than customization, it may still be a substantial challenge. As you will learn next, ERP systems offer thousands of alternative configuration options to flexibly meet clients' requirements. Making those choices is a challenging task, given the size and complexity of ERPs (some have thousands of tables) and initial options are sometimes nearly irreversible. Effective customization requires a combination of a deep knowledge of the software package and of the organization, typically requiring multidisciplinary teams where management accountants may have an important role to play.

Within traditional management accounting areas, such as product costing and profitability analysis, the need to create unique features requiring customization is typically less significant than in core business areas. On the contrary, unique production and sales processes are more likely to constitute distinctive competitive advantages and therefore to justify customization efforts. So, management accounting systems must be able to meet the specific needs of the operational areas and, in particular, must be flexible to adapt as operational areas change, in order to continue to capture and structure operational data to support reporting, analysis, decision making and knowledge creation.

Systems (de)coupling

Systems (including information systems) can be more or less connected, depending on how they exchange their inputs and outputs, either directly or through additional interfacing systems. The degree of **systems (de)coupling** depends on the interdependence between these systems: that is, on the extent that changes in one system affect the state of the other. For example, an accounting system is firmly coupled with the sales system if transactions entered by sales staff also produce accounting postings directly and immediately. On the other hand, if accountants need to manually post sales invoices in the accounting system, then the two systems are clearly decoupled. An intermediate degree of coupling could consist in, for example, an accountant reviewing sales transactions before they create postings in accounting; here, the reviewing process acts as a buffer between the two systems.

In the above example of strongly coupled systems, the dependency of the accounting system on the sales system requires close communication between the two, and sales staff must be aware of the accounting consequences of their activities. For example, 'expedite' workarounds by sales staff to solve particular invoicing problems (such as omitting or using a wrong product reference because the correct one was not readily available) may create serious problems for accountants and management accountants – for example, in inventory control and valuation or in sales profitability analysis. To prevent such problems, the company should provide training to increase awareness of accounting issues among sales staff. Should this approach not solve the problem, the company may consider making the two systems less coupled, for example, by adding verification buffers as the one described above (a manual reviewing process by an accountant). However, keep in mind that 'building-in' quality (doing things right at the first time) is typically preferable to inspecting later to look for defects, as you learned in Chapter 20.

The notion of coupling (or decoupling) among systems is fundamental to understanding the various types of information systems discussed next, in particular concerning the coupling between management accounting systems and other systems. In addition, the degree of coupling should be used to define policies concerned with disseminating accounting awareness among non-accounting staff and to identify potential roles for management accountants.

Types of information systems

This section analyses some types of information systems relevant to management accounting. Within the overall information systems architecture, a crucial decision concerns the scope and the interconnectedness of the various components of the information systems. Following the previous discussion of (de)coupling, you will start by analysing the two extremes of stand-alone systems and integrated systems. Then, we discuss spreadsheets, given their popularity in management accounting, and best-of-breed (BoB) systems, focusing on their role in accounting and how these solutions fit within the general IS architecture.

Stand-alone systems

A **stand-alone system** is largely decoupled from other organizational systems. A stand-alone financial accounting system might require, for example, the manual entry of sales invoice information from a separate sales system. Within the management accounting area, a stand-alone system involves gathering and typing information from different data sources manually. These sources may be highly diversified, ranging from financial accounting, production and human resources systems, to electricity meters measuring consumption of individual machines or plant sections. These low value-added activities take substantial amounts of time and are error prone, compromising more value-added activities such as data analysis and interpretation.

A stand-alone management accounting system can be based on several types of systems, such as specialized 'best-of-breed' systems or such general-purpose solutions as Microsoft Excel – see the section below for an analysis of both systems types. The decisive characteristic is to be largely decoupled from the remaining systems. Stand-alone systems were most common in the past, owing to the lack of alternative solutions with a larger scope and integration or to local IT initiatives, focused on solving a particular problem but without integration concerns. Stand-alone systems have been gradually replaced by integrated systems or have themselves developed the capability to integrate better with other systems. Nowadays, stand-alone systems are increasingly limited to smaller and less complex organizations – although here the shift towards integration is also felt, in particular towards ERPs.

Integrated enterprise systems

The late 1980s and the 1990s witnessed the rise of integrated systems, widely known as **enterprise resource planning (ERP) systems**. In its original sense, an integrated system aims to be *the* single system satisfying all information needs within an organization. They are the opposite of stand-alone systems. In their purest form, integrated systems go beyond the idea of having coupled (but different) systems. In an integrated system architecture, only one large system exists, made up of highly coupled subsystems specialized in particular functions. In recent years, ERPs' vendors have increasingly downplayed the requirement to provide the single system; instead, they are now more concerned with making the ERP the major backbone of the organizational IS, to which other systems (such as best-of-breed systems) can connect. For simplification, however, we retain for now the original vision of making the ERP the only IS. Enterprise resource planning systems are made of modules, each one supporting particular business processes and functions. These modules tightly integrate data and processes within a single system. Exhibit 21.2 describes, in a simplified way, the integrated functioning of financial accounting in SAP. You can see how postings in the general ledger are integrated with various operational, financial and business processes, involving internal departments (such as human resources and warehouses) and external organizations such as suppliers, customers and banks.

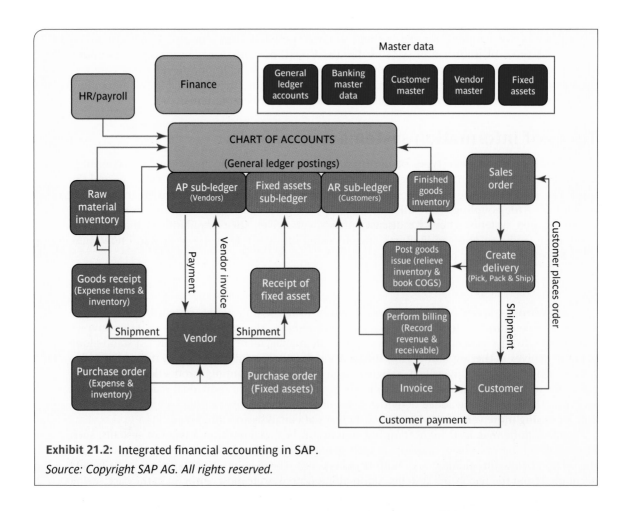

Exhibit 21.2: Integrated financial accounting in SAP.

Source: Copyright SAP AG. All rights reserved.

Integration, a core concept in ERPs, promotes greater and faster sharing and visibility of information and knowledge. ERPs address the long-standing problem of 'information silos' at functional, geographical and individual levels. ERPs also promote (but require) single data entry and a common database, to eliminate duplicated data and ensure consistency. Finally, ERP vendors seek to incorporate 'best practices' within their ERP products. Therefore, they promise improvements to those clients who adapt their business processes to fit the practices embedded in ERP packages – keeping in mind the ERP configuration and customization possibilities to achieve organization–IS alignment, discussed above.

The Germany-based vendor SAP has long been the ERP market leader, particularly among the largest companies (Panorama, 2011), and most empirical research on ERPs analyses SAP implementations. So, the following discussion draws on examples from SAP, although other ERP vendors, such as Oracle or Microsoft, should also be mentioned.

ERP systems: From large to small and medium companies

Enterprise resource planning systems first became popular among the largest companies. In the market segment of large companies, the existence of ERPs is almost a given, nowadays. They then spread to medium-sized and small-sized enterprises (SMEs). This expansion took into account smaller firms' business needs (typically less complex) and their limited financial capacity to support ERP implementation costs (traditionally very high). ERP vendors developed a range of products with varying levels of functionalities. For example, SAP offers three increasingly sophisticated ERPs for SMEs: SAP Business One; SAP Business ByDesign and SAP Business All-in-One, emphasizing faster and less costly implementation (for instance, an ERP up and running in 2–16 weeks, or even three days with a starter package).[2] In turn, other vendors traditionally focusing on SMEs or in other types of solutions (for example, Microsoft) have greatly enlarged their business management solutions, increasing their scope and functionalities, and now offer ERPs for both small and large companies. As a result, ERPs have also become ubiquitous in medium-sized companies and even in smaller companies above a certain size.

Given the remarkable evolution in information systems directed towards SMEs, nowadays even small businesses can obtain relatively sophisticated and detailed information from their information systems – including that in the management accounting area. Having more data in their information systems reduces a traditional obstacle for management accounting analysis: lack of data. However, the availability of raw data is not sufficient per se for the production, dissemination and usage of relevant information and knowledge (see the previous section). Therefore, the intervention of management accountants to guide and actually achieve this crucial evolution is essential.

ERPs: adapting to different industries and extending beyond the organization

Enterprise resource planning systems vendors have developed specific industry solutions. SAP offers dozens of industry packages, such as discrete industries (for example, car manufacturers), process industries (for example, chemicals or paper), consumer industries (for example, retail), financial services (for example, banks) and public services (for example, health care).[3]

Industry-specific packages coexist with cross-industry applications, dealing with processes such as customer relationship management (CRM), supplier relationship management (SRM) and supply chain management (SCM). The ERP system evolved from intra-organizational integration to inter-organizational integration, taking advantage of Internet development. Exhibit 21.3 analyses the distribution industry and depicts potential advantages of linking a distributor with its suppliers and with its customers and retailers, from a value-chain perspective. Linkages with suppliers improve procurement efficiency and cost savings. In turn, linkages with customers and retailers improve forecasting and planning, which optimizes inventory and meets demand and supply variations. In addition, better customer service and reliability promotes loyalty and quicker payments from customers, reducing days sales outstanding (DSO) and improving cash flow.

Enterprise resource planning systems' scope have stretched across company boundaries. They have created an 'extended enterprise', including both intranets (connecting users) and extranets (connecting organizations). Linking ERPs from suppliers and customers allows integrating purchasing, sales and financial processes across the supply chain. Inter-organizational exchanges of

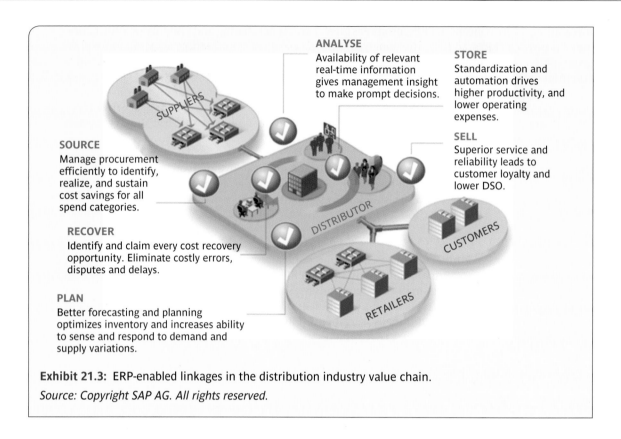

ANALYSE
Availability of relevant real-time information gives management insight to make prompt decisions.

STORE
Standardization and automation drives higher productivity, and lower operating expenses.

SOURCE
Manage procurement efficiently to identify, realize, and sustain cost savings for all spend categories.

SELL
Superior service and reliability leads to customer loyalty and lower DSO.

RECOVER
Identify and claim every cost recovery opportunity. Eliminate costly errors, disputes and delays.

PLAN
Better forecasting and planning optimizes inventory and increases ability to sense and respond to demand and supply variations.

Exhibit 21.3: ERP-enabled linkages in the distribution industry value chain.

Source: Copyright SAP AG. All rights reserved.

information support the comprehensive planning of the company's production activities and of the entire supply chain. They allow deeper financial analysis and control of relations within the supply chain. ERPs leverage the capabilities from on-line banking. *Management Accounting in Practice 21.4* and *21.5* illustrate this evolution. And as ERPs' scope widens and includes more and more externally provided information, they further contribute to overcoming the typical limitation's of lack of data.

21.4: Management Accounting in Practice

ERPs opening up doors – outside the company

The consumer products giant Procter & Gamble (P&G) is further strengthening its ties with suppliers and consumers in its digital revolution. For many years, P&G has been establishing electronic connections with retailers. This has allowed them to, for example, streamline financial relations and monitor stocks, hence preventing out-of-stocks. P&G's CEO, Robert McDonald, explains that P&G is now adopting a GDSN (global data synchronization network), a standardized data warehouse to do commerce with retailers 'in a totally automated way, with no human intervention'. It has been estimated that typically 70 per cent of orders have errors; however, with a GDSN, errors are virtually eliminated. In transport and logistics, an enhanced operational program, 'Control Tower', monitors all transportation, reducing 'deadhead' movement (when trucks are empty or not optimally loaded) by about 15 per cent, reducing costs and carbon monoxide. A similar interface for distributors, 'Distributor Connect', improves service and reduces inventory across the supply chain.

Leveraging on Web 2.0 to explore consumer feedback, P&G developed 'Consumer pulse' to scan and categorize comments across the Internet (for example, in blogs) and deliver the analysis to the relevant employee. This allows for real-time reaction, preventing that problems disseminated through the Internet spin out of control.

The integration of manufacturing and accounting systems has tremendous potential. P&G's CEO explains:

We're not there yet, but we envision a system where I could literally see, on my laptop, any product at any moment as it goes through the manufacturing line of any one of our plants. And what I'd love to be able to do is see the costs of that product at the same time. It's challenging because accounting systems aren't designed today for operations – they tend to look backward – but we're working on integrating our operational system with the financial system to move in that direction.

Source: McKinsey (2011).

Exercises

1) Discuss the kind of problems resulting from the order errors which are now avoided by the GDSN (consider both financial and non-financial perspectives).

2) Relate the criticism that 'accounting systems (...) tend to look backward' with the philosophy underlying the 'Beyond budgeting' movement (Chapter 10). Discuss how IS integration can improve the value provided by management accounting.

21.5: Management Accounting in Practice

ERPs opening up doors – inside the company

Companies can also benefit by using ERPs to open up their corporate doors and allow visibility into their own, internal processes. For instance, the global express package delivery company UPS allows customers to track their parcels along their way to the final destination, by introducing a reference in the company website.

Canon Europe, a subsidiary of Canon Inc. of Japan, a leading provider of imaging solutions such as photographic equipment, printers and scanners, made a similar move with regard to their internal financial processes related with suppliers. A self-service portal, developed by the consultancy firm Accenture, grants suppliers access to Canon's invoicing and payment activities. Each supplier can easily and independently access daily updated information to control and monitor the status of its invoices (Accenture, 2010). This transparency facilitates and strengthens the relationship with suppliers, saves costs by avoiding no value-added information requests and avoids potential processing errors – whose later correction is a costly and no value-added activity (see Chapter 19).

Source: Accenture (2010).

Exercises

1) Discuss whether providing information about internal processes to external entities, such as suppliers, may create problems to an organization.

2) Discuss how such openness may impact on corporate ethics.

Be aware that complaints about lack of information (including for management accounting) often miss the point. Common myths are that managers complain about a lack of information and suggest that more information would allow them to make better decisions. However, with ERPs, managers often have the opposite complaint: information overload and difficulty in locating, structuring and exploring relevant information. Reports from ERPs, especially with no or little customization, are often several pages long, where relevant information becomes lost among massive amounts of irrelevant information. Do not forget that information is data processed to suit a particular purpose. Poorly parameterized and/or customized ERPs often fail in structuring, aggregating or disaggregating, filtering and calculating data to actually produce useful information and, hence, support the production of knowledge.

Finally, remember that ERPs encompass multiple functional areas. So, ERPs are *not* accounting solutions – although there may be important influences between ERPs and management accounting. In addition, because ERPs are not focused in any particular area (for example, management accounting or business intelligence), they have been traditionally accused of being 'too generic' and limited in making more sophisticated or flexible analyses. This traditional limitation has been addressed by best-of-breed solutions (software specialized in particular areas). You will explore best-of-breed solutions below. Before that, we discuss what are sometimes viewed as victims of ERP systems: spreadsheets.

Spreadsheets: a pervading presence in management accounting

Spreadsheets are widely disseminated in organizations, with Microsoft Excel dominating the spreadsheet market (Webmasterpro.de, 2010). In everyday language, many people refer to a spreadsheet as 'Excel'. The management accounting area is no exception. Typical options in training and education leave little doubt about spreadsheets and Excel's popularity. For example, almost all CIMA courses on IT skills planned for 2012 involve Excel[4] and this book draws on Excel to illustrate various management accounting techniques.

However, critics argue that spreadsheets are no longer the best option for management accounting. Spreadsheets may even be a problem in organizations, rather than a solution. Why?

Microsoft Excel is a generic-purpose application and, basically, it is a stand-alone solution. Its flexibility and intuitive interface meet the needs of a wide variety of users, ranging from small children to managers. An average, non-expert user can develop or modify solutions in the Excel software installed in his/her own computer. Excel's flexible and autonomous development and usage are often considered an advantage. But it is also often considered a problem. Diverse solutions, locally developed and used by individuals or particular areas, often coexist within one organization and lead to a 'Babel Tower'. Different local languages and concepts, underlying local Excel-based solutions, make communication and comparisons across the organization difficult, misleading or even impossible (see the case study problem at the end of the chapter).

In management accounting, there is a particular risk that the same concept is given different names or is calculated in different ways, using different assumptions. For instance, the basic distinction between variable and fixed costs depends on the time frame (remember that in the long term all costs tend to be variable), and costs may be fixed with regard to produced quantities but not sold quantities, or vice versa. Suppose that two management accountants at different plants of the same company independently developed Excel-based reports, and that they enter data either manually or through interfaces also independently developed. There is a significant risk that figures in the two reports will end up by reflecting different criteria and assumptions. In addition, reports often omit such detailed (but important) assumptions. So, the final information may be misunderstood by people other than the spreadsheet producer. This inconsistency problem emerges as information travels in time (comparisons between different periods), space (comparisons between different organizational units, such as subsidiaries or plants) and systems (transferred across different systems). A typical difficulty, related to spreadsheets' non-integrated nature, emerges when transferring information from spreadsheets developed in plants or subsidiaries to consolidation solutions at headquarters: often, only the final figures are transferred. Visibility over local sites by headquarters is substantially reduced, in particular with regard to the assumptions and the ways to calculate the transferred figures. IBM (2010b, p. 4) points out: 'It's often difficult to understand or re-create the logic of the spreadsheet's creator.'

To support integrated solutions, ERP vendors emphasize the limitations of spreadsheets and, in general, of non-integrated IT architectures. In fact, the above problems are typical of non-integrated solutions in general, not of spreadsheets specifically; however, they are typical of many spreadsheet-based solutions widespread in organizations. The management accounting area is no exception. For instance, SAP presents its products for SMEs as fit for companies that 'have outgrown packaged accounting-only software and need to replace multiple, non-integrated applications' or that 'need to replace point solutions, manual processes, and *spreadsheets*'[5] (emphasis added). And companies around the world have indeed been moving towards increasingly integrated systems.

For educational purposes, the almost universal access to spreadsheets, unlike integrated systems, makes spreadsheets an adequate technological support to illustrate concepts and techniques such as management accounting ones. Spreadsheets are still a common solution in organizations – despite their limitations. IBM (2010b, p. 3) describes: 'Organizations of every size use spreadsheets for core financial functions such as strategic planning, financial reporting and consolidation.' Why? IBM answers: 'Despite the known risks, spreadsheets are here to stay and for good reason. They provide the control or lack of dependence from IT and are familiar, flexible and accessible throughout the organization.' Excel may still prevail in emerging areas where more sophisticated solutions have not been disseminated, or even developed, yet. In a survey on sustainability performance management, 66 per cent of respondents use Excel for data collection and 57 per cent for analysis (Accenture, 2009). The Chartered Institute of Management (CIMA, 2011a, p. 13) criticizes Excel-based processes as 'manual, inefficient and prone to data quality issues', in particular because integrated systems have already included these functionalities. In such situations, the flexibility and popularity of Excel promoted its usage as an immediate, quick-fix solution – although a short-term and temporary one.

Excel may also still remain adequate for relatively simple issues. An important issue does not necessarily require a complex system. One such example is CIMA's (2008) discussion on the role of information capture and usage in benefiting from management innovations. Even though the issue is important, CIMA acknowledged that, in less complex cases, Excel could provide an adequate solution. Finally, spreadsheets may continue to be used outside the globally designed IT architecture, when the replacing integrated systems fail to satisfy users. In those cases, users often turn back to their previous tools and practices, and Excel may continue to be used, even if in an 'unofficial' way. These outcomes are not uncommon and are examples of unsuccessful change processes, such as the ones you will read about in the next chapter.

Major business software vendors recognize this prevalence and popularity. Accordingly, they often announce their products' integration with Excel as a major selling point, developing strong interfacing capabilities (data import and export) and/or adopt the well-known, user-friendly Excel user interface. Rather than enemies, spreadsheets become partners or, at least, sources of inspiration. IBM, as a solution provider, again puts it thus: 'Especially at a time of budget belt-tightening, flexible and cost-efficient performance management can be achieved by leveraging the best of your existing spreadsheet investment with an integrated, full-featured planning, budgeting and forecasting solution' (IBM, 2010b, p. 3). These are important trends not only in ERP systems, but also in best-of-breed solutions, analysed next.

Best-of-breed (BoB) systems

Best-of-breed (BoB) systems are specialized in a particular area, attempting to offer the best possible solution in that field. There are BoB systems in virtually all areas, including ABC, BSC, consolidation, budgeting and other accounting techniques. They are promoted as offering more sophisticated solutions than ERP packages which, in their efforts to cover many or even all information needs, may end up by not offering the best possible solutions in particular areas.

Deciding between acquiring a BoB solution and an additional module of an already existing integrated system depends on a company's specific needs. The main potential advantage of BoB solutions is richer functionality, based on their exclusive focus on a specific area. However, each organization should decide whether they address relevant issues or even provide competitive advantages in its particular case. For example, a manufacturer with very high indirect costs may benefit greatly from a highly sophisticated activity-based costing BoB system; otherwise, it may settle for a more basic – and cheaper – solution, such as one provided by an additional module from its ERP vendor. In general, adopting BoB solutions makes much more sense for critical, high value-added areas, when compared with non-core areas. In addition, each organization should evaluate whether it can fully implement and explore the additional functionalities – many organizations cannot. Sophisticated BoB solutions risk having many 'bells and whistles' that end up unexplored. Also, solutions by integrated systems increasingly offer richer functionalities, reducing the gap towards BoB solutions. BoB solutions may also evolve faster to meet quickly changing requirements or emerging technologies. Rewriting a smaller piece of software (the BoB solution) is typically quicker than rewriting a larger one (entire integrated systems). However, integrated systems have also reduced the gap in this regard. Finally, BoB solutions may create less dependency by the client on the IS vendors, since the narrower scope of a BoB system makes shifting to a new vendor less difficult.

However, BoB solutions also have disadvantages when compared with integrated systems. The most typical disadvantage is a greater difficulty in interfaces and data sharing. For efficiency, timeliness and reliability, BoB solutions should be integrated with other systems – typically, the integrated system dealing with most or even all remaining areas. The difficulty of creating these interfaces and sharing data has traditionally been a major disadvantage of BoB solutions, when compared with the almost seamless integration between the entire ERP and particular additional modules by the same vendor. Finally, an IT architecture relying on BoB solutions is also more prone to data duplication problems.

Increased co-operation between ERP and BoB vendors has reduced these problems. Many BoB vendors have even become certified partners of ERP vendors, signalling easier interfacing and integration. In addition, as already mentioned, in recent years ERPs are increasingly presented as a major backbone to which other systems can connect – rather than being the single solution. This evolution has created an interesting paradox: while this interfacing characteristic of ERPs is typically considered an advantage of these solutions, this shift in ERP architecture has indeed facilitated the adoption of BoB solutions in very specialized areas.

Finally, BoB solutions may also imply higher costs. Although the entire package of an integrated system is usually quite expensive, implementing a BoB solution is typically more expensive than implementing an additional module to an ERP system. Increased costs include licences and personnel, through the additional need to create interfaces, as well as training and ongoing maintenance of the new BoB solution, which may also involve having to manage an additional relationship with a new vendor.

Cloud computing and impacts for management accountants

Fundamentals of cloud computing

Traditionally, companies installed software in their own servers. This physical hosting, within the company's domain, occurred regardless of having acquired the software (typically in less expensive products) or licensed it (for example, in ERPs). However, recent years have seen the emergence of a new business model: cloud computing.

Cloud computing may encompass software, hardware or both. This business model is based on the technology of virtualization, already available for a number of years. Regarding software, it allows delivering 'Software as a Service' (SaaS), rather than a product. Software is located in remote servers, typically in a location unknown to the end-user and owned by a third-party provider – either a completely external entity or, in the case of large groups, the group IT provider. The provider then makes the software available over the Internet. Other IT resources such as storage or processors can also be obtained as a service. Instead of acquiring additional capacity, clients can resort to remote servers and processors owned by cloud providers. Resorting to 'the cloud' may make sense in meeting both structural and, in particular, occasional resource needs. A clear example concerns processing capacity: most of it is traditionally wasted, since it is used at very low levels outside a few peak periods. Cloud computing relies on a client–server architecture, which means the data processing and storage occurs in a server (a large powerful computer) and the clients (such as desktop computers, notebooks or hand-held devices) connect to the server. There are more and more services available through cloud computing. We will now focus on software. You may already be using Google Docs, which enables access to basic word-processing and spreadsheets through any web connection. Google Docs dispenses with having your own software in your machine – and it is free. If you use products such as Google Docs, iCloud, Facebook and Twitter, then you are using cloud computing. Simple business solutions, such as payroll solutions, email or videoconferencing, are increasingly being adopted by companies, in particular small and medium-sized ones. Even large software solutions, such as ERPs, are now available through cloud computing. For example, for small and medium-sized companies, SAP offers SAP Business ByDesign (delivered exclusively on-demand as SaaS); other solutions targeted for SME also offer a remote hosting option for a monthly payment.[6] But cloud computing is experiencing wide adoption by large companies as well. Next, we analyse several advantages and disadvantages of cloud computing, including those from a financial perspective. Then, we discuss particular impacts for the finance function.

Advantages and disadvantages of cloud computing

With cloud computing, IT costs change substantially. Some resources may even be free, such as Google Docs which we described earlier. In other cases, resources are available for a monthly payment, either as a subscription or on a pay-as-you-go basis. Information technology costs behaviour changes fundamentally. Fixed costs become variable, particularly in the case of storage and processing resources, when payments depend on actual consumption. Up-front costs are reduced substantially: companies shift from capital expenditure (when buying the resources) to operational expenditure (the monthly payments). Cost reduction is the typical initial motivation for moving from an in-premises approach to cloud computing – although it is difficult to accurately calculate savings given the very different nature of the two approaches and the associated costs.

Second, IT maintenance and support issues are reduced. Accounting software in particular requires frequent updates due to regulatory changes. With cloud computing, updates are implemented by the cloud provider, dispensing with manual updates by each client and allowing it to provide all users and divisions with the latest versions. With fewer IT needs, additional cost reductions are possible.

Third, agility can be greatly improved. Deploying new solutions and changing existing ones becomes easier and faster. Local and central teams work with data shared across the organization and with the same system, increasing data reliability and avoiding time-consuming and difficult activities to verify and harmonize data from different sources. Employees can use a web browser anywhere to access information, making it more timely and valuable. Fourth, a cloud-based approach is highly scalable, allowing to better match the IS size, complexity and investment to evolving company needs.

The most fundamental advantage of cloud computing may be beyond direct cost savings. The main gains may come from its more flexible approach – but to whose financial value is even more difficult to estimate. New companies, with no or little IT infrastructure and resources and no software licences already paid, must seriously consider cloud computing, since they may avoid substantial investments in those items and they may build all their business on that basis from the start. Cloud computing should also be seriously considered by companies pursuing flexible business models, in particular through outsourcing business processes, or companies having very variable needs in IT resources.

A major disadvantage of cloud computing is security, including data protection, privacy and reliability, related to dependency on the service supplier. Risks emerge because resources, including valuable and sensitive business information, are located outside the company premises. However, concerns have been gradually diminishing, as more and more companies successfully migrate to cloud computing, increasing the confidence of the business and IT community in this business model. Another major obstacle concerns the legal issues involved in software licensing. Suppose that a customer has a licence for a software package installed in its servers. This licence may no longer be valid if this software is relocated to a public cloud provider. The cloud provider may need to negotiate licensing with the software vendor, increasing the final cost – particularly should the software be used by that customer alone, without spreading the cost among several customers.

A financial perspective on the cloud and cloud accounting

Above, you read of cloud computing benefits to be considered by management accountants, related to reduced or more flexible IT costs and the value-creation potential to be gained from greater flexibility and new forms of making business. In addition, there are particular advantages for the finance function, as highlighted by recent CIMA reports on cloud accounting (CIMA, 2010, 2011b, 2011c).

Cloud accounting, through cloud-based accounting solutions, enhances the dissemination of financial information, which can be made accessible by simply providing appropriate links to common data. Consolidation and the development of a central financial view of the organization greatly benefit from consistent data and systems and from cloud-enabled, collaborative work. These traditional challenges for large, diversified organizations were often addressed by adopting large and expensive ERPs, hosted within the organization. With cloud computing, these benefits become easier to achieve and at a lower cost. As CIMA (2010) concluded, cloud computing may enable not only substantial cost savings, but also create a more adaptive finance function.

Accountants should have at least a basic technical knowledge about the cloud. Accountants are especially sensitive to data protection, privacy and reliability issues and, additionally, may not grasp the cloud technical architecture well enough to understand and manage the risks involved. Greater knowledge will also help accountants to better evaluate cloud projects by adapting traditional models (such as TCO – total cost of ownership – and ROI – return on investment), considering the difficulty of estimating potential gains. Finally, this knowledge will also guide accountants to fully explore the radical opportunities opened up by cloud computing (CIMA, 2011b, 2011c).

Roles of management accountants in a changing information systems context

Profound developments in IT and IS have changed, and are expected to continue changing, the roles of management accountants. Some traditional activities have been eliminated owing to IS automation and integration, such as gathering data from different sources and then entering this data in management accounting systems, or creating and maintaining user-developed spreadsheets to perform cost calculations, budgeting and variance analysis. In addition, Caglio (2003) noted a bi-directional phenomenon of **hybridization** between accountants and IS and line staff, with professionals from each group assuming activities traditionally in the domain of the others. And research indicates that information systems such as ERPs are frequently promoters and facilitators (though not necessarily drivers) of these trends (Scapens and Jazayeri, 2003).

These developments in management accountants' roles shape this section. First, it analyses the transfer of traditional roles of management accountants to IS or to other professional groups. Second, it analyses an increased focus on more value-added accounting activities. Third, it analyses the enlargement of management accountants' roles into IT-related activities. Here, you will find some traditional accounting activities involved in IS design and maintenance and which are likely to be performed by management accountants.

Activities taken away from management accountants

Some activities traditionally performed by management accountants have been taken away from them for two major reasons: information systems and other professional groups from the managerial or IT area. Researchers such as Caglio (2003), Scapens and Jazayeri (2003) and Burns and Baldvinsdottir (2005) have noted these trends. Information systems have taken over an increasing number of activities whose nature allows automated performance. Tasks like calculations or manually gathering data from different sources have been largely taken over by IS. Spreadsheets had an immediate tremendous effect in calculation activities, and later also in data gathering, as their capacity to interface with other systems increased, transferring data in both directions. Later, ERPs (and other types of IS with integration capacities) eliminated many data-gathering activities, allowing data to flow seamlessly across functional and geographical areas.

Other professional groups are the second major reason. Some management accounting activities are increasingly carried out by line and IT staff – a trend strongly related to, and enabled by, advances in IS. Much accounting knowledge has become decentred across the organization. Some IT managers have acquired accounting skills to allow them to set up and maintain accounting IS – a competing trend with management accountants taking those roles, as you will see below. In addition, line managers are increasingly able to control their own budgets, analyse the variances automatically calculated by the IS and make forecasts, without having to rely on management accountants. These line managers become 'hybrid accountants'[7], perceiving these traditionally management accounting activities as managerial tasks (Caglio, 2003; Scapens and Jazayeri, 2003).

For this hybridization of management accounting, sophisticated management control solutions are crucial. They enable a quick and reliable collection of large amounts of information, and to calculate and analyse key performance indicators. Exhibit 21.4 provides a screenshot of a dashboard of such a solution, SAP BusinessObjects, calculating variances of key performance indicators and drawing graphics to facilitate analyses, according to criteria defined by the user.

While these trends are sometimes seen as a threat to the management accounting profession, they can also present advantages. Transactional activities taken over by IS were largely low value added. Although this transfer caused some professionals to be made redundant, it also allowed others to dedicate spared time to more value-added activities and taking more demanding roles. The decentring of management accounting to non-accountants has also opened up new possibilities for management accountants. We now analyse these exciting possibilities.

New value-added activities for management accountants

As IS offered more sophisticated capacities and freed up management accountants' time, many changed from typical 'bean-counter' activities to more value-added roles. Many chapters throughout this book have evidenced such examples: producing qualitative, business-grounded interpretations of variance analyses; uncovering insights into relevant drivers of costs, revenues and ultimate profitability, by, for example, analysing alternative portfolios of products or customers; contributing towards product design and continuous improvement through target costing and kaizen cost management; analysing financial impacts of alternative investment strategies and exploring sustainability analysis. There is an endless list of high value-added activities, both in

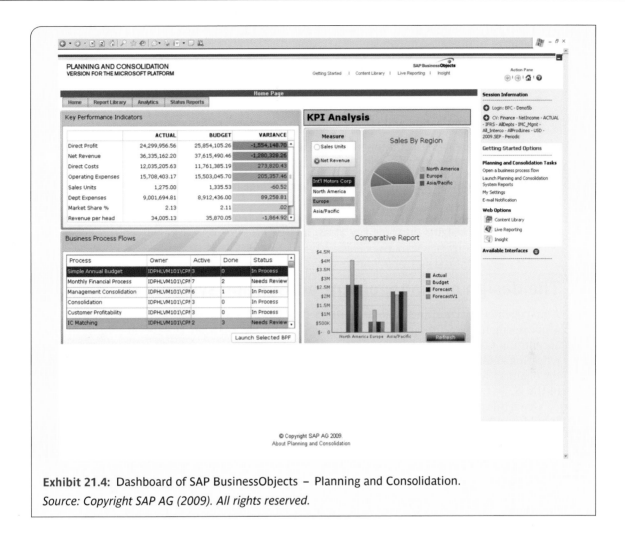

Exhibit 21.4: Dashboard of SAP BusinessObjects – Planning and Consolidation.
Source: Copyright SAP AG (2009). All rights reserved.

traditional and emergent fields of management accounting, which management accountants are now more capable of developing. Note that solutions which now allow non-accountants to perform accounting tasks, as in Exhibit 21.4, have also been indispensible in allowing management accountants to perform more value-added activities themselves.

Also, new training and consulting opportunities have arisen to meet the needs of the non-accounting professionals increasingly required to perform day-to-day accounting activities, as you read about decentring of accounting knowledge and activities. Finally, the business awareness gained by performing typical management accounting tasks in a more proactive, business-oriented way, combined with the resulting greater exposure to line managers, have also provided to some management accountants a career path into the management area.

IT activities for management accountants

Professional bodies have outlined IT roles for future accountants. While all accounting professionals are inevitably IS users, some may also be IS designers, managers or evaluators – or a combination of these roles (IFAC, 2007). We will focus particularly on IS evaluation and design. You will find an illustration of some traditional accounting activities involved in IS design and maintenance which are likely to be performed by management accountants. This section focuses on IS design because this is critical for management accountants' success and capacity to produce valuable insights to decision makers. Both routine, daily work and more creative, ad hoc activities of management accountants are greatly conditioned by the management accounting systems adopted by an organization.

The IFAC (2007) indicates that an accountant wishing to take a role in IS design should acquire competences in the following topics:

- Analysis and evaluation of the role of information
- Project management
- Systems investigation and project initiation
- User requirements determination, initial and detailed systems design and acquisition/development
- Systems implementation, maintenance, and change management.

You can find the detailed elements of competency for each topic in IFAC (2007, pp. 191–93). Now, you will explore insights on some key areas, linking back to concepts analysed throughout this book.

The design of management accounting systems

A management accounting system should reflect key organizational characteristics. Designing a management accounting system is therefore far more than an IT task, and more than an accounting task. Especially at the start, design is mostly a managerial activity. Design requires reflecting about what the organization is and how it operates, about what the designers envision the organization to become and how it should operate, and about options to embed these insights in the IS.

Given the managerial implications of the design of a management accounting system, the project should start by assessing current and future strategic directions and options. Senior consultants, combining a deep technical understanding of the software packages and mature strategic thought, can be highly useful at this stage to identify, as fully as possible, the repercussions of organizational strategies on the system design, and vice versa. Some system design decisions are structural (such as defining the organizational structure, as you will see next) and, once taken, they are difficult to revert – for example, in ERPs. Even the greater agility in cloud computing does not eliminate the importance of the design stage.

In addition to being managerially aware, IS roles beyond the user level, and particularly IS design, typically require management accountants to acquire programming skills or, at least, report-writing skills. The need for advanced IT skills varies among software packages and the context of each company (such as its resources and organization), but additional training is likely to be required in most cases.

The IT-related activities analysed next are likely to involve management accountants in multifunctional teams, potentially with both internal and external members. The precise role of particular management accountants will vary from case to case: they may have little or high involvement; they may, or may not, be involved in actually embedding the various options in the IS, and their decision responsibilities may range from none to very high. However, an awareness of issues such as these, and the capacity to work in a dynamic, multifunctional environment, is a likely common requirement for all future management accountants.

The selection of the IS and implementation options

Although the selection and design stages are often presented as separated, they are actually intertwined activities and share common reflections. Reflection on design options of future IS is required to orient the selection among packages with different capabilities. Management accountants can contribute to many vital decisions in the selection among alternative software packages, with different technological capabilities, and among alternative implementation options. Examples include:

- Should the IS provide permanently updated, online information? Or would information calculated periodically (for instance, at the end of the day or at the end of the month) be enough, or even more adequate?

- Should the IS provide extremely detailed information, in each area? Or would less detailed information still meet users' requirements for analysis?

- Should an integrated system be developed and adopted in one single step (a "big-bang" approach) or gradually (in terms of company processes, functions, locations or another criterion)?

- What post-implementation flexibility should the system have to meet future new requirements, such as new product lines, new distribution channels, entirely new businesses or profound internal reorganizations? How likely are those new requirements to emerge and what impact would they have in the adopted system?

- What are the advantages of cloud computing for the management accounting area and how can it be financially evaluated?

Answers to these questions have important consequences for the complexity (and cost) of the package and its implementation. These answers may also have important impacts beyond the management accounting area, since the IS of other areas may also need to be designed or implemented differently, according to the requirements of the management accounting system (see the end of chapter case study problem, regarding requirements for the ERP production module to meet product costing information needs). Management accountants' expertise may be vital in making correct decisions, with significant consequences concerning invested amounts, implementation time and the value provided by the selected system.

Information systems design involves embedding many management accounting concepts in the IS. As an illustration, we now discuss the definition of responsibility centres and charts of accounts; we also discuss challenges in obtaining and shaping information for management accounting purposes. Although the following analysis is not specific to a particular commercial solution, it adopts many terms from the ERP market leader, based on SAP (2006).

Mapping responsibility centres

A company's enterprise structure is mapped to SAP applications using organizational elements. Take the example of an international group. Organizational elements include the highest-level element 'client' (the entire enterprise/headquarters), controlling areas (for example, Europe, America and Asia), divisions (for example, a food division or a health products division), company codes (legal independent accounting units), plants, storage locations, distribution channels, functional departments and so on. Exhibit 21.5 illustrates the mapping of organizational units in SAP, ranging from the lower levels of individual plants, up to the global enterprise level.

Responsibility centres are based on organizational elements. As you read in Chapter 16, a responsibility centre may be defined as an investment, profit, revenue or cost centre. For example, a subsidiary possessing high autonomy for capital expenditures may be considered an investment centre. However, a plant whose director's responsibilities are mostly to manufacture products, according to orders from the sales division and using equipments and technology defined by headquarters, and then to sell them at predetermined transfer prices, is likely to be considered a cost centre.

Defining the kind of responsibility centre, for each organizational element, is a major managerial decision affecting the organization's (de)centralization, which then has to be embedded in the IS. Defining the perspectives that will be made visible, or invisible, by the IS has a huge potential to influence managerial action. Suppose that the IS is not designed to capture and report the revenue consequences of the actions of the cost centre responsible; this invisibility creates a 'blind spot' concerning revenues and promotes a greater focus on costs, rather than on generating revenues and profitability.

Defining charts of accounts and multiple valuation approaches

A chart of accounts structures accounting information within a ledger. Charts of accounts exist both in financial and management accounting. Using a single chart of accounts for both purposes improves data consistency, but should be detailed and flexible enough to satisfy both external and internal requirements. The structure and detail of a chart of accounts strongly influences the perspectives obtainable through data analysis. Owing to the high number of ledger postings in most companies, these companies often adopt sub-ledgers where individual postings are made; the general ledger then only contains collective postings, aggregating data from the sub-ledgers.

Companies may also need to produce multiple financial statements based on assumptions reflecting different national and international requirements. Multinationals have to produce financial statements to meet various national regulations. In both cases, companies need to adopt multiple valuation approaches. Nowadays, most financial accounting solutions are able to solve a task that, in the past, was challenging and error prone. Enterprise resource planning systems embed parallel accounting techniques to implement multiple valuation approaches. One approach to parallel accounting is adopting multiple charts of accounts: a leading chart of accounts (typically, the headquarters chart of accounts) is articulated with additional charts of accounts (for example, those of each subsidiary). Each posting in the subsidiary's chart of accounts is also posted to an account in the leading chart of accounts, thus building up the reports of the entire group. Keep in mind that, even when multiple charts of accounts exist for financial accounting purposes, the management accounting system should draw upon one single source of data, to allow meaningful comparisons.

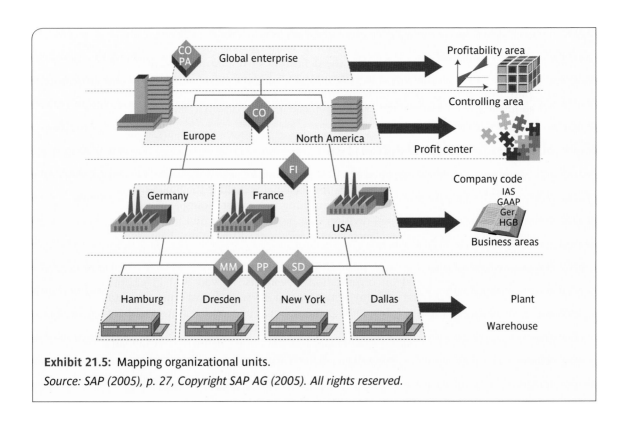

Exhibit 21.5: Mapping organizational units.

Source: SAP (2005), p. 27, Copyright SAP AG (2005). All rights reserved.

Obtaining and shaping information for management accounting

In an integrated system with a single data source, financial accounting is an important source of data for management accounting. Expense and revenue postings in financial accounting create costs and revenues in management accounting (in addition, as you learned in Chapter 3, management accounting also feeds financial accounting, for instance, by valuing finished products and works in progress at the end of the period). Then, costs (and revenues) are assigned to objects (SAP, 2006).

Key cost accounting concepts and techniques must be defined during the design of the management accounting system. Designers need to define the types of costs (for example, personnel costs) and cost behaviour. Cost behaviour includes the classic distinction between variable and fixed costs, but cost functions may be extremely complex, with non-linear behaviour. Constructing and applying complex cost functions require detailed production information (which, in an integrated system, may be provided directly by the production module) and requires the ability of management accountants to deal with non-trivial mathematics. Designers also need to identify and trace direct costs to products and services, and identify and assign indirect costs. The latter, overheads, can be allocated according to traditional or activity-based allocation bases, as you learned in Chapters 5 and 6. So, designers need to build, in the IS, appropriate models of internal activities, to accurately trace and assign costs. The design of profitability analysis should enable flexible internal and external perspectives. An internal perspective on profitability refers to internal profit centres, based on regions, functions or products. An external perspective analyses segments of the external market, based on products, customers, geographical areas or other criteria. In addition, the distinction between variable and fixed costs allows the calculation of profitability measures, including various contribution margins. Profitability analysis – and performance measurement more generally – are increasingly relying on analytical solutions, developing multidimensional views by flexibly drilling-in and slicing information cubes. Exhibit 21.6 represents how multiple ERP modules, depicted on the left (for example, FI – Financial accounting; CO – controlling; SD – sales and distribution) are sources of analysed data, including accounting-based data and costing-based data. Multiple internal and external segmentation criteria of data facilitate building information cubes – in this case, by regions, by product groups and by customer groups.

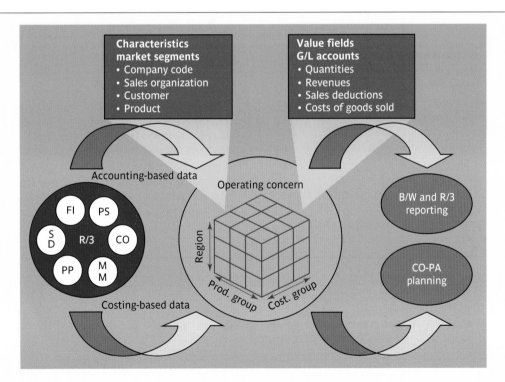

Exhibit 21.6: Data sources and analytical segmentation.

Source: Copyright SAP AG. All rights reserved.

Chapter summary

Information systems have dramatically changed the business world – and management accountants' world. The hybridization of management accounting, with cross-overs between accounting, managerial and IT activities, has challenged the relevance of past competences and has created the need for new ones. This chapter provided notions for a management accountant to approach the IT domain and highlighted the need to strengthen its IT skills. It sensitized future management accountants for many dilemmas related to IS and placed management accounting activities within an IS context, in particular concerning IS design. Hopefully, this chapter has persuaded the reader to further invest in this area which has created challenges and opportunities for today and tomorrow's management accountants.

Key terms

Best-of-breed (BoB) system Information system specialized in a particular area, attempting to offer the best possible solution in that field, traditionally with limited integration as typical of stand-alone systems (p. 569)

Big data Data with high volume, velocity and variety which is beyond the processing capacity of conventional systems and whose analysis may detect hidden valuable patterns and information (p. 560)

Cloud accounting Accounting carried out through cloud-based solutions (p. 571)

Cloud computing A business model in which IT resources (software and/or hardware) are provided as a service by a specialist provider, rather than individually owned and managed by the customer in its premises (p. 570)

Data Records of raw facts, without being organized or arranged to be meaningful for humans (p. 559)

Enterprise resource planning (ERP) system An organization-wide integrated system, originally aiming to be *the* single system satisfying all information needs, but increasingly repositioned as the IS backbone to which other systems connect (p. 564)

Hybridization (in management accounting) A bi-directional change in roles of accountants and IS and line staff, with professionals from each group assuming activities traditionally in the domain of the others (p. 572)

Information Data organized or modified in a way to become understandable and usable, and for a particular purpose (p. 559)

Information system A set of connected technologies and resources that collects, transforms and disseminates information (p. 555)

Stand-alone system A system highly or totally decoupled from the remaining systems (p. 563)

Systems (de)coupling (degree of) The extent to which changes in one system affect the state of the other (p. 563)

Review questions • • • • • • • • • • • • • connect • •

Level of difficulty:	BASIC	INTERMEDIATE	ADVANCED

21.1 Describe why information systems are important for management accountants. [LO1, LO7]

21.2 What are the three characteristics of big data? [LO2]

21.3 What is systems (de)coupling? [LO3]

21.4 Identify alternatives to achieve alignment between organization and information systems. **[LO4]**

21.5 What characterizes standalone systems? **[LO4]**

21.6 Indicate advantages and disadvantages of ERP systems. **[LO4]**

21.7 Indicate advantages and disadvantages of best-of-breed systems. **[LO4]**

21.8 Discuss the importance of cloud computing for management accountants. **[LO6]**

21.9 Give examples of how an accounting system interacts with the operational modules, when the two systems are highly coupled. **[LO3, LO5]**

21.10 What activities might be lost and gained by management accountants when an ERP system is introduced? **[LO7]**

Group discussion and activity questions ● ● ● ● ● ● ● ● ●

21.11 Gather information on two companies in the same industry: one with a mostly web-based business model, the other with a more traditional business model. Analyse their revenue and cost drivers. To what extent, and in what ways, do they differ? **[LO1]**

21.12 Students should be split into three groups. Each group should defend: (1) the addition of a management accounting module to an existing ERP system; (2) the adoption of a BoB solution for management accounting and (3) continuing to use spreadsheets for management accounting. **[LO4, LO5]**

21.13 Discuss whether lay-offs in the accounting function in the context of an ERP system implementation can be seen as the 'relevance lost' of management accounting. **[LO7]**

Exercises ● ● ● ● ● ● ● ● ● ● ● ● ● ● ● connect ● ● ●

E21.1 **Understanding information and information systems [LO1, LO2, LO3, LO4, LO5]**

Match the following descriptions with the correct terms provided below.

Descriptions	Terms
1. A comprehensive set of data which is organized in a logical manner and can be used for several purposes.	a. Information systems architecture
2. A system which is highly decoupled from the remaining systems.	b. Data
3. A single system, which aims to satisfy all information needs within an organization.	c. Stand-alone system
4. Formal definitions of how technology is used, how data is stored, how business processes are mapped and the functions of software within an organization.	d. Big data
5. Data that is beyond the processing capacity of conventional systems.	e. Best-of-breed system
6. Record of raw facts, without being organized or arranged to be meaningful for humans.	f. Systems (de)coupling
7. An information system that specialize in a particular area, attempting to offer the best possible solution in that field.	g. Database
8. The degree of interdependence between two systems.	h. Enterprise resource planning system

E21.2 **Systems (de)coupling [LO3]**

Amber Ltd is a mobile telephone service provider offering international SIM cards and data cards to people travelling from the U.K. to different countries. Amber uses a stand-alone accounting system for all its functional divisions. In an effort to achieve higher operational efficiency, it recently integrated the accounting and sales systems. Before the integration, the accounting team was manually posting sales invoices to the system. Now, new customer orders logged in by the sales team automatically result in an accounting entry.

Required:

Which of the following are potential problems that Amber might face as a result of the systems coupling? (Select all that apply).

a) The sales results may suffer as the sales division is now handling the accounting function too.

b) The sales team might not entirely understand the accounting implications of their actions.

c) The accounting team will have to perform less value-added activities.

d) The integration may lead to an increase in sales employees' training costs.

e) The integration will result in legal licensing issues for the company.

f) The company may require additional resources to manually review the accounting posts.

E21.3 **Drivers of success or failure in web-based companies and roles of management accountants [LO1]**

Identify companies in the social networking industry that did not succeed. Identify and discuss the key reasons for failure and how management accountants could have contributed to anticipate or avoid those problems.

E21.4 **Understanding information and information systems [LO1, LO2, LO3, LO4, LO5]**

Listed below are a number of terms relating to information systems:

a) Parallel accounting techniques

b) ERP systems

c) Information

d) Hybridisation

e) Blind spot

f) Big data

Required:

Choose the term that most appropriately completes the following statements.

1) _____ is a two-way change in the role of accountants and information systems and line staff, with professionals from each group assuming activities traditionally in the domain of the others.

2) A(n) _____ is created when the information system is not designed to capture and report the consequences of the actions of a particular responsibility centre.

3) _____ is (are) used in the in implementation of multiple valuation approaches in integrated systems.

4) As _____ are not focused in particular areas of business, they are considered to be generic.

5) When data is organized to make it more understandable and usable it is called _____.

6) Volume, velocity and variety are the three V's characterising _____.

E21.5 **Comparing best-of-breed (BoB) and integrated solutions [LO3, LO4, LO5]**

Search online to identify a vendor of a Best-of-Breed solution that is useful for management accountants. Identify and discuss the competitive advantages announced by the vendor. Then, research if vendors of integrated systems announce similar functionalities.

Required:

a) Are the advantages announced by the BoB vendor unique?

b) Do these advantages seem to add high value to the company? Do you think they are enough to convince potential customers to prefer the BoB solution instead of an integrated one?

c) What advantages announced by the vendor of integrated solutions seem to be most relevant? Do you think they are enough to convince potential customers to prefer the integrated solution instead of a BoB one?

E21.6 **The potential of 'big data' [LO2]**

Find companies which have already started to explore big data.

Required:

a) What challenges did they face?

b) What business benefits did they obtain?

c) Did you find reports of failure or, at least, disappointment, in exploring big data? What went wrong?

E21.7 **Understanding types of information systems [LO4, LO5]**

Listed below are features of Best-of-breed (BoB) systems and ERP systems. Identify the systems to which these features belong. (Select "X" in the applicable column.)

Features	BoB Systems	ERP Systems
1. These systems promote a single data entry and a common database to eliminate duplicated data and ensure consistency.		
2. These are generic systems limited in making more sophisticated or flexible analyses.		
3. These systems are more beneficial for critical, high value-added areas than for non-core areas.		
4. Their architecture allows only one large system that is made up of highly coupled subsystems specialized in particular functions.		
5. These systems are specialized in particular areas of business.		
6. These systems evolve faster to meet quickly changing requirements or emerging technologies.		
7. These systems are now aimed at being the backbone of the organizational information system, which connects to other systems.		
8. These systems have greater difficulty in creating interfaces and sharing data that is essential for integration.		

E21.8 **The business potential of cloud computing: the customers' view [LO6]**

Select a company that reports having made a previous 'business case' for adopting the cloud computing business model.

Required:

a)   What financial and strategic arguments were included in such business case?

b)   What challenges did this company face?

c)   What operational, financial and strategic benefits did it obtain?

d)   Did you find reports of failure or, at least, disappointment? What went wrong?

E21.9 **The business potential of cloud computing: the providers' view [LO6]**

Select two providers offering IT resources as a service, based on cloud computing. Examine the information they announce in terms of the discussion in this book's section, concerning cloud computing:

a)   Advantages

b)   Challenges

c)   Risks

E21.10 **Total cost of ownership and disadvantages of cloud computing [LO6]**

Clicker Ltd is an online travel agency. Clicker currently uses an in-premises server setup for all its IT needs. As the customer base of the company is increasing, the company is looking to implement a CRM system for a total of 15 users. Augustine, the IT manager, suggests having an in-premises CRM system that could be used for the next five years.

The up-front costs associated with having an in-premises CRM system are as follows:

User licenses	€85,000
Training costs	10,000
Additional infrastructure	20,000

The annual costs of operating the in-premises system will involve the following:

Technical support	€6,850
Hardware maintenance	3,500
License upgrades	4,000
Electricity costs for the infrastructure	1,200

The IT manager's assistant suggests cloud computing as a viable option. She says that the only upfront cost associated with cloud computing is the €10,000 that will be incurred for training existing employees.

The annual costs associated with a suitable hosted CRM are as follows:

User licenses	€250 per user per month
Technical support	€3,500
Premium license support	10% of total user license fee
License upgrades	€5,000

Required:

a) As the cost control manager of the company, you have been asked to determine which system is more cost effective. Prepare a total cost of ownership analysis for both the alternatives. Compare the two alternatives based on their total cost and ownership (i.e., all costs incurred by adopting each alternative).

b) Which of the following are disadvantages of cloud computing? (Select all that apply.)

   a) Maintenance and support costs increase substantially

   b) Safety of the company's sensitive data is questionable

   c) Scalability of the processing capacity is restricted

   d) Existing software licenses may no longer be valid

   e) Deploying new solutions and changing existing ones may be difficult

   f) Dependency on the service supplier increases

Case study problem • • • • • • • • • • connect • • •

C21.1 **ERP development in the financial area: SAP at Sonae Indústria [LO4, LO5, LO7]**

Sonae Indústria is a world-class manufacturer of wood-based panels. Sonae Indústria was founded in Portugal and now has plants in seven countries, while maintaining its headquarters in Portugal.

Adoption of SAP for financial accounting and the creation of a shared services centre

In 1999, Sonae Indústria adopted the first module of SAP, for Financial Accounting (SAP FI), to replace a legacy solution and adopt a common solution involving several subsidiaries. Although SAP FI improved information quality and speed, differences in practices across the plants still remained, leading to information inconsistencies and lack of comparability. In 2001, to further improve data quality and reduce costs, Sonae Indústria implemented a Shared Services Centre (SSC) to centrally perform transactional financial accounting activities, such as data posting and reconciliation. These activities, previously carried in each plant, began to be performed by the same accountants located at the SSC.

The development of SAP FI and the SSC was mutually reinforcing, as a SSC manager explains: 'It works both ways. Without a system and a technological platform, a SSC would never exist. But the SSC also allows uniformity in technological platforms and developments. Everything is a lot easier, because there is a global organizational platform here, the SSC.'

Changes in cost accounting

Shortly after the adoption of SAP FI, Sonae Indústria adopted SAP for Sales and Distribution and for Materials Management. In 2002, it started implementing the SAP Production module. However, there were still multiple solutions for management accounting.

Sonae Indústria traditionally performed product costing based on Excel spreadsheets. Management accountants at a plant level, called plant controllers, entered data in those spreadsheets, resorting to interfaces with a legacy production system and manually typing other information, such as energy consumption (manually obtained from the meters) and labour times and costs (manually obtained from the human resources systems). Plant controllers often used distinct Excel spreadsheets and ways to calculate, aggregate and present information in reports. Headquarters staff had difficulties in identifying and overcoming these differences. An IT manager acknowledged: 'There was a procedure manual for management control. But not all plant controllers did it in the same way.' Moreover, the spreadsheets did not ensure data reliability.

Changing the existing product costing system was a perceived need for some time, but it had never advanced. However, shortly after the launch of the project to implement SAP Production, a manager from the financial area proposed including the SAP Product Costing module in that project – which, until then, was exclusively focused on the production area.

Why adopt the SAP product costing module? And why at that moment?

Implementing the SAP Production module created a novel situation: most information needed for product costing was now available within one single system, SAP. A new costing system could take advantage of this new technical condition. Adopting a best-of-breed, non-SAP solution was never considered as an option. This option would reintroduce the need to obtain vast amounts of information from different systems (the other SAP modules) and would reintroduce interface difficulties similar to those that the company was now trying to eliminate. So, as in many other companies, choosing the ERP vendor solution was virtually inevitable, emerging as the only rational choice.

And why should the Product Costing module be implemented alongside the Production module, rather than later? Because implementing it later would require readjusting the Production module to meet product costing requirements. A major adjustment involved products bills of materials (BOMs, see Chapter 4), a part of the Production Planning module. Because the company always had to keep stocks of wood, enough for the needs of its continuous production process, wood supply did not have to be planned in very short periods of time (a few days). For this reason, until then, wood was not included in existing BOMs. However, product costing now required complete BOMs. Redefining BOMs of thousands of products is a massive project. So, simultaneously implementing both modules avoided duplication of efforts and was more efficient. According to a manager, not doing it would be a 'lost opportunity'.

With the integration of the two modules, product costing and variances began to be calculated automatically. This greatly strengthened data reliability, comparability and timeliness. An IT manager thus commented: 'With this new project, costing criteria won't be left to the liberty of each person any longer.'

In addition, since plant controllers no longer had to gather data and calculate costs manually, the plant controllers' role shifted towards more value-added activities, such as providing qualitative comments to variances based on field knowledge about the actual production processes. They were expected to leave their office and go to the shop floor, understand the business and know the problems, as well as providing support for both the plant director and headquarters' management controllers.

Required:

a) Discuss possible areas where different practices across plants could still persist before the creation of the SSC, even after a common SAP solution had already been implemented. Discuss possible reasons for such continuing differences.

b) Discuss possible implications on the SSC creation if a single system for financial accounting had not been previously implemented.

c) Take the position of a best-of-breed solution vendor. Outline possible arguments towards adopting a BoB product costing solution in the context described above. Then, critically discuss and, eventually, refute them.

d) 'Choosing accounting systems should be left to IT staff.' Use the above case study to critically discuss this statement.

e) 'Technology "speaks for itself" in technological options.' Critically discuss this statement, drawing from relevant insights from the text.

f) Compare the expected changes in the roles of plant controllers in this organization with the wider trends depicted in the literature, and highlight the influence of information systems in the changing roles of management accountants.

● ● ● # Recommended reading ● ● ● ● ● ● ● ● ● ● ● ● ● ● ● ● ● ●

● Dechow, N. and J. Mouritsen (2005) 'Enterprise resource planning systems, management control and the quest for integration', *Accounting, Organizations and Society*, 30(7–8), pp. 691–733.

This paper provides an alternative to Caglio's (2003) perspective on management accounting hybridization and a less optimistic view on the ERPs potential for management accountants. In an ERP context, management control becomes a collective affair; however, different perspectives on management control may be embedded in the ERP with different success. In a particular company, operational and logistic visions were simpler to sustain, and hence became more visible and acceptable, than the financial view. [Advanced reading.]

- Elias, N. and A. Wright (2006) 'Using knowledge management systems to manage knowledge resource risks', in M. J. Epstein and J. Y. Lee. (eds), *Advances in Management Accounting, Volume 15*, Oxford: Elsevier.

This article explores the emergent role of management accountants in the design and operation of knowledge management systems, in order to promote adequate usage and management of knowledge resources. It focuses on organizations whose primary product is knowledge. Knowledge management systems were only briefly mentioned in this chapter, but their distinctiveness and importance recommends reading this article.

- IBM (2010) 'Transforming spreadsheets: planning, budgeting and forecasting for midsize companies', http://www-01.ibm.com/software/analytics/cognos/express/library-whitepapers. html (requires free registration) (accessed on 15 May 2012).

This is an IBM white paper about a best-of-breed solution for midsize companies, including key accounting activities and supporting an initial business intelligence strategy. While keeping in mind its commercial nature, this publication is useful to identify a wide variety of limitations and risks of using Excel, particularly in complex, fast moving environments requiring the participation of multiple remote users.

- Magal, S. R. and J. Word (2012) *Integrated Business Processes with ERP Systems*, Hoboken, NJ: John Wiley & Sons.

This book, written with the support from SAP, analyses the key processes supported by modern ERP systems and examines the core concepts applicable in ERP environments.

- Rom, A. and C. Rohde (2006) 'Enterprise resource planning systems, strategic enterprise management systems and management accounting: a Danish study', *Journal of Enterprise Information Management*, 19(1), pp. 50–66.

This study is a survey about how ERPs and strategic enterprise management systems affect the ability to solve management accounting tasks. It concludes that different management accounting tasks are supported by different parts of the integrated system, hence recommending closer integration between the two types of systems.

● ● **References** ●

Accenture (2009) 'Optimizing sustainability performance management – a review of findings from Accenture's 2009 Sustainability Performance Management Survey', http://www.accenture.com/SiteCollectionDocuments/PDF/Accenture-Optimizing-Sustainability-Performance-Management.pdf (accessed on 19 July 2012).

Accenture (2010) 'Canon Europe pursues high performance by outsourcing finance and accounting', http://www.accenture.com/SiteCollectionDocuments/PDF/270Accenture_Business_Process_Outsourcing_Canon.pdf (accessed on 15 May 2012).

Amazon.com (2011) 'Annual Report' http://phx.corporate-ir.net/phoenix.zhtml?c=97664&p=irol-reportsannual (accessed on 15 May 2012).

Boczko, T. (2007) '*Corporate Accounting Information Systems*', London: Pearson.

Bughin, J., A. H. Byers and M. Chui (2011) 'How social technologies are extending the organization', *McKinsey Quarterly*, November, pp. 1–10.

Burns, J. and G. Baldvinsdottir (2005) 'An institutional perspective of accountants' new roles – the interplay of contradictions and praxis', *European Accounting Review*, 14(4), pp. 725–57.

Caglio, A. (2003) 'Enterprise resource planning systems and accountants: towards hybridization?', *European Accounting Review*, 12(1), pp. 123–53.

CIMA (2008) 'Don't blame the tools: the adoption and implementation of managerial innovations', http://www.cimaglobal.com/Thought-leadership/Research-topics/Management-and-financial-accounting/Dont-blame-the-tools-the-adoption-and-implementation-of-managerial-innovations/ (accessed on 15 May 2012).

CIMA (2010), 'Cloud computing could lead to a more adaptive finance function', *CIMA Insight E-Zine*, http://www.cimaglobal.com/Thought-leadership/Newsletters/Insight-e-magazine/Insight-2010/Insight-December-2010/Cloud-computing-could-lead-to-more-adaptive-finance-function/ (accessed on 15 May 2012).

CIMA (2011a) 'Sustainability performance management: how CFOs can unlock value', http://www.cimaglobal.com/Thought-leadership/Research-topics/Sustainability/Sustainability-performance-management-how-CFOs-can-unlock-value/ (accessed on 15 May 2012).

CIMA (2011b) 'The bright future for cloud accounting', http://www.cimaglobal.com/en-gb/Thought-leadership/Newsletters/Insight-e-magazine/Insight-2011/Insight-July-2011/The-bright-future-for-cloud-accounting/ (accessed on 15 May 2012).

CIMA (2011c) 'Cloud computing: benefits versus risks', http://www.cimaglobal.com/en-gb/Thought-leadership/Newsletters/Insight-e-magazine/Insight-2011/Insight-July-2011/Cloud-computing/ (accessed on 20 December 2011).

Dechow, N. and J. Mouritsen (2005) 'Enterprise resource planning systems, management control and the quest for integration', *Accounting, Organizations and Society*, 30(7–8), pp. 691–733.

Elias, N. and A. Wright (2006) 'Using knowledge management systems to manage knowledge resource risks', in M. J. Epstein and J. Y. Lee (eds), *Advances in Management Accounting, Volume 15*, Oxford: Elsevier.

IBM (2012) 'Bringing big data to the enterprise', http://www-01.ibm.com/software/data/bigdata/ (accessed on 15 May 2012).

IBM (2010a) 'Analytics: the new path to value', http://www-935.ibm.com/services/us/gbs/thoughtleadership/ibv-embedding-analytics.html (accessed on 15 May 2012).

IBM (2010b) 'Transforming spreadsheets: planning, budgeting and forecasting for midsize companies', http://www-01.ibm.com/software/analytics/cognos/express/library-whitepapers.html (requires free registration) (accessed on 15 May 2012).

IFAC (2007) International Education Practice Statement IEPS 2: Information Technology for Professional Accountants, http://www.ifac.org/sites/default/files/publications/files/ieps-2-information-techno-1.pdf (accessed on 15 May 2012).

McKinsey (2011) 'Inside P&G's digital revolution', *McKinsey Quarterly*, November, pp. 1–11.

Nixon, W. A. J. and J. Burns (2005) 'Management control in the 21st century', *Management Accounting Research*, 16(3), pp. 260–68.

O'Mahony, A. and J. Doran (2008) 'The changing role of management accountants: evidence from the implementation of ERP systems in large organizations', *International Journal of Business and Management*, 3(8), pp. 109–15.

Panorama (2011) '2011 guide to ERP systems and vendors: an independent research report', http://panorama-consulting.com/Documents/2011-Guide-to-ERP-Systems-and-Vendors.pdf (accessed on 15 May 2012).

SAP (2006) *SAP 01 - SAP Overview*, Walldorf: SAP.

SAP (2005) *SAPFIN – my SAP ERP Financials*, Walldorf: SAP.

Scapens, R. and M. Jazayeri (2003) 'ERP systems and management accounting change: opportunities or impacts? A research note', *European Accounting Review*, 12(1), pp. 201–33.

Webmasterpro.de (2010) 'International OpenOffice market shares', http://www.webmasterpro.de/postal/news/2010/02/05/international-openoffice-market-shares.html (accessed on 20 November 2011).

● ● ● Notes ●

1 http://ecohub.sap.com/store/mobility (accessed on 7 June 2012).
2 http://www.sap.com/solutions/sme/compare-bm-solutions.epx (accessed on 15 May 2012).
3 See http://www.sap.com/industries/index.epx for a full list of industry specific solutions (accessed on 15 May 2012).

4 http://www.cimaglobal.com/Events-and-cpd-courses/Events/Mastercourses/IT-Skills/(accessed on 19 November 2011).
5 http://www.sap.com/solutions/sme/compare-bm-solutions.epx (accessed on 15 May 2012).
6 http://www.sap.com/solutions/sme/compare-bm-solutions.epx (accessed on 15 May 2012).
7 See Dechow and Mouritsen (2005), summarized in the recommended readings list, about how ERPs may promote other losses for management accounting and its professionals.

When you have read this chapter

Log on to the Online Learning Centre at **www.mcgraw-hill.co.uk/textbooks/burns** to explore chapter-by-chapter test questions, links and further online study tools for Management Accounting.

CHAPTER 22

MANAGING CHANGE AND CHALLENGES FOR THE FUTURE

Chapter outline

- What is change, and why the concern at all?

- A framework for understanding management accounting change

- Unintended management accounting change

- Intended management accounting change

- Implementing management accounting change

- Challenges of change for the future

Learning outcomes

On completion of this chapter, you will be able to:

LO1 Appreciate management accounting change as cumulative, complex, and interconnected processes over time

LO2 Be familiar with the basics of an 'institutional' theoretical perspective on management accounting change

LO3 Identify characteristics of successful and unsuccessful change

LO4 Appreciate deep-set cultural and political aspects of change

LO5 Describe key considerations when implementing and managing accounting change

LO6 Give an overview of some of the possible drivers and challenges of management accounting in the future

LO7 Describe some of the emerging and future challenges for management accountants

Introduction

At the outset of this textbook we discussed the undercurrent theme of change in management accounting. Change is all-pervading in and around organizations, and management accounting is no exception. There is considerable and ongoing change in the business environment context within which management accounting operates; there are changes in the role of management accountants, and there are changes in the technical nature *and* the use of management accounting techniques and systems. Such background was discussed in Chapter 1, and the theme of **management accounting change** is a thread all the way through this book.

Management accounting change is complex, and can be viewed from multiple perspectives (Wickramasinghe and Alawattage, 2007). It is rarely predictable, is frequently irrational and is often brimming with the unexpected. Not surprisingly, the design, implementation and ongoing management of change have become a crucial part of the roles of today's management accountants. Indeed, many of this book's readers will likely become part of what shapes the path of management accounting in the future, as well as carving out future roles for management accountants. Thus, as we bring this textbook towards a close, it seems pertinent to more explicitly consider the notion of managing accounting change, and consider what is required when dealing with the multiple challenges that change management involves. We will also look at specific and probable areas for change in the future, and explore the possible ramifications of such change for management accountants and their profession.

In this chapter we give relatively little attention to the technical features of management accounting change, though preceding chapters have provided ample material on the technical (*and* non-technical) aspects of management accounting. In this chapter we are particularly interested in the non-technical aspects of the design and implementation of management accounting techniques or systems, and we will focus on such questions as:

- What is change, and are there different ways to view it? Is change predictable in its outcomes? And, why should we be concerned about change at all?

- Can theory assist us to make sense of management accounting change? Can theories help us design and implement change in practice?

- Is change always the 'right' thing to do? If so, why do so many organizations not change over long time periods?

- Is there a 'best' way to implement change? What are the potential pitfalls, and how might we prepare for these challenges?

- Why does some management accounting change fail to achieve its objective, what goes wrong, what types of unintended consequences occur?

- Can lessons be learned from organizations where change is viewed to be successfully implemented?

First we will discuss how we can view the phenomena of change. We introduce alternative thinking to the influential classical definitions of change, which present change as simply moving from one static state to another. Later in the chapter we will highlight an 'institutional' theoretical perspective of change (Scapens, 1994; Burns and Scapens, 2000), following which we then explore real case studies of both unsuccessful and successful management accounting change. We provide some narratives of the unfolding change 'story', and using theory we highlight some of the non-technical aspects of change in each case. Next, we cover issues that would seem important for managers who are personally engaged in designing and/or implementing management accounting change. Finally, having considered the nature and importance of change management, we will discuss some of the probable challenges of change in the future for management accountants.

What is change, and why the concern at all?

Change is nowadays part of the day-to-day fabric of organizations, including management accounting change. Multiple environmental pressures instigate changes in management accounting, because they create changes in managers' information requirements. There are also frequently internal pressures for management accounting change, for example via managers who desire change, or even assumptions that particular change would be the right thing to do.

So, that we should closely investigate management accounting change, and more specifically *managing* accounting change, needs little debate. It is only in relatively recent years that 'management accounting change' has become a notable concern. The common approach for a long time had been to view management accounting 'change' in a rather static sense; that is, the management accounting tools and techniques in use at any point in time were assumed to be 'best' practice. Such a view of management accounting was premised in rational-actor, equilibrium-based models that underpin neoclassical economics (see Scapens, 1994). According to this approach, any changes that did occur in management accounting merely reflected shifts to new solutions, part of organizations realigning with its environmental conditions.

Change can take place at different levels, not just unilaterally but interconnected, and not just in separate events but usually concurrently. For instance, we might consider change occurring at the following levels:

- *Environmental change* (for example, new policies or rules at the economy/society level, new and emerging world orders, new technologies or new social fads)

- *Organizational change* (for example, mergers and acquisitions, alliances and networks among and between organizations, or outsourcing)

- *Intra-organizational change* (for example, the implementation of new accounting techniques, redefining departmental structures or staff re-skilling)

- *Group/individuals change* (for example, the arrival and/or departure of staff, promotion or retirement)

Any aspect of organizational change, including management accounting change, can be described in terms of 'before the event' and 'after the event' descriptions. The mainstream view of management accounting change would normally be described as a shift to some new optimizing solution, and comparisons could be made between before and after the change event. But we can consider change in a much deeper way. Rather than simply comparing a situation before change with the situation after change, we would encourage students to think about less obvious but equally as important aspects of the **change process**, in particular how and why things evolved as they did.

We encourage the student to view change as being complex and part of cumulative processes over time. By thinking about management accounting change as part of cumulative processes, this will influence us to ask deeper and broader questions in respect of the change which takes place, for example we might be interested in:

- The historical background, and emergence of change – for instance, where did the (idea for) a new management accounting tool come from, and why? Were there any key catalysts of change?

- How was the implementation of this new management tool designed? Did certain managers or even outsiders (for example, management consultants) have an influence on the design?

- Did any unusual or unexpected features characterize the change process; in particular, were there any problems or tensions, and how were they dealt with?

- With the benefit of hindsight, what might we learn from this particular management accounting change process?

Following such a processual view of change, as briefly described above, we steer clear of assumptions that change necessarily brings about improved or 'best' situations. Although the intention underpinning most change is to make improvements on past and present situations, in practice the design and achievement of optimality is both difficult and subjective. This does not mean that improvement is unimportant. However, we recognize both the complexities and the unique attributes inherent in all management accounting change, and it is these complexities over time that we would like to shed more light on, and which more static approaches would not offer. In the next section we describe an institutional theoretical framework of management accounting change (see Burns and Scapens, 2000) which will assist us to investigate the inherent complexities of change as a process over time.

A framework for understanding management change

An **institutional theory of management accounting change** starts from a premise that management accounting constitutes a largely rules-based and routinized feature of day-to-day organizational life. Such management accounting rules and routines augment stability and continuity over time in organizational practice. In fact, rules and routines embodied in management accounting practices help bring order to organizations that otherwise could be far less organized given their very mixed and very complex make-up.

So, how does such order come about? We argue that for most organizations order is achieved through the interplay of rules, routines and shared assumptions within an organization about the nature of its activities. Below, these shared assumptions will be referred to as institutions (hence the name 'institutional theory'), but first we will consider the nature of rules and routines within organizations.

Rules and routines

Rules are necessary to co-ordinate and give coherence to the actions of groups and/or individuals within an organization. Rule-based behaviour can result from an explicit assessment of the available alternatives – for instance, there are different rules for what to do, when and how; and selected rules are then repeatedly followed so as to avoid undertaking such assessments on every occasion. By repeatedly following rules, organizational behaviour can become programmatic or automatic, and premised in the tacit knowledge that people acquire through experience, when people 'just know' what to do, when and how. At this stage, such rule-based behaviour can be described as a **routine**.

Management accounting practices are central to the web of rules and routines in most organizations – for example, consider budgeting. In most organizations, budgeting is underpinned by rules – budgeting is normally formalized in a rules manual which guides its users towards appropriate budgeting behaviour. For instance, there will be rules that schedule the establishment of an annual budget, as well as identifying when actual performance should be analysed against the monthly budget by the budget holder. There will be also rules that establish which people have authority to sign-off particular budgets, and/or which staff are accountable to particular budget figures.

Over time, rules get re-enacted, and begin to be performed automatically, but usually still in line with the original rule; at this stage, budgeting procedures can be said to have become routinized. Intra - organizational rules usually represent formalized statements of procedure, whereas routines represent the procedures actually in use. In the context of management accounting, rules comprise accounting systems as set out in the procedure manuals, whereas routines are the management accounting practices actually in use. Clearly, there is a relationship between rules and routines, but it is important not to confuse the two, as the management accounting systems in use within a particular organization may not always accurately mirror the systems actually set out in the procedure manuals.

Exhibit 22.1 portrays the interaction between budgeting rules and routines and how together they shape the actions of people within an organization, thereby facilitating co-ordination and a degree of stability in day-to-day organizational life. What people do in organizations is an enactment of the budgeting rules and routines.

The emphasis above on stability is not to say that change does not take place. Rather, as routines emerge and repeat, existing and original rules *can* be modified, as those people implicated in the relevant activities locate new and mutually acceptable alternatives, or change can also be imposed. For instance, we referred above to budgeting procedures, as defined in a rules manual. Let us assume that, for one organization, new rules are inherited when it is acquired by another organization.

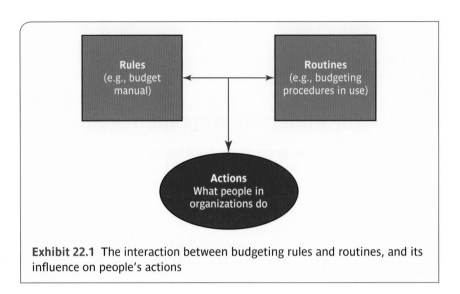

Exhibit 22.1 The interaction between budgeting rules and routines, and its influence on people's actions

As the new budgeting rules are implemented in the acquired organization, the modification (or even entire abandonment) of existing budgeting rules will take place. And, with repetition of the new rules, new routines will emerge.

Institutions

Institutions can be defined as shared and taken-for-granted assumptions in organizations – they are 'simply the way things are around here'. Staying with our illustration of budgeting, we have described budget manual procedures as being rules, and the actual doing of budgets as routines. If we take this a stage further, we can say that budgeting has become institutionalized in an organization when it is a generally accepted and unquestioned way of doing things.

Institutions form over time, with the ongoing re-enactment of rules and routines. They will encode rules and routines, though in a more abstract way, and they are very often tacit assumptions which people 'just know as being how we do things' without necessarily being observed in practice like rules or routines. So, institutions can be observed through the things that people do within organizations, although it is the rules and routines which shape the actions per se. We can extend our earlier exhibit to now incorporate the influence of institutions on rules and routines (Exhibit 22.2) and, through them, on the actions of people within organizations.

There is ongoing and self-reinforcing interaction between budgeting rules, routines and institutions, and over time the institutionalized nature of budgeting usually becomes stronger. This is important because as management accounting rules and routines, for instance budgeting, become more strongly institutionalized the harder they are to change. By definition when particular management accounting practices become institutionalized they are rarely questioned, and generally just assumed by all as 'the way things are done'. Furthermore, because institutions are a deep-set and ingrained aspect of organizations, it is seldom that people within such an organization will 'look outside the bubble' or blatantly investigate alternative ways of doing business.

For present purposes it is important to stress that an organization's rules, routines and institutions should be understood as far as possible *before* engaging in any change. More specifically, when an organization embarks on the introduction of a new management accounting tool or technique, the process of managing such change should give due attention to the existing rules, routines and institutions. While not wishing to overgeneralize it might be the case that management accounting change will stand a better chance of success when its technical content and underlying philosophy complements (rather than conflicts with) existing management accounting rules, routines and institutionalized ways. Further discussion of these sorts of issues relating to the management of change will emerge from our analyses of two (long) case study illustrations below. Both cases relate to real organizations although their identity is disguised.

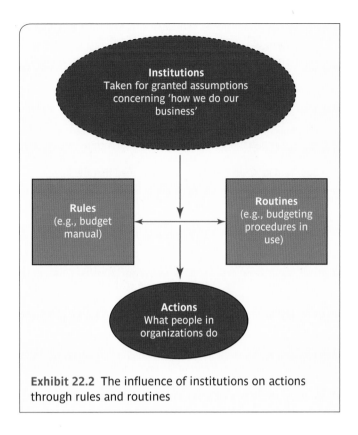

Exhibit 22.2 The influence of institutions on actions through rules and routines

Unintended management accounting change

In this section, we describe an organization that experiences unsuccessful management accounting change. In so doing, we adopt a broad view of 'successful' and 'unsuccessful' change, but recognize that there are difficulties in defining such terms. Our definition of 'success' is where the original intention of organizational change is broadly accomplished, and involves minimal resistance or conflict. We therefore define 'unsuccessful' as being where original intention is not fulfilled, and where there is most likely resistance and/or conflict involved.

The unsuccessful case study below, see *Management Accounting Insight 22.1*, describes resistance experienced when very simple accounting techniques were introduced in the research and development department of a small chemicals manufacturer in the UK. The case illustrates some of the difficulties when the implementation of management accounting change challenges the institutionalized assumptions embedded in this department. The latter prioritizes its chemical research activities, rather than the undercurrent financial implications of such activities and, as a result, there are considerable problems when introducing new, though seemingly quite simple, forms of accounting.

22.1: Management Accounting Insight

Nasty Stuff Ltd: an illustration of unsuccessful management accounting change

Nasty Stuff Ltd is a small specialist-chemicals manufacturer, comprising around 100 mostly skilled staff. In the years since it was established, production became locked-in to a small number of bespoke contracts with multinational customers, usually of five years' duration, and which they called 'captives' work. Captives business was so dominant that for many years it had consistently earned around 80 per cent of the company's total profits. However, although very profitable these contracts carried substantial risk, because they involved specialist plant and labour and because of the ongoing possibility that contracts might not be renewed when they came to an end.

Indeed, when two major captive contracts were terminated without renewal, this created a severe cash-flow crisis for Nasty Stuff Ltd. So significant was this cash-flow problem that it very nearly resulted in the company's demise. However, through negotiation of a new finance deal with a different bank, such demise was averted.

However, hard lessons had been learned. Crucially, the directors agreed that the business should attempt to redress the dominance of captives work. Accordingly, a new strategy was established which set a target for achieving a 50/50 turnover split between captives and 'other' products. These 'other' products were to be developed for a broader customer base, and were subsequently labelled as 'multi-client' work. The 50/50 turnover split was to be achieved within five years, an ambitious target. Importantly, it was the research and development (R&D) department which had responsibility for developing the new multi-client products.

Within Nasty Stuff Ltd there were common assumptions (that is, institutions) about the nature of the business, particularly concerning the importance of efficiencies, yields, working at (or near to) full capacity, and for generating good contributions (defined as sales less variable costs). The Managing Director (hereafter MD), probably the most influential and powerful individual in the organization, emphasized that it was these assumptions which underpinned what he called a 'results orientation' throughout the bulk of the organization.

Contribution-based information was used considerably in most management reports, not just accountants' reports, and was broadly understood across different departments and functional areas. Material costs were especially high in relation to other costs and, over time, contribution information came to underpin much of the day-to-day language used by the various managers to assess and convey performance in their part of the organization. For example, the Marketing Manager, the Operations Manager and the Chief Engineer all relied heavily on contributions-based spreadsheets for the day-to-day management of their functions within the business. Shift leaders and many operators just knew the contribution-earnings of individual products, and there was a widespread commercial awareness and 'results orientation' across the business.

However, following the cash-flow crisis, it became clear to MD that the institutionalized business assumptions, encompassing a 'results orientation', and grounded to a large extent in the recurrence of contributions-based routines, had failed to penetrate R&D. He believed that R&D was internally focused on 'playful chemistry', which R&D's highly qualified chemists generally characterized as being 'slow and painstaking'. The MD thus came to the conclusion that R&D was 'detached' from the rest of the business, and was more 'concerned with chemistry for the sake of chemistry, than in making money'. Critically, the MD feared that an absence of 'results orientation' in R&D could likely prove a significant barrier for developing the new multi-client products.

Management accounting change in the R&D department

Consequently, the MD began to investigate the past few years' general activity and performance in R&D. Alongside the Chief Chemist, head of R&D, he examined the latter's time sheets over a three-year period, in large part because these were the only tangible source of performance data that existed in that department! The examination revealed that time utilization in R&D had been 'unsatisfactory' – for example, only 60 per cent of highly qualified staff's time was actually spent on research activity, while the rest of the time was spent cleaning vessels or other non-direct research activity.

Moreover, the MD's investigation of past time sheets revealed that no overtime had *ever* been worked over the previous three years by R&D staff. This was also the situation during the cash-flow crisis, when many others (the MD included) had worked incredibly long hours for several months. This confirmed to the MD that there was no sense of urgency, and a complete absence of commercial astuteness or 'results orientation' in R&D.

On top of this, those products which the R&D department *had* spent time on and developed, over the past few years, and which *had* eventually reached the market, earned negligible contribution earnings. In other words, R&D's 'strike rate', as the MD put it, was 'quite abysmal'. Thus, six months after his initial investigation, the MD introduced a new and simple system of accountability within R&D. This new system comprised the formalization of weekly time sheets for individual research projects, as well as prioritization of new products which were to be 'brought to the market' by agreed dates, mostly within around three years. In terms of the institutional theoretical perspective discussed earlier, these new initiatives can be likened to the introduction of new rules within R&D.

The MD also worked closely with the Chief Chemist to develop new contribution-based reports and new reporting procedures (*cf*. more new rules), the primary intention of which again was to make R&D more results oriented and thus more in line with the rest of the business. The new relatively simple accounting practices and new forms of accountability rather rapidly became routine practice, for the Chief Chemist at least – for instance, the collection of time-sheet data, inputting the data, producing reports and holding monthly meetings with MD.

The MD especially played a key role in this implementation process of management accounting change. In particular, he assisted and shaped the process via his mobilization of:

1) *Staff perceptions* – for example, by utilizing various management-level meetings to convince others that change *should* take place within R&D. His presentations at these meetings were generally expressed in shock/crisis language (for example, highlighting the poor time utilization and the absence of any overtime), and threatened the potential for business closure if improvements could not be achieved in the multi-client product base.

2) *Resources* – for example, by drawing on the authority derived from his position, and reinforced by his strong and very persuasive personality, to take direct control of R&D.

3) *Decision-making* – for example, by establishing monthly performance meetings with the Chief Chemist.

The apparent ease and rapid speed with which the new accounting practices became routinized within R&D was also helped by the initial enthusiasm towards the change, embraced through the Chief Chemist. He appeared to accept the necessity of the new formalized time sheets, and expressed pleasure that he was working from systems of accountability which aligned with the accountability systems used elsewhere in the organization.

However, after two further years it became clear to the MD that there had actually been little change in the general ways of working within R&D. The accounting change had failed to reap any significant improvement in the development of multi-client products, thus Nasty Stuff remained exposed to the vulnerability of captives work. According to the MD, an intended results orientation had not become instilled into R&D's day-to-day activities, and 'there was no thinking in terms of making money'.

This, to a large extent, was because the Chief Chemist had acted as a buffer between his staff (in R&D) and the MD's broader concerns. More specifically, there was no delegation of the new accounting duties (rules, routines) within R&D, and new forms of accountability were not passed down to other members of staff within the department. The Chief Chemist undertook all the new rules and routines of accounting personally; in fact, the only difference for his staff was compiling time sheets each Friday afternoon, but without knowledge of why they were doing so. Significantly, one junior chemist within R&D confirmed that she and her colleagues in the lower ranks of R&D did not understand why these time sheets were being used, but that they had been just told to do them.

Thus, the new accounting systems in R&D had not changed R&D chemists' institutionalized ways of thinking concerning 'what they did' within the organization, nor had the change process come anywhere near to instilling a results orientation within this department. Despite the introduction of new rules, the dominant routines and taken-for-granted assumptions regarding R&D's business activities were still expressed in terms of chemistry, and which continued to be generally regarded as 'slow and painstaking'.

Source: adapted from Burns, J. (2000).

Exercise

If you had been in charge of the change programme in Nasty Staff Ltd, how might you have dealt differently with trying to instead a results orientation in R &D?

In the case study described in *Management Accounting Insight 22.1*, we learned about the difficulties of implementing management accounting change in an organizational setting where the new procedures challenged prevalent taken-for-granted assumptions concerning 'business activity' within R&D. On the surface, the implemented changes appeared relatively simple – time sheets analysis is not exactly sophisticated management accounting! However, on deeper reflection, the 'small' changes implemented in R&D had radical effects, because the new contribution-based rules and routines, and intended results oriented ways of thinking were fundamentally different to chemistry-oriented rules, routines and taken-for-granted assumptions in that department.

The new accounting systems were incompatible with existing institutions in R&D. 'If' a results orientation was to develop out from, or alongside these new accounting rules, institutional change was also necessary in R&D. In other words, the dominant focus on 'chemistry for chemistry's sake' needed replacing by general assumptions of 'making money' and a 'results orientation'. Such institutional change failed to materialize, however, and the change programme eventually became infused with conflict, and ultimately failed.

Intended management accounting change

Having just described a case where management accounting change did not emerge as was intended, and for which such failure was primarily due to incompatibility between the new rules/routines of accounting and existing institutionalized assumptions, a case study of intended management accounting change will now be described. In the case described in *Management Accounting in Practice 22.1*, we see change processes through which existing institutions were challenged as part of an intentional cultural change. Further, we explore how a new management accounting system was implemented in a way that supported rather than conflicted with the new and emerging organizational culture. Importantly, this cultural change was an extension of existing institutions, rather than representing an overhaul of existing institutions. We begin with some background to the broader organizational change of which management accounting change was an integral, but by no means the only, part.

22.1: Management Accounting in Practice

Polyfoam: an illustration of successful management accounting change

During the late 1990s, world-class manufacturing (hereafter WCM) represented a popular synthesis of management techniques for the contemporary manufacturing environment at that time. Its coverage s pans three broad areas – (1) people, (2) processes and (3) quality – and was premised on the notion that a world-class business is organized to serve the customer, and emphasizes non-financial measurement, continuous improvement, up-to-date information systems and 'responsive' management structures.

Particularly during the late 1990s, WCM had become a rallying call to spur improvement in products, internal operations, customer service and profitability. Furthermore, in some countries, governments' trade and industry incentive programmes had endorsed WCM. One of Polyfoam's operating units, Company A, introduced WCM as a result of one of these incentive programmes.

At the time, Polyfoam was one of the world's largest producers of polymer foam, and the largest supplier in Europe. Company A is a wholly owned subsidiary of Polyfoam and for most part had been a profitable unit since its acquisition. Its principal source of management information was the periodic 'Business Performance Report', which provided an overall evaluation of each business area – including cumulative results, current month/period results, available resources, capital expenditure and an operations review. The latter was probably the most important document, and was designed to provide in a simple two-page format the results and current state of the business.

Although annual budgets were prepared for each functional area, they were not considered a management commitment. Instead, they were regarded as an estimate of the likely profits, and failure to achieve the budget was not necessarily considered to be a reflection of poor performance. However, during the 1990s and particularly due to the impact of a world recession on its business, Polyfoam began to suffer a decline in its profitability. This subsequently led to reconsideration of the management information systems and, indirectly, of its management accounting systems, which we will now describe.

Manufacturing changes and cost control

The recession put severe pressure on all of Polyfoam's operating units, including Company A which suffered a major decline in demand for its products and incurred substantial operating losses. It responded by combining certain production facilities and seeking various ways to cut costs. Company A's management perceived their problems as stemming from significant competitive pressures in both domestic and overseas markets, poor delivery times and a lack of quality products. Inadequate management accounting, and poor management information systems in general, were cited by the senior managers as being key contributors to the company's problems.

Senior management decided to purchase a fully integrated, computerized management information system called 'Triton'. This system provided the database needed to track costs through to production, as well as to facilitate the introduction of new software to better control the production process. In essence, the new 'Triton' system integrated the financial and the manufacturing dimensions of the business. In addition, and with a view to attempting to improve product and service quality, total quality management (TQM) and just-in-time (JIT) systems were also introduced, along with statistical production control (SPC).

However, despite these changes in the manufacturing systems, business profits failed to increase. And, eventually, the managers began to realize that although they had been focusing on short-term cost reduction, the business still had not been achieving international competitiveness. They had focused on the mechanics and technical aspects of their new tools and techniques, rather than their substance or the skills required to enable the company to become internationally competitive.

In particular, Polyfoam had given a great deal of attention to the control of operating costs, without due consideration of what was required to be globally competitive, and without sensitivity towards customer needs. Polyfoam's response to the crisis had been too production centred and insufficiently customer focused. In time, however, it was acknowledged that what seemed to be required was a change in the company's overriding (that is, institutionalized) assumptions which, in this case, suggested a fundamental shift from a production orientation to a customer orientation.

Implementation of WCM

This recognition of a need to change taken-for-granted business ways emerged alongside, and in part was due to a growing awareness of the WCM programme. The Chief Executive Officer (CEO) of Company A had attended a WCM training course offered by a regional training agency, and he immediately encouraged the senior managers to do the same. As these senior managers came to recognize the potential of WCM, together they embarked on a widespread training programme for all levels of the company in an attempt to explain the benefits of WCM to everyone.

It took 12 months from the CEO becoming interested in WCM as a concept, to the shop-floor workers becoming sufficiently familiar with it, before implementation. It was then possible to develop a five-year long-range plan, together with a 'one-page strategy' for each business area. The latter outlined each area manager's vision for the business.

The implementation of WCM was achieved without any significant resistance from either the managers or other employees. Furthermore, the change programme had a remarkable impact on business performance. In addition to improving the reported profits, performance also improved over a range of indicators, from lead time and percentage of on-time deliveries to new product developments and employees' suggestions for improvements. The primary aim of most WCM programmes is to focus production on satisfying the requirements of customers. In Company A, there was a shift from manager-centred manufacturing to customer-focused manufacturing.

At the same time, a conscious effort was made to secure employee involvement in the change programme – that is, to utilize employees' skills in meeting customers' requirements and to ensure that employees' attitudes were customer-focused. In order to achieve this aim, incentives were changed from individual to group based, and a weekly 'Competitive Edge Report' was produced to provide the non-financial and financial measures required to control production.

Following the implementation of WCM, Company A's managers tended to focus more on actual costs and actual trends rather than standard costs, and to make greater use of *non*-financial measures. Furthermore, the production managers became their own accountants, as the new information systems enabled them to do much of their own local analyses. As a result, the information flow tended to run from production to accounting, rather than vice versa. In general, the so-called 'Competitive Edge Reports' were used for controlling operations, although the Business Performance Reports continued to be used for reporting purposes and for management control by senior managers. Finally, the number of people comprising the accounting function declined to only three, representing a significant scale-down, with the Financial Controller describing his new role as 'consultant to the production managers', and emphasising the importance of his understanding in production-related matters.

Source: adapted from a case study in Burns et al. (2003).

Exercise

Describe what you believe were the key factors of successful change in Polyfoam?

In the Polyfoam case described in *Management Accounting in Practice 22.1*, there appeared to be a number of steps taken by managers that were evidently important for the success of implementing WCM. These steps are displayed in Exhibit 22.3

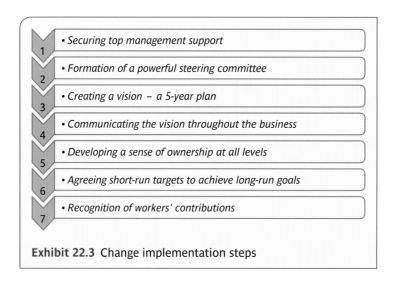

1. • Securing top management support
2. • Formation of a powerful steering committee
3. • Creating a vision – a 5-year plan
4. • Communicating the vision throughout the business
5. • Developing a sense of ownership at all levels
6. • Agreeing short-run targets to achieve long-run goals
7. • Recognition of workers' contributions

Exhibit 22.3 Change implementation steps

The first step was securing top management support. The decision to implement WCM was made by the CEO of Company A, and he then 'sold' the concept to his colleagues on the main management committee of Polyfoam. He had initially attended a WCM course, and all the members of his senior management team subsequently attended a similar course. Thus, as a result, broad support was gained for the project at the highest level of the company.

Second, was the formation of a powerful steering committee. The implementation of WCM was monitored by a steering committee, which comprised staff who held the necessary power and authority to take actions. For this purpose it is essential to have on the committee, not only those with sufficient hierarchical power, but also those who have power in relation to the day-to-day implementation of a project.

Third, Polyfoam created a vision, a five-year business plan. The desired outcomes of WCM were agreed and explicitly stated, prior to the implementation, in a 'vision statement', expressing what the business would be like in five years' time when WCM was firmly established. Although this provided a clear objective for the organization as a whole, it was also important in the sense that it let individuals know what WCM meant for them and what was expected of them.

The fourth step involved communicating the vision throughout the business. The vision statement was passed down the company and all parts of the business were required to produce 'one-page statements' which set out a strategy for local contribution towards this vision. As such, these statements expressed five-year plans for each area of the business and its processes.

Fifth, the change leaders worked to develop a sense of ownership at all levels of the organization. As the 'one-page vision statements' were prepared for all areas of the business, they served to encourage and nurture a sense of ownership throughout the organization. Furthermore, these statements were not just prepared to be then put aside and forgotten – instead, they became a major focus for the sixth step, which was agreeing short-run targets to achieve long-run goals. Each part of the business produced short-run targets, which were deemed necessary to achieve the five-year plan. Ongoing monitoring of performance against these targets became an important element of the management control systems, which were integrated within WCM.

Finally, for the seventh step, there was formal recognition of workers' contributions to a continuous improvement programme. The contribution of everyone within the organization, down to the individual shop-floor workers, was taken very seriously. As quality constitutes a core element of WCM philosophy, all workers were encouraged to take an active part in continuous improvement, and individual contributions were explicitly recognized. Further, a mixture of both individual *and* group rewards was built around quality-improvement targets.

The seven steps, above, should be considered in the context of unfolding institutional change in the Polyfoam case. As the initial manufacturing changes had not achieved their intention, and as profitability continued to be disappointing, the management of Company A recognized that they needed to challenge underlying and taken-for-granted assumptions about the nature of their business – that is, their production-orientation.

Importantly also, this need to change the institutionalized assumptions was recognized *before* the new WCM systems (and the new management accounting systems) were introduced. The initial training scheme 'sold' a need for such change per se, as well as 'selling' the concept of WCM, before these new systems were actually introduced. Thus, as the new systems were being implemented they were perceived as being part of, and an essential support to, the process of institutional change.

Furthermore, new ways of thinking which underpinned the new systems and a customer orientation were an extension (or modification at most) of the existing production orientation, rather than being a direct challenge to it. The centrality of 'production' to the company remained, but rather than focusing on merely the technical aspects of the production process, whereby costs would be cut and quality improved for their own sake, the business recognized a need to direct its production process towards meeting customers' needs. This, of course, differs to the nature of the change process in Nasty Stuff Ltd, where new accounting rules and routines conflicted with existing chemistry orientation.

The process of change in Polyfoam can thus be regarded as evolutionary in the sense that it builds on, and extends, existing and prevalent ways of thinking. The initial changes that were made, and the new manufacturing systems that were introduced, were compatible and aligned with underlying and long-established institutions. The external pressures of declining demand and increasing competition influenced the introduction of new production-centred management techniques, such as JIT and TQM (see Chapter 20). Thus, the ways of thinking underlying the new rules and routines were sufficiently compatible with the existing institutions within the company (that is, the production-based culture). But, as these changes failed to improve profitability, the need for a more customer-centred production culture was recognized, due largely to an external stimulus in the form of a government incentive programme. Furthermore, this need to change the existing institutional base was recognized before the introduction of the new WCM systems. Thus, when the new rules and routines were introduced, the institutions were already changing in a manner that was compatible with the underlying assumptions of WCM.

This case highlights evolutionary change which reaches its intentional goals. In the first instance new techniques, such as JIT and TQM, were successfully implemented, but only 'successful' in the sense that they were introduced without resistance, and came to be used in the organization. Here, the change was compatible with the existing institutions. However, in another sense, the change was also 'unsuccessful' in that it did not solve the profitability problems. So, a second change took place, and also addressed the profitability problem. In this second change, there was institutional change, which had begun before the new rules and routines were introduced. Thus, when the rules and routines were introduced, they were perceived as being in support of the new institutions (that is, the customer-centred production focus).

Implementing management accounting change

It was stated at the outset of this chapter just how complex management accounting change can be. We have considered broad conceptions of change, beyond simple movements 'from one situation to another', and used an institutional theoretical framework as insight to interpret the nature of management accounting change in two real organizations.

This section now summarizes some of the key messages from both case studies, once again drawing upon concepts and ideas from the institutional theoretical framework. In so doing, it is intended to provide useful pointers towards how 'best' to manage the design and implementation of management accounting change.

Institutions matter

A clear message from both case studies is that institutions matter. An organization's taken-for-granted assumptions can have a direct and important impact on the eventual outcome of a change programme. For instance, as we learned in the Nasty Stuff Ltd case, failure to question the nature of the existing institutions can create problems further down the line. To the contrary, in Polyfoam, because managers worked to understand and mobilize existing institutions before embarking on management accounting change, this helped smooth the change process and contributed towards successful outcomes.

The prospect of successful change implementation is likely to be enhanced if the new management accounting systems are compatible with existing taken-for-granted assumptions in an organization, which may or may not change during subsequent implementation process. Otherwise, conflict and resistance can develop, and ultimately failure. Again, the case of Nasty Stuff Ltd was an illustration of where new management accounting systems were incompatible with dominant institutions within the locale for change (R&D), and this incited resistance, blame, frustration, conflict and eventually failure. On the other hand, in Polyfoam there was sufficient compatibility between evolving customer-oriented institutions and the new management accounting systems. And, there was a questioning of, and changes in, extant institutions before the new systems were imposed.

Both case studies convey that management accounting change is complex and multidimensional, requires careful planning and thoughtful implementation, and extends significantly beyond the purely 'technical' focus. In fact the Nasty Stuff Ltd case study was especially illustrative of how failure in management accounting change can be to a large extent due to too much emphasis on technical aspects and insufficient consideration being given to the institutional context within which the new systems were being implemented.

Management accounting change which unduly focuses on the technical aspects of new systems is likely to create 'mechanical' routines, as happened in Nasty Stuff Ltd, with little or no accompanying change in dominant taken-for-granted business assumptions. Furthermore, acceptance and new ownership of accounting systems will not be achieved through an overly technical change programme.

Breaking the bubble

It is important to question an organization's existing settled assumptions before any significant changes to management accounting systems are made. By their inert and embedded nature, institutions will create a barrier to change, but institutions can and should at least be challenged. New management accounting systems can be designed (or bought) and changed relatively easily, but they can be very difficult to implement if they challenge existing taken-for-granted assumptions. Sometimes, change will demand breaking the bubble of taken-for-granted assumptions and this is not necessarily easy to do.

In respect of breaking the bubble, considerable responsibility must lie with the leaders of a change programme, who should seek to identify as far as possible the existing institutions within the organizational setting. They should also assess the extent to which new management accounting systems require institutional change. In so doing, it will be important to recognize institutional differences between organizations and different organizational units, as well as institutional differences between the individual departments within the same organization. (See Exhibit 22.4.)

Important questions which should be asked, when embarking on a programme of management accounting change, include the following:

- What are the taken-for-granted and generally unquestioned assumptions in your organization, and how internally consistent are they?

- Where do these taken-for-granted assumptions come from?

- How or by who are these assumptions reproduced and reinforced over time – for example, are they encouraged by the existing incentive schemes?

- Who are the powerful groups within your organization and what are *their* taken-for-granted assumptions?
- Are these assumptions potentially incompatible with the new management accounting tools or systems that are to be implemented?

Exhibit 22.4 What to consider when implementing management accounting change

For example, we might question whether different individuals or groups within the same organization think (or 'tick') in different ways. Does the marketing manager, for instance, have different assumptions about his/her business to those of the accountant? There are different mindsets within and across organizations, largely based on combinations of experience, qualifications, training and personalities. Such differences can have a significant impact on the relative success or failure of a management accounting change programme.

When considering such questions, it might be sensible for the leaders of a change programme to employ the assistance of an outsider to 'break the bubble' of an organization. Such a person will need to have a sufficient understanding of the business, while at the same time having a sufficient distance from it to be able to ask the necessary questions, which might not be raised by an institutionalized member of the organization. Although it is not impossible, it can be very difficult for insiders to actually see the taken-for-granted assumptions in their organization.

Institutional change

Once an organization's taken-for-granted assumptions have been identified, how do we go about managing institutional change? It would be naive to suggest that a predetermined set of procedures exist that can be used; however, as we saw in the Polyfoam case, good communication, education and training are paramount. Thus the nature and purpose of any management accounting change must be communicated to all relevant parts of an organization and, where necessary, the importance of changing the norm and unquestioned ways must be fully explained and openly discussed. Moreover, training in new procedures and assumptions should be both extensive and intensive – meaning that it should be given to everyone involved, and it should be of sufficient depth so that each person fully understands intended new ways of working.

As we witnessed in the Nasty Stuff Ltd case, 'mechanical' implementation of a new management accounting system is unlikely to change embedded ways of thinking (in that case, from a chemistry orientation). Management accounting change should be accompanied by clear explanations of why such change is taking place. And, this should encompass everyone who is involved in, or either directly or indirectly affected by the process of change. Otherwise, existing taken-for-granted assumptions are likely to remain unchanged and can create conflict and resistance, which can ultimately lead to failure in the change programme.

Challenges of change for the future

This chapter has explored, both conceptually and through researched-based examples, issues surrounding the design and implementation of management accounting (and more generally, organizational) change. This is such a key area for tomorrow's management accountants because change is about the most obvious and guaranteed process that will remain in and around organizations, but also most evidence suggests that management accountants are expected to be very involved in change management.

So what sorts of changes might we expect to witness over the next decade, and what might the roles for management accountants be? Or put another way, what are the emerging issues which promise to have major ramifications on the organizational world over the next 10 years or so? We briefly consider some of these emerging 'hot topics' in this final section of the book, although there are no doubt countless other issues we could have included (or just do not yet know).

Business partner role

A fair amount has already been included in the book (see Chapter 1, for example) about the recent emergence of a 'business partnering' role for management accountants, whereby the latter spend less time with mundane and routine accounting tasks, and work more 'out in the field' as advisory colleagues to business managers. Much written has been about this emergent role for management accountants, not least by the professional bodies (CIMA, 2009; CGMA, 2012a) who clearly wish to develop and promote such new and exciting roles for their members.

It will be interesting to see how this development pans out in the near future, and there is still much more to be understood and learned. How 'new' are these developments, or have some management accountants actually been advising business managers 'in native language' for longer than we think? What tools and techniques will management accountants adopt to facilitate this advisory role? What is the appropriate training and career path for moving into such advisory roles? What kind of professional competition might management accountants face in undertaking (or even assuming) such roles, and from whom?

22.2: Management Accounting in Practice

CIMA's critical agenda for 2012/13

In a recent report the Chartered Global Management Accountant (CGMA), a joint venture between two professional accountancy bodies CIMA and American Institute of Certified Public Accountants (AICPA), set out its short-term agenda for management accountants and the profession which they represented. They established themes and topics for 2012 and 2013, respectively, as follows:

	Theme	Topics
2012	Doing the right thing	● Applied ethics
		● Corporate social responsibility
		● Behaviours
		● Leadership
	Developing the skills and talent to succeed	● CFO priorities
		● Future of management accounting
		● Valuing talent – cost of losing and retaining talent
		● Tomorrow's finance talent and competencies
	Making it happen	● Contemporary performance management

2013	Risk versus innovation		• Strategy, risk and opportunity
	Resilient business models		• What they are and how to develop them
	Turning data into insights and action		• Managing mega-data
			• Cloud computing, IT
			• The Internet of things

Source: CGMA (2012b).

Exercise

Critically assess the themes and topics above; do you sympathize with CGMA's choice of themes and topics? (If you can, seek and read the whole report – (CGMA, 2012f) – though it is not absolutely essential.) Can you think of other more pressing matters for the short-term agenda of management accountants – explain your reasoning?

Accounting for networks

Organizations are collaborating and becoming interconnected more and more. The relationship between two organizations is no longer just about straightforward transactions. Collaboration through various networks is seen as a quick and flexible way to get hold of and use complementary resources and competences belonging to other organizations. It is working towards the achievement of common objectives that has driven many organizations to seek to form alliances, partnerships and other networked situations. Management information is shared between organizations – even competitors – and increasingly made more available to 'outsiders' in ways that would have been unthinkable not so long ago.

Immediately the concept of **accounting for networks** conjures up the potential for significant new roles for management accountants – in particular there would surely be a need for new control procedures, planning and more. The recent emergence of networks-based accounting has opened up the boundaries within which management accounting, and management accountants, operate. It creates new inter-organizational relationships, new structures and new cross-organizational processes, to name but a few of the impacts. All of this places huge demands on new information requirements but also accompanying control and measurement systems.

A CIMA-sponsored report by Caglio and Ditillo (2006) claimed that the impact of such developments on the roles of management accountants was actually not as significant as one might expect. They suggested that changes represented more of an extension of existing management accounting practice, across the expanded networks, rather than entirely new practices. However, one suspects that in the future the roles of management accountants will be significantly reshaped by further development of inter-organizational relationships.

Technological advance

The pace of technological advance over the past 20 years has been just staggering. In organizations, technology has for example completely changed ways of working in product design, operations, procurement, communication, and so much more. Even greater pace and magnitude of technological advance is guaranteed for the future, and it will be important that management accountants keep abreast of such developments (Rowan, 2012), not necessarily as a technical expert but as someone who can advise, and help the IT specialists and managers design and choose the appropriate information systems, tools and techniques for any specific information requirements.

We have already covered the implications of most recent and future technological advance, especially in Chapter 21, so we need not go into too much detail here. But it is important to recognize that technological advance will continue to have major implications in the future. One particular IT development in very recent years that is highly likely to have a significant, though as yet unknown, impact on the roles of management accountants, as guardians of organizational information, is cloud computing, alongside further advances in 'business intelligence' (CGMA, 2012c).

The age of 'big data' is truly upon us now (CGMA, 2012d), where technology exists to store, retrieve and potentially use an enormous amount of data for analysis and informing decisions on a scale previously unheard of. This is emerging technology that some data-reliant organizations such as Amazon, Google, Apple and Facebook have already begun to take advantage of.

Another potentially significant impact on management accounting will be **predictive analytics**, which is the use of a wide range of technological tools and techniques to retrieve, store and use external data, for instance data on customers, suppliers and other stakeholders (Cooper, 2012). Predictive analytics is about bringing the external context in, and facilitating powerful scenarios and 'what if' analyses. With a solid intelligence platform through good planning and forecasting tools, predictive analytics is said by its advocates to have extremely powerful forecasting abilities.

The main advantage to this technology (as, say, against business intelligence) is that predictive analytics uses external, not internal business-related information. It also has other powerful abilities such as being able to make linkages between economic indicators and internal business indicators. Management accountants will need to be up to speed on the development in such technology so that they can remain one of the first points of call for business managers to look to for assistance in retrieving and analysing appropriate information; the difference between this sort of thing and traditional roles however is that such information is entirely about the future not historical and much of the analysis will not only be potentially vast in quantity but also to a large extent experimental.

Ethics

Ethical business is high on the agenda for many organizations, especially organizations and industries which in recent times have been directly linked with the 2007 financial crisis, as well as those connected in any way to multiple corporate failures and scandals of the past decade. There has been a significant decline in societal-level trust towards organizations, and the response has included increased regulation and sweeping calls for more ethically grounded business practices.

A recent survey by the Chartered Global Management Accountant (CGMA, 2012e) investigated the extent of concerns over ethics in business, but also the enactment in practice of more ethical behaviour. Their conclusion was that although there have been some positive steps in terms of new regulation and intentions to be more ethical in business, the evidence suggests that actual practice was regrettably lagging behind.

The report argues that management accountants have a key role in the future for promoting ethical behaviour in organizations of all kinds but highlight that they themselves are in fact one of the most at-risk vocations for being under pressure to act unethically. There is clearly much work to be done in business ethics, and much trust restoration; management accountants promise to have a key role in such change processes but everything so far suggests that this will not be an easy role for them.

Sustainable development

No one could fail to notice the increased importance attached to sustainable development (see Chapter 19) in the past decade or so, in organizations but also in our society more generally. In this book we have tended to adopt the term 'sustainable development' rather than 'sustainability', as this gives more attention to the processes of attempting to *become* sustainable, as opposed to some static or final state (Milne et al., 2006).

Sustainable development is already having a considerable impact on organizations of all types. As we described briefly in Chapter 17, many organizations are nowadays including a society/environment perspective in their performance management tools such as the balanced scorecard or similar strategic performance management tool, and non-financial indicators pertaining to impact on society and the environment are on the increase. In particular, organizations need to be concerned about implications for the future, and 'do the right thing' for mounting problems such as climate change and water depletion; there is evidence that some organizations are starting to take such things very seriously (CGMA, 2012f) though there is still much scepticism around as to the amount of rhetoric and fake discourse involved in what organizations say they are doing and what they actually do in practice.

Water shortage and climate change, among other social and environmental challenges in the future, will continue to impose on organizations, and management accountants will be at the centre of producing and analysing information that will help these organizations not only to face such problems but also (hopefully) try at the same time to not contribute towards making such problems worse than they already are.

The adoption of integrated reporting (see Chapter 19) is seemingly on the increase and has some very powerful professional bodies behind it. Integrated reporting is a new approach to organizational reporting which seeks to link an organization's strategy, governance and financial performance to the social, environmental and economic context within which it operates. Unsurprisingly it includes the incorporation and elevation in importance of non-financial measures and indicators in an organization's annual report.

It is still relatively early days for the likes of sustainable development and integrated reporting in organizations, but it is most definitely an area that will further intensify in its use and application. If not already, it will become an integral part of an organization's strategising and hold an important place in its information base. Hence, management accounting and the roles of management accountants in this area are bound to become significant, while not necessarily alone in vying for the ownership of such information.

22.2: Management Accounting Insight

Integrated reporting and the ramifications for management accountants

Integrated reporting is still in its infancy, although there is some momentum in its adoption and diffusion. Early adopters include companies such as BASF, Philips, Novo Nordisk and United Technologies Corporation (UTC).

There is an interesting collection of case studies, commissioned by the Prince's Accounting for Sustainability Project (Hopwood et al., 2010) which explore how leading-edge organizations are trying to embed sustainable ways into their day-to-day operations, via accounting tools. Most cases show organizations to be at a very early stage, for various reasons, in trying to filter such ways into daily organizational life, although some were at least attempting to move in the right direction: the Novo Nordisk case, for example, by Dey and Burns explained how that company was using a balanced scorecard to try to promote responsible sourcing, as has been explained already in *Management Accounting in Practice 17.2*.

Source: Dey and Burns (2010); various organizational websites.

Exercise

Before tackling this exercise, do some research on integrated reporting – for example, try to find out what the organizations listed above are doing. Then, discuss the following:

a) Why do you think organizations adopt integrated reporting?

b) What do you think might be the main implications of adopting integrated reporting for an organization's management accounting practice?

c) What is the impact of integrated reporting on the roles of management accountants.

Chapter summary

In this chapter, we have explored the complexities of management accounting change, as well as teasing out the multiple challenges faced when managing change. By considering a broad and 'beyond optimizing solutions' perspective of change, and adopting an institutional theoretical view, we were able to explore research-based case studies of management accounting change which exposed much more than merely the 'before' and 'after' of particular accounting change processes. We have finished this chapter, and indeed the entire textbook, with a dip into the exciting if not rather unknown future of management accounting.

Key terms

Accounting for networks Accounting for the achievement of common objectives via alliances, partnerships and other networked situations (p. 603)

Change process A view of change as being part of an unfolding story rather than a simplistic shift from one optimizing state to another (p. 590)

Ethical business Doing what is the socially, morally and environmentally right thing to do (p. 604)

Institutional theoretical perspective of management accounting change One (of several) theoretical perspectives of management accounting change, focusing particularly on the important interactions

over time of organizational rules, routines and institutions (p. 591)

Institutions Unquestioned and taken for granted assumptions in an organization in regards to 'the way we do things' (p. 592)

Management accounting change The process by which management accounting practices become what they do (or not) over time (p. 589)

Predictive analytics The use of technological tools to retrieve, store and use external data, and predict multiple business scenarios and identify appropriate actions (p. 604)

Routine The re-enactment of rules, how things are actually done in an organization (p. 591)

Rules Formalized procedures of how things should be done in an organization (p. 591)

• • • Review questions • • • • • • • • • • • • connect •

Level of difficulty: BASIC   INTERMEDIATE   ADVANCED

22.1 How would you describe 'management accounting change'? **[LO1, LO2]**

22.2 What do you think is meant by viewing 'change as a process over time'? **[LO1, LO2]**

22.3 Describe the different levels at which management accounting change can take place. **[LO1, LO3]**

22.4 What is an 'institution'? **[LO2]**

22.5 Describe cloud computing. **[LO6]**

22.6 How much potential has predictive analyses? **[LO6]**

22.7 Define ethical business, and explain a management accountant's role in such things.**[LO6]**

22.8 Explain what integrated reporting is, and what it intends to promote. **[LO6]**

22.9 What is 'accounting for networks' and how will it involve the management accountant? **[LO6]**

22.10 What are some likely changes which management accountants may face in the near future? **[LO5, LO6]**

Group discussion and activity questions

22.11 Do you think that management accountants should rightfully be leaders of organizational change programmes, and if so, why? **[LO1, LO4, LO5, LO6]**

22.12 Critically appraise the usefulness of an institutional theoretical perspective for understanding the complexities of management accounting change. To do so, it might help if you read some of the key research papers such as Scapens (1994) and Burns and Scapens (2000). **[LO1, LO2, LO4, LO6]**

22.13 In your opinion, what will be the three most significant drivers of management accounting change in the next 10 years? Explain your reasoning. **[LO1, LO5, LO6]**

22.14 Do some research (read articles, search the web) on climate change, and describe some of the implications this will have on the future role of management accountants? **[LO7]**

Exercises   connect

E22.1 **Institutional theory of management accounting change [LO2]**

Institutions are the re-enactment of rules or in other words, how things are actually done in an organization: true or false?

E22.2 **Management accounting change [LO2, LO5, LO7]**

Listed below are a number of terms relating to management accounting change. Choose the terms that most appropriately complete the following statements.

> Business partnering
> Integrated reporting
> Rules
> What-if
> Breaking the bubble

a) _____ analysis is a predictive analytics tool used by companies.

b) _____ is a new approach to organizational reporting which seeks to link an organization's strategy, governance and financial performance to the social, environmental and economic context within which it operates.

c) The _____ role requires management accountants to spend less time with mundane and routine accounting tasks, and work more 'out in the field' as advisory colleagues to business managers.

d) _____ refers to challenging the existing taken-for-granted assumptions.

e) _____ refers to the formalized procedures of how things should be done in an organization.

E22.3 **Future challenges for management accountants [LO6, LO7]**

Which of the following roles do you *not* think will become more relevant to management accountants in the future?

a) Business ethics

b) Sustainable development

c) Systems design and change

d) Payroll and ledger management

E22.4 **Future challenges in management accounting [LO7]**

Fill in the missing words:

A new technology known as _____ _____ aims to *bring the external context in*, and to facilitate powerful predictive scenarios and 'what if' analyses.

E22.5 **Levels of change [LO1]**

Change can take place at different levels for example, environmental change, organizational change, intra-organizational change and group/individuals change.

Required:

Identify the level of change that each of these examples will fall into.

1) Cross training the line staff to enable them to perform accounting tasks

2) Introduction of the Sarbanes-Oxley Act of 2002

3) Introduction of new revenue recognition method by the management Intra

4) Merger of Brida Woods Ltd. and Myra Furniture Ltd.

5) Advent of social media as a strong advertisement tool

6) Retirement of the CEO of an organization

7) Outsourcing the production of a part which was being produced internally.

E22.6 **Management accounting change [LO2, LO7]**

Match the following terms with their descriptions.

Descriptions	Terms
1. Business practices that are socially, morally and environmentally right	a. Environmental change
2. These refer to mergers and acquisitions, alliances and networks among and between organizations, or outsourcing	b. Ethical business
3. The re-enactment of rules, how things are actually done in an organization	c. Predictive analytics
4. The use of technological tools to retrieve, store and use external data, and to forecast results in multiple business scenarios and identify appropriate actions	d. Routine
5. Unquestioned and taken for granted assumptions in an organization in regards to 'the way we do things'	e. Organizational change
6. These refer to new policies or rules at the economy/society level, new and emerging world orders, new technologies or new social fads	f. Institutions

E22.7 **Management accounting change [LO1, LO2, LO4]**

Is management accounting change simply about the introduction of a new tool, technique or system? Describe what other things management accountants should be concerned with.

E22.8 **Using predictive analytics [LO6]**

Star Symphony Ltd. is a producer of watches. The company has provided you with the following information:

Sales price per unit	£109
Variable costs per unit	£35
Total fixed costs	£37,000
Units sold	600

The company is planning to launch an advertisement campaign to increase the sales. This campaign will run for three months. The advertisement campaign will cost the company £8,000. The business intelligence reports show that such an advertisement could increase sales by 15–20%.

Required:

a) Perform a what-if analysis and show the effect of the advertisement campaign on company profits. (Show the impact for each 1% increase on sales)

b) As per the what-if analysis, what minimum percentage of increase in sales will justify spending on the advertisement campaign?

E22.9 **Implementing management accounting change [LO6]**

Imagine you have been asked to lead the implementation of a balanced scorecard in your local hospital:

a) What tasks would you undertake at the beginning of the change programme?

b) What potential hurdles and problems might you expect, and how would you deal with them?

c) Outline the process through which you intend to design and implement the balanced scorecard.

● ● Case study problem ● ● ● ● ● ● ● ● ● ● connect ● ● ●

C22.1 **ABC in ABB [LO1, LO4, LO5]**

In the late-1990s Asea Boveri Brown, UK (ABB) began the process of implementing activity-based costing. It took nearly two years into the change process before costs were even properly discussed or before an accountant started to (re)design the cost systems, but this was intentional.

At each UK factory: the first stage of the change programme was a gathering of around 15 representatives from different functions of the organization. This group met roughly every week, and spent six to eight months drawing up how they 'saw' the business. They mapped the business process on a large white board (reconfiguring when necessary), and captured a large portrayal of 'how the business is'. This portrayal 'told the story' of the business process and all the interconnections; so, from customer invoice through to delivery and after-sales-service, but also the interconnections with such other processes as stocks, finance, procurement and much more. After six to eight months the whiteboard was an interesting tale of flows of information, reporting lines, and much more.

The following six to eight months was spent by the group drawing up (on a large whiteboard again) 'how the business *should* be'; this version of ABB business tried to integrate operational efficiencies and common sense. The final six to eight months was devoted to how the factory might get from where it was at to where it should be.

It was only at this point that the change leader, an accountant, began to think about the new (activity-based) costing system. Until then, he had been ever-present in each of the group meetings described above, but intentionally had played an arm's-length role. Nearly two years on, and with much internal investigation into 'what we do' and 'what we should do', the factories were in a much better position to design and implement a new costing system.

Source: based on author's own research.

Required:

a) What were the advantages of the approach taken?

b) Would it be a surprise that very soon afterwards ABB launched into the implementation of activity-based management (ABM)? Why?

c) This was a successful change programme; what aspects of the change programme do you think helped achieve such success?

Recommended reading

- Busco, C., P. Quattrone and A. Riccaboni (2007) 'Management accounting: issues in interpreting its nature and change', *Management Accounting Research*, 18(2), pp. 125–49.

A thought-provoking, largely conceptual review of the management accounting change literature.

- Doherty, C. (2012) 'The world in 2022', *Financial Management* (CIMA), March, pp. 27–30.

An insightful article on what management accountants' roles might entail by the year 2022.

- Modell, S. (2007) 'Managing accounting change', in T. Hopper, D. Northcott and R. W. Scapens (eds), *Issues in Management Accounting*, 3rd edn, Harlow: Pearson Education.

A thorough overview of the academic literature covering the multiple issues and complexities surrounding management accounting change.

- Ribeiro, J. A. and R. W. Scapens (2006) 'Institutional theories in management accounting change: contributions, issues and paths for development', *Qualitative Research in Accounting and Management*, 3(2), pp. 94–111.

A useful overview of research on management accounting change which adopts an institutional theoretical perspective, with particular emphasis on the dynamics of power and politics.

- Scapens, R. W. (2006) 'Understanding management accounting practices: a personal journey', *Management Accounting Research*, 38(1), pp. 1–30.

Not only does this article provide an insight into what researchers have focused on over the past three decades in the management accounting area, but there are also interesting references to and discussion of the institutional perspective of management accounting change.

- Sulaiman, S. and F. Mitchell (2005) 'Using a typology of management accounting change: an empirical analysis', *Management Accounting Research*, 16(4), pp. 422–37.

A helpful typology of the various perspectives or types of change in management accounting, this paper offers a way to frame understanding of empirical observations on management accounting change.

- Wickramasinghe, D. and C. Alawattage (2007) *Management Accounting Change: Approaches and Perspectives*, Oxford: Routledge.

An excellent and thorough overview of different theoretical perspectives on management accounting change.

References

Burns, J. (2000) 'The dynamics of accounting change: inter-play between new practices, routines, institutions, power and politics', *Accounting, Auditing and Accountability Journal*, 13(5), pp. 566–96.

Burns, J. and R. W. Scapens (2000) 'Conceptualising management accounting change: an institutional framework', *Management Accounting Research*, 10(1), pp. 1–19.

Burns, J., M. Ezzamel and R. W. Scapens (2003) *The Challenge of Management Accounting Change*, London: CIMA/Elsevier.

Caglio, A. and A. Ditillo (2006) *Management Accounting in Networks: Techniques and Applications*, CIMA Research Executive Summary Series, 2(14).

CIMA (2009) 'Improving decision making in organizations – the opportunity to reinvent finance business partners', a report by the Chartered Institute of Management Accountants, July, CIMA, London.

CGMA (2012a) 'From ledgers to leadership: a journey through the finance function – 2012 update', report by the Chartered Global Management Accountant, January, http://www.cgma.org/Pages/default.aspx (accessed on 25 May 2012).

CGMA (2012b) 'Innovative outlook: framing the global management accounting agenda 2012/13', report by the Chartered Global Management Accountant, May, http://www.cgma.org/Pages/default.aspx (accessed on 25 May 2012).

CGMA (2012c) 'Improving decision-making in organisations: unlocking business intelligence', report by the Chartered Global Management Accountant, January, http://www.cgma.org/Pages/default.aspx (accessed on 25 May 2012).

CGMA (2012d) 'Big data analytics – where next?', online Magazine of the Chartered Global Management Accountant, May, http://www.cgma.org/Pages/default.aspx (accessed 25 May 2012).

CGMA (2012e) 'Managing responsible business: a global survey on business ethics', report by the Chartered Global Management Accountant, May, http://www.cgma.org/Pages/default.aspx (accessed 25 May 2012).

CGMA (2012f) 'Sustainable business: shared value in practice', report by the Chartered Global Management Accountant, April, http://www.cgma.org/Pages/default.aspx (accessed 25 May 2012).

Cooper, T. (2012) 'Predictive testing', *Financial Management* (CIMA Magazine), May, pp. 33–4.

Dey, C. and J. Burns (2010) 'Integrated reporting at Novo Nordisk', in A. Hopwood, J. Unerman and J. Fries (eds), *Accounting for Sustainability: Practical Insights*, London: Earthscan.

Hopwood, A., J. Unerman and J. Fries (2010) *Accounting for Sustainability*, London: Earthscan.

Milne, M. J., K. Kearins and S. Walton (2006) 'Creating adventures in wonderland: the journey metaphor and environmental sustainability', *Organisation*, 13, pp. 801–39.

Rowan, D. (2012) 'Opinion', *Financial Management* (CIMA), April, pp. 18–19.

Scapens, R. W. (1994) 'Never mind the gap: towards an institutional perspective on management accounting change', *Management Accounting Research*, 5(3–4), pp. 301–21.

Wickramasinghe, D. and C. Alawattage (2007) *Management Accounting Change: Approaches and Perspectives*, Oxford: Routledge.

When you have read this chapter

Log on to the Online Learning Centre at **www.mcgraw-hill.co.uk/textbooks/burns** to explore chapter-by-chapter test questions, links and further online study tools for Management Accounting.

Appendix A: Present value tables

This table provides the discount rates used to discount future cashflows. For example, if you have a discount rate of 3% and a single payment of £100, in five years time it will have a present value of £86.26.

Years	1%	2%	3%	4%	5%	6%	7%	8%	9%	10%
1	0.9901	0.9804	0.9709	0.9615	0.9524	0.9434	0.9346	0.9259	0.9174	0.9091
2	0.9803	0.9612	0.9426	0.9426	0.9070	0.8900	0.8734	0.8573	0.8417	0.8264
3	0.9706	0.9423	0.9151	0.8890	0.8638	0.8396	0.8163	0.7938	0.7722	0.7513
4	0.9610	0.9238	0.8885	0.8548	0.8227	0.7921	0.7629	0.7350	0.7084	0.6830
5	0.9515	0.9057	0.8626	0.8219	0.7835	0.7473	0.7130	0.6806	0.6499	0.6209
6	0.9420	0.8880	0.8375	0.7903	0.7462	0.7050	0.6663	0.6302	0.5963	0.5645
7	0.9327	0.8706	0.8131	0.7599	0.7107	0.6651	0.6227	0.5835	0.5470	0.5132
8	0.9235	0.8535	0.7894	0.7307	0.6768	0.6274	0.5820	0.5403	0.5019	0.4665
9	0.9143	0.8368	0.7664	0.7026	0.6446	0.5919	0.5439	0.5002	0.4604	0.4241
10	0.9053	0.8203	0.7441	0.6756	0.6139	0.5584	0.5083	0.4632	0.4224	0.3855
11	0.8963	0.8043	0.7224	0.6496	0.5847	0.5268	0.4751	0.4289	0.3875	0.3505
12	0.8874	0.7885	0.7014	0.6246	0.5568	0.4970	0.4440	0.3971	0.3555	0.3860
13	0.8787	0.7730	0.6810	0.6006	0.5303	0.4688	0.4150	0.3677	0.3262	0.2897
14	0.8700	0.7579	0.6611	0.5775	0.5051	0.4423	0.3878	0.3405	0.2992	0.2633
15	0.8613	0.7430	0.6419	0.5553	0.4810	0.4173	0.3624	0.3152	0.2745	0.2394
16	0.8528	0.7284	0.6232	0.5339	0.4581	0.3936	0.3387	0.2919	0.2519	0.2176
17	0.8440	0.7142	0.6050	0.5134	0.4363	0.3714	0.3166	0.2703	0.2311	0.1978
18	0.8360	0.7002	0.5874	0.4936	0.4155	0.3503	0.2959	0.2502	0.2120	0.1799
19	0.8277	0.6864	0.5703	0.4746	0.3957	0.3305	0.2765	0.2317	0.1945	0.1635
20	0.8195	0.6730	0.5537	0.4564	0.3769	0.3118	0.2584	0.2145	0.1784	0.1486
21	0.8114	0.6598	0.5375	0.4388	0.3589	0.2942	0.2415	0.1987	0.1637	0.1351
22	0.8034	0.6468	0.5219	0.4220	0.3418	0.2775	0.2257	0.1839	0.1502	0.1228
23	0.7954	0.6342	0.5067	0.4057	0.3256	0.2618	0.2109	0.1703	0.1378	0.1117
24	0.7876	0.6217	0.4919	0.3901	0.3101	0.2470	0.1971	0.1577	0.1264	0.1015
25	0.7798	0.6095	0.4776	0.3751	0.2953	0.2330	0.1842	0.1460	0.1160	0.0923
26	0.7720	0.5976	0.4637	0.3607	0.2812	0.2198	0.1722	0.1352	0.1064	0.0839
27	0.7644	0.5859	0.4502	0.3468	0.2678	0.2074	0.1609	0.1252	0.0976	0.0763
28	0.7568	0.5744	0.4371	0.3335	0.2551	0.1956	0.1504	0.1159	0.0895	0.0693
29	0.7493	0.5631	0.4243	0.3207	0.2429	0.1846	0.1406	0.1073	0.0822	0.0630
30	0.7419	0.5521	0.4120	0.3083	0.2314	0.1741	0.1314	0.0094	0.0754	0.0573
35	0.7059	0.5000	0.3554	0.2534	0.1813	0.1301	0.0937	0.0676	0.0490	0.0356
40	0.6717	0.4529	0.3066	0.2083	0.1420	0.0972	0.0668	0.0460	0.0318	0.0221
45	0.6391	0.4102	0.2644	0.1712	0.1113	0.0727	0.0476	0.0313	0.0207	0.0137
50	0.6080	0.3715	0.2281	0.1407	0.0872	0.0543	0.0339	0.0213	0.0134	0.0085

Appendix A (continued)

11%	12%	13%	14%	15%	16%	17%	18nb%	19%	20%	Years
0.9009	0.8929	0.8850	0.8772	0.8696	0.8621	0.8547	0.8475	0.8403	0.0833	1
0.8116	0.7972	0.7831	0.7695	0.7561	0.7432	0.7305	0.7182	0.7062	0.6944	2
0.7312	0.7118	0.6931	0.6750	0.6575	0.6407	0.6244	0.6086	0.5934	0.5787	3
0.6587	0.6355	0.6133	0.5921	0.5718	0.5523	0.5337	0.5158	0.4987	0.4823	4
0.5935	0.5674	0.5428	0.5194	0.4972	0.4761	0.4561	0.4371	0.4190	0.4019	5
0.5346	0.5066	0.4803	0.4556	0.4323	0.4101	0.3897	0.3704	0.3521	0.3349	6
0.4817	0.4523	0.4251	0.3996	0.3759	0.3538	0.3332	0.3139	0.2959	0.2791	7
0.4339	0.4039	0.3762	0.3506	0.3269	0.3050	0.2848	0.2660	0.2487	0.2326	8
0.3909	0.3606	0.3329	0.0375	0.2843	0.2630	0.2434	0.2255	0.2090	0.1938	9
0.3522	0.3220	0.2946	0.2697	0.2472	0.2267	0.2080	0.1911	0.1756	0.1615	10
0.3173	0.2875	0.2607	0.2366	0.2149	0.1954	0.1778	0.1619	0.1476	0.1346	11
0.2858	0.2567	0.2307	0.2076	0.1869	0.1685	0.1520	0.1372	0.1240	0.1122	12
0.2575	0.2292	0.2042	0.1821	0.1625	0.1452	0.1299	0.1163	0.1042	0.0935	13
0.2320	0.2046	0.1807	0.1597	0.1413	0.1252	0.1110	0.0985	0.0876	0.0779	14
0.2090	0.1827	0.1599	0.1401	0.1229	0.1079	0.0949	0.0835	0.0736	0.0649	15
0.1883	0.1631	0.1415	0.1229	0.1069	0.0930	0.0811	0.0708	0.0618	0.0541	16
0.1696	0.1456	0.1252	0.1078	0.0929	0.0802	0.0693	0.0600	0.0520	0.0451	17
0.1528	0.1300	0.1108	0.0946	0.0808	0.0691	0.0592	0.0508	0.0437	0.0376	18
0.1377	0.1161	0.0981	0.0829	0.0703	0.0596	0.0506	0.0431	0.0367	0.0313	19
0.1240	0.1037	0.0868	0.0728	0.0611	0.0514	0.0433	0.0365	0.0308	0.0261	20
0.1117	0.0926	0.0768	0.0638	0.0531	0.0433	0.0370	0.0309	0.0259	0.0217	21
0.1007	0.0826	0.0680	0.0560	0.0462	0.0382	0.0316	0.0262	0.0218	0.0181	22
0.0907	0.0738	0.0601	0.0491	0.0402	0.0329	0.0270	0.0222	0.0183	0.0151	23
0.0817	0.0659	0.0532	0.0431	0.0349	0.0284	0.0231	0.0188	0.0154	0.0126	24
0.0736	0.0588	0.0471	0.0378	0.0304	0.0245	0.0197	0.0160	0.0129	0.0105	25
0.0663	0.0525	0.0417	0.0331	0.0264	0.0211	0.0169	0.0135	0.0109	0.0087	26
0.0597	0.0469	0.0369	0.0291	0.0230	0.0182	0.0144	0.0115	0.0091	0.0073	27
0.0538	0.0419	0.0326	0.0255	0.0200	0.0157	0.0123	0.0097	0.0077	0.0061	28
0.0485	0.0374	0.0289	0.0224	0.0174	0.0135	0.0105	0.0082	0.0064	0.0051	29
0.0437	0.0334	0.0256	0.0196	0.0151	0.0116	0.0090	0.0070	0.0054	0.0042	30
0.0259	0.0189	0.0139	0.0102	0.0075	0.0055	0.0041	0.0030	0.0023	0.0017	35
0.0154	0.0107	0.0075	0.0053	0.0037	0.0026	0.0019	0.0013	0.0010	0.0007	40
0.0091	0.0061	0.0041	0.0027	0.0019	0.0013	0.0009	0.0006	0.0004	0.0003	45
0.0054	0.0035	0.0022	0.0014	0.0009	0.0006	0.0004	0.0003	0.0002	0.0001	50

Appendix B: Cumulative present value factors

Annuity table

This table provides the annuity factors to discount the value of future cash flows. For example, with a discount rate of 3% and with five annual payments of £100, the present value is £458.

Years 0 to:	1%	2%	3%	4%	5%	6%	7%	8%	9%	10%
1	0.990	0.980	0.971	0.962	0.952	0.943	0.935	0.926	0.917	0.909
2	1.970	1.942	1.913	1.886	1.859	1.833	1.808	1.783	1.759	1.736
3	2.941	2.884	2.829	2.775	2.723	2.673	2.624	2.577	2.531	2.487
4	3.902	3.808	3.717	3.630	3.546	3.465	3.387	3.312	3.240	3.170
5	4.853	4.713	4.580	4.452	4.329	4.212	4.100	3.993	3.890	3.791
6	5.795	5.601	5.417	5.242	5.076	4.917	4.767	4.623	4.486	4.355
7	6.728	6.472	6.230	6.002	5.786	5.582	5.389	5.206	5.033	4.868
8	7.652	7.325	7.020	6.733	6.463	6.210	5.971	5.747	5.535	5.335
9	8.566	8.162	7.786	7.435	7.108	6.802	6.515	6.247	5.995	5.759
10	9.471	8.983	8.530	8.111	7.722	7.360	7.024	6.710	6.418	6.145
11	10.368	9.787	9.253	8.760	8.306	7.887	7.499	7.139	6.805	6.495
12	11.255	10.575	9.954	9.385	8.863	8.384	7.943	7.536	7.161	6.814
13	12.134	11.348	10.635	9.086	9.394	8.853	8.358	7.904	7.487	7.103
14	13.004	12.106	11.296	10.563	9.899	9.295	8.745	8.244	7.786	7.367
15	13.865	12.849	11.938	11.118	10.380	9.712	9.108	8.559	8.061	7.606
16	14.718	13.578	12.561	11.652	10.838	10.106	9.447	8.851	8.313	7.824
17	15.562	14.292	13.166	12.166	11.274	10.477	9.763	9.122	8.544	8.022
18	16.398	14.992	13.754	12.659	11.690	10.828	10.059	9.372	8.756	8.201
19	17.226	15.678	14.324	13.134	12.085	11.185	10.336	9.604	8.950	8.365
20	18.046	16.351	14.877	13.590	12.462	11.470	10.594	9.818	9.129	8.514
21	18.857	17.011	15.415	14.029	12.821	11.764	10.836	10.017	9.292	8.649
22	19.660	17.658	15.937	14.451	13.163	12.042	11.061	10.201	9.442	8.772
23	20.456	18.292	16.444	14.857	13.489	12.303	11.272	10.371	9.580	8.883
24	21.243	18.914	16.939	15.247	13.799	12.550	11.469	10.529	9.707	8.985
25	22.023	19.523	17.413	15.622	14.094	12.783	11.654	10.675	9.823	9.077
26	22.795	20.121	17.877	15.983	13.375	13.003	11.826	10.810	9.929	9.161
27	23.560	20.707	18.327	16.330	14.643	13.211	11.987	10.935	10.027	9.237
28	24.316	21.281	18.764	16.663	13.898	13.406	12.137	11.051	10.116	9.307
29	25.066	21.844	19.188	16.984	15.141	13.591	12.278	11.158	10.198	9.370
30	25.808	22.396	19.600	17.292	15.372	13.765	12.409	11.258	10.274	9.427
35	29.409	24.999	21.487	18.665	16.374	14.498	12.948	11.655	10.567	9.644
40	32.835	27.355	23.115	19.793	17.159	15.046	13.332	11.925	10.757	9.779
45	36.095	29.490	24.519	20.720	17.774	15.456	13.606	12.108	10.881	9.863
50	39.196	31.424	25.730	21.482	18.256	15.762	13.801	12.233	10.962	9.915

Appendix B (continued)

11%	12%	13%	14%	15%	16%	17%	18%	19%	20%	Years 0 to:
0.901	0.893	0.885	0.877	0.870	0.862	0.855	0.847	0.840	0.833	1
1.713	1.690	1.668	1.647	1.626	1.605	1.585	1.566	1.547	1.528	2
2.444	2.402	2.361	2.322	2.283	2.246	2.210	2.174	2.140	2.106	3
3.102	3.037	2.974	2.914	2.855	2.798	2.743	2.690	2.639	2.589	4
3.696	3.605	3.517	3.433	3.352	3.274	3.199	3.127	3.058	2.991	5
4.231	4.111	3.998	3.889	3.784	3.685	3.589	3.498	3.410	3.326	6
4.712	4.564	4.423	4.288	4.160	4.039	3.922	3.812	3.706	3.605	7
5.146	4.968	4.799	4.639	4.487	4.344	4.207	4.078	3.954	3.837	8
5.537	5.328	5.132	4.946	4.772	4.607	4.451	4.303	4.163	4.031	9
5.889	5.650	5.426	5.216	5.019	4.833	4.659	4.494	4.339	4.192	10
6.207	5.938	5.687	5.453	5.234	5.029	4.836	4.656	4.486	4.327	11
6.492	6.194	5.918	5.660	5.421	5.197	4.988	4.793	4.611	4.439	12
6.750	6.424	6.122	5.842	5.583	5.342	5.118	4.910	4.715	4.533	13
6.982	6.628	6.302	6.002	5.724	5.468	5.229	5.008	4.802	4.611	14
7.191	6.811	6.462	6.142	5.847	5.575	5.324	5.092	4.876	4.675	15
7.379	6.974	6.604	6.265	5.954	5.668	5.405	5.162	4.938	4.730	16
7.549	7.120	6.729	6.373	6.047	5.749	5.475	5.222	4.990	4.775	17
7.702	7.250	6.840	6.467	6.128	5.818	5.534	5.273	5.033	4.812	18
7.839	7.366	6.938	6.550	6.198	5.877	5.584	5.316	5.070	4.843	19
7.963	7.469	7.025	6.623	6.259	5.929	5.628	5.353	5.101	4.870	20
8.075	7.562	7.102	6.687	6.312	5.973	5.665	5.384	5.127	4.891	21
8.176	7.645	7.170	6.743	6.359	6.011	5.696	5.410	5.149	4.909	22
8.266	7.718	7.230	6.792	6.399	6.044	5.723	5.432	5.167	4.925	23
8.348	7.784	7.283	6.835	6.434	6.073	5.746	5.451	5.182	4.937	24
8.422	7.843	7.330	6.873	6.464	6.097	5.766	5.467	5.195	4.948	25
8.488	7.896	7.372	6.906	6.491	6.118	5.783	5.480	5.206	4.956	26
8.548	7.943	7.409	6.935	6.514	6.136	5.798	5.492	5.215	4.964	27
8.602	7.984	7.441	6.961	6.534	6.152	5.810	5.502	5.223	4.970	28
8.650	8.022	7.470	6.983	6.551	6.166	5.820	5.510	5.229	4.975	29
8.694	8.055	7.496	7.003	6.566	6.177	5.829	5.517	5.235	4.979	30
8.855	8.176	7.586	7.070	6.617	6.215	5.858	5.539	5.251	4.992	35
8.951	8.244	7.634	7.105	6.642	6.233	5.871	5.548	5.258	4.997	40
9.008	8.283	7.661	7.123	6.654	6.242	5.877	5.552	5.261	4.999	45
9.042	8.304	7.675	7.133	6.661	6.246	5.880	5.554	5.262	4.999	50

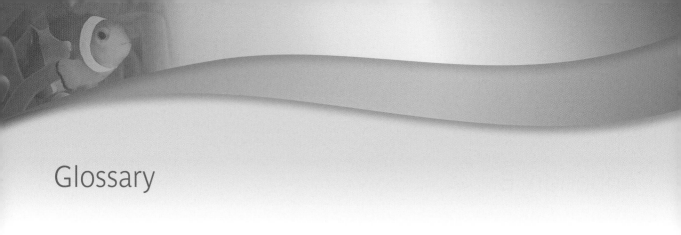

Glossary

ABC – a costing techniques that uses activity pools to store overheads, these are then traced to cost objects through the use of cost drivers.

Absorption costing – a method when all manufacturing costs are regarded as being inventoriable.

Accounting for networks – accounting for the achievement of common objectives via alliances, partnerships and other networked situations.

Accounting rate of return – a quick method of calculation the rate of return of a project – ignoring the time value of money.

Action/behavioural controls – are normally established when desirable (or undesirable) actions are known, and can also be observed in practice.

Activities – the name of a collection of tasks or processes which are linked in terms of overheads.

Activity pools – the collection point for overheads related to specific activities.

Activity/output base – the output level used to estimate costs.

Activity-based budgeting – budgeting based on activities rather than units, products, or departments. An extension of ABC.

Activity-based management – the use of ABC information to identify operational and strategic improvement possibilities.

Advisory accounting – where management accountants work as integral members of management teams, as 'business partners', using their financial astuteness and analytical skills to assist all kind of decision making.

Arm's-length principle – the OECD's preferred approach to transfer pricing, based on the price that would be defined between unrelated entities, keeping all other aspects of the relationship.

Attribute costing – estimation of expected costs of offering individual attributes in a product.

Attribute pricing – estimation of customers' willingness to pay for different product attributes, both individually and when integrated within particular product configurations.

Attributes of products or services – tangible or intangible features that characterize the product or service.

Backflush costing – a simplified costing technique for a JIT environment, with little or no inventories, without accounting for some flows in stages prior to recording goods sold (in particular, flows in and out of the work-in-progress account).

Balanced scorecard – a tool that uses financial and non-financial information, in an integrated and holistic way, to assist managers to map out and aim for strategic goals.

Bar-code – an optional display of data, the contents of which can be read by scanning devices. Their most commonly known application is in the automation of processing food and other products through supermarket checkouts.

Bar-coding – a means of gathering cost information at source, and works on the same (code and scanning) principles used in supermarkets.

Best-of-breed (BoB) system – information system specialized in a particular area, attempting to offer the best possible solution in that field, traditionally with limited integration as typical of stand-alone systems.

Beyond budgeting – a philosophy which seeks the abandonment of budgets. Using relative target measure this approach seeks innovation and value-added activities to measure the success of a department, under a devolved process.

Big data – data with high volume, velocity and variety which is beyond the processing capacity of conventional systems and whose analysis may detect hidden valuable patterns and information.

Glossary (continued)

Bottom-up budgets – budgets which are created through a process of negotiation with the operational managers.

Break-even point – the output/activity level at which neither a profit or loss is made.

Budget – a financial plan which considers the income and expenditures.

Budget committee – a formal committee within an organization who oversee the budgeting process and approval the final budgets.

Budget manual – a document explaining how all the budgets relate containing information on coding items within the budgets.

Budgeted utilization – the planned usage of the capacity of a production facility.

Business partners – a recent description of some management accountants' role, one of being adviser (consulting-like) to organizational managers outside of the accounting department.

Business process re-engineering (BPR) – a radical approach to organizational change, fundamentally questioning and re-engineering business processes, rather than merely improving them.

Capital allowance – the rate set by the tax authorities to calculate the taxable profit of an investment.

Capital budgeting – a set of normative theories which examines the most appropriate investment to be undertaken based upon a company's financial requirements.

Centralized – where responsibility rests mainly with senior management at the higher levels of an organization's hierarchical structure.

Change process – a view of change as being part of an unfolding story rather than a simplistic shift from one optimizing state to another.

Cloud accounting – accounting carried out through cloud-based solutions.

Cloud computing – a business model in which IT resources (software and/or hardware)

are provided as a service by a specialist provider, rather than individually owned and managed by the customer in its premises.

Coefficient of variation – a best fit measure, which indicates how well the values of the dependent variable are explained by the independent variable.

Committed fixed cost – a cost which is fixed and cannot be changed.

Conformance quality – the extent to which the actual characteristics of a product or service match its design specifications.

Continuous improvement (kaizen, in Japanese) – a company-wide approach of never-ending pursuit of improvements, typically small and incremental but adding up to significant cumulative improvements.

Contribution – sales revenue less variable costs.

Contribution margin ratio – contribution as a proportion of sales.

Control – the process of ensuring that what is actually done in an organization correlates with its objectives.

Control – the process through which managers seek to ensure that their plans are being put into action, for example through monitoring and reporting activities.

Controllable costs – costs which can be influenced by the actions of a particular person (or group) in relation to a particular undertaking.

Controls – are the package of tools, techniques and artefacts which produce and comprise the information necessary to assist the control process.

Conversion costs – all manufacturing costs other than direct materials costs.

Corporate steering wheel – an alternative version of the balanced scorecard but with similar and overlapping features.

Cost – typically, this is some monetary measure of the resources sacrificed or forgone in order to

Glossary (continued)

achieve a specific objective, such as acquiring a good or service. But, it is usually more complex than this – there are different costs for different purposes.

Cost accounting – a narrower application (subset) of management accounting, which concentrates on an organization's acquisition or consumption of resources.

Cost accumulation – where cost data is organized according to a classification system that identifies a group of costs in a particular (and usually obvious) way.

Cost allocation – a method to reasonably and accurately assign indirect costs to different cost objects.

Cost assignment – where accumulated costs are attributed to specific cost objects, via 'tracing' and allocating accumulated costs to a cost object.

Cost centre – a group which has responsibility for the costs incurred in a particular activity, normally headed up by a main responsibility manager.

Cost drivers – drivers that connect the activity pools and the cost objects. The cost drivers represent how the cost objects consume resources from within the activity pools.

Cost objects – something for which a separate cost measurement is required.

Cost of capital – the return that is required for an investment.

Cost or expense centres – responsibility centres where the manager has accountability against the costs which he or she has control over.

Cost plus pricing – a method whereby the cost of a product is estimated and a mark-up is added for profit.

Cost reduction – a process undertaken by an organization to decrease costs. This can involve a variety of strategies and target different measures of 'cost'.

Cost structure – the relative amount of fixed and variable costs in a business.

Cost system – a form of accounting system which captures cost data that will then form the basis of cost information for managers' use.

Costs of quality (COQ) – costs to achieve high quality and avoid failures, through prevention and appraisal activities, and cost consequences of poor quality, due to internal and external failures.

Cost-volume-profit – the term used to describe the technique of analysing how costs and profits vary according to changing output volumes.

Cost-volume-profit graph – a graph which shows all costs (fixed, variable, total) in relation to output.

Customer perspective – objectives, measures, targets and initiatives which focus on an organization's markets and customers.

Customer service – services provided to customers throughout the entire relationship – before, during and after the purchase.

Data – facts and figures.

Data – records of raw facts, without being organized or arranged to be meaningful for humans.

Database technology – information technology that supports the storage of vast amounts of data.

Decentring of accounting knowledge – a process whereby financial knowledge is spread through an organization, among managers and the workers, who can connect a 'bottom-line' effect' to localized activities.

Decentralized – where responsibility and accountability to one's own actions and decisions is passed out, downwards and outwards, from senior management.

Decreasing returns to scale – a term used by economists to describe increasing variable costs as output increases beyond capacity and inefficiencies occur.

Degree of operating leverage – a measure of the risk profile of a cost structure. Expressed as contribution divded by profit.

Glossary (continued)

Dependent variable – a variable (cost) whose change is dependent on other variables.

Design quality – the extent to which the designed characteristics of a product or service address clients' expectations.

Direct costs – costs which can be easily associated with a particular cost object.

Discount rate – the rate which is used to reduce the value of money into the present value based upon the rate of return and the time period.

Discretionary cost centre – where outputs cannot be measured in financial terms, and where there is difficulty in pinning down any obvious relationship between inputs (that is, resource consumption) and outputs.

Discretionary fixed cost – a cost which is at the discretion of managers.

Drivers of management accounting change – factors which cause shifts in the information requirements of business managers, hence affecting and potentially changing management accounting.

Economic value added (EVA®) – a type of residual income, adopting after-tax measures and adjusting several accounting measures of profit and assets to avoid distortions caused by Generally Accepted Accounting Principles (GAAP). These adjustments aim at approximating accounting measures to economic measures.

Elastic demand – where the demand of a product or service changes in relation to a change in the price.

Elasticity – the sensitivity of one variable against another.

Employee empowerment – where organizations give managers and workers the right to independently make local decisions.

Enterprise resource planning (ERP) system – an organization-wide integrated system, originally aiming to be *the* single system satisfying all information needs, but increasingly repositioned as the IS backbone to which other systems connect.

Ethical business – doing what is the socially, morally and environmentally right thing to do.

Expense – a cost that has been incurred when an asset is used up or sold for the purpose of generating revenues.

Experience curve – the ability to improve performance based on experience, represented by a downward sloping curve.

Favourable variances – variances that mean an increase in profit, due to: (1) actual revenues higher than budgeted, or (2) actual costs lower than budgeted; identified as 'F'.

Feasible region – the area of a linear programming chart (Simplex method) which satisfies all constraints.

Financial accounting – the process of collating information for the purpose of external financial reports, the most obvious of which would be the 'glossy' annual financial statements.

Financial perspective – conveys the financial performance objectives of an organization, plus associated measures, targets and initiatives.

Fixed costs – do not change (in total) as activity levels fluctuate.

Fixed overhead spending variance – difference between budgeted costs (BC) and actual costs (AC) in FOH items; valid in both variable and absorption standard costing.

Fixed overhead volume variance – (only in absorption costing) difference between flexed capacity utilization and budgeted capacity utilization, valued at the standard fixed overhead rate.

Flexible budget (or flexed budget) – budget produced after a period finishes, adjusting (flexing) the initial estimates to the *actual* volume of activity, in order to calculate flexed quantities and costs.

Flexible budget variances – comparisons between actual results and the flexible budget; these comparisons are meaningful because both budgets consider the actual activity level.

Glossary (continued)

Forecasting – using tools and techniques to make predictions about the future, as opposed to planning which is more about what the future 'should' look like.

Full-cost accounting (FCA) – a costing technique that includes the use of environmental and social resources in the full cost of production, in order to support management decisions promoting sustainable development.

Functional budgets – day-to-day operational budgets which focus on specific functions or aspects of the process or service.

Generally Accepted Accounting Principles (GAAP) – a combination of accounting standards and accepted conventions which define how accounting information is recorded and reported

High-low method – a cost estimation method which use two extremities of output (high and low).

Holistic – adopting a broad perspective of business activity, across multiple functions and through different levels of organizational hierarchy.

Hybridization (in management accounting) – a bi-directional change in roles of accountants and IS and line staff, with professionals from each group assuming activities traditionally in the domain of the others.

Increasing returns to scale – a term used by economists to describe decreasing variable costs as output increases.

Independent variable – a variable (output) which causes changes in the dependent variable.

Indirect costs – costs which evidently support more than one cost object.

Inelastic demand – where the demand of a product or service does not change with a change in the price.

Information – assists business managers in making decisions; a building block of organizational knowledge and learning, the production of which rests to a large extent with management accountants.

Information – data organized or modified in a way to become understandable and usable, and for a particular purpose.

Information – when raw data comes to be useful and meaningful to its owner(s), and subsequently has potential to influence their decision making.

Information integration – the bringing together of a broader business perspective, as expressed through both financial and non-financial measures.

Information overload – the potential danger of producing too much management accounting information to the extent that it becomes unmanageable, rather than focusing on relevant and useful information for managers' decision-making needs.

Information system – a set of connected technologies and resources that collects, transforms and disseminates information.

Information technologies – an array of computing and telecommunications tools which assist management accountants to collate, store, retrieve and use information in their day-to-day role.

Institutional theoretical perspective of management accounting change – one (of several) theoretical perspectives of management accounting change, focusing particularly on the important interactions over time of organizational rules, routines and institutions.

Institutions – unquestioned and taken for granted assumptions in an organization in regards to 'the way we do things'.

Integrated – where any particular perspective of organizational activity (for example, financial performance) is not to be viewed independently of alternative aspects of organizational activity (for example, customer-related or impact on the environment).

Internal business perspective – objectives, measures, targets and initiatives which an organization must do well internally in order to attain its strategic goals.

Glossary (continued)

Internal markets – a market which exists within an organization.

Internal rate of return – the rate of return which would produce an NPV of zero.

Investment – the purchase of an opportunity or physical asset.

Investment centres – where the manager has all the responsibility assigned to a profit centre (that is, sales revenues and costs) but also responsibility for working capital and capital investment decisions.

Job costing – a method which accumulates the costs incurred in the production of a single unit or a single batch of units.

Joint costs – common costs incurred before the split off point in a process.

Just-in-Time – a Japanese management philosophy which aims to produce/deliver products when required, and thereby reduce inventories.

Just-in-time (JIT) (or lean production) – a system that only purchases or produces when needed to address a customer order, in order to minimize waste (inventories and anything that does not add value). Just-in-tme philosophy requires JIT manufacturing + TQM + respect for people.

Kaizen budgeting – budgeting based on a continuous improvement philosophy. Seeking small improvements in the operating processes which are recorded within the budget statement.

Kaizen costing – cost management technique to reduce costs during the production stage, in a kaizen/continuous improvement approach to increase efficiency and reduce waste.

Labour efficiency variance – difference between direct labour flexed hours and actual hours used, valued at the standard wage rate.

Lag indicators – outcome measures, indicators of achievement in a particular perspective.

Lead indicators – performance drivers, activities which aim to assist the achievement of objectives in particular perspectives.

Lean manufacturing – an approach to manufacturing which aims to eliminate unnecessary process and production waste.

Learning and growth perspective – objectives, measures, targets and initiatives which focus an organization and its employees on continual learning and its resource capabilities.

Learning curve effect – see experience curve.

Least squares regression method – a mathematical formula can be used to calculate and draw a regression line rather than visual inspection or a scattergraph.

Life cycle costing – analyses costs throughout the entire life cycle of a product, from development to after-sales stages; an input for life cycle profitability analysis.

Linear programming – a technique used to find optimum solutions when multiple comstraints exist.

Loss-leader – a product sold at a loss to encourage customers to buy.

Management accounting – the provision of information to assist organizational decision making.

Management accounting change – the process by which management accounting practices become what they do (or not) over time.

Management control systems – systems which gather and use information to plan, control and monitor the actions of organizations.

Margin of safety – the sales volume (in units or monetary value) above break-even point.

Marginal costing – a costing technique in which only variable costs are attributed to products/services.

Marginal costs – the cost of increasing one unit of output.

Marginal revenues – the revenue gained in increasing one unit of output.

Margins – a measure of profitability.

Glossary (continued)

Master budget – a collection of all the data from all the individual functional budgets, typically in the form of the cash budget, predicted Incomes Statement and Statement of Financial Position.

Material *price* variance – difference between the standard price and the actual price per unit of material, applied to the actual quantity purchased.

Material usage variance – difference between the flexed quantity of materials required and the actual quantity of materials used, valued at the standard material price.

Mixed cost – a cost which has fixed and variable elements.

Multiple regression – a mathematical regression model with more than one independent variable.

Net present value – the sum of a time series of discounted cash inflows and outflows.

Non-financial information – information such as quality and customer satisfaction, and the management of which is deemed by some to be a precursor to financial success.

Non-financial quality indicators – indicators on customers, internal business processes and learning and growth that anticipate and drive the financial consequences of quality.

Normal utilization – the capacity of a production plant that is typically utilized under normal business/economic conditions.

Objective function – the function/equation to to solved (for example, maximize contribution) in a linear programming scenario.

Operating leverage – relative amount of costs that are fixed and variable in a business cost structure.

Opportunity cost – the value of something that a decision maker gives up as one decision option is selected over another.

Outsourcing – the transfer of an organizational activity/product/service to an external provider.

Pareto analysis – 80/20 rule that enables you to see what 20 per cent of cases are causing 80 per cent of the problems within a scenario, or how 20 per cent of cases are creating 80 per cent of the profits.

Payback – the length of time it takes to recover the initial investment of a project.

Performance management – a broadening of performance measurement to looking at the issues underpinning the *i* of performance

Performance management – a process of not just measuring an organization's performance, but also continually (re)designing, monitoring and acting upon such measures.

Performance measurement – seeing how an organization is doing, in comparison to its aims and targets.

Performance measurement – where managers assess an organization's actual performance against its planned activity, as well as continually gauging the likelihood of achieving organizational goals.

Period costs – costs that are not related to making or acquiring a product, or providing a service that generates revenues.

Personnel/cultural controls – are grounded in an underlying belief that organizations can mobilize and nurture solidarity and commitment towards organizational goals.

Plan-do-check-act (PDCA) cycle – a systematic, interactive approach to continuous improvement and problem solving, and a key tool in total quality management.

Planning – when organizations select from alternative options, such that all decisions combined will assist in the achievement of its goals.

Planning – where managers select from alternative options such that their decisions (combined) will assist towards achievement of organizational goals.

Practical capacity – the likely maximum possible output of a production facility, taking into account expected normal delays like down time.

Glossary (continued)

Predictive analytics – the use of technological tools to retrieve, store and use external data, and predict multiple business scenarios and identify appropriate actions.

Price – the value of a product or service that is used in the transaction process of selling to a consumer.

Pricing strategies – a portfolio of strategies that enable a company to target different markets or take advantage of the various stages of the life cycle of a product or service.

Prime costs – all the direct costs incurred when making a particular product.

Process costing – a method used when an organization's units of production are identical, or almost identical, in which case average per unit costs can be applied to product costing.

Process value chain – another way of viewing the internal business process, comprising: (1) the innovation process, (2) the operations process, and (3) the post-sales service process.

Product cost – a cost that is assigned to goods either purchased or manufactured for (re)sale.

Product life cycle – phases of a product life.

Profit centres – where managers are responsible for both revenues and costs.

Profit-volume graph – a variant of the CVP graph which reflects profits of varying levels of output.

Rate of return – the return which is required for an investment.

Real options – an investment which incorporates an opportunity to change the course of the decision at some point in the future.

Regression errors – the distance between a data point and the regression line.

Regression line – a line of best fit of multiple data points.

Relevance Lost – a milestone book published in 1987, which claimed that management accounting had ceased to provide business managers with useful information.

Relevant cost – a future cost affect by a decision.

Relevant costs – those costs which are pertinent to a particular decision in so far as they will influence which decision alternative is chosen.

Relevant range – the period over which the definition of variable and fixed costs is assumed to hold and can be relied upon.

Relevant range – the range of output at which costs are assumed to be stable.

Relevant revenue – a future revenue affect by a decision.

Residual income – an approach to performance measurement which holds that all measures of profit or surplus should take into account the cost of capital employed to generate it.

Residual income (RI) – operating profit minus a cost of capital charge on investment.

Residual value – the value of an investment at the end of its useful life.

Responsibility – the notion that when employees are empowered, they also become accountable for (and will have monitored) their actions and decisions.

Responsibility accounting – a process whereby the managers of subunits within an organization are assigned certain responsibility, and their performance against such responsibility.

Responsibility centre – an organizational unit for which a manager can be held accountable/responsible.

Results/output controls – are undertaken through measuring outcomes, and can be particularly worthwhile when the knowledge of (un)desirable action is sparse.

Return on investment (ROI) – profit divided by investment (profit and investment may be defined differently, depending on the purpose of the analysis).

Revenue centres – responsibility centres where managers are accountable to the financial outputs associated with generating sales (or, more specifically, sales revenues).

Glossary (continued)

Reverse engineering – engineering practice of disassembling competitors' products to obtain detailed insights about their design features, materials and production techniques.

Rewards – benefits which are aligned to performance, such as bonuses.

Roles – the ways in which accountants become involved in, and assist, organizational decision making.

Rolling forecasts – an approach to budgeting that uses a continuous updating approach to forecasting, the time period of the budget remains constant.

Routine accounting – tasks that nowadays are largely organized automatically via advances in IT and software – for example, financial reporting, transaction processing, ledger management, taxation and internal audit.

Routines – the re-enactment of rules, how things are actually done in an organization.

Rules – formalized procedures of how things should be done in an organization.

Sales margin volume variance – under variable standard costing, it is the difference between actual sales volume and budgeted sales volume, valued at the standard contribution margin; under absorption standard costing, it is the same difference, valued at the standard profit margin.

Sales mix – the relative proportion of a product sales to total sales.

Sales price variance – difference between the actual price and the standard price, applied to the actual sales volume.

Sensitivity analysis – a general term used in many business contexts to describe the analysis of how sensitive variables are to changes in conditions, for example how fixed cost increases effect profits.

Shared service centre – a centre that is responsible for specific tasks, providing expertise in one area to the remaining part of the organization.

Shared-services centre – an internal centralized service provider to an organization.

Shareholder approach – argues that financial performance measurement remains the most important measurement within organizations.

Simplex method – a graphical approach to solving linear programming scenarios.

Six sigma – a strategy to achieve an extraordinarily high conformance quality level, by reducing process variability that causes defects and undermines customer satisfaction.

Split-off point – the point in a process when separate products become identifiable.

Stakeholder approach – advocates that organizations adopt sufficient non-financial performance measures to supplement any use of financial measures.

Stand-alone system – a system highly or totally decoupled from the remaining systems.

Standard cost centre – where outputs of production are known and can be measured in financial terms, and the quantity of inputs necessary for producing one unit of output are also known.

Standard costing – the process of establishing cost standards that an organization expects to incur, then to monitor actual costs against such standards.

Standard costs – expected costs of one unit of output, under normal conditions.

Static budget – budget produced before a period starts, based on initial estimates.

Static budget variances – comparisons between actual results and the static budget, typically meaningless because they refer to different activity levels.

Step-variable costs – variable costs which increase in steps beyond certain levels of output.

Strategic – the ongoing process of endeavouring to achieve an organization's

Glossary (continued)

strategy. Being strategic gives some degree of fluidity and an underpinning notion of ongoing process to a strategy.

Strategic cost management – the application of cost management tools and techniques which simultaneously aims to improve an organization's strategic position and reduce its costs.

Strategic intent – the notion of cumulative strategizing, ongoing (re)formulation of organizational strategy in the context of changing external and internal conditions.

Strategic management – the process through which usually an organization's executive managers will devise plans, establish controls, monitor and use various tools and techniques to fulfil their organizational aims.

Strategic management accounting (SMA) – an amalgam of management accounting tools and techniques which assist managers to steer their organization in the direction of strategic intent.

Strategy – some form of grand scheme or plan which sets out a vision or aim for where an organization wants to be in the longer term.

Sunk costs – are associated with the past, and are unaltered by current and future decisions, so they are irrelevant to current and/or future decisions.

Sustainability assessment model (SAM) – a project evaluation technique to support decisions that promote sustainable development, based on full-cost accounting.

Sustainable development – a term which describes organizations attempting to develop its activities in a financially rewarding way but not at the expense of costs incurred on society or the environment.

Sustainable development (SD) – 'an approach to progress which meets the needs of the present without compromising the ability of future generations to meet their own needs' (World Commission on Environment and Development (WCED) (1987) *Tokyo Declaration*, Tokyo: WCED, p. 8)

Systems – the hardware and software which facilitates the collation of data and the processing of information.

Systems (de)coupling (degree of) – the extent to which changes in one system affect the state of the other.

Target cost – target price (based on market research) minus the target margin (based on corporate profitability objectives).

Target costing (or target cost management) – a cost management technique for the product development stage, to determine the maximum allowable product cost, based on customers' willingness to pay and corporate profitability objectives, and to design a product that can be sold at such maximum target cost.

Tax-compliant transfer price – transfer price that complies with applicable tax legislation.

TD-ABC – a version of ABC which works on estimating time rather than identifying cost drivers through lengthy surveys or interviews.

Techniques – an array of calculative methods that allow organizations to structure their problems and offer alternative actions.

The management accounts – an aggregated depiction of an organization's (monthly, year to date) financial and non-financial results.

Theoretical capacity – the maximum possible output of a production facility.

Throughput accounting – an alternative to traditional cost accounting which takes into account operational constraints which limit the capacity, and hence profitability, of an organization.

Top-down budgets – budgets which are formulated by top managers and imposed on the operational managers.

Total fixed overhead variance – (only in absorption costing) difference between flexed costs and actual costs for fixed overhead items.

Glossary (continued)

Total labour variance – difference between labour flexed costs and actual costs.

Total material variance – difference between material flexed costs and actual costs.

Total quality management (TQM) – permanent and integrated effort across the entire organization to excel in all customer-relevant quality dimensions of products and services.

Total sales margin variance – difference between actual contribution (based on standard costs) and budgeted contribution.

Total variable overhead variance – difference between flexed costs and actual costs for variable overhead items.

Tracing – the process of assigning direct costs to a particular cost object.

Traditional budgeting – an approach to budgeting that has set targets within a set accounting period. Generally using a line approach to detailing all the information.

Traditional costing method – an old business model where the consumption of overheads was typically absorbed on the basis of labour hours, machine hours or units.

Transfer price – price charged for flows of goods, intangibles, services or capital within an organization.

Uncontrollable costs – costs which cannot be influenced by the actions of an individual (or group) for a particular undertaking.

Unfavourable variances – variances that mean a decrease in profit, due to: (1) actual revenues lower than budgeted, or (2) actual costs higher than budgeted; identified as 'U'.

Value chain – the major activities that add customer value; it may be analysed at an organizational level or at an industry-wide level, from suppliers of basic raw materials through to the end customer.

Value engineering – a technique for product development oriented by customers' perceptions of value and expected costs of each product attribute.

Variable costing – when only variable manufacturing costs are inventorized, and fixed manufacturing cost is treated as an expense at the time period in which it is incurred.

Variable costs – change (in total) in proportion to the level of activity.

Variable overhead efficiency variance – difference between the allocation base flexed volume and actual volume, valued at the standard variable overhead rate.

Variable overhead spending variance – difference between the standard rate and actual rate of variable overheads, applied to the actual volume of the allocation base.

Variance analysis – technique of calculating variances and identifying their 'real-life' causes.

Wage rate variance – difference between the standard wage rate and the actual rate per hour of direct labour, applied to the actual number of hours used.

Writing down allowance – a yearly allowance, calculated to reduce the cash flow to a taxable profit value.

Zero-based budgeting – an approach to budgeting that starts with a blank piece of paper every accounting period. Resources are allocated on needs rather than past budgeted information.

Index

Index (continued)

Index (continued)

Index (continued)

Index (continued)

Index (continued)

Index (continued)

Index (continued)

Index (continued)

Index (continued)

Index (continued)

Index (continued)

Index (continued)

Index (continued)

Index (continued)

Index (continued)